Boston's First Nine
...The 1871-75 Boston Red Stockings...

Edited by Bob LeMoine and Bill Nowlin

Associate editor Len Levin

Society for American Baseball Research, Inc.
Phoenix, AZ

Boston's First Nine: The 1871-75 Boston Red Stockings
Edited by Bob LeMoine and Bill Nowlin
Associate editor Len Levin

Copyright © 2016 Society for American Baseball Research, Inc.
All rights reserved. Reproduction in whole or in part without permission is prohibited.

ISBN 978-1-943816-29-3
Ebook ISBN 978-1-943816-28-6
Cover and book design: Gilly Rosenthol

Front cover: Red Stocking images such as this one appeared as labels on
Nichols & MacDonald cigar boxes in the late 19th and early 20th centuries. (public domain)

Society for American Baseball Research
Cronkite School at ASU
555 N. Central Ave. #416
Phoenix, AZ 85004
Phone: (602) 496-1460
Web: www.sabr.org
Facebook: Society for American Baseball Research
Twitter: @SABR

TABLE OF CONTENTS

INTRODUCTION 1
Bob LeMoine

FORMING A FRANCHISE

When Boston Dominated Baseball 6
Mark Souder

Organizing the First Professional Base-Ball Team in Boston — *Boston Daily Advertiser* 24

The Boston Red Stockings Organizational Meeting 27
Richard "Dixie" Tourangeau

THE SEASONS

The 1871 Season 30
Bob LeMoine

The 1872 Season 35
Bill Ryczek

The 1873 Season 40
Bill Ryczek

The 1874 Season 46
Bill Ryczek

The 1875 Season 51
Bob LeMoine

THE PLAYERS

Bob Addy 57
Peter Morris

Ross Barnes 66
Gregory H. Wolf

Frank Barrows 74
Mike Richard

Tommy Beals 77
Mark S. Sternman

David Birdsall 80
Richard "Dixie" Tourangeau

Fred Cone 84
Mike Richard

Charlie Gould 88
Charles F. Faber

George Hall 93
Matt Albertson

Franklin "Heck" Heifer 99
Brian C. Engelhardt

Samuel Jackson 105
Bill Nowlin

Jumbo Latham 110
Scott Fiesthumel

Andy Leonard 112
Charles F. Faber

John E. Manning 116
David Nemec

Cal McVey 120
Charles F. Faber

Jim O'Rourke 123
William Lamb

Fraley W. Rogers 132
Richard "Dixie" Tourangeau

Henry C. Schafer 135
David Nemec

Al Spalding 138
Bill McMahon

Charlie Sweasy 142
Charles F. Faber

Deacon White 146
Joe Williams

George Wright 160
John Thorn

Harry Wright 170
Christopher Devine

THE BALLPARK

South End Grounds 175
Bob Ruzzo

TEAM ORGANIZATION

Boston Finances in the Early Professional Era..187
Richard Hershberger

Red Stockings Finances—
A Minor Observation..191
Bill Nowlin

THE FIRST PRESIDENT

Ivers W. Adams 192
Charlie Bevis

INTERESTING GAMES

Fast Day—Boston's Original Opening Day......196
Joanne Hulbert

April 6, 1871..200
Bob LeMoine

May 5, 1871 204
Bob LeMoine

May 16, 1871 208
Bob LeMoine

Homestand From Hell:
The Boston Red Stockings, May-June 1871 211
Richard "Dixie" Tourangeau

June 21, 1871...214
Jay Hurd

July 4, 1871 217
Michael R. McAvoy

August 3, 1871...220
Bob LeMoine

September 2, 1871..223
Bill Nowlin

September 5, 1871 225
Gregory H. Wolf

September 9, 1871..228
Mark Pestana

September 13, 1871..231
Jay Hurd

September 29, 1871..233
Gregory H. Wolf

May 11, 1872...236
Gregory H. Wolf

June 10, 1872...240
Richard "Dixie" Tourangeau

June 12, 1872...242
Paul E. Doutrich

July 20, 1872..244
Gerard R. Goulet

July 29, 1872..247
Gregory H. Wolf

September 20, 1872 250
Gerard R. Goulet

September 21, 1872..252
Mark Pestana

April 23, 1873 255
Matt Albertson

June 2, 1873...258
Terry Gottschall

June 3, 1873...260
Mark Pestana

June 14, 1873 262
Richard "Dixie" Tourangeau

July 4, 1873 (morning)..................................... 264
John Zinn

July 4, 1873 (afternoon)...................................266
John Zinn

July 26, 1873 268
Terry Gottschall

September 6, 1873..270
Bill Nowlin

October 2, 1873...272
Mark Pestana

A Rare First-Person Account of
What Nineteenth Century Ball Players
Did on An Unexpected Day Off 275
Richard "Dixie" Tourangeau

May 2, 1874...277
Richard "Dixie" Tourangeau

July 4, 1874 279
  Gregory H. Wolf

September 22, 1874 282
  Bill Nowlin

October 1, 1874 284
  Jim Wohlenhaus

October 7, 1874 286
  John Zinn

October 20, 1874 289
  Paul E. Doutrich

October 26, 1874 291
  Bill Nowlin

April 19, 1875 293
  Mark Pestana

April 29, 1875 296
  Gerard R. Goulet

May 18, 1875 299
  David Arcidiacono

June 3, 1875 302
  Bill Nowlin

June 28, 1875 305
  Michael R. McAvoy

August 4, 1875 308
  David C. Southwick

October 30, 1875 310
  John Zinn

The Rumors Begin About the 1876 Season 312

RED STOCKINGS BY RAIL OR BOAT

Hub Kids Bid Fans Anew:
The Red Stockings in Canada, 1872-1874 319
  David McDonald

Zane Grey and the Mystery of the
Winning Ball 328
  David McDonald

The 1874 Boston Red Stockings' World Tour 333
  Eric Miklich

Selections from the British Newspaper
Coverage of the Visit of the
American Baseball Players 340

Tim Murnane's Account of the
1874 Base Ball Trip to Europe 343

OTHER GAMES, OTHER FEATURES

Baseball On Christmas Day, 1873 353
  Bob LeMoine

Off the Beaten Path - Exhibition Games 354
  Bob LeMoine

Exhibition Games Played by the
Boston Red Stockings, 1871-75 362

Boston's "Home Games" Played
in Other Cities 368
  Bill Nowlin

McBride & Zettlein —
Thorns in Red Stockings' Side 371
  Richard "Dixie" Tourangeau

RED STOCKINGS IN PRINT

Following the Boston Red Stockings
in the Early 1870s 374
  Donna L. Halper

The Dawn of Athlete Endorsements 379
  John Thorn

Some Red Stockings Stats 385

Some Newspaper Coverage
of the 1874 European Tour
of the Red Stockings and Athletics 387

CONTRIBUTORS 388

INTRODUCTION

BY BOB LEMOINE

"It was a league of people: people with human foibles, people with no road maps to guide them as they tried desperately to further the growth of their beloved game."
— William Ryczek[1]

Remembering the 1870s

HE HAD JUST RETURNED FROM A world cruise, and must have shivered on his way to Braves Field on May 8, 1925. The weather was described as "none too soft or kind" by Burton Whitman of the *Boston Herald*.[2] Now 78 years old, George Wright was again stepping out onto a Boston baseball field. He was joined by old teammate Jack Manning and about 50 others who played, managed, or umpired from the 1870s or later. The occasion was the Golden Jubilee Game, celebrating the 50th season of the National League, founded in 1876. Wright and Manning played for Boston in 1876. This "was a day of reminiscence," wrote the Associated Press. "Grayed and stooped by the passing years, they came to the game despite the chill wind and the clouds that alternated with sunshine."[3]

Wright and Manning, as well as the contingent of old-timers and dignitaries, strode to the center-field flag pole with the modern Boston and Chicago teams and the 101st Regiment Band. The American Flag and Jubilee pennant were raised, and the band played the National Anthem. On the way back to the dugout, the old timers had a moment to acknowledge the cheers from the fans as the band played "Auld Lang Syne." They made their way to their reserved box seats, and as old-timers are known to do, they commented on the present game and contemplated the past.

"By gory," Manning blurted to Wright, "they say these fellows are faster than we were, George, but they make as many mistakes. See that, now, he's pitching outside to him, when it's a cinch he could not hit a ball in close."[4] Wright, however, was more interested in the number of foul balls becoming souvenirs for the fans. "We didn't have so many balls in those days," he recalled, "and when a ball went over a fence or into the crowd we would often halt the game for a few minutes until the ball was returned, then the ball would be put back into the game."[5] Noting that Jimmy Welsh had been purchased by the Braves for $50,000 the previous December, Wright joked, "One could buy a whole club for $50,000 in the '70s."[6]

"We hobnobbed with royalty out at Braves Field yesterday afternoon, meeting the grand old baseball veterans, now silvery haired and rapidly ageing ... old in years, but young in spirit," wrote Ford Sawyer of the *Boston Globe*.[7] The assemblage of stars was indeed impressive, but just as impressive was the longevity of the game, which arose from a time Sawyer called "the days when baseball playing was a rather precarious undertaking and one didn't know whether or not financial adversity would cause the league to toss up the sponge."[8]

George Wright, chatting with Boston Braves manager Dave Bancroft, at a game in Boston on May 8, 1925. Wright was in attendance to celebrate the "Golden Jubilee" Game for the 50th anniversary of the National League. (Courtesy of Muddy River Musings Blog).

The National League has survived even to our day, but Wright and Manning remembered a prior league which was never the subject of pageantry. Yet of the 22 players who played for the Boston Red Stockings over five seasons in that league, five are in the National Baseball Hall of Fame. This league and this time are worth remembering, in the opinions of those who have written, fact-checked, edited, and designed this book in front of you.

The NAPBBP: A Noble Experiment

The National Association of Professional Base Ball Players was baseball's first attempt to organize as a professional business and break away from its long amateur heritage. There had been professional players for a while; often they would get paid under the table or be listed as city laborers as a cover for being paid to play. But then the first openly professional team, the Cincinnati Red Stockings of 1869, took the baseball world by storm. They dominated whatever teams came into their path, and then traveled west on the newly-built Transcontinental Railroad. They went undefeated throughout 1869 and then finally met defeat at the hands of the Brooklyn Atlantics on an East Coast trip in 1870. They lost more games as the season concluded, as the world of professional baseball was changing. Other professional teams were catching up and proving stiff competition. The fans in Cincinnati lost interest in their now vulnerable team, and the owners decided that if the team was going to lose, they didn't need to *pay* them for the effort. The legendary team disbanded, and a Boston dynasty was on the horizon.

Boston businessman Ivers W. Adams had seen the Red Stockings play local Boston teams and imagined Cincinnati stars George and Harry Wright playing for a Boston professional team. Adams had the connections with some of the most prominent Boston business leaders of the day, with the cash to make a Boston team a possibility. They had the money and resources, and the Wrights had the baseball connections, bringing with them some of the greatest players of the day. The league and the new Boston team were set to begin in 1871.

Like any new startup company, it made a lot of mistakes along the way. There was no set schedule, so games had to be negotiated, sometimes at the last minute. The standings were always a mystery, with one newspaper sometimes showing a different leader board than a paper in the next town. Who won the championship at the end of the season was often a matter for discussion, with an unequal number of games played, and some teams that folded before the season ended. Boston, winner of the pennant from 1872 through 1875, arguably also won the 1871 pennant but for two games credited to Philadelphia over an illegal player playing for Rockford. The Rockford club signed Scott Hastings, who had started the season with a New Orleans club. Teams protested when he suddenly appeared playing for Rockford, a violation of league rules against raiding players during the season. Hastings was not eligible to play for Rockford until June 16. At the end of the season, all Rockford victories before June 16 were wiped out, including two wins over Philadelphia. Boston finished two wins behind first-place Philadelphia.[9]

These and many other irregularities make modern baseball researchers scratch their heads. But these were the 1870s, and for the game of baseball to evolve to where we are today, it had to emerge from a period in which the game was in a sort of adolescent identity crisis. The rules were changing, and who was going to umpire a particular game was anybody's guess. Players ran the teams and some teams were co-ops that depended on gate receipts to distribute payment after the game. Teams filled their schedules with exhibitions, hoping an extra game here or there would get them some extra cash on-hand. Other teams were desperate just to get train fare home.

Despite all of these obstacles, baseball survived and thrived, even though the survival of the fittest meant some teams disappeared off the map. But our focus is of course Boston, and the story of professional baseball from 1871-1875. The fans made sure the team had people to play in front of. Newspapers, even though some of the copies are either very brief or incredibly hard to read today, gave coverage to local Bostonians. Despite this entire era taking place almost 150 years ago, fans read the amazing stories of their home team in its journeys from Chicago to Canada and even the UK.

Harry Wright's Leadership

What should not be lost on the modern reader is the prominent place Harry Wright holds in professional baseball history. On April 13, 1896, baseball celebrated "Harry Wright Day" around the country to raise money for the late legend's memorial fund. Wright, hailed as the "Father of Professional Base Ball" by *Sporting Life* [10] and other publications, had died the previous October.

One such celebration was in Rockford, Illinois, where the old Forest City club once played. "Two thousand persons huddled together under the leaky roof of the grandstand at Riverside Park and withstood the torrent for half an hour," wrote the *Boston Globe*. The weather was terrible, but fans got to get a glimpse of some of the stars of the past. Businesses were closed and "blocks and residences were handsomely decorated and nearly everybody in town wore one or more of Harry Wright memorial badges." Carriages carried these legends through the streets to mass applause. Included in the carriages were George Wright, "millionaire" Al Spalding, and Fred Cone, with Spalding wearing his old Forest City uniform, Wright his old Cincinnati threads. Only one inning was completed, however, as a pouring rain settled in, ruining what could have been a most memorable day.[11]

Back in Boston, John Morrill, who played all but one of his seasons in Boston from 1876-1890, put together a Picked Nine to face the Harvard team. Tommy Bond and Candy Cummings were part of the nine, and Harry Schaefer, now a hotel manager, enjoyed some old chats with Cummings.[12] In Cincinnati Charlie Gould, who "played pretty fair ball, everything considered," and Deacon White, who heard "quite a bit of applause," played in an old-timer's game.[13]

Harry Wright's genius is what can be credited for the NAPBBP's moderate success. Baseball historian David Quentin Voigt's chapter on the NAPBBP is titled "Harry Wright's League."[14] Christopher Devine's biography of Wright notes how Wright was always the driving force behind the scenes even while on the field. "While he was known as the Cincinnati captain, manager, and center fielder, he operated in 1869 as General Manager, Traveling Secretary, and Public Relations Department. He arranged all the games and gate receipts percentages, set up the travel schedule, negotiated hotel and railroad bills, negotiated player salaries, bought equipment, directed the groundskeeping, handled the media, and promoted Red Stockings games."[15] It was this ingenuity on and off the field that he brought to Boston, bringing the city a championship-caliber professional team.

The Red Stockings were without a doubt Harry Wright's team, but the NAPBBP was also his league. It was a league that included teams in places that would never again have a major-league team: Troy, Fort Wayne, Rockford, Middletown, Elizabeth, New Haven, and Keokuk. Competition was a matter of the haves and have-nots, and the strong teams feasted on the weak ones, which often didn't last the season. The league saw teams bat under .200 for a season, and also pitchers who were 50-game winners. There were ridiculous statistics in which Boston players dominated the league. Spalding pitched $2,346\frac{2}{3}$ innings, an average of $469\frac{2}{3}$ per season, and had a winning percentage of .794 with a 204-53 record. Ross Barnes had a five-year batting average of .391, George Wright .350, Cal McVey .362, and Deacon White .352. The Red Stockings won 19 in a row in 1872, then 26 in a row to start the 1875 season.

It was Harry Wright's leadership that made this early professional league possible, as "he approached the game in a far more businesslike manner than did most of the other men associated with the pro game," wrote Benjamin Rader. "Wright not only carefully managed such details as club scheduling and finances, but above all, he firmly established his authority over the players. Acting as a paternalistic patriarch, he even dictated their living arrangements in Boston."[16]

"From its creation in 1871 to its crash five years later," wrote baseball historian John Thorn, "the National Association had a rocky time as America's first professional league. Franchises came and went with dizzying speed, often folding in midseason. Schedules were not played out if a club slated to go on the road saw little prospect of gain. Drinking and gambling and game-fixing were rife. … But from the ashes of the National Association emerged the Red Stockings' model of success and the entrepreneurial genius of Chicago's William Hulbert."[17]

This league and this era are not often recalled despite baseball's current emphasis on nostalgia, but without this great experiment of a league, the game may not have evolved as a professional sport at the time that it did. But baseball did grow as a professional sport, in large measure to Harry Wright and others who "got the ball rolling." "The National Association had its warts," writes Ryczek, "was poorly run, and generated only one worthwhile pennant race in five years. But it was the first major league, a noble experiment that served a necessary function in baseball's awkward transition from an amateur to professional sport."[18]

Part of Boston's Past

I was writing articles for SABR's Games Project describing the very first professional baseball games in Boston's history. I was curious as to why I had heard so little about these Boston Red Stockings or how all of this history came together. I mentioned this to Bill Nowlin, who amazingly, despite all of his Boston baseball writing and research over the years, admitted he too knew almost nothing about this era. He suggested we co-edit a SABR book on this team, gathering player biographies, articles on some of the most significant games, and other interesting things we would find. We definitely accomplished all of this, as we found a team of writers and researchers equally fascinated with this story.

On a frigid day in January of 2016, I was in Boston for a SABR meeting. I had never seen the site of the old South End Grounds, which is essentially seeing what hasn't been there for over 100 years. The *Boston Globe* on February 11, 1929, noted that the park, which even then was still referred to by its former name, the Walpole Street Grounds, was becoming a freight yard. "The old Walpole St. ball grounds," wrote the *Globe*, "of blessed memory to old Boston fans, is passing into oblivion." The *Globe* recounted the old names you will see in this book as well as the history of the park beyond the realm of these years. The park burned down in 1894, was rebuilt, then later was replaced by Braves Field in 1914. "Now it is all past and gone," the *Globe* lamented. "Where once the horsehide went whistling on its way over [the] left field fence the shifting engines will pant about playing their endless game over a network of rails."[19]

Today, the Ruggles Station subway trains also rumble through here, and the nearby Northeastern University keeps the area a continual high-traffic area. Besides a small plaque most would never notice, it is doubtful anyone today pauses to imagine what went on there. I tried to imagine Spalding on the mound and Harry Wright patrolling center field. I tried to imagine the fans crowding in to see their champion Red Stockings. But it was too cold, and too long ago.

We hope this book helps you to learn about Boston baseball in the 1870s, perhaps for the first time. Thanks to co-editor Bill Nowlin and a great team for putting this together, the stories of Boston's first nine.

Bob LeMoine
Co-editor

NOTES

1 William J. Ryczek, *Blackguards and Red Stockings: A History of the National Association, 1871-1875* (Wallingford, Connecticut: Colebrook Press, 1992), xi-xii.

2 Burton Whitman, "Young Braves Defeat Cubs, 5 to 2, in First Golden Jubilee Game," *Boston Herald*, May 9, 1925: 6.

3 Associated Press, "Old Timers Present. Players of Half Century Ago See Braves Defeat the Cubs," in the *St. Albans* [Vermont] *Daily Messenger*, May 9, 1925: 5.

4 "Little Change in Fifty Years, Old Brave and Ump Opine," *Boston Herald*, May 9, 1925: 6.

5 Ford Sawyer, "Veterans of Boston Teams of 70's At Golden Jubilee Celebration," *Boston Globe*, May 9, 1925: 8.

6 Ibid.

7 Ibid.

8 Ibid.

9 David Nemec, *The Great Encyclopedia of 19th Century Major League Baseball* (New York: David Fine Books, 1997), 10.

10 "Wright Is Dead. The Father of Professional Base Ball Called Out," *Sporting Life*, October 5, 1895: 3.

11 "Honor Wright. Memorial Fund Games in Many Cities," *Boston Globe*, April 14, 1896: 1.

12 "Memorial Sport. Games Played for the Wright Fund," *Boston Herald*, April 14, 1896: 3.

13 "Old 'Uns Played Pretty Good Ball," *Cincinnati Enquirer*, April 14, 1896: 2.

14 David Quentin Voigt, *American Baseball: From Gentleman's Sport to the Commissioner System* (Norman, Oklahoma: University of Oklahoma Press, 1966), 35-59.

15 Christopher Devine, *Harry Wright: The Father of Professional Base Ball* (Jefferson, North Carolina: McFarland & Co., 2003 [ebook edition]), 2.

16 Benjamin G. Rader, *Baseball: A History of America's Game* (Chicago: University of Illinois Press, 1994), 38-39.

17 John Thorn, "Our Game," in *Total Baseball*, 6th ed. (New York: Total Sports, 1999), 5.

18 Ryczek, 227.

19 "Walpole Street Grounds Passes," *Boston Globe*, February 11, 1929: 18.

WHEN BOSTON DOMINATED BASEBALL:

The Politics, Economics, & Leadership

BY MARK SOUDER

NOTHING OCCURS IN A VACUUM, not even in the green cathedrals of baseball. This is also true of the domination of the National Association of Professional Base Ball Players (NAPBBP) by the Boston Red Stockings. Baseball as we know it was created in New York, America's largest and richest city. Teams from Brooklyn and Philadelphia, the second and third largest cities of the era, competed with New York clubs in the domination of early baseball. So how did the Boston supplant the larger cities as well as the teams that dominated early baseball?

Baseball mirrors all of American society. Sustained success almost always is a combination of politics, money, and leadership wisely utilized by those in charge. Champions had been created before but with no reserve clauses, players constantly sought better opportunities. Boston now only held its powerful team together but improved, finishing in 1875 with a near "nuking" of the N.A.

This nearly total domination of the National Association by Boston required remarkable leadership in a turbulent time that was a combination of the competition outside Boston, the remarkable political and economic leaders of Boston who were united behind baseball, and the genius of Harry Wright in holding together a team of all-stars. A corollary question, in politics or baseball, is always: who did you beat? It doesn't diminish the success of the victor but helps understand why those victories are more impressive because the competition failed to achieve or attract the talent to win. Understanding the competitive context is also important to understanding Boston.

America in the early 1870s: The Challenges Facing All the Teams

There were a number of macro-issues challenging all baseball teams.

Fire

1871 was not a particularly noteworthy year in American history until fall. Then in October, Chicago burned. The fire began on the west side, then burned out the south side, the business core, and jumped the river to burn the north side. The courthouse, post office, major banks, the newspaper buildings, train stations, hotels, theaters, music halls and most commercial enterprises were annihilated. An estimated $180 million in damage was done, the coroner estimated 300 people had died, and 100,000 were homeless. Chicagoans bragged that it was so big that only the 1666 London Fire and Napoleon's burning of Moscow in 1812 could compare but "Chicago was twice as great as the total area destroyed by both of those fires."[1]

Chicago was the boom city of America, with railroads opening up agricultural and natural resources key to American growth. Boston was in the midst of a revival, trying to recapture its early leadership. Then on November 9, 1872 Boston caught fire.[2]

Chicagoans would point out that the Boston fire was far smaller than theirs. *Insureme.com* estimates the Great Chicago Fire loss at 2.9 billion in current dollars, the third most costly in American history, and the Great Boston Fire at sixth, costing 1.3 billion. The double shock of the back-to-back fires in Chicago and Boston stunned the insurance and finance industry in the U.S. which was centered in New York. I was a Congressman during the 9/11 disaster. Without action by Congress the industry could not have sustained the losses nor offered future coverage for terrorism. In 1872 the country did not have the equivalent gross domestic product or scale of government to stabilize the nation. The Panic of 1873 soon followed.

The Economic Panic of 1873

The Panic of 1873 was directly triggered by the collapse of Jay Cooke's bank in Philadelphia. Cooke had bailed out the Union Cause by selling bonds to maintain the northern forces on the fields of battle. He used his fame to secure funding for his ventures, including the proposed Northern Pacific Railroad. Other railroad lines also had been building rail capacity far beyond the ability to recover the investments. In 1872 the Credit Mobilier Scandal, involving bribes to Congress and massive fraud, wrecked the Administration of President Grant. In other words, the railroad chaos already had the financial markets reeling. Furthermore foreign investment, critical to growing America, was staggered by losses from the great fires and from the railroads. Capital became squeezed worldwide.[3]

Immigration

The immigration issue, and the politics of it (as well as the coming Irish domination of all of baseball), was only in its early stages in Boston. But it particularly engulfed the politics of New York, America's largest and richest city, during these years of the National Association and, along with the financial panic, destroyed its ability to consistently compete during this period despite its still overwhelming resources and population.

African-Americans and Reconstruction

The 1870s were a tumultuous transition period for American race relations. Reconstruction, the policy of federal military enforcement in the South to allow black voting and the beginnings of legal rights, was resisted by most (but not all) white southerners from the time it began. Opposition from southern sympathizers among northern Democrats who also opposed all rights for African-Americans, corruption rampant in Reconstruction, and lukewarm support among many northern Republicans of black rights beyond ending slavery all doomed the process by 1876. At this point in American history, looming industrialization had not yet resulted in massive migration north by former slaves so the large cities most impacted by the racial conflicts of the time were those nearest the Mason-Dixon Line (i.e. Philadelphia, Baltimore, and Washington).

Politics & Boston's Competition for Baseball Dominance

The baseball competitive environment can be summarized like this: 1) the major cities and 2) the others.

"The Others"

The "others" are handled most easily. Few investors were willing to gamble much money on the emerging professionalization of baseball, plus the smaller cities had a smaller resource base from which to draw. Thus they were referred to as "co-op" teams in which players were solely, or nearly totally dependent on revenue derived from game attendance to cover salaries and other expenses. They had no capital reserve.

Fort Wayne, Indiana; Rockford, Illinois; Middleton and New Haven, Connecticut; Elizabeth, New Jersey; Troy, New York; and Keokuk, Iowa were obviously just confident enough to begin a season but could not then or today compete with the largest cities in the nation. Even Washington DC, Hartford, and Cleveland did not yet have the resources or population to sustain real competition. The cities west of the Appalachian Mountains also had to deal with much higher costs of travel to go east (and even to play each other). Their smaller population size and less wealth also meant that the East Coast teams didn't like to play in those cities.

St. Louis was already a major city but lying west of the Mississippi in an East Coast League left it too isolated to be profitable. Two teams in 1875 began the change, but the Gateway to the West was not in factor in the N.A.

Chicago

In 1871, the championship competition was three-way among Chicago, Philadelphia and Boston.

Chicago then burned. In 1872 and 1873 they did not field a team. The powerful business establishment became pre-occupied with rebuilding Chicago. When Chicago returned for 1874 and 1875, they were decent but not yet as good. Both seasons they were just under a .500 team. Of course in 1876 Chicago led the creation of the National League and Major League Baseball as we know it today. But in the National Association, after the Great Chicago Fire, it wasn't competition to Boston dominance.

Baltimore

Baltimore, on the other hand, was America's sixth largest city, slightly larger than an unconsolidated Boston, but had never been dominant in the American psyche. Perhaps the War of 1812, when Frances Scott Key wrote the Star Spangled Banner while watching the harbor burn, was its high point. Babe Ruth grew up there but left. Edgar Allen Poe wrote poetry, which provided a great name for Baltimore's future NFL team. Symbolically, Baltimore was always a city with a harbor almost as good as the competition

German and Irish immigrant power was just ahead in Baltimore history, which ultimately impacted its politics and improved its baseball (e.g. Boss Sonny Mahon, Harry Von der Horst). But during the National Association era the powerful political duo of Arthur Gorman (a post-Civil War baseball pioneer) and Issac Raynor Rasin was just beginning to consolidate power in the Maryland Legislature and city of Baltimore. In 1872 the Democrat National Convention was held in Baltimore but the Party was still in disarray.

Baltimore, with its harbor and the resultant importance of railroads (especially the Baltimore & Ohio), was heavily influenced by the early form of black gold: coal. Ralph Waldo Emerson had referred to coal as "portable climate" in his book *Wealth*. Coal enabled industry to move beyond dependence on water falls for power.[4] Thus it is not surprising that coal dealer Robert C. Hall was the first President and organizer of the stock sales for the Lord Baltimores. They raised sufficient funds to field an all-professional team luring back home star pitcher Bobby Mathews from Fort Wayne.[5]

Baltimore baseball historian James Bready notes that the team was plagued by rumors of game-fixing. Team President Hall did not seem to be significant part of the Baltimore power structure, though he was a leader in the horse racing establishment. Pimlico Race Course opened in 1870, with the Preakness Stakes beginning in 1873 (second-leg of the famous Triple Crown of horse racing). Horse racing, gambling, and "fixing" have always been closely tied, as has boxing. Baltimore's Bobby Mathews, one of baseball's greatest pitchers, is still not in Baseball's Hall of Fame likely because of his links to infamous game fixing in Baltimore and New York.

Baseball, with prominent early examples like New York's John Morrissey, struggled for decades to separate itself from those popular sports of the era as a "clean game." Baltimore didn't help.

New York

New York had multiple problems that kept it, and Brooklyn, from providing consistent competition to Boston. As noted earlier, Chicago Fire followed by the Boston Fire nearly wiped out the insurance industry centered in New York City. This, followed by the financial collapses in the Panic of 1873, short-circuited any New York City financial advantages. The political and business powers were pre-occupied with things far more significant to the future of New York. Furthermore, still NYC was so large, it was never as obsessed with its marketing image as were the cities that tried to compete with it. New York knew it was the biggest.

The politics of New York City were particularly brutal during the N.A. era. Boss Tweed, the original godfather of the New York Mutuals baseball team, was under intense investigation during this period. His political world began to fall apart in 1871. In 1873 he first avoided conviction but in the November retrial Tweed was convicted on 204 of 220 counts. He escaped to Europe. In 1876 he returned to New York and prison.

In 1872 to replace Tweed, the aforementioned John Morrissey—infamous former head of the Dead Rabbits Gang, champion boxer, Congressman, baseball game fixer, former financier of the Troy Haymakers (who just happened to fold that year with some players going to the Mutuals) and still notorious gambler—emerged as co-leader of Tammany Hall with John Kelly. Through his connections with Cornelius Vanderbilt and others, Morrissey had become a somewhat respectable gambler and politician as opposed to a fascinating but crooked thug.

New York was still New York, the largest city, the center of finance, home to the most powerful media, and the original home of "New York" baseball. In other words, New York City was hardly irrelevant to baseball. Three years of star pitcher Bobby Mathews, and one from Candy Cummings, kept them near the top. But during the N.A., a simple fact stands out: New York City could not topple Boston or the Philadelphia teams. In the five years their record against Boston was 12-30 (skewed by their 0-10 futility in 1875) and 31-34 against the three teams from Philadelphia. They were never quite good enough. You could bet on it.

Brooklyn

Brooklyn was an even more tangled mess. During this period Hugh McLaughlin was the Democrat political boss who dominated Brooklyn politics. He was both an internal rival to and ally of Manhattan Tammany before NYC consolidated. The bridge was completed in 1883, after the Tammany rings on both sides were paid off. It is little wonder that the baseball teams in Brooklyn were not necessarily known for probity during this era (obviously the Manhattan teams weren't either). The major institutions were corrupt so it is not surprising that the baseball teams weren't models of good behavior. During the era of the National Association, neither city could muster any sustained baseball threat, or consistent integrity even by the lower standards of the time.

Philadelphia

Philadelphia was the primary, consistent competitive threat to Boston. If Boston's moment as the center of America's political universe was pre-Revolutionary War through the abandonment of Boston by the British, Philadelphia's dominant moments were from 1776 to 1787, when the Constitution was completed. From that time on, Philadelphia—like Boston—had periods of time when it dominated a category such as baseball but like Boston, it was mostly in New York's shadow. Boston just complained about it more whereas Philadelphia seemed more resigned to its fate.

In the 1870s, however, Philadelphia was hoping for resurgence. Heading toward 1876 even Independence Hall was getting a makeover. The clout of Philadelphia is illustrated by the fact that two other Philadelphia teams were still playing in 1875. Philadelphia had split into two teams in 1873. They literally split, with the White Stockings taking five of the nine top players. The Athletics continued as a top team because they retained a core of pitcher Dick McBride, Al Reach, and Cap Anson with Elias "Hicks" Hayhurst as its leader.

So why, in the 1870s, did Philadelphia split whereas Boston did not? The racial divide we alluded to earlier became ground zero in Philadelphia during the Reconstruction Era until its demise in 1876. The politics were intense in these major cities of the era, but Philadelphia was the only one where black/white controversy split the city.

In the fall of 1871, the year the National Association was organized, a local black educator and civil rights leader Octavius Cato was gunned down on the first election day in which newly-enfranchised African-American voters were going to have a major determination in selecting the new Mayor. In other words, the Republicans were going to win if they voted. Two local Democrat Party henchmen assassinated Catto and were aided in escaping town. Catto was also a Republican Ward leader and the head of the famous black Philadelphia Pythians baseball team.

This tumult from 1871 to 1876 spilled into Philadelphia baseball very directly. The Republican Ring, dominated by powerful gas interests, ruled the city. Mayor William Stokely governed the city during the era of the NA. Among the loyal Republican Ring city councilmen was Hicks Hayhurst, who also was appointed head of the Police Committee. It oversaw the cleaning up the police department which had been at least partly responsible for killing Hayhurst's friend Catto. Dick McBride, the star pitcher of the

Athletics, was also a political appointee who had a "flexible" job in the city clerk's office.[6]

Philadelphia's sparring Republican factions (Athletics leaders Col. Thomas Fitzgerald and Hayhurst earlier divided the Athletics over this issue) appeared prevent Philadelphia from becoming an equal competitor to Boston except in 1871 season which was prior to the tumult exploding in gunfire. It may, in fact, have helped fuel the internal rivalry as well as the opportunity to earn revenue through intra-city competition. What is clear is that the Boston Red Stockings traveled to England with the Athletics in 1874. In other words, Boston was aligned with the traditional Republican power team of Philadelphia.

When one analyzes the competition, it makes the astounding consistent success of the Boston Red Stockings even more extraordinary.

The Wright Brothers' Flight to Boston

It is not without some irony that Boston in the early 1770s was the cradle of American liberty, with the Adams family among the leaders in the early events that led to the creation of our Republic, and then in the early 1870s that Boston led the early stages of the professional of our National Pastime. It could be argued Boston, along with Philadelphia, pulled the rest of America along in both ventures.

It is also clear that in both revolutions, the keys were talent and leadership. And politics, both of the traditional kind and the Harry Wright version. In fact, Harry Wright may have been the best "politician" in that era as he worked with local leaders to keep his team together through fire, economic panic, and change that roiled the rest of the nation.

Harry Wright was a cricket player but America wasn't England. The New York style of baseball began to be widely played, accelerated by young men with idle time between the Civil War bloodbaths. Younger brother George Wright, the more skilled player, was wooed to the Washington Nationals with a government "job." The Nationals 1867 Western Tour was tremendously successful, as the Nationals defeated the greatest power of the West, the Cincinnati Red Stockings headed by Harry. Their only defeat was the result of great pitching in Chicago by Albert Spalding.

The Cincinnati Red Stockings were the most powerful example of a young leader's organization that decided to contract with players to help promote a City's image while hopefully also making money for the owners. Or perhaps the goals were the other way around, but there were dual goals.

The Nationals were actually a professional team as well, just a government-subsidized one. Cincinnati was the first private sector professional team. Harry convinced his brother to join him in Cincinnati (along with Asa Brainerd) as Washington politics broke up the Nationals. The Cincinnati club owners were the rising sons of many of the Cincinnati political, media and economic power structure. Most of them were already successful but their relatives even more so, and their own careers were rapidly rising. Baseball was not their focus.

Harry Wright used touring, both in the West and the East, to achieve multiple goals including to earn revenue, promote Cincinnati and the Red Stockings, provide attractive travel to players who otherwise would not have had financial resources like the upper classes, and to recruit (i.e. poach) other players. He also, obviously, had his eye open for other opportunities if things went bad in Cincinnati. Things did go bad in Cincinnati: after two years of conquering American baseball. The owners of the club didn't make money, to hold the top players Wright insisted they needed more not less money, and the leaders decided they could make more money and promote Cincinnati in better ways than baseball. Their great rival Chicago soon soared past it in standing, though likely it would have happened even if Ohio had held onto the first set of Wright brothers.

A key part of the story is a match the Red Stockings played in Boston to a large crowd of 2,000 people on the Boston Commons. Wright, like most Americans who traveled and followed the news, already realized that Boston was undergoing a major overhaul and revival. He could also see that, in spite of the crowd for the Cincinnati game and the successful amateur baseball teams in the city, the Boston Commons was not suited for professional baseball. Harry Wright's biographer, Christopher Devine explained what happened this way:

> "The Boston Common was primarily used for Boston games because it was the only level grounds that could hold a large crowd. But because it was public property, permission was needed to play on it. Before play began in May 1869, the Common was rendered unusable for ball playing, leaving the Boston clubs to find new grounds. Delegates of city ballclubs decided eventually to build a field in the South End in an ideally accessible field location. In the fall of 1869, all city government candidates in favor of improving the field, generically christened the Union Grounds, won their races, defeating all the candidates opposed.[7]

The political battles in the election of 1869 were not just about baseball but rather part of a continuum of progressive change by an aggressive new emerging leadership in the Boston area that had decided to remake the city. The principal annexations that created today's Boston were done from 1868 to 1874, with the most important being Roxbury in 1868 and Dorchester in 1870.[8] The political goal of the Roxbury and Dorchester annexations was to give Boston further room for expansion, more area for improved housing as opposed to the downtown density, and green space for parks and community development. In the late 1850s a decision had been made to proceed with a massive landfill project to turn the Back Bay area into usable land. Land sales proceeded into the 1860s and 1870s. In 1870 when Oliver Wendell Holmes vacated his Beacon Hill for a Back Bay residence, he labeled his abandonment of the old house "a case of justifiable domicide."[9]

The building of the South End Grounds was the beginning of a larger park vision that won nationwide media attention. America's most first landscape engineering firm was founded by Frederick Law Olmstead in Boston. Olmstead had developed the most of the famous city parks in America including Central Park in New York. As the newly expanded Boston developed its green space, Olmstead conceived Boston's famed "emerald necklace" of connected parks. The South End Grounds were near the southeastern end.

In the midst of the progressive Boston revival, of which baseball domination was about to become another prong, was an extraordinary event never again repeated in American history except for a second, less dramatic effort in Boston. The annexations, the landfills, and the parks development had been also part of a cultural push in Boston. This period also led to expansion and creation of educational institutions and new cultural leadership including the creation of Boston's famed Museum of Fine Arts in 1870.

An Irish immigrant named Patrick S. Gilmore conceived the idea of a National Peace Jubilee and Music Festival to be held in Boston in 1869. His dream was big. The constructed wooden facility, located around Copley Square including the land where the Fairmont Copley Plaza Hotel is now located, could hold 50,000 people and was the largest structure in the country.[10] Gilmore's plan was not to display new manufacturing breakthroughs or discoveries like the Ferris wheel or ice cream: he organized a five-day music festival.

It wasn't just any music festival. It featured classical music including the "anvil chorus" with a hundred firemen striking anvils, the William Tell Overture and the Messiah. Patriotic, religious and children's days were included. There was an orchestra of 1,000 and a chorus of 10,000. President U.S. Grant attended, in spite of memorably stating that he only knew two tunes, "One is Yankee Doodle and the other one isn't." The incredible success and fame of the Jubilee solidified Gilmore's place in history as the father of concert music.[11]

But it is one thing to conceive an idea as a dream, and quite another to make it happen. Gilmore was hardly an unknown at the time he proposed the massive, unprecedented undertaking. He was the director of the Boston Brass Band which organized the first large American concerts, the forerunner of the Boston Pops. Gilmore is nationally recognized as the father of concert bands. At the outbreak of the Civil War in 1861, Gilmore and his band joined the Massachusetts 22nd Regiment. He was became the bandmaster of the

Union Army (and also served, for example, as stretcher bearers at the Battle of Gettysburg). Gimore is a famed songwriter whose inspirational music included the most famous Union tune of the Civil War, "When Johnny Comes Marching Home." He is also credited with putting to music a tune he heard a Union soldier singing known as "John Brown's Body." Julia Ward Howe rewrote the lyrics, now known as "The Battle Hymn of the Republic."[12]

Gilmore worked the press, and pounded on doors trying to raise funds for the Jubilee. Finally, as the date drew alarmingly close, Eben Jordan, the co-founder and leader of the rising (and soon to be nationally famous) retailer Jordan, Marsh & Company, decided to go "all in" with Gilmore. Jordan agreed to be treasurer, then organized community leaders and raised the necessary funds. Without Eben Jordan, Boston today would be a different city. In 1873 a 27-year old Civil War colonel, young Republican politician named Charles Taylor purchased a struggling small newspaper named the *Boston Globe*. During the panic of 1873, every stockholder but Eben Jordan pulled out. Jordan saved Taylor and the *Globe*. Taylor and his son later became the first Boston owners of the American League's Red Sox.[13]

Professional baseball came to Boston because of everything else that was happening. Everything else didn't happen because of baseball. The rising leadership, many of whom played baseball on the Boston area clubs themselves or were fans, saw the opportunity to make baseball a part of making Boston a nationally celebrated city as well as a better place to live.

When Harry Wright walked into the Parker House (now the Omni Parker House), it was already the distinguished hotel for the elite of Boston. Internationally celebrated writer Charles Dickens had made it his Boston residence for five months just two years earlier. Even Boston Cream pie originated there. It was also Boston's political hangout since it was located right across from City Hall and near the state capitol building. Wright likely felt important just walking into the hotel.

The Boston new ballpark was essential but Wright also needed to know whether the proposed ownership would provide the financial resources to not only keep his preferred Cincinnati players together but also hire additional stars (in particular, raiding Chicago). Wright also wanted more control. To establish this, Wright needed to meet the proposed leadership and look them in the eyes to see if there was enough clout, as well as the commitment to sustain a team. After what happened in to him Cincinnati Wright wanted some stability.

When he met the men in the room, he had to be impressed just as they were with him. It wasn't just the influential young men of Boston often the sons of political leaders or business titans (like in Cincinnati), but also present were the powers behind them. Through the hindsight of history we can now understand just how extraordinary this group was because these men in Boston were the cutting edge of a transfer of power from the classic elite of America to a much more diversified mix of leadership committed to remaking American cities and commerce which included annexation, parks, and improved governmental services like decent sewers and water.

Who Were These Merchant Kings & Politicos Behind Boston Baseball?

It is unclear how the introductions were handled at the initial meeting with Harry Wright. Henry Lillie Pierce perhaps was the first introduced because he was a twofer: a merchant king and a powerful politician. His father had been a state legislator, and Pierce served multiple terms in the 1860s. When his home of Dorchester was annexed into Boston, Pierce was elected Mayor of the newly consolidated Boston in 1872. Thus at this meeting, it was likely that people in the room likely knew that Pierce had a very good chance to be the political king at the City Hall across the street the next year. In fact, it is likely that they were a key impetus behind putting him there.

After a one-year term as mayor, Pierce was elected to Congress for two terms. In 1877 he left Congress to again seek, and win, the Mayor's office. In other words, during the years of the National Association, Pierce was the Boston Mayor at the beginning and end, and was the Congressman during the years in between.

But Henry Lillie Pierce was first a chocolate man, as in building up Baker Chocolate Company into one of the most famous chocolate companies in America. Baker won the highest awards for chocolate and cocoa at the Vienna Exposition in 1873 and in Philadelphia at the 1876 Centennial. The company existed until 1927 when it was absorbed into General Foods, and then became part of Kraft. In other words, it was a stable product and company.[14]

Pierce was a powerful man in politics and business. He wasn't the son of a politician, like the Cincinnati group. He was a real one. So was attendee Charles Augustus Burditt, who was an active Republican leader and member of the Boston Common Council.

While Pierce was the pre-eminent politician present, everyone present also knew who Eben Jordan was. Jordan was not just known to them as the successful retailer but as the financial man behind the nationally famous and profitable Peace and Music Jubilee two years earlier. In fact, those present included Alderman and businessman Edward Augustus White, who had played a prominent role in the Jubilee. So did attendee James Horatio Freeland. John C. Haynes—later treasurer of the Red Stockings—worked for the music business of Oliver Ditson, later becoming the president of Oliver Ditson & Co. Ditson was on the Jubilee Executive and the Finance committee with Jordan. The firm Burditt & North, of which Councilman Charles A. Burditt was a senior partner, were managers of the Boston Symphony and in some contemporary articles Burditt was personally listed as the "popular manager." These music supporters all worked in concert, so to speak.[15]

To a significant degree, the established financial powers present at the initial baseball meeting suggest that it was a re-convening of the Jubilee leaders who were joined by younger, rising baseball enthusiasts (much like Jubilee organizer Gilmore was a music enthusiast). These leaders backed "enthusiasts" who could promote Boston.

Perhaps Frank George Webster was introduced next. He was a financial power and a leader of Kidder, Peabody & Co. In the book *Gentlemen Bankers*, the firm is described as having reached prominence "during the railroad boom of the late 1870s."[16] "Kidder, Peabody participated in the postwar funding of treasury short-term obligations in the 1870s."[17] In other words, we earlier noted that the Chicago and Boston fires, plus the over-building by many railroads had resulted in the Panic of 1873, which had been triggered by bank closings and shortages of capital. Kidder, Peabody & Co helped "bail out" the federal government by buying treasury notes. It is one of the more effective ways to accumulate political power. Webster was a formidable force behind the Red Stockings ownership. These men were able to pull lots of strings and made financial and political deals together beyond just promoting Boston. They logically viewed the success of Boston and their personal success as one and the same.

In the 19th Century, especially during this baseball transition when some teams were backed by young men's clubs, some by governments, and some by opportunistic investors hoping to make a quick buck—not to mention gamblers—the good teams came and went. In most cities, an event like the Boston Fire would have finished off baseball. Chicago, with an admittedly bigger fire, took years to recover. The Economic Panic of 1873 finished off others. The combination sent Boston reeling as well. The follow-up economic crisis (and opportunity for others) distracted some of this first group. First year President Ivers Adams, for example, withdrew as leader when his firm was pummeled by the fire. The Red Stockings themselves had income drop precipitously in 1872 and their survival was threatened. But Boston survived. The owners reorganized and proceeded ahead. Their collective goal was to make Boston dominant and they did.

The Red Stockings Presidents

In the five years of the National Association, the Boston Red Stockings had four Presidents—Ivers Adams in 1871, John Conkey in 1872, Charles Porter in 1873, and Nicholas Taylor Apollonio. The frequency of change would seem to suggest instability but other facts illustrate why the franchise kept increasingly its dominance, as opposed to collapsing.

Ivers Whitney Adams has a name that fits well with the Cabots, Lodges, and Saltonstalls of WASP domination but actually Ivers's father was a carpenter in rural Ashburnham. Ivers Adams never attended college. He was not those Adamses.[18]

Ivers Adams was a rising retail merchant, a profession built upon personal salesmanship especially back when there were not yet dominant chain stores. John H. Pray, Sons & Company was a significant retailer in downtown Boston. It was founded in 1817. Eben Jordan of the classic Boston retail institution Jordan Marsh did not begin in the retail jobbing business until 1851, over thirty years later. An article in the *Cambridge Tribune* in 1892 refers to Pray & Sons as the finest firm in the carpets trade, also noting its wholesale business and widespread reputation.[19]

Boston was an important carpet market in the 1870s, having "always enjoyed a large scale of the Mediterranean trade (e.g. Turkish and Persian carpets). An 1877 *Carpet Trade Review* states that John H. Pray, Sons & Co took over much of the business from the earliest founders of the trade. John H. Pray "was a gentleman of courtly presence" who was "ably seconded by his two sons John A. and William H., who in connection with Mr. I.W. Adams, still retain the old style of the firm." (In business, if you read between the lines, the father felt Adams was needed to oversee things, not just his sons.) When American carpet production (as opposed to imported rugs) began with the introduction of "Lowell" and "Bigelow," the Pray firm became the promoter and wholesaler of those brands across the United States.[20]

Erastus B. Bigelow of Lowell was the most important individual in the creation of the American carpet industry including not only the manufacturing but the key patents to make carpets. Bigelow carpets greeted the first baseball meeting invitees to the Parker House in Boston, as well as top establishments across America including the Capitol, the Senate, the U.S. House of Representatives and the White House.[21]

The early textile industry was centered in Boston and New England, as Americans desired more control and cheaper goods than imports from England. Carpet was a logical outgrowth from the textile industry. Most of the industry moved to the Carolinas and then to Asia, but the Lowell National Historic Site is the primary historic resource of the National Park Service to highlight early American manufacturing. Canal Place I at the historic park is the largest of the Bigelow/Lowell buildings still standing.[22] The importance here is to note that Ivers Adams was a leader in what was then the most important regional manufacturing industry as well in national commerce and international trade. He wasn't just a baseball guy.

Adams was the original organizer but the Boston fire caused him to focus with the survival of the John H. Pray & Co. at that point, not the baseball team. He was the leader of the Red Stockings for only one year but Adams set up the ownership team.

John Conkey succeeded Adams in 1872. Conkey was 32 when he attended the baseball organizing meeting in Boston. When in his twenties, he became a partner in a business that focused on the China trade business of the powerful Augustine Heard & Company. Heard had settled in Canton, China in 1830 where he was a partner of the Samuel Russell & Co, the leading American opium dealer in China (among other things). Heard eventually formed his own firm with partners John Coolidge and, most significantly, financial powerhouse John Murray Forbes. It became the third largest American firm dealing with China.

Forbes was also an active politician. He was an abolitionist and early Republican leader who provided funding and support to Abraham Lincoln and Union causes during the War. His son married the daughter of Mr. New England, writer Ralph Waldo Emerson.[23] One of his ancestors, John Forbes Kerry, became a United States Senator from Massachusetts, a Presidential candidate, and United States Secretary of State.[24]

The economic problems drove the Augustine Heard & Company Chinese trading business into bankruptcy by 1875, which resulted in Conkey losing his business. He re-organized it at that time but it is highly likely that the events including the Boston (and Chicago fires of 1872) were already squeezing the capital markets. 1872 had also been a bad year for the Red Stockings revenues, forcing a re-organization and supplemental capitalization of the team. The combination of issues, but likely more the economic problems of his own business, resulted in Conkey serving just one year. The next President had also been part of the original group, suggesting that it was a re-organization as opposed to a revolution.

Charles Hunt Porter was directly involved in the activities of the Base Ball Club, having played and organized the Quincy Actives baseball club the decade before. One of the final pieces in making the Red Stockings so dominant was the adding of James "Deacon" White. Porter was personally involved in signing White in Corning, New York the year White had become "church struck." White, according to Porter, was a "clerical-looking man with a tall hat" but Porter recognized that White was the sought after catcher because of a smashed finger and his hard-looking hands. Having a skilled catcher in the days before the invention of full gloves and all the protective equipment was essential to sustained success.[25]

Porter, like many of the other Boston leaders (and a high percentage of young leaders across the nation) had been an officer during the Civil War. Porter's hometown, Quincy, was the home of the distinguished Adams family, including Presidents John Adams and his son John Quincy Adams (JQA). During the 1870s Charles Francis Adams Sr. (JQA's son) was a national leader in the abolitionist movement. Porter could not have been involved in education, park and water department issues—eventually becoming the Quincy's first mayor—without intense political involvement since Quincy would obviously have been ground zero of many of the intense conflicts as they played out in Massachusetts led by Charles Frances Adams. Porter, like the other young leaders, loved baseball but had a career of increasing importance outside of baseball.

Before moving to the fourth Red Stockings President in four years, it is worthwhile to again note some continuity of leadership amongst the change. The *Boston Post* story about the annual meeting of the 1874 Boston Base Ball Club meeting notes the Treasurer's annual report given by John C. Haynes, who was re-elected to that post for 1875. Haynes, as earlier noted, was a leader in the Oliver Ditson music company that had been closely connected to the Boston Jubilee.[26]

Another key transition figure—Arthur Soden—was elected to the Board of Directors of the Club at the same meeting. Soden had been drafted into the Union Army in July, 1863. He was a hospital steward in the 22nd Massachusetts Regiment.[27] This was the same Regiment to which Patrick Gilmore, creator of the Jubilee, and his Boston Band belonged. As noted earlier, the Boston band had helped man the hospital stretchers at major battles. It is not clear that Gilmore met Soden, but it is quite the coincidence nevertheless. Soden was also a young baseball enthusiast, who in 1876 led the takeover of the Red Stockings when they joined the National League. Again, in Boston there was change but continuity in leadership.

Nicholas Taylor Apollonio held the Presidency of the Boston Club for the longest period during the National Association years, though that is not saying all that much. It is impossible to separate Nicholas from his father Nicholas A. (N. A.) Apollonio. The younger Apollonio was a comparative unknown, while his father was a prominent government official. Nicholas worked as a clerk in his father's office, and only has a track record of other jobs later in his life, including, interestingly, working with foreign trade with China. He was defined by this father more than himself, except for baseball. He, like many of the other younger key leaders of the Red Stockings was not just club President but also a baseball fan who enjoyed playing the game.

N.A. Apollonio was elected as Registrar for Boston by the Alderman and City Council (the process varied over the years). The position is among the first listed in city government sections of Boston directories, and was among the best paid. The Registrar was the superintendent of burial grounds and funerals and was responsible for records of the births, deaths and marriages as well as granting certificates for intentions of marriage.[28] N. A. Apollonio earned $3000/year from 1872 to 1876. In 1870 the average worker in manufacturing and construction made an estimated $378/year according to the Bureau of Economic Research.[29]

In other words, the Apollonios were not among the very rich typical of the more senior part of the Red Stockings leadership, nor were they going to become as wealthy as most of the others in the group, but they were in an economic class—the political class - far above most citizens of the time. Government leadership minus graft did not lead to great wealth, but it did lead to a very comfortable life. The Registrar received a budget for clerks approximately equal to his salary. It varied by year. Assistants were added after annexations and as the city grew. His son Nicholas's salary as a clerk was clearly very good but far short of his father's. In other words, he was not a potential dominant financial owner of the team.

Both Apollonios have gone down in American history as unique contributors to Italian-American history: the father was the first Bostonian of Italian heritage to hold a high-profile political position and the son was the first Italian to have a significant position in professional baseball. After his death in 1891, N. A. Apollonio was described as having taken "a great interest in all the affairs of the Italians in our community, which grew out of a love for his father, who was Italian by birth." For his first job, young N.A. Apollonio left his family in Connecticut for New York City. In the 1840s he was a contributor to the *Spirit of the Times* (one of the first newspapers to cover sports, including early baseball) which was owned by the company that also reprinted the British newspaper *Albion* for American subscribers. His skills led to his being hired by the Rev. J.F. Himes in 1845 to print the *Advent Herald* in Boston.[30]

The Advent was not your typical newspaper. It was the publisher for the Seventh Day Adventist Church. Rev. Himes was the best friend of William Miller, to whom the sect traces its founding. There was a problem in 1845 when N. A. Apollonio was hired, since Miller had identified the Church with the prophecy that Jesus Christ would return no later than October 22, 1844.[31] The Church's focal points were reconfigured, and abolitionism became one of its identifiable missions.

N. A. Apollonio was at the very center of the movement in Boston. In 1848 he was selected as a member of the City Committee core of the Free Soil Party of Boston, on which he remained until 1854 when he was elected to public office.[32] In 1848, the year Apollonio joined its leadership, Charles Francis Adams, Sr. of Quincy was selected as the Free Soil Party's candidate for Vice-President of the United States.

In the years prior to the Civil War, the northern states were divided between those who focused on keeping the United States unified (such as Daniel Webster of Massachusetts) and those who demanded abolition of slavery (such as William Lloyd Garrison of Boston). Anti-immigration and anti-Catholic sentiment (roughly the same thing for the next 80 years) caused further chaos. Massachusetts was ground zero in this conflict.

The Know-Nothing Party was a northern coalition of anti-immigrant, anti-Catholic, anti-alcohol, and anti-slavery parties. (Its name arose from its members answering "I know nothing" when asked about their "secret" organization.)[33] Their overwhelming sweep of Massachusetts in 1854 was not matched in any other state. The Governor, all state officials, the entire state senate, and all but three state representatives were elected as Know Nothings. However, Adams and others such as Wendell Phillips who focused primarily on abolitionism spoke out against the Know Nothings. Adams, for example, said their program was "immoral" and "antisocial."[34]

In 1854, when the Know Nothings were about to sweep the state, the incumbent Boston registrar died. C. H. Brainard as well as other unidentified friends of Apollonio encouraged him to seek the office. Apollonio won. Since Brainard was the only ally cited, it raises the obvious question: who was Brainard? He was prominent in Boston and beyond in the printing and artistic community. He is most remembered for his lithograph of abolitionist leaders titled "Heralds of Freedom."[35] Included among the portraits were Garrison, Phillips, Theodore Parker, and Ralph Waldo Emerson. It was publicized and sold throughout the nation.[36] Clearly Apollonio was put forward by the abolitionists, and his political success was tied to them.

The Know Nothing Party soon fell apart. In Massachusetts the Whigs had already split between the "Cotton Whigs" (i.e. tied to the textile industry dependent upon southern cotton) and "Conscience Whigs" (i.e. abolitionists tied to Adams and Apollonio's allies). The Free Soil Party and the Conscience Whigs were wiped out by the Know Nothings. The Conscience Whigs/Free Soil remnant were the early core of the Republican Party that backed John Fremont for President in 1856, Nathaniel Banks as the first Republican Governor in 1858, and John Andrew's election in 1860 as the second Governor of Massachusetts. Brainard, Apollonio's sponsor, helped promote Andrew with another widely dispersed lithograph.[37]

The Apollonio family was part of the fabric of the Free Soil and abolitionist movement, not a shiny button added for decoration. In fact, a quick review illustrates the depth of the connections to abolitionism among key leaders. Nicholas Apollonio was the fourth and longest serving Red Stockings President during the National Association years. The third President, Charles Porter, was a politician from Quincy, dominated by Charles Francis Adams, Sr. The second President, John Conkey, career began with and continued to be tied to Free Soil leader and Republican Party founder John Murray Forbes. And the first President was Ivers Whitney Adams, from a different branch of the Adams family but clearly comfortable working with the abolitionist leadership. The most powerful politician in the original meeting, Henry Lillie Pierce, was a fierce abolitionist. He served as Mayor of Boston during part of the NA years, and as the Congressman representing Boston during the other years.

We previously discussed how the National Peace Jubilee and Music Festival of 1869 knit together the Red Stockings key leadership. Of course the "peace" being celebrated was the triumph of the North, which resulted in the abolition of slavery. Even the original musical connection was anchored in politics. John Andrew, second Republican Governor (who Apollonio's sponsor Brainard promoted), was responsible for enlisting Jubilee founder Patrick Gilmore in the 24th Massachusetts regiment specifically to reorganize military music making. The first Republican Governor, Nathaniel Banks, was one of the first major generals appointed by President Abraham Lincoln. General Banks then chose Gilmore not just to reorganize music for Massachusetts regiments but named him bandmaster for the entire Union Army.[38] "It's a small world" isn't just a theme song for a Disney attraction.

While Apollonio remained interested in the team after he left the Club's Presidency, as shown by his continued correspondence with Harry Wright, Apollonio did not have the wealth to continue in the position. He had interest but no power. Boston joined the new National League. A revitalized Chicago franchise hired away many of the Red Stockings stars. Boston began bleeding a different kind of red: red ink. But it is also true that by 1876 many other things had radically changed. It is unclear why the businessmen who had quietly funded the team disappeared, but there were likely multiple reasons including the successful establishment of baseball as a promotional tool for Boston. Others had significantly advanced in their business careers. Politics, however, is seldom not a factor.

1876 was one of the most politically tumultuous in American history. The Presidential candidate who won the popular vote lost in the Electoral College by a single vote because of a deal that resulted in the end of Reconstruction in the South. In Massachusetts Charles Francis Adams Sr. ran as a Democrat for Governor, and other abolitionists flipped parties as well. N. A. Apollonio survived as Registrar of Boston by a single vote, the only serious challenge in his long career. One of the few who publicly defended him, seemingly incongruently given past history, was Democrat Alderman Hugh O'Brien. O'Brien was elected the first Irish mayor of Boston in 1884.[39] The Red Stockings changes may have been more than just about money but this book is about the National Association years of 1871-1875, not 1876 and beyond.

There is one more relevant footnote to the founding meeting of the National League. William Hulbert of Chicago was the organizer of the NL. He wanted the first President to be from the East. In the 1850s, when the Aetna Insurance Company was becoming a national power in the industry, it was led by Eliphalet Bulkeley. Eliphalet was a Free Soil leader and one of the founders of the Republican Party. On his Aetna board was the Boston abolitionist and Apollonio political sponsor, C. H. Brainard. Eliphalet's son

Morgan and N. A's son Nicholas—the sons of leading abolitionists and early Republican leaders—were the two most influential Eastern owners. Apollonio turned the position down.[40] Bulkeley, who historically is more famous as a politician than as a baseball man, was chosen as the first National League President and ultimately as a member of Baseball's Hall of Fame.

To adapt a famous expression, in politics "what you know" (e.g. abolitionism) leads to "who you know."

Money & Love: Other Ways Boston Held Its Stars

Baseball, Boston & Liverpool

While the geographical and ancestral connections between Boston and Liverpool, England are superficially obvious due to the importance of U.S. and British oceanic trade in the 1870s. Powerful British political leader William Gladstone was born in Liverpool and served his first term as Prime Minister of the United Kingdom during this period from late 1868 to 1874. Liverpool was the primary port city and fought for financial independence from London, before London achieved dominance by 1900.[41]

Massachusetts was the penultimate English colony in the early settlement of North America, though Boston had led the revolt against England during the Revolution. After the United States was created, New England became staunchly Federalist and its leaders were once again known as "Anglophobes."

The financial center of the United States was first Philadelphia and ultimately moved to New York City, but Boston's strategic port, manufacturing industries and connections to England meant that it continued as a critical conduit for British investment in the United States. The European economy did not offer the dramatic financial gain (or risk) that was present in America. At the cusp of the industrial revolution, one industry that boomed was insurance.

The insurance expansion in the 1860s and 1870s in England was not led by London but Liverpool. A British researcher noted that it "accounted 1/5 of the home fire market in 1869, the last year that fire duty, the tax that obligingly measured that market, was levied. Two of the four largest British fire insurers were Liverpool companies. Their exploits in promoting the enormous insurance trade to the U.S.A. were far more dashing than anything achieved in London." Royal Insurance of Liverpool (later Royal Globe) was the most important of those firms.[42]

It is clear that it wasn't just the baseball salaries that kept the stars in Boston. Wright held together the team in many ways. Boston's baseball fame was obviously personal point of pride and had marketable value. But pride, as is true today in baseball, only goes so far in replacing cash. But players took pay cuts and freezes partly because, as noted, the competition wasn't in great shape either. Boston also offered opportunities beyond baseball, including supplemental employment.

Boston's most essential players were Spalding and the Wright Brothers. William Ryczek has noted that in 1874, "the pitcher (Albert Spalding), along with George and Harry Wright, were passing the winter months as clerks in the office of Foster and Cole, agents for the Royal Liverpool Insurance Company, to supplement the $1,800 salary each earned during the baseball season."[43]

The national insurance newspaper of the United States in 1872 included this item: "Foster & Cole, 15 Devonshire Street, Boston; Marine and Fire Insurance Effected in First Class Companies, in Boston, New York and Philadelphia. Losses adjusted and paid in Boston. Geo E. Foster; Chas H. Cole; Gideon Scull; July 1, 1872."[44]

A Boston genealogical history includes this important tidbit about Royal Insurance agent Foster & Cole: "It is one of the oldest as it is the largest house in its line in Boston and New England, employing about seventy people in its office at 85 Water Street, Boston, and maintaining a branch office at 65 Warren Street, Roxbury.[45]

The importance of these examples is twofold. The first note says that losses were adjusted and paid in Boston. The second pointed out that most of the firm's employment was in Boston. The Wrights, both experienced in handling monetary decisions with sporting goods stores and Harry with the Red Stockings budgets, and Spalding, whose long history also proves his financial acumen, could have been financial clerks or salesman. It is likely, however, that the bulk of the needs in the Boston office in 1874—especially considering the Boston Fire of 1872 and the frenetic pace of rebuilding the city over the next few years—were for fire "adjustors" (pre- and post-evaluation of assets). Such responsibilities would have greatly expanded their already apparent financial skills.

Of course, another fringe benefit of playing for Harry Wright were traveling opportunities far beyond what the average American could ever dream of taking. Wright managed teams back in Cincinnati and took "join the Red Stockings and see the world" to levels far beyond any other team. Patterned after the Western Tour of the Washington Nationals in 1867, the Cincinnati Red Stockings toured the East. Then they went to California, which was the ultimate Western Tour (just four months after the final stake at Promontory Point in Utah had completed the Transcontinental Railroad). In Boston, they went to Canada for their summer break. Then Wright sent Spalding to scout and prepare for a baseball tour to Wright's English homeland.[46]

Wright wanted to show the Brits how to play the more entertaining game of baseball. Since the English played cricket not baseball, the Bostonians needed to bring along some baseball opponents as well. Wright first mentioned the possibility of the Philadelphia Athletics joining Boston on the Tour in a January 5 letter to their club president. On January 24 he sent Spalding to England. Why Philadelphia, and why the Athletics? While Philadelphia was rather obvious (for the competitive reasons we discussed earlier), why not the White Stockings who were the better team during this period?

Wright's personal ties were greater to the more established Athletics. In 1873 Harry Wright wrote to Hicks Hayhurst, when the White Stockings lead the NA at the summer break: "Let us get our second wind, then look out Philadelphias."[47] The Republican political compatibility among the leadership was a factor as well. As noted earlier, pitcher and on-field manager McBride, for example, worked in the Republican clerk's office and Athletics board member Hayhurst was a city councilman aligned with the Republican Ring.

But there were business ties as well. For example, Thomas Cope was the premier trader in Philadelphia and he had specific Liverpool ties. A book about early ports of entry into the United States notes that "Thomas Cope had died in 1854, though Cope company ships remained busy in the 1850s, bringing English and Irish emigrants from Liverpool to Philadelphia."[48]

The Athletics and the Red Stockings departed to Liverpool for their English tour from Philadelphia, not Boston. Cope's line had been superseded by the American Line of steamers tied to the Pennsylvania Railroad. "The popularity of the American Line steamers was underlined during the summer of 1874 when the *Ohio* sailed for Liverpool with more than 400 passengers, including members of the Athletic and Boston Baseball Clubs, who were crossing for some exhibition games."[49]

There were obviously things below the surface driving major decisions. In this case, some interesting facts stand out.

1. When Spalding went to England, and Wright was planning for the trip, both were on the winter payroll of the primary New England agency of the Royal Insurance Company of Liverpool. This was not likely an accident.

2. I own a stamped 1874 insurance document of the Royal Insurance Company of Liverpool. It was a policy sold in Philadelphia (Boston was where the finances and adjusting were handled, not all sales) to a dry goods firm named Evans & Kennedy ("dry goods" merchandising, in port cities, was generally dependent upon trade).[50] In other words, Royal Insurance was also important in Philadelphia.

3. The Evans and Cope families were intermarried (e.g. the Cope histories are written by Evans family members). Evans and the Athletics most important leader, Elias Hicks Hayhurst, were also partners in a small trading firm located on the Philadelphia docks prior to Hayhurst becoming a city councilman. In addition to all this, Alfred Cope had been Chairman of the

school which had employed Octavius Catto, the famed baseball leader of the black Phythians Base Ball team who had been assassinated in 1871. The Athletics leader Hayhurst - an advocate, friend and ally of Catto - obviously had familiarity with both Cope and Evans families.[51]

The Royal Insurance Company of Liverpool thus had strong connections in both American cities as well as in Great Britain. Their agents obviously had to sign off on employees Wright and Spalding planning the baseball trip. Philadelphia was also important to Royal Insurance. Many Philadelphia businessmen traveled with the Athletics to England as did some Boston businessmen. Had the Royal Insurance Company been heavily invested in the Tour, the promotion effort would likely not have been so lackluster. Baseball was not their focus. In the scheme of things for their company, baseball (even counting some supplemental salaries of baseball players) was a financial cipher. However, promoting good will in the business and political establishments of two important American trading cities was very important.

What is incredibly ironic—stunningly so—are the purchases of John William Henry II. His group purchased the Boston Red Sox in 2001 and the *Boston Globe* in 2013. The *Globe* had been made into a great newspaper by Charles Taylor, the first Boston owner of the American League's Red Sox. In between, in 2010, Henry's group added the Liverpool F.C. to its sports ownership collection. The Red Sox only trail the New York Yankees in Facebook and Twitter fans and followers with a combined total of over 7.2 million.[52] The Liverpool soccer team, however, has a combined total of over 24.2 million followers and fans. So it is rather obvious that in spite of the efforts of Wright and Spalding, the Brits never took to baseball.[53] But the Boston-Liverpool connection lives on.

The Sporting Goods Stores: Profiting from Baseball Celebrity

With the rise of leisure time and affordable products, the market for sporting goods greatly expanded. In 1866 Peck & Snyder Sporting Goods opened in New York City, billing itself as the "largest dealers in games of sports in the world."[54] New York was, by far, the dominant population center of the U.S. and the city where the style of baseball played today originated ("New York style baseball") so it makes sense that baseball manufacturing and retailing was centered there.

Harry Wright's biographer Christopher Devine states that in February, 1871 George Wright moved the store that he and Harry had established in New York while they played in Cincinnati to Boston because of poor sales in New York City. The Wright family had been associated with cricket in New York City from the time they had arrived in the U.S.[55] Harry Wright had awarded his brother the contract to provide the Red Stockings uniforms. In spite of this, Wright's business struggled so he moved it to Boston. There George Wright bought the patent for the first catcher's mask in 1875 from its inventor Fred Thayer, a baseball player at Harvard. In 1879 George Wright accepted the manager's job of the Providence Grays but soon moved back to Boston to manage his growing sports business. He had taken Henry Ditson as a partner, who also had a sporting goods store, and re-named it Wright & Ditson. It became the premier sporting goods company for tennis equipment, as well as for baseball and other sports.[56]

There is confusion about whether Wright & Ditson began in 1871, not the least being from the Wright & Ditson official site which states their beginning year as 1871. This likely refers to the separate precursor Boston retail operations. Evidence is clear that the firm Wright & Ditson was created after they merged in 1879. The city of Boston Landmarks Commission in the historical research necessary to certify a house George Wright once owned for landmark status, states that Wright & Gould (Charles "Charlie" Harvey Gould, another Boston player) operated under their joint name in 1871 and 1872, and then just under Wright's name until he merged with Ditson.[57]

Harry Wright also re-appeared as a purveyor of sporting goods with a firm called "Wright, Howland & Mahn" on 26 Kneeland Street in Boston. George W. Howland is listed as a manufacturer of steel plate spikes and L. H. Mahn as manufacturer of the Mahn baseball.[58] In 1872 Louis Mahn had purchased a patent from John Osgood for baseball designed so if one stitch broke, the entire baseball would not unravel. It became the official baseball for both the National Association and the National League. Mahn lived in Jamaica Plain, now part of Boston, just south of the ballpark. The Wrights also lived there for a time, though when Orator Jim O'Rourke joined the Red Stockings for the 1883 season he boarded with Harry and Carrie Wright at their home in the Highland section. Brother George, sporting goods partner Charlie Gould, and O'Rourke all boarded with the Harry and Carrie Wright.[59]

However, it was Albert Spalding who became the ultimate sporting goods monopolist. He learned the trade from the Wright brothers.

Boston & the Loves of Albert Spalding

Helping Boston keep such a collection of stars together on one team, without a reserve rule, was romantic "love." George Wright, for example, married a Boston Irish girl in 1872 which supplemented his sporting goods store as an anchor keeping him in Boston, where he died at age 90. But the case of Albert Spalding's love life is the most unusual.

A 1901 *Boston Post* feature story titled "Al Spalding's Romance" states Spalding had fallen in love as a teenager in his adopted hometown Rockford, Illinois. "They became engaged, fixing for the time when Spalding should have enough money to support a wife. But there came a lover's quarrel and Spalding left Rockford to go to Boston."[60] In other words, supposedly Wright was able to recruit Spalding because of romantic love lost. But even buried in this love story is money—the lack of enough income to support his youthful flame.

In Boston, Spalding married Sarah Josephine "Josie" Keith. Her father, Henry Snell Keith, was a respected farmer and local Republican politician. He, like many others in the area, was a shoemaker for the shoe factory of Elisha Holbrook of Holbrook, part of the Abington area factories.[61] The area provided nearly half of the footwear provided to the Union Army during the Civil War. That is a lot of shoes and boots.[62]

It is apparent from all the sporting goods manufacturing activity that occurred around Boston, with superior equipment including baseballs, that there was an inter-relationship between the mills of Lowell (e.g. carpet, textile), the manufacture of leather shoes, and other industrially produced items (e.g. a tack factory was the original catalyst that consolidated footwear around Abingdon; Howland of Wright, Howland & Mahn manufactured cleats). These skills led to pre-eminent stitching designs for the "Mahn" baseball, the first catcher's masks, tennis rackets, baseball gloves and other sporting goods.

In Peter Levine's book about Spalding, he notes that in young Spalding's personal scrapbook—before Wright had approached him about joining the Red Stockings—an article that included a notice that Wright and his brother had opened "a store in New York for the sale of bats, balls, bases and all the paraphernalia needed for outdoor games."[63] It hints that lost love was not the only motive for joining the Wright brothers in Boston. Spalding was planning ahead.

In 1876 Spalding, with his eye obviously on developing sporting equipment and his future empire, bought the patent for the Mahn ball from Mahn.[64] The company Spalding created eventually bought up all his baseball rivals—Wright & Ditson, Peck & Snyder in New York City, and Al Reach's company in Philadelphia. Boston connections taught Spalding how to be a successful capitalist in multiple ways.

William Hulbert offered Spalding $2,000 and promise of 25% of the gate receipts for the coming season to join the Chicago White Stockings of the newly created National League. For Spalding, money trumped love. Sort of. His former Rockford sweetheart had also been married to another. When Josie Spalding died in 1899, Spalding soon married his first Rockford love, Elizabeth Churchill (Mayer). They had actually been secret lovers for years. Elizabeth was involved in a cult of sorts, which led to their building a home at Point Loma in San Diego on the compound. There Spalding became involved in California politics as he had been in Chicago, which included a failed attempt to become United States Senator. Spalding clearly was a man of multiple loves: women, baseball, politics, and, greatest of all, money.[65]

When one understands the business and political connections of the Boston ownership group, the travel that came with playing for Harry Wright, the sporting goods business opportunities presented, the personal lives of key players, the satisfaction of being recognized as baseball's best team, and the struggles of competing cities during the National Association era it is easier to understand why the star players were reluctant to leave the greatest power in the baseball world.

NOTES

1. Donald L. Miller. *City of the Century: The Epic of Chicago and the Making of America* (New York: Simon & Schuster, 1996), 160.
2. Stephen Puleo, *A City So Grand: The Rise of the Metropolis, Boston 1850-1900* (New York: Beacon Press, 2010), 174-175.
3. Thomas Kessner, *Capital City: New York City and the Men Behind America's Rise to Economic Dominance, 1860-1900* (New York: Simon and Schuster, 2003), 159-160.
4. John F. Stover, *History of the Baltimore & Ohio Railroad* (West Lafayette, Indiana: Purdue University Press, 1984).
5. James H. Bready, *Baseball in Baltimore: The First Hundred Years* (Baltimore: Johns Hopkins Press, 1998), 18.
6. Peter McCaffery, *When Bosses Ruled Philadelphia* (University Park, Pennsylvania: Pennsylvania State University, 1993), Chapter 2: Ring Rule, 17-45; Daniel R. Biddle and Murray Dubin, *Tasting Freedom: Octavius Catto and the Battle for Equality in Civil War America* (Philadelphia: Temple University Press, 2010).
7. Christopher Devine, *Harry Wright: The Father of Professional Base Ball* (Jefferson, North Carolina: McFarland, 2003), 85-86.
8. "Principal Annexations of Territory," City of Boston website, at http://www.cityofboston.gov/archivesandrecords/facts/annexations.asp
9. Puleo, *A City So Grand*, 98.
10. "National Peace Jubilee 1869; http://www.celebrateboston.com/events/national-peace-jubilee.htm
11. "Peace Jubilee Coliseum," goodoldboston.blogspot.com/2011/07/peace-jubilee-coliseum.html; Puleo, *A City So Grand*, 168.
12. Tom Lee, "Gilmore, Patrick S.: America's First Superstar!" Irish Cultural Society of the Garden City Area; http://www.irish-society.org/home/hedgemaster-archives-2/people/gilmore-patrick-s; Michael Quinlin, *Irish Boston* (Guilford, Connecticut: Globe Pequot Press, 2004), 73-76.
13. James Morgan, *Charles H. Taylor, Builder of the Boston Globe* (Boston: published by the Boston Globe on the Fiftieth Anniversary of his leadership, 1923), 59.
14. Anthony M. Sammaro, *The Baker Chocolate Company* (Charleston, South Carolina: The History Press, 2009).
15. Patrick Sarsfield Gilmore, *History of the National Peace Jubilee and Great Music Festival, Held in the City of Boston, June 1869*; (published by the author Gilmore and distributed by Lee and Shepard; Boston and New York); 206-207; "Descendants of Solomon Peirce 46. Oliver Ditson" (includes information on Haynes); *Solomon Peirce Family Genealogy compiled and arranged by Marietta Peirce Bailey*, (Press of George H. Ellis Co., Boston; 1912), 25; Burditt & North as Boston Symphony Managers, for example, appeared in an ad for a Symphony appearance in *The Washington Critic* on March 21, 1890.
16. Susie J. Pak, *Gentlemen Bankers: The World of J. P. Morgan* (Cambridge, Massachusetts: Harvard University Press, 2013), 99.
17. Alan D. Morrison and William J. Wilhelm Jr., *Investment Banking: Institutions, Politics, and Law* (New York: Oxford University Press, 2007).
18. Charlie Bevis, "Ivers Adams," SABR BioProject.
19. "Advertisement for carpeting and upholstery, John H. Pray, Sons & Co., 646-658 Washington St., Boston, Mass., undated," www.historicnewengland.org/collections-archives-exhibitions/collections
20. "Chat Concerning Carpets" *Carpet Trade Review*, June 1877: 84.
21. "A Century of Carpet and Rug Marking in America" by the Bigelow-Hartford Carpet Company; Livermore & Knight Co., 48.
22. "Canal Place One: Building History," http://www.canalplaceone.com/history.html
23. "John Murray Forbes," uudb.org/articles/johnforbes.html
24. Tulsa Brian, "Were John Kerry's Ancestors Drug Runners?"; www.freerepublic.com/focus/f-news/1242224/posts
25. James B. Jackson; "The Hall of Famer," *www.slate.com/article/sports/sports_nut/2013/07*
26. "About-Home Matters: Base Ball," *Boston Post*, December 3, 1874.
27. Brian McKenna, "Arthur Soden," SABR BioProject.
28. *The Boston Almanac and Business Directory* (Boston: Sampson, Davenport and Company, 1875), 75.
29. Clarence D. Long, *Wages and Earnings in the United States, 1860-1890* (Princeton, New Jersey: Princeton University Press, 1960), 41.
30. "City Registrar Dead, N. A. Apollonio Passes Away in His Roxbury Home, Was Elected to His Responsible Office in the Year 1854" *Boston Globe*; October 30, 1891: 13.
31. http://www.catholic.com/tracts/seventh-day-adventism
32. "City Registrar Dead," *Boston Globe*.
33. John R. Mulkern, *The Know-Nothing Party in Massachusetts* (Boston, Massachusetts: Northeastern University Press, 1990), 201 footnote 3.

34 http://www.sec.state.ma.us/mus/exhibits/guest/Irish_Immigration_and_the_Know-Nothings.pdf

35 Devon Proudfoot, *From Border Ruffian to Abolitionist Martyr: William Lloyd Garrison's Changing Ideologies on John Brown and Antislavery* (Bowling Green, Ohio; Bowling Green State University, 2013), 10.

36 "Heralds of Freedom," *The Liberator* (Boston, Massachusetts) November 14, 1856: 3.

37 "Portrait of John A. Andrew, Esq.," *The Liberator* (Boston, Massachusetts); September 28, 1860: 3. Lithographs were particularly important prior to advanced photography including in political campaigns. They were framed in people's homes and offices, as well as widely promoted in newspaper advertising and/or supplements to articles.

38 Bryan S. Bush, *Louisville's Southern Exposition, 1883-1887: The City of Progress* (Charleston, South Carolina: The History Press, 2011), 57.

39 "Board of Aldermen…The City Registrar's Office-Reported Irregularities-Election of Mr. Apollonio-Orders Passed, Etc., Etc.," *Boston Post*, March 14, 1876: 3.

40 "Base Ball: Convention of Managers in Cleveland," *Louisville Courier-Journal*, December 14, 1876.

41 Charles P. Kindleberger, "The Formation of Financial Centers: A Study in Comparative Economic History," Princeton Studies in International Finance No. 36, 17.

42 Neil McKendrick, *Business Life and Public Policy: Essays in Honour of D.C. Coleman, Edition 1* (Cambridge: Cambridge University Press, 2002), 144.

43 William J. Ryczek, *Blackguards and Red Stockings: A History of Baseball's National Association 1871-1875* (Wallingford, Connecticut: Colebrook Press, 1992), from the *New York Clipper*, January 3, 1874, 136.

44 *United States Insurance Gazette & Magazine;* Vol. 36; November 1, 1872 to May 1, 1873: 470.

45 William Richard Cutter, A.M., *Genealogical and Personal Memoirs Relating to the Families of Boston and Eastern Massachusetts Volume IV* (New York: Lewis Historical Publishing, 1908).

46 Devine, *Harry Wright: Father of Professional Baseball*, 104-105.

47 Ryczek, 115.

48 M. Mark Stolarik, editor, *Forgotten Doors: The Other Ports of Entry to the United States* (Philadelphia: Balch Institute for Ethnic Studies, 1988), 41.

49 William H. Flayhart, *The American Line (1871-1902)* (New York: W.W. Norton & Company, 2000), 53.

50 Royal Insurance of Liverpool insurance contract for merchandise with Evans & Kennedy of Philadelphia, November 3, 1874.

51 "Hayhurst & Evans, Wholesale Dealers in Foreign and Domestic Produce at No. 30 North Wharf; E. Hicks Hayhurst and Morris J. Evans" period advertising trading card (undated); Biddle & Durbin, *Tasting Freedom: Octavius Catto*, 403.

52 http://fivethirtyeight.com/datalab/everyones-still-chasing-the-yankees-and-red-sox-on-facebook-and-twitter/

53 caughtoffside.com/2014/07/19/top-ten-most-supported-football-teams-in-Europe/5/

54 "Peck and Snyder: The Company" by Rich Mueller; February 17, 2010; a re-post of an article by Jerry Houseman; www.sportscollectorsdaily.com/peck-and-snyder-the-company

55 Devine; *Harry Wright: The Father of Professional Baseball*, 101.

56 David L. Fleitz, *More Ghosts in the Gallery: Another Sixteen Little-Known Greats at Cooperstown* (Jefferson, North Carolina: McFarland; 2007), 11-12.

57 Kehew-Wright House: Boston Landmarks Commission Study Report, Petition #246.12; City of Boston.

58 www.sheaff-ephemera.com/list/odds_ends_album/wright_howland_mahn.html; Wright, Howland & Mahn Christmas advertising trade card with listing sporting goods for sale on the back; owned by the author

59 Jamaica Plain Historical Society; www.jphs.org/victorian/baseball-in-jamaica-plain.html; Mike Roer, *Orator Jim O'Rourke* (Jefferson, North Carolina: McFarland, 2005), 34.

60 "Al Spalding's Romance," *Boston Post*, December 15, 1901.

61 "Henry Snell Keith," *Representative Men and Old Families of Southeastern Massachusetts*, Vol. I (J. H. Beers & Co.), 269.

62 "Abington/North Abington" from the Atlas of Plymouth County, Massachusetts, 1879; www.mapsoantiquity.com/store

63 Peter Levine, *A.G. Spalding and the Rise of Baseball* (New York: Oxford University Press, 1985), 10.

64 *www.jphs.org/victorian/baseball-in-jamaica-plain.html*

65 Levine, Chapter 7: Retirement to California: Theosophy and the United States Senate, 123-142.

ORGANIZING THE FIRST PROFESSIONAL BASEBALL TEAM IN BOSTON

The following article appeared in the *Boston Daily Advertiser* on page 4 of the January 21, 1871 issue.

THE BOSTON BASE-BALL CLUB
MEETING OF THE SHAREHOLDERS—A HISTORY OF THE ENTERPRISE—ORGANIZATION OF THE ASSOCIATION AND ELECTION OF OFFICERS

A meeting of the stockholders of the Boston Base-Ball Association was held yesterday afternoon at the Parker House. Twelve or fifteen gentlemen attended, representing ninety shares of stock. I.W. Adams was chosen president, and J.A. Conkey secretary. On taking the chair Mr. Adams addressed the meeting as follows:—

Gentlemen of the Boston Base Ball Association:

You have been called together this evening to take the first step toward a permanent organization of our club, and as some of you are not fully acquainted with the several steps which have been taken, with the consent and hearty cooperation of you all, as far as was possible up to the present time. I propose to give you in as few words as possible a history of my efforts in that direction. Twelve months ago the idea of a professional nine for Boston first entered my mind, and at that time I determined, provided the right men could be secured as players, and also, and of equal importance, the right men could be induced to assist me in carrying out this project, our city should have a nine and a club she would be proud of.

I determined it should be first class in every particular, that the greatest care should be exercised that men of good character and temperate habits only should belong to its nine, that they should be men of unquestioned ability as players, and, therefore, good teachers of the sport, that they should agree to conform to all the rules and regulations of the club, and should be under the complete control of the captain of the nine.

I determined further, from satisfactory information which I possessed myself of, that I should secure Messrs. Harry and George Wright first, and failing to secure them should let the whole matter drop. This position was taken from a firm conviction that they were the only two men possessing the knowledge and the ability to manage and discipline a nine known to myself, and in whose honesty and integrity I could place implicit confidence. It is unnecessary to inform you the measure of success attending my efforts in this direction, as those gentlemen are now present with you and their presence prevents me from speaking further of them. Here I wish to thank you who so heartily stood by me during the further negotiations for players and other steps necessary to be taken, making those labors comparatively easy, considering the discouraging news received at this time of the breaking up of the Cincinnati club, with the circular of the executive committee of that club, deciding (in the language of one of the dailies of that city) "to flop out of existence," after holding the highest position in the base ball world for two successive seasons, and with the reasonable hope of still holding it for a longer time had they dealt liberally and at the proper time with their deserving men. I repeat, I thank you for "sticking," for I have some reason for believing this action of that executive committee was intended, partly at least, for us here, as cold water thrown upon our enterprise; but we knew our men, and, instead of giving up the Wright brothers, whom they accused of impossibilities for such men, or of taking one step backward, I took one step forward and secured two more of the

"Red Stocking" nine—Messrs. Charles H. Gould and Calvin A. McVey –being just the four players, and those only, the Cincinnati Club had proposed to re-engage, and because the executive committee of that club chose to dictate terms which were not acceptable to these men; and because they succeeded in making satisfactory engagements elsewhere, that committee attempted to veto one of the chief amusements of the times, to do what the founders of the old "Red Stocking" club never would have done so long as the athletic sport of base ball was national.

But without delay, and believing in the success of our enterprise, irrespective of other parties, and with the advice and constant council of the two Wrights, further steps were taken, and Messrs. Albert G. Spalding, Roscoe C. Barnes, and J.F. Cone of the Forest City, of Rockford, Ill., respectively filling the positions of pitcher, short stop and left field of that nine, were added to the four already secured of our nine. Next was engaged a young and comparatively unknown player, but one whose record as an amateur has been a good one both as a player and a gentleman, and gives promise of proficiency second to none, Samuel Jackson, from the Flower City club, of Rochester, New York.

Harry C. Shafer, formerly of the Athletic club, of Philadelphia, and David S. Birdsall, of the Union club, of Morrissiana, complete the playing members of our nine secured.

Their position in play at all times will be determined and controlled by their captain, Harry Wright, and by him alone.

With these men secured and one more it is proposed to engage, we feel we shall have a nine, the utility of which, if for nothing else, cannot be excelled for the season of 1871; for we shall have, to fill the position of pitcher, three distinct changes, for that of catcher the same, at the first base two changes, second the same, third, two also. For the important position of short stop, we have three men, two of whom have played with distinguished ability. In the field there is plenty of talent, perfectly at home in the several positions, and these men have been selected not alone for their ability as base ball athletes, but because they are known to be strictly temperate, industrious and gentlemanly in their conduct at all times, besides honest lovers of our national game. We also believe that men with these qualifications only can attain that physical condition and base ball proficiency necessary for such exhibitions of the exercise at all times, as all true lovers of our national sport delight to see.

Having completed our nine, the place to play it was the next important consideration, and, while we have not concluded arrangements where to play, preferring to confer with you before taking definite action, we have decided a much larger ground must be secured than any very near, or in our city, and negotiations are now pending for accommodations on the line of the Boston and Providence Railroad, where better facilities for playing and seeing the game than any yet enjoyed can be had.

We would suggest the erection of a covered building capable of seating about a thousand people, with reserved seats for ladies, shareholders, members of the club and those of our friends who may take sufficient interest in the success of this enterprise to assist us at any time.

We would further suggest, immediately following our organization, application be made to our legislature, now in session, for a special act of incorporation.

We wish it distinctly understood, at the commencement of the season, the middle and the end of it, and throughout the country, the Boston Nine will play to win every match made for it by honest efforts, and none other, and games lost will be lost honorably and squarely.

One word in reference to professional base ball playing.

There is really not the slightest reasonable objection which can be made to professional base ball playing pursued in its integrity; on the contrary, much can be said in its favor. It is only through the medium of a disciplined, well-trained, professional nine, that the fielding beauties of the game can be fully presented. In the field meetings of such a nine, managed with a view solely to developing the attractive features of base ball, and presenting to the pleasure-seeking public an exciting out-door sport, free from the objectionable surroundings and evils connected with nearly every other of our great public sports, our people of both sexes can find the source of the most exciting contests and interesting displays of manly skill, to a degree which no other sport or game presents. It is about time that the erroneous notion which some people have got into their heads that professional ball playing means gambling and rowdyism, and that to have anything to do with that class of ball players is to countenance betting ring contests, and "hippodrome" matches for gate-money, should be given up as a mistaken idea. The gentlemen who composed the great majority of the members of the Cincinnati club in 1869 and 1870 found it no difficult task to organize a professional nine which has done more to bring the national game into favor and to fully develop its most attractive features than any amateur nine could possibly do. Not a breath of suspicion, not a blot upon the fair escutcheon of the Cincinnati club can be charged to its honorable professional nine known as the "Red Stockings," from the beginning to the close of their brilliant career. The fact is, if the admirers of the game in this city desire to see base ball played as it should be, they must look to a well-managed professional nine to gratify them; for though our amateurs may have all the needed abilities to excel, no doubt, the very fact that they cannot spare the time or attention to the requisite training and practice is sufficient to prevent them from attaining success at the command of a well-organized professional nine, such as we trust Boston will have this coming season under the leadership of Captain Harry Wright.

A draft of a constitution was presented at the conclusion of the chairman's address, and the various articles were adopted *seriatim*. According to this instrument the association is to have a capital stock of $15,000 divided into 150 shares. The officers will be a president, vice-president, a secretary, a treasurer, and a board of directors consisting of the officers named and one member chosen from the stockholders. Tickets, not to exceed two hundred in number, are to be sold annually to persons selected by the association or stockholders therein, constituting the holders members of the association for one year and entitling them to admission to the association's grounds and club house and to reserved seats at matches on the ground, but not to participation in the government of the club or admission to meetings of the association. Having adopted the constitution by a unanimous vote, the association elected offers for the ensuing year as follows:—

President—I.W. Adams

Vice-president—J. A. Conkey

Secretary—Harry Wright

Treasurer—Harrison Gardner

Directors—The president, vice-president, secretary and treasurer, *ex officio*, and G.H. Burditt.

THE BOSTON RED STOCKINGS ORGANIZATIONAL MEETING

January 20, 1871, Parker House, Boston

BY RICHARD "DIXIE" TOURANGEAU

IVERS WHITNEY ADAMS HAD A SPEcific plan and friends with the money to back it up—if he could secure their help. He was certainly the instigator behind Boston's having a representative baseball team if there was to be an organized "league" in 1871. Adams called his Congress, State, and Washington Street merchant pals to the famed Parker House for a luncheon meeting on Friday, January 20, 1871. His special guests were Harry and George Wright, formerly the star brothers of the Cincinnati Red Stockings, whom Adams saw play in 1869 and 1870 in Boston as they traversed the country beating nearly all opponents.

Adams's urgings and comments to his well-heeled friends were in the *Boston Journal* and *Boston Daily Advertiser* the next day, while other papers had shorter accounts. Even the *New York Clipper* printed Adams's speech in its January 28 issue.[1] He was simply asking them to contribute to a $15,000 stock-buying venture that would back his dream baseball team's creation and foundation.

The local press printed a few names, those who were elected to front-office positions, but it was left to historian George V. Tuohey, 26 years later, to name everyone who got a Parker House invite in his iconic *A History of the Boston Base Ball Club*.[2]

In 1948 Harold Kaese's book *The Boston Braves, An Informal History* was published as part of the famous G.P. Putnam and Sons baseball series. On page 5 he listed Adams's wealth roster again, but not without error. He wrote that an F.G. Welsh became a stockholder. There was no such person, but on hand was Canton's affable Frank George Webster, "The Dean of State Street." The various newspapers, historian Tuohey, and finally sportswriter Kaese each mixed up an initial or two but a little research has easily corrected those minor glitches.

Though not quite all at the apex of their final wealth as 1871 began, it was an extremely impressive bunch that Adams, 33, had gathered.

John Adams Conkey (1839-1903) was an orphan by 1852. His father, John Q.A. Adams Conkey, was in the crockery business, but died in 1843; his mother, Martha Howe (Bird) Conkey, passed in 1851. The family physician, Dr. Henry E. Townsend, was Conkey's guardian and sent him to the finest schools. As a young man Conkey clerked for Tuckerman-Townsend, noted tea merchants. Then he dealt in the China Trade for August Heard, later becoming a customs broker and forwarder, estate trustee, and bank notary. A talented thespian, he was a Newton Player and a member of the New England Historic Genealogical Society. Conkey was chosen as team vice president and became the Red Stockings' second president in 1872, when Adams returned full-time to his businesses and outdoor sporting interests.

Harrison Gardner (1841-1899) served in the Civil War as a lieutenant in the 45th Massachusetts Regiment. Gardner worked at several prosperous firms before being named a partner of commercial merchants Smith, Hogg, and Gardner. Among his many club memberships around the city were those of the Longwood Club and the Boston Athletic Association. He was the Red Stockings' first treasurer.

Charles Augustus Burditt (1835-1926) was in the hardware business with his brother George, who was ensconced in the western part of the state. Confusion concerning which Burditt was in on the Red Stockings deal plagued news stories. But George almost never came to eastern Massachusetts before 1885. Charles was a senior partner in the Burditt & North firm and a founder of the Burditt and Williams Hardware Co. He was a fixture in the Dock Square part of Boston. Burditt was elected to the club's Board of Directors.

John Franklin Mills (1823-1876, born in Vermont) was the oldest of those at the lunch and maybe the most "strategic" invitee since he was the partner of Harvey D. Parker, who started the Parker House eatery/hotel. Mills worked for Parker as a waiter at a small restaurant at age 21, proved his considerable worth and ability, and when Parker opened the Parker House, Mills was the main operator. He continued in that job until just before his death.

Eben Dyer Jordan (1823-1895, born in Maine) was likely the wealthiest man at the table at that time. Despite growing up on a farm, he partnered with Benjamin L. Marsh to create the famed Jordan-Marsh retail store in the 1860s. In 1865 his store, woolen mills, and printing company were worth more than an unprecedented $27 million in annual revenues.[3]

Henry Lillie Pierce (1825-1896) was a member of the Massachusetts House of Representatives, a two-term US congressman in the 1870s, and was elected mayor of Boston in 1873 and 1878 before going into the insurance business. His first employment was with the Walter Baker & Co., a chocolate producer, which he took over by 1854 (when Baker died) and of which he was the sole proprietor the rest of his life. He was a trustee of the Museum of Fine Arts and had membership in several other clubs including the posh Algonquin Club. Among the dozens of causes he was involved in, one was to repeal the state and national law that prevented the enlistment of "colored soldiers" into the State militia or US Army.

Edward Augustus White (1825-1891) was in the clothing and real-estate businesses. He became an alderman and was on the Boston Common Council and Water Board, and became a fire department commissioner.

James Horatio Freeland (1827-1902) partnered early on with his brother C.W. Freeland in men's clothing manufacturing in Worcester. He later shared ownership in three other companies, one supplying cloth goods for the Union Army in the Civil War. The Great Fire of 1872 burned Freeland out but soon he rebuilt in the form of the Continental Clothing House with Silas W. Loomis on Washington Street. He was a member of the Ancient and Honorable Society, the Central Club, Boston Art Club, and Commercial Club, among many fraternal groups.

Frank George Webster (1841-1930) was likely the richest of the group when claimed by death. As a young man he was a bookbinder, wallpaper clerk, and bank teller before his service in the Civil War. Postwar, he was in on the ground floor at the opening of Kidder, Peabody & Co. Eventually he became known as the "Dean of State Street," where over the years he amassed his considerable fortune. Webster's summer home at Squam Lake, New Hampshire, is on the National Register and he owned various Canadian preserves and clubs and was a member of the exclusive Union and Algonquin Clubs and The Country Club of Brookline.

Charles Hunt Porter (1843-1911) became the third president of the Red Stockings in 1873.[4] Conkey, like Adams, went back to real business endeavors after one season of baseball activity. Colonel Porter, too, had fought in the Civil War (more than a dozen notable battles) and later became the first mayor of Quincy, Massachusetts, in 1889 when the town became a city. Prior to that he was also park commissioner and organized the Quincy Actives Base Ball team and played on it in the 1860s. During his entire life he was involved in politics in the "City of Presidents," taking seats on the school board and fire department, and he formed the Quincy Water Co.

Nicholas Taylor Apollonio (1843-1911, born in Brooklyn, New York) was not listed as being at the Parker House but became the fourth Boston Red Stockings president (1874). His father was Italian immigrant Nicholas Alessandro Apollonio, a printer and City of Boston registrar for 40 years. With special permission, young Nick entered Boston English High School at age 11. He was an accountant and clerk by trade and directed operations for the Great Falls Manufacturing Co. for 35 years. Likely the first Italian to be connected with big-time baseball, he eventually became a Winchester resident and was involved with the Winchester Savings Bank, and always cared deeply about the town's well-being. As Red Stockings president in 1876, Apollonio oversaw the transition from the chaotic National Association to the much more "organized" National League, but even more crucial to Boston fans, the sudden departure of the "Big Four" of Albert Spalding, Deacon White, Ross Barnes, and Cal McVey for Chicago in 1876. Arthur H. Soden joined the Red Stockings toward the close of that first NL season in 1876 and took over as president before the 1877 campaign began.

SOURCES

The sources for material on these men is largely gleaned from their obituaries, though some other sources have been consulted as well. The sources are listed here, alphabetically, by each man.

APOLLONIO: *Winchester* (Massachusetts) *Star*, April 7, 1911. See also Nemec, David, *The Rank and File of 19th Century Major League Baseball* (Jefferson, North Carolina: McFarland and Company, 2012), 285.

BURDITT: *Boston Globe*, September 18, 1926.

CONKEY: *The New-England Historical Genealogical Register*, Vol. LIX. *Memoirs*, Section 1903 Deaths (supplement to April 1905), lxxi. (Boston: New England Historic Genealogical Society, 1905).

FREELAND: Supreme Council of the Ancient Accepted Scottish Rite, "In Memoriam, Illustrious Brother," *Proceedings of the Annual Session Held in Boston, June 26, 1903* (Boston: Massachusetts Council of Deliberation, 1903), 31-33.

GARDNER: *The* (Brookline, Massachusetts) *Chronicle*, February 18, 1899.

JORDAN: *Boston Herald*, November 16, 1895.

MILLS: *Boston Globe*, April 10, 1876, and *Boston Daily Advertiser*, April 10, 1876.

PIERCE: *Boston Globe*, December 18, 1896.

PORTER: *Quincy* (Massachusetts) *Patriot*, August 12, 1911, and *Boston Globe*, August 11, 1911.

WEBSTER: *Boston Globe*, January 23, 1930.

WHITE: *Boston Evening Transcript*, May 14, 1891.

NOTES

1. *New York Clipper*, January 21, 1871: 338.

2. George V. Tuohey, *A History of the Boston Base Ball Club* (Boston: M.F. McQuinn & Co., 1897), Part III, 62.

3. It has been difficult to determine whether or not this referred to annual revenues or net worth, though mentions of the sum appear to suggest annual revenues, which would be truly astonishing.

4. In George V. Tuohey's book, he begins Chapter V, "The Club's Presidents," by saying (his information came from J.C. Morse of the *Boston Herald*) that all five Red Stockings presidents were then alive and living in Boston. Tuohey via Morse writes that Charles H. Porter was the third president and held office for two seasons. Then Nicholas T. Apollonio became the fourth president for both 1875 and 1876. The years attributed to each man were incorrect. The *New York Clipper* of December 27, 1873, printed a letter from "President" Porter on the subject of professionalism in the Association. It was dated December 15 and appeared on the bottom of the sixth column of page 306. In the very next column, at the bottom, was a one-paragraph item, "Boston Baseball Association," which gave the "recent vote" for officers for the Club. Apollonio was elected president and Porter became a director for the coming 1874 season. Sometime between December 16 and Christmas Eve the vote had taken place and Porter was no longer president.

THE 1871 SEASON

BY BOB LEMOINE

"BOSTON CAN NOW BOAST OF POSsessing a first-class professional Base Ball Club," declared the *Boston Journal*, "as all the efforts tending to establish an institution of this kind here culminated yesterday."[1] Professional baseball in Boston began on January 20, 1871, through the efforts of Ivers W. Adams, who had been working toward this achievement for at least a year. While baseball in Boston dated to 1854 with amateur games played on Boston Common,[2] several factors kept the city as the only major urban area in the Northeast without a serious baseball team. For one, it took time for the New England Game version of baseball (which included a smaller diamond and consequent shorter distance from home plate to the pitcher's mound, more players on the field, and outs being recorded by "soaking," or plunking a runner with the ball) to give way to the more prevalent New York Game.[3] Another factor was the lack of an adequate playing field, which was solved when the Union Grounds (later called the South End Grounds) were built in 1869 in Boston's South End. But besides these, people with big pockets were needed to fund a professional team, and Adams was the one with connections to do so.

Adams was in attendance when the Cincinnati Red Stockings visited the Boston area in 1869-1870, and he began dreaming of a professional baseball club in Boston. He began having correspondence with George and Harry Wright. George Wright came to Boston to meet with Adams in November of 1870, once the Cincinnati team was officially disbanded. Now the door was open for Adams's dream to come true.

Harry Wright had the influence to assemble a new team. Three players came with him from Cincinnati: his brother George, Charlie Gould, and Cal McVey. Harry Wright then brought Dave Birdsall from the Union Club of Morrisania, Harry Schafer from the Philadelphia Athletics, and Al Spalding, Ross Barnes, and Fred Cone from the Rockford, Illinois, team.

The Massachusetts Legislature incorporated the team with $15,000 capital, made possible by several prominent businessmen.[4] Adams met these fellow Boston-area entrepreneurs at Boston's Parker House, and in his remarks to them emphasized that these Wright brothers "were the only two men possessing the knowledge and the ability to manage and discipline a nine ... and [in] whose honesty and integrity I could place implicit confidence."[5] Two hundred memberships in the club were sold, granting the purchasers free admission to games all season long as well as use of the clubhouse.[6]

The next step involved joining a league of professional teams, which had been on the horizon as the worlds of amateur and professional baseball were coming to a parting of the ways. The 1870 fall meeting of the National Association of Base Ball Players had been "a fiery affair marked by hot words between the two camps, and it ended with the amateurs staging a walkout," wrote David Voigt.[7] It was clear that baseball would be expanding from the world of fun and recreation to fun, recreation, and big business. Possessing the vision of a new professional league but little time to properly organize and hammer out specifics, these new pioneers quickly created a new league on March 17, 1871.

As the rain pattered on the roof, delegates from 10 teams met at the Collier's Rooms Saloon at Broadway and 13th Street in New York City. Eight delegates reached for their billfolds and submitted the $10 fee to join the new league. The charter teams were the already established franchises of the Philadelphia Athletics, New York Mutuals, Washington Olympics, Troy (New York) Haymakers, Chicago White Stockings, Rockford (Illinois) Forest City, Cleveland Forest City, and one newcomer: the Boston Red Stockings. Two delegates were stingy with their money, so the

Brooklyn Eckfords and Washington Nationals did not join. A few days later, a ninth club, the Fort Wayne (Indiana) Kekiongas, paid the fee and joined. So that they didn't have to reinvent the wheel, the founders adopted the same constitution and bylaws from the existing National Association, "as far as the same did not conflict with the interests of professional clubs," the *New York Clipper* reported. "'The National Association of Professional Base Ball Players' thereby sprang into existence," the *Clipper* declared.[8] The word *professional* was simply inserted into the league name they were familiar with, moving from the NABBP to the NAPBBP. "The formation of the new professional league," wrote William Ryczek, "was accompanied by little fanfare. Ten men on a rainy night in a New York City saloon had set the course for professional sports in America, an imperfect beginning to be sure, but a beginning."[9]

Harry Wright was responsible for all the scheduling of the Boston team since the NAPBBP did not have a set schedule. It was generally agreed upon that teams would play one another five times before the season ended on November 1, with three of the first five being counted as "championship" games. "This was an extremely time-consuming process, often requiring extensive negotiation. Fully 90 percent of Wright's correspondence from 1871 to 1875 consisted of inquiries or responses to inquiries about possible games," wrote Warren Goldstein.[10]

While today a famous baseball phrase is "Who's on first?" the NAPBBP season of 1871 could have made a skit called, "Who's *in* first?" The NAPBBP never set clear guidelines on how the standings would be structured: Would teams be ranked according to number of games won or by the number of series won? Because of the lack of clarity, you could pick up a newspaper on a given day and see a different team in first place than in the newspaper in the next town, and often the same newspaper was inconsistent from day to day. These issues were left to be sorted out at the end of the season. "This led to an early brand of parity," wrote Ryczek, "as virtually any team could claim possession of first place by choosing the method which best suited their circumstances."[11]

An 1871 pinback, most likely worn as a season pass to Red Stocking games. (Courtesy of the Andy Leonard Collection, Heritage Auctions).

On April 6, 1871, Boston played an exhibition game against a picked nine, winning 41-10. It was the first professional baseball game played in Boston.

On April 8 Boston played the Lowell, Massachusetts, club. The *Boston Journal* noted that Boston was "improving in their play wonderfully, so much so as to make it not improbable that they will at the very outset rank as the foremost club in the country."[12]

Boston's first regular-season game was played on May 5 against the Washington Olympics in Washington, D.C. Washington had five former Cincinnati Red Stockings players to Boston's four, and the game generated national interest. If not for a rainout, this game would have been the first official game in the National Association and in professional baseball, and justifiably so. Instead, the Fort Wayne Kekiongas, who would disband before the season was over, hosted the first official game.

On Monday, May 8, Boston faced the Brooklyn Atlantics in an exhibition game at Brooklyn's Capitoline Grounds, the same location where Cincinnati's winning streak had come to a sudden end the previous June. Despite the raw, chilly cold, 2,000 spectators turned out even though "no one expected the Brooklyn Nine to win the game." The Brooklyn pitcher was wild, and the Boston strikers weren't able to "punish" him because "it was rare that they could get a ball from him within any far reach of the bat." The umpire stayed true to the rules of calling balls early on, however, "if he had followed the rules very closely and called balls in the order of delivery, the Bostonians would still be on their first inning." Boston won 25-0.[13]

On May 9 Boston won 9-5 at Troy, despite losing George Wright to a leg injury. Wright and Fred Cone collided on a fly ball when Cone couldn't hear Wright call for the ball because of the blare of a train whistle.[14] Significant also is the *Journal's* mention that the Boston club was "now quite as well known by the name 'Red Stockings' as by their original title. …"[15]

Boston returned home May 16, and played Troy in the first home opener in Boston professional baseball. Both "nines made their appearance on the field, and were greeted with hearty cheers by the large crowd of spectators in attendance, numbering some 2500," the *Journal* wrote.[16] But sloppy play ruined the Red Stockings' inauguration of the Boston grounds, and the *Post* commented, "(W)e could have wished it were played elsewhere."[17] Boston lost, 29-14. On May 20 the Red Stockings got back on track and defeated the Philadelphia Athletics 11-8 before a crowd of 3,000. The next game, on May 24 against the Olympics, ended in a 4-4 tie, "not satisfactory to a large amount of spectators."[18] Only about 500 spectators came out for the next two games, against Rockford, as the Boston temperature hit the rare 90s at the end of May. The Boston bats were hot as well; they won 25-11 on May 29 and 11-10 on May 30.

"The financial success of the venture was in doubt for some time, but local pride in the team grew stronger, with each successive game," wrote George Tuohey, a 19th-century sports historian, "and many of the contests, especially those with the Athletics of Philadelphia, attracted thousands of people."[19]

Then the Red Stockings endured their longest losing streak of the season, three straight, albeit over the course of two weeks from June 2 to June 17. George Wright returned on June 17, but the Red Stockings "rather disappointed their friends, as it was thought they would make a better show with the Mutuals," wrote the *Journal* of the 9-3 loss.[20] They broke out of their slump in a big way on June 21, defeating Fort Wayne 21-0 on a shutout by Spalding, "one of the most remarkable games of record," the *Boston Advertiser* opined.[21] A 20-8 loss at Philadelphia put the Red Stockings' record at 6-6 at the end of June, and they would spend July and August on the road.

The Red Stockings would be nearly unstoppable from then on, however, going 14-4 to finish the season and outscoring their opponents 249-159. The streak began as America celebrated its 95th year of independence. The "two branches of the old Red Stockings—the Boston club and the Olympic club of Washington," met before a crowd near 5,000 on July 4.[22] Boston won 7-3. In three straight victories over Rockford, Fort Wayne, and Cleveland, the Red Stockings pounded out an amazing 63 hits and 63 runs. Boston lost 15-11 on August 22 at the New York Mutuals, ending the road trip. They were 12-9 and 4½ games behind Philadelphia.

Fort Wayne played its final game on August 29, hobbled by player defections. The Kekiongas were a co-op club whose players shared gate receipts. Star pitcher Bobby Mathews and infielder Tom Carey, "the two in whom the most confidence had been placed, willfully broke their plighted word and became in the eyes of our citizens dishonored Messrs," leaving for greener pastures. "The course adopted by these young men is very reprehensible," a hometown newspaper said.[23] The Brooklyn Eckfords replaced the Kekiongas so as not to disrupt the schedules of contending teams, although the Eckfords themselves would not have an official record in the standings.

Back in Boston, the Red Stockings found home cooking a delight, winning six straight games. A 31-10 thrashing of Cleveland on September 2 saw Boston score 23 runs in the last two innings. The game was halted after eight innings; because Cleveland "had not a ghost of a chance for winning, they requested that the contest end there."[24] The Red Stockings defeated Philadelphia 17-14 on September 9, moved to within 2½ games of first-place Chicago, and were suddenly gaining ground in the standings. They trailed by only one game after a victory on September 27 that gave them a record of 18-9. The only loss in September was in Chicago, the last game played at Lake Front Park before it was destroyed in the Great Chicago Fire. Boston lost 10-8 despite having two runners on in the ninth and Ross Barnes smashing two long foul balls with home-run distance.

After the tragic fire, Chicago played the remainder of its schedule on the road. Its players, who had lost everything in the fire, depended on donated uniforms from other teams and "not two of the nine were dressed alike, all their uniforms having been consumed in the fire. They presented a most extraordinary appearance from the parti-colored nature of their dress. All who could get white stockings did so, but they were not many. One man wore a Mutual shirt and Eckford hose; another an Atlantic shirt, Mutual pants, and Flyaway hose, and so on; each man being obliged to borrow a shirt from anyone who was willing to lend," wrote the *Chicago Tribune*.[25] Philadelphia defeated Chicago 4-1 on October 30 in Brooklyn before a scarce 500 fans. The *Boston Herald* reported that "it is generally believed that it sends the whip pennant to Philadelphia, though nothing is certain until several points are decided by the committee."[26]

A fitting end to this thrown-together season was confusion about who actually won the pennant. The NAPBBP met in Philadelphia on November 3. James Kerns, president of the Philadelphia club, said "the rules governing the championship were faulty, and considerable doubt existed whether they were to be interpreted as meaning the most number of *games* won or *series* won," reported the *Clipper*. "He suggested that the rules be changed so that each club would be obligated to play five games with every other contestant, and all games to count, the club winning the most and losing the least number of games be declared the champions."[27] Another issue was the number of exhibition games played, since teams saw the opportunity to draw crowds and played games which didn't count in the standings. Sometimes patrons paying full price at the gate did not know the game was only an exhibition, "a circumstance not conducive to good public relations."[28] Sometimes the teams themselves didn't agree on whether a completed game was official or not.

From that point forward, most wins were the governing factor, but in 1871 it was ruled that the team with the most series wins was the champion: Philadelphia, which had one more victory than Boston. The nine unfinished games of Fort Wayne were ruled as forfeited victories for their opponents. The league also decided that four victories by Rockford didn't count and their victories went to their opponents (two of them to Philadelphia, because of an "illegal" player). Rockford had acquired Scott Hastings, a member of the New Orleans Lone Stars, who had played Rockford in an exhibition game before the season. Hastings liked Rockford so much that he decided to join the team. Other teams protested, citing the NAPBBP rule that a team could not "raid" players from another team during the season. The rule restricted a player from playing for a new club within 60 days of departure.

"The Boston Nine have just completed their first season, and it has been very successful," wrote the *Boston Traveler*. "Though they did not secure the emblem of championship, they have shown themselves the real champions of 1871, having defeated the winners of the pennant three out of four legal games, and as they also, at the close of the season, show a better average than the Athletics, to whom a mere accident gave them the whip pennant."[29] Harry Wright sent an official letter on behalf of the NAPBBP on November 23 "declaring officially that the Athletics were the champions of the United States for 1872."[30] Unlike today, the championship year represented not the season in which the championship was one, but the following year in which the pennant flapped in the breeze to the pride of its fans.

At the December 7 meeting, the Boston Base Ball Association was incorporated. Adams was re-elected president of the club, but declined, so John A. Conkey was elected in his place. "If we have been instrumental in elevating the standard of our national pastime, to the accomplishment of which object we have turned our special attention, then we have cause for satisfaction," Adams remarked "We look forward to the coming season with confidence."[31]

With a year of experience under their belts, the new Red Stockings were now primed to dominate the NAPBBP, winning four straight pennants from 1872 to 1875. Their dominance actually led to the end of the league itself, and the more structured National League was formed in 1876.

NOTES

1. "The Boston Base Ball Club. A Permanent Organization Effected. All the Players Engaged," *Boston Journal*, January 21, 1871.

2. Harold Kaese, *The Boston Braves, 1871-1953* (Boston: Northeastern University Press, 1954), 4; John Thorn, "Early Baseball in Boston, Part 2," ourgame.mlblogs.com/2012/07/07/early-baseball-in-boston-part-2/. Accessed July 6, 2015.

3. Christopher Devine, *Harry Wright: The Father of Professional Baseball* (Jefferson, North Carolina: McFarland & Co, 2003), 79 [Google E-book Edition].

4. George V. Tuohey, *A History of the Boston Base Ball Club ... A Concise and Accurate History of Base Ball From Its Inception* (Boston: M.F. Quinn & Co., 1897), 61. [Google Books version].

5. Ibid.

6. "The New Boston Club," *New York Clipper*, January 28, 1871: 338.

7. David C. Voigt, *American Baseball: From Gentleman's Sport to the Commissioner System* (Norman, Oklahoma: University of Oklahoma Press, 1966), 35.

8. "Base Ball. The Professionals in Council. A National Association Organized," *New York Clipper*, March 25, 1871: 402.

9. William J. Ryczek, *Blackguards and Red Stockings: A History of Baseball's National Association, 1871-1875* (Wallingford, Connecticut: Colebrook Press, 1992), 14.

10. Warren Goldstein. *Playing for Keeps: A History of Early Baseball* (Ithaca, New York: Cornell University Press, 2009, 20th Anniversary Edition), 143. [Google E-Book Edition].

11. Ryczek, 55.

12. "Base Ball. The Boston-Lowell Match. The Former Victorious, Score, 40 to 1. Gossip," *Boston Journal*, April 10, 1871.

13. "Base Ball," *Boston Journal*, May 10, 1871: 4.

14. "Boston and Vicinity," *Boston Journal*, May 11, 1871: 4.

15. Ibid.

16. Ibid. Actual attendance accounts in newspapers ranged from 2,500 to 8,000.

17. "Base Ball. Match Between the Boston Nine and the Haymakers, of Troy—the Boston Club Badly Beaten," *Boston Post*, May 17, 1871: 3.

18. "Base Ball. The Boston-Olympic Match," *Boston Journal*, May 25, 1871: 4.

19. Tuohey, 62.

20. "Base Ball: the Mutual-Red Stocking Match—Defeat of the Bostons by a score of 9 to 3," *Boston Journal*, June 19, 1871: 1.

21. "Base Ball. The Visit of the Kekiongas—Their Defeat by the Boston Nine," *Boston Advertiser*, June 22, 1871: 1.

22. "Base Ball. A Victory for the Boston Wing—Bostons Defeat the Olympics by 7 to 3," *Cincinnati Commercial Tribune*, July 6, 1871: 5.

23. "Kekiongas," *Fort Wayne Sentinel*, September 6, 1871: 4.

24. "Base Ball. Saturday's Matches—Bad Defeat of the Clevelands by the Bostons," *Boston Journal*, September 4, 1871: 4.

25. *Chicago Tribune*, November 3, 1871: 1.

26. "Base Ball," *Boston Herald*, October 31, 1871: 2.

27. "Special Meeting of the Professional Association," *New York Clipper*, November 11, 1871.

28. Ryczek, 57.

29. "Season Record of the Boston Nine," *Boston Traveler*, November 16, 1871: 2.

30. "Base Ball," *Philadelphia Inquirer*, November 27, 1871: 2.

31. "The Boston Club—Annual Meeting—Election of Officers," *Boston Journal*, December 8, 1871: 1.

THE 1872 SEASON

BY BILL RYCZEK

HARRY WRIGHT WASN'T A SORE loser, but as captain of the Cincinnati Red Stockings, he'd been unaccustomed to losing. After his Red Stockings went through the 1869 season without losing a game, and finished the following year with just a handful of losses, Wright expected that the team he brought to Boston in 1871 would win the first National Association pennant. He'd taken the Red Stockings he believed to be the most reliable, and supplemented them with outstanding young talent like pitcher Al Spalding and second baseman Ross Barnes of Rockford.

The Red Stockings were not only talented; under Wright's leadership they were perhaps the most respected team in the NA, and in early 1872 the *New York Clipper* stated, "Boston sets a good example for other teams with their gentlemanly conduct and honorable play."[1] Betting, one of the albatrosses of the NA, was not allowed on Boston's Union Grounds, which meant that gamblers had to ply their business quietly and couldn't openly abuse those players whose efforts were harmful to their investments.

Despite its talent and character, Boston hadn't won the 1871 pennant, in part due to injuries to George Wright and others, but Harry was certain that, absent the misfortune that dogged his club the previous year, he would win in 1872. He therefore retained essentially the same players, adding only Fraley Rogers, a 22-year-old outfielder from Brooklyn, and Andy Leonard, one of the old Cincinnati Red Stockings who'd played in Washington the previous season.

The NA presented an unbalanced lineup in 1872, almost equally divided between stock clubs and cooperatives. The former paid its players a regular salary while those who played for co-ops received a share of the gate receipts. Nearly all players preferred a guaranteed salary and the most marketable signed with the stock clubs. For the most part, the co-ops were left with players who couldn't win a spot on the stock clubs.

It's hard to beat teams with players who weren't good enough to make those teams, and the presence of such a large number of uncompetitive co-op nines wasn't good for the NA. Harry Wright was to blame for the entry of at least one of the weak sisters. When Benjamin Douglas of the Middletown Mansfields wrote looking to schedule exhibition games, Wright suggested that Douglas pay the NA's $10 admission fee, which would obligate all NA teams to reply in the affirmative to Douglas's requests.

Ten dollars and a box of stationery do not make a major-league team, a fact that would become painfully apparent when the stock clubs met the co-ops on the diamond. At the Union Grounds in Brooklyn, the admission fee was 50 cents when stock teams were playing, but it cost just 25 cents to watch a game involving a co-op team. In mid-May, the *New York Clipper* noted that stock and co-op teams had played each other 18 times, and each time the stock club had won.[2] Eventually the *Clipper* began publishing separate standings for each class, even though they were in the same league.

The Red Stockings had gotten off to a sluggish start in 1871, but in 1872 they left the gate like a lightning bolt, winning 22 of their first 23 games, a pace reminiscent of Wright's old Cincinnati juggernaut. Boston ran roughshod over the co-ops, scoring 20 or more runs seven times in the 23-game span, each time against a co-op team. The only loss was to the Athletics of Philadelphia on May 4. By July 4, when Boston won its 22nd game, the Athletics were second (on a percentage basis) with a 13-3 mark.

On July 27 the Red Stockings (22-2) met the Athletics (14-5) in a game that, if Boston won, would give them a commanding lead. The Athletics shuffled their lineup, and the new combination won the game, 9-1, keeping the Philadelphia club in the race.

As the summer wore on, the NA's weaker teams fell by the wayside, one by one. The Nationals of Washington played their final game on June 26, finishing with an unblemished 0-11 record. There was no official announcement of disbandment; the Nationals simply vanished and played no more. The Olympics, also of Washington, lasted just nine games, although they managed to win two of them.

The Haymakers of Troy, which had been one of the league's better teams in 1871, and which had a 15-10 mark by late July 1872, ceased operations after a game with the Mansfields on July 23. The Troy stockholders, facing expenses of $500 per week, stopped paying the players, who took the field a couple of times on a cooperative basis before ending the career of the venerable organization. A number of the Troy players came from Brooklyn, and when the Haymakers folded, several of them went back to their home city to play for the Eckfords, a co-op that had difficulty putting fans through the gate and nine players on the field.

Cleveland had also fielded a respectable team in 1871. In 1872, they were able to beat the co-ops but not the stock clubs, and that shortcoming prevented them from drawing crowds large enough to pay salaries. After some poor performances in late May, the Forest City club aborted a road trip and returned home to Cleveland. After a lengthy hiatus, they took to the road again in late June. After a 20-1 loss to the Mutuals, Cleveland pitcher Rynie Wolters disappeared, forcing his teammates to take the field shorthanded.

Remarkably, Wolters' eight teammates managed to defeat the Eckfords, an indication of the ineptitude of the Brooklyn club. For a second time, the discouraged Cleveland players crept back to the shores of Lake Erie. In mid-August, with no money left in the treasury of the stock organization, the Forest Citys took the field against the Red Stockings under a cooperative format. Two one-sided losses marked the end of the Cleveland team.

The Mansfields, coming from little Middletown, Connecticut, managed to last until mid-August, when they folded with a 5-19 record, having lost their last 10 games. With their passing, the only co-op teams left in the field were the Atlantics and Eckfords, both of Brooklyn. On the date of the last Cleveland game, the NA's survivors lined up as follows:

	W	L	Pct.	GB
Boston	30	3	.909	—
Athletics	20	5	.800	6
Baltimore	21	13	.618	9½
Mutuals	20	13	.606	10
Troy*	15	10	.600	11
Cleveland*	6	16	.273	18½
Atlantics	5	16	.238	19
Olympics*	2	7	.222	16
Mansfields*	5	19	.208	20½
Eckfords	2	13	.133	19
Nationals*	0	11	.000	19

*Disbanded

Boston, after the fire, November 9th and 10th, 1872 by Joshua Smith. (Library of Congress)

A quick perusal of the standings reveals a number of troubling aspects. First is the sharp divide between Troy and Cleveland, indicative of the uncompetitive nature of the 1872 NA. A second unsettling development is the fact that by mid-August five of the 11 teams—nearly half—were no longer in the field. Further, the paring of teams had not made the NA any more competitive. The six remaining clubs were divided in a rigid class structure: Boston and the Athletics were the aristocracy, Baltimore and the Mutuals represented the middle class, and the Atlantics and Eckfords stood at the bottom of the social ladder.

Finally, one notes the discrepancy in the number of games each team had played. Apart from the troubles of the disbanded clubs, first-place Boston had played 33 games while its closest pursuer, the Athletics, had played just 25. With no formal schedule, each team could dictate its pace, which was a problem throughout the life of the NA. Clubs canceled engagements if one of their players was injured or if a more lucrative opportunity arose. The disbandments created another problem, necessitating an increase in the number of games to be played in each series from five to nine. Many series remained unfinished at the end of the season, as the top teams played exhibitions against each other after they'd finished their quotas, rather than play championship games with the Atlantics and Eckfords, who drew poorly. A game between Baltimore and the Atlantics at Brooklyn's Capitoline Grounds attracted only 100 fans and another between the Red Stockings and Atlantics just 200.

The Red Stockings had six games remaining with the Athletics in September and October, games that would determine the championship of the NA. In the first game, which took place on September 5, the first inning set the tone. The Athletics, batting first, loaded the bases with none out, but couldn't score. The first five Red Stocking batters got hits, leading to three runs. Four more Boston runs in second began the rout that ended with a 16-4 win, leaving the Athletics 7½ games behind.

It looked as though the pennant race was over, for not only had the Athletics fallen further behind, they had played sloppily. At one point, Andy Leonard of Boston fell while running from third to home, but shortstop Denny Mack of the Athletics wasn't paying attention and held the ball while Leonard scrambled to his feet and scored.

With nearly half its teams out of commission, two of the remaining clubs uncompetitive, and the pennant race decided, the NA faced a dilemma. There was no postseason competition to whet fan appetites, and the fact that only six teams remained active encouraged the playing of exhibitions after quotas were completed. Exhibition games were notoriously suspicious, with many fans believing they were decided based upon the gamblers' wishes. Prior to the start of the season, the Red Stockings and Athletics had stated they would not play exhibition games against NA teams, a stand heartily supported by the *Clipper*. When the number of teams dwindled, however, the noble intentions of the Red Stockings and Athletics dissipated.

In order to stimulate interest, William Cammeyer, proprietor of the Union Grounds in Brooklyn, proposed a tournament at his facility and put up $4,000 in prize money. Cammeyer's idea was not original, for in July a Philadelphia sporting gentleman had offered a similar amount if the top five teams in the NA would play one game against each other. His offer was not accepted, but the Red Stockings, Athletics, and Mutuals agreed to compete in Cammeyer's tournament for a first prize of $1,800, a second prize of $1,200, and a third prize of $1,000.

The tournament began on October 8 and 9 with two exciting games. On the 8th, the Mutuals and Red Stockings played a 10-inning 7-7 tie that was called due to darkness and a disabling injury suffered by Boston catcher Dave Birdsall when he was hit by a foul tip. The following day, the Athletics beat the Mutuals 9-7 in 12 innings.

Despite the exciting baseball being played at the Union Grounds, the fans didn't seem interested. Attendance was disappointing, and it looked as though Cammeyer might not recoup his investment. His prospects weren't helped by the fact that Boston, which was not playing in the tournament on the 9th, played the Atlantics at the nearby Capitoline Grounds, siphoning a few potential spectators from Cammeyer.[3]

Charles H. Porter, president of the Red Stockings in 1872. (Courtesy of the Quincy Public Library).

	W	L	Pct.	GB
Boston	39	8	.830	—
Athletics	30	14	.682	7½
Baltimore	35	19	.648	7½
Mutuals	34	20	.630	8½
Troy	15	10	.600	
Cleveland	6	16	.273	20½
Atlantics	9	28	.243	25
Mansfields	5	19	.208	22½
Olympics	2	7	.222	18
Eckfords	3	26	.103	27
Nationals	0	11	.000	21

Note: Although the NA based its standings on number of wins, the table above has been adapted to the modern standard of percentage of wins.

Under the tournament's round-robin format, the Athletics and Red Stockings qualified to play for the championship, but the game ended in a 10-10 tie called due to darkness after 12 innings. Since Cammeyer was dissatisfied with the gate receipts, he continued to amend the format, allowing the Mutuals, who'd been eliminated, to re-enter the fray, and set up a second championship game. That contest was postponed due to rain and Boston, which had a number of injured players, declined to play further. After 10 days and nine games, there was no champion. It was rumored that the teams had agreed in advance that the Athletics and Red Stockings would get $1,500 each and the Mutuals would get $1,000. Despite the muddled results in New York, the same three teams went to Philadelphia to partake in a similar affair, which proved as unfulfilling as Cammeyer's disappointing tourney.

With the pennant in hand, the Red Stockings fell off the torrid pace they'd maintained for most of the season, going 7-5-1 in their last 13 games. Still, they won the pennant handily.

Boston's success on the field was not accompanied by a happy pecuniary result. Harry Wright was one of the most financially astute managers in baseball, and he was as unaccustomed to losing money as he was to losing games, but the mismatched league, the unsuccessful tournament, and the fans' skepticism over the integrity of the games led to a $5,000 deficit at the end of the year. With cash in short supply, the Red Stockings had been unable to pay its players in full when the team disbanded for the winter.

A catastrophic fire ravaged downtown Boston in October 1872, and in combination with the losses suffered by the Red Stockings, it was questionable whether Wright would be able to place a team on the field in 1873 to defend the NA title. He spent much of the winter attempting to convince his players that if they signed for the 1873 season, the club would pay the salary arrearage as well as salaries for 1873.

Perhaps it was Harry's formidable rhetorical ability, or maybe it was the lack of viable alternatives, for there were only a few stable stock organizations, and none of the players wanted to take their chances with a cooperative nine. Whatever the reason, virtually all of the Red Stocking players agreed to play in 1873.

On December 11, 1872, more than 150 supporters of Boston baseball met in Brackett's Hall and developed a plan to save the Red Stockings. A new organization, called the Boston Base Ball Club, was formed and the Boston Association, which had operated the team in 1872, was dissolved. The new entity took control of the team, raised money through the sale of stock, and assumed the debts of the Boston Association, including the unpaid salaries. There would be major-league baseball in Boston in 1873, and it would be winning baseball, for the 1872 club was the first of four consecutive championship teams.[4]

NOTES

1 *New York Clipper*, March 9, 1872.

2 *New York Clipper*, May 18, 1872.

3 Remarkably, the Atlantics beat the first-place Red Stockings.

4 In its November 30, 1872, issue, the *New York Clipper* reported receipt of a letter from Thomas Hall of Boston stating that it was almost certain that the Red Stockings would take a trip to England during the summer of 1873. The supposition was correct but a year premature.

THE 1873 SEASON

BY BILL RYCZEK

THE 1964 PHILADELPHIA PHILLIES are known for staging one of the most precipitous collapses in the history of major-league baseball, squandering a 6½-game lead with 12 games to play. Nearly a century earlier, another Philadelphia team, the White Stockings, also lost a seemingly insurmountable lead and gave the National Association flag to Harry Wright's Red Stockings of Boston.

Boston had captured the pennant in 1872, and since the core of the team returned intact, the Red Stockings were favored to repeat in 1873. The White Stockings were a new organization, but in the 1870s, newly formed teams did not face the same obstacles as those encountered by 20th-century expansion clubs. With no reserve clause, the White Stockings were able to use their substantial capital to sign talented veterans, including a number of players induced to defect from the rival Athletics. The new club sent its $10 entry fee to Harry Wright, chairman of the Championship Committee, and prepared to battle for the pennant. Upon receiving the funds, Wright responded to Philadelphia president David Reid, "May the best club win is the wish of yours truly."[1]

The White Stockings were an artistic and financial success from Opening Day. On June 11 they played the Athletics, and the rivalry, plus the presence of a number of former Athletics in the White Stockings nine, attracted a crowd of 8,000 to 10,000, yielding about $5,000 to the White Stockings treasury. For the season, the White Stockings won eight of nine games with the Athletics, and by mid-July they were 27-3 and in first place by a whopping 8½ games.

The Red Stockings were in second place with a 16-8 record, not bad but leaving them well in arrears of the new Philadelphia club. Boston had lost a game to the Atlantics, one of the league's poorer teams, and another to the pathetic Resolutes of Elizabeth, New Jersey, who won just twice all season. On June 5 the Red Stockings lost to Philadelphia by the embarrassing score of 22-8. The 1872 champions looked awful in the field and on the bases, and Al Spalding pitched so poorly that Harry Wright took his place in the box. Harry was even worse, giving up eight runs in the ninth inning.

Boston usually started the season strongly, for Harry Wright had each player join the local YMCA and work out daily, but in 1873 they left the gate haltingly. George Wright, the Red Stockings' best player, was suffering from rheumatism. Jim O'Rourke, who'd been a rookie the previous season with the Mansfields of Middletown, signed late and had taken some time to get in fighting trim. James White, who seemed to have an annual period of indecision regarding his desire to play professional baseball, likewise was dilatory in getting to Boston.

In mid-July, following a Red Stocking loss to the mediocre Mutuals of New York, the *New York Clipper* stated, "[I]t is evident that [Boston] will not be the champions this year. In fact, if they do not show improvement in September, they will hardly reach second place."[2]

In the 1870s it was common for teams to take a hiatus from their schedule during the dog days of summer. Crowds were typically smaller during the heat of July and early August, as many people left the city for the cooler countryside, and NA teams frequently took extended tours. They played in towns and cities that rarely saw big-league ball, where people were more likely to endure a bit of sun and humidity for the rare opportunity to see major leaguers in action.

At the beginning of August, the Red Stockings embarked on a lengthy tour scheduled to take them to Allegheny, St. Louis, Keokuk, Chicago (where the White Stockings of that city were inactive following the great fire of 1871), Rockford, Detroit, Guelph, Toronto, Ottawa, and Ogdensburgh. In addition to giving Canadians an opportunity to fill the Boston coffers, the tour would allow the Red Stockings to benefit from the cooler Northern climate. The Philadelphia White Stockings, eschewing a tour, repaired to the resort town of Cape May, New Jersey, for rest and recuperation. Once they were fully rejuvenated, they expected to coast to the pennant in September.

In early June the White Stockings had released veteran infielder Bob Addy at his own request.[3] Addy returned to his home in Rockford, Illinois, where he'd previously played with that city's Forest City club. Harry Wright thought Addy could help the Red Stockings and wrote to him, "Telegraph you will join us in St. Louis, and we will go for them all, raising the standard of the mighty Reds higher and higher until we—just say you will come, that's all."[4] Henry Chadwick and the *Clipper* may have given up on the Red Stockings season, but Harry had not. He had earlier written to Hicks Hayhurst, manager of the Athletics: "Let us get our and your second wind, then look out Philadelphias."[5]

When the White Stockings returned from Cape May, they did not seem to be the same nine that left Philadelphia three weeks earlier. The team that had won 27 of its first 30 games before the break lost its first five afterward. Meanwhile, the Red Stockings came off the road red-hot, and closed the gap to 4½ games by September 15, when they faced the White Stockings in a key game at Philadelphia's Jefferson Street Grounds.

On the day of the game, Philadelphia pitcher George Zettlein was reported to be feeling poorly. He might have been ill, he might have been hung over, or perhaps he was simply not in the mood to play. Whatever the cause, he pitched poorly, yielding 15 hits in a 7-5 Boston win. The Red Stockings were now just 3½ games behind with six weeks to play.

Since there was no fixed schedule in the NA, team managers could arrange their games in any order they chose, as long as they completed their quota. Harry Wright's correspondence is filled with letters attempting to book games with other NA clubs, and in 1873 he seemed to encounter more difficulty than usual. The delays in booking worked to Boston's advantage, for during the final six weeks, they had six games against the Nationals of Washington, who finished the season 8-31.

After beating the White Stockings, Boston defeated the Atlantics and Mutuals, while Philadelphia lost to the latter club. The defeat was harmful, but the manner in which it occurred was even more telling, for the White Stockings completely broke down. The Mutuals scored five unearned runs in the second inning on four Philadelphia errors. Zettlein was so ineffective that he was removed in midgame. Fergy Malone and Ned Cuthbert became embroiled in an argument when Malone suspected that Cuthbert was not giving his best effort. The flurry of errors, desperate position switches, and shouting matches on the field were indicative of a club in disarray. Still, the *Clipper* kept the faith. "Philadelphia will almost certainly win," it reported, "unless they fall flat on their faces in the next four weeks."[6]

That, however, is exactly what they did. Zettlein had done something to cause management to lose confidence in him, and he was replaced in some critical games by George Bechtel, whose later banishment by the National League indicates that he was probably not the most reliable player in the NA. Bechtel pitched against the Nationals on the first day of October and allowed the Washington club to jump out to a 14-2 lead. For a bad team like the Nationals, however, a 12-run margin was not a sure thing, and by the ninth inning, the lead had shrunk to 14-13, with Philadelphia's Jim Devlin on second with the tying run. Unwisely trying for third on an infield grounder, Devlin was thrown out and the game was over. Despite 18 Philadelphia hits and 19 Washington errors, the White Stockings had lost, and dropped into a virtual tie with the Red Stockings.

The following day, Boston and Philadelphia met in the latter city in a game that would put the winner in first place. With the Red Stockings leading 7-5 in the fourth inning and two Bostonians on base, Al Spalding hit a fly ball to short center field. Center fielder Fred Treacey came in, Captain Jimmy Wood went out from second base, and the ball fell safely as the two men stood looking at each other. While the ball lay harmlessly on the grass, Treacey and Wood

1873

Memorandum of Agreement between the Boston Base Ball Association of Boston, and Andrew J. Leonard.

Witnesseth! That the said A. J. Leonard hereby agrees to play Base Ball and other Athletic Sports and exercises with said Association and with or for no other Association, person, or body whatever for the term commencing March 16th 1873, and ending November 15th of the same year for which labor and services the Association agrees to pay the said A. J. Leonard the sum of Sixteen Hundred Dollars ($1600.00)

The said A. J. Leonard further agrees to obey all orders and regulations which are now in existence or which may hereafter be established by said Association or its officers for the conduct of himself or of the members of said organization.

The said A. J. Leonard from the signing hereof untill the expiration of said term, promises and hereby agrees to comport himself in a quiet, temperate, and gentlemanly manner at all times Violations of any of the terms of this contract

If not a success financially will forfeit One Hundred Dollars ($100.00)

Andy Leonard's 1873 player contract, two pages. Courtesy of Heritage Auctions, Dallas. The contract was tendered to the auction house by Leonard's grandson, Charles McCarty. Thanks to Kesha Holmes-Smith of Heritage.

will nullify and destroy the whole of the said association so desire and choose.

In witness whereof the said Boston Base Ball Association and A. J. Leonard have hereunto set their hands and seals this 11th day of January 1873.

C.H.P.   Chas. H. Porter
         Prest. Boston Base Ball Asso.

A.J.L.   A. J. Leonard

H.W.   Harry Wright Secy. B.B.B.A.

began screaming at each other while both Boston runners scored.

Later in the inning, Wood dropped a throw at second base and fired the ball to the ground in disgust, as another run crossed the plate. The next inning, Wood, apparently having lost confidence in some of his players, made a number of changes in the lineup. The final score was 18-7, and Boston, after a long run, was in first place. It was the Red Stockings' 10th straight win.

Two days later, the White Stockings lost 5-4 to the Mutuals, as Devlin again ended the game by being thrown out after a poor baserunning decision. Devlin, like Bechtel, was later banned from the National League, although there is no evidence he was playing to lose in 1873. Treacey and Zettlein were also suspect characters who were later accused of crooked play, and in retrospect the sorry performance of the White Stockings in the latter stages of the 1873 season took on a somewhat sinister air.

Boston continued to win and finished the year with victories in 26 of its final 31 games. The White Stockings, after their 27-3 start, had finished 9-14. The final standings were as follows:

	W	L	Pct.	GB
Boston Red Stockings	43	16	.729	—
Philadelphia White Stockings	36	17	.679	4
Lord Baltimore	34	22	.607	7½
Philadelphia Athletics	28	23	.549	11
New York Mutuals	29	24	.547	11
Brooklyn Atlantics	17	37	.315	23½
Washington Nationals	8	31	.205	25
Elizabeth Resolutes	2	21	.087	23
Marylands	0	6	.000	16½

Note: Although the NA based its standings on number of wins, the table above has been adapted to the modern standard of percentage of wins.

When the games concluded, two controversies lingered. The first had become public knowledge in August, when a number of contracts, supposedly signed in secret, became public. After a two-year hiatus, the city of Chicago was ready to re-enter the Association under the management of Norman Gassette and a local businessman named William Hulbert. Chicago did everything in a big way, and what better way to re-emerge on the scene than with the best players from the NA's top team. In August, that team was the Philadelphia White Stockings, and Gassette and Hulbert signed seven White Stocking players to 1874 Chicago contracts. Included among the seven were Zettlein, Wood, Treacy, Cuthbert, and Devlin, all of whom had played poorly, and in some cases suspiciously, in the latter stages of the 1873 season. There was a rule prohibiting players from signing for a subsequent year prior to the end of the current season, but NA rules, like latter-day records, were made to be broken. The *New York Times*, in late September, listed 43 players who had signed for the 1874 season, and all of the newspapers listed 1874 rosters long before the 1873 season had ended.[7]

While these major rules violations went unpunished, the second controversy, based on a minor alleged technical violation, kept the pennant from Boston until deep into the winter. As noted, when Bob Addy had been released by the White Stockings, he repaired to Rockford, where he played in a pickup game on July 4. The NA had a rule stipulating that a player could not play for a new team within 60 days of appearing in a game with another team. The intent was to prevent revolving from team to team, but no one seriously believed that the rule covered pickup games.

No one except the Philadelphia White Stockings, whose hands were far from clean and who should have been ashamed to claim the pennant after the way they had finished the season. The White Stockings asked that all 31 games in which Addy appeared for Boston be forfeited, which would give the pennant to Philadelphia.

The Championship Committee, which had the duty of officially awarding the title, consisted of Harry Wright and two Philadelphians, Hicks Hayhurst of the Athletics and Frank McBride of the White Stockings. Both Wright and McBride had a direct interest in the outcome, and Hayhurst was a rival of both. Parochialism was a continual thorn in the collective side of the NA, one that would contrib-

The 1873 Boston club. (Courtesy of Ars Longa Cards).

ute to its ultimate demise two years hence when the Philadelphians conspired to award shortstop Davy Force to the Athletics.

In January 1874 McBride said the Championship Committee could not award the title until the Judiciary Committee ruled on the legality of Addy's participation in Boston games. Wright sent a number of letters to the members of the Judiciary Committee urging them to meet, but also wrote to Philadelphia president Reid, "Independent of any action you may see fit to charge the Judiciary Committee with, we consider ourselves justly and honorably entitled to the championship honors for 1873. Not from a single source other than the Philadelphia Club have we heard a doubt expressed as to the fairness of our title."[8]

Although a prompt meeting would have disposed of the groundless charges, the Judiciary Committee dawdled and did not convene. Finally, Wright convinced Hayhurst, with whom he had a good relationship, to sign the resolution declaring Boston the champion, thus carrying the day by 2 to 1. Reid protested that Hayhurst had been coerced by Wright, but he had been defeated at his silly game, and Boston officially claimed the 1873 pennant of the National Association.

NOTES

1. Wright Correspondence, Wright to Reid, April 4, 1873.
2. *New York Clipper*, July 26, 1873.
3. In his biography of Addy for the SABR BioProject, Peter Morris indicated that he believed the reason Addy asked for his release was to be present at the birth of his son, who was born, Morris believed, on August 1.
4. Wright Correspondence, Wright to Addy, date illegible.
5. Wright Correspondence, Wright to Hayhurst, June 23, 1873.
6. *New York Clipper*, September 27, 1873.
7. *New York Times*, September 21, 1873.
8. Wright Correspondence, Wright to Reid, February 12, 1874.

THE 1874 SEASON

BY BILL RYCZEK

FOR THE BOSTON RED STOCKINGS, the 1874 campaign bore a great similarity to baseball's strike season of 1981; each year's pennant race was divided into two segments, separated by an interruption of roughly two months. In 1981, the players union, under the leadership of Marvin Miller, initiated a work stoppage, while in 1874 the Red Stockings and Philadelphia Athletics, under the leadership of Harry Wright, sailed across the Atlantic to bring the American game of baseball to England. Miller's group had a better financial outcome, but the trip to Europe was a historic journey that was well worth the monetary loss.

Boston, winner of the previous two National Association championships, took the field with a lineup virtually unchanged from 1873. The only departing regular was right fielder Bob Addy, who had played such a controversial role in the 1873 pennant race. Addy's replacement was Cal McVey, an original 1871 Red Stocking who spent the 1872 and 1873 seasons in Baltimore. McVey was a much better hitter than Addy, and in 1874 he led the team in batting average, runs, hits, and runs batted in.

A second addition to the team was 25-year-old outfielder George Hall, who arrived from the Canaries of Baltimore to spell Harry Wright in center field. Baltimore had a strong team in 1872 and 1873, but in 1874 the Canaries were reduced to cooperative status, which made it difficult for them to retain their players. Wright, 39, was in his last season as an active player (except for token appearances during the next few years) and was no longer able to play every game.

As always, there had been turnover during the off-season, and the NA would field just eight teams in 1874, the smallest number in its five-year life. The limited quantity, however, did not substantially improve the quality. Baltimore, as a co-op that couldn't afford top talent, was in for a rough year. The Blues of Hartford were a new team with experienced but mediocre talent and would battle the Canaries to stay out of last place. The Atlantics had played poorly since joining the NA in 1872, and the Mutuals were almost as bad in 1873. The Philadelphia White Stockings' roster had been eviscerated by the raid of Chicago, which was back in the major leagues for the first time in three years. It appeared that Boston's primary challenge for the 1874 pennant would come from their old rivals, the Athletics.

At the end of the 1872 season, Boston had been in financial distress, but by the time the 1874 campaign got under way, the fiscal ship had been righted. Even after paying roughly $4,000 in 1872 expenses in 1873, the treasury, buoyed by stockholder contributions of $3,700, showed a surplus of $700. Despite two championship seasons, the payroll had been reduced from $16,700 in 1872 to $15,800 in 1874. With a cushion in the treasury and lower expenses, the financial outlook for 1874 was relatively bright, despite the pall cast by the financial panic of the previous September. Wright hoped that the European venture would provide an additional boost to the exchequer.

The start of the season was delayed by unseasonably cold weather, and Boston's home opener, scheduled for April 25 against the Philadelphia White Stockings, was postponed when a spring storm dropped six inches of snow on the city. Although the skies cleared, the Union Grounds remained unplayable, and a second game against the White Stockings was called off, as was a match against Hartford scheduled for the 29th.

Finally, on May 2, the Red Stockings were able to open the season, and their 12-3 victory over the Mutuals was the first of 13 consecutive wins. Two losses in late May—shocking defeats at the hands of the Atlantics—were followed by five more victories to bring Boston's record to 18-2, giving the Red Stockings a 6½-game lead over the second-place Athletics.

The Atlantics weren't a great team, but they provided a few surprises in 1874. The most important addition to the Brooklyn club was 18-year-old pitcher Tommy Bond, who late in the season came within a single out of pitching the first no-hitter in major-league history. Harry Wright liked what he saw, and after Al Spalding left for Chicago, Bond pitched Boston to National League pennants in 1877 and 1878.

Despite their two wins, the Atlantics were not a threat to dislodge the Red Stockings from the top slot. Neither was Hartford, despite a strong start, nor Baltimore. Philadelphia had lost too many top players to contend, and the Chicago team those players joined was plagued by the same suspicious play that sank Philadelphia in 1873. The White Stockings had a disastrous road trip in early June that proved the undoing of the team.

In Philadelphia, Chicago dissipated a 6-1 lead and lost 15-6 to the other White Stockings, their collapse marked by a number of suspicious errors. Concerned about the integrity of their players, the White Stockings held some of them out of the lineup for a game against the Mutuals. The new lineup played far worse than the old, and Chicago sustained an ignominious 38-1 defeat, a debacle caused by numerous errors (the teams combined for 36) and 34 Mutual hits. Catcher Ferguson Malone, the former Philadelphia player now with Chicago, became disgusted with his pitcher's erratic delivery, and after several wild pitches, he made only a perfunctory effort to chase the errant heaves. The margin of defeat was the largest ever for a professional team.

The 1874 Red Stockings club. Top row (L-R): Cal McVey, Al Spalding, Deacon White, Ross Barnes; Seated (L-R): Jim O'Rourke, Andy Leonard, George Wright, Harry Wright, George Hall, Harry Schafer, Tommy Beals (Public Domain).

The Red Stockings continued to hold first place, but fell off their torrid early pace. George Wright missed a month with an injury variously described as a sprained ankle and an injured knee. Second baseman Ross Barnes was below par due to a bad hand. In early July Harry Wright took time out from the NA schedule to take his team on a tour that included a swing into Canada which, according to Wright's reports, was a great financial success.[1] On July 15, after their return from the north, Boston lost to the Athletics, 6-4, a defeat that cut their lead over the latter club to 4½ games. The contest was billed as the farewell game, for afterward the two teams embarked for Europe, and the Red Stockings did not play another championship game for nearly two months.

Current teams occasionally travel to Japan for regular-season games, complain about the 14- to 15-hour flight, and often play poorly upon their return. In 1874 travel was much more grueling, and it took the Red Stockings and Athletics 11 days to sail from Philadelphia to Liverpool. The return journey was plagued by four days of stormy weather and the death of a passenger (not one of the baseball entourage).[2]

Because of the heat, most clubs played a light schedule in August, and the absence of the NA's two best teams created an additional problem. The six remaining clubs had to play each other far too frequently to sustain fan interest, and a crowd of more than a thousand spectators was rare. Philadelphia had the White Stockings, but Boston was without baseball for two months, so the Hartford and Philadelphia nines scheduled games there on August 12 and 13. Only 500 attended on the 12th, and the next day's game was postponed by rain.

Finally, on September 10, the Red Stockings and Athletics, who had spent a month in England and Ireland playing baseball against each other, did the same thing on US soil. After an enthusiastic welcome in Philadelphia, Boston won 5-4 in a game marked by a controversial call of umpire Theodore Bomeisler that went in favor of the Red Stockings. After Bomeisler left the field under police protection, the two teams boarded the New York Express on the Albany Road and received a second rousing reception in Boston, where the Athletics reversed the result of the previous game and defeated the Red Stockings by a single run.

While the two top teams were away, the Mutuals had feasted on weak competition to lift themselves into the thick of the pennant race. After the games of September 10, the standings were as follows:

	W	L	Pct.	GB
Boston	31	8	.795	—
Athletics	23	11	.676	5½
Mutuals	30	17	.638	5
Philadelphia	23	20	.535	10
Chicago	22	25	.468	13
Hartford	12	22	.353	16½
Atlantics	11	28	.282	20
Baltimore	7	28	.200	22

The Mutuals were the most unpredictable team in the NA, and certainly one of the most suspect. The club had been connected with Tammany Hall since its inception in the 1850s, and politicians like John Wildey and Alex Davidson had been active in management. The infamous William M. "Boss" Tweed was also involved with the club, and on at least one occasion helped it obtain funds from the City of New York. During the amateur era, many Mutual players were employed by the city's coroner's and street-cleaning departments.

Gamblers followed the Mutuals wherever they played, and in early August 1874 the club had been involved in a suspicious affair. Betting odds before a game with the White Stockings were puzzling, and when the Mutuals removed star pitcher Bobby Mathews with an alleged groin injury after one inning, those who had backed them believed the fix was in. Nothing was ever proven, and a doctor certified to Mathews' disability, but there had been so many shady episodes involving the Mutuals that any unusual circumstance was grounds for suspicion.

The Mutuals had played horribly in 1873, and many were convinced that their poor performance was not accidental. In 1874, however, they were playing better than they'd played in several years. When the Red Stockings and Athletics left for England in mid-July, the Mutuals were just 17-16. While the two teams were away, they won 13 of 14 games to move within 5½ games of the Red Stockings with nearly two months of the season remaining.

The Mutuals and Red Stockings were scheduled to play each other on September 22 and 24, and by that time the New York nine had crept to within three games of the lead. In the first game, Harry Wright was the starting pitcher for the first time all season. Al Spalding had pitched the day before and lost and perhaps Harry, who was more conscious than most NA managers of his pitcher's workload, wanted to spare him a few innings.

Harry turned over a 4-3 advantage to Spalding when the latter took over the pitching chores in the fifth, but Boston's ace couldn't hold the lead. The Mutuals scored three times in that inning, and although Boston rallied to tie the game, the Mutuals scored the winning run in the ninth inning on a sacrifice fly by Dick Higham—the same Dick Higham who later became the only major-league umpire ever banished for dishonesty. The lead was down to two games.

Two days later, the margin was reduced to a single game when the Mutuals beat Boston 8-5. The Mutuals had won 19 of 20 games, while Boston had lost five of seven since returning to the United States.

	W	L	Pct.	GB
Boston	32	13	.711	—
Mutuals	34	17	.667	1

Nothing could rejuvenate a faltering team like three home games against the last-place Baltimore club and, as expected, the Red Stockings won all three. Boston, due to the interruption caused by the European tour, had played several fewer games than their pursuers. In order to complete their full quota of games (they would be the only NA team to do so), the Red Stockings had to endure a grueling October schedule. NA teams generally played no more than three or four games a week, but during the last 19 days of the 1874 season, Boston played 16 championship games.

As in 1873, much of Boston's stretch run was scheduled to be played against the NA's weaker teams, the same teams the Mutuals had feasted upon. At one point, 28 of New York's 36 wins were at the expense of Chicago, Hartford, the Atlantics, and Baltimore. During the final month, they had to test their mettle against the top clubs. Of Boston's final 26 games, 17 were against Hartford, Baltimore, and the Atlantics. The quality of the competition was reflected in the results. Following the second loss to the Mutuals, Harry Wright's crew finished 20-5, while the Mutuals were just 8-6. Boston won its third consecutive pennant by a comfortable margin.

	W	L	Pct.	GB
Boston	52	18	.743	—
Mutuals	42	23	.646	7½
Athletics	33	22	.600	11½
Philadelphia	29	29	.500	17
Chicago	28	31	.475	18½
Atlantics	22	33	.400	22½
Hartford	16	37	.302	27½
Baltimore	9	38	.191	31½

Good had triumphed over evil. The Mutuals and their Tammany backers had fallen to Boston in what the *New York Clipper* described as a "triumph of good training, discipline, and earnest, united efforts to win."[3] On November 6, to celebrate a third consecutive pennant, the Boston stockholders held a banquet for the players. After dinner, Albert Spalding stood up and proposed a toast "to the Boston Baseball Club—may we fly the pennant in 1876."[4] The Red Stockings would indeed fly the pennant that year, but Spalding would see it only when he visited Boston with his Chicago teammates.

Late in the 1874 season, there were rumors that Spalding planned to sign with the White Stockings for 1875. Teammate James White had supposedly turned down a Chicago offer of $2,000 per year. "Chicago has become the last city a professional wants to go to," said the *Clipper*. "Players strive to get engagements in Boston, where they meet with considerate treatment."[5] A year later, however, White, Spalding, McVey, and Barnes decided to move to the city where the weather was cold, the press was critical, and the fans were demanding, but the money was right. They had one more year in Boston, and that year they would lead the

Red Stockings to perhaps the most dominant season of any team in major-league history.

NOTES

1. *Hartford Courant*, July 4, 1874.
2. The tour is covered in a separate chapter.
3. *New York Clipper*, November 7, 1874.
4. *New York Clipper*, November 14, 1874. The team that won a pennant was considered the champion of the subsequent season. Therefore, by winning in 1874, Boston was entitled to fly the pennant in 1875.
5. *New York Clipper*, July 11, 1874.

THE 1875 SEASON

BY BOB LEMOINE

"In no other major league campaign did a team's superiority show as it did in 1875."
— David Quentin Voigt[1]

IN 1975 CINCINNATI, DUBBED "THE Big Red Machine," visited Boston in the World Series. It is doubtful anyone remarked "Well, it's nothing like the 'Big Red Machine' Boston had in 1875." Those 1875 days were long forgotten, but Boston did have a Big Red (Stocking) Machine that dominated baseball, going 71-8 with an .899 winning percentage, simply unheard of in the modern day.[2] Very few ever mention such a feat, and some only consider the "modern" era of baseball from 1901 on.

The 1875 season saw unique attempts at expanding the National Association of Professional Base Ball Players. To use the language of modern business, several startup companies tried and failed, and lack of management and structure created great gaps between the haves and the have-nots. The NAPBBP was baseball's first experiment with a professional league, and it would die a slow death in 1875 while Boston dominated yet again. This was the end of an era.

This would be the final year for the Boston Red Stockings – Harry Wright would give up the name to Cincinnati when it re-entered professional baseball in 1876. Four core players of the team would leave for Chicago, as owner William Hulbert opened his wallet and Midwest charm for these Boston stars. But his action also included ending the National Association itself, which somehow survived a five-year run despite major organizational flaws. It was the end of player-dominated teams. Baseball was now organized under a group of business owners determined to escape the transient nature of the National Association. Baseball was moving into big business. Just around the corner was 1876 and the new National League that is still with us today.

The 1875 season saw six new clubs pay the user-friendly $10 fee and join the National Association, pushing the league total to 13 teams, with disastrous results. Three of the new clubs were located in the West; though ambitious, they proved to be financially unsustainable. Much of Boston's success was due to the total lack of talent now entering the league. If the season were being replayed in a video montage, perhaps the best background music would be Queen's "Another One Bites the Dust." "Given the economic depression of the times and the obvious superiority of Boston, it was unrealistic for newcomers to hope for large crowds," wrote historian David Quentin Voigt.[3]

The Philadelphia Centennial club was created on the assumption the City of Brotherly Love could support three clubs. That was not the case. The Centennials went 2-12 and were outscored 138-70. They did manage a huge upset of their city rival Athletics, which the *Philadelphia Times* called "one of those freaks that baseball is subject to."[4] They followed their surprising win with a 20-1 loss to the same team the next day. The final game of their short existence resulted in a 5-0 shutout loss to Albert Spalding and Boston on May 24 upon which the *Times* commented, "(H)ad they wished their heartiest to lose they could not have done worse."[5] About 100 devoted fans were there to see the grand finale, and the *Times* summed up that despite the franchise's doing okay financially, "better to disband ere money was lost."[6]

The breakup of the Centennials also led to a first in baseball history. Knowing the team would not be able to survive the season, the stockholders sold George Bechtel and Bill Craver to the Athletics for $1,500. This reportedly is the first known club-to-club player transaction in baseball history, "and the future possibilities of such a tactic captured the imagination of more mercenary promoters," wrote Voigt.[7]

The only major-league club ever located in Iowa was the Keokuk Westerns, which had the distinction of a

1-12 record and a .180 team batting average. The White Stockings traveled to Keokuk to begin the season, made only $68 on the trip from the low gate attendance, and "will not pay another visit there for a long time," the *Chicago Tribune* wrote.[8] Boston made the trip to Iowa on June 10, won 6-4, and decided to forfeit their games on June 12 and 14 and head for Chicago "on account of their many games and their recent hard traveling," the *Boston Globe* reported.[9] Boston made more money playing in Chicago. Keokuk soon disbanded, and the hopes that professional baseball would spread west would have to wait.

The new Washington Nationals also struggled, batting .193 as a team, and were outscored 338-107, being shut out five times. Of the 338 runs the Nationals allowed, only 105 were earned, the result of 285 errors. Eight players had 20-plus errors for the season. Washington started the season 0-11; in five consecutive losses their opponents scored more than 20 runs (including 22-5 and 24-0 routs by Boston). They finished their miserable season 5-23, dropping out of the league after a July 4 game. It was reported that the club's business manager made off with team funds and the players were left without two dimes to rub together over 1,000 miles from home.[10] More likely, however, the players concocted the story themselves to solicit funds to pay their way home.[11]

That July 4 contest was also the final game for the St. Louis Reds, who played Boston only once, losing 10-5 on June 3 in St. Louis. Boston's win on that date put them at 26-0, the last win in their season-opening undefeated streak dating back to April 19, while St. Louis fell to 2-8. The average age of the St. Louis players was just under 23, and the team batting average for the season was .199. They were outscored 161-60 with 150 errors making only 50 of those runs earned. They finished the season 4-15. Because of poor gate attendance, the club was given no invitations to travel east.

New Haven was Connecticut's second attempt at fielding a professional baseball club. Boston defeated the Elm City club in the first two games of the season, 6-0 and 14-3. New Haven went on to lose its first 15 games, and a surprise win on July 2 against Boston

The Red Stockings and Philadelphia Athletics in 1875, in a rare glimpse at the original South End Grounds. (Boston Public Library).

only pulled the team's record up to 3-24. New Haven's final record of 7-40 caused less of a stir in the league than did players Henry Luff and Billy Geer, who were arrested for leaving hotels with more luggage than they had entered with.[12] Extra luggage didn't amount to better play on the field, however, as Luff and Geer had 50 and 49 errors respectively, on a club that committed 447, was outscored 397-170, and had a .218 team batting average.

The final new club to join in 1875 was the other St. Louis club, the Brown Stockings. They were the most respectable new club, going 39-29, good enough for fourth place, led by Lipman Pike's .346 batting average and George Bradley's 33 wins. While being outscored by Boston 77-35, the Brown Stockings did pull off two victories: 5-4 and 5-3 victories on June 5 (Boston's first loss after 26 victories) and August 21. Those two victories accounted for 25 percent of Boston's losses for the season. This St. Louis club would spend two seasons in the National League, and then disband in 1877.

Then there was the legendary Brooklyn Atlantics club, who were a shell of their former selves. Founded in 1855 and one of the founding clubs of the National Association of Base Ball Players, the club's fate in 1875 was a sad ending to a storied franchise. This Atlantics team batted .195 as a team, with 432 errors contributing to 299 unearned runs. The team was outscored 438-132. Not surprisingly, Boston was undefeated against Brooklyn, going 6-0 and outscoring the Atlantics 74-22. Even using 35 players did not help the Brooklyn cause. The Atlantics won their second game on May 26 to go 2-11, but then lost their last 31 games to finish a horrendous 2-42.

The Philadelphia Athletics were the not-so-close second-place finishers to Boston. The Athletics were a formidable 53-20, led by four players in the starting lineup batting over .300 (Bill Craver, Davy Force, Ezra Sutton, and Dave Eggler) and one at .299 (George Hall). Twenty-three year-old Cap Anson batted .325 and pitcher Dick McBride won 44 games with a 2.33 ERA. Still, Philadelphia finished 15 games behind Boston.

Hartford finished a strong third (54-28) with a rare feature at the time of two strong starting pitchers, Candy Cummings (35-12, 1.60) and Tommy Bond (19-16, 1.43). The Philadelphia Whites (or Pearls) brought in a young pitcher who didn't want his father to know he played baseball for a living, so he took the name Joe Josephs. Facing Chicago on July 28, the pitcher, whose real name was Joe Borden, threw a no-hitter, the first in professional baseball history, mostly disregarded by those who do not count the National Association as a "major league."

Stories happening off the field are commonplace today, but not so much in the 1870s. Yet, two major off-the-field stories dominated the baseball world during the season.

While the 1874 season was still in progress, the Chicago White Stockings had signed infielder Davy Force to an 1875 contract dated September 18. When the 1874 season ended, the Philadelphia Athletics also signed Force to a contract, dated December 5. National Association rules forbade a player to sign a contract with a team while under contract with another, but newspapers frequently posted late in the season a "who's who" of player changes for the coming season. Even though the Chicago signing was legally November 2 and not September 18, the Association's Judiciary Committee ruled that Force belonged to Chicago. However, politics were at play, and the committee was to give its report in the evening of the general session.

In the meantime, new officers for the National Association had been elected, and Charles Spering of the Athletics was voted in as president. Not surprising, Spering refused the committee's report and attempted to persuade the delegates that Force belonged in Philadelphia. He then postponed the decision until the next morning. The next day was also when the newly elected members of the Judiciary Committee would meet. One of the newly elected members, from the Keokuk club, declined to accept the position, so Spering found it in the best interests of all to fill the position himself, placing three men from Philadelphia on the five-man committee. The ruling on Force was reversed. Chicago was, of course, irate, as was Harry Wright, over the injustice. Unruly crowds followed Force and the Athletics, and the Philadelphia fans countered. A June 28 extra-inning game at the Athletics saw Boston leave with a 10-10 tie and an unruly mob on the rain-drenched field.

Boston made only three personnel moves before the 1875 season. Outfielder Jack Manning, a member of the 1873 club, returned, and along with his glove he also threw 144 innings from the pitcher's box, starting 18 games. Utilityman Frank Heifer spent his entire 11-game career with Boston and also pitched in relief. First baseman Jumbo Latham appeared in 16 games. Harry Wright also officially retired as a player in 1875, at the age of 40, although he did allow himself to play in one game a year in 1875, 1876, and 1877. Manning filled the role Wright had provided as relief help for Al Spalding, but still the workhorse threw 570⅔ innings, going 54-5 with a 1.59 ERA. The top 10 batting averages for the league included five by Red Stockings: Deacon White (.367), Ross Barnes (.364), Cal McVey (.355), George Wright (.333), and Andy Leonard (.321). The same "fab five" also led the league in hits and total bases.

The team scored 831 runs and allowed 343, with a team batting average of .321.

The 1875 Red Stockings were one of the first teams to play professional baseball below the Mason-Dixon Line. Playing the Washington Nationals on April 29 and May 1 before a hostile crowd in Richmond, Virginia, Boston won 22-5 and 24-0. On May 18 Boston (16-0) played at Hartford (12-0) in a battle of undefeated teams. A huge crowd that included Mark Twain packed the stadium and the entire city seemed to close in anticipation. Boston struggled for a 10-5 win, and Twain's umbrella was stolen.

The second big off-the-field story of 1875 was the impending breakup of the Red Stockings, leaked to the press in July. Imagine the look on Harry Wright's face at the restaurant in Taunton, Massachusetts, when he was given the news, recounted in the *Boston Daily Advertiser* on July 23. "While the Red Stockings were dining at Taunton, on Tuesday last, McVey said to Captain Harry that he had concluded not to play in Boston next year. Harry laughed, thinking it merely a jest, but his amusement was turned into surprise after dinner, when White told him, in answer to a question about playing here next season, that he had given his word to go to Chicago, and that Spalding, Barnes, and McVey had also bound themselves verbally to the same club. The managers of the Boston club were naturally astonished at this intelligence."[13]

A *Worcester* (Massachusetts) *Spy* report showed that already in the 1870s biblical allusions were being used by New Englanders to describe their local baseball team. "Like Rachel weeping for her children, she refuses to be comforted because the famous baseball nine, the perennial champion, the city's most cherished possession, has been captured by Chicago."[14] One could imagine a modern scenario of four Red Sox stars signing with the New York Yankees and the phone lines on Boston sports talk shows lit up with irate fans. Even in 1875, passion for the Hub team was strong. A *Boston Globe* reader named "Grand Stand" wrote a letter to the editor asking, "Why didn't these men, when offered, 'fancy prices,' go to the managers of the Boston club and tell them, and then, if Boston could not pay these prices, they could accept the situations with good grace? Not one of them ever said a word, for if they had they could have had the same prices, if they were so disposed, and remained in the [sic] Boston. All of them owe their present position to Captain Harry Wright, he having brought them out of an obscure country village in Illinois, and this is the reward the 'old man' receives."[15]

"The time is out of joint," declared the *Boston Daily Advertiser*. "Tweed is escaping from the penalty of his crimes, there are bad crops in Europe, the democratic party is marching rapidly under its soft money flag, the monarchists are gaining victory in the French Assembly, – and now the famous Boston nine has been assaulted and captured by Chicago. There is probably no paragraph of news this week that has caused so much real vexation out of doors in Boston as this last. The pride of Boston in its base ball team has been something unique."[16]

Despite the shocking news and the groans of the fans, the 1875 Boston Red Stockings never let the distractions get to them on the field, and despite the negativity launched at Spalding, he was still able to have winning streaks of 22 and 24 games during the season.

Even while contractually bound to leave for Chicago, Boston's big four continued to dominate the 1875 season with the Red Stockings. Chicago owner William A. Hulbert had first approached Spalding and convinced the pitching ace that a boy from the Midwest would be better off pitching in the Midwest. "I would rather be a lamppost in Chicago than a millionaire in any other city," Hulbert pitched to him.[17]

The *New York Clipper* bemoaned the breakup of the Red Stockings, who in its view represented class and integrity. "Having tried in vain for years to defeat the Boston Red Stockings on the field, it would appear as if an effort were to be made to break up the club altogether, as the only way of ever being able to get hold of the coveted pennant. Is there no law of fair dealing that suggests to club-managers that this violation of the spirit of an Association rule is discreditable?"[18]

There was talk at the winter convention in March 1876 of expelling the defecting Boston players from the league.[19] Hulbert had an ax to grind with teams in the East over the Force case, and also thought the preponderance of gambling and other evils in the National Association meant the league itself should dissolve anyway. So before there was a chance his players could be banned, he and Spalding drafted the constitution for a new National League of Professional Base Ball Clubs. Note the "clubs" instead of "players" in the organizational title, for this was not mere verbiage. The structure of professional baseball was changing. The National Association's five-year run was a player-driven endeavor; now, power would be in the hands of the owners. Gone were the days of Harry Wright giving a player what he felt he deserved. Gone were the days of games played in small towns with mismatched schedules with umpires pulled off the street or a team bench. Harry Wright, sensing Hulbert's business sense, went along with the new league, as did Hartford, the St. Louis Brown Stockings, and the New York Mutuals. The two new clubs came from the west: Cincinnati and Louisville. The National League was born, and a new chapter in baseball history had begun.

There was still one final game to play in 1875, however, and it was truly the end of an era.

At the South End Grounds on October 23, Boston and Chicago played an exhibition game at 3 P.M. with the four "defectors" wearing Chicago uniforms. "One of the largest crowds of the season," according to the *Boston Daily Advertiser*, came to see Borden, still going by the name Josephs, pitch for Boston. Spalding refused to pitch against his former teammates, instead playing left field, "either not daring to set his reputation 'on a cast and stand the hazard of the die,' or for some other reason," wrote the *Springfield Republican*.[20] The crowd was not happy, "the game being deprived by it of about half its interest, and furthermore, it involved a breach of good faith on the part either of the Boston club managers with the public or of Spalding with the managers," wrote the *Daily Advertiser*.[21]

McVey actually did the pitching and "surprised all his friends and was apparently as much at home in his new position as he was in his own place with the Bostons," wrote the *Boston Journal*.[22] Chicago players obviously felt they had something to prove, scoring four in the first inning, then three in the second, fourth, and fifth innings and one in the sixth for the 14-0 win. Yet, none of the runs against Borden were earned, all coming as a result of 23 Boston errors. "It was muffing from beginning to end," the *Advertiser* wrote, and the fans "indulged in the despicable practice of 'chinning' and booing at the umpire for calling strikes on Boston batsmen."[23]

The Boston Red Stockings era was over, as was that of the National Association. This was baseball's first experiment with a professional league, and served as a "time between the times" of baseball history. Baseball was moving away from being a purely amateur sport, as more teams and players were turning professional. People worried that paying players would ruin the "purity" of the game. We are now 145 years and counting from the earliest days of professional baseball. The game has changed along with the ebb and flow of time. But these were professional baseball's pioneers who, through their amazing successes and glaring mistakes, paved the way to the National League and a lasting structure for professional baseball.

Boston was not without a professional baseball team come 1876. Though outside our brief survey here, Harry Wright pulled together another team going by the name Red Caps (disgruntled Boston fans apparently still called them Red Stockings) in the new National League. The team included brother George and former National Association players Leonard, Manning, O'Rourke, and Schafer, adding Joe Borden and others to the mix, perhaps most notably Foghorn Bradley and Tim Murnane. The 1876 team finished in fourth place, but finished first in 1877 and 1878. In 1883 it became known as the Boston Beaneaters, and eventually the Boston Braves. It is the same franchise that today plays in Atlanta.

For the full story on the Boston National League club from its beginnings in 1871 until its move to Milwaukee in 1953, see Harold Kaese's *The Boston Braves 1871-1953*. For an interest in the history of Braves Field in Boston and the great games played there from 1914 to 1953, see SABR's *Braves Field: Memorable Moments at Baseball's Lost Diamond*.

SOURCES

In addition to sources cited in the Notes, the author consulted the following:

Batesel, Paul. *Players and Teams of the National Association, 1871-1875* (Jefferson, North Carolina: McFarland, 2012).

Nemec, David. *The Great Encyclopedia of Nineteenth-Century Major League Baseball* (New York: David I. Fine Books, 1997), 65-84.

Special thanks to SABR members Bill Nowlin and Dixie Tourangeau for suggestions on information to include in this article.

NOTES

1. David Quentin Voigt. *American Baseball: From Gentleman's Sport to the Commissioner System* (Norman, Oklahoma: University of Oklahoma Press, 1966), 51.
2. There were also three tie games, all played in Philadelphia.
3. Voigt, 50.
4. "Centennial Club Dissolved," *Philadelphia Times*, May 27, 1875: 4.
5. "The Base Ball Field," *Philadelphia Times*, May 25, 1875: 4.
6. "Centennial Club Dissolved."
7. Voigt, 58.
8. Quoted in the *Hartford Courant*, May 19, 1875: 2.
9. "Base Ball. The Champions Defeat the Keokuks," *Boston Globe*, June 11, 1875: 1.
10. "Base Ball," *Cincinnati Daily Gazette*, July 7, 1875: 1.
11. William J. Ryczek, *Blackguards and Red Stockings: A History of Baseball's National Association, 1871-1875* (Wallingford, Connecticut: Colebrook Press, 1992), 194.
12. Ryczek, 195-196.
13. "The Boston Nine. Secession of Spalding, White, Barnes, and McVey – Their Engagement by the Chicago Club for 1876," *Boston Daily Advertiser*, July 23, 1875: 1.
14. *Worcester* (Massachusetts) *Spy*, July 24, 1875, cited in Peter Levine, *A.G. Spalding and the Rise of Baseball: The Promise of American Sport* (New York: Oxford University Press, 1985), 21.
15. "The Seceding Players – How They Came to Secede," *Boston Globe*, July 28, 1875: 8.
16. "A Base Capture," *Boston Daily Advertiser*, July 23, 1875: 2.
17. Voigt, 62.
18. "Breaking-Up the Boston Team," *New York Clipper*, July 31, 1875: 139.
19. Harold Kaese, *The Boston Braves, 1871-1953* (Boston: Northeastern University Press, 2004), 15.
20. "The New Reds Defeated By the Old," *Springfield* (Massachusetts) *Republican*, October 25, 1875: 8.
21. "Out-Door Sports. A Notable Game on the Boston Base Ball Grounds," *Boston Daily Advertiser*, October 25, 1875: 1.
22. "Out Door Sports. Base Ball," *Boston Journal*, October 25, 1875: 4.
23. "Out-Door Sports. A Notable Game on the Boston Base Ball Grounds."

BOB ADDY

BY PETER MORRIS

"A CELEBRATED BASE BALL CHARACter" was A. G. Spalding's succinct description of Bob Addy, who was his teammate on three separate clubs.[1] Others who knew Addy well referred to him as a philosopher or as a wag or as the "Honorable Bob." The reasons behind that last tag remain unknown, but it certainly sounds like the sort of inside joke that always swirled around Addy. Fred Cone recalled that his teammate "could say the funniest things while on the field without cracking a smile. Many a game he won for us by keeping up our spirits when the opposing team had a big bunch of runs to the good."[2] Another contemporary described him as "big hearted, bow legged, profane Bob Addy."[3]

For better or worse, everyone had a favorite memory and an opinion of Bob Addy, even when their views seemed contradictory. Cap Anson famously described him as an "odd sort of genius" because, to the horror of the single-minded Anson, Addy "quit the game because he thought he could do better at something else."[4] Yet others found his passion for baseball unsurpassed. "Bob Addy is the modern wonder," declared one sportswriter. "If base ball ever dies out, we believe Bob will want to die. His whole soul is wrapped up in the sport. To see him run in from the extreme field, and hear him beg for a high in-field ball, like a child begging for a bun, is amusing."[5] Cone agreed that Addy's "temperament was such that he could never miss seeing a game."[6]

On one point there was no dispute: that he was unforgettable. "Everybody remembers Bob Addy," declared a *Hartford Courant* reporter in 1886 — *twelve years* after Addy had spent a mere six months playing ball in that city.[7] More than three decades after Addy had played his last major league game, the nickname of rookie Shoeless Joe Jackson prompted a sportswriter to recall that "the famous second baseman, Bob Addy, did that very often, as he was much troubled with sore feet."[8]

But it was not just his eccentricities and his wit that made Bob Addy so memorable. For one thing, he was one of the best players of his era in spite of being very late to take up baseball. In addition, he played the game with a spirit of reckless abandon that led teammate George Bird to call him "about the toughest fellow I ever saw. He would go after anything, any way, and his hands were broken and battered out of shape."[9] Finally, Bob Addy was the first Canadian major leaguer and, unlike many early Canadian-born players, he had actually grown up there.

When and where Bob Addy was born has long been a disputed issue, with most sources indicating that he was born in Rochester, New York, in 1845. Addy seems to have given this information out in his later years, but there is overwhelming evidence that he was actually born in Canada. He was living in Port Hope, Ontario, when the 1861 Canadian census was taken—his birthplace was listed as Upper Canada (Ontario), and his age was given as 19. Nine years later, he was living in Rockford with many of his baseball teammates and was reported to have been born in Canada around 1842. It was not until the 1880 census that he was first listed as being born in New York.

While the census data points to a Canadian birthplace, it is other evidence that clinches the matter. A. G. Spalding, who knew Addy from their days on the Forest City Club of Rockford, described Addy as "originally a Canadian cricketer."[10] Canada was also given as Addy's birthplace in an 1874 book written by George Wright.[11] Finally, when the Forest City Club stopped in Hamilton, Ontario, during an 1870 tour, the locals learned of his Canadian birth and Addy became "the object of special pride on the part of the Canucks, they claimed him from the start as one of them." This made Addy the subject of kidding from his teammates and he finally declared: "I don't care nothing for them, I tell you I don't care nothing about 'em.'"[12]

Exactly when he was born remains unclear. Late in life he began claiming an 1845 year of birth, but the evidence suggests otherwise. His tombstone has 1838, which would be very intriguing if true, but the source of this information is not known. The 1860 and 1870 censuses suggest that he was born around 1842, and that seems most plausible.

Bob Addy reportedly "belonged to several cricket clubs in the Dominion," but any details are lost to history.[13] Nor is much known about his early years except that he was born shortly after his parents emigrated from Ireland and that his father, whose name appears to have been James, had died by 1857.

It becomes easier to follow Addy's trail in 1861, when he appears in Port Hope on the Canadian census, already working in his lifelong profession as a tinsmith. Listed with him are his mother Ellen (age 44, born Ireland), his younger brother James (17, born Upper Canada, a saddler), and his older brother George (25, born Ireland, a clerk). George's presence in Port Hope is a bit odd, since he had been listed in Ogle County, Illinois, on the 1860 U.S. census and got married in that county in February of 1861. So perhaps he was still in the process of relocating to the United States.

By 1866 George Addy was a well-established Ogle County produce dealer with two young children, and Bob had followed him there. Both brothers also started playing on the Clipper Base Ball Club of the nearby town of Rochelle. While the club itself had limited success, Bob Addy made the sort of indelible impression that he so often did. A. G. Spalding would later recall paying a fateful visit to Rochelle in June of 1866 with the Forest City Club of Rockford, during which "Robert Addy startled the players of the Forest Citys by a diving slide for second base. None of us had ever witnessed the play before, though it may have been in vogue. Certainly we were quite nonplussed."[14]

On the basis of Spalding's comments, Addy has often been credited with inventing the slide. It would be nice to report that this was true, but baseball innovations are rarely that clear-cut. Slides seem to have gradually evolved from accidental slips while trying to make a sudden stop at a base into deliberate evasive maneuvers. While a slide in 1866 would still have been

Bob Addy, ca. 1869 w. Forest City (Spalding Collection, New York Public Library)

a novelty, there is no way to definitively pinpoint the first intentional slide.[15]

What we can be sure of is that Addy's play made a vivid impression the visiting players. "He showed wonderful ability as a ball player in this game," recollected Spalding, "by practically playing the whole game, captain of the team, pitcher, catcher, and, in fact, took every position where the player had developed weakness by making an error."[16] Both his standout play and his tendency to try to cover the entire field would become recurring themes of the career of the "celebrated base ball character."

Addy was soon offered a place on the Forest City Club and a job at a Rockford hardware store, both of which he accepted. It was a coup for the Forest Citys and the start of the club's highly successful policy of recruiting players from the surrounding countryside.

The Forest City Club was still experimenting with lineups, and Addy played all four infield positions during the remainder of the 1866 season. He began a two-year stint as a club director in 1867, and it was during these years that the Forest Citys began using a regular lineup in which Addy played second base and batted leadoff. The new stability paid off on July 25, 1867, when the Forest Citys traveled to Chicago to face the Nationals of Washington, a seemingly invincible club that was making a historic tour of the South and Midwest. Spalding recalled that "we were all frightened nearly to death, with possibly the exception of Bob Addy, who kept up his nerve and courage by 'joshing' the National players as they came to bat with witticisms."[17] Addy also launched his reputation as a clutch performer by scoring four runs and turning a key double play as the Forest Citys pulled off a stunning 29-23 upset that put the club on the national map.[18]

The Forest Citys made a gradual transition from amateurism to professionalism over the next three years, a process that entailed the replacement of several starters. Only three players remained fixtures in the club's lineup: Spalding, Addy, and a young protégé of Addy's named Roscoe Barnes. Spalding and Barnes went on to become superstars in the first major league, the National Association (1871-1875). Addy is much less remembered today, in large part because his National Association statistics are not on a par with Spalding's and Barnes's gaudy numbers. But those who saw him play, especially during his years in Rockford, believed that he too was a star of the first magnitude.

George Wright wrote that Addy was "a thorough ball-player, and a most earnest worker; a splendid base runner, a good batter, and a lively fielder. He is a valuable member of any organization from the fact of his steady play having [a] tendency to infuse confidence into the minds of his fellow-players."[19] Anson recalled Addy as "a good, hard, hustling ballplayer, a good base runner and a hard hitter."[20] As late as 1876, he was still considered "one of the hardest working players and best run-getters in the country."[21]

Such judgments do not mean much when they are not supported by the statistical record, and a superficial look at Addy's National Association and National League statistics suggests that he was a run-of-the-mill major leaguer. But that conclusion can only be drawn by overlooking the key fact that by the time those leagues were formed, Bob Addy was already on the downside of his career—exactly how far past his prime he was again depends on the knotty issue of his correct age. While we have less extensive statistics from the 1869 and 1870 seasons, when Addy was in his prime, the available records show that he deserved to be regarded as one of the game's best players.

In 1869 Addy averaged well over five hits per game, a figure that ranked him first among all the players on the more than 400 clubs that were members of the National Association of Base Ball Players.[22] While the absence of at-bats make the comparison from club to club an imperfect one, he also easily topped a club that included Ross Barnes and many other future major leaguers in both hits per game and total bases.[23] Barnes was only 19 that year, but the following year, it was again Addy who led the star-studded Forest City Club in batting, collecting 204 hits in 56 games.[24]

These two glorious seasons almost never happened. As the start of the 1869 season approached, Addy was talking seriously about heading west to "seek his fortune."[25] But in the end he decided to stay in Rockford for another summer, and he enjoyed a season that has to be ranked as the best of his career, since his five-plus hits per game were compiled while making the switch to the game's most demanding defensive position.

Forest City catcher George King had chosen to retire after the 1868 season, so Addy moved behind the plate. Catchers wore no equipment except a rubber mouthpiece, making the position extraordinarily dangerous, and they also needed great dexterity to prevent passed balls. Working with a hard-throwing pitcher like Spalding was especially onerous, but Addy made a seamless transition to the new position. Even more impressively, when he saw Doug Allison of the "Red Stockings" of Cincinnati standing close to the plate to catch, he immediately made the same decision.[26]

The 1869 season is remembered as the undefeated season of the "Red Stockings" of Cincinnati, but it was also a memorable campaign for the Forest Citys. The Rockford club, although still ostensibly amateur, lost only four games all season—all of them to the openly professional Red Stockings. In one of those contests, the Forest Citys came within two outs of pulling off an upset that would have changed baseball history.

The match was played in Cincinnati on July 24, and "Addy was the hero of the game in every way. Not only was he catching directly behind the bat, something he had done only at critical moments until two weeks before, but he allowed only two passed balls to [Cincinnati fill-in catcher Asa] Brainard's five, scored four runs in five times at bat, one a home run, and continued the game after having been knocked flat by a foul in the sixth inning."[27] Addy's insistence on remaining in the game after the gruesome injury led a Cincinnati paper to praise his "commendable pluck."[28]

More than half a century after the fact, Addy's brother-in-law Victor Wheeler still remembered the game vividly. "Bob was absolutely unafraid," he recalled. "He would step into the fastest ball and it didn't seem that anything could get away from those twisted fingers of his, strong as steel cables. Down in Cincinnati that day they carried him to the players' tent on the grounds, with part of his teeth knocked loose, and sent for a doctor. Addy wouldn't stay. He came back on the field and took up his place behind the batter. Then the game had to stop while Cincinnati stood up and cheered him for ten minutes."[29]

Led by Addy's heroics, the Forest Citys were clinging to a 14-12 lead as the game went to the bottom of the ninth inning. But after the first batter was retired, the Red Stockings mounted a three-run rally to preserve their undefeated season.

Bob Addy left Rockford at the conclusion of the 1869 season and announced that he would not be returning. But "the week before the election Bob was back again, swearing to locate permanently, and establishing himself in a tinning and jobbing shop opposite the court house."[30] He returned to second base in 1870 as the Forest Citys completed the transition to open professionalism. The club compiled a 42-13-1 record during a prolonged schedule that included Addy's previously mentioned return to Canada and that climaxed with an October 15 victory over the Red Stockings. On one of the club's few off-days, on August 13, Addy found time to get married in Rockford.

The winter following the 1870 season saw the birth of the National Association and the departure of three club stalwarts, as Spalding, Barnes, and Cone all chose to sign with Boston. The Forest Citys nonetheless decided to enter the new league, and Addy thus became the club's longest-tenured member (with the exception of Al Barker, who played sparingly). A much younger lineup resulted, with Addy the grizzled veteran among a group of newcomers who included the nineteen-year-old Cap Anson.

Scott Hastings is now listed in record books as the manager of the 1871 Forest Citys, but there seems to be no basis for this designation. Most baseball clubs of the 1870s did not have anyone whose role resembles that of today's manager, so listings of this sort are just an exercise in futility. Hiram Waldo, a Rockford bookseller, was the man who signed players and made player personnel decisions, while Addy was named the club's captain and made in-game decisions.[31]

Addy got off to a sizzling start, pounding Asa Brainard, the former Red Stockings pitcher, for four hits in the club's second National Association game and then collecting five hits two games later to lead the Forest Citys to a thrilling extra-inning come-from-behind victory over the Kekiongas of Fort Wayne. But then he cooled off, and so did his teammates. The season was not a success, but neither was it anywhere near as bad as the 4-21 record that appears in the record books—the club actually won eight of its 25 games but had to forfeit four wins when Hastings was ruled to have been ineligible.[32]

The Great Chicago Fire put a temporary halt to professional baseball in the region then known as the West and a permanent end to the brilliant career of the Forest City Club of Rockford. For a while, it appeared it would also mark the end of Bob Addy's career, as the newlywed elected to remain in Rockford and pursue business.

He returned to the diamond in 1873 with the White Stockings of Philadelphia (one of two National

Association entries from that city that year). His new club won seventeen of its first nineteen games to grab a commanding lead in the pennant race. But in early June, Addy requested and received his release. Despite his short stay in Philadelphia, he had made such a vivid impression that he was "he was presented with a magnificent gold watch by the directors of the club, and was tendered a dinner."[33]

Business concerns were said to have been the reason for his return to Rockford, but a more personal matter may have been the determining factor. Bob and Ida Addy's only son was a boy named George. Following in the family tradition, George would later give contradictory information about his date of birth, but it appears most likely that he was born on August 1, 1873.

Shortly after that date, following a two-month absence, Bob Addy signed to join Spalding and Barnes with Boston. The Red Stockings were nine games behind his old team at the time of the signing, but he provided a much-needed spark. He batted .355 in 31 games, and Boston won 26 of those games to cruise to the pennant. Tim Murnane later credited Addy with having "pulled the Bostons through for the championship by his fine work at right field and timely hitting and baserunning in 1873."[34]

The hard-won pennant was jeopardized by claims that Addy was ineligible because of having played for a club in Rockford after leaving Philadelphia. But former Forest City Club officer A. N. Nichols attested that Rockford had no club of any kind, and that Addy had merely taken part in a contest involving "little boys." The controversy simmered down, and Boston was awarded the pennant.[35]

Addy spent the 1874 season in Hartford, his last year as a regular infielder. At season's end, it was announced that he planned to organize a new professional club in Springfield, Massachusetts. But he was slow to sign players, prompting speculation that he would only enlist the services of a pitcher and catcher and would cover the rest of the field by himself.[36] Eventually plans for the Springfield Club were abandoned, and Addy instead returned to the White Stockings of Philadelphia where, according to one rather far-fetched retrospective article, he pretty much ended up fulfilling the prediction that he would have to cover the entire field.

The roster of the White Stockings was strewn with talented players who had suspect reputations. According to this article, "in one game eight of the players were fixed to lose. The one true man was Bob Addy … It was thought by those who were engineering the 'skin' that it would not be necessary to buy Addy, and besides he had the reputation of being a square player." Throughout the contest, Addy did "great work in the field and was striving to win, covering a wonderful amount of ground," even while his teammates were conspiring to lose. Finally, at a pivotal moment Addy made a long run and saved the game by catching a ball that a teammate intended to let drop. When the teammate realized what had happened, "his disgust was supreme, and in a tone of contempt and scorn he remarked: 'Look here, Bob Addy, do you want to play the whole game?'"[37]

The story is at the very least exaggerated, and may be pure fabrication. Yet it is fascinating how well it captures two of the characteristics that were at the heart of Bob Addy's reputation as a "celebrated base ball character": his tendency to venture into the territory of teammates and his scrupulous honesty in an era when rumors of game-fixing were rampant. As Anson would say, "He was honest as the day is long."[38]

After the 1875 season the National League was formed as a successor to the National Association. The main motive for this coup was that it legitimized Chicago's William Hulbert's signing of Boston's four best players, the so-called "Big Four" of Spalding, Barnes, Jim "Deacon" White, and Cal McVey. From Rockford's perspective, the development was most ironic: five years earlier, the National Association had been launched when Boston had signed Spalding and Barnes, and the two young men who had grown up in Rockford had led Boston to four straight pennants. So their return to Illinois seemed a case of turn-about being fair play.

The demise of the National Association left the fate of many players, including Addy, up in the air. It was at first reported that he would remain in Philadelphia with a club that would combine some of the most talented and unsavory players from a city swarming with men who embodied both traits. The *New York Times* reported with dark irony that the managers of the new club had "engaged such able and honorable players as Dick Higham, John Nelson, George Zettlein, Billy Craver, Treacy, Meyerle, Bob Addy, and Shafer [sic]. Mr. Bob Addy will officiate in the capacity of Captain. The one great advantage in having a nine of this kind is that they always play to win—perhaps. As an evidence of the high standing of this club, it is only necessary to state that at a recent election all the officers were required to subscribe an oath to the effect that they would not countenance the selling of a single game. Some people are curious to know why the imposing of such an oath was necessary."[39]

But as the *Chicago Tribune* was quick to point out, the *Times* had done an "injustice to Addy in classing him with such a gang."[40] Like many of his teammates, Addy was owed money at the end of the 1875 season and was anxious to leave Philadelphia.[41] Meanwhile, Spalding had been named captain of the new club in Chicago and Anson had been added to the club's contingent of Forest City alumni. Spalding soon offered Addy a spot on the team and the two men who had already been teammates in Rockford and Boston were reunited for the third time.

Upon his arrival in the Windy City, Addy made his usual indelible impression and displaying the now-familiar traits. An account of the team's home opener reported, "every man was where he belonged, from impassive White around to the agile Addy, and from the sure-handed Iowa infant [Anson] down through the grades of height to Capt. Bob Shorty, who teetered all over the infield as he thought there was occasion."[42]

His wit also remained conspicuous. When a July exhibition game to raise funds for an orphanage was rained out, the *Tribune* observed that "the orphans were unlucky—in fact, to use the words of that venerable philosopher, Robert Addy, it was to have been expected that they would be unlucky, for if they hadn't been unlucky they wouldn't have been orphans at all."[43]

Exactly how venerable Addy was by this time can only be estimated, but he was most likely nearing forty and now exclusively played the outfield. Nevertheless, he was as energetic as ever, and several game accounts describe slides like the one that had startled Spalding a decade earlier. According to one of these reports, "Addy opened the second inning and took his base on called balls. He at once stole second in his usual underground manner, and to the great detriment of his good clothes."[44]

Chicago won 36 of its first 43 games to take a commanding lead in the race for the National League's inaugural pennant. But Addy got off to a slow start at the plate and found himself sharing time in right field with Oscar Bielaski and Fred Andrus. His benching apparently was not Spalding's decision; a *Cincinnati Enquirer* sportswriter maintained after the season that "a higher authority than Spalding laid Addy off the nine and put Bielaski in his place—Bielaski, whose batting shows him eighty per cent weaker than Addy, and five per cent weaker as a fielder."[45]

But the pennant race suddenly tightened up in August when the White Stockings were swept at St. Louis. Addy was reinstalled in right field and again showed his knack for clutch performances. He pounded out four hits in a crucial game against St. Louis and continued to swing a hot bat as Chicago maintained its lead.[46]

In September, with the pennant within sight, Boston came to town for a game that featured numerous players from the old Red Stockings-Forest City rivalry. Addy, Spalding, and Barnes all took the field for the home side, while the visitors included Andy Leonard and both Wright brothers. For good measure the umpire was Fred Cone, the third player who had left the Forest Citys after the 1870 season to play for Boston.

Boston jumped to a six-run lead, but Chicago roared back and finally pushed across two decisive runs in the ninth inning for a 12-10 win. According to a game account, "Addy and White carried off the honors very easily, both in fielding, batting, and run-getting. The former made five wonderful catches, those off [Jim] O'Rourke, [Jack] Manning, and [Harry] Schafer being as fine bits of play as ever were seen in any game. Addy's base-running also drew out great applause." The dramatic win allowed Chicago, in the words of the *Tribune*'s reporter, to reach "a step in the championship race which is next door to the absolute securing of the pennant."[47]

The labyrinthine phraseology was necessary because of some disputed games, but there was now little doubt about the league's first pennant-winner. Four days later, the last shred of doubt was eliminated when Chicago defeated Hartford. Once again, Addy was the hero in the clincher, making "a couple of extraordinary catches" in the ninth inning of the 7-6 nail-biter, one of which seemed "fairly impossible until taken."[48]

Bob Addy had now played an important role for championship teams in both the National Association and National League, but his mid-season benching still rankled, and he was not interested in returning to Chicago.[49] He instead signed with Cincinnati, prompting a reporter to offer this satirical warning to the fans of that city: "whatever happens on your ball-field the Hon. Bob will have part and lot in it; if a man is to be run out between third and home, Bob will show up and take a hand in it like as if he had been standing there all the while."[50]

Upon his arrival in Cincinnati, Addy made the same kind of impression that he had made throughout his career. Before played his first league game with his new team, it was reported that "The Hon. Bob Addy seems to be a sort of demi-god in Cincinnati; if he stubs his toe the fact is recorded with due solemnity; if he tumbles down while fielding the ball, it is immediately telegraphed throughout the entire country, headed, 'Sad disaster;' and if he makes a base hit, the local reporters spoil their entire reserve of lead-pencils, in making a half-column note of it."[51] Alas, it was Cincinnati's season that proved a sad disaster. After a 3-11 start, Addy took over as captain, only to see the team disband a few days later. Following a two-week hiatus, the team was reassembled, but the club finished with a dismal 15-42 record in a season that ended Addy's major league career. In an odd twist, he also played a role in the end of Spalding's pitching career—on June 5, Addy smashed a line drive that hit his old batterymate in the chest and literally knocked Spalding out of the box in what proved to be the final start of his illustrious major-league career.[52]

In November, Cincinnati announced that it was releasing Addy on the ground of drunkenness.[53] But whether this was the real reason remains open to doubt. A Chicago sportswriter quipped that the charge, "sounds oddy," and pointed out that "Bob, though never a reliable player, has always been considered an honest man."[54] More to the point, Addy had a two-year contract, and the allegation enabled parsimonious Cincinnati owner "Si" Keck to avoid paying him for its second year.[55]

"Philosopher Bob" returned to Chicago that winter and opened a skating rink on the corner of Madison and Ada streets. To drum up business, he even organized a game of baseball on ice.[56] Addy's new enterprise prompted one reporter to quip that "Bob stands up better on ice than he does on land."[57]

But Addy soon gave up the skating rink business and finally did what he had so often talked of doing by heading out west, where he remained for the rest of his life. He brought along his young son George but not his wife Ida. She was still alive according to Bob's listing the 1880 census, but otherwise she remains a mysterious figure. Her marriage record gives her name as Ida Belle Seeley, while her son's marriage record says that it was Ida Enose, but she cannot be identified under either name. Nor is anything known about what became of her after Bob moved west.

Even after permanently settling in the West, Addy's doings continued to be chronicled in the eastern press. In 1879 he was reported to be playing baseball in Salt Lake City for a team known as the Gentile Club.[58] Seven years later, a claim that he had become a Mormon with twelve wives was widely reprinted.[59] Other unfounded reports had him in Oregon and California.

The reality seems to have been more prosaic. By the time of the 1880 census, he was living in Evanston, Wyoming, and he was still there at the end of the decade. Around 1891, he moved to Pocatello, Idaho, where he opened a hardware store and, on the first day of 1892, was remarried to a much younger woman named Louise Emma Clark. The marriage produced one child, a daughter named Ellen Louise, who was born on December 1, 1897.

As we have seen, Bob Addy continued to be remembered with great fondness in baseball circles long after his retirement. His feelings toward the game are more difficult to ascertain, but it certainly appears that he retained his passion for baseball. As late as 1890 he was still playing for the town team in Evanston.[60] His last known involvement with baseball came in 1899 when he took part in a "fat versus lean" game in Pocatello. Appropriately, the man who had been known for roaming the field at will started the contest with the "fat" side but ended it with the "leans."[61] One can imagine one of his fellow players exclaiming, "Look here, Bob Addy, do you want to play the whole game?"

Bob Addy died in Pocatello on April 9, 1910, after a severe attack of apoplexy.[62] His widow passed away in 1929, and their daughter died in 1974. At least one grandson is still alive as of 2009. His son from his first marriage moved to Spokane, Washington, and then to Oregon, where he is believed to have died in 1957. His brother George was last heard from in 1900, when he was living in Philadelphia and made news by making a desperate trip to England. The purpose of the voyage was to prevent his youngest daughter Arlan, a soprano who was singing with the D'Oyly Carte Opera, from marrying Dr. Henryk Arctowski, the Polish explorer who had recently returned from heading the celebrated Antarctic Expedition. But after meeting Arctowski, George Addy dropped his opposition and gave his blessing to the wedding.[63]

SOURCES

Coverage of the Forest City Club is usually based upon A. G. Spalding's fascinating but unreliable *America's National Game: Historic Facts Concerning the Beginning, Evolution, Development, and Popularity of Base Ball, with Personal Reminiscences of Its Vicissitudes, Its Victories, and Its Votaries* (1910) (reprint, Lincoln: University of Nebraska Press, 1992). I have instead relied primarily on two sources: an extraordinary 44-part history of the club that was written by Horace E. Buker and published serially in the *Rockford Republic* in 1922 and a five-part series by John Molyneaux that appeared in *Nuggets of History*, a publication of the Rockford Historical Society ("The Sinnissippi Base Ball Club," 43: 1 (March 2005); "The Forest City Base Ball Club: The Amateur Years," 45: 1 (March 2007); "No Longer Amateurs: The Forest City Base Ball Club in 1868," 46: 2 (June 2008); "'We Can Beat the Spots Off the Best Club That Ever Lived': The Forest City Base Ball Club in 1869," 46: 3 (September 2008); "The Eastern Tour—The 1870 Season of the Forest City Baseball Club," 47: 3 (September 2009)). Other sources that were of help included coverage of the 1896 Harry Wright Day celebrations in the *Rockford Register-Gazette* on April 13 and 14, 1896; the reminiscences of Fred Cone ("Baseball Thirty Years Ago," *Lima News*, July 15, 1899) and Charles Page (E. C. Bruffey, "Bruffey Tells of Charles T. Page, *Atlanta Constitution*, August 10, 1919: A4; *Atlanta Constitution*, March 14, 1909); "Spalding's Start," *Sporting Life*, June 20, 1908, 16; Harriet Spalding, *Reminiscences of Harriet I. Spalding* (East Orange, New Jersey: Spalding, 1910); Peter Levine, *A. G. Spalding and the Rise of Baseball* (New York: Oxford University Press, 1909); a history of baseball in Rockford written by James McKee that appeared in *Sporting Life* on April 9, 1884: 4; Harvey T. Woodruff, "Forest Citys a Noted Team," *Chicago Tribune*, March 31, 1912: C2; Adrian C. Anson, *A Ball Player's Career* (1900: reprint, Amereon), and William J. Ryczek's *When Johnny Came Sliding Home: The Post-Civil War Baseball Boom, 1865-1870* (Jefferson, North Carolina: McFarland, 1998). Joe Overfield's profile of Addy in *Nineteenth Century Stars*, eds. Robert L. Tiemann and Mark Rucker, (Kansas City: Society for American Baseball Research, 1989) was also very valuable. Coverage of Addy's time in the National Association and National League is mostly based on contemporaneous newspaper accounts and on William J. Ryczek's *Blackguards and Red Stockings: A History of Baseball's National Association, 1871-1875* (Jefferson, North Carolina: McFarland, 1992). Specific sources are cited in the notes.

NOTES

1 *Chicago Inter-Ocean*, April 12, 1896.

2 "Baseball Thirty Years Ago," *Lima News*, July 15, 1899.

3 *Bismarck Daily Tribune*, July 7, 1891.

4 Adrian C. Anson, *A Ball Player's Career*, 51.

5 *St. Louis Globe-Democrat*, April 1, 1877: 7.

6 "Baseball Thirty Years Ago," *Lima News*, July 15, 1899.

7 *Hartford Courant*, July 27, 1886: 2.

8 *Sporting Life*, September 5, 1908: 7.

9 *Rockford Republic*, September 6, 1922: 10.

10 *Chicago Inter-Ocean*, April 12, 1896: 10.

11 George Wright, *Record of the Boston Base Ball Club, Since Its Organization: With a Sketch of All Its Players for 1871, 72, 73 and 74, and Other Items of Interest* (Boston: Rockwell & Churchill, 1874), 15

12 John Molyneaux, "The Eastern Tour—The 1870 Season of the Forest City Baseball Club," *Nuggets of History*, 47:3 (September 2009), 3

13 George Wright, *Record of the Boston Base Ball Club, Since Its Organization: With a Sketch of All Its Players for 1871, 72, 73 and 74, and Other Items of Interest*, 15

14 A. G. Spalding, *America's National Game*, 480.

15 See my *A Game of Inches* (Chicago: Ivan R. Dee, 2006), volume 1, entry 5.2.1, for an extended discussion of the origins of the slide.

16 *Chicago Inter-Ocean*, April 12, 1896.

17 A. G. Spalding, *America's National Game*, 111.

18 *Rockford Republic*, May 3, 1922: 1 and 10.

19 George Wright, *Record of the Boston Base Ball Club, Since Its Organization: With a Sketch of All Its Players for 1871, 72, 73 and 74, and Other Items of Interest*, 15.

20 Adrian C. Anson, *A Ball Player's Career*, 51.

21 *St. Louis Globe-Democrat*, December 12, 1876: 5.

22 Marshall D. Wright, *The National Association of Base Ball Players, 1857-1870* (Jefferson, North Carolina: McFarland, 2000), 241.

23 Ibid., 255.

24 *Rockford Republic*, August 12, 1922: 9.

25 *Winnebago County Chief*, April 15, 1869.

26 *Rockford Republic*, June 21, 1922: 9.

27 Ibid.: 9.

28 *Cincinnati Dispatch*, quoted in *Rockford Republic*, June 21, 1922: 9.

29 *Rockford Republic*, June 21, 1922: 9.

30 *Rockford Republic*, June 28, 1922: 14.

31 *Rockford Republic*, August 16, 1922: 10.

32 William Ryczek, *Blackguards and Red Stockings*, 45-46.

33 Unspecified Philadelphia paper, reprinted in George Wright, *Record of the Boston Base Ball Club, Since Its Organization: With a Sketch of All Its Players for 1871, 72, 73 and 74, and Other Items of Interest*, 46.

34 *Sporting Life*, March 24, 1886: 5.

35 *New York Clipper*, February 21, 1874; William Ryczek, *Blackguards and Red Stockings*, 117-118.

36 *Chicago Tribune*, November 22, 1874: 16; *Chicago Tribune*, December 6, 1874: 2.

37 *Philadelphia Times*, reprinted in *St. Louis Globe-Democrat*, June 25, 1886: 5.

38 Adrian C. Anson, *A Ball Player's Career*, 51.

39 *New York Times*, January 30, 1876: 2.

40 *Chicago Tribune*, February 6, 1876: 12.

41 *Chicago Tribune*, February 27, 1876: 9.

42 *Chicago Tribune*, May 11, 1876: 8.

43 *Chicago Tribune*, July 18, 1876: 5.

44 *Chicago Tribune*, April 28, 1876: 5; for other instances of Addy sliding, see *Chicago Tribune*, June 9, 1876: 5, and *Chicago Tribune*, September 24, 1876: 3.

45 *Cincinnati Enquirer*, reprinted in *St. Louis Globe-Democrat*, February 4, 1877: 7.

46 *Chicago Tribune*, September 17, 1876: 7.

47 *Chicago Tribune*, September 23, 1876: 6.

48 *Chicago Tribune*, September 27, 1876: 5.

49 *St. Louis Globe-Democrat*, November 21, 1876: 5.

50 *St. Louis Globe-Democrat*, March 18, 1877: 7.

51 *Providence Dispatch*, quoted in *Chicago Tribune*, April 22, 1877: 7.

52 *Chicago Tribune*, June 6, 1877: 2.

53 *St. Louis Globe-Democrat*, November 11, 1877: 5.

54 *Chicago Inter-Ocean*, November 17, 1877: 8.

55 *New York Times*, November 15, 1877: 1.

56 *Chicago Inter-Ocean*, January 17, 1878: 8.

57 *Cincinnati Enquirer*, no date, quoted by Joe Overfield in *Nineteenth Century Stars*.

58 *St. Louis Globe-Democrat*, April 20, 1879: 10.

59 *Sporting Life*, August 4, 1886: 5.

60 *The Sporting News*, April 12, 1890: 5.

61 *Salt Lake Herald*, September 5, 1899: 3.

62 *Deseret Evening News*, April 16, 1910: 28.

63 "Face Which Won Arctowski: Portrait of Miss Caroline Addy, Party to the Romance of a Magazine Picture," *Chicago Tribune*, December 5, 1900: 7.

ROSS BARNES

BY GREGORY H. WOLF

"NO MATTER HOW GREAT YOU WERE once upon a time—the years go by, and men forget," wrote W. A. Phelon in *Baseball Magazine* in 1915. "Ross Barnes, forty years ago, was as great as [Ty] Cobb or [Honus] Wagner ever dared to be. Had scores been kept then as now, he would have seemed incomparably marvelous."[1] One might be shocked at such a lofty judgment, or simply brush it off as empty hyperbole from a sportswriter for whom everything was better a generation or two earlier. But was it accurate?

A pioneer of baseball, the right-handed Ross Barnes was one of the best hitters over a six-year stretch (1871-1876) that the sport has ever seen. He was the undisputed master of the fair-foul hit, a speedy and innovative base stealer, and a daring second baseman with a rifle arm in an era when fielders did not wear gloves. A cornerstone of the great Boston teams in the first professional baseball league, National Association of Professional Base Ball Players (1871-1875), Barnes batted over .400 in three out of five seasons helping his club capture four consecutive championships. In the inaugural campaign of the National League the following season, Barnes topped the circuit in almost every offensive category, including hitting (.429) to lead the Chicago White Stockings to the title. Barnes's end came quickly. Struck with a debilitating illness at the height of his career in 1877, he played only three more, mostly ineffective seasons and retired in 1881 as a shell of his former self.

Testimonials about Barnes's accomplishments abound in the sports pages of the late 19th and early 20th centuries. In 1887, the *Chicago Tribune* reported that Bob "Death to Flying Things" Ferguson, a longtime former player and respected manager in the NA and NL, regarded Barnes as the "best batter and ball player that ever lived" and also noted that the generation of players following Barnes drank too much.[2] *The Sporting Life*, in an 1898 article, considered Barnes, along with George Wright and Cap Anson "one of the fellows who built the foundations of the game as it is played."[3] Barnes was the "king of second baseman, as well as the finest batsman and run-getter of all time" pronounced former NA ballplayer-turned-nationally-syndicated sportswriter Tim Murnane in 1903.[4] Mike Scanlon, a Washington, D.C. baseball institution who wrote about the sport for 50 years beginning in the 1860s, opined in the *Washington Post* in 1906, "I believe [Barnes] was a greater player than [Nap] Lajoie is to-day."[5] Hall of Fame pitcher and sporting goods pioneer Al Spalding, whose transformation from a sandlotter in a Midwestern town to the era's most acclaimed hurler was closely tied to Barnes for about a decade, named Barnes the second baseman on baseball's all-time team in multiple issues of the *Spalding Guide* prior to World War I.[6] A more impartial arbiter, William Connelly, writing for *Baseball Magazine* in 1914, selected Barnes to baseball's third all-time team, after Nap Lajoie and Eddie Collins.[7]

Phelon's observation about fading memories was prescient. Barnes's accomplishments and contributions to the game gradually began to a fade as those with memories of him passed. By the 1950s Barnes had been consigned to a footnote in baseball history. In light of renewed interest in 19th century baseball and with the efforts of the Society for American Baseball Research, Barnes's legacy has attracted more attention. In 2013 SABR's Nineteenth Century Baseball Committee selected Barnes as the "Overlooked 19th Century Baseball Legend."[8]

Roscoe Charles Barnes was born on May 8, 1850, in Mount Morris, a small town in upstate New York, about 45 miles southwest of Rochester. For many decades well after his playing career ended, Ross Barnes was often misidentified as Roscoe Conkling Barnes. The mistake arose because of his middle initial and the name of a well-known US representative and later US senator from New York from 1867 to 1881,

Ross Barnes (Spalding Collection)

Roscoe Conkling. Ross Barnes's parents were Joseph, a farmer, and Mary (Weller) Barnes, both native New Jerseyians, who married in 1832 and subsequently welcomed at least eight children into the world between 1834 and 1854 (five boys, John, Fletcher, Joseph, Ross, and Franklin; and three girls, Lucy, Sara, and Martha). According to the 1860 US Census, the family resided in Lima, about 20 miles northeast of Mount Morris. By 1865 or 1866, the Barnes clan had relocated to Rockford, a fast growing industrial city of about of about 8,000, located 90 miles west-northwest of Chicago.

During four unimaginably destructive years of civil war which claimed approximately 620,000 lives (about 1 in every 25 males), many Union and Confederate soldiers were exposed to baseball. When they returned to their respective towns across the country after the war, they brought "base ball" with them, thereby increasing its popularity. No longer just a sport played predominantly in the East, baseball was emerging as a national pastime. The *New York Times* described Rockford of the 1860s as "the cradle of the great American sport in the West."[9] Though it is difficult to determine when young Ross began to play baseball, by 1866 he was a member of the Pioneers, a local 16-and-under amateur team on which another famous Rockford resident, Al Spalding, also played. By late 1866 or early 1867, the Rockford Forest Citys, an adult amateur team signed both Barnes and Spalding, whose fates would be linked for the next decade.

Playing shortstop for the Forest Citys from 1867-1870, Barnes established a reputation as one of the best all-around, young players in the game. Three games deserve mention. Barnes, Spalding, and the Forest Citys gained national exposure in what baseball historian John Thorn considered among the most, if not the most important, games in baseball history.[10] Rockford upset the seemingly invincible National Club of Washington, which had embarked on one of the first tours in baseball history, 29-23, on July 25, 1867 in Dexter Park, Chicago. The Forest Citys subsequently enjoyed "phenomenal success" and also toured nationally.[11] On June 24, 1869, the Rockford amateurs were on the verge of handing the Cincinnati Red Stockings, the first openly professional baseball team, their first loss in a game described by the *Chicago Tribune* as "the most exciting and hotly contested game of base ball ever played" in Cincinnati.[12] Trailing 14-12 after eight innings, Cincinnati, led by player-manager Harry Wright, his brother George, and Charlie Gould scored three runs in the ninth to win and thus preserve the first and only undefeated season in professional baseball history. Rockford avenged the loss the following season when the defeated Cincinnati 12-5 on October 15, handing the professionals one of their six losses in 74 contests.[13]

Harry Wright did not forget Barnes or Spalding when he was hired to form the first professional baseball team in Boston in early 1871. In addition to taking several of his own players from Cincinnati, notably his brother, Gould, and Cal McVey, as well as the club's name, the Red Stockings, he traveled to Rockford and signed Barnes and Spalding. The core of the club that would eventually dominate the National Association was in place.

Founded on March 17, 1871 in New York City, the National Association was the first professional baseball league; however, neither Major League Baseball nor the Baseball Hall of Fame (as of 2016) considers it one. Over the course of its five-year existence, the NA was marred by franchise instability. The league consisted annually of eight to 13 teams; however, there were at least 23 different clubs, but only three, the Boston Red Stockings, New York Mutuals, and Philadelphia Athletics fielded a team for all five seasons. The league also lacked a central authority, like the National Commission (1903-1920) or its replacement, the Commissioner of Baseball, to oversee baseball and ensure its integrity. Consequently the NA was plagued by contact jumpers as well as gamblers.

Boston, considered among the favorites to win the NA's inaugural championship, got off to a rough start, winning just seven of its first 15 games (one tie), which were often scheduled just days in advance. Signed as a second baseman, Barnes moved back to shortstop when George Wright, widely regarded the best player in the county at the time, was injured. Once Wright returned, the Bostons went on a roll, winning 13 of their last 16 to battle the Chicago White Stockings and the Philadelphia Athletics in what proved to be the only pennant race in the NA's history. A crushing 10-8 loss to Chicago on September 29 ended Boston's hope for a title. Though Harry and George Wright, as well as Spalding grabbed most of the attention, Barnes was arguably the most exciting offensive player in the league. The 21-year-old scored the most runs (66 in 31 games) and totaled the most bases (91). He also ranked second in extra-base hits (19), third in batting average (.401), and tied for fifth in RBIs (34).

Boston dominated the National Association over the next four years, running away with the title each year with records of 39-8, 43-16, 52-18, and 71-8. Unlike other teams, Boston benefitted from uncharacteristic continuity among its players. Barnes, George Wright, McVey, Andy Leonard, and Harry Schafer started for all four seasons; Spalding notched an unfathomable 185 of the team's 205 victories. In 1873, Boston acquired catcher Deacon White, perhaps the best offensive and defensive catcher in the NA.

In his second season in the NA, Barnes gradually emerged from George Wright's shadow to become the league's most feared hitter. In this era, pitchers stood 50 feet from the mound and threw underhand; batters, known as strikers as in cricket, called for either low or high balls, and were not penalized for fouling pitches (unless they were caught). Described by William Connelly of *Baseball Magazine* in 1915 as a "demon with the bludgeon,"[14] Barnes batted a league-high .430 and .431 in 1872 and 1873 respectively, as well as pacing the circuit in slugging percentage, extra-base hits, and total bases in both seasons; in 1873 he scored a league-record 125 runs in 60 games. After missing 19 games in 1874, yet batting .340 and finishing sixth in runs scored (the top six and eight of the top 10 run scorers were from Boston), Barnes returned in 1875 to set the NA record for hits (143) and led the league in runs (115). He owns the career record for a number of offensive categories in the NA, including batting average (.391), runs scored (459 in 265 games), doubles (101), and slugging percentage (.518), while batting primarily in the leadoff position.

What made Barnes a feared hitter? At 5-foot-8 and 145 pounds, Barnes was of average height and weight, and about the same size as George Wright. Spalding, for example, was the tallest at 6-foot-1. Barnes excelled by taking a cerebral approach to the game, augmenting his natural athletic abilities. During his career and in the few decades thereafter, Barnes was often described as a scientific hitter, for example by the *New York Clipper* in 1878.[15] Barnes was "not of the class of chance hitters who, when they go to bat simply go in to hit the ball as hard as they can without the slightest idea where it is going," wrote the *Boston Globe*. "He studied the position and made his hits accordingly."[16]

As a scientific hitter, Barnes mastered the art of hitting "fair-fouls," a legal hit during all five years of the NA and the first year of the NL. According to Peter Morris in his ground-breaking study *A Game of Inches*, Dickey Pearce is credited for having developed the practice in the 1860s.[17] Fred Cone, a native Rockford resident who played with Barnes on the Forest Citys, and with the Boston Red Stockings in 1871, provided an excellent description of the fair-foul hit in *Baseball Magazine* in 1899. "The trick was to cricket the ball with a hard swing so that it would strike fair and bound off into foul territory," said Cone. "If the ball could be cut hard down near the base line, it would get away from the fielder and roll on for two or three bases."[18] Some researchers have dismissed Barnes's batting accomplishments, suggesting that he took advantage of a loop-hole. Bill James, for example, argued in the *Historical Baseball Abstract* that Barnes is not among the 125 best second basemen in the history of the sport because he was primarily a fair-foul hitter.[19]

A closer examination of Barnes career might suggest a different conclusion. Robert H. Schaefer, in his insightful article on fair-foul hitting in the *National Pastime*, provided a compelling argument that players in the 1870s did not consider a fair-foul a "second-rate means of attaining first base or that it was a cheap hit" on the contrary, "it was universally regarded as requiring exceptional finesse. Only the most highly skilled strikers were able to execute it with consistency."[20] The fair-foul was almost impossible to defend against; however, few batters were able to hit them hard like Barnes. Far from being a one-trick pony capable only of fair-foul hit, Barnes was a complete hitter who sprayed balls to all fields as attested by countless game summaries from Boston and Chicago newspapers. If anything, Barnes took advantage of defensive shifts. If the third baseman played close to the bag in an attempt to defend against the fair-foul, Barnes hit the ball in the gap between second and third base. When the National League banned the fair-foul prior to the 1877 season, few players, managers, or executives felt Barnes, widely hailed the best hitter in the sport, would suffer. "I don't think it [new rule] will affect his average in the least," said Charles E. Chase, vice president of the Louisville Grays. "He can bat equally well to any portion of the field," but also added, "He undoubtedly gained many runs for his club last year by his scientific fair fouls."[21]

In addition to his hitting exploits, Barnes might have been the NA's most dangerous player on the base paths. According to Tim Murnane, who played against Barnes in both the NA and NL, Barnes "had no superior as a baserunner."[22] Barnes holds the single-season stolen base record (43 in 1873) as well as the career-record (103) in the NA. Murnane, whose 30 steals in 1875 were one better than Barnes's 29, also noted that Barnes was the "first player to throw himself wide of the base and hold onto the bag."[23]

Teammate Fred Cone claimed that Barnes's "fielding was the cleverest ever seen."[24] Barnes played during an era when fielders did not wear gloves (they became standard equipment in the 1880s), and infielders and catchers (who wore no mask) were especially prone to injury. Fielding errors were a major part of the game. Games averaged approximately 14-16 errors during the five years of the NA; and more than two-thirds of all the runs scored were considered unearned. The second baseman was arguably the most active infielder; he covered all of the ground from second to first, short center and short right field, and second base on steal attempts. The *New York Clipper* lauded Barnes's "shrewd judgment" as a fielder and considered him a "base-playing strategist" with no equal.[25] Once described as the "Johnny Evers of his day,"[26] Barnes teamed with George Wright to form the most formidable infield in the NA. Barnes "could cover more ground than any man I ever saw," wrote Tim Murnane. "He had a long reach and could pick up ground balls when on the dead run from either side."[27] With his strong, whip-like throws, Barnes led second basemen in assists for four consecutive seasons (1872-1875), and in double plays three times. Perhaps most tellingly, Barnes led all second sackers in fielding percentage from 1872-1874, and again with Chicago in the inaugural season of the NL.

Throughout his playing career, Ross was described as honorable and a gentleman, good-looking, well-dressed, and concerned about his appearances.[28] He had a medium complexion, with dark hair and dark eyes, and typically sported a fashionable moustache, often a thick walrus one. Despite his outwardly aristocratic appearance, Barnes supposedly had a prickly personality and gave the impression of a prima donna. William Ryczek, in his study on the history of the

National Association, noted that Boston manager Harry Wright often used harsh words to keep Barnes in his place.[29] During Boston's four-year stranglehold on the NA championship, the club was anything but a harmonious group. According to Al Spalding, "there was a time when the whole infield wouldn't speak to Ross Barnes."[30] The *Chicago Tribune* reported that for the entire 1872 season Barnes and first baseman Charlie Gould "never exchanged a word, and glanced at each other like opposing game chickens,"[31] leading some to conclude that their feud led to Gould's retirement at season's end.[32]

In 1874 Boston and the Philadelphia Athletics, the most prominent baseball clubs of the NA, interrupted their season on July 16 to depart on a historic goodwill trip to England to foster interest in the sport by playing exhibitions among themselves and against English cricket teams.[33] Discovering little interest for baseball in Old Country, the teams finally returned stateside on September 9, and resumed play in the NA. But the mood in Boston was not as jovial as when they departed.

During Boston's almost eight-week absence, speculation had arisen that the club might not field a team the following season. Rumors persisted through the offseason and into the 1875 campaign when the *Chicago Tribune* made an earth-shattering announced in mid-July that the Chicago White Stockings' president William Hulbert had signed Barnes, Deacon White, Cal McVey, and Al Spalding.[34] Boston, which had largely been spared of debilitating contract jumping, was dealt a death blow. The signings "shook the baseball world by its very centre" and were "greatest sensation in the history of baseball" wrote Harry Palmer in *Outing*.[35] Some wondered if the "Big Four," as they were described thereafter, would depart in midseason, but they didn't, and led Boston to what proved to be the last title in the NA.

Hulbert's signing of the "Big Four" was a calculated move in an effort to stack his own team in what he hoped would be a new professional league, organized and run by business men for the sake of earning profits. The result was the founding of the National League on February 2, 1876. The eight-team league consisted of six teams (Chicago, Boston, Philadelphia, Hartford, St. Louis, and Mutual of New York) from the NA and two new teams (Cincinnati and Louisville). No longer was the Eastern seaboard the epicenter of the baseball world.

Playing a prearranged schedule of 66 games from late April to late September, Chicago cruised to the championship. Barnes led the league in practically every offensive category, including batting average (.429), slugging percentage (.590), runs scored (126), hits (138), doubles (21), triples (14), extra base hits (36), and total bases (190), while playing in every game. Had there been an MVP award, it would likely have been a toss-up between Barnes and Spalding who won 47 games in his final, full season.

Barnes made history on May 2 at Avenue Grounds in Cincinnati when he hit the first home run in the history of the National League in Chicago's 15-9 defeat of the Reds. With two outs in the fifth inning, Barnes smashed what the *Chicago Tribune* called "the finest hit of the game, straight down the left field to the carriages for a clean home run."[36] In his next at-bat

Ross Barnes, 1871. (Public Domain)

Barnes almost repeated his feat by lining one to the fences for a triple.

In the offseason, team owners engaged in a heated discussion about fair-foul hits and bunting. According to the *Chicago Tribune*, there were several proposals for rule changes: eliminate bunting altogether; require a batter to take a full, hard swing at the ball; ban fair-foul hitting completely; or a combination of all three.[37] There is no proof that rule changes were directed at Ross Barnes. The *Tribune* noted that requiring batters to swing forcefully at the ball would almost certainly curtail bunting, as well as fair-foul hitting (which were often hit like a bunt); however, Ross Barnes would not be affected by such a change. Indeed the daily offered yet more proof of his overall hitting ability. "[Barnes] always hits [the fair-foul] with a full swing of the bat, and just as hard as he strikes any other kind of ball."[38] Ultimately, the fair-foul hit was banned.

A career .399 hitter over his first six seasons in professional ball (1871-1876), Barnes's batting average dropped precipitously to .272 in 1877 leading many researchers in the latter half of the 20h century and beyond to conclude that Barnes was indeed just a fluky fair-foul hitter who was unable to adjust to the rule change. That judgment seems incorrect.

The 27-year old Barnes left the Chicago White Stockings in mid-May 1877, suffering from a mysterious illness. On May 19 the *Chicago Tribune* reported that "Barnes has been physically incapable of exertion; he is as weak, debilitated and worn as would be any strong man after six month' sickness."[39] He returned to his home town of Rockford to recover, and was expected back in June.[40] However as June came and went, and Barnes was unable to play, rumors also spread. The *Tribune* refuted claims by their rival paper, the *Chicago Times*, that Ross was fabricating his illness and should be released. "The slam at Ross Barnes is scandalous and utterly unfounded," wrote the *Tribune*. The paper also published a telegram purportedly from Barnes, "I seldom leave the house now. I don't feel badly, but I grow weaker every day."[41] When Barnes showed up at Chicago's ball park, the Twenty-Third Street Grounds, on August 7 for the first time since his last game on May 17, the crowd gave him a "hearty round of applause."[42] However, "the King of the Game" could not rekindle his old magic. The *Cincinnati Enquirer* reported that Barnes "showed the effects of sickness" upon his return;[43] and subsequently, that Barnes "seemed to have lost all of his former vim, and played without energy or life."[44]

SABR member Robert H. Schaefer has argued compellingly that Barnes suffered from the ague, a malaria-like chronic disease which caused fevers, chills, and debilitating muscle aches and pains.[45] Contemporary newspapers reported about rumors that Barnes never fully recovered from the illness which apparently sapped his natural athleticism and speed, prematurely ending his professional baseball career after two more ineffective seasons (1879 and 1881).[46]

Chicago did not offer Barnes a contract for the 1878 season; however, the ball player was not yet finished with business in the Windy City. In early 1878 he became the first professional ballplayer to file a lawsuit against the club to redress a contract grievance. Barnes claimed that he was not paid for three months of his $2,500 salary when he was sick and could not play. According to the *Chicago Tribune*, the "case is a new one in the experience of ball clubs, and the outcome will be looked forward to with the interest of the professional ballclubs."[47] Ultimately Judge M. B. Loomis in the Cook County Courts ruled against Barnes later that year.[48]

Barnes was a baseball nomad in his final years as an active player. In 1878 he signed as a player-manager with the London (Ontario) Tecumseh of the International Association. Some researchers consider the IA to be the first "minor league" or even a rival to the NL. In 1879, Barnes joined his former teammates Cal McVey and Deacon White on the Cincinnati Reds. Barnes batted .266 for the fifth-place club in an eight-team league. Out of baseball the following season and reported to be a "commercial traveler for a Western wholesaler" according to the *Chicago Tribune*, Barnes's career came full circle when he accepted manager Harry Wright's offer to rejoin Boston.[49] Now 31 years old, Barnes played primarily shortstop (as he had for Cincinnati). Described as "useless as a fifth leg on a horse," Barnes batted .271 and tied Tom

Burns to lead all shortstops with 52 errors while the Red Stockings finished in sixth place.[50]

After the 1881 season with Boston, Barnes returned to his home in Rockford. He occasionally played in amateur games with the Forest Citys, and even contemplated a few comebacks, but the most prolific hitter in the first few years of baseball never donned another uniform. In nine professional seasons, Barnes batted .360, collected 860 hits, and scored 698 runs in 499 games.

Barnes was apparently in good financial position after his playing career. The extended Barnes family was well established in Rockford. Brothers John, Fletcher, and Franklin became successful industrialists and bankers. Newspapers reports in the 1880s claimed that Ross Barnes had a net worth of $100,000, and was a successful member of the Chicago Board of Trade.[51]

Barnes returned to baseball in 1890 as an umpire in the newly formed Player's League. Founded by baseball's first union, the Brotherhood of Professional Base-Ball Players led by John Ward, it lasted only one season, but included many of the stars on the NL. Barnes soon discovered that "umpiring isn't as pleasant as he expected it to be" and "came in for a regular kicking roast at the hands of the players."[52] The experience was a bitter one for Barnes, who felt as though he had been manipulated into becoming an umpire.[53]

A bachelor, Barnes spent the rest of his life in the Windy City, as well as maintaining a regular presence in Rockford.[54] He was reportedly involved at one time in the hotel business and also worked as an accountant for the Peoples Gas Light and Coke Company. On May 5, 1915, Barnes died at the age of 64 in his apartment in the Hotel Wicklow on 666 N. State Streetv in Chicago. The cause of death was reported as both a dilation of the aorta and stomach problems.[55] He was buried in his parents' plot at Greenwood cemetery in Rockford.

According to the rules of the Baseball Hall of Fame (as of 2016), only players with a minimum of 10 years of major-league experience are eligible for induction. Barnes falls one year short. Unlike some of his teammates, Barnes was not involved in the game as a manager, owner, or organizational pioneer which would allow him to be considered for induction as a non-player. For example, teammate Harry Wright played only four full seasons (all in the NA), but is considered the father of professional baseball by many; and Al Spalding pitched only six full seasons, yet went on to found a sporting goods empire, and served as an executive of the Chicago White Stockings. There have been efforts, led by social media sites like Facebook, urging the Hall of Fame to reconsider its rules in light of Barnes's contributions to baseball in its earliest professional phase. Perhaps one day, Ross Barnes, will join his teammates, the Wright Brothers and Spalding, and those to whom he was so favorably compared, such as Ty Cobb, Honus Wagner, Nap Lajoie, and Eddie Collins, and be enshrined with baseball's best in the Hall of Fame.

NOTES

1 W. A. Phelon, "The Month's Parade," *Baseball Magazine*, April 15, 1915: 123.

2 *Chicago Tribune*, June 5, 1887: 13.

3 *The Sporting Life*, May 23, 1898: 14.

4 Tim Murnane (1903) quoted from "One of the Greatest Players of All Time Was 'Ross' Barnes," *Boston Globe*, February 6, 1915: 5.

5 "Old Fans Recall Days of Nationals Triumph," *Washington Post*, June 10, 1906: 2.

6 See for example, *Spalding's Official Baseball Guide. 1907.* Henry Chadwick, ed. (New York: American Sports Publishing, 1907).

7 William Connelly, "The Greatest Baseball Team of All History," *Baseball Magazine*, May, 1914.

8 "SABR 43: Ross Barnes Selected as Overlooked 19th Century Baseball Legend for 2003," SABR.org. http://sabr.org/latest/sabr-43-ross-barnes-selected-overlooked-19th-century-baseball-legend-2013.

9 "Diamond Find Veterans," *New York Times*, April 12, 1896: 3.

10 John Thorn, "July 25, 1867: The most important game in baseball history?," SABR.org. http://sabr.org/gamesproj/game/july-25-1867-most-important-game-baseball-history. And "Base Ball. The Great Tournament. Opening Game Between the Nationals and Forest City Club—A Close and Exciting Outcome," *Chicago Tribune*, July 26, 1867: 4.

11 "Diamond Find Veterans," *New York Times*, April 12, 1896: 3.

12 "Base Ball. Rockford Boys at Cincinnati," *Chicago Tribune*, July 25, 1869: 1.

13 "The Sporting World. The Rockford Amateurs Defeat the Cincinnati Professionals," *Chicago Tribune*, October 16, 1870: 3.

14 Connelly.

15 "No. 4—Roscoe C. Barnes, Second-Baseman," *New York Clipper*, 1878. [Undated article].

16 "One of the Greatest Players of All Time Was 'Ross' Barnes," *Boston Globe*, February 6, 1915: 5.

17 Peter Morris. *A Game of Inches: The Stories Behind the Innovations that Shaped the Game* (Guilford, Connecticut: Ivan R. Dee, 2006).

18 E.G. Westlake, "Baseball Thirty Years Ago," *Great Bend* (Kansas) *Weekly Tribune*, July 21, 1899: 6.

19 Bill James, *New Bill James Historical Baseball Abstract* (New York: Free Press, 2001), 533.

20 Robert H. Schaefer, "The Lost Art of Fair-Foul Hitting," *The National Pastime*, Number 19, 1999: 5.

21 *Chicago Tribune*, March 4, 1877: 7.

22 Tim Murnane (1903) quoted from "One of the Greatest Players of All Time Was 'Ross' Barnes," *Boston Globe*, February 6, 1915: 5.

23 Ibid.

24 *The Sporting Life*, May 23, 1898: 14.

25 "No. 4—Roscoe C. Barnes, Second-Baseman," *New York Clipper*, 1878. [Undated article].

26 "Barnes was the Johnny Evers of his day," *Arizona* (Phoenix) *Republic*, July 28, 1911: 12.

27 Tim Murnane (1903) quoted from "One of the Greatest Players of All Time Was 'Ross' Barnes," *Boston Globe*, February 6, 1915: 5.

28 Sam Crane "Sam Crane Writes Series of Stories on Fifty Greatest Ball Players in History." Undated article. Player's Hall of Fame file.

29 William J. Ryczek, *Blackguards and Red Stockings. A History of Baseball's National Association, 1871-1875*. (Jefferson, North Carolina: McFarland, 1992), 26.

30 *The Sporting Life*, January 15, 1898: 7.

31 *Chicago Tribune*, January 19, 1879: 12.

32 Ryczek, 26.

33 John W. Bauer, "Summer 1874: New game in the Old World. US teams tour England," SABR.org, http://sabr.org/gamesproj/game/summer-1874-new-game-old-country-us-teams-tour-england.

34 "Base Ball. The Nine Next Year," *Chicago Tribune*, July 20, 1875: 5.

35 Harry Palmer, "America's National Game," *Outing*, July 1888,:354.

36 "Sporting News. Fourth Game and Victory of the Chicago White Stockings," *Chicago Tribune*, May 3, 1876: 5.

37 "Base-Ball. More About the New Rules," *Chicago Tribune*, November 26, 1876: 7.

38 Ibid.

39 "Base-Ball," *Chicago Tribune*, May 19, 1877: 2.

40 "Base Ball Topics," *The Times* (Philadelphia), May 31, 1877: 2.

41 *Chicago Tribune*, July 22, 1877: 7.

42 "The Six league Clubs Engage in Championship Contests," *Chicago Tribune*, August 8, 1877: 5.

43 *Cincinnati Enquirer*, August 29, 1877: 7.

44 *Cincinnati Enquirer*, October 8, 1877: 5.

45 Robert H. Schaefer, "The Lost Art of Fair-Foul Hitting," *The National Pastime*, Number 19, 1999: 6.

46 See *Cincinnati Enquirer*, January 11, 1879: 6 and *Chicago Tribune*, June 15, 1879: 7.

47 *Chicago Tribune*, November 10, 1878: 7.

48 Ibid.

49 *Chicago Tribune*, December 5, 1880: 7.

50 *Cincinnati Enquirer*, October 2, 1881: 9.

51 *Pittsburgh Daily Post*, April 20, 1887: 6 and *Pittsburgh Dispatch*, February 1, 1889: 6.

52 *Sporting Life*, May 3, 1890:10.

53 *Sporting Life*, January 3, 1891: 2.

54 It appears as though Ross Barnes was married for 14 months. According the marriage indexes in Cook County, Illinois, Barnes married Ellen F. Welsh on August 14, 1900. The couple was granted a divorce in October 1901. "Mrs. Barnes is divorced," *Rockford Morning Star*, October 22, 1901.

55 *Sporting Life*, February 13, 1915 and March 6, 1915.

FRANK BARROWS

BY MIKE RICHARD

WHILE THE BOSTON RED Stockings of 1871 had many players who would go on to distinguished baseball careers, outfielder Frank Barrows was not one of them. In his only year in the new National Association of Professional Base Ball Players, Barrows played in 18 games for Boston, batted .151 (13 hits in 86 at-bats), and drove in 11 runs.

Franklin Lee Barrows was born on October 22, 1844, in Hudson, Ohio, to Rev. Elijah Porter and Sarah (Lee) Barrows. The family moved to the Boston area when his father was appointed professor of Hebrew language and literature at the Andover Theological Seminary in Newton, just outside Boston. Franklin attended nearby Phillips Academy in 1859 and then remained in New England, where he developed his interest in baseball.[1]

Barrows played for the Boston Tri-Mountains in the National Association of Base Ball Players (NABBP), the first national baseball organization, from 1867 to 1870. Tri-Mountain was first established in 1857. "From an historical perspective," wrote one commentator, "The Tri-Mountains are important because they were the first of the organized clubs playing the 'Massachusetts game' to abandon it in favor of the 'New York game.' This was an inevitable step on the path to victory for the latter and it is the New York version that modern baseball descended from."[2]

During Barrows' tenure with the team, for which he played second base and occasional shortstop, Tri-Mountain posted records of 19-3 in 1867, 12-9 in 1868, and 7-9 in 1869. Barrows occasionally was mentioned in newspaper accounts of games. Playing on the Boston Common on August 6, 1867, against the challengers, the Annawan Club of Mansfield, the Tri-Mountains, lacking three of their usual nine, were edged, 28-27. Barrows was singled out for praise by the *Boston Journal*: "Barrows' fielding was excellent, he having caught five flies, besides putting out two on bases."[3]

In a New England Tournament held in September 1867, Barrows hit a "home run by a splendid strike to centre field" in the fifth game.[4] Tri-Mountain won the deciding game over Lowell, 42-22, on September 29 before 3,000 to 4,000 spectators and won the silver ball. Barrows pulled off a double play in the game, tagging the baserunner and then throwing to first, and he also "made the best hit of the day, sending the ball over Rogers head at left field, on which he made a clean home run."[5]

The team opted to go professional in 1870 with somewhat disastrous results. While its overall record was 6-7, it was 0-4 against the four professional teams it played. Tri-Mountain lost to the Philadelphia Athletics 45-4, the Cincinnati Red Stockings 30-6, the Mutuals of New York, 25-11, and the Chicago White Stockings 36-16, and never played another pro season.

Barrows was one of only two members of the team to play a professional career, along with a 1868 teammate, pitcher Tom Pratt, who played in only one major-league game, for the Philadelphia Athletics, on October 18, 1871. (He had two hits in six at-bats.) He was later joined by Elvio Jiménez and Clarence Dow as the only players to have six at-bats in their only major-league baseball game.

In the spring of 1870, "Mr. Frank Barrows" was listed as one of the umpires of several baseball games between Harvard University and the Boston Red Stockings.[6] It was likely through that association that he became acquainted with Harry Wright and joined the Red Stockings for the 1871 season. He also umpired a game between Harvard and the Athletic Club of Philadelphia in May.

The Red Stockings signed Barrows in mid-January of 1871; he and Harry Schafer were the last two players signed.[7] The team played its opening game on April 6 at the Union Grounds, against a "picked nine," beating them, 41-10. Barrows played for the picked nine as did Dave Birdsall. The two played in another

Frank Barrows (Ars Longa Cards)

game, as opponents, six days later. Near the end of the month, Barrows was named as the 11th man on the Red Stockings.[8] The team went on the road and played a few preseason games, among them a game on May 2 in Washington against the Olympics. Barrows didn't play when the Red Stockings played the franchise's first game, on May 5 in Washington, but served as one of the two scorers in the game.

Barrows made what would today be considered his major-league debut on May 20, 1871, when he batted leadoff (flying out to second baseman Al Reach) and went 1-for-5 in an 11-8 win over the Philadelphia Athletics. After collecting his first professional hit in the fifth inning, singling over the head of second baseman Reach, he scored along with Roscoe Barnes on a single by Dave Birdsall.

It's not known whether Barrows was right-handed or left-handed, either as a batter or in his throwing. His height and weight are likewise unknown.

While baseball reports of this era were sparse in their depiction of the games, Barrows did capture the attention of the fans when he made a fine defensive play in right field against the Chicago White Stockings on June 2. In the fourth inning, Chicago's Jimmy Wood "sent a hot fly to right field, which Barrows … took most handsomely, making one of the best catches ever seen on this grounds, and for which he received loud applause."[9]

For much of the season Barrows shared left field with teammate Fred Cone. However, there were few other highlights reported to the newspaper. On August 7 he played center field and had a double in a 23-7 win over the Philadelphia Athletics, while on September 13 he had one hit and scored a run in a 20-17 victory over the Troy Haymakers. One of the most dramatic moments of the season came in a September 9 game against the Athletics, which drew an estimated 5,000 to the Boston grounds. The Red Stockings were down 14-11 after eight innings. Boston, batting first in the game, rallied in the top of the ninth and took a 15-14 lead when Barrows came up and added another insurance run by singling in Al Spalding. One more run scored behind him, and then the team shifted to defend its three-run lead. Barrows speared a ball hit by Ned Cuthbert for the first out. Birdsall caught a foul tip for the second out. Then John Radcliff lofted a ball to Barrows. The crowd held its breath, but he caught it and "a series of shouts ensued, exceeding any demonstrations of the kind ever witnessed here. The crowd fairly yelled, and hats went up into the air, while their owners danced about apparently frantic, while the ladies waved their handkerchiefs, evidently as much pleased as anyone over the victory snatched by the Reds from the very jaws of defeat, who won not only the game but the championship series with the Athletics."[10]

Barrows played his final game on October 7, a 12-3 win over the Haymakers. He singled once.

The Athletics placed first in the National Association standings at year's end, with both the Chicago White Stockings and the Boston Red Stockings two games behind.

The Red Stockings' batting average in 1871 was .310. Barrows' .151, was by far the lowest on the team. (Sam Jackson was second lowest at .224.)

Barrows did not return to the Red Stockings for the 1872 season, nor did Cone or Jackson, but Barrows' name did crop up in a box score for the Middletown (Connecticut) Mansfields in 1872 when he played in the first game of an intrasquad doubleheader. "In the first game, the Seniors whitewashed the Juniors 24-0. Frank Barrows, who had played with the Boston Red Stockings in 1871, manned right field for the Mansfields. This may have been a tryout for Barrows, who had been spotted with the club for several weeks, or perhaps he was a last minute replacement for Buttery, who was home visiting family."[11]

Barrows was also listed as a substitute umpire in the National Association for that 1872 season. One of the games he umpired was the July 20 game when the Red Stockings hosted the visiting Troy team.

In 1897, when he was 52 years old, Barrows played in an exhibition game along with other old-time major leaguers, against a team from Australia. Playing right field on a team that featured former Red Stockings teammates George Wright and Albert Spalding, Barrows scored a run for the "Old Boston" team against the Australian All-Star team.[12]

In his career after baseball, Barrows entered the wool trade. The Boston City Directory of 1880 listed his occupation as wool buyer, wool sorter, and overseer of a worsted mill.[13]

Barrows moved to the Central Massachusetts city of Fitchburg where he worked as an overseer at the Star Worsted Mills for several years. He was also a noted champion bowler in that city.

After spending much of his life as a bachelor, the 56-year-old Barrows met Josephine F.G. (Gulliver) Gould, a widowed Falmouth bookkeeper, a native of Pittsburgh. Mrs. Gould had a son, William, by her first marriage. The couple married in Boston on December 17, 1902, and lived the rest of Barrows' life at 72 Grove Street in Fitchburg.

On February 6, 1922, Barrows was stricken with a heart ailment and died at the age of 75. He was buried in Oak Grove Cemetery in Falmouth, Massachusetts.

NOTES

1. Thanks to Bob Richardson for helpful suggestions regarding Barrows' family background.
2. Patrick Mondout, "Boston TriMountains," baseball-chronology.com/baseball/leagues/NABBP/Clubs/Boston-Tri-Mountains.asp.
3. *Boston Journal*, August 7, 1867: 4.
4. *Boston Herald*, September 27, 1867: 2.
5. *Boston Journal*, September 30, 1867: 4.
6. *Harvard Advocate*, May 27, 1870: 134.
7. *Springfield* (Massachusetts) *Republican*, January 16, 1871: 8.
8. Rosters were considerably smaller at the time. *Boston Journal*, April 24, 1871: 4.
9. *Boston Post*, June 3, 1871.
10. "Another Victory Achieved By the Red Stockings," *Boston Journal*, September 11, 1891: 1.
11. David Arcidiacono, *Major League Baseball in Gilded Age Connecticut* (Jefferson, North Carolina: McFarland, 2009), 85.
12. Paul Batesel, *Players and Teams of the National Association 1871-75* (Jefferson, North Carolina: McFarland, 2012), 43.
13. Ibid.

TOMMY BEALS

BY MARK S. STERNMAN

A VERSATILE MAN WHO LIVED ON both coasts, played multiple positions for different teams in different leagues, and even went by different names, Tommy Beals played reserve roles for three championship teams in the last three seasons of his six-year professional career. A subpar hitter, Beals on defense "was an exceedingly active player and covered an immense amount of ground."[1]

On June 18, 1845, two Connecticut natives, Albert Beals (born in 1820 or 1821), a photographer, and Fannie (or Fanny, born in 1822 or 1823) Lamb, married. In August 1850 in either Hartford or New York City,[2] they had a son named Thomas Lamb Beals. The Beals family lived in Watervliet, New York, north of Albany, in 1860 and in Gold Hill, Nevada, in 1870.

Beals first received notice in 1867 when, playing right field for the Union Club of Morrisania, he "made the most brilliant catch of the game"[3] in the eighth inning of a 14-12 win over the Brooklyn Atlantics. Beals "distinguished himself … when he played for the Unions, for it was then in the time of lively ball games, when an outfielder had more work to do than the present time."[4]

At the age of 20 in 1871, Beals, playing under the name W. Thomas (he played as W. Thomas from 1871-1873), made his National Association debut for the Washington Olympics in a July 27 game against the Troy Haymakers. He got his first hit (a single) and made his first error on July 28 in a 10-6 loss to Troy. He finished his rookie season batting .194 in 10 games. In 1872, he started the season batting 4-for-21, but finished on an 8-for-19 run to close the season with a .306 batting average. Beals hit ninth in the order in all 19 games he played in 1871 and 1872.

The Olympics franchise lasted just two years, and the Washington Blue Legs took over the Olympic Grounds for 1873. Beals played for this new team, his last season in Washington, and hit .272 in 37 games.

Over his career Beals split his time almost evenly between the infield (58 games) and outfield (60 games), but in 1873 he caught for the only time in his professional career, putting in 13 games behind the dish.

Beals joined the Boston Red Stockings in 1874 and enjoyed his best day with the bat that year in his first game for his new team on May 9. Still batting ninth, he went 5-for-7 with a triple, three runs scored, and four RBIs as Boston rolled, 28-7, over the Baltimore Canaries at the South End Grounds. The performance earned him a promotion to the second slot in the batting order, which he would occupy more than any other over the rest of the season.

Along with the Philadelphia Athletics, Boston took a European tour in the middle of the 1874 campaign. As the last man on the roster, Beals took tickets at one game[5] and umpired another.[6] Back from Europe, Beals also drove in four runs in a home game on October 24 as Boston beat the Hartford Dark Blues, 11-8. As a team, Boston had just seven RBIs in this game because the visitors committed an astounding 21 errors.

The primary spare outfielder in 1875, Beals received more playing time in his last year in Boston than he did in 1874. In a 16-2 rout of Philadelphia on May 11, "The principal feature of the game on the side of the Bostons was the extraordinary play of Beals in the centre field, who caught three very difficult flies in splendid style and was loudly cheered."[7]

Beals seemed to have a mixed relationship with teammate George Wright. While one source asserts, "George Wright and Tommy Beals went many a day without the interchange of a friendly word,"[8] another reports that Wright, later a member of the second class of inductees to the Hall of Fame, named his oldest son Beals after Tommy.[9]

In 1876 Beals left Organized Baseball and moved to Colorado, where he worked as a miner. He later headed to the West Coast, where he would spend his post-baseball career. SABR's Minor League Database reveals that Beals played for the San Francisco Mutuals and the Oakland Pioneers of the California League in 1879, but his name appeared on a list of retired players at the end of that year.[10] Another report two months later had Beals "and the management of the Chicago Club … in correspondence … on … an engagement [in Chicago for the 1880] season."[11]

Ross Barnes, Cal McVey, Al Spalding, and Deacon White, four Boston players, left for the Chicago White Stockings in 1876, the first season of the National League. The Red Stockings, aware of Chicago's interest in Beals, asserted that Boston still controlled the rights to him.

Spalding, now secretary of the White Stockings, unsurprisingly disagreed, telling a reporter, "I don't believe Boston has any desire to raise such a foolish question as the expulsion of Beals five years after their difficulty with him, and, under the verbal agreement which he had with them about the matter, they have no chance to argue the case."[12]

The imbroglio seemed to present an awful lot of fuss about a player of the caliber of Beals, who not surprisingly struggled after missing four years of professional play. While only 29, Beals nevertheless was the oldest player on Chicago's squad of 13.

The 1880 season began on May 1, but Beals did not crack the lineup until July 13, when he played second base and batted eighth, oddly one spot higher in the order than star slugger Cap Anson.[13]

In 1880, the last season Beals played, he hit just .152, but at least had a more mixed record in the field. After a 9-4 win over the Worcester Ruby Legs on August 26, a report on the game lauded Beals, who had "played the base as well as it could be played. He was particularly strong on thrown balls, and cooperated with [catcher Ned] Williamson in a style that is not surpassed by any second-baseman living. He has a clever way of receiving the ball and at the same time standing in the way of the runner—a thing which requires some nerve, but is the way to play second base."[14]

After three off days, the same two teams met, with decidedly poorer results for Beals, "who played as though he had never seen a ball-field before.… It may

Tommy Beals (Spalding Collection)

well be doubted whether Beals should be permitted to play second base again."[15]

A little more than one month later, "Beals … declared his intention of abandoning the ball-field once more, and this time for good, although he has had advantageous offers to play in League clubs next season."[16]

Beals "quit the game to enter business"[17] but for a time ended up in government. After marrying Emma MacGregor in Virginia City, Nevada, on September 2, 1884, Beals served in the state legislature from 1894 to 1896 as a Republican member of the Assembly representing Virginia City. He put in a year on the Judiciary Committee.[18] According to the US Census, Beals worked in San Francisco as a photographer (like his father, who had died on December 4, 1884) in 1900 and as a railroad conductor in 1910, the job he held when he died.[19]

A widower at the end of his life, Tommy Beals died in San Francisco on October 2, 1915, at the age of 65.

His ashes are interred at Cypress Lawn Memorial Park in Colma, California. In 1979 a member of the cemetery staff wrote the following letter to the late Bill Haber, one of the 16 founding members of the Society for American Baseball Research: "Replying to your letter of April 6th regarding information on relatives of the late Thomas L. Beals who was cremated at our cemetery on October 4, 1915, we are sorry to advise that we have no way [of] checking out any survivors."[20]

NOTES

1. Henry Chadwick, *Spalding's Base Ball Guide 1896* (New York: American Sports Publishing Company, 1896), 162.
2. The death certificate of Beals and an October 4, 1915, obituary from an unidentified newspaper lists his birthplace as Hartford; baseball-reference.com and Census records show New York as his place of birth. Likewise, Census records from different years give different dates of birth for both of his parents as well as different spellings for his mother's first name. Thanks to reference librarian Cassidy Lent of the National Baseball Hall of Fame and Museum for scanning the Hall's file on Beals.
3. James L. Terry, *Long Before the Dodgers: Baseball in Brooklyn, 1855-1884* (Jefferson, North Carolina: McFarland, 2002), 66.
4. Harold Kaese, *The Boston Braves 1871-1953* (Boston: Northeastern University Press, 2004), 13.
5. William J. Ryczek, *Blackguards and Redstockings: A History of Baseball's National Association, 1871-1875* (Jefferson, North Carolina: McFarland, 2002), 159.
6. "The American Base-Ball Players in London," *New York Times*, August 4, 1874: 2. Beals umpired in eight National Association games from 1872 to 1875. See retrosheet.org/boxesetc/B/Pbealt101.htm (accessed August 5, 2015).
7. *Boston Daily Globe*, May 12, 1875: 4.
8. "Base-Ball," *Chicago Daily Tribune*, January 19, 1879: 12.
9. Jacob C. Morse, "Hub Happenings," *Sporting Life*, August 6, 1898: 19. "Beals and Wright were such close friends that the latter named a son after him: Beals Wright (1879-1961), who like his father George and his uncle Harry made it to the Hall of Fame … the International Tennis Hall of Fame. Elected in 1956, Beals won gold medals in singles and doubles at the 1904 St. Louis Olympics, and the U.S. Championship the following year." John Thorn, "The Unions of Morrisania," April 10, 2013, ourgame.mlblogs.com/2013/04/10/ (accessed August 5, 2015).
10. "Base-Ball," *Chicago Daily Tribune*, December 28, 1879: 12.
11. "Sporting," *Chicago Daily Tribune*, February 15, 1880: 7.
12. "Sporting News," *Chicago Daily Tribune*, March 23, 1880: 5.
13. "Sporting Events," *Chicago Daily Tribune*, July 15, 1880: 8.
14. "Sporting Events," *Chicago Daily Tribune*, August 27, 1880: 5.
15. "Sporting," *Chicago Daily Tribune*, August 31, 1880: 8. Beals made three errors in this game, more than in any of the other 44 games for which the author found defensive data in either online or newspaper accounts.
16. "Base-Ball," *Chicago Daily Tribune*, October 10, 1880: 7.
17. "Boston Stars of '77 Famous Ball Team," *The* [New London] *Day*, July 13, 1904: 2.
18. leg.state.nv.us/dbtw-wpd/exec/dbtwpub.dll?AC=CHANGE_REPORT&XC=/dbtw-wpd/exec/dbtwpub.dll&BU=http%3A%2F%2Fwww.leg.state.nv.us%2Fdbtw-wpd%2FLegSim.htm&TN=Legislators&SN=AUTO2964&SE=1481&RN=0&MR=20&TR=0&TX=1000&ES=0&CS=2&XP=&RF=Expanded%20Record&EF=&DF=Expanded+Report&RL=1&EL=1&DL=1&NP=3&ID=&MF=MYWPMSG.INI&MQ=&TI=0&DT=&ST=0&IR=104&NR=0&NB=0&SV=0&SS=0&BG=e9f0e8&FG=000000&QS=&OEX=ISO-8859-1&OEH=ISO-8859-1 (accessed August 4, 2015). Beals had two sons, Thomas and Albert. The October 4, 1915, obituary of Beals from an unidentified publication in the National Baseball Hall of Fame mentions only Albert.
19. Paul Batesel, *Players and Teams of the National Association, 1871-1875* (Jefferson, North Carolina: McFarland, 2002), 23.
20. The National Baseball Hall of Fame and Museum file on Beals includes a copy of this letter.

DAVID BIRDSALL

BY RICHARD "DIXIE" TOURANGEAU

"HE WAS A FAITHFUL, CONSCIENtious player, who always worked to win and could always be depended upon."[1] To have something very complimentary said about you at your passing is gratifying, but the person who says it can be as telling about your life. This testimonial was made by 1870s star ballplayer (and future Hall of Famer) George Wright upon the death of Dave Birdsall, his friend of more than 30 years and teammate on both the original 1871 Red Stockings and the first Boston championship squad in 1872.

David Solomon Birdsall was born on July 16, 1838, in New York City's Lower East Side, to Solomon and Sarah Birdsall. He was the oldest of four children, with siblings Eliza Jane, John, and Sarah E. coming later. David's father is listed as a policeman in the 1860 US census and in the few City Directories in which his name appears. By 1860 David had left the family and was working as a store clerk, living on Second Avenue in 1867, not far from his parents. It is likely he joined the base ball craze sweeping New York City in the 1850s, playing for various neighborhood teams. Officially Birdsall played one game in 1858 at second base for the Metropolitans.[2] The 1890 Civil War Veterans Census indicates that David enlisted in the war effort in July 1861 and served four years as a private. Such duties seemed not to interfere with his occasional ballplaying; he "is first prominent with the Harlem team for three years" (1860-62), and the (Bronx) Unions of Morrisania in 1863.[3] It was with Morrisania that Birdsall got his reputation as a dependable player. Through the 1860s he caught and pitched for the Unions as they slowly became a respected club. When position-player teammate Charlie Pabor started pitching in the mid-1860s, the Unions improved. In 1866 they compiled a 25-3 record, the same year cricketeer-turned-baseballist George Wright first crossed diamond paths with Birdsall. Wright played nine games for the Unions.

In 1868 infielder Wright played in all 43 Union games as did Birdsall—behind the bat. At 37-6 the Union amateurs ranked behind only the Athletics of Philadelphia (47-3) and New York Mutuals (47-7), while edging out Harry Wright's Cincinnati Red Stockings by one victory. Morrisania had won 29 straight games before losing 13-12 to the pre-iconic Cincinnati Red Stockings in late August. Harry then coaxed brother George to Porkopolis to help create what became the unbeaten juggernaut Red Stockings of 1869 and most of 1870.

Birdsall also moved in 1869, taking his talents to the Washington Nationals, who finished 13-13 but were only 4-12 against the best amateur clubs.[4] The Wrights and Cincinnati (57-0) beat the Nationals 24-8 in June 1869; Birdsall managed one hit. At age 32 Birdsall returned to his Morrisania mates in 1870 and caught 18 games in their 20-19 season (7-18 versus "professional" teams). He met his old friends the Ohio River Wrights on June 15. Asa Brainard surprisingly shut out the usually strong Unions, 14-0. It was the day after the Red Stockings' extraordinary win streak had been suddenly snapped by the Brooklyn Atlantics, 8-7 in 11 innings. In Brainard's "chicago" win, Birdsall had one of the five Union hits, walked twice and lined into a double play started by his quick-handed pal George Wright.

Having shown his worth playing with and against the Wright brothers, it is no surprise that when the signings for the new professional league were announced in late January of 1871, Birdsall was inked with the Boston club. The *New York Clipper* of January 28, 1871, under a story dateline of January 21, listed all team rosters to that date.[5] It was the day after Ivers Whitney Adams held his Parker House lunch, announced his grand intention of fielding the finest team in the new National Association and asked some deep-pocket friends to buy stock in it. Starting with manager Harry Wright and his stellar brother

Dave Birdsall, 1872 (Spalding Collection)

George, down to Birdsall, all were in the fold before there was an actual team. It is not difficult to figure that because George and Harry knew of Birdsall's worth firsthand, they picked him as "insurance" for the Red Stockings roster. Twenty-five years later, at his death, *Sporting Life* surmised that Boston acquired Birdsall because of "his successful catching of the wild and swift left-handed Pabor" of Morrisania.[6]

Reasons for employing Birdsall might not have been that evident to the unschooled base ball masses. He was the second oldest Red Stocking (only player-manager Harry Wright was older) and had the slightest physical stature of anyone on the team. At 126 pounds, he did not have a catcher's physique, but he had been a nimble and notable backstop his entire 12-year amateur career. Cincinnati right fielder Cal McVey would do the bulk of catching for the 1871 Reds, but resting him was of prime importance to the team, and Birdsall was key to that plan. Durable Dave caught the preseason games and most Reds exhibitions, giving McVey days off but allowing the club to make side money. Birdsall, who most often played right field, and Cal often traded positions in some one-sided Association games.

Birdsall batted third in front of cleanup slugger McVey in most of the 1871 games, and his hitting was a surprising plus for the Reds. Except for an early twisted ankle (missed two games), at 33 Birdsall held up well. With all the other better-hitting, younger players in the league, Birdsall (.303) finished second in runs scored (51) to teammate Ross Barnes (66) and third in team hits behind McVey and Barnes. A strategically rested McVey benefited greatly, leading the league in hits (66), finishing second to Athletic star Levi Meyerle in batting average, .492 to .431, and McVey was second in RBIs to New York Mutual pitcher Rynie Wolters, 44 to 43. But with shortstop George Wright injured for half the Reds' games, the Scott Hastings contract fiasco (his NA Commission-determined ineligibility culminated in forfeits giving Philadelphia two wins in games they lost to Hastings' Rockford, Illinois, club) and the blowing of four "safe" leads, the Reds finished second to Philly (20 wins to 21), dampening Birdsall's productive season.

In the very first game, on May 5 in Washington (Olympics), Dave accounted for four runs in the 20-18 win, despite being struck out twice by loser Asa Brainard. On May 29 his four hits and four runs aided a 25-11 win over the Rockford Forest Citys. His "career high" day also came versus Rockford, when on July 10 his five hits and five runs off loser Bill "Cherokee" Fisher helped whip the host Westerners, 21-12. Back at the South End Grounds on September 2, Birdsall scored five runs on three hits against the hapless Cleveland Forest Citys, in a 31-10 victory.

Things changed a bit in 1872 as Birdsall began to wear down. He played in 16 of 48 games and hit just .211. But he was McVey's energy-saving substitute again, catching two or three games each month, all exhibitions and the final innings of some slaughters, saving Cal from the continuous chore of catching Al Spalding's speedballs. But reliable Dave still had his offensive moments. On May 9 Birdsall helped pound new Brooklyn Eckfords pitcher Jim McDermott, 20-0, with three doubles and three RBIs, a combined two-hitter for Spalding and Harry Wright. Later Birdsall contributed a run and an RBI to a ninth-inning rally that edged the tough Mutuals, 4-2. The Reds won the first 10 games he played in, giving them a 33-4 record. He caught the year's finale, against the Eckfords, a 4-3 win for Spalding over Reds nemesis George Zettlein. Dave was an important cog in the first Boston championship season (39-8-1).

Birdsall might have retired in 1873 because of Association-wide faster pitching, but instead stayed on to help his club as best he could. Though much less evident, his "insurance policy" talent was again illustrated, as he caught most of the April exhibitions. It took two young "Jims" bound for stardom to replace him. McVey left Boston and new catcher James "Deacon" White (formerly of Cleveland, inducted into the National Baseball Hall of Fame in 2013) needed time to get settled.

Birdsall started the first three games of the season and those were the last of the total 48 he played in official Association competition. The defending champion Red Stockings lost two of those first three games before Deacon White stepped in for good and helped capture a second straight NA championship. Bridgeport, Connecticut, native and 1872 Middletown Mansfield budding star James "Orator" O'Rourke replaced Birdsall in right field. Birdsall, however, was a fixture in moneymaking exhibitions throughout the year, playing in more than 20, catching in half of those. On occasion when the opposing team would be minus a player, stalwart catcher Birdsall would fill the toughest position for the amateurs, allowing the game to be played and the gate to be collected.

Birdsall's final game with his Red Stockings comrades was one of spontaneous fun. In late December, Harry Wright assembled what was left of his team in wintry Boston, gathered some top local amateurs and announced in the Christmas Day *Boston Daily Advertiser* that there would be a game that morning at the South End Grounds, no admission to be charged. It was to be 10 innings with 10 players to a side. The temperature hovered at 34, and the wind was calm under a partly cloudy sky. On a hard, bumpy, but dry field the Wrights faced the Spaldings as the "pick up" teams battled to an 18-16 Wright brothers victory. The two winning runs appropriately scored in the intended 10th frame. Dave caught Spalding for the final time and scored three runs. Harry, George, and younger brother Sam Wright played with Bob Addy, Charlie Sweasy, and Jack Manning, while Spalding's group included Birdsall, future National League Beaneaters owner Art Soden, Fred Cone, and Jamaica Plain baseball manufacturer Louis H. Mahn. About 500 hearty holiday souls attended.[7]

During the 1873 season, "impartial" Dave Birdsall was called upon to umpire one July game, in Brooklyn, as he and the Reds traveled with the Athletics from Philadelphia to Boston. The Atlantics beat the Athletics, 14-7. Choosing to remain a Boston resident, yet no longer a member of the team in 1874, Birdsall kept his hand in the game he loved by umpiring three South End games. Boston won two.

The 1880 US census has Birdsall at 222 Harrison Avenue with his wife and child. He had married a woman (Fanny from either Eastern Canada or Vermont) in 1872. Daughter Carrie (Caroline Sarah) was born on January 8, 1873. There is no Massachusetts record of the marriage or any clue as to what happened to Fanny. The daughter's birth is recorded under Caroline "Bird." At her birth the Birdsalls lived on Oxford Street (now part of Chinatown), before moving to 222 Harrison, where Dave would stay until his death.

Proudly listed with the "Boston Base Ball Club" in the City Directories of 1872 and '73, Birdsall was a clerk starting in 1874 and for the rest of his working days. He was involved in several businesses, the first being with the Melodeon Billiard Hall, then owned by John Henry Flack. There were a dozen pool halls along lower Washington Street then, the Melodeon, a former theater, being the most lavish. Flack was a tournament player in Massachusetts who died suddenly in 1880. He owned a second billiard establishment at which Birdsall also worked.

Birdsall then briefly joined Elisha A. Holbrook at his billiard business before becoming employed by the Old Colony Railroad at its Kneeland/South Street depot/ticket office. In the mid-1880s he hooked up with Causeway Street liquor dealer John M. Benson.

By 1894 and until his death, Birdsall was a clerk at 56 Kilby Street, Humphrey Dyer's restaurant in bustling Liberty Square. Back during his 1870s billiard parlor days on Washington Street, Birdsall's location was between the sporting-goods stores of both Wright brothers, so he likely saw them frequently.

Only six weeks prior to Birdsall's death, *Sporting Life* reported that he had a "recent hospital stay and was hobbling around with the aid of a stick."[8] The prognosis of his "coming out all right" was wrong; Birdsall died on December 30, 1896, leaving his daughter. The *New York Clipper* ran a nice obituary lauding his playing career and adding that had Birdsall lived in pain since an operation in 1895.[9] Birdsall was an Elks Lodge member, and was listed as one of the mourners, and perhaps an usher, at the funeral of baseball icon Mike "King" Kelly in November 1894, since the near-destitute King was buried by that organization.

Dave Birdsall is buried five headstones (15 feet) from Kelly in the Order of Elks Plot at Mount Hope Cemetery in the Mattapan section of Boston. A miffed *Sporting Life* writer complained that only two old ballplayers attended his funeral, local Jack Manning (1873 and 1875 Reds) and the Stockings' only third baseman, Harry Schafer, who devotedly came up from his native Philadelphia. A *Sporting Life* blurb revealed that in 1871 both George Wright and Birdsall met Schafer in New York and they all boated up to Boston to begin training for their first Red Stocking season.[10]

Over the decades Birdsall's daughter, Caroline, lived in Boston and Cambridge, working for a clock company until she died in 1951 in Allston.

SOURCES

In addition to the sources cited in the Notes, the author also consulted Retrosheet.org, census information, city directories from Boston and New York, and numerous daily Boston newspapers.

NOTES

1 "Another Veteran Gone," *Sporting Life*, January 9, 1897: 9.
2 Marshall D. Wright, *The National Association of Base Ball Players 1857-1870* (Jefferson, North Carolina: McFarland, 2000), 21.
3 *Sporting Life*, January 9, 1897: 9. The Morrisania section of the Bronx begins about 0.7 miles east of Yankee Stadium and is bound by Webster and Prospect Avenues (east to west) and 161st St. to 169th St. (south to north). It is less than a square mile.
4 Wright, 251.
5 *New York Clipper*, "Players Who Have Signed Papers," January 28, 1871: 338.
6 J.C. Morse, "Recollections Awakened by the Death of Birdsall," *Sporting Life*, January 9, 1897: 7.
7 "A Ten Inning Game," *New York Clipper*, January 3, 1874: 315.
8 "Another Vet Gone," *Sporting Life*, January 9, 1897: 9.
9 *New York Clipper*, January 9, 1897: 719.
10 "Recollections …," *Sporting Life*, January 9, 1897: 7.

FRED CONE

BY MIKE RICHARD

WHILE FRED CONE DIDN'T HAVE much of a career at the plate with a mere 20 hits in his only season, he banged out one-quarter of those hits in one memorable game for the 1871 Boston Red Stockings.

In the team's July 12 game against the Fort Wayne Kekiongas, Cone collected five hits in a lopsided 30-9 victory.

Joseph Frederick Cone was born in May of 1848 in Rockford, Illinois, to Mander and Sarah (Odell Bushnell) Cone. He is listed in baseball records as growing to 5-feet-9 with a playing weight of 171 pounds. We do not know whether he was right- or left-handed.

Young Fred grew up on his parents' farm in the village of New Milford, four miles south of Rockford, with brothers Edward and Hiram Cone. As a boy he played for a junior club called the Unions and then joined another local team, the Sinnissippis (derived from an area near Rockford called Sinnissippi), for the 1866 season.

Cone became the regular first baseman for the Forest City juniors in 1867.[1] The club had been established two years earlier and made a successful transition from an amateur squad to a professional team. During that 1867 season, Forest City made quite a name for itself by defeating the Nationals from Washington, 29-23.

Cone went on to play first base for two seasons with Forest City (1868 and 1869) before first baseman Joe Doyle was signed for the 1870 season. Cone then played left field, where "he gained a good reputation."[2]

Said Cone regarding the signing of Doyle, "He wore no big glove to protect his hands, yet he was lightning on thrown balls, no matter how badly they broke. Up in the air, down in the ground, in fact any old way, he would get them and save many an error. In getting into fast double plays he was a wonder."[3]

Cone's reminiscences about his playing days with the Forest Citys appeared in a July 15, 1899, issue of the *Lima News*: "All players in those days were social lions, the old-timers say. Carriages were provided for them whenever they went to other cities to play and all sorts of invitations were extended to them. The fans were enthusiastic as they are to-day and the spectators used to become familiar and take the players into their confidences. Batting and fielding averages formed the small talk at sociable and dinner parties. An astonishing amount of loyalty to the home team was displayed by businessmen, lawyers, judges and the profound thinking economists."[4]

Cone also recalled the popularity of the sport when the champion Unions of Morrisania, New York, made the trip from the East to play the Forest Citys in Rockford: "The banks closed, business men shut up their stores and the judge of the county court gravely informed his lawyer friends that the court had to sit en banc with a number of other estimable judges—of baseball—in a well-known stand out in the remote part of the city given over to the baseball players."[5]

"That game with the Unions was one of the best we ever played, although we lost," said Cone.[6]

During that period, future Hall of Famer Albert Spalding and another future Red Stockings teammate, Ross Barnes, also starred for the Rockford club.

Cone also noted memories of a game played by the Forest Citys in Rockford on October 15, 1870, against the Red Stockings:

"Mr. Spalding has preserved in a scrapbook the score of that never-to-be-forgotten game at Rockford in which the gaudy pennant of the famous Red Stockings was trailed in the dust of defeat by the score of 12 to 5. Each side made three home runs and not a Red walked to first on 'called balls' which showed that Spalding had great control in that contest. The scrapbook also noted, '(Bob) Addy, (Ross) Barnes, (Tom) Foley, (Gat) Stires, (Joe) Simmons and Cone played great ball.'"[7]

After the 1870 season managing the Cincinnati Red Stockings, Harry Wright was enticed to Boston to head the first professional baseball team there, and he raided the Rockford Forest City team to bolster his lineup. As the *Rockford Weekly Register-Gazette* put it, "(H)e has paid the Rockford Forest City Club the high compliment of engaging Barnes, Spalding, and Cone; whereat the *Chicago Tribune* laments that these were not secured for the White Stockings."[8] Wright brought the men to play for the Boston version of the Red Stockings for the 1871 National Association season.

Originally, Wright had only intended to take Barnes and Spalding, but "a great catch which Cone made in left field, followed by a throw to the plate which retired a runner, was witnessed by Mr. Wright and he immediately added Cone's name to the list of recruits that he wanted."[9]

Barnes, Spalding, and Cone lived in a rooming house on Heath Street in the "Boston Highlands" section of the city, about a mile from the grounds and next door to the one where Harry Wright boarded. Al Spalding wrote the Rockford newspaper in late April, before the season began, that "as we are all together, we don't get very lonesome."[10]

The Red Stockings' first game of the season was played in Washington on May 5. Cone played left field and batted eighth in the order, as he did in almost every game of the season, only occasionally batting seventh. Boston won the coin toss and sent the Olympians to bat first; the Red Stockings came from behind with five runs in bottom of the ninth inning, to win 20-18. Every player on the team scored at least one run; Cone and Cal McVey were the only players to score just once. Cone singled over second base in the eighth and came around to score after a walk and an errant throw to second base on an infield grounder. Cone had walked twice earlier in the game, but was stranded both times.

In a game with the Troy Haymakers on May 9, Cone was involved in a play which that caused severe injury to shortstop George Wright. On a fly ball hit into short left field in the sixth inning, Wright called for the ball but the hard-charging Cone did not hear him because of a passing train and the two players collided.

The injury did not seem serious at first, but it was the same leg Wright had injured in 1870, and after a 20-minute delay he was sent to the hotel in a carriage. He was slow to heal, causing him to miss 16 games (half the team's total of 31).[11]

The play also affected Cone, who injured a wrist and missed several games. Cone shared an outfield spot with teammate Frank Barrows, who played in 18 games.

The Haymakers and Red Stockings squared off again on May 16, and Cone was one of six Red Stockings to score in the first inning, but Troy got its revenge and won, 29-14.

In his only major-league season, Cone played in 19 of the 31 games, as well as several exhibition games. He batted .260 (20-for-77) with 16 runs batted in and 17 runs scored. He had three doubles and a triple, but

Fred Cone (Ars Longa Cards)

was more of a threat on the bases as he stole 12 bases while being caught only once. His .260 batting average ranked him ninth on the team, but his .329 on-base percentage placed him fifth.

Defensively, Cone committed seven errors in 48 chances, for an .854 fielding average, which would seem abysmal by later standards, but was in fact tied with Ross Barnes for third-best on the squad. The Red Stockings as a team recorded an .834 fielding average. Cone had two outfield assists.

Where the 1871 Boston team had fielded a roster of 11 players, the 1872 team made do with just 10 players all season long. Fraley Rogers, Andy Leonard, and Harry Wright were the outfielders. Cone was not needed. He was in Boston as late as April, and was the umpire in a couple of games between the Red Stockings and Harvard, but was not retained for the ballclub.

He was considered for a Chicago professional team in 1873, but nothing seems to have come of it.[12] In 1876 he signed with Chicago as "assistant manager, and substitute."[13] No more is known about his possible play that season.

After his baseball career, an opportunity arose for Cone to work as a hotel clerk and he left the game to go into the hotel business. While playing for Rockford, he had been a hotel clerk and worked for a man named Harry Starr in the Holland House. The *Rockford Daily Register* reported in 1883 that "Cone is now one of the best hotel clerks in Chicago and flashes his diamond studs behind the Grand Pacific counters."[14]

Cone married Elizabeth (Munger) Holley on December 2, 1881. The couple had no children.

In later years, he became the night manager of the Grand Pacific and later worked for the Wellington and Great Northern hotels in Chicago.[15]

Shortly after Harry Wright died, a "Harry Wright Day" was held in several cities on April 13, 1896. Cone was among those who traveled to Rockford, reuniting in an exhibition game with Spalding, George Wright, Addy, and a number of others from the Forest City teams of the 1860s.

Cone became quite opinionated about the progress of the game of baseball and in an 1896 interview with the *Rockford Daily Register* expressed his disdain for the way the game was being played in the professional ranks.

"From what read in the papers I have come to the conclusion that they don't play ball nowadays. I don't want to see the time-honored game dragged in the dust," the paper quoted him as saying.[16]

Cone noted that the current crowds, estimated at 6,000, were a far cry from the cozy crowds of his day.

"I did not feel at home among the crowd. It was no good-natured, howling crowd, but they all sat there with a long look on their faces, as if something terrible was about to take place. What do people go to a ball game for if it is not for a good time?" he said.

Cone also expressed surprise at the "gloves" worn by the players in the field, as opposed to playing barehanded as many players in his day did.

"Try as hard as I could I was unable to pick out the catcher among the crowd of players. All because they had a big bunch of cotton on their hands. Even the fielders wore them," he said.

"After the game was started the first batter knocked a little weak fly over third base and the crowd yelled. I could not see what they yelled for, as I was ashamed of the batter. Then I found the catcher. Oh, what a sight he was. On his breast he wore a mattress that was large enough for a family of six to sleep upon, and talking about gloves, it was a corker, big as a large pillow. Around his head he wore enough steel to keep all the firm of the 'Long, Short & Co.' in confinement for years to come. How that poor, imposed upon fellow could see is more than I can make out."[17]

A note in an 1896 issue of the *New York Times* regarding an old-timers game said, "Fred Cone, who made his advent into Rockford in 1868 with his overalls in cowhide boots, as a member of the Stillman Valley 'Plowboys,' now wears a gorgeous diamond in his shirtfront and is the day clerk of the Victoria Hotel."[18]

After an illness of seven weeks, Cone died at his home on Oakwood Boulevard in Chicago of apoplexy at 6 A.M. on April 13, 1909 at the age of 61. He was survived by his wife of 30 years and a brother E. Frank Cone. Funeral services were held at Graceland Chapel in Chicago, where he was buried.

NOTES

1. Peter Morris, William J. Ryczek, Jan Finkel, Leonard Levin, and Richard Malatzky, *Base Ball Pioneers, 1850-1870: The Clubs and Players Who Spread the Sport* (Jefferson, North Carolina: McFarland & Co., 2012), 230.

2. "The National Game," *Rockford Weekly Register-Gazette*, March 25, 1871: 8.

3. *Base Ball Pioneers*, 230.

4. "Baseball Thirty Years Ago—What Has Become of the Members of the Forest City Ball Team of 1870," *Lima* (Ohio) *News*, July 15, 1899: 24.

5. Ibid.

6. Ibid.

7. Ibid.

8. "The National Game," *Rockford Weekly Register-Gazette*, January 21, 1871: 9.

9. "J. Fred Cone Buried Today," *Daily Register-Gazette* (Rockford, Illinois), April 15, 1909: 2.

10. "Our National Game," *Rockford Weekly Register-Gazette*, April 29, 1871: 8.

11. William J. Craig, *A History of the Boston Braves: A Time Gone By* (Charleston, South Carolina: The History Press, 2012), 78. Initial reports had Wright, "the acknowledged King of the Base-ball Field," suffering a broken leg. See "George Wright Injured," *Cincinnati Enquirer*, May 10, 1871: 8.

12. "Base Ball," *Chicago Tribune*. July 24, 1972: 6.

13. "Base Ball," *Rockford Weekly Register-Gazette*, January 7, 1876: 3. The November 3, 1875, *Boston Journal* mentions Cone as a "business manager" as well.

14. "A Man About Town," *Rockford Daily Register*, July 14, 1883: 3.

15. *Base Ball Pioneers*, 230. See also "Fred Cone Makes Changes in Place of Employment," *Rockford Morning Star*, March 17, 1904: 2.

16. "The World of Sport," *Rockford Daily Register*, August 29, 1896: 3.

17. Ibid.

18. "Diamond Field Veterans: Stars of a Quarter of a Century Ago to Play a Ball Game," *New York Times*, April 12, 1896: 3.

CHARLIE GOULD

BY CHARLES F. FABER

THE BOY LOVED BASEBALL. AS A teenager he was the best baseball player in his hometown. But Charlie Gould probably never dreamed of playing baseball for a living. His future career was more likely as a clerk or perhaps as a bookkeeper. At that time, there were no openly all-professional baseball clubs, where a young man could earn a living. That changed when Charlie was 20 years old; he went on to play and manage in the major leagues for six seasons.

Charles Harvey Gould was born in Cincinnati, Ohio, on August 21, 1847, the fourth child of Elizabeth Fisk and George W. Gould, a produce merchant who started by selling butter and eggs along the Ohio River waterfront and built the enterprise into a thriving wholesale business. As a youngster, Charlie worked as a clerk in his father's business. At the age of 15 he was playing first base for the Buckeyes, the best ball club in the Queen City. He stayed with the Buckeyes from 1863 through 1867 and earned a reputation as an outstanding fielder. It is said that he won a baseball-throwing competition by throwing a ball 302 feet 3 inches, quite a feat considering the condition of the balls used in the contest.[1]

In 1866 Aaron B. Champion, a Cincinnati lawyer and entrepreneur, formed the Cincinnati Base Ball Club. The club won two games and lost two during its initial season, both losses coming at the hands of the Buckeyes. The team played its home games on the grounds of the Union Cricket Club. One of the cricketers, Harry Wright, had been a star player for the famed Knickerbocker baseball club in New York before becoming a professional cricket player. Wright decided that baseball had a brighter future than cricket, so he accepted Champion's offer to join the Cincinnati Base Ball Club, as captain and center fielder. Soon Wright was named manager, with duties that today would be considered responsibilities of the field manager, general manager, traveling secretary, and scout.

In 1867 the Cincinnatis were a strong aggregation, augmented by several paid performers Wright had brought from the East. The club won 17 games, while losing only one. Among the victories was a 109-15 drubbing of the Holt Baseball Club in Newport, Kentucky. The one loss was a 53-10 beating at the hands of the Washington Nationals. The defeat was a particularly bitter pill for Harry Wright, as Washington's star player was shortstop George Wright, Harry's brother.

Champion and Wright were determined to make the club not only the strongest in the Midwest, but one that could compete successfully with the powerful teams in the East. In order to accomplish this they had to obtain the best players in the country, which meant they had to pay the price. In 1868 the National Association of Base Ball Players still had a rule against pay for play, but the rule was frequently violated, sometimes openly, more often by subterfuge, such as providing salaries for sham jobs in a sponsor's business (The rule was repealed during the winter of 1868-69). Champion and Wright took full advantage of any opportunities to acquire star players. Champion remained president of the club, responsible for players' salaries. Wright became his man for all seasons.

Before the 1868 season began Wright hired seamstress Bertha Betram to create new uniforms. She made white flannel jerseys, with a bright red C stitched on the front; white knickers with a clasp below the knee, and long, bright red stockings, giving rise to the clubs new nickname—the Red Stockings. The 1868 club won 41 of the 48 games they played that season, including two victories over their Queen City rivals, the Buckeyes, 28-10 and 20-12. Local bragging rights clearly now belonged to the Red Stockings.

Seven losses were seven too many for Champion and Wright. They were in pursuit of perfection.

Charlie Gould (Spalding Collection)

In 1869 they fielded the first openly all-professional club in the history of baseball. Most prominent among the acquisitions was Harry Wright's brother, George, perhaps the best ballplayer of his era. Also prominent among the new professionals was Charlie Gould, the ex-Buckeye who had been hired away from his former team. At six feet, Gould was the tallest player on the squad. At a time when most first sackers were anchored to the bag, Gould, with his height, his unusually long arms, and his agility, was able to play off the base and still get back to the bag in time to catch a throw from a fellow infielder. So adept was he at catching balls thrown his direction that his teammates said throwing to him was as easy as throwing a ball into a bushel basket. Bushel Basket became Gould's nickname.

The only native Cincinnatian on the team, Gould was popular with Queen City cranks (as fans were called in those days.) He was affable, fun-loving, and accessible to the cranks. He enjoyed practical jokes, as long as they were not malicious. He did not participate in the rowdy behavior that characterized some of his teammates.

On April 17, 1869, the Red Stockings played their first exhibition game as an all-professional club, defeating a local team of amateur all-stars, 24-15. Charlie Gould started at first base and collected four hits. On May 4 the Red Stockings met another Cincinnati squad, the Great Western Club, in their first official game of the season, and trounced their opponents, 45-9. After defeating all the local opposition, the Red Stockings embarked on a trip to the East. Gould played first base in every game, batted second in the lineup, and was frequently a star of the game. One of his more outstanding games came at Springfield, Massachusetts, when he accumulated six base hits and eight stolen bases, as the Red Stockings defeated the Mutuals, 80-5

The undefeated Cincinnatis steamed into New York City, prepared to meet three of the strongest teams in the nation. On June 15 they defeated the New York Mutuals in a hard-fought contest, 4-2. The next day they routed the Brooklyn Atlantics, 32-10. The Red Stockings completed their three-game sweep of Gotham's finest by trouncing the Brooklyn Eckfords, 24-5. They continued their victorious swing through the East with wins in Philadelphia, Baltimore, Washington, and wherever a game could be scheduled. The final game on the tour came in Wheeling, West Virginia. The Red Stockings were leading the Baltic Base Club by the score of 53-0 before the game was halted because of rain. Gould collected six hits in the four innings played before the rains came.

Returning to the Queen City, the Red Stockings continued their winning ways, highlighted by a 71-15 blowout of their erstwhile rivals, the Buckeyes. To prove it was no fluke, the Stockings prevailed in a rematch, 103-8. On August 26, the Troy Haymakers visited Cincinnati. The result was one of the most controversial games ever played. With the score tied, 17-17, Troy's president pulled his team off the field to protest an umpire's decision. The umpire, John

Brockway, awarded the game to Cincinnati on a forfeit. However, the NABBP Judiciary Committee held that the game was officially a tie—the first blemish on the Red Stockings' 1868 record.[2] It was later revealed that the protest had been staged. Haymaker owner John Morrissey had wanted the game to end in a tie so that he could collect on his bets that Cincinnati would not win the game. After the season ended the Troy club apologized for its disgraceful behavior.[3]

Having defeated the best in the East and the Midwest, the Red Stockings had only one more world to conquer. They went west. They won games in St. Louis, Omaha, San Francisco, and Sacramento by huge margins and returned home undefeated. Harry Wright listed the club's record as 56 wins and one tie. Various newspapers reported the victory total as 57, 58, or 61, depending on whether rain-shortened contests were included.[4] The average score was something like 40-10. Charlie Gould was fourth on the team with 21 home runs.

His salary for 1869 was $800. In addition, every man on the team received a $50 bonus for completing an undefeated season.

In April 1870 the Red Stockings boarded steamboats and headed South. They defeated the Louisville Eagles, 94-7, and headed for New Orleans. The Cincinnatians defeated the five teams they faced in the Crescent City by scores of 51-1; 80-6; 39-6; 26-7; and 24-4. On the way back the Red Stockings stopped in Memphis long enough to demolish the Oriental Base Ball Club, 100-2. Returning home the club continued winning by huge margins, the most lopsided being a 108-3 blasting of the Union Base Ball Club of Urbana, Ohio. By the fifth inning of this game Gould already had collected 11 hits. The next day the Red Stockings whipped the Dayton Base Ball Club, 108-9. They defeated the Forest City club of Cleveland and headed east, handily beating teams in upstate New York and Massachusetts. When they reached New York City, they defeated the Mutuals, 16-3, for the 27th consecutive victory of the 1880 season.

On June 14 they faced the Brooklyn Atlantics. At the end of nine innings, the score was tied, 5-5. The Atlantics began to leave the field, satisfied with a tie. Wright and Champion both protested, citing the rule that in case of a tie at the end of nine innings the game must continue "unless it be mutually agreed upon by the captains of the two nines to consider the game as drawn."[5] Rather than lose the game by forfeit, the Atlantics allowed the game to resume. In the top of the 11th inning, the Red Stockings scored two runs to take the lead, 7-5. The Atlantics came back in the bottom of the frame and tied the game at 7-7. With Bob "Death to Flying Things" Ferguson on first base, pitcher George Zettlein came to the plate. He smacked a hard grounder to the right of Charlie Gould at first base. The Bushel Basket, reputedly the best fielding first baseman of his time, unexpectedly muffed the ball. Retrieving the ball and seeing Ferguson heading for second base, Gould fired the ball wildly toward second. The ball bounced into left field, and Ferguson scored the winning run. The Red Stockings' long winning streak had come to an end on an error by the Bushel Basket.

During the season, dissension struck the club. Two major cliques emerged, divided over opinions about drinking and discipline. The Wright brothers, Gould, and McVey opposed what they considered rowdy behavior; the others had a different view about off-field conduct.

On August 2, 1870, Aaron Burt Champion unexpectedly resigned as president of the club. The vice president and secretary also announced their resignations. Under new leadership in the front office, the Red Stockings finished the 1870 season with a record of 68 wins, six losses, and one tie. However, Stephen D. Guschov quotes from a pamphlet issued by Champion's successor A. P. C. Bonte noting that the executive board decided that they could not afford to pay the "enormous salaries now demanded by professional players" and would revert to amateur status in 1871.

On November 30, Harry Wright announced that he had agreed to become the manager, captain, and secretary of the new professional club being organized in Boston. Less than two months later George Wright joined his brother in the Hub. Charlie Gould and Cal McVey soon were on their way to Beantown.

Boston ownership asked Wright if he could bring any other former Cincinnati players to the fold, but Wright demurred. He wanted no drinkers, growlers, or shrinkers on his team.

On St. Patrick's Day, 1871, a new organization was formed. Called the National Association of Professional Baseball Clubs, it is generally considered baseball's first major league. Boston became a charter member. Wright christened the team the Boston Red Stockings and led it to a second-place finish in the circuit's inaugural season, two games behind the pennant winning Philadelphia Athletics. Wright righted the ship the next season and won the league championship in each of the four remaining years of the loop's existence. In the *Baseball Encyclopedia*, Pete Palmer and Gary Gillette paid tribute to Wright: "In a league with questionable organization, officiating, and, in some cases, honesty of its participants, British-born Harry Wright was the pillar of class and professionalism."[6]

Gould was Boston's regular first baseman in 1871 and 1872. He had moderate success as a batter, hitting .285 in 1871 and finishing in the league's top 10 in doubles and home runs. His average declined to .255 in 1872, but he led the league in triples and made the top 10 in extra-base hits. In the field he continued to excel, twice leading the league in putouts and double plays He finished second or third each year in range factor. On the negative side, he led the loop's first basemen in errors both years.

Unsigned in 1873, Gould caught on with Baltimore in 1874, but had a miserable year at the plate, hitting only .224. In 1873 or 1874 Gould married a young Ohio woman, Laura Netherly. The couple had five children. Twin girls, Laura and Laulie, were born in July 1874. Laura died in infancy. A son, Morton, was born in 1876; a daughter, Florence, in 1879; and another son, Charles, in 1886.

In 1875 Gould joined the New Haven Elm Citys as a player-manager for the club's only big league season. His first managerial experience was not a good one. New Haven folded in mid-season with a record of seven wins and 40 losses.

Despite the debacle in Connecticut, Gould was given another chance to manage. Cincinnati had joined the new National League in 1876, reclaimed the name Red Stockings, and hired its former home town hero Charlie Gould as its first National League manager. He had even less success in Cincinnati than he had in New Haven. The Red Stocking finished in last place with a record of nine wins and 56 losses. That was the end of Gould's managerial career. He played a few games in 1877, appearing in his final game on July 12 at the age of 29.

For the remainder of 1877 and the next two seasons, Gould remained with the Red Stockings, acting for a time as the team's assistant secretary, taking minutes at stockholders' meetings, and making travel arrangements. In 1879 he was a groundskeeper and equipment manager, purchasing brooms, buckets, and balls and seeing that the ball park was kept in shape.[7]

By 1880 Gould's employment by the Red Stockings had ended. Over the next several years he held various positions with the Cincinnati Police Department and the Sheriff's office. He later worked briefly in such jobs as streetcar conductor, insurance agent, clerk and storeroom manager for the Pullman Palace Car Company.[8]

In 1913 Gould left his hometown and went east to live with his son, Charles. He died at his son's home in Flushing, New York, on April 10, 1917, at the age of 69. Gould's body was brought back to Cincinnati and buried in the family plot in Spring Grove Cemetery. A tombstone was not placed on the grave until 1951, when Warren Giles, general manager of the Reds, had a monument erected to honor Gould as the Reds' first National League manager. Ironically, Gould was not a very good manager. He was a fair hitter and a superb fielder. He should be remembered as a baseball pioneer with the Red Stockings and as the first major leaguer born in the Queen City.

NOTES

1 Stephen D. Guschov, *The Red Stockings of Cincinnati: Baseball's First All-Professional Team.* (Jefferson, North Carolina: McFarland, 1998), 31.

2 *Ibid.*, 79.

3 *Ibid.*

4 *Ibid.*, 92-93.

5 George Bulkley, "The Day the Reds Lost," *The National Pastime*, 1983, 8.

6 Pete Palmer and Gary Gillette, *The Baseball Encyclopedia*. (New York: Barnes and Noble, 2004), 1363.

7 Kevin Grace, "'Bushel Basket' Charlie Gould of Red Stockings." *SABR Research Journal Archives.*

8 *Ibid.*

GEORGE W. HALL

BY MATT ALBERTSON

BASEBALL FANS GENERALLY REmember players who are involved in some of game's most famous events. The same can be assumed of players who are the first to accomplish a particular feat in the game. However, George Hall was both a central figure in one of major-league baseball's earliest scandals and the first major-league player to earn the title of "home run king," but is all but forgotten by the average baseball fan. Hall's career ended abruptly in 1877 and he essentially vanished from the modern historical record. He was one of the better hitters of the era. His batting skill, involvement in some of early baseball's famous events, and subsequent fall from grace make him one of the more colorful players in the 19th century.

George William Hall was born on March 29, 1849,[1] in Stepney, England, to George R. and Mary Hall; he was the third of five children. Hall's father, an engraver, emigrated from England to the United States around the time Mary birthed their fourth child, Edwin. Mary and her four children immigrated to the United States soon thereafter and arrived at New York on July 26, 1854.[2] George developed an affinity for baseball in his adolescent years in Brooklyn and proved to be an adequate fielder and skilled with the bat.[3]

Hall began his baseball career as an amateur and played for the Excelsior Juniors of Brooklyn in 1868 and as a first baseman for the Cambridge Stars (New York) in 1868 and 1869.[4] In 1870 he joined the Brooklyn Atlantics and was responsible for ending the most famous undefeated streak in professional sports history. On June 14, 1870, the Cincinnati Red Stockings brought their unblemished 57-0 record to the Capitoline Grounds in Brooklyn to face the Atlantics. Henry Chadwick's *Base-ball Manual* for 1871 estimated that nearly 10,000 people watched as the Atlantics and the Red Stockings played an intense match. Cincinnati led 3-0 after three innings, but the Atlantics rallied to score four runs in the following three innings. "The game now began to get quite exciting, and every movement of the players was watched with eagerness."[5] The teams traded the lead and were tied 5-5 after nine innings. Cincinnati refused to accept a tie-game outcome and sought to finish the match. In the 11th, the Atlantics tied the score again. Charles Ferguson was on second and George Zettlein at first. Hall batted next but what unfolded next is unclear.

Hall stepped up to the plate and hit Asa Brainard's pitch to George Wright, who tossed the ball to Charlie Sweasy. At this point, the reports begin to differ. Cincinnati newspapers agree that Sweasy muffed the ball and hurried a throw to catcher Doug Allison, who did not catch the ball. "Hall hit to Wright, who threw to Sweasy, who muffed and threw to Alison, who missed it, and Ferguson scored the winning run. [Long and tremendous cheering.]"[6] The *New York Tribune* simply states that "Hall closed the game in triumph for the Atlantics; his hit released Ferguson, who ran over the plate, winning the game by one run."[7] The *Brooklyn Daily Eagle* held that Hall got a hit. "Hall batted Zettlein out at second, and was nearly put out at second himself, but Sweasey dropped the ball passed in by George Wright, and Fergy got home, making the winning run."[8] Most newspapers held that Sweasy dropped the ball and threw the ball errantly to home plate, allowing Ferguson to score but it was Hall's action that initiated the play that ended Cincinnati's unbeaten streak. Chadwick's guide called the game "The Match of the Season of 1870."[9]

Despite the incredible victory, the Atlantics reorganized as an amateur club in 1871. Because of this, Hall decided to take his services elsewhere and found a home as a center fielder for the Washington Olympics of the newly christened National Association. Hall batted .294 in 1871 and continued to impress fans and players with his speed. In 1872 the Olympics reorganized as a co-op team and Hall again decided to move on, this time to Baltimore. He spent 1872 and 1873 as a member of the Baltimore Canaries (also known as the Lord Baltimores). Hall batted .340 in his two years with Baltimore and ranked third in the league in doubles and triples in 1872. Baltimore folded in 1874 despite strong second-place finishes in 1872 and 1873. The Panic of 1873 affected Baltimore's proprietors and the funds for the Canaries quickly vanished.[10] Financial uncertainty led Hall to leave Baltimore before the 1874 season and sign with the Boston Red Stockings for half of his 1873 salary.[11]

George Hall's experience highlights the volatility and financial unease of 19th century baseball clubs. Prior to the formation of the National League, clubs, and especially their players, were at the mercy of gate receipts in order to stay afloat. An ambitious schedule and the need to travel from city to city made it difficult to remain financially stable and profitable on a consistent basis. Thus, players like Hall found it difficult to make a living playing the game they loved. However, players made important—and at times detrimental—personal connections when they jumped from club to club. Hall is no exception, as he met a shady character named Bill Craver and was likely introduced to his future wife, Ida Layfield, a Maryland native, while a member of the Canaries.[12] George and Ida were married in 1876 while George played for the Athletics of Philadelphia.[13]

In 1874 Hall joined the best baseball club in the National Association, the Boston Red Stockings. The Red Stockings were crowned National Association champions in 1872 and 1873 and fielded a roster that included five future Hall of Famers— George Wright, Harry Wright, Jim O'Rourke, Deacon White, and Al Spalding. Although Hall's career hitting statistics suggest he was a slightly above-average player, his addition to the best professional squad in the National Association speaks volumes. Both Wright Brothers, Andy Leonard, and especially Cal McVey knew how dangerous Hall could be with the bat. Additionally, McVey was Hall's teammate in Baltimore in 1873, where the two batted .380 and .345 respectively. It's possible that Harry Wright signed Hall at McVey's urging. With Boston Hall split time in the outfield with the aging legend Harry Wright and others.

George Hall, 1874 (Spalding Collection)

Combined with his offensive skill, Hall's defensive prowess improved the Boston outfield. The *New York Clipper* commented, "Hall was the crack player south of Philadelphia at centre field."[14] Hall's versatile defensive talents blended nicely with the evolving understanding of outfield play. Prior to 1874, the right fielder was considered the weakest of the three, with the best outfielder playing in left field. By 1874 the *Clipper* opined that right field was the most active due to the lack of a shortstop on that side, but all outfield positions essentially required equal skill.[15] "As a general thing, however, the three positions required the same qualities, viz., long-distance throwing, sure catching, and good judgment in the guaging [sic] of balls."[16] Pitching improved in several ways so fewer balls were hit to the outfield. Thus, by 1874, outfielders were standing much closer to the infield than in the game's early days. Hall's speed helped him in this style of play because he could quickly track a ball down if one were hit well, deep into the outfield. His arm was likely good to above average because he played all outfield positions successfully.[17] Outfielders like Hall had to be incredibly athletic to succeed. "It will not do, therefore, to put any but the best men in those positions," the *Clipper* opined.[18]

The Red Stockings' first National Association game of 1874 was against the New York Mutuals on May 2. Hall's first professional contest played with Boston was a significant one as he replaced Harry Wright in the lineup, "filling (Wright's) position acceptably at centre-field."[19] He had one hit, scored a run, and made two putouts in center field. But Hall's season was mediocre– actually the worst of his professional career. This is possibly due to his limited playing time; Hall played in only 47 of the 71 scheduled league games. His role on the club was again as a rotating outfielder, splitting most of his time with Harry Wright. Hall batted .288 and had 64 hits, one home run, and 34 RBIs, all figures either career lows or close to them. Still, Hall played a role in one of baseball history's grandest tours: the 1874 World Base Ball Tour.

The *Clipper* called the tour "The Grand International Tour."[20] In the winter of 1873 Harry Wright proposed that the Red Stockings and Athletic of Philadelphia sail across the Atlantic in the summer of 1874 and expose Europeans to the American game. Hall returned to his country of birth on July 27, 1874, and played his first game on July 30 at the Liverpool Cricket Grounds in front of 500 onlookers. He scored two runs in the 14-11 loss to Athletic. On July 31 Hall hit one of Boston's five home runs as the Red Stockings beat the Athletic, 23-18. This trend continued for the entire tour as he proved to be an offensive force. He hit in every game but one and belted at least two home runs.[21] The *London Times* noted that Hall was a good fielder.[22] He established himself as one of the best players on the tour. The teams returned to America on September 9. The tour proved to be a financial failure; the English reacted indifferently to the American game. "Some American athletes are trying to introduce us to their game of base-ball, as if it were a novelty; whereas the fact is that it is an ancient English game, long ago discarded in favour of cricket," the *Times* lectured.[23] The Red Stockings completed their season on October 30 with a loss to Hartford. Boston finished 1874 atop the National Association standings with a 52-18-1 record.

Despite playing for a champion, Hall signed with the Athletic of Philadelphia for the 1875 season. The reasons are unknown but Philadelphia may have offered a higher salary to Hall, who hit extremely well against the Athletic in Europe. In his first season with Philadelphia, Hall hit .299, with 107 hits, 4 home runs, and 62 RBIs. His play was above average (2.3 WAR) but Philadelphia finished a distant third to Boston in the final standings. The Red Stockings were a major catalyst in the National Association's collapse in 1875—they were simply too good and attendance waned. Chicago businessman William Hulbert formed the National League officially in February 1876. He viewed the National Association as corrupt, mismanaged, and, worst of all, weak. Hall decided to stick with Philadelphia for 1876, a decision that set up his best season in professional baseball.

The National Association's best clubs from 1875 squared off against one another on April 22, 1876, in Philadelphia.[24] Hall had several clutch at-bats that kept Philadelphia in the game. Regardless, the Athletics dropped the opener to the Red Caps, 6-5. Once again Hall was at the center of baseball history as he played a crucial role in the National League's origin story. Although the game is now a famous first, Hall's play in a forgotten game later that season was arguably his best performance.

The Cincinnati Reds arrived in Philadelphia and began a three-game series against the Athletics on June 14. (The first game was scheduled for June 13 but was rained out.) Both teams were bad; the Athletic carried a 5-15 record into the set while the Reds sported a balmy 4-17 record; no wonder that "the attendance was small."[25] Despite their poor record, Philadelphia put on a powerful offensive display. "The extraordinary batting of the Athletics on this occasion has perhaps never been equaled, and certainly, has not been excelled. … Hall's wonderful batting was *the* feature. …"[26] During the game, Hall tallied five hits in six plate appearances, "once making a clean home-run by driving the ball over the right-field fence, and making, besides, three three-basers [triples]."[27] It is likely that his omitted fifth hit was a single because the *Clipper* noted all Athletics who registered extra-base hits that day. Thus, George Hall was probably a double away from being the first major-league player to hit for the cycle.[28] His home run—one of his league-leading five in 1876—was rare for two reasons: 1) He hit a home run in the fifth inning and 2) the ball bounded over the fence (a legal home run at the time). Such home runs were rare in the 19th century. That he hit a dead ball deep enough to bound over the fence in the middle of a game in which the Athletics notched 20 runs on 23 hits is even more impressive. The ball was surely a misshapen blob at that point. Three days later Hall hit two home runs off Amos Booth of the Reds, becoming the first player to hit more than one in a game.[29] The veteran had his best offensive season in 1876, batting .366 with 98 hits, 5 home runs, and 45 RBIs in 268 at-bats. His league-leading five home runs crowned him professional baseball's first "home run king."

Despite Hall's success, the 1876 Athletics were a bad team, mostly young and inexperienced.[30] Financial woes hit the club hard, and it failed to complete its scheduled final Western road trip, no-shows for series in Chicago and St. Louis. The club also owed every player between $200 and $500 in back pay. Rumors circulated in Philadelphia that a new club would be organized, using the players from 1876."[31] Hall told the team management that he would stay,[32] but, the Athletics were barred from the National League for the 1877 season, leaving him without a team.

Hall soon found a home along with former teammate Bill Craver on the Louisville Grays. The Grays were a formidable team with pitching ace Jim Devlin on the roster. While Chicago and Hartford failed to translate their 1876 success into the 1877 season, Louisville transformed itself from a mediocre team in 1876 to pennant contenders. On August 13 the Grays had a four-game lead over St. Louis with a 27-13 record. St. Louis offered Hall a contract for 1878. (He also expressed interest in joining the Cincinnati nine for 1878.) For whatever reason, he had no interest in signing again with Louisville, even though his salary was a healthy $2,800.[33] Hall was a major catalyst for Louisville's success in 1877, batting .323, but he was also a major factor in the club's downfall.

The Grays were leading the pennant race by 3½ games midway through August. Suddenly, with 20 games left in the season, Louisville began to drop games. Between August 17 and September 26, the Grays went 2-11-1 and ended the season on October 6 with a 35-25 record, good enough for second place, but a distant seven games behind. Hall led the team in hitting on August 17 but hit just .143 on the final road trip.[34] His performance and that of a few teammates increased suspicion that games were being fixed. John A. Haldeman, a baseball writer for the *Louisville Courier-Journal*, learned that four players, including Hall, had been persuaded by gamblers to throw games.[35] Furthermore, after the ill-fated Eastern road trip, Hall sported a new diamond pin and cluster diamond ring.[36]

Speculation about the purported Louisville scandal increased at season's end. Club owner Charles Chase interviewed Jim Devlin, who said he played loosely only during exhibition games. "Hall had seen Devlin enter Chase's office that morning and was now filled with anxiety that he had blown the whistle on him."[37] Hall offered to tell Chase about the scandal's mechanics if Chase "promised to let [him] down easy."[38] Eventually Hall admitted to fixing games. On October 26, at a meeting of the Grays' board of directors with the entire team to discuss the Grays' last 20 games, Hall maintained that he accepted payment only to throw non-League games.[39] Four days later, the directors expelled Hall and others from the Louisville club. Despite that, and the League rule barring players convicted of disreputable play from signing with other National League clubs, St. Louis signed both Devlin and Hall for the 1878 season.[40] On December 5 the National League Board unanimously banned Hall, Devlin, Bill Craver, and Albert Nichols from signing with any National League club until reinstated.[41]

The National League never reinstated Hall, and he eventually faded into obscurity. Rumors spread that he continued to play for nonleague teams, but no evidence of that has been founed. Hall moved back to Brooklyn with his wife, Ida, and took up steel engraving, his father's trade. The couple had six children. Ida died of acute nephritis in 1912 and was buried in Brooklyn's Evergreen Cemetery. In his later years, George either quit or retired from the engraving profession and became a clerk in a New York art museum. He died of heart trouble on June 11, 1923, and was buried next to his wife.

Hall was involved in some of professional baseball's earliest key moments and established himself as one of the era's better players. Baseball historian and statistician Bill James labeled him baseball's "Least Admirable Superstar" of the 1870s.[42] Hall's role in baseball's largest scandal of the 19th century continues to overshadow his skill as a player. He completed his career with a .322 batting average with 13 home runs, 252 RBIs, and 538 hits.

NOTES

1. Hall's birth date is disputed. Most sources claim March 29, 1849, as his date of birth while his death certificate states that it was June 22, 1849.

2. They immigrated to the United States aboard the *Sir Robert Peel*. Year: *1854*; Arrival: *New York, New York*; Microfilm Serial: *M237, 1820-1897*; Microfilm Roll: *Roll 143*; Line: *22*; List Number: *928*.

3. James D. Smith III, "George William Hall," from the archives of the National Baseball Hall of Fame and Museum.

4. Ibid.

5. Henry Chadwick, *Chadwick's Base Ball Manual*, baseballchronology.com/baseball/Books/Classic/Henry-Chadwicks-Baseball-Manual/Page-2.asp#70RedStockings1stLoss.

6. "Base-Ball: The Atlantics of Brooklyn Beat the Champions by a Score of 8 to 7 in a Game of 11 Innings, the Rest on Record," *Cincinnati Daily Enquirer*, June 15, 1870.

7. "Base-Ball: Atlantics vs. Red Stockings," *New York Tribune*, June 15, 1870.

8. "The Atlantics Triumphant," *Brooklyn Daily Eagle*, June 15, 1870.

9. *Chadwick's Base Ball Manual*.

10. Joe Tropea, "Your Baltimore Canaries: A Very Brief History of Baltimore's Second Professional Base Ball Team," Maryland Historical Society, April 3, 2013. mdhs.org/underbelly/2013/04/03/your-baltimore-canaries-a-very-brief-history-of-baltimores-second-professional-base-ball-team/.

11. George V. Tuohey, *A History of the Boston Base Ball Club* (Boston: M.F. Quinn & Company, 1897), 68; Baseball-reference.com cites, per Preston Orem, that Hall's salary was $1,000 with Baltimore in 1873 and $500 with Boston in 1874. If this is true, then the financial situation must have been truly perilous for Hall to accept half his salary with an employer 400 miles north of Baltimore.

12. Borough of Brooklyn, New York. Death Certificate number illegible (1912), Ida Aurelia Hall; Bureau of Vital Records, New York.

13. The 1900 US Census states that George and Ida were married for 24 years (1876). 1900 U.S. census, Kings County, New York, population schedule, New York City (page 16), dwelling 280, family 340, George W. and Ida A. Hall; digital image, Ancestry.com, Accessed September 25, 2015.

14. "Baseball: The Players of 1873. Outfielders," *New York Clipper*, March 28, 1874.

15. Ibid.

16. Ibid.

17. As an outfielder, Hall's career fielding percentage (.856) was slightly above the league average (.824). His Range Factor per 9 innings of 2.17 and Range Factor per Game of 2.19 were also above the league average (RF/9: 1.99, RF/G: 2.01). Per baseball-reference.com, baseball-reference.com/players/h/hallge01.shtml.

18. "Baseball: The Players of 1873. Outfielders."

19. "Boston vs. Mutual," *New York Clipper*, May 9, 1874.

20. "Baseball: The Grand International Tour," *New York Clipper*, March 7, 1874.

21. Box scores are available for only 9 of the 15 games played in Europe. Eric Miklich, "1874 World Base Ball Tour," 19cbaseball.com/tours-1874-world-base-ball-tour.html.

22. "Base Ball." *Times of London*, August 7, 1874.

23. GRANDMOTHER. "Base-Ball." *Times of London*, August 13, 1874.

24. On the first major-league game, see John Zinn, "April 22, 1876: A New Age Begins With Inaugural National League Game," in Bill Felber, ed., *Inventing Baseball: The 100 Greatest Games of the 19th Century* (Phoenix: Society for American Baseball Research, 2013), 97-99.

25. "Baseball: Athletic vs. Cincinnati," *New York Clipper*, June 24, 1876.

26. Ibid.

27. Ibid.

28. Not enough substantial evidence exists to credit Hall with hitting the first cycle in professional baseball. In addition to the *Clipper*'s account, the June 15, 1876, *Cincinnati Enquirer* states that Hall totaled 14 bases (four for a home run, nine for three triples, and one for a single). The *Times* of Philadelphia, June 15, 1876, credits Hall with a home run, two triples, a double, and a

single (totaling 13 bases). Major League Baseball Historian John Thorn agrees with the information provided in both the *Clipper* and *Enquirer*. The accepted first cycle in the major leagues was completed by Curry Foley in 1882.

29 David Vincent, *Home Run: The Definitive History of Baseball's Ultimate Weapon* (Dulles, Virginia: Potomac Books, 2007), 6.

30 William A. Cook, *The Louisville Grays Scandal of 1877: The Taint of Gambling at the Dawn of the National League* (Jefferson, North Carolina: McFarland & Company, Inc., 2005), 78.

31 Ibid.

32 Cook, 84.

33 Cook, 124.

34 Cook, 130.

35 Ibid.

36 Cook, 137.

37 Cook, 139.

38 Ibid.

39 Cook, 139-141. George Hall's testimony: "About three or four weeks after Al Nichols joined the Louisville Club, he made me a proposition to assist in throwing League games, and I said to him: 'I'll have nothing to do with any League games.' This proposition was made before the club went on its last Eastern trip. He made the proposition to throw the Allegheny [Pittsburgh] game, and I agreed to it. He promised to divide with me what he received from his friend in New York, who was betting on the games. Nichols and I were to throw the game by playing poorly. While in Chicago, on the club's last Western trip, I received a telegram from Nichols, stating that he was $80 in the hole, and asking how he could get out. I told Chapman that this dispatch was from my brother-in-law, who lived in Baltimore. I did not reply to the dispatch. Devlin first made me a proposition in Columbus, O., to throw the game in Cincinnati. He made the proposition either in the hotel or upon the street. We went to the telegraph office in Columbus, and sent a dispatch to a man in New York by the name of McCloud, saying that we would lose the Cincinnati game. McCloud is a pool-seller. The telegram was signed 'D & H.' We received no answer to this telegram. I did not know McCloud. Devlin knew him. McCloud sent Devlin $50 in a letter, and Devlin gave me $25. One of us sent a dispatch to McCloud from Louisville saying, 'We have not heard from you.' He sent then sent the $50 to Devlin; this was the 1-0 Cincinnati game. We telegraphed to McCloud from Louisville that the club would lose the Indianapolis game. I never received any money for assisting in throwing this game. I think it was the 7 to 3 game. Devlin said that he did not want to sign the order to have his telegrams inspected; said it would ruin him. There was another game Nichols and I threw. It was the Lowell Club of Lowell, Mass. He and I agreed to throw it. He did all the telegraphing. Never got a cent from Nichols for the games he and I threw. My brother-in-law has often said I was a fool for not making money. He has said this for several years past. His talking this way caused a coldness between us. When I was in Brooklyn the last time he asked me if we could not make some money on the games, and I told him I would let him know when we could. He bet on the Allegheny game and lost. Telegraphed him from here about the Indianapolis game. Had a talk with him in June, I think in Brooklyn, about selling games. Have sent two or three telegrams to him—not over three. His name is (Frank) Powell, and he lives (at 865 Fulton Street) in Brooklyn. Nichols first approached me about throwing games. Nichols asked me, on the last trip, if I could get somebody to work Brooklyn for me. I can't tell you where it was that Nichols first approached me about throwing league games. When I told him that I would have nothing to do with League games, I meant that I would go in with him on outside games. I made the proposition about the Cincinnati game to Devlin. Last night I said he made it to me. I made the proposition in Columbus. Nichols spoke to me in Cincinnati about selling the Cincinnati game, and I said I would see about it. Nichols said: 'George, try and get Jim in.' He suggested that I should write a letter to Devlin. Devlin was not in the room when I wrote it. In the note to Devlin I think I said: 'Jim how can we make a stake?' I left the note on the marble-top table in our room at the Burnett House, Cincinnati. When I next saw Devlin he was in the room putting on his ball-clothes, and it was there that he said: 'George, do you mean it?' And I said: 'Yes, Jim.' After Devlin accepted the proposition I told Nichols that Jim was in it. Nichols was not in with us on the Cincinnati game. Think I wrote the letter to Devlin in Columbus, but won't be certain. Think I destroyed the note at that time. Did not take it out of his pocket two or three days afterwards and destroy it. Am certain of this. Never got a cent for the Indianapolis game. Devlin said that he had never heard from McCloud about the money for it. Received but $25 from Devlin."

40 "Baseball: The League and Its Work," *New York Clipper*, January 20, 1877.

41 "Baseball: League Association Convention," *New York Clipper*, December 15, 1877.

42 Bill James, *The New Bill James Historical Baseball Abstract* (New York: Free Press, 2001), 15.

FRANKLIN "HECK" HEIFER

BY BRIAN C. ENGELHARDT

THE BRIEF MAJOR-LEAGUE career of Reading, Pennsylvania, native Franklin "Heck" Heifer consisted of 17 appearances (15 as a position player and 2 as a pitcher) with the 1875 Boston Red Stockings of the National Association of Professional Base Ball Players. After his time with Boston, Heifer's professional career consisted of playing for a number of minor-league teams over the course of the next 12 years, several of which were in Reading. During that time he was among the prominent figures on the Reading baseball scene, not only because of his skill on the field but also because he was the second native of Reading to play in the major leagues.

Described as being "very fond of athletic sports and particularly baseball"[1] during his childhood, Heifer was born in Reading on January 18, 1854, and was the only boy of the four children of Daniel and Elizabeth Heifer.[2] By the time he was 20, Heifer had developed his talents on the diamond to the extent that during the 1874 season he was a member of the starting lineup of the Active Baseball Club of Reading, the top team in the area, which played as the Actives. Significantly, in that season the Actives changed their schedule from competing against only Reading area teams to playing teams from outside the area as well. With the expanded range of opponents, the team achieved a great degree of success[3] against such Pennsylvania opponents as the Centennials of Lebanon, the Modoc and Alpha clubs of Philadelphia, the Resolute club of Renovo, the Morgan club of Lancaster, the Expert club of Harrisburg, the Antelopes of Allentown, and the Lewisburg club.

Playing primarily in the outfield, but also occasionally filling in at shortstop and pitcher, Heifer established himself as the most talented member of the Actives, and was said to have the attitude of a player who "always played to win."[4] Exact statistics as to the Actives' record in 1874 are not available, but their success is evident from their having begun their season with a June 6 game against Lebanon and, while playing a few games a week, not suffering their first defeat until nearly two months later, on August 3, an 11-6 loss on to the Easton Baseball Club before a crowd of about 4,000, the largest crowd ever to witness a baseball game in Reading up to then.[5]

According to the *Reading Eagle*, the Easton Club was "regarded by knowing professional players to be the very best club in the country not on the professional lists." Coincidentally, a major factor in the success of the Easton team was its pitcher, Reading native George Washington Bradley, who was a year away from starring for the St. Louis Brown Stockings of the National Association.[6]

The *Eagle* described Easton's victory as "one of the most closely contested (games) that either club has ever played," with Bradley's pitches, coming in "very swiftly and during the first part of the game … not hit."[7] However, with the score tied at 4-4, Easton broke the game open with five runs in the eighth inning. (The game account in the *Reading Times* attributed the rally to Easton's "doing some heavy batting," while the *Eagle* blamed Easton's runs to be the product of "bad luck, overthrows and a general demoralization" on the part of the home team.)[8] Playing in the outfield that day for the Actives, Heifer scored a run but was otherwise not mentioned in the game accounts in either the *Times* or the *Eagle*—probably a good thing, since those accounts focused for the most part on various errors by the Actives.

Heifer's two hits and "several admirable catches"[9] in the outfield were among the few bright spots for the Actives in a 31-12 loss to Easton a week and a half later that was described by the *Eagle* as "the worst game of base ball ever played."[10] While the Actives' bats were for the most part again held in check by Bradley (eight of their runs were scored in the ninth inning when the team was already down by 19 runs), their play in the field was characterized as being full of "inglorious muffs and wild overthrows … (making it) startling the score against them was not nearer one hundred."[11]

On September 26, 1874, the Actives invited the Philadelphia Whites (Pearls) of the National Association of Professional Base Ball Players to play an exhibition game and help the Actives dedicate their new "ball grounds" at 19th and Perkiomen Avenues in Reading. In the first game played in Reading by a major-league team (the National Association being the major league at that time), the Actives lost, 15-0. Managed by Bill Crane (three years before his banishment from baseball for throwing games), the Whites rode the pitching of future Hall of Famer Candy Cummings, who "delivered a … curve ball which is very deceptive."[12] The Whites were declared to have "Chicagoed" the Actives—the slang term at that time for a shutout.[13] Heifer provided the offensive highlights for the home team, being the sole Active to get as far as third base.[14]

A week later, on October 1, the Actives hosted another National Association team, the Chicago White Stockings (referred to by both the *Eagle* and the *Times* as the "Giants"). With White Stockings pitcher George "Charmer" Zettlein holding the Actives' bats in check, the White Stockings won, 13-5.[15] Notably, this time the Actives avoided being Chicagoed by a major-league team, as Heifer led their offensive attack with two hits and two runs batted in.

The next time a National Association team played an exhibition in Reading was the afternoon of May 21, 1875, when the Boston Red Stockings played the Actives, who by that time were captained by Heifer. Whatever drama Heifer experienced over the course of his brief major-league career later that season, it was less than the drama surrounding the events that led to his signing by the Red Stockings that day.

Noting that the Red Stockings "had not lost a game to any of their professional brethren this season," (their league record at that point was 19-0), the *Reading Eagle* contrasted the Actives and the Red Stockings "as being like a cooking stove compared with an iron furnace."[16] Reporting on the arrival of the Red Stockings in Reading for the game, the *Eagle* mentioned that the Red Stockings had "vanquished the Philadelphia (Whites)" the day before in a league game by an 8-6 score[17] and predicted that the Boston team would "walk away with everything during 1875."[18] (The *Eagle's* prediction proved correct, as the Red Stockings went on to win the Association championship with a sterling 71-8 record in what would be the league's last season.)

The Red Stockings' manager, future Hall of Famer Harry Wright, watched the Actives go through their pregame warmups, focusing his attention on Heifer. Wright's scouting of Heifer was rewarded; Heifer made "some wonderful catches in left field."[19] Wright continued to focus on Heifer during the game, noting his "nerve, coolness, and steady play."[20]

As for the game itself, in front of a crowd of 1,000 the Red Stockings won, 27-11. It was only the Actives' second game of the season, and they demonstrated some rust as they made an unspecified number of errors in the first two innings and spotted the visitors to a 13-0 lead.

Whatever drama existed in the events of Heifer's brief career with the Red Stockings, it did not match the drama in the circumstances that led to his signing. Heifer's play throughout the game involved anything but rust as he "batted the Boston pitchers with great ease," getting four hits including a double, driving in two runs and scoring two. He also pitched part of the game, then moved to the outfield, where he made a "thrilling one handed catch that startled (Wright)."[21]

Aside from what Heifer had shown in the game of his power, fielding, speed, and great arm, what no doubt excited Wright even further was that at 5-feet-10 and 175 pounds, Heifer was a big man for the times. All of these factors led Wright to sign Heifer to a contract immediately after the game as a means of strengthening the Red Stockings' bench in preparation for a trip to St. Louis.

During his first few weeks with the Red Stockings, Heifer's activities were limited to practices and pregame drills on the road trip to St. Louis. Heifer some years later said that "those Boston men fired balls (at me) as a caution" as "they were testing (my) ability as a (first) baseman."[22] This process in the days before fielder's

Frank Heifer (Reading Area Fire-Fighters Museum)

gloves left Heifer with a pair of sore hands, but his performance in the drills evidently satisfied Harry Wright, and on June 3 in the sixth inning of Boston's 10-5 victory over the host St. Louis Red Stockings, Heifer, who had started the game in right field, was moved to first base when catcher Deacon White injured his thumb. White moved to right field and first baseman Cal McVey replaced him behind the plate. In its account of the game, the *Boston Globe* said that Heifer "played very acceptably," although the paper referred to him throughout as "Franklin."[23]

Two days later, in a June 5 game against the other St. Louis team, the Brown Stockings, Heifer was again in the starting lineup, playing first base and facing fellow Reading native George Washington Bradley, who had made his debut with the Brown Stockings on May 4. Earlier that week, Boston had handed Bradley his first loss of the season, 10-3. On June 5, Bradley avenged his first loss by pitching the Brown Stockings to a narrow 5-4 victory, the Boston team's first loss of the season. The *Boston Globe* wrote that Bradley and "the 'Brown Sox' were carried off the field on the shoulders of their friends." Playing first base, Heifer was credited with seven putouts but got no hits and wasn't mentioned by the *Globe*. (Two days later, with Heifer not in the lineup and with St. Louis fans alive with Brown Stocking fever, a crowd described by the *Globe* as "the largest ever seen on a ball field in this city, about 8,000" saw the Red Stockings pound Bradley for 24 base hits on the way to a 15-2 victory. Bradley was said to be suffering from an attack of vertigo that day.)

Heifer played in 15 more games for the Red Stockings that season, until he was released in mid-September. He played nine games at first base and six in the outfield, and pitched in two games. In 50 at-bats he had 14 hits for a .280 batting average of .280 with three triples and five RBIs. In Heifer's final game with Boston, a 10-4 Red Stockings victory over the Brooklyn Atlantics on September 9, he hit a single scored twice and was credited with 14 putouts at first base.[24] Despite his solid batting statistics, Heifer's release was attributed to a decision by Red Stockings directors to cut payroll, "with Heifer being dropped because the other but inferior players had more local influence with directors."[25]

Heifer had earned Wright's respect as a player; the manager called him "a ballplayer that could be depended upon every time."[26] The respect grew into a friendship between the two; indeed, at any game where Wright was managing and knew Heifer was in attendance, he would invite Heifer to sit with him on the bench with the players.[27]

Back in town "for a visit" (according to the *Eagle*'s game account), Heifer was inserted back in the Actives lineup for an October 8 game in Reading against the Burlington Club of New Jersey. The Actives won, 15-3. According to the game account, Heifer, who was in town "for a visit," played second base for "his old and first love club ... and filled that position very creditably."[28] "(H)e has improved wonderfully in appearance, and his style of play has greatly changed for the better," the *Reading Eagle* gushed.[29]

With the Actives for the entire 1876 season, Heifer was playing a prominent role in a highly successful campaign during which the team barnstormed on a Western trip, playing semipro or professional teams in Harrisburg, Altoona, Hollidaysburg, Johnstown, Pittsburgh, and New Castle, Pennsylvania; Mansfield, Columbus, and Cincinnati, Ohio; Wheeling, West Virginia; and Covington and Louisville, Kentucky.[30] Named captain of the Actives early in May before the team embarked on the trip, Heifer played shortstop for most of the games, filled in from time to time in the outfield, and pitched on occasion. Several game accounts in the *Eagle* over the course of the Western tour singled him out as a leader of the club, usually writing something like "Heifer played a good game," with little elaboration. (Individual Actives statistics do not appear to ever have been published.)

That season the Actives also played two exhibition games in Reading against teams in the newly formed National League. Heifer played in both. The first was a 9-2 loss to the Chicago White Stockings on June 9. The White Stockings arrived in Reading with a league record of 17-3, and went on to win the first National League pennant with a record of 52-14. Heifer was familiar with a number of the White Stockings, who were his former teammates on the Red Stockings, most notably manager-pitcher Al Spalding, who held the Actives to six hits. In its headline the *Reading Times* termed the game an "Honorable Defeat."[31] The Actives stayed close until Chicago scored five runs in the ninth. The *Eagle* described Heifer as having "showed himself to good advantage" playing second base, where he was involved in turning a double play.

The other National League team the Actives faced in 1876 was the Cincinnati Reds, and in this game, played on September 1, the Actives won, 8-4. A notable contrast to the White Stockings, the Reds arrived in Reading with a league record of 7-45, on their way to a 9-56 final record (proof that teams didn't have to be good to barnstorm).[32] Although Heifer made an error in the course of the victory, his "fine playing in the entire game made up for (his) few slip ups."[33] The visitors were said to have commented that "they had never met a finer amateur club of ball players."[34]

On July 3 the Actives played the St. Louis Red Stockings, an independent team comprised mostly of former St. Louis Browns who did not sign with any National League team, the most notable being 19-year-old future Hall of Famer James "Pud" Galvin, the team's primary pitcher. Galvin, who eventually won 365 major-league games, was not at his best against the Actives, giving up nine hits in a 5-0 loss. Heifer led the Actives' attack with three hits. The *Eagle* said, "The visitors seemed astounded at the terrific batting and the sharp fielding of the home champions," adding, "The home team has not played a better game this season and the fielding of … Heifer … (and several other Actives) was the most brilliant ever to be seen" at the Actives' field.[35] The Actives' Len Lovett allowed only five hits to the visitors. (Presumably smarting from the beating by the Actives, Galvin took the mound again the next day and threw a no hitter against the Philadelphia Athletics.)[36]

Heifer began the 1877 season with the Actives until economic hard times forced the team to disband in July. After this, he began a baseball odyssey in which he played for 10 teams over 11 seasons, with his first stop being with Erie of the League Alliance. In August, Erie disbanded, and Heifer signed with another League Alliance team, Buffalo. It is likely that one of Heifer's Buffalo teammates was 17-year-old infielder John Montgomery Ward, who was at the beginning of a Hall of Fame career.

With no team in Reading, Heifer began the 1878 season with the Binghamton Crickets of the International Association, but the team disbanded on July 19 after playing 12 games. Heifer moved to the Syracuse Stars in the same league, the league's eventual second-place finisher with a record of 26-10.

After beginning the 1879 season with Worcester Grays of the National Association, Heifer retired because of issues with rheumatism after playing in only 11 games. In 1884 he returned to the game to manage the Actives, now playing in the Eastern League, but the team disbanded on August 4 after going 28-27. Heifer played in 23 games, batting .307 and playing several positons.

In 1886 and 1887, Heifer played for three teams that didn't finish their seasons. He began the 1886 season with the Providence Grays of the Eastern league, appearing in eight games, until the Grays disbanded on June 2 after compiling a 7-14 record. At the outset of the 1887 season he played for the Oswego Starch Boxes of the International Association, but the team disbanded on May 31 after compiling a 3-23 record. Heifer then joined the rejuvenated Reading Actives in the Pennsylvania State Association, but the Actives were not rejuvenated for very long; the entire league disbanded on July 20, with the Actives having a final record of 20-23.

That 1887 season was Heifer's last year playing or managing baseball. He entered the contracting business, performing excavation as well as hauling of heavy materials for the Reading Traction Company. His business was an apparent success; according to the *Eagle*, it involved "many wagons, carts and horses."[37] His success was relatively short-lived. On August 28, 1893, Heifer died of typhoid fever contracted after he had been suffering from malaria.

After his death an unnamed former teammate told the *Reading Eagle*, "Of all the old Active club players no one on the nine ever inspire more confidence than did 'Heck' Heifer. He had an encouraging smile and words of advice for all, (with) a great deal of the teamwork of the Active club (being) due to his points and suggestions."[38] The teammate recalled Heifer as having a "good keen eye. With bat well raised in motion he waited for a high ball over the plate, and the ball generally went safe into the field." He described Heifer as hitting generally to straightaway center field, but "then again he excelled in right-field hitting."[39]

The teammate most fondly remembered Heifer for the intangibles he brought to his teams, describing him as a "great leader" and "a man of few words while on the ball ground … never known to question (the) umpire's decision. … He would simply say 'that settles it' and there was no more said."[40] The former teammate concluded, "It would be well for the younger generation of ball players to take a pattern of this modest excellent young man and follow in his footsteps. He was kind, modest, quiet, quick to hear and slow to speak; never used profane language; never (indulged) in coarse talk; never insulted anyone, but was a gentleman at all times and under all circumstances and a novel man in every respect."[41]

Heifer was survived by his wife, Esther, and a son, Frank. Heifer's great-grandson Frank Heifer, until his retirement in 2000, was superintendent of the Pottstown, Pennsylvania, School District. A picture of Heifer, a former volunteer fireman, hangs in the Reading Area Fire-Fighters Museum.

Acknowledgments

The author would like to thank Frank Heifer, Heifer's great-grandson, and Andrew Heifer, Heifer's great-great-grandson, for taking part in interviews that assisted in the preparation of this article.

Also thanks to the Reading Area Fire-Fighters Museum for allowing the use of Heifer's picture.

SOURCES

In addition to the sources noted in this biography, the author also accessed Heifer's player file from the National Baseball Hall of Fame, and the following sites:

baseball-reference.com.

retrosheet.org.

news.google.com/newspapers.

SABR Bioproject: sabr.org/bioproj/.

Much of the material in this article, as well as the sources, were also used were used in "Days of Grin and Heck: Berks County's First Two Major Leaguers," which appeared in *The Historical Review of Berks County*, Summer 2014, Volume 79, Number 5.

NOTES

1 *Reading Eagle*, "Obituary," August 29, 1893: 1.

2 Ibid.

3 Bruce K. Gehret, "Early Baseball in Reading," *Historical Review of Berks County*, July 1943, 105.

4 *Reading Eagle*, "The Actives at Easton Yesterday," August 14, 1874: 1.

5 Ibid.

6 Bradley debuted with the Browns on May 4, 1875, less than a month before Heifer's debut, making Heifer the second native of Reading to play in the major leagues.

7 *Reading Eagle*, "The Actives First Defeat."

8. Ibid.; "Baseball: An Exciting Game Yesterday," *Reading Times*, August 4, 1974: 2. No statistics were provided, nor have any been found as to the Actives' record that season or at that point in the season.

9. *Reading Eagle*, "The Actives at Easton Yesterday."

10. Ibid.

11. Ibid.

12. *Reading Eagle*, "The Visit of the Philadelphia Club," September 28, 1874: 1.

13. *Reading Times*, "Baseball: Philadelphia vs. Actives." September 28, 1874: 11.

14. Ibid.

15. *Reading Eagle*, "A Brilliant Game of Baseball Yesterday," October 1, 1874: 1.

16. *Reading Eagle*, "The Champion Ball Team in Reading," May 21, 1875: 1.

17. Ibid.

18. Ibid.

19. *Reading Eagle*, "Heifer as a Ball Player," September 10, 1893: 1.

20. Ibid.

21. Ibid.

22. Ibid.

23. *Boston Globe*, "The Bostons Again Victorious in the West," June 4, 1875.

24. *Boston Globe*, "The Bostons Defeat the Atlantics," September 10, 1875.

25. *Reading Eagle*, "Heifer as a Ball Player."

26. Ibid.

27. Ibid.

28. *Reading Eagle*, "Actives Defeat the New Jersey Champions," October 9, 1875: 1.

29. Ibid.

30. Charles J. Adams III, "The 1876 Reading Actives Kicked Off the Great American Pastime in Berks," *Historical Review of Berks County*, Summer 2012, Vol. 77, No. 3, 39.

31. Reading Times, "Actives Sustain Honorable Defeat," June 10, 1876: 1.

32. The game account did not include a box score, nor even any of the names of those who played for the visiting Reds, who were managed by Charles Gould. It is likely that Dory Dean pitched for the Reds, who would finish the season with a 4-26 record and a .133 winning percentage, which, according to David Nemec's *The Great Encyclopedia of 19th Century Major League Baseball*, is the worst winning percentage of any pitcher with at least 20 decisions. (Joe Harris of the Boston Americans claimed the distinction, come the twentieth century.) Dean took over as the team's primary pitcher when Cherokee Fischer, who held that role at the beginning of the season, was released in July due to repeated incidents involving drunkenness.

33. *Reading Eagle*, "The Boys Stock Up Again," September 2, 1876: 1.

34. Ibid.

35. *Reading Eagle*, "Actives Very Best Game," July 4, 1876: 1.

36. Charles Hausberg, *Pud Galvin*, SABR Bioproject, sabr.org/bioproj/person/38c553ff.

37. *Reading Eagle*, "Obituary."

38. *Reading Eagle*, "Heifer as a Ball Player."

39. Ibid.

40. Ibid.

41. Ibid.

SAMUEL JACKSON

BY BILL NOWLIN

OF THE 22 MEN WHO PLAYED FOR the Boston Red Stockings over the five years from 1871 through 1875, 17 were American-born and the other five were born in other countries. There was one Canadian, one Irishman, and three from England. George Hall (Stepney) and Harry Wright (Sheffield) were both English natives. So was Samuel Jackson.

Jackson was born on March 24, 1849, in Ripon, Harrogate Borough, North Yorkshire West Riding, England. The actual birth register confirms that he had no middle name. His parents were John Jackson, who milled corn for a living, and Jane Jackson. At the time of the census of England in 1851, they had four children, all boys, of whom Samuel was the youngest. They lived with John's widowed mother, Mary, and had a 19-year-old servant from Leeds, Harriet Place.

In 1853 the family immigrated to the United States, but seemed to live near the border with Canada. Their fifth child, Mary, was born in 1855, in Canada.

Rochester, New York, baseball historian Priscilla Astifan reports, "Sam Jackson first appears in the baseball accounts in 1865, at the apparent age of 15, playing with the Pacifics. He continued to play with them in 1866 and then played with the Alerts, a significant junior team, in 1867 through 1869. Jackson helped his teammates achieve one of the best scores against the 1869 Cincinnati Red Stockings on their historic tour which included a stop in Rochester on June 4. Sam's brother William played right field on the same Alerts team, while Sam played first base. The Alerts, including Jackson, played against the Cincinnati Red Stockings another time that year when they made a western tour which included Cincinnati. In 1870 Jackson again played here with the Flower City, a consolidation team."[1]

Sam Jackson was 22 when he first played for the Boston Red Stockings. When Boston "finally determined to secure a base ball club second to none in the country… Mr. Adams, the proprietor of a hotel in that city," approached George Wright in 1870. Wright, unable to come to terms with the Cincinnati Red Stockings, responded to Adams's interest, signed on, and began to recruit players. George and Harry Wright, Charlie Gould, and Cal McVey were said to be "the nucleus of the Boston nine," with Ross Barnes, Al Spalding, and Fred Cone—all from the Rockford, Illinois, Forest City club—"three of the best players in the Western country." The seven were supplemented by Harry Schafer and Samuel Jackson, described by the *Cincinnati Daily Gazette* as "a No. 1 player in all respects."[2]

Red Stockings president Ivers W. Adams had described Jackson to fellow stockholders in the Boston Base-Ball Association as "a young and comparatively unknown player, but one whose record as an amateur has been a good one both as a player and a gentleman, and gives promise of proficiency second to none, Samuel Jackson, from the Flower City club, of Rochester, New York."[3] The *New York Tribune* dubbed Jackson "a promising amateur of the Flour*(sic)* City Club of Rochester."[4]

Manager Harry Wright wrote to Jackson, in Rochester, on January 9 urging him to report to Boston during the first week of March. "As your terms are satisfactory, you may consider yourself engaged," he wrote, adding that his contract would be ready for him when he arrived in Boston but that in the meantime he was sending a few lines to Jackson that he wanted Jackson to countersign before announcing that he had been hired.[5]

Jackson's first game in Boston was on Fast Day, April 6, 1871. He played right field and batted eighth against a picked nine in front of 5,000 spectators at the team's home field, the Union Grounds. The Red Stockings won, 41-10. Jackson scored seven runs, the most on the team. Some other games were played in Cambridge, and against the Harvard club at the

Union Grounds, in April. Jackson tripled in the first inning in the April 26 game, and doubled in the fifth.

He made his regular-season debut on May 9, at Troy against the Troy Haymakers. He had himself quite a day, taking over for George Wright at shortstop after both Wright and Fred Cone collided going after a fly ball to left. Wright's leg was injured so badly he had to leave, transported by carriage to the hotel. Both Wright and Jackson had three at-bats, and each was 2-for-3. Both of Jackson's hits were for extra bases, a double and a triple, and he drove in two runs as Boston beat Troy, 9-5. The *Boston Journal* said that Jackson "did the best batting of the game."[6]

When the Red Stockings arrived back from Troy on May 10, a crowd of some 300 met them at the Boston and Albany railroad train depot in Boston. The whole team went on to the club's headquarters at 18 Boylston Street, save for the Wrights. George's leg could not bear weight, so Charlie Gould and Fred Cone carried him to another carriage which transported him to brother Harry's home. The rest of the team enjoyed a dinner at the Parker House.[7]

Wright didn't come back until June 17, and just for that one game. Ross Barnes took over most of the work at shortstop.

Jackson's next game was a full week later, against Troy in Boston. He batted ninth, played center field, and was 1-for-4 with a first-inning RBI. On May 24 the Olympics of Washington came to Boston. This time Jackson led off, playing second base. He was 0-for-5 and committed his second error of the season. The game ended in a 4-4 tie.

Asa Brainard may have had his number; Jackson was 0-for-4 in a rematch with Brainard and the Olympics on May 27.

The Rockford Forest Citys came to Boston on May 29 and got hammered, 25-11. Jackson was again playing second base and leading off. He was 4-for-7, with a double and a triple, an RBI, and three runs scored. Three days later the two teams played again on Decoration Day; though Jackson was 0-for-5, he got on base and scored three times in Boston's 11-10 win. Rockford committed eight errors.

In the June 2 game Jackson batted ninth. He was 2-for-4 with a double and an RBI in the second inning, but the Chicago White Stockings beat Boston, 16-14. He was 0-for-5 against Cleveland on June 14 and 0-for-4 against the Mutuals of New York on June 17, batting third. That said, Jackson was considered to be a threat. Describing the June 14 game, the *New York Clipper* correspondent wrote that Jackson had come to bat in the ninth inning, down by two runs: "Jackson to the bat amid much excitement, as he had not yet made a first base hit and as he has a peculiar faculty for saving games the crowd looked for something from him in that line."[8]

Four days later, the Fort Wayne Kekiongas came to Boston. This time, Jackson was again in the middle of the order, batting fourth. He was 1-for-6 in the game, with another run batted in.

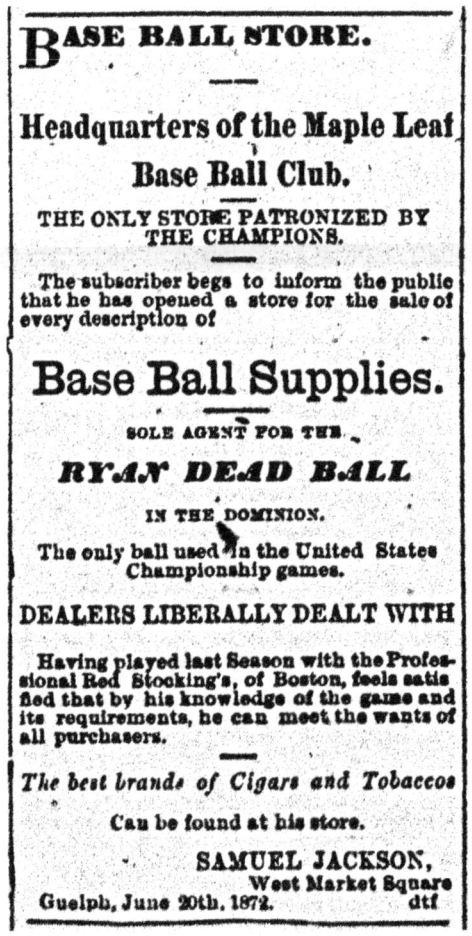

June 1872 advertisement in the Guelph Mercury *for Samuel Jackson's Base Ball Store.*

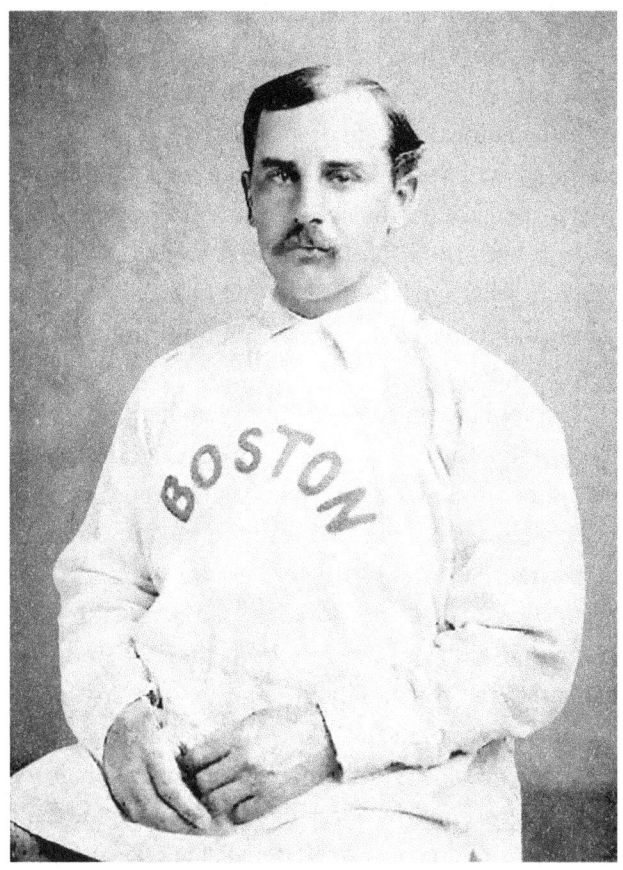
Sam Jackson (Ars Longa Cards)

There was a nonchampionship game against Brown University on June 23, which the Red Stockings won, 24-3. Jackson scored three runs. (The two teams played again on June 30.) On the 26th Boston played Philadelphia at the Jefferson Street Grounds. Jackson was 1-for-5 with an RBI; the Athletics won, 20-8.

The team traveled north of the border for a nonscheduled game against the Resolutes of Hamilton, Ontario, on June 30. They won, 27-0.

On the Fourth of July in Washington, Boston beat the Olympics, 7-3. Jackson was 0-for-4 with two errors, and was also caught off base in the first inning—not for the first time in 1871. He was also 0-for-4 with another error, his 17th of the season, at Lake Park in Chicago on July 7. His average had dipped to .188.

He had a better day on July 10 in Rockford: 2-for-5 with an RBI.

The best day of Jackson's career was his 4-for-7 game at Fort Wayne on July 12. He scored five times and drove in three; Boston won, 30-9.

The very next day, in Cleveland on July 13, he played his last championship game for the Red Stockings in 1871. He was 0-for-4 with an error.

After July 13, the team didn't play another championship game until August 3. That's the very day George Wright came back; Ross Barnes shifted over to second base.

Jackson, however, played at least one other game for the Red Stockings, working second base (with Barnes at short) on July 14 in Troy.

He had played in 16 games, batting .224, with 11 RBIs and 17 runs scored. He'd walked once and struck out four times (tied with Dave Birdsall for the most on the club), and had been caught stealing the one time he tried. He had five doubles and three triples. Jackson committed 18 errors in all, in the 14 games he played second base, and committed one at shortstop the one game he played there. The game he played in center field, he was error-free.

Though he was not in any more championship games in 1871, he hadn't entirely left the club. He's seen in an intramural match, playing second base for Harry Wright's nine against Spalding's nine, on August 1 at the Boston grounds. With only 11 players on the Red Stockings roster all season long, the teams were both supplemented by players from local amateur clubs. And on September 12, he played left field in a "practice game" in Boston against the Unas.[9]

The *Chicago Inter Ocean* acknowledged Jackson late in September, noting that Ross Barnes had taken over at second base and "Jackson has dropped out altogether."[10] The circumstances of his departure are unknown. It probably wasn't due to his card-playing, but there's a story he told a Buffalo newspaper. Harry Wright apparently "insisted that the players go to sleep at 10 P.M. One night, four of them were playing cards around midnight. When he called to them, the players, with their doors locked, did not respond. The next day they could tell from Wright's looks that he knew they had been awake."[11] Jackson told the *Buffalo Express*, "After that, we utilized a light-proof curtain when we remained up after hours."[12]

The *Chicago Tribune* foresaw Jackson working in 1872 as a reserve for the Brooklyn Atlantics.[13] He was the left fielder for Brooklyn at the start of the season, playing in the inaugural contest against the Middletown (Connecticut) Mansfields on May 2. He went without a base hit in four at-bats, but was 2-for-4 the following day in Troy. On May 6 the Troy team paid a visit to Brooklyn's Capitoline Grounds; Jackson played left field and swapped positions with John Kenney, taking over second base while Kenney went to left field. He was 0-for-3 and committed two errors on top of one he'd made on May 3.

Then the Boston Red Stockings came to town and beat Brooklyn 23-3. The Atlantics committed an astonishing 23 errors. Three of them were Jackson's, and he'd only come in midway through the game to take over for Bob Ferguson at third base. He'd now made six errors in four games. That said, teammates Barlow, Burdock, Ferguson, and Remsen had all committed seven on more, and (despite neither team committing a recorded error in Brooklyn's first game) the Atlantics had committed 52 errors in the succeeding three games. The *Boston Journal* succinctly observed, "The defeated Nine played very poorly throughout the game."[14]

Jackson was hitless in his two at-bats on May 7; he was batting .167. He'd neither scored nor driven in a run, nor drawn a base on balls.

Less than a full calendar year after he'd begun playing, Jackson's career came to an end. He appeared in only those first four games for Brooklyn. There was no reported injury. It may simply be that he didn't measure up. The Atlantics didn't do any better without him; they lost their next five games, too. There was quite a lot of reshuffling, dropping, and adding of Brooklyn players over the following month, and as late as August 5 the team had only won two championship games. Brooklyn cycled through 23 players in 1872 (the Boston Red Stockings only used 22 players in total from 1871 through 1875), but remarkably used just one pitcher all season long—Jim Britt. He started every game, and every start resulted in a complete game. Britt finished the season 9-28 (4.53 ERA). Fourteen Brooklyns played outfield at one time or another.

Jackson's career in baseball had come to an end. A little over a month later, he is found operating a retail store in Guelph, Ontario, named Ryan's Dead Ball Distributorship.[15] He sold cigars and tobacco, but also "every description of Base Ball Supplies." He proclaimed himself the sole agent in the Dominion of Canada for the Ryan dead ball, "the only ball used in the United States Championship games." Jackson's newspaper advertisement said that "Having played last Season with the Professional Red Stocking's *(sic)*, of Boston, feels satisfied that by his knowledge of the game and its requirements, he can meet the wants of all purchasers."[16]

In 1873 Jackson married Mary Estelle Bell, a New York native born to a father from England and a mother from New York. Jacob Dunn Bell had been born in Liverpool in 1811. He arrived in New York as a teenager, in 1827. His wife, Hannah Sprague, was from New York. Jacob worked as a machinist in 1850 but was listed as a farmer in both the 1860 and 1880 censuses. The Bell family lived near Rochester.

At the time of the 1865 New York State census, John and Jane Jackson and their family lived in Rochester, too. John continued work as a miller. That was the trade Sam Jackson took up after baseball. He appears in the 1880 census living in Niagara, New York, with Mary and their three children, Mary (who became known as Minnie), Frank, and Laura. Twenty years later, they still lived in Niagara and Sam was still working as a miller. Daughter Mary was a teacher, living with them. A younger daughter, Laura, born around 1883, lived in the household as well. It was in 1900 that Samuel Jackson became a naturalized American citizen.

Ten years later the family had moved to Plainsville (now Gypsum), New York, near Gypsum Springs on the eastern edge of the Town of Manchester, some 25-30 miles southeast of Rochester. Sam purchased and worked at a grist mill. In January 1928 Sam's wife, Mary, died. Sam and his daughter Mary were living in the same home at the time of the 1930 census.

Jackson's grandson David VanGelder talked with Tim Munn in 2004 and said that "his grandfather was always a physical man right up to the time of his death. ... David said he played catch with his elderly grandfather when an errant throw broke the front porch window. [David] thought he would be upset but to the contrary [Jackson] dismissed it with laughter. He described his grandfather as a person of tremendous work ethic—worked up to the day he died, a Mark Twain mustache and loved to smoke his pipe."[17]

Not long afterward, Samuel Jackson died at home on August 4, 1930, at Clifton Springs, New York, just about five or six miles from Manchester. He is buried nearby at the Gypsum Cemetery in Gypsum, New York.

SOURCES

In addition to the sources noted in this biography, the author also accessed Jackson's player file from the National Baseball Hall of Fame, Retrosheet.org, and Baseball-Reference.com. Thanks for help on this article to Priscilla Astifan, and to Richard Astifan, Paul Batesel, Bob LeMoine, and Tim Munn. Thanks as well to genealogy research volunteer Barbara Hill, and to Wilma Hill, curator from the Ontario County Historical Society. And thanks to Craig Bacon, Deputy County Historian at the Niagara County Historical Society.

NOTES

1 Emails to author from Priscilla Astifan, March 28 and June 10, 2016. From 1990 through 2002, Ms. Astifan produced a series of five booklets on "Baseball in the 19th Century" for the Rochester Public Library.

2 "Base Ball," *Cincinnati Daily Gazette*, January 19, 1871: 2.

3 "The Boston Base-Ball Club," *Boston Journal*, January 21, 1871: 1.

4 "Base-ball Nines for 1871," *New York Tribune*, January 27, 1871: 3.

5 Letter from Harry Wright in Cincinnati to "Friend Jackson," January 9, 1871. The letter is in the Samuel Jackson player file at the National Baseball hall of Fame.

6 "Base Ball at Troy, N.Y.—The Bostonians Defeat the Haymakers," *Boston Journal*, May 10, 1871: 4.

7 "Boston and Vicinity," *Boston Journal*, May 11, 1871: 4; "Base Ball at the Hub," *Cincinnati Commercial Tribune*, May 14, 1871: 1.

8 "Cleveland vs. Boston," *New York Clipper*, June 24, 1871: 93.

9 "Base Ball," *Boston Journal*, September 13, 1871: 1.

10 "White Over Red," *Chicago Inter Ocean*, September 30, 1871: 4.

11 Howard W. Rosenberg, *Cap Anson 2: The Theatrical and Kingly Mike Kelly* (Tile Books, 2004), 265, 266.

12 *Buffalo Express* of July 29, 1888, cited in Rosenberg, 266.

13 "The Sporting World," *Chicago Tribune*, January 21, 1872: 2.

14 "Base Ball," *Boston Journal*, May 8, 1872: 4.

15 Timothy Munn and Matthew F. Vitticore, *From Backyards to Big Leagues: Ontario County Baseball 1850-2004* (Canandaigua, New York: Ontario County Historical Society, 2005), 59.

16 Newspaper advertisement dated June 20, 1872, in unknown newspaper, clipping found in Jackson's player file at the National Baseball Hall of Fame.

17 Email from Tim Munn to Priscilla Astifan, June 3, 2016.

JUMBO LATHAM

BY SCOTT FIESTHUMEL

GEORGE WARREN "JUICE" LATHAM was born September 6, 1852, in Utica, New York, to Amy Victory Latham and Charles Latham, a constable and one of Utica's first patrolmen. Growing up, George attended Utica's South Street School and then the Advanced School while playing ball for amateur teams, including the Lightfoots and the Actives. At some point early in his playing days, he received the nickname "Juice," apparently a reference to the energy he displayed while playing and coaching. Later, he would also be called "Jumbo," an obvious reference to his stocky 5' 8" and eventually 250-pound build. Regarded as one of the most vocal coaches in the game during the nineteenth century he was known to most baseball fans as "Juice."

As one of baseball's first professional players, Juice Latham was well-known and respected in his hometown. His long career as a player, manager, and umpire brought him into contact with some of the legendary names in baseball history. In 1869, Latham played in Ottawa, Ontario. Where he spent the next four years isn't known, as he next turns up playing in New Haven, Connecticut in 1874. In a newspaper interview just before his death, Latham mentions the many places he played, but makes no mention of any teams from 1870 to 1873. In 1875, Latham was a member of the Boston entry in the first organization of professional teams, the National Association's Boston Red Stockings. Baseball pioneer Harry Wright ran the Boston club, and because Juice had been with the New Haven Elm Citys the year before, after playing first base in 16 games for Boston, Wright sent Latham to New Haven to help that club out as a player/manager. The 1875 New Haven club, a new entrant in the National Association that season, had two wins against 21 losses when Latham arrived, so while their record of 4-14 under his leadership may not appear that good, it was a definite improvement. The following year he started in Canada as player/manager of the Tecumseh club of London, Ontario, but finished the season in Binghamton, New York.

Latham made his National League debut in 1877 with Louisville, but he maintained a residence in Utica, and the 1877 Utica City Directory listed his occupation as "baseballist." The 1877 Louisville team would go down in history as the club with the first great gambling scandal in professional baseball. The team was having a successful year, winning a vast majority of their games until late in the season several games were lost under questionable circumstances. While four Louisville players would eventually be banned from baseball for throwing games, Juice Latham was never accused of any wrongdoing. In fact, he was so well thought of that when the club's board met hoping to re-organize the team for 1878, Latham was the first player considered to be brought back. Unfortunately, for financial reasons Louisville was not able to field a team that season.

Latham did not play in the NL in 1878 because he went home to become a member of the first professional team representing his hometown of Utica. The only Utica native on the team, the well-respected and popular second baseman helped the Utica club to a third-place finish in the International Association. The following season, Latham played for minor-league teams in Springfield and Washington.

After spending two years with the Treasury Department in Washington, Latham returned to the major leagues in 1882. That year, Philadelphia fielded a team in a new major league, the American Association. Latham served as player/manager for the Philadelphia Athletics, guiding the team to a third-place finish with a 41-34 record. He spent the 1883 and 1884 seasons in the American Association with the Louisville Eclipse, playing a majority of his big-league games at first base, although he did play every infield position at least once.

Jumbo Latham, January 1875 in Utica (Spalding Collection)

In 1885, Latham split time between Trenton and Richmond in the Eastern League. In 1886, he was playing for Jersey City, and Utica was in a tight International League pennant race. Utica asked Juice to secure his release from Jersey City so that he could help them down the stretch drive. When Latham joined the team on July 7, the club's record was 23-16 (.590 winning pct.) After that date, Utica was 39-18 (.684 winning pct.), and Juice was voted team captain in August by his teammates in recognition of his leadership. Utica's 1886 International League championship was the first pennant in the city's history. Latham returned to play for Utica in 1887, with much different results. The team struggled on the field and at the gate before the club was eventually sold and transferred to Wilkes-Barre.

The now 35-year-old Latham's playing career was winding down. He was with Columbus, Ohio, for part of 1887 and played or coached for New York State clubs such as Oneida and Elmira over the next few years. He still could be found playing an occasional first base for semipro teams around Richfield Springs when he was over 40. When not playing, he umpired in numerous amateur, charity, and professional games in the Utica area.

Being well-respected in the community didn't prevent Latham from being arrested in 1891 when he was umpiring a game being played on Sunday in apparent violation of "blue laws." The issue of Sunday ballplaying in New York State was a complicated one that took three decades for the legislature to decide, but suffice it to say that occasionally the clergy and members of a community would raise the issue, and it would result in the local police arresting some combination of players, managers, ticket takers, owners, or, as in this case, an umpire. Latham and several players were arrested by Utica's Chief of Police Charles Dagwell. There was a one-day trial, with the jury returning with a verdict in their favor in just 15 minutes. Chief Dagwell certainly knew who Juice was because Dagwell had been a member of the Utica Base Ball Club a quarter century earlier and Juice's brother John was a Utica policeman.

After his days in baseball ended, Latham worked as a driver on the Utica Belt Line street railway, as a mason (an accident while working this profession cost him the sight in his right eye), and with the Utica Gas & Electric Company. Juice Latham died of uremia on May 26, 1914 at the age of 61. He never married and had no children. Even though he had other careers, it is entirely appropriate that his death certificate lists his occupation as "Retired Base Ball Player."

SOURCES

Cook, William A. *The Louisville Grays Scandal of 1877: The Taint of Gambling at the Dawn of the National League* (Jefferson, North Carolina: McFarland, 2005).

Shiffert, John. *Base Ball in Philadelphia: A History of the Early Game* (Jefferson, North Carolina: McFarland, 2006).

Albany Knickerbocker Press, and the following Utica newspapers; *Sunday Tribune, Saturday Globe, Daily Press*, and the *Observer*.

ANDY LEONARD

BY CHARLES F. FABER

HE WAS BORN IN IRELAND DURING the Potato Famine, named for an American president, and crossed the ocean as an infant to become a star in a game that was unknown in his native land at the time. Eventually, baseball came to flourish in Ireland. In the present Irish Baseball League the most outstanding player annually receives the Andy Leonard League Most Valuable Player Award.

Andrew Jackson Leonard was born on June 1, 1846, in County Cavan, Ireland, a son of Ann Liddy and Andrew Leonard. One might wonder why Irish parents named a baby after an American president. Actually, such a thing was not all that unusual. Old Hickory was the first president of the United States of Irish ancestry, and was exceedingly popular in Ireland at the time. County Cavan was suffering in the late 1840s. Starvation was rampant, caused by the failure of the 1845 potato crop, on which the county's economy was dependent. Ann Leonard, her youngest son, Andrew, and his two sisters, Ann and Catharine, fled to America, sailing from Liverpool on the ship *Milan*, which arrived in New York on June 13, 1848. They settled in Newark, where they were joined by the family's three oldest sons, John, Thomas, and Richard. No record can be found of what happened to their father.

Growing up in Newark, Andy Leonard quickly took to the game of baseball. It has been reported that he joined the Hudson River Club of Newburgh, New York, in 1866 at the age of 18.[1] After playing two seasons in Newburgh, the youngster returned to New Jersey and joined the strong amateur club in Irvington, a suburb of Newark. Leonard and his teammate, Charlie Sweasy, earned considerable attention for the quality of their play during their two years in Irvington. Sweasy was from the same Newark neighborhood where Leonard had learned the game. In 1868 the two went west together to Cincinnati, where they joined the Buckeyes, the strongest team in the Queen City. It is likely they received some inducement to go to Cincinnati. Probably they were not paid under the table. In the amateur era, it was common practice for supporters of a club to secure players well-paying jobs that allowed them the opportunity to play baseball in their off-duty hours. Sweasy and Leonard both found employment as hatters,

Meanwhile A.B. Champion and Harry Wright were creating the Cincinnati Base Ball Club, soon to be known as the Red Stockings, to challenge the Buckeyes for baseball supremacy on the Ohio River. The Red Stockings became the first openly all-professional baseball club in history. In 1869 Leonard and Sweasy jumped to the Red Stockings. For a salary of $800, Leonard became the first Irish-born professional baseball player.

In his earlier years, Leonard had been an infielder, usually playing at shortstop. Harry Wright's brother George was going to be the shortstop for the Red Stockings and the other infield positions were filled as well, so Wright placed Leonard in left field. Andy mastered the position and played in the outer garden the rest of his career, with only occasional assignments in the infield. In his history of baseball in Cincinnati, Harry Ellard noted that Leonard was a brilliant left fielder but he "ranked the best as a batsman."[2] Ellard called Leonard a "jolly, good-natured fellow."[3]

The praise of Leonard as a batsman was justified by some of his accomplishments during the Red Stockings' remarkable 1869 season. In a July 22 game against their crosstown rivals, the Buckeyes, Leonard came to bat three times in the fourth inning and hit a single, a triple, and a home run, almost hitting for the cycle in a single inning.[4] On the Red Stockings' tour of the West, the Cincinnatians played the Pacific Ball Club in San Francisco on September 29. Leonard hit three homers, including a grand slam, in the rout. A California reporter described the slam: "The striker

Andy Leonard (Spalding Collection)

carefully measured the ground with his eye and sent the ball whizzing along the grass out past right field and over the graveled outside walk, enabling every man on base to get safely home and the striker himself to make a home run. It was a very effective strike."5 Yes, it was — very effective!

In an 1870 mismatch against the Union Base Ball Club in Urbana, Ohio, Leonard collected at least one hit in each of the nine innings played.6 Even considering the 1870 rules favoring the batter and the quality of the opposition that day in Urbana, it was quite an accomplishment.

Praise for Leonard's fielding started when he was a shortstop in Irvington and continued throughout his career until his vision started failing. One newspaper called him "one of the 'Class A' of outfielders. In all respects he is superior, being a perfect judge, a sure catch, and a wonderful long thrower."7 Another paper opined that "as regards accuracy of throwing, Leonard at left field has no superior. He has so repeatedly thrown in the ball from that position to the home plate with such unerring precision that the runner on third base has not dared attempt to reach home.8

Leonard was lauded by future Hall of Famer Cap Anson, one of the 19th century's top performers, as "a splendid judge of high balls, a sure catch ... a swift and accurate long-distance thrower ... a good batsman and a splendid base runner."9

Apparently Leonard developed a high opinion of himself as an outfielder. Wright complained about Leonard and right fielder Cal McVey saying how they "dislike exceedingly, when playing in the field, to be told to change their positions when certain players come to the bat ... seemed to think it was a reflection on them or their judgment as players, when told by the pitcher or captain to change or move in the field."10

After the 1870 season the Cincinnati Red Stockings reverted to amateur status. The National Association, often considered baseball's first major league, was formed in 1871. Harry Wright took several Cincinnati players, not including Leonard, with him to Boston, where he called the new club Red Stockings. Why Wright did not take Leonard with him to Boston is not known. However, Wright wanted no drinkers on the team, and it was said that Leonard "would occasionally kick over the traces."11

Leonard and teammates Asa Brainard, Doug Allison, Charlie Sweasy, and Fred Waterman joined the Washington Olympics of the National Association. On May 5, 1871, the 5-foot-7-inch, 168-pound, right-handed Leonard became the first native of Ireland to play in the major leagues. He spent only one season with the Olympics. His most notable performance during his season in the nation's capital came on July 7, when he scored three runs in one inning in a game against the Fort Wayne Kekiongas. In 1872 he was reunited with his former manager, Harry Wright, in Boston. He hit over .300 in each of his four years with Boston in the National Association. Wright had a powerful aggregation in Boston. The Red Stockings won the league championship each year that Leonard played for them in the National Association.

Anti-Irish prejudice was rife in Boston in the 1870s. Signs "No Irish Need Apply" were common in shop windows. Jim O'Rourke, a talented young outfielder, was offered a contract to play for Boston in 1873, on the condition that he change his name. Wright requested the young man to drop the O from his surname to mask his otherwise obvious Irishness. To his credit the player refused. "I would rather die than give up any part of my father's name. A million would not tempt me."[12] Wright relented and signed O'Rourke anyway. (O'Rourke went on to a long and distinguished major-league career. He was inducted into the National Baseball Hall of Fame at Cooperstown in 1975.) Soon the Red Stockings added more players of Irish descent. Most prominent were Leonard, John Morrill, Tim Murnane, and Tommy Bond. They led Boston to championship after championship.

In July 1874 the Boston Red Stockings and the Philadelphia Athletics were given a three-week break from the National Association schedule, so they could introduce the game to the British Isles. The British showed little interest in baseball, and few fans showed up at the games. The highlight of the trip turned out to be a cricket match between the Americans and the Marylebone club, one of the strongest in England. Harry and George Wright were experienced cricketers, but most of the Americans knew little about the game. The Wrights conducted a crash course for their countrymen on rules and strategy. When the game commenced several of the Americans forgot the defensive strategy, crushing the ball as far as they could hit it. The Americans won the match 107-105, with Andy Leonard scoring 12 runs. The Americans spent two days in Ireland, defeating an all-Ireland team in cricket, 165-79. Leonard scored 26 runs in a match at Cavan, the place where he had been born 28 years earlier.

Leonard's grandson, Charles McCarthy, said his grandfather made a triumphal return to his native country: "Oral family history has him returning triumphantly to his hometown, Cavan, as both an American champion ballist and as a native-born Irishman, survivor of the Great Hunger (or Famine), who had battered the English cricket champions silly at their own game."[13]

During the same year as the British trip, 1874, Andy Leonard married Alice Nugent, the 22-year-old daughter of Irish immigrants. They eventually had six children, four of whom—Andrew, William, John, and Alice—survived to adulthood.

In 1876 the National Association was replaced by the National League. Wright took his Red Stockings into the new circuit. On April 22, 1876, Leonard became one of two Irish-born players to appear in the first National League game. Despite anti-Irish prejudice, Leonard was extremely popular in Boston, particularly among the many fans of Irish ancestry. The Red Stockings won the National League pennant in both 1877 and 1878.

With his skills starting to decline, Leonard spent the 1879 season in the minor leagues. He reverted to shortstop, the same position in which he had starred

Andy Leonard, 1872 (Spalding Collection)

as a youth. He played this demanding position for the Rochester Hop Bitters in the National Association (now reconstituted as a minor league) and hit .302 in 20 games.

In 1880 Leonard attempted a comeback in Cincinnati, the scene of so many of his earlier triumphs. Failing eyesight forced his retirement in midsummer. He played his final major-league game at the age of 34 on July 3, 1880. His errors allowed Providence four earned runs as the Reds lost, 6-4.

After retiring from baseball, Leonard returned to Newark, where he worked for the Water Department for some time. He then went to Boston to work as a sales clerk in a sporting goods store opened by his former teammate, George Wright. Leonard continued in that employment until shortly before his death from a gastric ulcer at the age of 57. Andrew Jackson Leonard died in Roxbury, Massachusetts, on August 22, 1903. He was buried in the New Calvary Cemetery in Boston.

NOTES

1. "Andy Leonard," wikipedia.com.
2. Harry Ellard, *Baseball in Cincinnati: A History* (Jefferson, North Carolina: McFarland, 2004), 101.
3. *Ibid.*
4. Reported by Stephen D. Guschov, *The Red Stockings of Cincinnati* (Jefferson, North Carolina: McFarland, 1998), 70-71.
5. *Daily Alta California,* September 30, 1869, cited by Guschov, 86.
6. Guschov, 101.
7. *St. Louis Republican,* June 1, 1875, cited by Guschov, 34
8. *New York Clipper,* 1874 PreSeasonGuide, cited by Guschov.
9. Cited by Bob Richardson and Jim Sumner, "Andrew Jackson Leonard," in Robert L. Tiemann and Mark Rucker, eds., *Nineteenth Century Stars* (Kansas City: Society for American Baseball Research, 1989), 77.
10. Harry Wright, letter to Henry Chadwick, January 2, 1875. Cited by Guschov, 34.
11. *The Sporting News,* December 18, 1886.
12. David L. Fleitz, *The Irish in Baseball* (Jefferson, North Carolina: McFarland, 2009), 7-8. Fleitz says the story may be apocryphal. It had been reported in *The Sporting News,* February 10, 1948.
13. The account of the trip to Britain is taken from Fleitz, 8-9.

JOHN E. MANNING

BY DAVID NEMEC

AFTER BEGINNING HIS MAJOR-league career in 1873 as a versatile utilityman with a strong claim to being the first notable relief pitcher,[1] in the 1880s Jack Manning developed into an outfielder whose primary asset was his strong arm. In his final four major-league seasons (1883-86) he tabulated 100 outfield assists, ranking him fourth among the leaders during that period, trailing only Hugh Nicol (123), Mike "King" Kelly (122), and Jimmy Wolf (102).

Born on December 20, 1853, in Braintree, Massachusetts, Manning was the son of Irish-born parents James and Mary Manning. At the time of Manning's birth his father was a papermaker, but he later became a stone mason and well-off enough to keep a 14-year-old servant, Mary Boyd, in the family home by 1880. Also still living in the family home at that time were four of the Mannings' six adult children, including Jack, who never married.

In Jack's childhood the Mannings moved to nearby Boston, where Jack attended public schools. Rather than finish his schooling, he left short of graduation from high school to clerk in a store and play baseball for the store team on his days off. After Harry Wright, the player-manager of Boston's National Association powerhouse, discovered the 5-foot-8½-inch, 158-pound Manning playing second base for the highly regarded Boston Juniors amateur nine late in the 1872 season at age 18, he was signed to a contract calling for $800 with Wright's Red Stockings for the following year.[2] The right-handed batter and thrower made his major-league debut with Boston on Opening Day in 1873, playing first base and going 1-for-4 on April 23 in an 8-5 loss to George Zettlein of the Philadelphia Whites at Boston.

Manning then spent the next half-dozen years bouncing back and forth between the Red Stockings and other teams, struggling to find a place in the talented lineup of the strongest club in the National Association and later the National League. Although he played a fair amount of infield, he did not really have the defensive skills to excel there in top competition, and in Boston he was primarily employed in right field, where he specialized in throwing runners out at first base on ordinary groundballs and one-hop line drives, plays made possible because outfielders in the 1870s played very close to the infield by modern standards.

Manning also utilized his arm strength to pitch. The rules of the day allowed substitutions only in case of injury, so a replacement pitcher had to be summoned from another position when the situation warranted a change. Harry Wright, an outfielder-pitcher himself, was very aggressive in the use of "change pitchers" (believing, and correctly so, that forcing opposing batters to see a variety of pitching deliveries and styles in the course of a game would keep them off-balance) and frequently brought Manning in from right field to pitch in midgame. So often was Manning substituted for Boston's starting pitcher, usually either Al Spalding or Wright himself, that baseball historian John Thorn credits him with being in all probability the game's first bona-fide relief pitcher.[3]

Saves were not a statistic in those days, but retrospective calculations credit Manning with a total of 11 saves in 23 relief appearances with Boston during the seasons of 1875 and 1876, by far the leading number for the era. In 1874 Manning spent the season with the lowly Baltimore Canaries after Boston did not tender him a new contract following his rookie 1873 campaign, freeing him to sell his services elsewhere. His record as a pitcher with Baltimore was an abysmal 4-16 in 20 starts, but Wright saw enough promise in his arm to rehire him for 1875. Once back in a Hub uniform, he was 16-2 in 18 starts and added six saves in his nine relief appearances as Boston swept to its fourth consecutive National Association pennant.

The following year, Boston's first as a member of the fledgling National League, which in 1876 replaced

Jack Manning (Spalding Collection)

the floundering National Association as the game's lone major league, Manning played in all 70 official league games, pitching in 34 of them, 20 as a starter and 14 in relief. Long before the end of the 1876 season, he was dubbed the "saver" by the Boston press[4] as he finished with a perfect 4-0 record with five saves and a glittering 0.68 ERA in the 40 innings he worked in relief.

Yet, with all that, no thought appears to have ever been given into turning Manning, who was never more than an adequate hitter, into a full-time pitcher. After the 1876 season, in fact, he was loaned by Boston to Cincinnati in a unique transaction for its time and seldom appeared in the box thereafter. In his 13 pitching appearances in 1877-78 he posted a 1-4 record with just one save and an ERA of 8.48 that was nearly double that of any other pitcher who worked more than 20 innings in that time frame. Earlier Manning had earned a reputation for violating the then-extant rule that required underhand pitching, and it may well be that the rest of the league simply caught up with him once other pitchers acquired the knack of throwing undetected from a higher position and were able to do so with more velocity.

Manning's odd loan to Cincinnati for the 1877 season merits some discussion as it provides insight into how loose business practices sometimes were in professional baseball's infancy, when clubs and even entire leagues struggled mightily to remain solvent. In 1876 Boston's four-year pennant run was interrupted, largely because four of its stars were signed by other National Association clubs midway through the 1875 season for 1876 delivery. The brazen theft played a large hand in the dissolution of the NA and the formation of the National League in its stead. Among the four stars Boston lost after the 1875 campaign was Deacon White, who went to Chicago along with three other Beantown mainstays, Al Spalding, Cal McVey, and Ross Barnes. All were instrumental in bringing Chicago the inaugural NL pennant and were offered Chicago contracts for 1877. White, however, chose to return to Boston but only with the proviso that his younger brother Will be signed as Boston's change pitcher. When Harry Wright acceded to White's demand and Boston then also garnered Ezra Sutton from the disbanding Philadelphia NL club, Manning became a likely bench warmer in 1877—and a costly one at that as he had been signed in 1876 to a three-year contract at $1,800 per year, according to David Ball's Trade Log.[5]

To rid itself of at least some unnecessary expense, Boston, as can best be determined at this late date, worked out an arrangement with Cincinnati owner Si Keck whereby Boston would pay part of Manning's salary (accounts differ as to how much) if Keck's club would temporarily take him off Boston's hands. Manning thereupon became a member of the last-place Queen City entry in 1877 and was reclaimed by Boston after he had his last good season at the plate, batting .317 with a .767 OPS, second on the Cincinnatis only to one of the game's greatest sluggers in its early years, Charley Jones.

Back in a Boston uniform in 1878, Manning was once again on a pennant winner but fell off markedly offensively, hitting just .254 with a .585 OPS. When he was not offered a contract renewal and no other NL club showed interest in him, he signed for 1879 with the Albany Capital Cities of the National Association, which had earlier been reformed as a minor league. Except for the 1880 season with the rapidly sinking Cincinnati NL franchise, Manning spent the remainder of the late 1870s and the early 1880s in the minors. His sojourn in the bushes was distinguished only by a postseason West Coast tour he made with Rochester at the finish of the 1879 season after the Flour Cities took the place of the Albany club in the NA.[6]

In 1883 Manning returned to the majors as the right fielder of the new Philadelphia NL entry. There he was reunited with Harry Wright, who became the Quakers manager in 1884. It was not a happy reunion, however, as the two engaged in acrimonious offseason battles over salary, with Wright publicly denigrating Manning's fielding and baserunning. Manning's defenders replied by suggesting that if Wright valued Manning so lightly he might just as well release him, but Manning remained the Philadelphia right fielder through 1885. At the tag end of the 1884 season he enjoyed his major-league career highlight on October 9 in a game at Chicago when he became the first member of a visiting team to hit three home runs in a game. (His three circuit blasts off John Clarkson at the White Stockings' tiny Lake Front Park were all but for naught as the Quakers suffered a 19-7 shellacking. The 12-run deficit remains the largest ever by a team in which one of its players went deep three times in the contest.)

Just before the start of the 1886 season, Manning escaped Wright at last when he was waived out of the NL and acquired by Baltimore, the American Association's perennial cellar dweller. Manning batted only .223 for Billy Barnie's Orioles, but with an exceptionally weak ballclub playing in a park that heavily favored pitchers, he led the team's qualifiers in hits, total bases, batting, slugging, and on-base percentage. Nevertheless, he was released after the season, probably because of his diminished speed and weakened fielding; his 1.32 range factor was the lowest that year among all outfielders in both major leagues in a minimum of 100 games. His major-league coda occurred on October 14, 1886, at Philadelphia when he played right field and went 0-for-4 in a 5-1 loss to the Athletics' Cyclone Miller.

Manning claimed, possibly with tongue in cheek, that "early piety" had turned his hair prematurely gray, which led managers to think he was older than he really was. Major-league clubs refused to buy his story, however, even though he actually was the age he claimed to be (33), and he finished his career playing for New England minor-league teams. Probably his most memorable post-major-league day on the diamond came on September 15, 1887, when a benefit game was held for him at Boston's South End Grounds between a local club called the Pioneers and select members of Boston's first National League team in 1876, including Manning himself. The Pioneers won 12-5 in a contest abbreviated to six innings in front of a crowd of around 2,000. The affair netted Manning around $1,000.[7] Still to be determined is precisely why the benefit was held. Manning, from all outward appearances, was never without work or in need of money; yet *Sporting Life* in 1889 reported that he was "said to be in very needy circumstances" and Ed Andrews, a former teammate of his on the Quakers, had "started a subscription" for him.[8]

In any event, soon afterward Manning landed a job as a groundskeeper for the Boston Players League club in 1890 and later worked variously as a clerk, a theater stagehand, and a janitor. On February 2, 1925, he was among the six surviving players from the National League's yearling 1876 season to attend the league's "Golden Jubilee" celebration in New York's Broadway Central Hotel, the same location where the NL had been founded 49 years to the day earlier.[9] The lifelong bachelor died in Boston on August 15, 1929, at age 75 and was interred at Boston's New Calvary Cemetery.

NOTES

1 John Thorn, *The Relief Pitcher: Baseball's New Hero* (New York: E.P. Dutton, 1979).

2 Doug Pappas research reported on Baseball-reference.com.

3 William F. McNeil, *The Evolution of Pitching in Major League Baseball* (Jefferson, North Carolina: McFarland & Co., 2006), 38.

4 Ibid.

5 David Ball's 19th Century Player Transaction Register, SABR site; addenda sent by Ball to David Nemec 2007-11. Thanks to David Ball for help in gathering information used in this biography.

6 *New York Clipper*, July 31, 1880.

7 *Boston Globe*, September 16, 1887.

8 *Sporting Life*, February 6, 1889.

9 *Brooklyn Eagle*, February 3, 1925.

CAL MCVEY

BY CHARLES F. FABER

MILLIONS OF BOYS HAVE GROWN up dreaming of becoming a professional ballplayer. For a young Iowa farmboy named Calvin McVey playing ball for a living was the furthest thing from his mind. There were no openly professional ballclubs during his childhood. However, he was to become one of the first to play for pay, a member of the team that forged the longest winning streak in the history of the sport.

Calvin Alexander McVey was born near the village of Montrose in Lee County, Iowa, the southeastern-most county in the state, on August 30, 1850. He was a son of Caroline and William McVey, natives of Indiana, who had moved to the Hawkeye State when it was still on the frontier. Iowa had been admitted to the Union less than three years before Calvin was born. William was a farmer, and not a particularly successful one, who moved from place to place in southern Iowa and northern Missouri until he gave up farming and returned to Indiana, where he secured employment as a tax collector and later as a piano tuner. Calvin was first mentioned in the Indianapolis City Directory in 1867 as a student at North Western Christian University and as a piano maker for the Indianapolis Piano Manufacturing Company, an enterprise owned by a relative.

As a boy Calvin had been a nimble athlete, known for his cartwheels and handsprings. He had been a capable bare-knuckle pugilist. In Indianapolis Mac, as he was called, was introduced to baseball, which he soon came to love. He played for two different amateur clubs, the Actives and the Westerns. In 1867 the latter club took on the powerful Nationals of Washington, D.C., in a highly publicized match of one of the best teams in the East against the best of the West. McVey's team lost, but the teenager earned a national reputation as a competitive player.

In 1869 A.B. Champion formed the nation's first club of all openly professional players—the famous Cincinnati Red Stockings. Most of his players were imported from the East. (Only one was a Cincinnati native.) Harry Wright had been a member of the famous Knickerbockers in New York. He came to Cincinnati to play cricket, but Champion named him manager of the Red Stockings. Wright had heard about the exploits of the youngster with the Indianapolis Westerns and signed him to a contract. (Actually William had to sign for his son, as 18-year-old Calvin was considered a minor, too young to sign a legally binding document.) Mac was younger and less experienced than his teammates, and Wright was unsure of the best position for him to play, but he knew the youngster could hit, so he put him in right field. Calvin McVey became the youngest player in professional baseball, the first salaried player born in Iowa, and the first pro born west of the Mississippi River.

At 5-feet-9 and 170 pounds, Mac was probably about the size of the average player of his day. He batted and threw right-handed. It is said that he brought his athletic agility with him to the professional ranks, frequently turning flip-flops on the field after his club posted another victory.

After defeating a number of Midwestern teams, the Red Stockings took off on a tour of the East on May 31, 1869. To the surprise of many, the Cincinnati club defeated all of its opponents, with only one club making it a close contest. After a game in Washington, where the Red Stockings routed the Nationals, the club was invited to the White House. It was quite a thrill for the 18-year-old erstwhile Iowa farmboy to meet the president of the United States, Ulysses S. Grant. Having defeated all the best teams in the East and the Midwest, the Red Stockings headed for the West Coast. They took a stagecoach from St. Louis to Omaha, with Cal McVey and the manager's brother George Wright sitting next to the driver. Then they boarded a train for San Francisco, with McVey being a member of the first ballclub ever to travel on the

Cal McVey (Spalding Collection)

new transcontinental railroad. The Red Stockings demolished all of their opponents in San Francisco. The winning streak continued until June 14, 1870, when the Red Stockings lost in extra innings to the Brooklyn Atlantics.

The 1870 census showed Calvin McVey living with his parents in Indianapolis. His occupation was listed as baseballist.

Two factions emerged on the team during 1870, divided largely by their attitudes toward drinking and discipline. McVey, the Wright brothers, and Charlie Gould (the team's only native Cincinnatian) favored teetotaling. Despite all their success on the field, the club was not a money-making proposition. Champion resigned as president, and the club's directors voted to return to amateur status. In March 1871 the first professional league was formed—the National Association of Professional Base Ball Players (NA). Harry Wright became the captain of the Boston entry, which he named the Red Stockings after the famous Cincinnati club. From Cincinnati he took with him three players—his brother George, Charlie Gould, and Calvin McVey. The fact that Cal was the team's best hitter was probably the principal reason he was included in this elite group, but Wright's perception of the youngster's exemplary character may have played a part in the decision.

In his first year in the NA, Cal batted .431 and was runner-up to Levi Meyerle for the league's first batting title. He was used primarily as a catcher, but logged a few games in right field. Before his major-league career was over, he had played all nine positions, including pitcher. After two seasons in Boston, McVey departed for Baltimore, where at the age of 22, he became the league's youngest manager. He spent only one year with the Lord Baltimores (or Canaries, as they were sometimes called) before returning to Boston for two more seasons. In 1874 he married a 22-year-old Indiana woman named Abbey. In 1876 and 1877 he played (mostly first base) for the Chicago White Stockings of the newly formed National League. Mac helped the Chicagoans win the first NL pennant, but after two years he was on the move again. This time it was back to Cincinnati, where he played third base for the Reds in 1878 and 1879. He had played nine years in the two leagues, averaging .362 for his five years in the National Association and .328 for his four seasons in the National League.

McVey had been impressed with California during his 1869 visit to San Francisco with the Red Stockings, so he moved to West and tried his hand at minor-league ball in the Bay Area. Caroline and William McVey also succumbed to the lure of the Golden State and joined their son in California. They were living in the same household as Abbey and Calvin in Oakland at the time of the 1880 census. In California William worked from time to time in his former occupations of farmer and tax collector. Cal played for two different San Francisco teams in the California League in 1880—Bay City and the Californias. He may have organized, managed, and played for the San Francisco Pioneers in 1885, but no records of his involvement with the Pioneers are currently retrievable.

As soon as the 1880 baseball season was over, the McVeys relocated to Tulare County, southeast of San Francisco. When he registered to vote that November, Calvin gave his occupation as an R.E. agent. In 1884 Calvin again registered in Tulare County, as did his father. Cal's occupation was given as an agent and William as farmer. In 1890 Cal registered to vote in San Diego, again giving his occupation as an agent. In 1893 he was back in Tulare County. In 1896 he registered in Fresno. On the registration forms he was described as being of fair complexion, with brown hair and blue eyes. Identifying features were "baseball marks on fingers."

Most of the 1890 census schedules, including all those from California, were destroyed by a fire in the Commerce Department Building in January 1923. Voter registration records are the only official guide to Mac's activities between 1880 and 1900. Of course, women were not allowed to vote at that time, so no account of Abbey's whereabouts is available.

In the 1900 census Calvin was shown as a resident of a boarding house on Powell Street in San Francisco. Although he was listed as married, Abbey was not with him at that time. The 1901 San Francisco City Directory lists Mac as a special policeman, residing at 209 Eddy Street, and also as a watchman at 17 Powell Street. According to John Liepa, a historian in Iowa who has researched McVey's career, Calvin's wife was seriously injured and his home destroyed by the calamitous San Francisco Earthquake in 1906. Liepa wrote that McVey was reduced to living in a small shack and depending on charities for food and clothing. In 1908 his address was 139 14th Street in San Francisco; no occupation was given in the city directory. Seven years after the earthquake the ex-ballplayer was working in a mine in Nevada, when a 30-foot fall crippled him. Liepa wrote that despite his injuries McVey was able to work as a night watchman for a lumber company for ten years. (Curiously, the city directory in 1913 named McVey as the manager of San Francisco's Central Amusement Company.) A former Red Stocking teammate, Doug Allison, petitioned the National League for medical and financial assistance, and minimal aid was provided, but not enough to lift McVey out of economic hardship.

A final moment of glory came for Cal McVey in 1919 when he was invited to come to Cincinnati as an honored guest at a celebration of the 50th anniversary of baseball's first professional team. He proudly rode in a festive parade prior to the opening of the World Series between the Reds and the Chicago White Sox.

Calvin Alexander McVey died in San Francisco at the age of 69. His remains were cremated. In 1968 he was inducted posthumously into the Iowa Sports Hall of Fame. The best biographical sketches are by Liepa and Frederick Ivor-Campbell. Not many modern baseball fans are familiar with the exploits of Cal McVey, but 19th-century aficionados acknowledge him as one of baseball's great pioneers.

SOURCES

Frederick Ivor-Campbell, "Calvin Alexander McVey," in Robert L. Tiemann and Mark Rucker, eds., *Nineteenth Century Stars* (Kansas City: Society for American Baseball Research, 1989).

John Liepa, "The Cincinnati Red Stockings and Cal McVey, Iowa's First Professional Baseball Player," *Iowa Heritage*, 87:1 Spring 2006.

www.ancestry.com.

www.baseball-reference.com.

JIM O'ROURKE

BY WILLIAM LAMB

During a playing career that spanned a remarkable six decades, Jim O'Rourke did much to advance baseball as our national pastime. A key member of championship teams in both the National Association and the National League, O'Rourke was a versatile performer in the field and a reliable .300 hitter at the plate. Thereafter, as his playing days wound down, O'Rourke assumed the role of baseball executive, particularly in his native Connecticut, where he established a thriving minor league. O'Rourke was also a figure of some cultural significance, rising to prominence in an era when anti-Irish prejudice still flourished in many quarters. Unlike the stereotypical brawling, hard-drinking wastrel of King Kelly stripe, O'Rourke was a sober, well-educated ballplayer whose dignified bearing both on and off the diamond was punctuated only by a proclivity for grandiloquence. In time, these rhetorical flights of fancy, which amused and bewildered his contemporaries, gave rise to the moniker by which Jim O'Rourke is known to this day: Orator.

He was born James Henry O'Rourke in Bridgeport, Connecticut, on September 1, 1850.[1] He was the second of three children surviving to adulthood born to Hugh O'Rourke and his wife, Catherine (nee O'Donnell), Irish Catholic immigrants from County Mayo who arrived in Bridgeport around 1845.[2] Jim's youth was spent attending local schools, working on the small family farm, and playing baseball, often with older brother John, himself destined to become a major leaguer. A right-handed thrower and batter, young Jim O'Rourke began his formal playing career in 1866 as a member of the Bridgeport Ironsides, a recreational team for boys 12 to 15 years old. The following summer, he played for the Unions, another local youth team. In 1868 Jim advanced to the Stratford Osceolas, a top-notch semipro team for which he saw duty mostly as an outfield substitute.[3]

O'Rourke's ascension in baseball ranks was temporarily stalled by the untimely death of his father in December 1868.[4] Staying close to home to assist on the family farm, he returned to the Unions for the 1869 season. In 1870 he was back with the Stratford Osceolas as an outfield regular and backup catcher, his name often appearing as *Rourke* in print accounts and box scores of Osceolas games. That year, an otherwise successful season ended on a down note when the Middletown Mansfields swept Stratford to win the championship of Connecticut. But a season later, the Osceolas returned the favor, upsetting Middletown in a state championship rematch.[5]

In 1872 the Middletown Mansfields, entering the one-year-old National Association, sought to upgrade their roster by signing the Stratford battery of O'Rourke and pitcher Frank Buttery. According to popular lore, O'Rourke's joining the Mansfields was conditioned upon the team procuring a replacement to perform his chores on the O'Rourke farm.[6] Shortly after the season began, O'Rourke also took on the responsibilities of husband, marrying sweetheart Anna Kehoe, a recent arrival from Ireland. While the marriage would prove a long and happy one, the same could not be said of the O'Rourke experience with the Middletown Mansfields. A small-bore operation with shaky financial underpinnings, the Mansfields posted a 5-19 log in the National Association before the team folded in mid-August. Jim thereupon returned to the farm in Bridgeport.

Although he had batted only a modest .273 while alternating between shortstop and catcher for Middletown[7], O'Rourke had made a favorable impression in National Association circles. In December 1872 he was invited to join the Boston Red Stockings by team leader Harry Wright, renowned for his stewardship of a Cincinnati nine that had gone undefeated during an 1869 nationwide tour. With Annie now pregnant with the first of the eight O'Rourke children,

Jim accepted—but only after receiving written assurance from Wright that his salary was guaranteed by club backers.[8] An early photograph of him in Boston colors depicts the 5-foot-8 O'Rourke standing erect in the batter's box and already sporting the luxuriant handlebar mustache that would become his personal trademark. Under the tutelage of Wright, a seminal baseball strategist and a man of principle[9], the 22-year-old O'Rourke blossomed, hitting a robust .350 for a 43-16 Red Stockings pennant winner.

O'Rourke's sophomore season in Boston (which saw him moved to first base) was a solid one. He posted a .314 batting average with a league-leading five home runs as the Red Stockings breezed to a second consecutive league crown. The highlight of the 1874 campaign, however, was a midseason exhibition tour of Great Britain. There, O'Rourke's powerful arm won him a distance throwing contest.[10] He also displayed a surprising natural aptitude for the national game of the host country, cricket.[11] Apart from overseas adventure and continued good play, the 1874 season also saw the first incidence of a recurring event in the O'Rourke career: difficulty with management. Jim rebelled against club owners' attempt to recoup the purported financial loss incurred by the Great Britain trip via $100 assessments on Red Stockings players. Eventually Harry Wright persuaded O'Rourke to accept the deduction from his paycheck. But resolution of the dispute marked the first, last, and only time that Jim O'Rourke would capitulate in a fight with his baseball employers.

The 1875 season would see the Boston Red Stockings at the zenith of their success and the five-year-old National Association at the end of its run. Alternating between the outfield and catching, O'Rourke had a mixed year offensively. He batted a somewhat off .296 but led the Association in home runs (6) while finishing third in runs scored (97) and RBIs (72). With four of the circuit's five top batsmen (Deacon White .367; Ross Barnes .364; Cal McVey .355, and George Wright .333) and A.G. Spalding posting an incredible 54-5 log on the mound, the Red Stockings (71-8) waltzed to the 1875 pennant, 18½ games ahead of second-place Hartford. At season's end, however, the Boston team

Jim O'Rourke (The National Pastime Museum)

was gutted, with stars Spalding, White, Barnes, and McVey defecting to Chicago. Shortly thereafter, the National Association disbanded, replaced by a new, owner-dominated circuit, the National League.

Despite expectations to the contrary, Jim O'Rourke did not join his former teammates in Chicago. Nor would he sign with the National League franchise in Boston, holding out for a salary increase as Opening Day 1876 approached[12]. This time, it was club management that caved in, inking O'Rourke to a $1,600 pact that doubled his previous salary.[13] The signing came just in time for Jim to hustle to Philadelphia for the team's National League debut. There, a first-inning single off Athletics pitcher Lon Knight accorded O'Rourke the distinction of recording the first base hit in National League history. During that inaugural season, Jim amply repaid his employers' largess, playing in all 70 league games and batting a team-leading .327. But the Boston Red Caps (as the team was now called) were no match for the star-laden Chicago club, which captured the first National League flag handily. Red Caps fortunes—and the course of baseball history—underwent a change in December 1876. Ascending to the club presidency at the winter meeting of team stockholders was Arthur H. Soden, a prosperous roofing contractor and baseball enthusiast. For the next 30 years, the aloof and tough-minded Soden reigned over the franchise, marshaling the talent that brought eight championships to Boston while spearheading team owner efforts to curtail player freedom of movement and salaries.[14]

In 1877 O'Rourke had a breakout season, batting a career-high .362 while pacing the National League in runs scored (68), walks (20), and on-base percentage (.407). He was among the leaders in hits, total bases, and slugging percentage. With first baseman Deacon White returned to Boston and leading the league in most of the other offensive categories, and pitcher Tommy Bond posting all but two of the team's 42 victories, the Red Caps rallied to capture the pennant—an achievement subsequently diminished by the discovery that players from the second-place Louisville club had dumped crucial late season games.[15] The 1877 season also occasioned the first of Jim O'Rourke's clashes with team boss Soden. With many National League franchises operating in red ink, the league had imposed a $30 fee for uniforms on the players. O'Rourke refused to pay it and, after much wrangling, Soden relented, exempting him from the charge. The following season, Soden levied a $20 charge on his players for laundering their uniforms while they were on the road. And again, O'Rourke balked at paying the charge, precipitating another dispute with Soden.[16] Jim also had his problems between the foul lines in 1878, slumping to .278 with reduced run production. Still, Boston managed a successful pennant defense, its 41-19 record four games better than that of runner-up Cincinnati.

Unhappy in Boston, O'Rourke joined Red Caps mainstay George Wright in a move to Providence for the 1879 season. Once with the Grays, O'Rourke quickly regained his batting stroke. His .348 batting average and 126 hits were second only to the league leader, teammate Paul Hines (.357 and 146), while Jim's .371 on-base percentage was the league best. More importantly, O'Rourke and his mates had the satisfaction of winning the pennant, their 59-25 record five games better than that of a Boston nine that featured a standout rookie outfielder named John O'Rourke.[17] Shortly after the 1879 season ended, the league's magnates adopted the first version of the reserve clause, a contractual restraint that bound five designated players from each team to the club they had played for the previous season. The owners of the Providence club, however, chose not to reserve Jim O'Rourke for the 1880 campaign. And Jim, anxious to play alongside his older brother, signed with Boston, his previous difficulties with team owner Soden notwithstanding. Sadly, the season was a disappointment to all concerned. John, seriously shaken up in a late-May crash into the outfield fence at Troy, saw his bating average plummet 66 points from the previous season's .341 and posted reduced numbers across the board. Jim also had an off year, matching his brother's .275 batting average but with a league-leading six home runs. Arthur Soden, meanwhile, had to endure a sixth-place finish for his Boston team and the reduced revenue at the gate that came with it.

Boston placed neither O'Rourke on its reserved list for the 1881 season, and the brothers were soon entertaining offers from other National League clubs. But John, now 32 years old, chose the security of a position with the New Haven Railroad over another diamond campaign.[18] Jim, meanwhile, joined the Buffalo Bisons as playing captain/manager. Under O'Rourke's direction, the club, a sad-sack 24-58 the previous season, posted a respectable 45-38 record. Like that of the franchise, Jim's own performance rebounded. Playing mostly third base, he batted .302 with 71 runs scored, fourth best in the league. The 1881 season also featured delivery of perhaps the most celebrated exemplar of O'Rourke grandiloquence. In response to a request by shortstop Johnny Peters for a $10 advance on his salary, the Orator replied:

"The exigencies of the occasion and the condition of our exchequer will not permit anything of that sort at this period of our existence. Subsequent developments in the field of finance may remove the present gloom and we may emerge into a condition where we may see our way clear to reply in the affirmative to your exceedingly modest request."[19]

Dealing with cash-strapped players fell to O'Rourke because, in addition to leading the team on the field, he also performed the tasks of club bursar, traveling secretary and prefect of discipline. A number of the pleasure-seekers on the Buffalo team—most notably mound stalwart Pud Galvin—chafed under the governance of their chief, a nondrinking, nonsmoking taskmaster who took his leadership responsibilities very seriously.[20] But like him or not, the Bisons continued their competitive play under O'Rourke, posting winning records in both the 1882 and 1883 seasons, if not challenging for the National League pennant. Nor did the press of his off-field obligations appear to take a toll on O'Rourke. For on July 3, 1883, he appeared in his 319th consecutive game, setting a new league standard. By mid-September, Jim was near the close of a season that would see him hit .328. Then tragedy struck. On September 15, 1883, second daughter Anna died from a sudden illness. She was only 9 years old. Upon receiving the news, a grief-stricken Jim O'Rourke immediately left the team for the funeral in Bridgeport. Four days later he returned to Buffalo to guide the Bisons to the finish of a 52-45 campaign.

During his time in Buffalo, O'Rourke, an implacable foe of the reserve clause, had operated without one in his contract. Rather, he and the club owners proceeded under a yearly gentleman's agreement that O'Rourke would maintain allegiance to the Bisons franchise. But in the spring of 1884 Jim served notice that this would be his last season in Buffalo. Despite his impending departure, he continued to serve the club diligently. Before the season's start, he alleviated playing-field problems by locating more suitable grounds and superintending the construction of Olympic Park, a handsome new venue for the Bisons. O'Rourke then led the team on the field by example, batting .347 and pacing the National League with 162 base hits.[21] At season's end the Bisons were in third place, their 64-47 record closing the O'Rourke ledger as Buffalo field leader with a four-year mark of 206-169 (.549).

The year 1885 proved a watershed in the professional life of Jim O'Rourke. After Anna's death he was determined to find a club close enough to Bridgeport to allow him to spend Sundays at home with the ever-expanding O'Rourke brood.[22] Using a bidding war among interested teams to his advantage, Jim extracted a $4,000 contract from the New York National League club. He also negotiated the now standard player reserve clause out of his 1885 deal. In New York O'Rourke joined the Hall of Famers—Buck Ewing, John Montgomery Ward, Tim Keefe, Roger Connor, and Mickey Welch—being aggregated by team owner John B. Day and manager Jim Mutrie[23] and reached the pinnacle of his playing career. His time in New York had other ramifications as well. He formed a close and lasting friendship with Connor, a fellow Connecticut (Waterbury) Irishman as taciturn as O'Rourke was loquacious. After their major-league days were over, the two played pivotal roles in the establishment of minor-league ball in their home state. Of perhaps more consequence, the signing with New York reunited O'Rourke with former Providence teammate Ward, a baseball visionary who would shortly put into practice the fundamental employment principles that O'Rourke held dear. In the fierce Players League War to come, O'Rourke (and Tim Keefe) would serve as commander Ward's primary lieutenants. In the short term, however, the reconnection to Ward had more immediate effect. Emulating Ward's example, Jim enrolled in law school during the offseason, his tuition at Yale being underwritten by the Giants.[24] In time the practice of law would provide a congenial outlet for the Orator's delight in speech.

The 1885 New York Giants ran roughshod over the opposition, posting an 85-27 record. Its .759 winning percentage is the highest ever recorded by a major-league team—that finished in second place. With Cap Anson, John Clarkson, and the irrepressible King Kelly at the peak of their Cooperstown-bound careers, the Chicago White Stockings (87-25) were two games better than New York. Still, the season was a good one for O'Rourke. He batted .300, with 119 runs scored and a league-best 16 triples. But trouble for O'Rourke and his playing brethren was on the horizon.

Shortly after the 1885 season was over, National League magnates adopted a $2,000 ceiling on player salaries. Within days the Brotherhood of Professional

Base Ball Players was formed, with Giants Ward, O'Rourke, and Keefe being the prime movers in this new union movement.[25] New York owner Day, an outspoken opponent of the salary ceiling, promptly ignored it, signing O'Rourke to a $3,000/no-reserve-clause contract for the 1886 season. Other club bosses likewise disregarded the ceiling. But the well of magnate/player relations had been poisoned, with consequences that would manifest themselves in due course. In the meantime, Jim O'Rourke continued his dependable play in a Giants uniform, batting .309 and patrolling center field when not spelling Buck Ewing behind the plate. But in 1887, a walks-as-hits-inflated .344 batting average did not camouflage a fall-off in the performance of the now 37-year-old O'Rourke.[26] Nor was the team maintaining standards, having slid to fourth place. Indeed, for Jim O'Rourke the year's highlights occurred mostly away from the diamond: graduation from Yale Law School in June, followed by his passing the Connecticut bar examination and admission to the practice of law on November 5, 1887.[27]

In 1888 a resurgent Giants nine, with relatively minor contribution from a .274 hitting O'Rourke, captured the National League crown, their 84-47 record nine games superior to that of the runner-up White Stockings. The Giants then claimed the title world champions, defeating the American Association St. Louis Browns in a postseason match of league standard-bearers, but again with little help from O'Rourke (.222/1 RBI in 10 games). But suspicions that the Orator was finally slowing down were confounded during the 1889 campaign. Jim's .321 batting mark included 46 extra-base hits and, although never swift afoot, the 39-year-old also managed to steal 33 bases. The Giants, meanwhile, repeated as world champions, nipping Boston at the wire for the National League pennant and then besting the Brooklyn Bridegrooms of the American Association in a "World Series" that saw Jim O'Rourke bat a robust .389, with two homers and seven RBIs.

The success of the 1889 Giants' season had been accompanied by simmering player discontent in New York and elsewhere. Long resentful of the reserve clause, the players were further aggrieved by the implementation of a rigid salary-classification scheme by National League club owners. Shortly after the 1889 baseball championship had been decided, the players struck back, announcing the formation of an employee-controlled major-league operation, the Players League. The brainchild of John Montgomery Ward, the new circuit would raise havoc on the baseball scene, successfully recruiting virtually all the front-line players in the National League and a number of American Association standouts as well. The Giants were particularly hard-hit, losing their entire lineup save for aging pitcher Mickey Welsh and outfielder Mike Tiernan, to the Players League. A combative John B. Day retaliated by seeking injunctive relief against Ward, O'Rourke, Keefe, and Ewing, but to no avail. Jim and the others prevailed in court and, except for Ward, player-manager of the Players League team in Brooklyn, commenced the 1890 season playing for the Players League Giants in a new ballpark (Brotherhood Field) separated from the National League operation in the New Polo Grounds (later Manhattan Field) by no more than a ten-foot-wide alley and the stadium walls.

Playing for the Ewing-led Big Giants, Jim O'Rourke registered exceptional numbers during the 1890 season. In addition to a .360 batting average, the 40-year-old posted career-best figures in hits (172), doubles (37), home runs (9), RBIs (115), slugging (.515), and on-base percentage (.410), all achieved while playing in only 111 games. O'Rourke's performance, however, was not duplicated by his team (third place). Nor did the Players League prosper as a whole. In fact, the season had been a catastrophe for the new circuit's financial backers. That fall they were outmaneuvered in peace settlement negotiations by A.G. Spalding, the hard-nosed de-facto leader of the National League, and bluffed into dissolving the Players League. In New York, National League owner Day and his Player League counterparts merged operations, precipitating the return of O'Rourke and others to their former club.[28] By virtue of the terms of the consolidation agreement, O'Rourke also became a small shareholder in the reconstituted New York Giants franchise. He then resumed his post in the Giants' outfield, posting respectable batting averages for the 1891 (.295) and 1892 (.304) campaigns.

Jim O'Rourke's tenure as a New York Giant ended on a sour note. Late in the 1892 season manager Pat Powers began cleaning house. Among the veterans released by the Giants was the 42-year-old O'Rourke, his contract assigned to Washington for the 1893 season, As recounted by one Giants historian:

"O'Rourke was outraged. In a clubhouse scene, he denounced Powers as a fool who was running the team into the ground. John Day, supporting his manager, suspended O'Rourke for insubordination and outrage to authority. After thinking it over, the Orator apologized to Powers and was reinstated. But he did not return to the lineup."[29]

His association with the Giants severed at season's end, O'Rourke assumed the post of player-manager for the Washington Senators, a former American Association franchise admitted to the National League in 1892.[30] Appearing in all but one of the Senators' 130 games, O'Rourke batted a creditable .287, with 95 RBIs. But his supporting crew was hapless, the team's last place 40-89 finish prompting the release of manager O'Rourke and the end of his career in the major leagues. Including the one-year debacle in Washington, manager Jim O'Rourke posted a 246-258 (.488) record in five seasons as a major-league field leader. Far more distinguished were his accomplishments as a player: a .313 batting average over 22 seasons in the National Association, National League, and Players League, with 2,678 base hits[31], the most of any 19th-century big-league ballplayer not named Anson. He had also been a member of eight league champion teams.

With his major-league career over, O'Rourke returned to Bridgeport, where he practiced law and oversaw his real-estate interests. But he was unable to get baseball out of his system. A brief turn as a National League umpire during the 1894 season gave O'Rourke a taste of the abuse that the men in blue were forced to endure. By mid-June he had had enough, pronouncing the duties of an umpire "too trying" for him to continue[32]. Thereafter, he again took to the field as a player, making appearances for the St. Joseph T, B&L Association, a crack semipro team that played near home. Long active in parish and civic affairs, Democrat O'Rourke stood for election to the Connecticut legislature that fall but fell victim to the Republican landslide that swept the nation.[33] In 1895 he attempted to organize a professional league in Connecticut but the effort was stillborn. His newly formed Bridgeport Victors team was therefore obliged to play as an independent, with O'Rourke himself in uniform for eight of its games.[34] More noteworthy than his own play, however, was O'Rourke's engagement of Harry Herbert, a black outfielder and Bridgeport resident who would spend the next four seasons playing for O'Rourke teams.[35]

In 1896 Jim assembled eight Connecticut teams into the Naugatuck Valley League. With its 46-year-old catcher-manager leading the way with a .437 batting average, the Victors captured the league pennant. Reorganized once again and renamed the Connecticut State League, the circuit soon included a team from Waterbury sponsored by old O'Rourke teammate and friend Roger Connor.[36] For the next eight seasons Jim O'Rourke's name would regularly appear in the Bridgeport lineup, the team renamed the Orators in 1898 in his honor. In addition to his role as player, manager, and chief league official, O'Rourke subsequently became active in the National Association of Professional Base Ball Leagues, a minor-league protective organization that he helped found in 1902. As if the above were insufficient to occupy his time, O'Rourke also attended to various local responsibilities. From 1901 to 1903, he was a Bridgeport fire commissioner, a post that often brought him into heated disagreement with Denis Mulvihill, the city's hard-drinking mayor. As reported by O'Rourke authority Bernard Crowley, "On occasion, police intervention was needed to end their debates."[37] Later O'Rourke served on the Bridgeport Paving Commission. He was also an active member of the Royal Arcanum, the Connecticut Bar Association, the Bridgeport Elks, and the Knights of Columbus.

In 1903 a proud O'Rourke was joined in the Orators lineup by his son Jimmy, an infielder who later played for the New York Highlanders.[38] The following season, 54-year-old Jim O'Rourke, still the regular Bridgeport backstop, appeared in his 1,999th and final major-league game. With the New York Giants on the verge of their first pennant since 1889, manager John McGraw summoned O'Rourke, the last active member of that old championship team, to catch the title clincher. And the old warrior did not disappoint, handling Joe McGinnity over all nine innings of a 7-5 victory over Cincinnati.[39] He even went 1-for-4 at the plate.[40]

Before the 1906 season, Connecticut State League President James H. O'Rourke, erstwhile nemesis of player salary limitations, announced that the league's $1,800 ceiling on player salaries "will be strictly enforced" by the league office.[41] O'Rourke himself remained the everyday catcher (93 games) for the Orators that season but thereafter his playing time began to dwindle. Still, in January 1910 he told a reporter that the secret to his perpetual youth and vigor was "baseball. It is the real elixir of life."[42] But shortly thereafter, he gave up the Bridgeport franchise, selling the club to H. Eugene McCann, a friend who had once managed a minor-league team in Jersey City.

Baseball was not the only thing taking a smaller place in Jim O'Rourke's life. His children were now mostly married and out of the house. So was his mother, Catherine O'Donnell O'Rourke, who had died in 1907, aged about 85. But the real blow came on June 14, 1910, when Annie, Jim's wife of 38 years, died from the lingering complications of a fall. A year later that loss was compounded by the death of brother John, felled by a heart attack while handling baggage on a Boston railway platform. Jim endeavored to fill the void by remaining engaged in the affairs of the National Association of Professional Baseball Players and the Connecticut State League. And on September 14, 1912, Connecticut State League president O'Rourke donned the pads a final time, catching nine innings for the New Haven Wings in a game against Waterbury. He was then 62 years old.

Jim's last years in baseball were not happy ones. In February 1916 he lost a protracted battle with New England League President Tim Murnane over the direction of minor-league baseball in the region. Among the casualties of the New England Baseball War was an O'Rourke/Murnane friendship that dated to when the two had been young teammates on the Stratford Osceolas. Withdrawing from Organized Baseball, Jim devoted his remaining years to his law practice and doting on his grandchildren. He also remained busy with parish and professional duties, serving on the executive committee of the Park City Knights of Columbus World War I fund and handling matters as a member of the National Board of Arbitration.

On New Year's Day 1919, O'Rourke braved a blizzard to consult a client and then caught a severe cold on the walk home from his office. Pneumonia quickly set in. He died seven days later, aged 68 and deeply mourned in the Bridgeport community. A locally published obituary extolled him as "a kindly father, a splendid citizen, a true friend," and a man who would be remembered by baseball fans for "his great skill as an exponent of the national game."[43] After a funeral Mass at St. Mary's Church, Jim's remains were buried in the family plot at St. Michael's Cemetery in nearby Stratford. He was survived by his seven children and his sister, Sarah O'Rourke Grant.

In 1945 the memory of Jim O'Rourke was permanently preserved via his enshrinement in the National Baseball Hall of Fame. His Cooperstown plaque tersely summarizes his career but is far too small to reflect the scope of his contributions to the game. As a pioneer player, union organizer and early minor-league executive, James Henry "Orator" O'Rourke was an exemplary figure, one eminently worthy of baseball's highest accolade.

SOURCES

In addition to the sources specifically cited in the notes below, the following works were consulted during the preparation of this profile:

Marty Appel, *Slide, Kelly, Slide: The Wild Life and Times of Mike "King" Kelly, Baseball's First Superstar* (Lanham, Maryland: Scarecrow Press, 1999).

Christopher Devine, *Harry Wright: The Father of Professional Baseball* (Jefferson, North Carolina: McFarland & Company, Inc., 2003).

Bill James, *The New Bill James Historical Baseball Abstract* (New York: The Free Press, 2001).

David Nemec, *The Great Encyclopedia of 19th Century Major League Baseball* (New York: David I. Fine Books, 1997).

Harold Seymour (with Dorothy J. Mills), *Baseball: The Early Years* (New York: Oxford Univ. Press, 1960).

David Stevens, *Baseball's Radical for All Seasons: A Biography of John Montgomery Ward* (Lanham, Maryland: Scarecrow Press, 1998).

The writer is indebted to O'Rourke experts Mike Roer and Bernie Crowley for their generous assistance in the preparation of this profile.

NOTES

1. O'Rourke himself usually gave his birthday as August 24 and early biographical sketches often have him born in 1852 or 1854. The September 1, 1850, birthday given above as well as other biographical information about O'Rourke is derived from various US censuses, material contained in O'Rourke's file at the Giamatti Research Center, National Baseball Hall of Fame and Museum, Cooperstown, New York, and, especially, Mike Roer's thorough and informative biography *Orator O'Rourke, The Life of a Baseball Radical* (Jefferson, North Carolina: McFarland & Company, Inc., 2005), and the O'Rourke family genealogical chart accessible at www.MikeRoer.com. E-mails from O'Rourke expert Bernard Crowley also provided the writer with helpful information on the O'Rourkes.

2. Roer, 8. Jim's siblings were brother John (1849-1911) and sister Sarah (1854-1931). An elder brother named Patrick (1837-1852) died when Jim was a toddler and other O'Rourke children, now lost to history, may not have survived infancy.

3. Roer, 8-16.

4. Hugh O'Rourke, a farmer and part-time night watchman, died of tetanus on December 31, 1868, about age 56. Cause of death per e-mail from Bernie Crowley to the writer, dated October 10, 2011.

5. Roer, 17-24.

6. Ibid., 25-26. O'Rourke's salary for the 1872 season was $500.

7. Statistics cited in this profile are taken from www.baseball-reference.com.

8. For almost a century, no account of the O'Rourke signing with Boston was complete without reference to Wright's alleged request that Jim drop the O' from his surname, lest offense be given to the "Puritan" backers of the Red Stockings club. To this, Jim gallantly replied that he "would rather die than give up my father's name. A million dollars would not tempt me." See e.g., the O'Rourke obituary in the *Bridgeport Evening Post*, January 9, 1919, or Bernard J. Crowley, "James Henry O'Rourke," in *Baseball's First Stars* (Cleveland: SABR, 1996), 324. O'Rourke's biographer, however, suspects the anecdote is apocryphal, tracing its print origins to a 1906 column by Boston sportswriter (and former O'Rourke teammate) Tim Murnane. See Roer, 33. The writer is also skeptical, as the business entrepreneur/sportsmen who backed the Boston club (Ivers Adams, John Conkey, N.T. Apollonio, et al.) were hardly Puritan or Boston Brahmin types. And whatever anti-Irish prejudice they may have harbored privately would have been more than offset by the financial attraction of drawing the city's burgeoning Irish population to the ballpark. Perhaps to that end, the 1873 Boston Red Stockings would occasionally feature an all-Irish-Catholic outfield, with O'Rourke in center flanked by Andy Leonard and Jack Manning.

9. During the 1873 and 1874 seasons, O'Rourke boarded at the South Boston home of Harry Wright and family. This daily exposure to Wright's dignified conduct and professionalism would have a lifelong effect on young O'Rourke. Wright also taught Jim, previously a dead pull hitter, how to hit to right field.

10. O'Rourke's winning heave covered 369 feet on the fly, as reported in the *Boston Herald*, August 30, 1874.

11. Roer, 43-48. The cricket playing abilities of Harry, George, and Sammy Wright, the sons of an English-born cricket professional, came as no surprise. But apart from O'Rourke and pitching ace A.G. Spalding, the other Americans were pretty much hopeless at the game.

12. Roer, 49-50, citing the Harry Wright Correspondence, Vol. I, 1874-1875, preserved in the Spalding Collection at the New York Public Library. See also William J. Ryczek, *Blackguards and Red Stockings: A History of Baseball's National Association, 1871-1875*, (Wallingford, Connecticut: Colebrook Press, 1992), 203-204.

13. O'Rourke had not seen a salary increase in three years, playing the 1874 and 1875 seasons for the same $800 stipend that he had received in his first year in Boston. Roer, 62.

14. Soden succeeded N.T. Apollonio as club president. With the assistance of team secretary William Conant and treasurer James Billings—known, with Soden, on the sports pages as the Triumvirs — Soden asserted absolute control over the Boston franchise. He was also a major force in NL executive councils. For more, see Brian McKenna's excellent BioProject profile of Arthur H. Soden.

15. After a postseason investigation, star Louisville pitcher Jim Devlin and teammates George Hall, Bill Craver, and Al Nichols were permanently expelled from baseball by National League President William Hulbert.

16. Roer, 67-71. Throughout his long playing career, O'Rourke's uniform would always be kept in immaculate condition, courtesy of the women in his household.

17. John O'Rourke, a left-handed batter and thrower, matched his younger brother's production, batting .341, with a .521 slugging average and a league-leading 62 RBIs.

18. John would play a few games for the Philadelphia Athletics of the minor-league Eastern Championship Association in 1881 and then sit out the 1882 diamond season entirely. He returned to the majors in 1883, batting .270 for the New York Metropolitans of the American Association. At the close of that season, John retired from baseball, working the rest of his life as a railway baggage handler.

19 As recounted by sportswriter Sam Crane in a profile of O'Rourke published in an unidentified circa 1911 article, preserved in the Jim O'Rourke file at the Giamatti Research Center. O'Rourke did not confine such rhetorical extravagance to his baseball charges, According to his daughter Edith, he also corrected misbehaving O'Rourke children "in five- syllable words." Lee Allen column, *The Sporting News,* February 10, 1968.

20 Player discontent with manager O'Rourke was periodically noted in the press. See e.g., *Sporting Life,* July 16, 1884, and April 22, 1885.

21 For 85 years O'Rourke was deemed the 1884 National League batting titlist. But in 1969 revision of player statistics by the MLB Records Committee conferred the championship on King Kelly (.354). Then in 1999 the MLB reversed course and returned the crown to O'Rourke. But the authoritative baseball-reference.com sticks with Kelly as the batting champ. For more on the controversy, Roer, 114-115, and John Thorn et al., eds., *Total Baseball,* 7th ed., (Kingston, New York: Total Sports Publishing, 2001), 528-531.

22 Wife Annie O'Rourke ultimately gave birth to eight children: daughters Sarah, the late Anna, Agnes, Ida, Lillian, Irene, and Edith, and son James Stephen, known as Queenie. As the National League did not then play games on Sunday, Jim would only be a train ride away from home most weekends if he signed with a team that played in New York, Providence, or Boston.

23 Technically, the team, as well as the New York Metropolitans of the American Association, was operated by the Metropolitan Exhibition Company, the corporate alter ego of Day and junior partners Joseph Gordon, Charles Dillingham, and Walter Appleton.

24 In June 1885 Ward earned a law degree from Columbia University. At about the same time, the New York club, formerly called the Gothams or simply the New-Yorks, acquired the moniker Giants, the name that the team soon made famous.

25 For more on Giants involvement in the players union movement, see James J. Hardy, Jr., *The New York Giants Base Ball Club, The Growth of a Team and a Sport, 1870-1900* (Jefferson, North Carolina: McFarland & Company, Inc., 1996), 92-94.

26 For one peculiar season, a base on balls was counted as a hit. Elimination of this scoring anomaly reduces O'Rourke's 1887 batting average to .285.

27 Roer, 124-132. While attending the law school, O'Rourke also coached the Yale baseball team.

28 Genuinely fond of the generous and genial Day, Ward had attempted to avoid injury to the Giants owner by offering him a lucrative position in the Players League executive offices. Ever the National League loyalist, Day refused and waged a stubborn battle against the Players League that ultimately precipitated his financial ruin.

29 Hardy, 143-144; *New York Times,* September 14, 1892.

30 Washington was one of four American Association teams that survived that league's demise at the end of the 1891 season. To accommodate Washington and the other new arrivals, the National League expanded to 12 teams in 1892.

31 Adjusted to eliminate the walk/base hit aberration of the 1887 season, O'Rourke's career numbers are a .310 batting average with 2,639 hits.

32 Roer, 195-199. On occasion thereafter, O'Rourke umpired college games.

33 Roer, op. cit, 201-202. Biographer Roer relates that Jim O'Rourke described himself as a "Theodore Roosevelt Democrat." But another O'Rourke authority identifies him as a Republican. See Bernard Crowley's sketch of O'Rourke in *Columbia, The Knights of Columbus Magazine,* May 1994, 14.

34 As per www.baseball-reference.com. O'Rourke batted .429 in 35 at-bats.

35 Roer, 208. While reflective of O'Rourke's fair-mindedness, the move was not particularly groundbreaking, as Herbert had played the 1894 season with Pawtucket in the New England League.

36 Connor remained involved in Connecticut minor-league ball for years, playing for the Waterbury team himself until the age of 47.

37 Crowley, *Columbia,* 14.

38 A career minor leaguer, Queenie O'Rourke appeared in 34 games for the Highlanders in 1908, hitting .231. The origin of his nickname is a mystery but both Mike Roer and Bernie Crowley hypothesize that it may have come from growing up the only male child in a household full of O'Rourke women.

39 For a fuller account of the circumstances, see Benton J. Stark, *The Year They Called Off the World Series: A True Story* (Garden City, New York: Avery Publishing Group, Inc., 1991), 156-157.

40 For decades, the 54-year-old O'Rourke was considered the oldest player to record a base hit in MLB history. Recent research by SABR members Cliff Blau and Richard Matalzky, however, has transferred the honor to St. Louis Browns coach Charlie O'Leary, 59 years old when he delivered a pinch hit late in the 1934 season.

41 *The Sporting News,* February 24, 1906. Age and a change in occupational station had also transformed the attitude of former union firebrand John Montgomery Ward. Now a corporate lawyer, Ward had as a client the National League, whose once-hated reserve clause Ward had no compunction about defending in court.

42 *New York Herald,* January 11, 1910.

43 *Bridgeport Evening Post,* January 9, 1919.

FRALEY W. ROGERS

BY RICHARD "DIXIE" TOURANGEAU

SPORTSWRITER/HISTORIAN George V. Tuohey hastily put together his famous *A History of the Boston Base Ball Club—1871 to 1897* in mid-1897. It was published to help celebrate Boston's National League Beaneaters capture of the 1897 pennant after three unsuccessful seasons. Though weighted toward teams and players from the 1890s, the book does have blurbs about players from the Hub's first two decades. The 1870s section recounts the team's calculated organization by Ivers W. Adams and the Wright brothers' superb leadership of the National Association's Red Stockings dynasty. Of the 30-plus players with short biographies (including photos), nine are from that era. Only three have photos, Harry and George Wright, of course, and one-year right fielder Fraley W. Rogers. Aside from his name being included in the 1872 roster, Rogers is not mentioned anywhere else in the volume.

Born in Brooklyn on December 25, 1850, Fraley Rogers grew up in a baseball-crazed family. He was the youngest of five children of Albert and Abbie Rogers. Albert is listed briefly as being a hotel employee and a saloonkeeper but later had a steady job at the Fulton Fish Market in Manhattan. Oldest brother Albert H. played ball in the early 1860s as did the middle son, the more famous sibling, Mortimer Maxson Rogers, one of the most gregarious and cleverest entrepreneurial personalities connected with early base ball. Both boys can be found in Brooklyn Resolute lineups as early as 1861, and in one game both Albert and Mort hit home runs to help beat Niagara, 23-13. Fraley was the youngest child, being born at a perfect time to later join the Red Stockings in 1872 for their first championship campaign.

Following the basepaths of his brothers, teenager Fraley played for various Brooklyn teams. Box scores show that Mort got to play with both brothers, but the trio cannot be found playing in a game together.

By 1850 the Rogers residence was at 35 South Sixth Street and it was soon a neighborhood mecca for anything concerning base ball in the Williamsburg section of Brooklyn. Fraley's first amateur games of note were with the Resolutes in 1865. Mort was there, too, before heading to Boston to play for the Lowells and to start his various businesses. The Rogers boys could not prevent the Resolutes from losing all seven games they played. In 1866 Fraley graduated to the Brooklyn Stars and continued to play with them for the next six seasons, 87 percent of the games. On occasion there were borough "all-star" games, and Fraley, like his siblings, was usually on the Brooklyn squad. He was an outfielder mostly although he did play all the infield positions at one time or another. Bob Manly and Herb Worth were two of his longer-lasting teammates and in 1868 pitching phenom William Arthur "Candy" Cummings came to the Stars. In most Brooklyn Stars box scores from 1868-71, Fraley was the leadoff batter. In 1871 he played right field, first base, and sometimes catcher, while brother Mort was in center field and first. Albert H. was a team director.

Despite his young age Rogers was always in the top echelon for Brooklyn in most hitting categories, hits, runs, and total bases, and he was a better-than-average fielder. The Stars played against George Wright and Dave Birdsall in New York (Unions of Morrisania) before George went to Cincinnati in 1869. In June 1870 the Wright-led Red Stockings beat the Stars handily at the Capitoline Grounds but the game gave the Wrights another chance to see Fraley in action. By 1872 Reds flychaser Birdsall was just too old for the speedy National Association pitching so the Stockings went looking for an agile young replacement. Excelling in the rugged New York base ball wars was to Fraley's credit and being the brother of Mort Rogers only enhanced his résumé. The 1871 Stars whipped their amateur opponents (22-1) but were 1-12 against professional teams, though most of those games were close. According to the *New York Clipper*'s February 10 final Stars stats, Fraley had the most at-bats and was second in hits and fourth in team average in his 32 games.

Fraley and 1871 Washington Olympic (and ex-Cincinnati Red Stocking) Andy Leonard were the big additions in the Hub Stockings' 1872 roster. The two replaced veteran Birdsall and three mediocre fly chasers, Fred Cone, Frank Barrows, and Sam Jackson, in the South End pasture. Combined, the trio had hit .212 and scored 47 runs in 1871. In 1872 Leonard (.349/57 runs) and Fraley (.275/39) easily improved those numbers.

Fraley is listed as 5-feet-8 and a stocky 184 pounds. Though very nice, the picture in Tuohey's history book doesn't make clear whether Fraley swung right- or left-handed.

Rogers' signing by the Stockings may have seemed smooth but staying there was bumpy. Philadelphia-born John Joseph Ryan was also brought into camp, coming north in April from a team in Savannah, Georgia. Rogers (his first name was often written as "Franey") was unlucky from the start of spring practice, first damaging a finger (thought broken) and then badly spraining an ankle. Ryan (three hits/three runs) was in the lineup on April 4, Fast Day, the first game that saw the Reds clobber a "Picked Nine," 32-0. In ensuing exhibitions Ryan and Rogers were in and out of the lineup. Though Ryan's stats were good, as Boston got closer to starting the season Rogers was more often in right field and batting eighth.

Ryan never played for the Red Stockings in any championship games, but in 1873 played two games for the Philadelphia Whites. Ryan (156 games, .208, outfield and pitcher) was in professional ball for the next four years—each season for a different team. After Philadelphia, he played in succession for NA Baltimore and New Haven, then NL Louisville and Cincinnati.

The Reds began their 1872 championship quest on April 30 with a 26-3 stomping of the Washington Nationals, as they opened with seven road contests. In his first 10 Association games, Rogers hit only .188, with his best coming in the only loss, 10-7 to the Athletics in Philadelphia. He got two hits, scored, and knocked in a run against ace Dick McBride. The Reds started 22-1, but lost to host McBride again on July 27, 9-1. Fraley's two hits/RBI (eighth inning) prevented a brilliantly pitched "chicago" for Philly.

By September it was clear that the Reds (32-3) were going to be the Association's second champion. Rogers had been only an average hitter (.275). Omitting his .230 efforts in 18 games versus McBride and old Stars teammate Candy Cummings (Mutuals), Fraley hit .302. His best games were: May 7, back at his "home" Capitoline Grounds, when he had four RBIs in a 23-3 win over the Brooklyn Atlantics; July 4 at Mansfield, Connecticut, as his five scores helped beat the hosts, 25-12; and August 2 versus the Atlantics at the South End Grounds, when he smashed four hits (three runs/three RBIs, and his only triple), in a 26-3 victory. During June and July Rogers averaged two hits per game, hitting in 14 of 15 tilts. His only home run

Fraley Rogers, 1872 (Spalding Collection)

came in Cleveland on September 19, off "Uncle Al" Pratt, in a 12-7 win (he also had a double). On June 10, Rogers' two hits and two runs off Cummings forced the game into extra innings, a first for Boston. They won 3-2 in 11 frames.

Fielding was not Rogers' forte; in 62 outfield chances in 1872, he committed 13 errors for a fielding percentage of .790. He played outfield in 41 games and 6 at first base, sometimes both in the same game.

The Reds (39-8-1) were the champs of 1872 and Rogers was a solid part of Boston's first pennant-winning club. He played in 45 of 48 games and hit better (.275) than Charlie Gould or Harry Wright (both .255). Though he chose to retire in 1873, he was inserted in the lineup for two games, but no news outlet explained why. On July 4 at the South End Grounds, Boston split a doubleheader with the Resolutes of Elizabeth, New Jersey, a short-lived franchise. Rookie Jack Manning played first base in both games. The next day Fraley Rogers appeared at the first sack (the 23rd Reds game), got two hits, and scored in a 13-2 win. On July 16 the Reds traveled to Springfield, Massachusetts, for a "home" game at that city's Hampden Park. McBride's Athletics provided Boston with a 21-13 victory on a rutty, unlevel field. In addition, former Brown University pitcher A.J. Jennings was called to umpire when Atlantics manager Bob Ferguson failed to show up. Jennings' competency was questioned but the game was completed. Fraley got two more hits, scored, and committed two errors, and the final out ended his baseball career.

Rogers stayed in Boston for a few years. He married Anne Maria Cole, daughter of a Boston tailor, on October 20, 1874. The couple moved back to New York by the late 1870s. The *New York Clipper* of May 21, 1881, confirmed news that astounded baseball fans.[1] On May 10 in his Harlem apartment (119 West 126th Street) and without any warning, Fraley Rogers, 31, took a revolver and shot himself in the head. The *Herald Tribune* said he suffered financial difficulties while the *New York Times* claimed the sad ending was due to a delirious, insane reaction to malaria, which Rogers had contracted in 1880. He was a head clerk for fruit magnate Leopold Schepp, and widowed Anne Maria with two children. In the 1990s, SABR historian and former Hall of Fame Library senior researcher Bill Deane made a study of ballplayer suicides. Rogers remains the first such case on his list. With his wife, who remarried in 1883, having connections to Central Massachusetts, Fraley is buried in her family plot at Pine Grove Cemetery in Westborough, about 10 miles east of Worcester, south off Route 9. His name is not on the tall white monument that marks the plot. The fallout of the tragedy was quick, as ill brother Mort, living five miles south in Lower Manhattan, died three days later, leaving wife Eliza and three children. Because her name also disappears from the Brooklyn City Directory at that time, it is possible that Abbie Rogers, their mother, also died in 1881.

Very disappointingly, the *Brooklyn Daily Eagle* did not print any notice of the deaths of two of the borough's most popular Stars of only a decade before. The *Herald Tribune* did mention that he was a former star athlete and expert billiard player.

SOURCES

Boston Courier, Boston Daily Advertiser, Boston Globe, Boston Herald, Brooklyn Daily Eagle, New York Clipper, New York Times, New York Herald Tribune.

US Census, 1850, 1860.

City Directories of Boston, Brooklyn, and New York City.

Massachusetts State Vital Records.

Pine Grove Cemetery administrative records.

Retrosheet.org.

Tuohey, George V. *A History of the Boston Base Ball Club* (Boston: M.F. Quinn, 1897).

Wright, Marshall D. *The National Association of Base Ball Players, 1857-1870* (Jefferson, North Carolina: McFarland, 2000).

Members of the Rogers family are difficult to trace as they managed to elude most censuses and city directories as a rule and the common name doesn't help. Fraley's initial "W" though often used has not been found transcribed as a name and there are no "W" ancestors in the family. Often times Fraley Rogers has a "W" listed as a middle initial but in one place only is there a reference clue as to what it might stand for. The *Clipper* listed the election of team officers and players engaged for the 1872 Red Stockings. An F. "Winslow" is among the group, with Winslow appearing as if it were a surname. All of the other players are mentioned with their regular last names, his is the only odd one. See "Boston Club," *New York Clipper*, December 16, 1871: 290.

NOTES

1   *New York Clipper*, May 21, 1881: 138.

HENRY C. SCHAFER

BY DAVID NEMEC

HENRY SCHAFER WAS THE FIRST major-league player to spend a career spanning eight or more seasons entirely with the same franchise. He was called Harry, probably from early childhood, but had two more colorful baseball-related nicknames. One was Silk Stockings, but he was known best to fellow players as Dexter, the name of the most famous racehorse in North America in the late 1850s and the 1860s.[1] Both nicknames remain without explanation; Schafer was neither particularly fast on the bases nor the scion of a notable family. Too, he was relatively colorless in all and is probably the least remembered regular on the Boston club's dynasty in the 1870s.

Born in Philadelphia on August 14, 1846, the 5-foot-9½, 143-pound right-handed hitter and thrower developed his game on Philadelphia's Parade Grounds along with Bill Hague and Tom Miller. The son of teamster George Schafer, he was one of five children, among them three sisters (Mary, Eliza, and Ann) and a brother, John. His mother's name appears to be missing from the 1850 census, suggesting that she may have been deceased by then, perhaps a victim of childbirth complications.[2]

Schafer began playing organized ball in 1867 with the local Arctic club and then joined the esteemed Philadelphia Athletics the following year, remaining with them through the 1870 season. His last game with the Athletics came on October 19, 1870, at Philadelphia when he played right field in place of West Fisler, who normally occupied the spot, and went 3-for-3 in a 15-3 win over the Brooklyn Atlantics.[3]

When the National Association was formed in the winter of 1870-71, the Athletics were among the first teams to enlist in the first all-professional league, but had no use for Schafer, whose best position was third base. They had already signed Levi Meyerle, one of the strongest hitters in the game at the time, to man third base. Schafer, in contrast, was considered only a mediocre hitter but a respectable fielder and a very accurate thrower, though reportedly a trifle slow at getting rid of the ball.

Left unattached for the coming 1871 season, Schafer eventually signed with the Boston National Association entry, managed by the venerable Harry Wright, the chieftain of the fabled undefeated 1869 Cincinnati Red Stockings. He was in time to join the club in its inaugural spring training tune-up, a 41-10 drubbing in Boston of a local picked nine on April 6, "Fast Day," in which he played third base.[4] In his first official National Association game as a member of Wright's cast on May 5, 1871, at Washington, Schafer again served at third base and bagged two hits in a loosely played 20-18 victory over the Olympic club's Asa Brainard, who had been Wright's pitching ace two years earlier on the Cincinnati Red Stockings.

Schafer ultimately participated in all of Boston's 31 league games and finished with a .282 batting average, 28 points below the club's final composite mark. At that, it was arguably his best season at the plate. In addition to his being the first to serve an eight-year career with the same team, Schafer was also the first position player to log as many as eight full seasons in the majors without ever batting .300. His peak year actually came in his rookie season when he achieved a .692 OPS thanks to a .296 on-base percentage and a .396 slugging average, both career highs. As might be expected, Schafer, after batting in the seventh slot in his initial major-league appearance, from then on generally batted last or next to last in the order.

After achieving regular status at third base in each of his five NA seasons with Boston, Schafer played every inning of every game at the hot corner in 1876 after the club moved to the fledgling National League once the NA disbanded; it was the ultimate tribute to his durability and the third and final time he had either led or tied for the league lead in games played. The first professional league's dissolution was attributable in part to Boston's dominance—four successive pennants after finishing second in 1871, and most by a gigantic margin.

When the Red Stockings returned to their winning ways in 1877 and copped the first of two successive National League pennants, Schafer suddenly found himself demoted to scrub status, playing in only about half of the team's official games while versatile John Morrill saw the most duty at Schafer's former sinecure, third base. Most of Schafer's appearances were in the outfield, where his strong arm came in handy, but he showed little range and fielded an execrable .621, making 11 errors in the 29 chances that came his way.

When all of Boston's regulars—including pitcher Tommy Bond—played almost every inning of every game in 1878, Schafer frequently appeared in exhibition affairs, playing a wide variety of positions, but saw action in only two official contests, both in the outfield, even though he was on the team all season.

His big-league finale in an official National League contest came on August 31, 1878, at Chicago, when he played right field and went 0-for-4 in a 5-2 win over Chicago's rookie star, Terry Larkin. Exactly a month later, on September 30, in Boston's last championship game of the year, Schafer, if he was in the park at all that day, was on the bench at Providence in a 2-1 loss to the Grays' vaunted rookie John M. Ward. Assuming his presence at the game, since his contract was still in force until the season ended, it was his final day of active status as a big leaguer. Though the Bostons launched their annual fall exhibition tour of the East on October 2, just two days after the close of the official season, Schafer seems no longer to have been with the club. There is no evidence of him in any of Boston's 1878 postseason box scores.

Since Schafer was so seldom employed in his last two seasons with Boston, there is good reason to speculate that he may have been kept on the team solely because he was among the several players Harry Wright signed to multiyear contracts after raiders from other National Association teams signed four of Wright's biggest stars to contracts for the 1876 season while the 1875 campaign was still under way, and Schafer's contract was a three-year deal that expired

Harry Schafer (Spalding Collection)

in the fall of 1878.[5] In any event, Wright clearly made no effort to retain Schafer once the 1878 season was in the books. Seeing no more future for himself in the National League, Schafer joined several other former Boston players, including Andy Leonard and Tim Murnane, on the Albany club of the National Association (by then a minor league) in the spring of 1879, and later that season he played briefly with the Rochester Hop Bitters of the same loop. Toward the end of the summer the *Cleveland Plain Dealer* reported that he was "now manager of a Boston club room."[6]

As late as 1886, Schafer considered making a comeback with the Rochester International Association team under manager Frank Bancroft, but wisely refrained in view of his age; he was by then nearing 40.[7]

Three years later, Schafer was listed among the many ex-Boston players the *Chicago Tribune* cited for being owed back pay from 1877 when Boston's tightfisted owner, Arthur Soden, taxed the entire Boston team 50 cents a day for expenses while on the road and $30 per year for uniforms, and held the assessed amount out of their last pay checks. Although the players agreed to it at the time because Soden cried poor and claimed club was losing money, they later learned differently.[8] Not surprisingly, nothing came of the Chicago paper's plea for belated retribution.

Over the next 30 years Schafer frequently appeared at old timer's events in Boston and was a close follower of both Hub major-league teams, the National League Braves and the American League Red Sox. On one such occasion, when he was spotted in attendance at a local game, *Sporting Life* observed: "The veteran Harry Schafer, of the Bostons of the early days, scarcely ever misses a game and a better preserved and more genial chap one would scarcely want to meet. ..."[9]

At some point during his playing days, Schafer married Delphine Knower, who predeceased him. The couple had one child, a daughter, Bertha. In May 1921, on the anniversary of Boston's first major-league game 50 years earlier, he was among the four players from the team still alive, joining Cal McVey, Frank Barrows, and George Wright.[10] Schafer was residing by then in Philadelphia with his daughter, having moved there from Boston several years earlier. He died in the city of his birth on February 28, 1935, at age 88 of chronic myocarditis, leading to mesenteric thrombosis, and was buried in Philadelphia's Fernwood Cemetery.[11]

NOTES

1 *The Sporting News*, January 4, 1896.
2 Ancestry.com.
3 *New York Clipper*, October 20, 1879.
4 *New York Clipper*, April 7, 1871.
5 Among them was Joe Borden who was stripped by Wright of his pitching duties during the course of the 1876 season and fulfilled the remaining time on his multiyear contract as a groundskeeper for the club.
6 *Cleveland Plain Dealer*, November 29, 1879: 1.
7 *The Sporting News*, June 21, 1886.
8 *Chicago Tribune*, February 3, 1889.
9 *Sporting Life*, June 29, 1907.
10 *Boston Globe*, April 17, 1921.
11 *The Sporting News*, March 7, 1935.

AL SPALDING

BY BILL MCMAHON

ALBERT SPALDING'S LIFE STORY could have been written by Horatio Alger. He had three careers—as a baseball pitcher, a club owner, and a sporting-goods tycoon—and was very successful at all of them. A fourth career, in politics, was just getting under way when he died. And despite an initial setback, ultimately he might well have been successful there, too.

The first of three children, Spalding was born on September 2, 1850, in Byron, Illinois, near Rockford, to James and Harriet Spalding. The family was fairly affluent, owning land and horses. However, James Spalding died when Albert was 8 years old, and the family subsequently moved to Rockford. Albert preceded them, living with an aunt, and it is said that he began playing baseball as a defense against loneliness. He became good enough at it to be asked to join the leading amateur team, the Forest Citys.

In 1867 the Chicago Excelsiors sponsored a tournament that featured the Washington Nationals, regarded as the best team in the country. The Nationals routed the Excelsiors, 49-4, but Spalding pitched the Forest Citys to a 29-23 victory over them. He was hired away by the Excelsiors, but soon returned to Rockford, where he worked at various jobs while continuing to pitch. While on tour with Rockford in 1870, Spalding defeated the famous Cincinnati Red Stockings.

Harry Wright, who had managed the Red Stockings, moved to Boston and worked to organize the first professional league, the National Association. He signed players for his own team, the Boston Red Stockings, including Spalding, Ross Barnes, and Fred Cone from Rockford. Wright was an important formative influence on Spalding, imparting organizational skills to the young man.

From the start, Spalding dominated National Association pitching, leading the league in wins for every year of its five-year existence. In 1871 he was 19-10, winning one more than the two second-place pitchers. The following year, Spalding put up a record of 38-8, winning five more than second-place Candy Cummings. He won even more games in 1873—41 wins against 14 losses. Increasing his wins total again in 1874, Spalding was 52-16. Remarkably, Spalding appeared in every one of the Red Stockings' games in 1874. The team played in a total of 71 championship games (excluding exhibitions), and Spalding started 69 of them (65 were complete games), while relieving in the other two. His ERA for the season was 1.92; his career ERA is calculated at 2.13. In 1874 he worked an astounding 617⅓ innings, far more than would ever be assigned to any pitcher in a 162-game season.

In 1874 Wright sent Spalding to England to organize the first foreign tour by American baseball players. The participants were players from the Boston and Athletic (Philadelphia) clubs. They departed July 16, arriving at Liverpool on the 27th. In addition to Liverpool they played games at Manchester, London, Sheffield, and Dublin. There were 14 baseball exhibitions, in which Boston won eight, but also seven cricket matches against top British teams. The Americans astonished the locals by winning six and losing none, the other being drawn because of rain. The victors sailed from England on August 27, returning home September 9.

Spalding had a record of 204-53 in five years, topped by a 54-5 record in 1875, when he had 24 consecutive wins. Not only did he lead in wins for every year of the National Association's existence, he also increased the number of wins each year over the year before. Overall, he had 91 percent of Boston's victories in the Association.

After finishing in second place in 1871, the Red Stockings won the next four pennants. Spalding's performance is described thus by Robert Tiemann: "In the pitcher's box, Spalding was in complete control, using a fine fastball and change of pace. He was a master at keeping hitters off balance, either by quick-pitching

Albert G. Spalding (Spalding Collection)

or by holding the ball while the batter fidgeted. In addition, he was a good batsman, adept at opposite field hitting, and a savvy fielder who helped perfect the dropped-popup double play."[1]

In addition to his work on the mound, Spalding also played 64 games in the outfield and 52 at first base. He was a very good hitter, too, with a career batting average of .313. In 411 games, he batted in 338 runs.

Because he disapproved of drinking and gambling, Spalding was sympathetic to William Hulbert's proposal to organize a new league with stricter discipline. Hence Hulbert was able to lure Spalding, as well as other stars, to his Chicago White Stockings. To prevent the Eastern clubs from retaliating, Hulbert formed the new National League; this meant for Spalding a "promotion" to captain/manager. In the National League's inaugural year, 1876, Spalding again led the league in which he pitched with 47 wins, but George Bradley of St. Louis, who had a 5-4 record against Spalding, was probably a shade better. Spalding was 47-12, and Chicago won the pennant. In 1877 Spalding abandoned the mound for first base. Bradley was hired to replace him, but the team dropped from first to fifth place. Spalding gave up the captaincy and played in only one game in 1878; he was through as a ballplayer at age 27. It appears that his other interests had taken precedence over ballplaying.

After retiring as a player, Spalding became secretary of the White Stockings, becoming president when Hulbert died in 1882. Spalding believed in strict separation between players and management, with the latter handling financial matters. He built a team that dominated the early 1880s, as the White Stockings won pennants in 1880, 1881, 1882, 1885, and 1886. He was determined to have a clean game that drew respectable citizens to the ballpark. He was innovative, starting the practice of spring training when the team went to Hot Springs, Arkansas, in 1886, and he sponsored a world tour of players in 1888-89.

Cap Anson chronicled this trip as follows: Spalding organized a round-the-world tour with exhibition games between the Chicagos and a picked team, called the All-Americas, from the rest of the league.[2] Among the All-America players were John M. Ward, Ned Hanlon, Fred Carroll, and Egyptian Healy. They left Chicago via the Burlington Railroad on October 20, 1888. For about a month they toured the West, playing in such places as Minneapolis/St. Paul, Des Moines, Omaha, Denver, Salt Lake City, and San Francisco. On November 18 the players sailed for Hawaii, arriving a week later. In addition to Honolulu they played in Auckland and a few Australian cities. In January they sailed to Ceylon, where they also played, but they avoided India for health reasons.

On February 7, 1889, the players arrived in Egypt, where they had a game in the shadow of the pyramids. From there they proceeded to Naples, Rome (playing before the king of Italy), Florence, and Paris. In the latter city, on May 8, Ned Williamson tore his kneecap in a game, virtually ending his career. They crossed the Channel that evening, playing in London (before Edward, Prince of Wales) and other British cities, as well as Glasgow, Belfast, and Dublin. In all there were 28 games abroad, the All-Americas winning 14, the Chicagos 11, with three ties. The weary travelers sailed from Queenstown on March 25, arriving in New

York on April 6. Two days later there was a game in Brooklyn followed by a banquet at Delmonico's, at which Chauncey Depew was the speaker, with Mark Twain also in attendance. After further exhibitions at Baltimore, Philadelphia, Boston, Washington, Pittsburgh, Cleveland, and Indianapolis, the touring players arrived back in Chicago on April 19 for a banquet at the Palmer House. The final game was played on the 20th at West Side Park, six months after they had started out.

Meanwhile, Spalding had undergone a career change from player to team owner and sporting-goods magnate. In February 1876 he opened a sporting-goods store, in partnership with his brother Walter, at 118 Randolph Street in Chicago. Within a few years they had a four-story building in Chicago, a five-story store in New York, and outlets across the country from Oregon to Rhode Island. Spalding was able to use his influence to supply balls, bats, uniforms, and other equipment to the league. He published semiofficial guides and instruction manuals, carrying this practice over to other sports to promote his merchandise.

Spalding became the National League's most influential owner, promoting the reserve clause and its system of "indentured serfdom," i.e., keeping salaries down and controlling where men could play. He assumed a moral authority over the players, railing against drinking in the pages of his *Guide*.[3] He set up what many consider the second "World Series," against the Association's St. Louis Browns, but Chicago only achieved a tie in 1885 and then lost four of six the following year.[4] This induced Spalding to break up his team. First to go were the drinkers. Mike Kelly was sold to Boston for $10,000, and Jim McCormick and George Gore were axed. The following year star pitcher John Clarkson brought another $10,000 from Boston. Thus ended the Chicago dynasty.

By 1890 the players had a union, the Brotherhood, and rebelled, forming a rival league. Spalding led the effort to undermine the Players Association and ultimately turned Organized Baseball into a monopolistic trust. But he began to tire of baseball and turned over the presidency of the Chicago team to James Hart in 1892. According to Francis Richter, who regarded Spalding as "the greatest man the National game has produced," Spalding put the game above selfish interests.[5] This caused him to come out of retirement to oppose the syndicate scheme of Andrew Freedman and John T. Brush. He ran for the league presidency against old friend Nicholas Young and actually "won" through a flawed process that was challenged in the courts. When it appeared that he would ultimately lose, he resigned the NL presidency in April 1902.

Spalding then sold out completely and retired to Point Loma, California. He devoted himself to proving baseball a uniquely American game, promoting the myth of its invention by Abner Doubleday.

From a baseball standpoint Spalding's most significant relationship was that with Adrian "Cap" Anson. They had started out with Rockford, came to Chicago in 1876, and worked to build up the White Stockings. Anson shared Spalding's views and enforced his values on the field. However, Anson and James Hart had differences dating back to the world tour, and when Hart took over the team the friction escalated until

Spalding, apparently in an old-timers game (Spalding Collection)

Anson was dismissed after the 1897 season. On the one hand, it was time for a change. On the other, Anson felt stabbed in the back by his old friend. Spalding tried to placate Anson with a testimonial said to be worth $50,000 (over $1 million today), but Anson was too proud to accept. In Anson's autobiography the envy is clear: They started out together; Spalding prospered, while all of Anson's investments turned sour.[6]

Spalding was married twice, first to Josie Keith in 1875; they had a son Keith. Josie died in 1899, and in 1901 Spalding married the widow Elizabeth Mayer Churchill. They had been clandestine lovers for some time and had a son (Spalding Brown Spalding, later changed to Albert Goodwill Jr.) out of wedlock. After marrying Elizabeth, Spalding acknowledged the paternity and also adopted her other son, Durand Churchill. He also took an interest in the career of his nephew Albert Spalding (1889-1953), a world-class violinist. Elizabeth was devoted to theosophy, and the Spaldings moved to Point Loma to be part of the community founded by Katherine Tingley. Spalding had been in the second echelon of Chicago society, but in the San Diego area he was a civic leader. This led to his campaign for the Senate in 1910. Although he was the popular choice, the insiders in the state legislature chose his opponent, John D. Works. Spalding died of a stroke on September 9, 1915, leaving an estate of $600,000 to his wife and three sons. Twenty-five years later, in 1939, he was named to the National Baseball Hall of Fame by the Old Timers Committee.

SOURCES

In addition to the sources in the notes, the author also consulted:

Chicago Tribune, September 10, 1915: 1; September 15, 1915: 13.

Gold, Eddie, and Art Ahrens. *The Golden Era Cubs, 1876-1940* (Chicago: Bonus Books, 1985).

Golenbock, Peter. *Wrigleyville, a Magical History Tour of the Chicago Cubs* (New York: St. Martin's, 1996).

Levine, Peter. *A.G. Spalding and the Rise of Baseball, the Promise of American Sport* (New York and Oxford: Oxford University Press, 1985).

Nemec, David. *The Great Encyclopedia of 19th-Century Major League Baseball* (New York: Donald Fine Books, 1997).

Nineteenth Century Notes. Newsletter of the Nineteenth Century Committee, Society for American Baseball Research, No. 99 (1999): 2, 2.

Smith, Duane A. "Spalding, Albert Goodwill 'Al.'" *Biographical Dictionary of American Sports: Baseball*. Revised and expanded edition (Westport, Connecticut: Greenwood, 2000).

Spalding, Albert G. *America's National Game* (New York: American Sports, 1911).

Spalding's Official Base Ball Guide. Various editions. (Chicago and New York: A.G. Spalding & Bros.)

NOTES

1. Quoted in William E. McMahon, "Albert Goodwill Spalding," in Frederick Ivor-Campbell, Robert L. Tiemann, and Mark Rucker, eds., *Baseball's First Stars* (Cleveland: Society for American Baseball Research, 1996), 154.

2. Adrian C. Anson, *A Ball Player's Career, Being the Personal Experiences and Reminiscences of Adrian Anson* (Chicago: Era Pub. Co., 1900), 140-285.

3. *Spalding's Official Base Ball Guide* (1886), 14-16.

4. The first world's series is now often considered to be the 1884 one between Providence and New York.

5. Francis C. Richter, "Heroic Figure Passes From the Stage," *Sporting Life*, September 18, 1915: 3, 7.

6. Anson, 306-314.

CHARLIE SWEASY

BY CHARLES F. FABER

FOR A FEW YEARS AS A YOUNG MAN he was the most noted second baseman in all of baseball. But a combination of factors prevented Charlie Sweasy from fulfilling the promise of his youth. He played his final major-league game at the age of 30 and is all but forgotten today.

Charles James Sweasy[1] was born in Newark, New Jersey, on November 2, 1847, youngest of the six children of Margaret Rachel Meeker and John Sweasy, a brick mason. During his boyhood he was part of a group of Newark boys who became very skilled players.[2] As teenagers Charlie and his friend Andy Leonard were good enough to be paid under the table as professionals.[3] In 1866 18-year-old Charlie and his friend Andy joined the strong Irvington club in a Newark suburb. A second baseman, young Charlie became known for his exceptional fielding. Playing without a glove and on sometimes rough infields, he made occasional errors on groundballs, but he excelled in catching balls hit into the air.

According to his obituary in the *New York Times*, in 1868 Sweasy joined "the noted Lancaster Red Stockings, managed by the late Harry Wright."[4] This is inaccurate. The Lancaster Red Stockings did not exist in 1868; they were organized in 1884. Harry Wright never managed a team in Lancaster. What actually happened is that Sweasy and Leonard traveled to Ohio and joined Cincinnati's strongest amateur club, the Buckeyes. What induced the young men to go west is not known, but if they received under-the-table pay, it would have been the height of hypocrisy. In 1869 the Buckeyes blasted the Red Stockings for going all-professional and said "You may be assured the Buckeyes will not be troubled with 'revolvers' who carry their pockets filled with offers from other clubs."[5] More likely, supporters of the Buckeyes found employment for Sweasy and Leonard in jobs that allowed them time to play baseball on the side. Such a practice was common among amateur clubs at the time. It has been reported that both Sweasy and Leonard were employed as hatters before joining the Red Stockings.[6] It could be that both young men were recruited to play for the Buckeyes and were provided jobs by the same employer.

We may not know why Sweasy and Leonard joined the Buckeyes. But we know for certain the reason they left. It was money. In 1869 Harry Wright, manager of the Cincinnati Red Stockings, lured Sweasy and Leonard away from his crosstown rivals by offering a salary of $800 for the season's play.[7] The Buckeyes' best player, Charlie Gould, had already agreed to accept the same salary to switch to the Red Stockings.[8]

As the Cincinnati Red Stockings swept through their undefeated 1869 season, Charlie Sweasy was clearly one of the stars. Although he is remembered today as an outstanding fielder, he had some notable exploits as a hitter and baserunner. In 1869 Sweasy clouted 30 home runs, second on the club to George Wright's 49. Some of his homers came in bunches; some were game-winning blows. For example, in a game against the Forest City Baseball Club on July 24, 1869, the Red Stockings were facing defeat for the first time, trailing 14-12, in the last of the ninth. Cincinnati tied it up, and Sweasy knocked in the winning run in a 15-14 victory to keep the streak alive. In an incredible performance in San Francisco on October 1, Sweasy hit for the cycle in one inning—two singles, a double, a triple, and a home run in five appearances in the fourth inning of a game against the Atlantic Base Ball Club. Even more amazing were his baserunning exploits against the Baltic Base Ball Club in Wheeling, West Virginia, in a game that was rained out in the fourth inning. In four innings Sweasy stole six bases, including three steals of home.

Competition was a little tougher in 1870, but Sweasy still hit 18 home runs to lead the club in that department. However, he fell out of favor with Harry Wright for some unacceptable (to the strict manager)

— 142 —

Charlie Sweasy (Public Domain)

behavior. Dissension was developing on the club with two cliques emerging. Harry and George Wright, McVey, and Gould on one side; Sweasy, Leonard, Asa Brainard, Fred Waterman, and Doug Allison on the other. The latter group thought that manager Wright was too strict and had no business censuring their off-the-field activities; the first group objected to rowdy behavior and heavy drinking by some of their teammates.

The problem came to a head on August 26, after a game in which Sweasy had been the hero. Trailing the Riverside Base Ball Club, 27-23, in the ninth inning, the Red Stockings mounted an improbable comeback. With two outs and the bases loaded the Cincinnati club had cut the lead to 27-25. Sweasy hit a grand slam to win the game, 29-27. On board a steamship for a trip back to the Queen City, Charlie Sweasy, probably inebriated, got into a fight with a couple of unnamed teammates. The players got so unruly that the captain threatened to run the boat ashore and throw the troublemakers off. When they got back to Cincinnati, Sweasy was expelled from the club for his disgraceful conduct. The club president announced that the club would be purged of all intemperate, insubordinate, and disorderly members.[9]

Sweasy was soon reinstated, but his behavior was neither forgiven nor forgotten. There were too many other examples of unacceptable conduct. Meanwhile, the Red Stockings were in financial difficulties. The executive board decided they could not afford to pay the salaries of professional players. In November 1870 the officers decided to return to an amateur status. When baseball's first openly all-professional team disbanded, Harry Wright was employed as the manager of the Boston Red Stockings in the new National Association of Professional Base Ball Players. Wright soon induced his brother George and former teammates Cal McVey and Charlie Gould to join him in Beantown. Boston's ownership expressed interest in obtaining Sweasy and other Red Stockings, but Wright demurred. He wanted no drinkers, growlers, or shirkers on his team.

Other clubs were willing to take a chance on Sweasy and some of his fellow drinkers. The Washington Olympics signed him for 1871, but he lasted but one season in the nation's capital before jumping to the Cleveland Forest Citys in 1872. After one year on Lake Erie Sweasy signed with Boston for 1873. However, he played only one game for Harry Wright's squad before he had another falling-out with his once and present manager. Wright released Sweasy and allowed him to join the Brooklyn Atlantics with a warning to his new employers: "When you draw up his contract you cannot make it too strict. He will do well if kept well in hand and looked after sharply. ... I have talked to Sweasy very plainly and should he fail this season, it would be his last."[10]

In 1874 Sweasy played only 10 games for the Atlantics before moving to Baltimore, where he played eight games for the Canaries. In 1875, the final year of the National Association, he was the player-manager in 19 games for the St. Louis Red Stockings, the third Red Stockings team for which he had labored in his brief career. In his five seasons in the National Association he had appeared in only 55 games while toiling for six different clubs. After his heroics in

1869 and 1870, his subsequent career must have been a huge disappointment for him. Sweasy failed to hit a single home run in his five seasons in the National Association or his two seasons in the National League, and his career batting average was a paltry .194.

There are several possible explanations for Sweasy's decline in productivity. In 1874 he began suffering from rheumatism, which plagued him the rest of his career. Excessive drinking may have also contributed to his declining skills. The much higher level of competition in the professional leagues was also a factor. But the main cause of his diminished productivity was undoubtedly the change in baseball rules. Early rules heavily favored the striker (batter) over the pitcher. The old rules required the ball to be pitched with the arm straight and not jerked or thrown to the bat. The striker could tell the pitcher exactly where he wanted the ball placed, high or low, inside or outside, across the letters, or however the striker wanted it. Strikes were called only after the batter had been warned for not offering at well-placed pitches. Three balls entitled the striker to a base. Balls hit into fair territory but rolling foul before reaching first or third base were considered fair balls. This led to the corner infielders positioning themselves at the bag or even in foul territory, making huge gaps in the infield.

The National Association revised the rules to redress the imbalance between hitting and pitching with dramatic impact. In 1871 the National Association's first season, 2,659 runs were scored in 258 games, an average of slightly more than 10 runs per game. Only 47 home runs were struck in 1871 by all clubs combined in the entire league.

In 1876 the new National League replaced the defunct National Association.

Cincinnati fielded a team, again known as the Red Stockings, in the new circuit. Sweasy's former teammate Charlie Gould was named manager of the club. Sweasy returned to Cincinnati as the club's regular second baseman. Although he performed reasonably well in 1876, his contract was not renewed. In 1877 he played a few games for the Rhode Island club in the New England League. In 1878 he returned to the majors as a member of the National League's Providence Grays. He played his final major-league game for Providence on September 30, 1878, at the age of 30.

In 1879 Sweasy played for the Manchester club in the National Association (now a minor league.) After that stint, he was out of professional baseball for a few years. In 1881 he was employed as a jeweler and played for a strong semipro team in Attleboro, Massachusetts, "The Jewelry Capital of the World." Rheumatism soon caused Sweasy to give up the sport temporarily. He tried a comeback with his hometown Newark Domestics of the Eastern League in 1884, but appeared in only two games in his final season in Organized Baseball.

In reminiscing about the 1869 Red Stockings, Harry Wright told *The Sporting News* in an 1886 conversation, "That team was rather easy to handle, although Sweasy and Leonard would occasionally kick over the traces, and Doug Allison had to be treated very gingerly at times. … All the members of the club are alive today. … Sweasy is, I think, working at his trade in New York, he is a hatter."[11]

Whether Sweasy actually resumed his work as a hatter is doubtful. Other sources say that after retiring from professional baseball, Sweasy returned to Newark. He played some ball with local teams, but it is said that his body was worn out and sobriety continued to be an issue.[12] For many years he made a living selling oysters. One report is that in his declining years Sweasy "regaled the denizens of various watering holes with tales of his glory days with the Red Stockings."[13] The 1900 census listed his occupation as watchman at the town hall in Irvington, New Jersey.

In 1876 Sweasy married Ellen[14] Robertson of Boston, the 26-year-old daughter of Jane and William Robertson, a carpenter. (Both of the Robertsons were born in Nova Scotia and came to the United States in the early 1800s.) Charlie and Ellen had four children, only two of whom survived to adulthood. Their first child, a daughter named Effie, was born in 1876 and was still living in 1930. A son named Charles, was born in 1877 and died in Providence on August 11, 1878. A daughter, Fanny, was born August 11, 1881, in Attleboro. She died on June 20, 1882. The second son,

Howard Tipper Sweasy, was born on June 26, 1879, in Providence and died in Quincy, Massachusetts in 1927. By 1900 Charlie and Ellen had separated, but they never divorced.

Charlie Sweasy died of consumption in a Newark hospital on March 30, 1908. His obituary mentions no survivors, although Ellen, Effie, and Howard were all still living. Baseball historians honor Charlie Sweasy as one of the game's pioneers, a fine-fielding, power-hitting, base-stealing member of baseball's first openly all-professional club. His reputation is somewhat tarnished by the belief that he had "a rather ornery disposition at times, an irascibility brought on by frequent imbibition."[15] Be that as it may, he was an outstanding contributor to the growth of our nation's pastime.

SOURCES

The author wishes to express his appreciation to Sharon Meeker for the information about Sweasy's wife and children, which she provided in a series of email communications in March 2015.

In addition to those cited in the notes, the following sources were useful:

Palmer, Pete, and Gary Gillette, eds. *The Baseball Encyclopedia* (New York: Barnes & Noble, 2004).

ancestry.com.

baseballchronology.com.

baseball-reference.com.

cincinnativiews.net.

sabr.org.

NOTES

1. In early records the surname is sometimes spelled as Swasey, Sweasey, and other variants. The name was transcribed Smeasu by ancestry.com in its report on the 1900 census.
2. njsportsheroes.com.
3. Ibid.
4. *New York Times,* March 31, 1908.
5. Stephen D. Guschov, *The Red Stockings of Cincinnati* (Jefferson, North Carolina: McFarland, 1998), 26.
6. cincinnativiews.net.
7. Guschov, 31.
8. Ibid.
9. Ibid., 123.
10. Harry Wright letter to Charles Hadel, April 8, 1874, cited by Guschov, 142.
11. *The Sporting News,* December 18, 1886.
12. njsportsheroes.com.
13. Ibid.
14. Her name was sometimes spelled as Ellen, sometimes as Helen. Her middle name may have been McGregor.
15. Guschov, 31.

DEACON WHITE

BY JOE WILLIAMS

DEACON WHITE WAS A BASEBALL pioneer. He caught baseball fever after the Civil War and played until the 1890s. His baseball career spanned the end of the amateur era and the start of professionalism, the establishment and demise of the National Association, the founding of the National League, and a players' revolt that led to the creation of the Players' League. He was the best catcher in baseball when the most important players in the game were catchers. He played for six championship teams and was a two-time batting champion. He was well respected by teammates, opponents, writers, and fans. History pushed White aside for many decades until he was finally elected to the National Baseball Hall of Fame on December 3, 2012, solidifying his place as a baseball legend.

James Laurie White was born on December 2, 1847, in the rural town of Caton, New York.[1] The Steuben County town, west of Elmira and a few miles from the Pennsylvania border, was the home to roughly 1,000 residents at the time of his birth. Jim was the son of Lester S. and Adeline (Hurd) White. Lester was a farmer born in nearby Tompkins County around 1820. Adeline was a Caton native born around 1823. The family was of English stock but Jim's grandparents were born in America.[2]

Jim was second-born, with an older brother, and six younger siblings. Living nearby were Lester's brother Benjamin and his family, including future ballplayer Willard Elmer White.

Prior to the start of the Civil War, baseball was largely a city-based sport. The widespread growth of the game didn't come until after the Civil War and a popular view was that returning soldiers taught rural folks the new game of baseball that they learned during the war. This is exactly what a 91-year-old Jim White stated a few weeks before his death in an interview with *The Sporting News*. "I learned to play ball from a Union soldier ... in 1865, and taught the boys the new game of baseball they had played in the Civil War."[3] If this is the case, it is quite possible the soldier who taught him the game was his older brother, LeRoy, who joined the Union cause in September 1864 and returned home the following year.[4]

In 1866 Jim helped form a team in Caton. The next year he and LeRoy joined the Monitor Base Ball Club of Corning. On August 8, 1867, the Monitors played in Hornellsville against the Ellicotts of Jamestown for the championship of the Southern Tier of New York counties. Jim played catcher and LeRoy was the left fielder. In the third inning, LeRoy took over as pitcher with a 13-6 lead, forming an all-brother battery. In the end, Jamestown defeated Corning, 23-21. A summary of the game included the following statement: "The Monitors are weak in their short-stop, catcher and in general fielding." Jim's day behind the batter may not have been his best; he had seven passed balls. Still, Jim White must have been a pretty good player because the following year he made his way to Cleveland to work and play semipro baseball.[5]

The Forest City Base Ball Club of Cleveland, comprising mostly local players, was formed in August 1865, becoming the city's first established team. Jim and LeRoy joined the team in 1868. Jim White, 5-feet-11 and around 175 pounds, instantly became the team's best player.[6]

White's first game in Cleveland was on June 4 against the local Railway Union Club. Forest City lost 21-14 as Jim played shortstop and LeRoy pitched. In Jim's first at-bat, he "put up an easy one" to the pitcher which was "gracefully accepted." The *Cleveland Daily Leader* was impressed with the new player: "While we say that the playing was good on both sides, we would like to make special mention of the play of J. White, the shortstop for the Forest City Club. His record at the bat is very good, but his fielding is better."[7]

On July 25 both Jim and LeRoy hit home runs and scored six times each in a 59-25 trouncing of the Railways in LeRoy's last game with the club.[8]

On July 31 Forest City lost to the Unions of Morrisania; White started the game at shortstop, moved to catcher, and then pitched. The *Leader* wrote, "White played very prettily and well in the position of catcher. He is quick and throws swiftly and with precision." Comments followed on his pitching: "White pitches a swift ball, much swifter than it looks to be, but he needs to practice to pitch the ball where he wants it."[9]

At season's end, Forest City's record was 11-11-1. White played in all 23 games, leading the team with 73 runs scored while hitting at least seven home runs. He split his time between shortstop and catcher, with at least three pitching performances.[10]

White did not play with Forest City the first half of the 1869 season. There were inaccurate reports that he played for the Central City Base Ball Club of Syracuse.[11] It can be surmised that he had simply left the team and gone home to New York to farm. This could have been his first "retirement" from the game, something he would become known for in coming years.

White returned to the club in August and took over catching duties.[12] A month later, Forest City played Central City in Syracuse on September 14, winning 39-11. White stroked four hits and scored four runs for Forest City. The *Syracuse Daily Standard* wrote, "[A]s for White, their catcher, we think we never saw a better."[13]

The 1869 Forest City Club showed tremendous improvement over the 1868 team. The added professionals helped the team double its win total while losing only six games to some of the best teams in the country. After rejoining the team, White played in at least 15 games, mostly behind the batter with the occasional pitching relief appearance.

The battery of Al Pratt and White proved to be among the best in the game, and other teams and spectators took notice. After the "Blue Stockings" defeated the Niagara Club of Buffalo on September 16, a Buffalo paper praised the men: "The specialty in the playing of the Cleveland club, is that of the pitcher and catcher. We have seldom seen these positions played more harmoniously."[14]

White had signed in November to play for Forest City in 1870 but rumors as late as March claimed he also signed with the White Stockings of Chicago.[15]

White stayed in Cleveland. One of his new teammates on the now completely professional nine was Ezra Sutton, a 20-year-old third baseman who had played for the Alert Club of Rochester, New York, in 1869. Sutton would challenge White as the top hitter on the club.

In the season's first game, Forest City pounded the Eurekas of East Cleveland, 86-6, with White hitting two home runs and scoring 13 runs.[16] After a victory against Oberlin, Forest City played two losing games against the undefeated Cincinnati Red Stockings, then followed with wins in their next six games, including a 46-5 defeat of the junior club Eastern Rocks, who gave up three homers to White.[17] The win streak ended on May 31 with a loss to the still undefeated Red Stockings.

When the Forest City Club of Rockford came to town in mid-June, the *Cleveland Plain Dealer* reported, "White, the catcher, had a very bad hand, so bad that he was forced to wear buckskin gloves, yet he played superbly."[18] Al Pratt later reminisced that the barehanded catcher's hands began to turn black and blue so he wore gloves.[19] White wasn't the first catcher to wear gloves in a game but this instance is notable.

In the second game against the "Green Stockings," White's hands were badly sore so he switched to pitcher in the fourth inning with Sutton as his catcher. The *Plain Dealer* wrote, "White is probably the swiftest pitcher in the world," and used one play to illustrate his speed as a pitcher: "An idea of the swiftness of his delivery may be obtained from the fact that during this inning, while Sutton was close behind the bat, the striker tipped the ball, which glanced upward, struck Sutton squarely on the forehead just over the left eye, and rebounded with such force that White caught it on the first bound in the pitcher's box and put the striker out."[20]

In mid-June Jim's first cousin, Elmer White, was brought in to be the change catcher and play right field, debuting on July 21 versus the Eastern Rocks.[21]

In August, the club went on an Eastern tour with White splitting time at catcher and pitcher. On the 11th he pitched the club to a 26-5 victory over the Niagaras of Buffalo with Elmer as his backstop. The next day he hit a clean homer while pitching the Forest Citys to a 29-2 win over Flower City of Rochester. After three games behind the batter and three losses, White returned to pitch a 13-0 gem on August 18 against the Eckfords of Brooklyn.[22]

The 1870 season was White's breakout year. He led the team with 184 total bases and finished second to Sutton with 108 hits while pitching 74 innings with the team's best average of 1.06 runs per inning.[23] The *Clipper* wrote, "[W]e never saw a catcher so quick and expert in his movements behind the bat. ... A cat after a mouse is not quicker than James is after a foul ball. ... [H]e is fearless of the hottest balls. ... White is what Creighton was—a natural ball player."[24]

On April 24, 1871, White married Marium Van Arndale of Caton. The newlyweds arrived in Cleveland the next day to get ready for the first season of the National Association of Base Ball Players, which formed on March 17 in New York City.[25] Forest City became a charter member of the first professional league when it paid its $10 entry fee.

The Forest City club traveled to Indiana to play in the first game of the new league against the Kekiongas of Fort Wayne on May 4. Pitching for the Kekiongas was 19-year-old Bobby Mathews. White led off the game and stroked a double, thus getting both the first hit and first double in professional league history. He then became part of the first double play when he didn't get back to second after a Gene Kimball fly out to second baseman Tom Carey, who touched the base. Mathews threw a four-hit shutout, outdueling Pratt 2-0 in a game that was "unpreceded in the annals of base ball."[26] Jim White led all hitters with two hits. Elmer played right field and struck out three times.

The Opening Day loss was a good indication of what was coming for the team. Forest City also lost

Deacon White, with Detroit (Spalding Collection)

its home opener on May 11 despite White hitting his first league homer.

On June 22 Elmer broke his left arm in the first inning of a game after falling down trying to get a foul ball.[27] He was out until August 30.

Forest City finished the season 10-19 in seventh place. White caught all 29 league games while batting .322 for the season. He was tied for the most games caught in the NA and led the league in putouts.

Before the 1872 season, tragedy struck the White family. Elmer died, likely of tuberculosis, on March 17 in Scio, New York.[28] The 22-year-old became the first professional league player in baseball history to die.[29]

The Forest City club began the season on May 14 in Washington. White led a 19-hit attack against the Nationals with four hits as Rynie Wolters pitched a complete-game 13-10 victory, but the team was 5-12 until July 6, when it clobbered the woeful Eckfords, 24-5. White, playing left field, had a huge day with four hits and five runs scored. However, after two more losses, the Forest City Base Ball Association canceled the contracts with the players. A compromise was made between the officers of the association and the players that allowed the players to form a co-operative club, keep the same team name, finish out the championship season, play on the old association grounds and split the gate receipts among themselves. White was named captain and manager.[30] But in mid-August, the team disbanded.[31]

White played in all 22 games for the 6-16 Forest City club in 1872, batting .339 with the league's sixth-best on-base percentage (.363). The *Clipper* said he didn't distinguished himself as he did in the previous two seasons as a catcher but passed the blame off on his supporting cast: "[N]o catcher can play with the ability his skill and experience warrant unless he works with a supporting team in the field, willing and able to back up his own strenuous exertions to win." The paper also commented on White's character: "We have never known him to growl at an umpire, and his record for integrity is untarnished by even a suspicion."[32] The foundation for White's famous nickname had begun to be laid.

Despite being one of the top players in the country, White decided to retire from the game. The Boston Red Stockings sent a director of the club to his home to pry him out of retirement. He was reportedly retained but had not reported when play began. In a letter to the *Clipper* on April 11, captain Harry Wright said, "James White has not arrived. He has been converted [to religion], and thinks at present that he would not be doing right if he should play baseball."[33] Philadelphia's *Sunday Dispatch* was less polite in its description of White's absence: "Mr. James White, who was engaged for the Boston Club, evidently does not think it *wicked* to break a contract and seriously inconvenience that organization by doing so at the last moment. It seems that James has "got religion," and thinks … [that playing ball would] jeopardize his future happiness."[34]

In fact, White reported on April 19, having "very properly concluded that a man can play ball in a reputable professional nine despite the fact of a recent conversion to religion."[35] White made his debut against Harvard the next day.[36]

The 1872 Boston championship team was in need of a catcher after Baltimore scooped up Cal McVey during the offseason. White's signing was even more important. Before he reported, the Red Stockings were left with weak-hitting backup Dave Birdsall or an inexperienced Jim O'Rourke. The season started in Boston on April 23 with an 8-5 loss to the White Stockings of Philadelphia. The club said in a letter to the *Clipper*: "James White will not be in good condition for a week yet, but he played his position finely."[37]

White joined a team stocked with talent: Ross Barnes at second, George Wright at short, Andy Leonard in the outfield, and Al Spalding as the pitcher. The team played well and was in a three-way race for second place, behind the White Stockings.

While Boston was fighting to get back into the championship hunt, the *Clipper* reported on September 6 that McVey would catch for Boston in 1874 and that "Jim White is as yet undecided about playing, but in case he should remain he will play right-field and change-catcher."[38] The Red Stockings closed the gap and defeated Philadelphia 18-7 on October 2 to take possession of first place. The win gave both teams 34 wins for the season with Boston having two fewer losses and one tie. Philadelphia went 2-2 the rest of the season while Boston played 12 games, winning nine, to capture the pennant.

Jim White had an outstanding season, leading the league in games played (tied with 60) and RBIs (77). He batted .392 and slugged .508, both good for third. On defense, he led all catchers in games played and putouts, and was tied in double plays. The *Clipper* named him the top catcher for 1873 and once again praised his character: "[H]e stands A No. 1 as a thoroughly honest and reliable player, and he is one whose daily habits of life show that his honesty is not simply policy, but a principle inherent in the man."[39]

White returned to Boston in 1874 for a salary of $1,800, the same as Barnes, Spalding, and both Wrights.[40] He played right field and was the change catcher before taking over full-time behind the batter on May 13, with McVey moving to right field for most of the season.

The Red Stockings finished the first half of the season with a 30-8 record; the Athletics were second at 23-10. The Athletics beat Boston on July 15 in Philadelphia, and the next day both teams boarded the American Line steamer *Ohio* and headed for England to play ball. White passed up the trip due to the "express wish of his family."[41] Harvard player John F. Kent took White's spot on the tour. When the teams returned to Philadelphia on September 9, White was on the dock among the crowd to greet his teammates.[42] On September 22 the Mutuals moved one win ahead of Boston and remained neck-and-neck with the Red Stockings until Boston started to pull away on October 14. Boston ended the season with 10 more wins than the Mutuals and once again was the champion.

The *Clipper* rated "honest Jim White" as the best catcher in 1874, calling him "agile in his movements as a cat, and as plucky withal as a bulldog."[43] He once again led the league in games caught while finishing second in putouts. At the plate he batted .301 and was a top-10 hitter in many offensive categories, including tied for second with three homers. The *Clipper* article pointed out White's style of barehanded catching as "yielding to the ball in catching it" by using a "spring-like movement" instead of letting the ball hit the hands at full force to stop it.[44]

Boston opened the 1875 NA season on April 19 with a 6-0 win over New Haven, grabbing first place from the start with no looking back. The team was primed to win a fourth championship in a row, starting the season 26-0. White injured a thumb on June 3 so switched to right field, with McVey moving to catcher. The Red Stockings' first loss was to the St. Louis Browns, 5-4, on June 5, with White not in the lineup. The *Clipper* attributed the loss to the "ill-luck" of losing White: "Now, McVey is a fine catcher, but he is not Jim White, for James stands alone; and when Spalding found that he had not Old Reliable behind the bat, he began to feel less confident as to results; and finally, when the Reds came to play their second match with the St. Louis nine, things were not as they were before."[45] White returned to the lineup the next game and had five hits as Boston soundly beat the Browns, 15-2.[46]

On July 10 Boston's "Big Four" of Barnes, McVey, Spalding, and White, met with the management of the Chicago club and agreed to play for the "fancy" prices the Boston club would not offer.[47] As the team dined in Taunton, Massachusetts, 10 days later, McVey said he was not playing in Boston next season. Harry Wright took it as a joke but discussed it with White after the meal. White admitted that the "Big Four" agreed to play for Chicago next season.[48] In a letter to the *Boston Herald*, White said he had met with the president of the Boston club, N.T. Apollonio, a month earlier before the team's Western trip and that Apollonio told him the Red Stockings could not compete with the "fancy Western prices" he might be offered on the trip. White promised he wouldn't accept any offers on *that* trip, but did admit to accepting Chicago's offer when they were in Boston and said he didn't want to force Boston to increase its offer.[49]

Spalding was the first to accept Chicago's offer, agreeing to be the team's captain and to recruit the others. The *Clipper* was quite harsh: "The spirit of the Association laws on the subject of engaging players for the ensuing season is that no club-manager or agent shall approach players to negotiate for their services for the next year until the close of the present season."[50]

Despite the news, Boston continued to play outstanding ball. After a 15-3 victory over the Athletics of Philadelphia on October 11, the team was 16 wins ahead of the second-place Athletics. The next day Boston played the Lynn Live Oaks. Jim faced brother Will White and got a couple of hits in the game as Boston won, 14-12.[51]

Eleven days later, after finishing the season series with Chicago in Boston, the teams' putative 1876 squads faced each other. The "Big Four" joined the Chicago players on the field and defeated the rest of the Boston club, 14-0. The *Clipper* said the crowd was one of the largest of the season. McVey pitched while Spalding played left field. White scored three runs and had eight putouts as catcher.[52]

At season's end Boston was 71-8-3, with 17 more victories than second-place Hartford. White led the league with a .367 batting average, finished second in on-base percentage (.372) and doubles (23), and was third in hits (136). On defense he led all catchers in putouts and assists. He was given a silver water pitcher after the season that was inscribed "Won by Jim White as most valuable player to Boston team, 1875."[53]

William Hulbert, president of the Chicago club, set up a meeting at the Grand Central Hotel in New York City on February 2, 1876, with representatives of seven other clubs. The meeting led to the formation of the National League of Professional Base Ball Clubs. Hulbert's signing of the "Big Four" and Cap Anson from the Athletics was a violation of the NA's rules, and the players potentially could have faced expulsion from the league. The formation of the new league eliminated that possibility.

White arrived in Chicago in early April. He brought along his brother Elmer, who went by the nickname Melvin, to take care of the team's grounds. As for Will, he joined the Cricket Base Ball Club of Binghamton, New York, for the 1876 season.[54] On April 25 Chicago played its first NL game against Louisville, winning 4-0. White caught and had one hit. Chicago had some competition during the year from Hartford and St. Louis but was in first place most of the season.

In one notable game, on July 22, White pitched for the first time in many years. Chicago beat up Louisville 30-7, and White pitched the last two innings just for fun. He gave up one hit, struck out three batters, and didn't allow a run.[55]

White's play on the field in 1876 showed he had little trouble adapting to his new team. He was once again the best catcher in the game playing for another championship. He led the league with 60 RBIs. He batted .343 and finished fourth in runs while leading all catchers in games caught for the fifth time. The team finished 52-14, winning the championship, and beating Boston nine out of 10 games.

After the season, both Jim and Will signed with Boston. On April 2, 1877, Jim, Will, and Melvin left for Boston. Melvin was to be responsible for the Boston ball grounds.[56] Jim's role was to split time at first base and the outfield with occasional appearances as catcher.

The team also added Hartford's 31-game winner of the previous season, Tommy Bond, and Jim's former Cleveland teammate Ezra Sutton.

White's return to Boston ended a four-year period of dominance by the best battery in the game. From 1873 to 1876, Spalding won 194 games while losing only 47. White was behind the plate for most of Spalding's games. Without White, Spalding would start and win only one more game as a pitcher.

After a victory on July 18, Boston was 19-10-1, with two more wins than the St. Louis Brown Stockings. On July 20 Will made his major-league debut, against the Red Stockings in Cincinnati. Jim caught his younger brother; thus forming the first all-brother battery in major-league history. Will pitched the first seven innings before Bond came in from center field to relieve the 22-year-old. Jim White was praised by the *Cincinnati Daily Gazette*: "His stops of wild balls were fairly marvelous, and evoked constant applause from the crowd."[57] But Cincinnati won with Will suffering the loss.

In its last 21 league games, Boston went 20-1, including two wins by Will, one a 14-0 shutout over Cincinnati. For the season, Boston (42-18) had seven more wins than Louisville (35-25). Jim had played for a championship team in five straight seasons. If an MVP award were given out for the 1877 season, White would have easily won it. He finished first in batting average (.387), hits (103), triples (11), extra-base hits (27), RBIs (49), total bases (145), slugging (.545), and OPS (.950). The decision to limit White's use as catcher saved his hands so Boston could take advantage of his heavy hitting.

Rumors began to emerge in November that the White brothers would sign with Cincinnati for 1878. The death of Jim's father-in-law on November 20 left him another valuable farm, and he said he knew he should give up ballplaying to tend to his farms, horses, and cattle but that he had a strong fascination with the national game.[58] Once referred to as a silver-tongued orator, White was starting to be called "The Deacon" by his peers.[59]

Jim and Will White joined a Cincinnati team that also included sluggers Charley Jones, Lip Pike, and rookie King Kelly, who would catch a quarter of the games during the season, allowing Deacon a break.

With Deacon batting cleanup, the team started the season 6-0 and was 15-5 after its first 20 games, but succumbed to Boston for the NL championship. The Reds won 10 of their last 11 league games and were declared the champs of the West by the *Clipper* after "their brilliant rally under the Brothers White during their September matches."[60] The team finished second with a 37-23-1 record, four wins behind Boston.

Hopes were high for the Reds in 1879. The *Clipper* said the Whites "have proved themselves to be the equals of the best catching and pitching pair who have ever played in a league nine together."[61] Deacon was named manager and captain.

Despite a 5-0 start, the team stumbled. After 18 games and a 9-9 record, White resigned his captaincy. The *Clipper* wrote that he gave up managing the team because he was being used as a "catspaw" by team president J. Wayne Neff. White said he had "accepted the management and captaincy with the agreement that he was to have sole control" of the club. White was told to read a threatening note to his players but refused. The team was demoralized.[62]

The team struggled under new manager Cal McVey a good portion of the season but did manage to win more games than it lost. White finished the season with a .330 batting average, 110 hits, and 52 RBIs, all fifth best in the league. He was among leaders in several defensive categories as a catcher but his days as the primary catcher of a team had come to an end. In the years to come, White would primarily start elsewhere on the field. He closed out the 1870s with the most games caught, 409. At the plate he ranked second in hits (846) and RBIs (422), third in total bases (1,069), fourth in on-base percentage (.358), and fifth in games (525), runs (504), and batting average (.345).[63] White was easily the premier catcher of the decade. Historian Peter Morris said, "The good catchers of the 1870s were few: Deacon White was far and away the best, because he alone was a standout in the field and at the bat."[64]

Though White had declared 1879 as his last season, he was persuaded to sign with Cincinnati for 1880. His wife became ill, and his father died in late July. It wasn't until August 6 that Deacon appeared in his first game, playing right field at Troy, which happened to be Tim Keefe's first major-league game and first victory. Keefe held White hitless.[65] The season did not end well when White found out he had been fined $10 by manager John Clapp for not going to third in a game against Buffalo on September 27. The team had deducted it from his paycheck without telling him. Deacon followed with a $55 claim for traveling expenses for his wife that he said he was promised. The claim was denied.[66]

Deacon White, fielding at third base (Library of Congress)

Cincinnati finished the 1880 season last in the National League with a 21-59-3 record. Deacon did not play catcher and hit .298 in 35 games, breaking a string of nine straight seasons batting over .300. His time in Cincinnati officially came to an end when the team was kicked out of the league for playing Sunday games and selling alcoholic beverages at games.

Deacon signed with Buffalo for the 1881 season. The 33-year-old played almost every day but was used as a utility man, playing primarily at first, second, and the outfield. The next season he shifted to third and remained there for most of the rest of his career, although he was the change catcher during the 1882 and 1883 seasons. On May 16, 1884, White set a record by having 11 assists in a nine-inning game while playing third.[67]

As a batter, Deacon was no longer the hitter he was in the 1870s, but he was still solid. In 1881 he batted .310 and was fourth in RBIs. After two below-.300 seasons in 1882 and 1883, White had a renaissance year in 1884, batting .325 and finishing in the top 10 in many offensive categories.

White and his wife, Marium, had a daughter, Grace Hughson White, on September 8, 1882. It was written that her favorite play object when she was 8 months old was a NL regulation baseball.[68]

Deacon's years in Buffalo included significant developments in baseball. The competing American Association began play in 1882. White's brother Will joined the Cincinnati Association team and become the league's best pitcher, going 40-12 while leading his team to the league's first championship. The reserve clause limit, tying players to teams, was increased from five players to 11 in 1883. The National Agreement between the AA, the NL, and the minor-league Northwestern League led to a peaceful time among the leagues and to the creation of the United States Championship series in 1884, baseball's first World Series.

Buffalo never won a pennant during White's tenure. Before the 1885 season he decided to retire once again, for fear that the NL would start allowing Sunday games.[69] When the championship season started, however, the third baseman was unexpectedly in the lineup.[70]

The 1885 club was not competitive, falling to 15-34 by July 10, with poor attendance and deepening financial troubles.[71] Rumors that the team would disband emerged and discussions with teams for its players were taking place. Managers from other teams were in Buffalo "bidding for these men in about the same manner that slaves were sold during the rebellion [Civil War]." It was said that Deacon and Dan Brouthers were headed to Baltimore. When the players got word that they were being sold like cattle, they "kicked" and "smashed the whole scheme."[72]

Despite the commotion, the team survived. White batted in the fourth spot most of the season and had an outstanding year on defense. The *Clipper* wrote on August 29: "Jim White has not made an error at third in ten straight games. No one can call the Deacon "old" yet. In batting and fielding he leads them all at third."[73] At season's end, his .888 fielding percentage was second best among the league's third basemen.

In September the Detroit Wolverines purchased the Buffalo franchise for $7,000 so they could obtain the "Big Four" of White, Brouthers, Hardy Richardson, and Jack Rowe.[74] New York manager Jim Mutrie said he would not let his team play if the Buffalo foursome was on the field for Detroit, calling the transfer an illegal act.[75] League President Nick Young agreed and ruled that they could not play for Detroit. He ordered umpire Bob Ferguson to forfeit the game to New York if the quartet played.[76] The players did not join Detroit. They also refused an order to rejoin Buffalo, saying they were granted their release by Buffalo and were free to sign with any team for 1886.[77] The four embarked on a fishing tour of Lake Erie while Buffalo finished the season with 16 straight losses.[78]

On October 17 the NL and AA signed a new National Agreement, and also agreed that the foursome were free to contract with any league team but could not sign for more than $2,000. The players were expecting between $3,500 and $4,000 from Detroit.[79] On November 19 a special committee composed of John Day, Spalding, and Young ruled that the four players belonged to Detroit. Manager Bill Watkins declared that he signed Brouthers, Richardson, and Rowe that evening and was heading to Corning in the morning to sign White.[80]

During the 1886 season, Detroit (87-36-3) finished 2½ games behind the White Stockings for the pennant. The true difference was the season series, which Chicago won 11 games to 7. White finished eighth in the NL in RBIs (76) and 10th in hits (142). The *Detroit Free Press* wrote, "Deacon White has a very refreshing custom of hitting the ball when there are men on bases."[81] White led the league in games played at third with 124 and was still being praised for his defense, with the "agility of a colt [who could] give many of the younger pretentious players pointers."[82]

As the 1887 season began, White was now the oldest player in the NL at 39. He was benched on June 7 for poor play, replaced by 26-year-old Billy Shindle.[83] He didn't stay benched for long, and batted .303 for pennant-winning Detroit.

Detroit followed up its NL dominance with a 15-game "World Series" defeat of the American Association's pennant-winning St. Louis team, winning 10 of 15.[84] Deacon hit .207 with eight runs scored in the series. Despite the poor offensive performance, the *Clipper* wrote, "The veteran "Deacon" White has become an immense favorite in Detroit, especially since the world's championship series, in which he did such yeoman service."[85] It was White's sixth championship.

The 1888 championship season saw Detroit finish in fifth place. The *Clipper* wrote: "Hard luck never before had such a cruel grip on any National League club."[86] The 40-year-old White, however, had an outstanding year. He had a career-high 157 hits, ranking fifth in the league. He finished fifth in RBIs (71), sixth in average (.298), seventh in doubles (22), and ninth in total bases (201) while playing the second-most games at third (125).

On October 16, 1888, Sam Thompson was sent to Philadelphia, Jack Rowe and Pete Conway were sent to Pittsburgh, and White, Charlie Bennett, Dan Brouthers, Charlie Ganzel, and Hardy Richardson were sent to Boston. The Beaneaters agreed on an estimated $30,000 for the five ballplayers.[87] The "Big Four" was no more.

White tried unsuccessfully to convince the other four players not to sign with Boston.[88] On December 18 White and Jack Rowe purchased a controlling interest in the International Association's Buffalo Bisons. White was named president of the club and Rowe vice president. Both planned to play for the Bisons.[89] The deal sent shock waves throughout the baseball community with White and Rowe being labeled as rebels.

The Detroit franchise would lose the cash it agreed upon with both Boston and Pittsburgh for the players' services if they didn't sign. On December 19, speaking with a reporter for the *Detroit Free Press*, White, asked if he was attempting to break the reserve clause, responded, "Not at all. The reserve rule is all right. It is the bulwark of the national game. What I protest against is the selling of a player without his knowledge or consent. I am quite willing to break up the custom."[90]

The players had not yet agreed to terms with the clubs they were released to, so both were still on Detroit's reserve list. NL President Young ruled that the players still belonged to the league and could not play in Buffalo. The players argued that they signed with Detroit and not the NL. Since Detroit was not going to be in the NL in 1889, the players felt they were free to do as they pleased and play in Buffalo.[91]

White said, "Our contract states that when a club loses its membership the right to reserve ceases. Detroit has sold its franchise, and I have not yet been transferred, I don't see what claim the Detroit club has on me."[92] Rowe argued that they were not fighting the reserve rule, instead they "simply object to a defunct club selling us like slaves to some other club regardless of our personal feelings."[93]

On March 2, 1889, White moved his family from Detroit to Buffalo with the intention of remaining there.[94] However, a few days later, White and Rowe were put on the reserve list for Pittsburgh.[95] After a few months of on-and-off negotiations, the players agreed to go to Pittsburgh. They each received $1,250 from their release money, and a salary of $500 per

Jim White (Spalding Collection)

month.[96] Deacon exclaimed, "I don't want a man to sell my carcass without I get half."[97] Will White, Buffalo's manager and starting pitcher, took over the operations of the club to allow the owners (Jim White and Rowe) to play for Pittsburgh.

White and Rowe played for Pittsburgh, which finished 61-71-2 in fifth place. White batted mostly fourth but hit just .253 in 55 games, the worst average of his career. His Buffalo franchise didn't fare so well either, finishing seventh in an eight-team league. The season finished in the middle of a baseball war between the NL owners and players that led to the formation of the Players' League.

In December 1889 the Buffalo Club of the Players' League was incorporated. Rowe and White were among the incorporators.[98] Quickly White and Rowe sold the franchise to "capitalists of (Buffalo)" for over $10,000.[99] An initial roster of Buffalo players included White and Rowe. Also listed were Ed Beecher, Dummy Hoy, Connie Mack, and Sam Wise, the nucleus of the Buffalo Brotherhood team.[100]

Buffalo was not expected to do well. White split time between third base and first base. On July 9 Deacon entered a game against New York in the second inning as a pitcher with Buffalo losing 3-0. He pitched eight innings and allowed 18 hits and 15 runs as the team lost, 18-4.[101] He didn't play for almost two weeks after that outing, which was the last pitching appearance of his major-league career.

Buffalo was losing money and in July the league took control and awarded new players to the team.[102] The new players did not make the team any better.

Deacon's last major-league game came on October 4 against Brooklyn. The Bisons were shut out.[103] The League's weakest hitting crew and worst pitching staff ended the season in last place with a 36-96-2 record, 46½ games out of first. White went 0-for-4 at the plate. It wasn't a storybook ending to a career that started shortly after the Civil War. He finished his career ranked second all-time in RBIs (988), fourth in games (1,560), plate appearances (6,973), at-bats (6,624), hits (2,067), outs (4,574), and total bases (2,605), seventh in runs (1,140), and ninth in extra-base hits (392) and batting average (.312).[104] After the season White was able to get the league to pay the final salaries of the Buffalo players.[105] When the Players' League was no more, so was Deacon's major-league career.

In June 1891 White signed with Elmira (New York-Pennsylvania League) for around $300 a month to manage, captain, and play catcher for the Gladiators.[106] After a few weeks of mixed team success, on July 4, by mutual consent, White left Elmira to retire from the game and go back to Buffalo to "spend the remainder of his days enjoying the fortune of $40,000 which he has accumulated on the diamond."[107] In 10 games with Elmira, Deacon batted .229 with eight singles and no extra-base hits. The team could not afford to pay White for his name alone. It was time to walk away from the game.

Once his playing days were over, White continued to live in Buffalo while maintaining his farm and creamery in Steuben County. He owned a broom factory and livery business in Buffalo and partnered with Will in owning the Buffalo Optical Company. He also continued his spiritual life and in September 1896,

White along with his brother-in-law Henry L. Davis and Rev. H.H. Hickok certified the incorporation of the Advent Christian Church of Buffalo.[108]

White's brother Will died unexpectedly on August 31, 1911, at the age of 56. He was teaching his 12-year-old niece how to swim and suffered a heart attack and drowned.[109]

Jim and Marium moved in 1909 to Mendota, Illinois, to be with their daughter, Grace, who was attending Mendota College. Marium died on April 30, 1914 at the age of 62. She was buried in Restland Cemetery in Mendota. Deacon eventually rekindled an old romance with Alice Melissa (Force) Thurber, with whom he had attended Country Day School in Caton. The couple were married on April 10, 1917, in Rochester, New York.

In the 1920s and 1930s, Deacon continued to be involved with the church, worked for his son-in-law's printing company, listened to major-league baseball games on the radio, and attended games and practices of the Aurora College baseball team. He lived with his daughter and eventually apart from Alice, who moved to New York and then Winston-Salem, North Carolina. She died on August 21, 1944, at the age of 95.

In June 1936 National League President Ford Frick invited White to attend the All-Star Game on July 7 in Boston. Frick wrote: "Yourself, Mr. Tom Bond and Mr. George Wright are, so far as we know, the only surviving players who appeared in the National League at the time of its organization, and we feel that your presence at the All Star game would be a distinction and honor which the National League would much enjoy."[110]

It is probable White's daughter, Grace Watkins, declined on his behalf. Responding to a similar invitation on July 1, she wrote: "Nothing would please Mr. White more than to be able to participate with you in this very interesting celebration. At present Mr. White is quite feeble being nearly 89 years of age and is practically confined to his room. He has always maintained a very great interest in baseball especially in the clubs in which he played. This would have been a great pleasure to him to have accepted your Invitation and had it been a year or two earlier, I believe he would have made the effort to have been with you."[111]

Before the National Baseball Hall of Fame election announcement in 1939, *The Sporting News* wrote: "Plans for the celebration of the centennial of the game at Cooperstown, N.Y., this year would be incomplete if they did not include the installation of a plaque bearing the name of James (Deacon) White, and a special invitation for him to attend the ceremonies as the official representative of the major leagues."[112] When White failed to be elected, the paper wrote: "Baseball passed up a great opportunity to capitalize on sentiment in ignoring this grand old man of the game, now in his 90's, whose waning years could have been glorified by personally seeing his name inscribed in the Hall of Fame, which is dedicated to the sport he so long adorned."[113]

Twenty-five days after the celebration in Cooperstown, Deacon White died of uremic poisoning on July 7, 1939.[114] He was said to have been deeply disappointed that he wasn't elected to the Hall of Fame. He died at his daughter's summer cottage at Camp Rude on the Fox River near St. Charles, Illinois, north of Aurora.[115]

White had been the oldest living former major-league ballplayer since George Wright died on August 21, 1937. John McKelvey was slightly more than three months older than White but only played in 1875 before the NL was formed.

Despite White's passing, the campaign for his election continued for many years, but to no avail.

In December 2008 White received 41.7 percent of the vote from the Veterans Committee, not enough for election. In 2010 the Hall of Fame had revamped the Veterans Committee structure, forming three "era" committees that would rotate each year: Expansion Era (1973-Present), Golden Era (1947-1972), and Pre-Integration Era (Origins-1946). The Pre-Integration Era Committee was third in the rotation and announced its first results on December 3, 2012, electing three new members: Jacob Ruppert, Hank O'Day, and Deacon White. The wait was finally over!

Jerry Watkins, White's great-grandson, spoke at the induction ceremony on behalf of the family on July 29, 2013.

SOURCES

In addition to the sources cited in the Notes, the author also consulted Ancestry.com, Baseball-Reference.com, and Retrosheet.org.

Egan, James M. *Base Ball on the Western Reserve: The Early Game in Cleveland and Northeast Ohio, Year by Year and Town by Town, 1865-1900* (Jefferson, North Carolina: McFarland, 2008).

Maas, David. Files and Notes. Family Friend of Jerry Watkins, great-grandson of Deacon White.

Morris, Peter. *A Game of Inches: The Game Behind the Scenes: The Stories Behind the Innovations That Shaped Baseball* (Chicago: Ivan R. Dee, 2006).

Morris, Peter. *A Game of Inches: The Game on the Field: The Stories Behind the Innovations That Shaped Baseball* (Chicago: Ivan R. Dee, 2005).

Morris, Peter. *Catcher: How the Man Behind the Plate Became an American Folk Hero* (Chicago: Ivan R. Dee, 2009).

Roer, Mike. *Orator O'Rourke: The Life of a Baseball Radical* (Jefferson, North Carolina: McFarland, 2005).

Seymour, Harold. *Baseball: The Early Years* (New York: Oxford University Press, 1960).

Spink, Alfred H. *The National Game* (St. Louis: National Game Publishing Co., 1910).

NOTES

1 Though many sources listed his birthdate as December 7, White's headstone, his Hall of Fame player questionnaire, and other sources list it as December 2. It appears an error was made in the mid-1970s, changing it to December 7, the same birth date as his cousin Willard Elmer White.

2 D.H. Watkins, Letter to Lee Allen, July 23, 1956.

3 Gene Kessler, "Deacon White, Oldest Living Player, at 92 Recalls Highlights of Historic Career That Started in 1868," *The Sporting News*, June 22, 1939: 7B.

4 "Aged Civil War Veteran Is Dead: O. LeRoy White Passes Away at 88; Was Professional Baseball Player," *Evening Leader* (Corning, New York), February 17, 1934: 12.

5 "Championship of the "Southern Tier!" Jamestown Takes the Belt!" *Jamestown* (New York) *Journal*, August 16, 1867: 3.

6 Peter Morris, "Forest City Base Ball Club of Cleveland," *Base Ball Pioneers, 1850-1870: The Clubs and Players Who Spread the Sport Nationwide* (Jefferson, North Carolina: McFarland, 2012), 125-33.

7 "Railway Union Victorious—Champions Beaten—Exciting Game—Interrupted by Rain—Score, Railway, 21; Forest City, 14," *Cleveland Daily Leader*, June 5, 1868: 4.

8 "Forest City Victorious," *Cleveland Plain Dealer*, July 27, 1868: 3.

9 "The Unions Still Champions—A Beautifully Played and Most Interesting Game," *Cleveland Daily Leader*, August 1, 1868: 4.

10 Marshall D. Wright, *The National Association of Base Ball Players, 1857-1870* (Jefferson, North Carolina: McFarland, 2000), 203-04. Home-run and pitching appearance totals from author's research of daily game accounts.

11 The *Cleveland Daily Leader* wrote on July 28 of the coming match between Forest City and the Central City Club, "The game will derive additional interest from the fact that James White, the Forest City catcher of last season, now plays that position in the Central City Club." However, just two days later, the newspaper provided the following: "It turns out that the James White of the Central City club is not the Forest City catcher of last year, but another man of the same name." The "White" on the Syracuse team was Horatio Stevens White.

12 "Base Ball," *Cleveland Daily Leader*, August 2, 1869: 4.

13 "City Items. Base Ball," *Syracuse Daily Standard*, September 15, 1869.

14 "Buffalo against Cleveland—The Game Between the Forest Citys and the Niagaras—Score 32 to 22 in Favor of Cleveland," *Evening Courier & Republic* (Buffalo), September 17, 1869.

15 "Base Ball," *Cleveland Plain Dealer*, March 2, 1870: 3, and March 8, 1870: 3; *Cleveland Daily Leader*, March 15, 1870: 4.

16 "The Forest City Club of Cleveland," *New York Clipper*, May 14, 1870: 43.

17 "The Game Saturday," *Cleveland Daily Leader*, May 23, 1870: 4.

18 "The Game Yesterday—Forest City vs. Forest City—Cleveland Wins—Score 21 to 12—Miscellaneous," *Cleveland Plain Dealer*, June 14, 1870: 3.

19 "An Older Timer. Al Pratt Tells of His Base Ball Career," *The Sporting News*, March 23, 1895: 2. Pratt was the pitcher on June 13, 1870. He said the incident took place in 1872; a probable case of misremembering.

20 "The Return Game Between the Two Forest City Clubs—Cleveland Defeated—Score 24 to 18," *Cleveland Plain Dealer*, June 15, 1870: 3.

21 "Base Ball," *Cleveland Daily Leader*, July 21, 1870: 1; *Cleveland Plain Dealer*, July 21, 1870: 3.

22 Gene Kessler, "'Deacon' White, 84 Years of Age, Recalls How First Professional Baseball Was Played as Early as 1868," *The Sporting News*, November 6, 1930: 7. White recalled, "[M]y windup motion puzzled them," and gave a demonstration of his delivery: "He twisted his shoulders and zipped his arm in a perfect arch. The knuckles almost touched the floor, but we noticed he had used a stiff arm without bending the wrist, had kept his feet flat and face forward."

23 Wright, 301-02.

24 "The Professionals of 1870. Review No. 1," *New York Clipper*, January 21, 1871: 333.

25 "At Home," *Cleveland Daily Leader*, April 26, 1871: 4.

26 "The Finest Game on Record," *New York Clipper*, May 13, 1871: 42.

27 "Almost a Defeat—Elmer White Breaks His Left Arm—Game With the Athletics To-day," *Cleveland Plain Dealer*, June 23, 1871: 3.

28 "Died," *Corning (New York) Journal*, March 28, 1872: 3.

29 Scio town historian Marlea Robbins, telephone interview, March 15, 2016. Historian Frank Russo was also helpful with his insight into the death of Elmer White.

30 "Amusements. Base Ball," *Cleveland Daily Leader*, August 5, 1872: 4.

31 "Funeral of the National Game in Cleveland—The Muffers Disband To-day," *Cleveland Daily Leader*, August 20, 1872: 4.

32 "The Players of 1872. The Catchers—No.2," *New York Clipper*, December 21, 1872: 301.

33 "The Boston Club Games," *New York Clipper*, April 19, 1873: 20.

34 "A Whimsical Freak," *Philadelphia Sunday Dispatch*, April 20, 1873.

35 "Baseball. Notes," *New York Clipper*, April 26, 1873: 26.

36 "Base Ball," *Boston Herald*, April 21, 1873: 4.

37 "Philadelphia vs. Boston," *New York Clipper*, May 3, 1873: 34.

38 "Baseball Gossip," *New York Clipper*, September 6, 1873: 178.

39 "The Players of 1873," *New York Clipper*, February 21, 1874: 373.

40 George V. Tuohey, *A History of the Boston Base Ball Club* (Boston: M.F. Quinn & Co., 1897), 68.

41 "Short Stops," *New York Clipper*, July 25, 1874: 131.

42 William J. Ryczek, *Blackguards and Red Stockings: A History of Baseball's National Association* (Wallingford, Connecticut: Colebrook Press, 1999), 165-66.

43 "The Professional Season of 1874. Fourth Article. The Play and the Players," *New York Clipper*, December 19, 1874: 299.

44 Ibid.

45 "The Championship Record. Defeat of the Bostons," *New York Clipper*, June 12, 1875: 83.

46 "Base Ball," *Daily Evening Traveller* (Boston), June 8, 1875: 1.

47 "Boston Baseball Association," *New York Clipper*, December 25, 1875: 307.

48 "The Chicago Nine for 1876," *Chicago Daily Tribune*, July 24, 1875: 2.

49 "Jim White Rises to Explain," *New York Clipper*, August 7, 1875: 149.

50 "Breaking-Up the Boston Team," *New York Clipper*, July 31, 1875: 139.

51 "Boston vs. Live Oak," *New York Clipper*, October 23, 1875: 237.

52 "Chicago, '76, vs. Boston, '76," *New York Clipper*, October 30, 1875: 242.

53 Gene Kessler, "Deacon Jim White Won First Most Valuable Player Award 55 Years Ago as Boston Star," *The Sporting News*, November 20, 1930: 6.

54 "Local Matters," *Addison (New York) Advertiser*, May 4, 1876.

55 "The Home Willow-wielders Slaughter Devlin and His Varied Phenomena," *Chicago Daily Inter-Ocean*, July 24, 1876: 3.

56 Uri Mulford, *Pioneer Days and Later Times in Corning and Vicinity, 1789-1920* (Corning, New York: U. Milford, 1922), 272.

57 "The Cincinnati Red Stockings Victorious Over the Bostons," *Cincinnati Daily Gazette*, July 21, 1877: 10.

58 "Base Ball," *Cincinnati Commercial*, December 20, 1877: 3.

59 "Baseball. Ball Talk," *New York Clipper*, March 9, 1878: 394.

60 "The League Arena," *New York Clipper*, September 21, 1878: 202.

61 "The Cincinnati Club," *New York Clipper*, November 2, 1878: 253.

62 "The Cincinnati Club," *New York Clipper*, June 21, 1879: 101.

63 Baseball-Reference.com Play Index used to calculate 1870s totals.

64 Tim O'Shea, "Peter Morris on His Catcher Book," *Talking with Tim*, May 20, 2009, talkingwithtim.com/wordpress/2009/05/20/peter-morris-on-his-catcher-book/ (accessed June 12, 2016).

65 "Troy vs. Cincinnati," *New York Clipper*, August 14, 1880: 163.

66 "Later Baseball Notes," *New York Clipper*, October 16, 1880: 238.

67 "Philadelphia vs. Buffalo," *New York Clipper*, May 24, 1884: 152.

68 "Notes," *Cincinnati Commercial*, April 1, 1883: 3.

69 "Sporting Matters," *Detroit Free Press*, April 23, 1885: 3.

70 "Detroit vs. Buffalo," *New York Clipper*, May 9, 1885: 116.

71 "The Buffalo Club," *New York Clipper*, July 18, 1885: 274.

72 "Dots from Other Diamonds," *New Orleans Daily Picayune*, July 25, 1885: 8.

73 "Base Hits," *New York Clipper*, August 29, 1885: 378.

74 "Bought Another Club. The Detroit Management Purchase the Buffalo Franchise," *Detroit Free Press*, September 16, 1885: 8.

75 "A Big Four Puss. The New Yorks Say They Won't Play if the Buffalo Men Do," *Detroit Free Press*, September 19, 1885: 4.

76 "Detroit vs. New York," *New York Clipper*, September 26, 1885: 441.

77 "Baseball. The Big Four," *New York Clipper*, October 3, 1885: 458.

78 "Base Ball," *Washington Sunday Herald*, October 4, 1885: 4.

79 "Detroit's Heavy Disappointment," *St. Paul Daily Globe*, October 21, 1885: 4.

80 "The Big Four Are Ours," *Detroit Free Press*, November 20, 1885: 8. Deacon signed a two-year deal for $7,000.

81 "Piling Up Victories. Base Ball. Liners," *Detroit Free Press*, June 16, 1886: 5.

82 "Tuesday's Great Game," *The Sporting News*, May 24, 1886: 1.

83 "Detroit vs. Pittsburg," *New York Clipper*, June 18, 1887: 217.

84 "Delighted Detroit," *Sporting Life*, October 26, 1887: 5.

85 "National League Record," *New York Clipper*, November 12, 1887: 559.

86 "An Interesting Review of the Peculiar Situation in the Lake City," *New York Clipper*, September 1, 1888: 397-98.

87 "Our Boston Budget. The Deal with Director Stearns for Some of the Detroit Talent," *New York Clipper*, October 27, 1888: 530.

88 "Base Ball Notes," *The Times—Philadelphia*, November 4, 1888: 14; "Boston's Ball Schemes," *New York Times*, November 12, 1888: 5.

89 "Jack Rowe and Deacon White Surprise the Natives. They Buy Buffalo Out," *Buffalo Courier*, December 19, 1888: 3; "Baseball. The Buffalo Deal," *New York Clipper*, December 29, 1888: 673.

90 "Boston's Treachery," *Detroit Free Press*, December 20, 1888: 8.

91 "The Buffalo Deal," *New York Clipper*, December 29, 1888: 673. See also "Among the Ball Men," *New York Herald*, December 21, 1888: 6.

92 "Boston's Treachery"; "Base Ball News," *The Times—Philadelphia*, December 23, 1888; 16.

93 "Stray Sparks from the Diamond," *New York Clipper*, January 5, 1889: 689.

94 "'Deacon' White's Settled Plans," *New York Herald*, March 4, 1889: 9.

95 "The Base Ball World," *Philadelphia Inquirer*, March 11, 1889: 6.

96 "Short Stops," *New York Times*, July 4, 1889: 3; Joseph Overfield, "James "Deacon" White," *The Baseball Research Journal* 4 (1975): 10.

97 "Jim White Talks Business," *Cleveland Leader and Morning Herald*, June 29, 1889: 3.

98 *New York Clipper*, December 28, 1889: 700.

99 *New York Clipper*, January 4, 1890: 716; *New York Clipper*, December 6, 1890: 617.

100 *New York Clipper*, December 28, 1889: 700.

101 "The Players' League. The Western Clubs Playing Their Second Eastern Series of Games," *New York Clipper*, July 19, 1890: 297.

102 "Bracing Up Buffalo. Secretary Brunell Reorganizing the Players' League Club," *The News* (Frederick, Maryland), July 28, 1890: 5; *New York Clipper*, August 2, 1890: 330.

103 "Players' League. Buffalo vs. Brooklyn," *New York Clipper*, October 11, 1890: 490.

104 Baseball-Reference.com. Play Index used to calculate career totals.

105 "Ward, Hanlon and Irwin Added to the General Conference Committee," *Pittsburgh Post*, October 22, 1890: 6.

106 "Six Men Released," *Elmira Daily Gazette and Free Press*, June 13, 1891: 8.

107 "Deacon White Has Gone," *Elmira Daily Gazette and Free Press*, July 6, 1891: 8.

108 "New Church Incorporated," *Buffalo Courier*, September 27, 1896: 11.

109 "Will White, Famous Old Redleg Twirler, Dead at Port Clinton, Ontario," *Cincinnati Enquirer*, September 1, 1911: 2; Ruth Holmes McKee, Letter to Lee Allen, September 6, 1962.

110 Ford Frick, Letter to James L. White, June 3, 1936.

111 Grace Watkins, Letter to L.S. MacPhail, July 1, 1936. MacPhail had invited White to a Reds game to celebrate the NL's 60th anniversary.

112 "An Honor Due Deacon White," *The Sporting News*, April 20, 1939: 4.

113 "Six Hits and An Error," *The Sporting News*, May 11, 1939: 4.

114 D.H. Watkins, Letter to Lee Allen, July 23, 1956.

115 "James White, 92, Ex-Baseball Star," *New York Times*, July 8, 1939: 20.

WHEN JIM WHITE PLAYED

The baseball cranks all sneer at me
    An' poke a lot o' fun,
Because I praise the sort o' plays
    They made in seventy-one,
An' yet who care for fun an' sneers?
    By gum, I know I'm right!
Somehow the game ain't played the same
    As 'twas by old Jim White.

They talk about their great Lajoie,
    Their Wagner an' their Bay;
To hear 'em yarn you'd think, by darn,
    Nobody else could play
An' yet I seem to call to mind
    Those scenes o' wild delight
When 'cross the fence some hit immense
    Was smashed by old Jim White.

An' Lordy! How old Jim could catch!
    He'd stand an' dodge the bat,
'Thout mask or mit—it took some grit
    To snatch 'em in from Pratt.
He'd nail 'em high an' scoop 'em low –
    It was a thrillin' sight;
No player dared—he'd be too scared –
    To catch like old Jim White.

So when you sing o' big Lajoie –
    Don't call the old-uns slow;
The game they knew an' played it, too,
    Some thirty years ago,
An' while, o' course, the players now
    Are men o' grit an' might,
Somehow the game ain't played the same
    As 'twas by old Jim White.

Cleveland Plain Dealer
(*Boston Post*, August 30, 1903)

GEORGE WRIGHT

BY JOHN THORN

"Whenever he would pull off one of those grand, unexpected plays that were so dazzlingly surprising as to dumfound his opponents, his prominent teeth would gleam and glisten in an array of white molars that would put our own Teddy Roosevelt and his famed dentistry establishment far in the shadow."
—Sam Crane[1]

WHO WAS GEORGE WRIGHT? That fans should ask such a question today is unfathomable, but fame can be fleeting, even when memorialized in a plaque at the Baseball Hall of Fame. Wright was elected in 1937, did not live to see his plaque installed, and after all these years has been the subject of no book-length biography. Yet he was *honored in his generation, and was the glory of his times.*

As the greatest player of the period before professional league play, he was the game's first revolving free agent, selling his services to the highest bidder in each of five successive seasons following the Civil War. In 1869 he was the shortstop and batting star of the undefeated Cincinnati Red Stockings, who took on all comers coast to coast. In 57 contests that the Red Stockings played against National Association clubs—established amateur and professional teams—George Wright's bat produced an average of five hits and 10 total bases per game, with 49 home runs among his 304 hits and a batting average of .629. (To the argument that the opposition was frequently soft: in the club's 19 games against fellow professionals—the Reds won all, of course—he hit 13 home runs and batted .587.)

Wright revolutionized the style of playing shortstop, taking advantage of his magnificent arm to play beyond the baselines, an innovation. He led the Boston Red Stockings to six championships in the 1870s, then moseyed down the road to Providence at decade's end and won another. He began a sporting-goods empire that involved him his whole life long; championed the new sports of golf and tennis in this country; played top-rank cricket in baseball's first two international tours (1874 and 1888-1889) and remained active in that sport well into his 50s. He was an enthusiastic golfer in his twilight years and remained a lifelong proponent of exercise and competition.

There's the summary, for one who must run as he reads. But the details of George Wright's epic life are certainly not as well-known as those of Babe Ruth, and he may fairly be called the Babe Ruth of his time. Chronology is God's way of telling a story, so let's begin at the beginning.

As with Ruth, who believed that he was born in 1894 until it was revealed to him, 40 years later, that he was one year younger, George Wright has had his debut botched to this very day. Most sources (including the Hall of Fame) assert that he was born in the Westchester County city of Yonkers, New York, on January 28, 1847.

But in fact George was born in the northern region of New York City known as Yorkville or Harlem.[2] More specifically, he was born into a cricket family whose home was at Third Avenue and 110th Street, easy walking distance to the Red House Grounds, where his father, Samuel, was the resident professional for the St. George Cricket Club (SGCC), which welcomed British expatriates but not players of American birth.

Samuel had been born in Sheffield, Yorkshire, in 1812 and with his wife, Ann (Tone) Wright, and young son, Harry (born in 1835), he came to the United States via Liverpool in 1836, lured by an offer from the Dragon Slayers. The other Wright children were all born in New York, including George's older brother, Daniel, and younger brothers, William and Samuel Jr. Harry trained as a silversmith (and George as an engraver) but, like his brothers, in turn took to cricket under their father's tutelage and, in the case of Harry and

George, went on to become assistant professionals with the SGCC.

In 1854 the St. George's Cricket Club—which had begun life in the 1830s with grounds at Manhattan's Bloomingdale Road (today's Broadway) and 30th Street before relocating to the Red House Grounds—accepted the invitation of the New York Cricket Club, whose players were all American-born, to share their space at the Elysian Fields, across the Hudson River.³ The Wright household relocated to Hoboken and Sam Sr. continued as instructor, groundskeeper, and principal bowler. Harry became a formidable cricketer, playing his first contest with the SGCC in 1850.⁴

Little Georgie, "when scarcely taller than a wicket," also displayed a great aptitude for the game, and by his own account began play with the junior club in 1857, at the age of 10. By the time he turned 13, in 1860, he began to play alongside the men of St. George.⁵ When he was 16 years old, in 1863, he played in first-eleven matches with men twice his own age. Let George tell his own cricket story:

I first commenced playing cricket when about ten years of age in the rear of the house where I lived at Hoboken, N.J. Under a long grape arbor my father first placed a cricket bat in my hands and taught me the way to handle it, as well as the way to bowl. The first match I played in was at the age of thirteen, as one of the St. George's junior eleven against the Newark Juniors, at Newark (I then being not much higher than the wickets). I bowled well in this match, taking five wickets, for which the president of the St. George Club gave me a silver quarter dollar for each wicket captured. During that season I also played in several second eleven matches, after which I commenced to play on the first eleven at different times, and when sixteen years old I became a regular first eleven man. I visited Boston with the club, and no doubt many of the old cricket members of the Boston Club will remember me as little Georgie, as I was then called. In this match, against the Boston Club, I made double figures and bowled well, for which I was presented with a silver mug. After the match I threw a cricket ball one hundred and fifteen yards, which was considered a very long throw in those days. The Boston cricketers took my cap and placed in it many silver dollars. … During the two seasons I was with the Cincinnati Reds, I played one cricket match, that was when the club visited California, we [played] a picked eleven of San Francisco, defeating the cricketers easily. I made 50 runs in this match. During the time I was a member of the Boston Baseball Club, the team played three or four matches a season, generally defeating all comers, owing to the good fielding of our ball players, and the bowling of my brother, Harry, and myself. In 1872 I was selected as one of the Massachusetts Twenty-two to play against Grace's Eleven, which game was played on the baseball grounds. … After retiring from baseball in 1880, I became a regular member of the Longwood Club, of Boston, playing with them ever since. Cricket was my first game, and I always enjoyed playing it, and I look forward to continue playing it for a number of years to come.⁶

The Wright brothers had become infatuated with baseball, too. Both had been exposed to the American game and played with verve on fields adjoining the cricket grounds at the Elysian Fields. "There were, of course," George recalled in 1888, "other base ball clubs in existence in Brooklyn, notably the old Atlantics, Stars, Excelsiors, Enterprise, etc., but the real center of base ball was at Hoboken. Here there were located three grounds, where from six to eight clubs would play practice games on various afternoons of the week, and it was here, while a member of the Gotham club, that I first learned to play ball."⁷

Harry had become a member of the Knickerbocker Base Ball Club in 1858 and was instantly deemed so proficient that he was named to play in the first of the summer's Fashion Race Course all-star games, a three-game series pitting the best of New York clubs against their counterparts from Brooklyn. Continuing to divide his attentions with cricket, Harry remained with the Knickerbocker club until 1863, when he joined the equally venerable but by that time more competitive Gotham club. Sixteen-year-old George played catcher and outfield for the Gotham Juniors

George Wright (Spalding Collection)

but by midseason he also played with the first-class club. On September 11, against the Star of Brooklyn, both played in a match game for the Gothams: according to the published box score, Harry at catcher and George in left field but it is possible that their positions were in fact reversed.[8]

For 1864 the Wrights returned to the Gotham club but by the following year both were on the move. George accepted a position as the professional of the Philadelphia Cricket Club. He took part in baseball games, too, with the Olympic Club, which had been founded as a town-ball club in 1833 but recently converted to the new game of baseball. Harry, too, left the Gothams for a job as a cricket pro—fatefully, as events would unfold—with the Union Cricket Club of Cincinnati; he had seen no way to earn a living in baseball. But the cricket post he would soon exchange for an opportunity to manage and captain, at the same salary, the Cincinnati Base Ball Club. Oddly, Philadelphia and Cincinnati had been the two enduring hotbeds of town ball and had taken to baseball with a near frenzy.

A book in the Hall of Fame's collection, *Felix on the Bat*, supplies a fine memento of the Wright family's cricket heritage. Beautifully illustrated, the book was a classic instructional written and illustrated by the great Kent and All-England batsman of the 1840s, Nicholas Wanostrocht, whose pen name was "N. Felix." Sam gave the book to George when the boy was 18, but George had long studied it at his father's knee. In later years he wrote on the flyleaf: "This book I prize very highly as it was given to me by my Father in the year 1865. Often I have viewed its contents when a boy looking forward to some day to play the game of cricket well. G.W."

Though employed in Philadelphia in 1865, George returned to the Elysian Fields of Hoboken for a benefit game staged for his father on September 20. Advanced in years, Sam Sr. nonetheless would continue to play cricket even after his departure to Boston in the 1870s, where Harry and George would make their fortunes.

In 1866 George returned to New York City and assumed his first (covertly) paid baseball position as shortstop and sometime third baseman of the Union Club of Morrisania. This was a celebrated early team, of interest for such other professionals as Dave Birdsall, who went on to play with George for Boston in the National Association, and Charlie Pabor, longtime pitcher and outfielder with the most inexplicable of all baseball nicknames: "The Old Woman with the Red Cap."

But peripatetic George left the champion Unions after the 1866 campaign to join the subsidized Washington Nationals as they planned their tour of the West (what is today termed the Midwest). George was supposedly earning his living as a government clerk, but the address of his "employer" as listed in the City Directory was a public park. Below are the Nationals and their nominal occupations and places of employment. No one seemed to mind their extended absence from their desks during the tour.[9]

W.F. Williams, law student.
F.P. Norton, clerk in Treasury.
G.H.E. Fletcher, clerk in Third Auditor's Office.

E.A. Parker, clerk in Internal Revenue Department.

E.G. Smith, clerk in Fourth Auditor's Office.

Geo. H. Fox, graduate (July 3), Georgetown College.

S.L. Studley, clerk in Treasury.

H. W. Berthrong, clerk for Comptroller of the Currency.

George Wright, clerk, 238 Pennsylvania Avenue.

H.C. McLean, clerk in Third Auditor's Office.

A.N. Robinson, clerk, Washington D.C.

The Nationals traveled as far as Illinois, where they were upset—in their only loss of the tour—by the Forest City of Rockford and their boy pitcher, Albert Spalding. George "played short, and his style of meeting a ground ball with his heels, brought together as the ball came within handling distance, and meeting it well in front to deaden it by giving with it, was something new," and, as described in 1897, "has never been improved on to this day."[10]

In a game against the Cincinnati Red Stockings, Harry's expected pleasure in playing against his brother's club soon was dashed: After initially holding their own against the Nationals, tied at 6-6 into the fourth inning, the Reds ultimately were humiliated by a count of 53-10. Although this would be their only loss of the year, it came against their lone opponent from outside the tristate area, and so a lesson was there to be drawn. At the end of the season, the Red Stocking club directors instructed Harry to follow the Nationals' model and begin recruiting professionals from distant places.

Returning to New York in 1868, George was welcomed back by the Unions of Morrisania. In a little noted sidelight, the return to New York enabled George, with the distant participation of brother Harry, to establish a "base ball and cricket depot."[11] In the 1869 New York City Directory, George Wright is listed as being in the business of "balls," at 615 Broadway, residing at 300 Willow in Hoboken. Harry is listed in the same place of business, though with an unlisted residence; we of course know he resided in Cincinnati.[12] The venture lasted only this one year, but would be resumed in Boston in 1871 as [George] Wright & [Charles] Gould at 18 Boylston Street and, later on, as the long-lived [George] Wright & [Henry A.] Ditson firm. In between, George had a solo operation, selling "cigars and base ball goods," at, first, 18 Boylston; then, 591 Washington Street; and, next, 39 Eliot Street. Harry Wright's later partners in Boston-based sporting goods would be George Howland and Louis Mahn.

We have seen that Harry felt the need to improve his Red Stockings after their thrashing by the Nationals. The arrival in 1868 of pitcher Asa Brainard from the 1867 Nationals—he had been the successor to Jim Creighton with the Excelsior of Brooklyn—and local first baseman Charlie Gould strengthened the club. Harry also signed New Yorkers John Van Buskirk Hatfield and Fred Waterman, and brought in catcher Doug Allison from Philadelphia. For 1869, he embraced the Nationals' model of total professionalism. In short order, Harry turned away all the club's local lads except for Gould; relinquished the revolver Hatfield back to the Mutuals, his former club; and signed Cal McVey from Indianapolis. He also reached terms with Charlie Sweasy, Andy Leonard, and Dick Hurley from the local Buckeyes, the first two having come to Cincinnati by way of their former club, the Irvingtons of New Jersey, the last named by way of Columbia College in New York.

But Harry's great coup was to secure the perpetually available services of his brother George, unbound by long-term contract or a not-yet-dreamed-of reserve clause. Thus were the 1869 Red Stockings set to become the most accomplished club in the land and, at $9,300 in salaries alone, the most profligate. George was paid $1,400, even more than Harry, whose $1,200 salary was second highest. The money made the team powerful, but no one could have imagined that they would be literally unbeatable. George Wright became baseball's first nationwide hero.

The Red Stockings took on all comers, from Maine to California, in 1869, and never tasted defeat. They won 84 consecutive games in 1869-1870 before getting their comeuppance from the venerable Atlantics of Brooklyn, the champions of several earlier 1860s campaigns.

On June 14, 1870, at the Capitoline Grounds in Brooklyn, the Reds jumped off to a 2-0 lead in the first, but the Atlantics held a lead of 4-3 after six frames. The Reds regained the lead with two tallies in the seventh, but the Atlantics knotted the contest at 5-5 in the eighth, and there things stood at the conclusion of nine innings. Captain Bob Ferguson of the Atlantics agreed to a draw, as was the custom, but Harry Wright of the Reds insisted that the game be played to a conclusion, "if it took all summer."[13] Backed up by Reds president Aaron B. Champion, he ordered his men back on the field. Ferguson then did the same for his Atlantics.

After a scoreless 10th, the Reds appeared to settle the issue with two runs in the top of the 11th. But Brainard's nerve was wearing thin, according to the *New York Clipper* report.[14] He allowed a leadoff single to Charlie Smith, then followed with a wild pitch that sent Smith all the way to third. "Old Reliable," first baseman Joe Start, drove a long fly to right field, where Cal McVey had difficulty extricating the ball from the standing-room-only crowd. Smith scored, and now Start was on third. At this point Ferguson came to the plate and, seeing how his men had been foiled by George Wright's brilliant plays time and again, the right-handed hitter turned around to bat from the left side, simply to keep the ball away from the Reds' shortstop—thus becoming the game's first documented switch-hitter.

Ferguson drove the ball past the second baseman to tie the score. When George Zettlein drove a liner toward first base, Charlie Gould blocked it, but threw hurriedly and wildly to second base in an attempt to force Ferguson. The ball skittered into left field, and Ferguson scampered home with the winning run. Additional batters came to the plate, for the rules did not yet call for the game to end until three outs were registered in the final half-inning, but no further scoring ensued. After the contest, Champion telegraphed the following message back to Cincinnati: "Atlantics 8, Cincinnatis 7. The finest game ever played. Our boys did nobly, but fortune was against us. Eleven innings played. Though beaten, not disgraced."[15]

Interest in the Red Stockings waned in the second half of the 1870 season as they had the temerity to lose six of that season's 74 contests. Cincinnati fans, their passions stoked by the club's directors, accused the players—the Wrights in particular—of sabotage.[16]

During the various tours our club made through the country the past season, these players [the Wrights], it is said, convened councils of the best and most prominent members of opposing nines. In these councils they took pains to impress upon the minds of their fellow professionals the great value of their services, and the limited compensation they were receiving. ... The result of all this maneuvering has been that the players whose services are desirable hold themselves at such enormous figures as to preclude the possibility of an established club engaging them with any hope of meeting expenses with the receipts of games. ... The officers of the Cincinnati club are, of course, highly indignant at this procedure upon the part of the Wrights, and with characteristic independence, will not submit to be dictated to. ... The members of the late first nine, with their inflated ideas of their market value, will be permitted to drift wherever chance or self-interest may lead them.[17]

Has it not been ever thus? The Cincinnati directors withdrew their support, the club disbanded, and the ballpark was razed, with the lumber and the Red Stocking trophy bats and balls hammered down at auction.

Harry "drifted on" on to form the Boston Red Stockings as a charter member of the newly formed National Association of Professional Base Ball Players, bringing along fellow Cincinnati alumni McVey, Gould, and brother George. To this nucleus he added Rockford stars Al Spalding and Ross Barnes and, in 1873, Cleveland's Deacon White. The rest of the 1870 Reds—Brainard, Leonard, Sweasy, Waterman, and Allison—went to Washington to play with the Olympics.

Despite its imposing lineup, Boston fell short of the winning the flag in 1871 as George suffered a leg injury in an outfield collision that kept him out of all but 16 of the club's 31 games. The collision was due to Fred Cone not hearing George call him off, because of a train whistle; the New York, New Haven, and

Hartford Railroad tracks ran along the third-base stands. Second baseman Barnes was compelled to play shortstop, with the light-hitting Sam Jackson taking over at the keystone sack.

The league provided no mandated slate of games, but instead left it to the clubs to schedule five games with each competitor with three victories ending the series—so the teams played varying numbers of games. Although all games played were recorded in the standings, winning percentage did not determine the champion. But the major innovation of the National Association, besides its very existence, was the establishment of a pennant race. The Philadelphia Athletics captured the flag in that inaugural season, by virtue of a defeat on October 30 of the demoralized Chicago White Stockings, playing in borrowed uniforms of various hues and styles because their equipment (and their ballpark) had been destroyed in the Great Fire three weeks earlier.

The Wrights and Boston, however, rolled over the competition in the next four years, winning by increasingly grotesque margins, thus hastening the demise of the National Association. George, who hit .413 in his curtailed season of 1871, went on to hit .337, .387, .329, and .333 while fielding his position brilliantly.

After Boston went 71-8 in 1875, winning the pennant in a cakewalk, the Chicago White Stockings, upset that such Western stars as Spalding and Cap Anson were playing for clubs in the East, staged a coup that exploded the National Association. Because Chicago owner William Hulbert entered into surreptitious negotiations with Spalding—as well as White, Barnes, and McVey—during the 1875 season, he feared that revelation of his plan would lead to Chicago's being expelled from the National Association. Instead, he withdrew from the circuit and enlisted the strongest clubs to join him in a new National League.

The Wrights stayed in town, but Boston's "Big Four," along with Anson of the Philadelphia Athletics, were indeed lured back to the region of their youth. After Chicago won the league's inaugural flag in 1876, Boston resumed its winning ways with pennants in 1877 and '78. George's batting began to slip in his National League years, and his range decreased to the extent that he moved to second base in 1877, the year of his father's death. In 1878 he returned to shortstop and Boston won, but he batted only .225; it looked like the end of a glorious trail.

In his heyday, there wasn't "an infielder in the game today who had anything on George Wright when it came to playing shortstop, and certainly there was none during his time," Deacon White later said. "George fielded hard-hit balls bare-handed, gathered them up or speared them when in the air with either hand. He was an expert and accurate thrower, being able to throw with either hand."[18] Added Sam Crane: "George Wright was about 5 feet 10 inches tall and weighed about 160 in his prime. I remember him; he had a thick crop of dark curly hair, a small mustache and a dab on either cheek for a bluff at 'siders' [a.k.a. burnsides, today known as sideburns]. He was slightly bowlegged, and I never knew a bowlegged ballplayer who was not a crackerjack—a la Hans Wagner."[19]

George's heyday may have been past, yet he had one last hurrah on the playing field. In 1879 he left Boston for Providence, taking with him outfielder Jim O'Rourke, and George's Grays won the championship by five games over brother Harry's Red Stockings.

In 1880 George wished to return to Boston to be nearer his now thriving sporting-goods business. But National League owners had instituted a reserve clause in 1879, ostensibly concerned about the annual revolving of players from club to club, and the snatching of players from lower classifications in midseason; in truth the reserve clause was greeted by some players, grateful for the security, and reviled by others, as its effect was to tamp down salaries.

As I wrote in *Baseball in the Garden of Eden*:
At first the reserve clause applied only to five players per club, who by and large were pleased to be so designated, for to be reserved meant to be assured of a job. Within four years, however, the reserve clause came to apply to nearly all the players on a roster, binding them to one employer for life and providing management with a cudgel to keep player conduct and salary demands in line. … It did not take long for the problems attendant to the reserve clause to manifest. George Wright,

who had been the greatest player in the land for a decade, with the Red Stockings of Cincinnati and then Boston, in 1879 led the Providence Grays to the championship. On April 21, 1880, however, he declined the club's final contract offer, perhaps preferring to stay in Boston and mind his sporting-goods business. As a reserved player, however, he was obligated to play for Providence and no other; he elected to sit out the season (although he did inexplicably play in a game for Boston on May 29). For 1881, no longer under reserve, he signed to play with Boston.[20]

George did manage to play in seven games for Boston in 1881, but he was clearly finished. When brother Harry became manager of the Grays for 1882, George joined him for one last pennant race, but the Grays finished second to the Chicago White Stockings by three games. After batting .162 in 46 games at shortstop, George left baseball for a return to business life and an occasional game of cricket … or so he thought.

In 1884 he became an owner of the Boston franchise in the Union Association, a rival major league—a second rival, actually, after the founding of the American Association in 1882—that "granted" to Wright & Ditson the supply of its official ball. When the Unions folded after one season, Wright returned his attention to his business, which Albert Spalding purchased in 1892 along with the sporting-goods firm of Al Reach—secretly in each case so as to avoid possible antitrust action under the new (1890) Sherman Antitrust Act. Both of the acquired firms appeared to act independently for years thereafter. Both Wright and Reach retained cordial relations with Spalding, and accepted his offer to serve on the Mills Commission of 1905-1907, which was responsible for determining the origin of baseball.

In 1888 Spalding invited George to come along on the baseball world tour of 1888-89, especially for his ability to play cricket, which the baseballists would be expected to play in England. Both of the Wrights and Spalding—indeed, the entire Red Stocking and Athletic clubs—had interrupted the 1874 regular season for two months to make baseball's first such expedition.

Sam Crane observed that "while the introduction of baseball to our English cousins was not a pronounced success, still the ballplayers taught the Britishers some few points about their own game—cricket. It was always eighteen ball-players against eleven cricketers, but the Americans were never defeated at the English game, and George Wright was the crack batter of the American eighteen."[21]

In 1922 Wright & Ditson issued a booklet celebrating its 50th anniversary, prompting some latter-day historians to claim that Ditson joined the firm in 1872, when he was 16. But the golden jubilee was for George Wright alone, who had conducted his sporting-goods business continuously since 1871. Henry A. Ditson did not join him until sometime in 1879, after four years in a provisions (grocery/general) business in which he became a partner, [Lewis P.] Bird & Ditson. One may understand why George wished to return to Boston in 1880 and did so, despite being compelled to sit out from baseball for a year because of the reserve clause.

The combination of Wright's celebrity and Ditson's backroom skills soon led to an expansion of operations and the location of new retail stores in New York City, Chicago, and San Francisco, in addition to Providence and Cambridge. The company began to offer not only baseball goods but also uniforms and equipment for lawn tennis, cricket, lacrosse, football, bicycling, polo, camping, and fishing.

Ditson's particular passion was lawn tennis, which he correctly predicted would be the bellwether of the business. By 1883 the company was manufacturing the sport's regulation tennis balls and publishing the official rules of the game. Wright & Ditson lawn tennis racquets became the gold standard.

Wright, on the other hand, while continuing an active playing regimen in cricket, attached his company's efforts to the rising sport of collegiate football. In 1882 the company secured the right to publish the American Intercollegiate Association's "Foot-Ball Rules" as compiled by Walter Camp, the "Referee's Book" and the "Foot-Ball Record Book." Publishing the books for the Association enabled Wright & Ditson to put their catalog in the hands of nearly every football player in the country.

On November 15, 1891, the 35-year-old Ditson died of heart disease. He had been responsible for the day-to-day operations of the company and replacing him would be difficult. By February 1892, Wright had made his decision; he quietly sold the controlling interest in Wright & Ditson (9,997 of the 9,999 company shares) to A.G. Spalding. Spalding brought in John Morrill, Wright's former Boston Red Stockings teammate, to oversee Wright & Ditson's retail department. Perhaps the most important acquisition by Spalding in 1892 was control over Wright & Ditson publications. By the mid-1890s, official Spalding guides replaced almost all of the major sports annuals previously produced by Wright & Ditson. A decade later, after the consolidation had fully taken hold—adding the Victor company into the consortium—Spalding would become the primary supplier of football equipment, Reach dominated in baseball offerings, and Wright & Ditson's tennis and golf lines were considered the best in the nation.

As great a cricketer, baseballist and businessman as he was, George may be best known today for his contributions to golf. On one of his trips abroad in the 1880s he found some golf equipment in a store. He didn't know what the implements were for, but concluding they were in the sporting line, he purchased a set. In Boston he put the clubs on a shelf and let them gather dust. Soon along came a Scotchman by the name of Findlay who wondered what they were doing there. Wright explained that he was at a loss to know how to use the things. The Scotchman enlightened him. They got their heads together, and not long thereafter, as none is more zealous than the convert, George Wright established, in October 1890, the first public nine-hole golf course in the United States at Franklin Park in Boston. (This "first" is challenged by Van Cortlandt Park, a layout in the Bronx, which may have beaten Franklin Park to the proverbial punch by a matter of months.)[22]

The *New York Times* obituary in 1937 referred to Wright as "the father of the ancient game [of golf] in this country," having been one of the first to popularize the Scottish sport on American shores.[23] Wright and Ditson imported and sold golf clubs; none other than US Open champion Francis Ouimet worked at the store while pursuing his amateur career. He would later say that George Wright "...did as much toward developing the game of golf in this country as any man," even if Wright's greatest gift was to approve of giving Ouimet additional vacation time so he could enter the 1913 Open.[24] The 20-year-old caddie defeated the British "old guard"—Harry Vardon and Ted Ray—in a playoff, becoming the first amateur to win the title.

George left baseball as an active player in 1882 but, still fit from his play at cricket, tennis, and golf, donned a uniform again a couple of times, in 1896 and 1897. The first instance was to honor his recently deceased brother Harry, in a National League sponsored "Harry Wright Day," marked with games in several venues to raise money for a suitable burial monument. For Harry Wright Day at Rockford, Illinois, Al Spalding squeezed into his old uniform and pitched for a team of his Forest City playmates. On the opposing side in a Boston uniform was George Wright.

George's second and final time in baseball togs was on June 21, 1897, when he played shortstop at the South End Grounds against a touring Australian baseball team. This game was notable as well for an exhibition of Professor Hinton's new automatic pitching machine. After the game, George Wright organized a banquet in the visitors' honor.

In 1925 he attended the Golden Jubilee celebration of the founding of the National League. In 1935 when the National League instituted the award of lifetime passes to veterans of long service, he was given pass number 1. Serving Commissioner Landis, Wright took part in the Centennial Committee that conceptualized the plans for the National Baseball Hall of Fame; in 1937 he was honored as its 12th inductee and the first player whose entire career was in the nineteenth century. (Connie Mack, also honored in 1937, could be thus described but he was not inducted on account of his playing credentials.)

George Wright died at his home in Dorchester, Massachusetts, on August 21, 1937. His resting place is the Holyhood Cemetery in Brookline. He was preceded in death (1913) by his wife, Abigail, whom he had married in Boston in 1872, and was survived by his three children: sons Irving and Beals and daughter Elizabeth. Both his sons were noted tennis players and Beals, as a member of the International Tennis Hall of Fame, forms with his father a unique two-sport Hall of Fame tandem.

NOTES

1   Undated clip, part of a series on "The Fifty Greatest Ball Players in History" by Sam Crane that ran in the *New York Evening Journal* in 1911-12.
2   Wright's marriage record and passport, available on Ancestry.com, say he was born in New York City. See also Bill King, *Lewiston Daily Sun,* January 27, 1937.
3   "NYCC lets St. George Come to Hoboken," classified advertisement in *New York Herald,* May 9, 1854.
4   Lindsey Flewelling, "*The Wright Family, Cricket in America, and the First Professional Baseball Team,*" britishandirishhistory.wordpress.com/2016/04/06/THE-WRIGHT-FAMILY-CRICKET-IN-AMERICA-AND-THE-FIRST-PROFESSIONAL-BASEBALL-TEAM/.
5   George Wright, *Record of the Boston Base Ball Club, Since Its Organization: With a Sketch of All Its Players For 1871, '72, '73, and '74 and other items of interest* (Boston: B.B.B.C., Rockwell & Churchill, 1874.)
6   *New York Clipper,* April 25, 1891.
7   *Boston Herald,* June 18, 1888.
8   *New York Clipper,* September 19, 1863.
9   *Ball Players' Chronicle,* August 8, 1867: 2, in letter from Frank Jones, club president.
10 George V. Tuohey, *A History of the Boston Base Ball Club* (Boston: M.F. Quinn, 1897), 198.
11 *Ball Players' Chronicle,* March 3, 1868: 77; also, advertisement in *Clipper,* April 18, 1868.
12 New York City Directory, 1869 directory listing.
13 Harry Ellard, *Base Ball in Cincinnati: A History* (Cincinnati: self-published, 1907), 188.
14 *New York Clipper,* June 25, 1870.
15 Ellard, 189.
16 *Cincinnati Daily Gazette,* November 23, 1870.
17 Ibid.
18 baseballhall.org/hof/wright-george.
19 Sam Crane.
20 John Thorn, *Baseball in the Garden of Eden* (New York: Simon & Schuster, 2011), 172-173.
21 Sam Crane.
22 W.D. Whitman, "George Wright," *Canton Commercial Advertiser,* September 14, 1937; nyshistoricnewspapers.org/lccn/sn85054395/1937-09-14/ed-1/seq-3/
23 Obituary, *New York Times,* August 22, 1937.
24 Francis Ouimet, *A Game of Golf* (Boston: Houghton Mifflin, 1932), 45.

HARRY WRIGHT

BY CHRISTOPHER DEVINE

WILLIAM HENRY WRIGHT, BETTER known to the baseball community as Harry Wright, strikes historians as, in the words of Bruce Markusen of the National Baseball Hall of Fame, an "especially underrated Hall of Famer."[1] He was regarded in his time as "The Father of Professional Base Ball," but Wright's modern legacy pales in comparison, though many of his innovations mark the game that we know today.

The time and place of Wright's birth to Samuel Wright Sr. and Annie Tone Wright (married in 1830) is not certain, but it is most often recorded as January 10, 1835, in Sheffield, Yorkshire, England. The age listed on Wright's birth certificate, however, implies that he was born on December 13, 1834, while genealogical records from the Mormon Church suggest that he was born on November 8, 1832, in Leeds, England.[2] Nonetheless, it is most likely that Wright was born in 1835; he never disputed this date during his lifetime, and it is supported by US Census records.

Further mysteries surround Wright's early life. The exact date of his arrival in the United States also is uncertain, although it appears that Samuel, a "fancy wood turner" by trade, came to New York City with his family in 1836 to become a professional cricketer for the St. George's Dragonslayers. This year also witnessed the birth of Dan Wright, mostly unknown to baseball historians because he was the only one of the four Wright brothers not to take up the game professionally. (Dan moved to San Jose, California, sometime between 1861 and 1877.[3]) Subsequent additions to the Wright family included George (born January 26, 1847); Samuel Jr., or Sammy (November 25, 1848); and Mary (1858).

A rumor later circulated that George Wright was, in fact, a Hall of Fame half-brother to Harry. Its source was a statement by George's housekeeper on his 1937 death certificate that he was the son of a woman named Mary Love. There is no evidence to support such a claim, nor is it clear that Love actually existed or was connected to the Wright family.

Harry Wright dropped out of public school in 1849, at the age of 14, to apprentice as a jeweler at Tiffany's. The following year, he joined the Dragonslayers, the team for which his father—one of the most revered cricketers of his day—played until 1869. By 1857 Harry began receiving money for his performance as a cricketer. It was during that year, while coaching George in cricket on the Elysian Fields in Hoboken, New Jersey, that he looked over to an adjoining field and witnessed his first game of baseball.

Wright quickly adapted to, and grew to love, the sport. At 5-feet-9¾ and 157 pounds, the right-hander distinguished himself as a formidable athlete. He and George were regarded by the *New York Dispatch* as "the best exponents of batting as a science in the country," and the *Detroit Post* once labeled Harry as "the finest, safest, best, and least showy player in America."[4]

Wright played his first game for the New York Knickerbockers on July 8, 1858, after joining the club the previous year. Later in July, he participated in the historic Fashion Course Matches, which for the first time charged money for admittance. In 1863 he possibly became the first player to (openly) receive money for a game when a "benefit" was held by the Knickerbockers for him, his father, and others. Harry, the only one to actually make money from the benefit, received $29.65.

The Civil War so decimated the Knickerbockers' schedule—to say nothing of the United States, of course—that Wright decided to join the New York Gothams in 1864. But by the next year he had left the Gothams, and baseball altogether, to accept a position as instructor and bowler for Cincinnati's Union Cricket Club.

In March 1865 Wright went west with his wife of four years, Mary Fraser, and their children, 4-year-old Charles, young Lucy Louise, and newborn George

Harry Wright (Spalding Collection)

William, or Willy. Mary soon died of unknown causes, and on September 10, 1868, Harry married Caroline Mulford. They had six children: Hattie (born March 30, 1869), Stella (1870), Harry II (August 4, 1871), Carrie (January 27, 1874), Albert (December 20, 1874), and William (July 13, 1876). The two sets of children resented each other, and Mary's children later lived with Harry's brother Sammy as well as with his sister, Mary.

In Cincinnati Wright quickly returned to baseball in much the same way he first came to it, after witnessing a game on an adjoining field as he played cricket. After talking with Cincinnati Base Ball Club president Aaron Champion, he initiated a mass exodus of Union Cricket Club players to the base-ball club that took the field together in the fall of 1866. Wright adapted his bowling techniques from cricket to become an effective pitcher known for his offspeed pitches, in contrast to the hard-throwing pitchers of the day. He took advantage of this contrast when taking over pitching duties in the middle of a game from fireballer Asa Brainard—an early instance of what now is known as relief pitching. Wright was also prolific at the bat. While playing for Cincinnati in 1867, he hit 22 home runs and scored 112 times over a 17-game stretch. This included a game on June 23, in Newport, Kentucky, in which Wright hit an unfathomable seven home runs. He also pitched the game, and won.

A visit to the West in 1867 by the dominant Washington Nationals, for whom George Wright played shortstop, inspired Harry and the Cincinnati Base Ball Club to consider launching a tour of their own. The Red Stockings, as the team was called from its attire, were in need of such an idea since their dominance of local teams had made it difficult for them to turn a profit. A tour to other parts of the United States might bring such profits if the Red Stockings were good enough to compete against the nation's best clubs.

To make such a tour feasible, the Red Stockings would field an openly all-professional team in 1869— the first of its kind. Originally, club officials intended to sign every player who won an 1868 Clipper Medal, the equivalent, one might say, of a modern All-Star selection. But when this plan proved unrealistic, Wright was given the task of recruiting the necessary talent; a combination scout and general manager. Wright put together a team of young players who, even if not individually outstanding, would function well as a team. His emphasis on teamwork earned him recognition from sportswriter Tim Murnane as the originator of the very concept itself.[5] Supporting this lofty designation was Wright's remarkable record of innovations that helped the team to function as an integrated unit—chief among them the use of hand signals to fielders, calling balls in the air, having one fielder back up another, platooning, and the hit-and-run.

The results of Wright's efforts were impressive, to say the least; the Red Stockings dominated at home and abroad throughout the 1869 season. During a tour of the East against the heralded teams of New York, Philadelphia, and elsewhere, the club went undefeated, shocking the sports world. The fame of the Red Stockings became so great that they were asked to tour the Western United States as well, particularly California. No such trip ever had been undertaken. But the Cincinnatis swept the competition, helping to spread the popularity of baseball nationwide in the process.

The Red Stockings impressed not only with their quality of play, but also with their upstanding conduct. This was particularly important because, many suspected that the Red Stockings, as the first professional baseball club, would prove to be a corrupting influence on what had been a purely amateur, gentleman's game. Yet the team earned a reputation for honesty, discipline, and fair play that can easily be traced to the leadership of its manager, center fielder, and effectively its general manager: Harry Wright.

Wright's reputation as the most ethical gentleman in the game—"There was no figure more creditable to the game than dear old Harry," said *The Sporting News* [6]—defied the money-grubbing stereotype of what an exponent of professionalism was expected to be. Instead, he emphasized the necessity of fair play and high ethical standards for the advancement of the game, and exemplified both through his own conduct. In one 1868 home game, he reversed the blatantly errant ruling of an umpire seeking to curry the favor of the Cincinnati crowd. Owing largely to this action, the Red Stockings lost the game. In later years Wright even was entrusted to umpire games within his own league.

The Red Stockings eventually met defeat in a close and controversial game against the Brooklyn Atlantics on June 14, 1870. From there, the club unraveled after further losses and the desertion of the Cincinnati fan base. The once-adoring press sharply turned on the club, which by the end of the year officially splintered in an ugly public drama.

Wright took the team name and several of its players to Boston, to take part in the new National Association of Professional Base Ball Players (NAPBBP, often shortened to NA), baseball's first all-professional league, formed only two years after Cincinnati, through Wright's leadership, fielded the sport's first all-professional team. By the end of its run in 1875, the National Association came to be known as "Harry Wright's League" because his Boston club so thoroughly dominated it. After a disappointing 1871 season, in which it finished second to Philadelphia, the club rebounded to capture four consecutive titles, a feat unequaled in the sport for several decades.

The Boston Red Stockings also extended the concept of a professional baseball tour to reach outside the United States' borders—first, to Canada, then with an 1874 tour of the British Isles conceived by the ever-innovative Harry Wright. Alas, it was an ill-conceived venture from the start, seemingly more of a personal dream of Wright's than a wise professional plan, and it resulted in financial disaster. The ever-frugal and business-minded Wright had to accept financial loss in his desire to see the game that he championed catch fire in the land of his birth. That hope failed for two reasons: the incompetent work of an agent paid to arrange and promote games in England; and Englishmen's reticence to abandon their beloved cricket for the inferior American stepchild called "base ball." Upon his return, Wright was despondent: "We had an early frost," he wrote a friend. "I feel frosty." [7]

The financial impact of the tour was devastating to the National Association, mostly because it removed from competition the Association's two strongest clubs, Boston and the Philadelphia Athletics. In 1876 the league was supplanted by an upstart organization, the National League, that proved to have far more staying power. Wright did not resist the new league, and in fact had an integral role in its founding. He realized that the NA was financially weak and too dominated by Eastern clubs to be viable in the long term. The NL, on the other hand, included strong Western clubs and thus seemed capable of functioning as a truly national baseball league.

Reminiscent of the beginning of the NA, the Boston club underachieved in the National League's inaugural year and then went on to win two consecutive championships. The clubs were noted for their accomplishments despite a weak lineup, furthering Wright's status as a superior manager. As one newspaper article put it in 1886: "It is true Mr. Wright is not infallible, and he is apt to err, just as any other person in his particular profession will blunder, but Mr. Wright will make 49 good ones to every bad one."[8]

By 1881 the club's fortunes had eroded, and Wright felt underappreciated in Boston. So he moved to nearby Providence to head the Providence Grays. Wright would not have the same level of success in Providence as in Boston, but his tenure there was significant. In particular, it was there that he introduced to baseball the concept of a farm system. With club management concerned about its players' high salaries, Wright thought it would be beneficial to assemble a club of amateurs to play on the Providence grounds while the first nine played away games. Essentially, his idea was to use the second nine as a breeding ground for talent that could replace senior members in case of injury or poor play, for less money than it would cost to lure players from Providence's National League competitors. Though such an institution was not to be popularly adopted for several decades, *Sporting Life* plainly stated in 1883 that Wright was "the father of the 'reserve club' system."[9]

In 1884 Wright left Providence to take over the woefully young Philadelphia Quakers. He instantly helped to improve the club, but never won a championship during his 10-year tenure there. Philadelphia's management failed to pay the players—or, for that matter, its manager—appropriately, leaving Wright to do his best with a limited talent pool.

One way Wright improved the club's talent was by taking them on what was then known as a "Southern trip"—the equivalent of what we know today as spring training. Wright first took his club south in 1886 with the idea that such a warm-up would give the Philadelphias an advantage over other teams by starting off with six weeks of play under their belts as opposed to entering the season fresh. The plan worked just as he expected, and other teams began to follow suit so that by 1890 every club went south in the spring.

In late May 1890, Wright was suddenly struck with what was described as catarrh of the eyeballs and was rendered temporarily blind. It would take until the next March for him to regain his eyesight. The period in-between was very painful and emotional for Wright, his family, and the baseball community. When he came back to manage with partial sight late in the 1890 season, he was received with great affection, but privately pitied for his weathered appearance.

To make matters worse, Carrie was struck by illness and confined to bed shortly after Harry went blind. After a long illness and unsuccessful surgery, Carrie died on February 5, 1892. Harry's grief was tremendous. However, by July 1893 he was engaged to be married to a woman named Isabella (or Isabelle, according to some accounts), a teacher who was later noted for "organizing classes for crippled children" and for being "a pioneer in the movement to provide lunches to school children at nominal cost."[10] The two were married in 1894. Family legend has it that Carrie Wright's children did not get along well with their stepmother and regarded her as "nasty."[11] Perhaps this was because Isabella was the sister of first wife Mary Fraser; the *Dictionary of American Biography* reports their relation, but it has not been confirmed elsewhere.

Matters weren't going well with the Philadelphias, either. Throughout his tenure in the city, Wright had always had trouble with the management of Al Reach and especially Colonel John I. Rogers. Rogers micromanaged the club and publicly and privately attacked Wright's disciplinary tactics, despite much evidence against his criticisms. After the 1893 season the Philadelphias chose not to renew Wright's contract, a move loudly protested by the Philadelphia press and fans.

The National League also regretted this move, and sought to compensate Wright by creating for him the token position of "Chief of Umpires." It was understood that Wright would hold the position for life, and that it would be abolished thereafter. Officially, his charge was to monitor umpires and evaluate their performance. However, the league apparently did not supervise Wright's work, and it is doubtful that it had any substantive significance.

Wright died on October 3, 1895, after contracting a serious illness in his lungs. After being diagnosed on September 21, he tried to relieve the problem by inhaling the salty air of Atlantic City, a favorite vacation spot, but he died there the day after an operation.[12]

Harry Wright (Spalding Collection)

"No death among the professional fraternity has occurred which elicited such painful regret," lamented sportswriter Henry Chadwick.[13] He added: "[Harry Wright was] the most widely known, best respected, and most popular of the exponents and representatives of professional baseball, of which he was virtually the founder."[14] This was not merely an exaggeration upon the occasion of Wright's passing; an 1886 newspaper also referred to Wright as "undoubtedly the best known baseball man in the country."[15] Even Rogers, Wright's bitter adversary in Philadelphia, declared, "It has therefore truly been said, that so identified was he with the progress and popularity of the game its history is virtually his biography."[16]

Wright's contributions to baseball are highly regarded now, as they were in his day. Indeed, a 1999 poll conducted among members of the Society for American Baseball Research ranked Wright as the third greatest contributor to nineteenth-century baseball, behind only Chadwick and Albert Spalding. Interestingly, in November 1893 *The Sporting News* noted that Wright's only competitor for such a title was Cap Anson.

To honor his memory, the National League held a Harry Wright Day on May 13, 1896, from which all proceeds were to go toward building a memorial at Wright's gravesite. Wright himself had tipped his hat to the old league before his death by decreeing in his will that his personal writings be donated to its archives.

Wright was elected to the National Baseball Hall of Fame in 1953 by the Veterans Committee, 16 years after his brother George was admitted. Many of Harry Wright's admirers thought he had been made to wait too long. Chief among them was his son, Harry II. Baseball, he claimed, had come to value sluggers and men of brawn too highly by the 1950s, over the scientific batter and great mind of an earlier era that his father epitomized.[17]

SOURCES

In addition to the sources cited in the Notes, the author consulted the following:

Devine, Christopher. *Harry Wright: The Father of Professional Base Ball* (Jefferson, North Carolina: McFarland & Co., 2003).

NOTES

1. Author's correspondence.
2. Family records provided by Halsey Miller Jr.
3. Henry Chadwick Scrapbooks.
4. Both quotations are from clippings in the Chadwick Scrapbooks.
5. Ibid.
6. *The Sporting News*, December 12, 1895.
7. Harry Wright correspondence, to William Cammeyer, September 15, 1874.
8. Henry Chadwick Scrapbooks.
9. *Sporting Life*, December 12, 1883.
10. *Brooklyn Daily Eagle*, January 26, 1933.
11. Author's correspondence with Halsey Miller Jr., great-grandson of Harry Wright.
12. Chadwick Diaries, Volume 23.
13. Henry Chadwick Scrapbooks.
14. Ibid.
15. Ibid.
16. Ibid.
17. Author's correspondence with Halsey Miller Jr.

SOUTH END GROUNDS

BY BOB RUZZO

The End of the Beginning

WHEN THE BOSTON BRAVES LEFT the field at the South End Grounds on Tuesday, August 11, 1914, the glorious opening chapter of professional baseball in Boston passed into history without notice. After a frustrating 13-inning, 0-0 tie with the Cincinnati Reds, all that mattered that day was that the Braves had fallen a half-game behind the second-place St. Louis Cardinals in their quest to track down John McGraw's league-leading New York Giants.[1]

There would always be another game tomorrow, although the forecast for the next day's contest seemed somewhat dubious for Boston cranks contemplating a trip via the Tremont Street streetcar to the city's South End. Fans of the franchise had been making a similar journey for decades, first by horse-drawn car, then by electric streetcar.[2]

For the South End Grounds, the third iteration of a ballpark on the same city block, however, tomorrow never came. Major-league baseball was never again played on the 4½ acre site.[3]

With Wednesday's game postponed because of rain, the Braves left town the next day on an extended road trip, never to return to the location that served as their home for longer than any other facility in the more than 140-year history of the franchise. Upon their return to Boston in September, Fenway Park, less than two years old and still sparkling, beckoned. After the Braves started the following season in Fenway with the permission of their American League cousins, in August 1915, Braves Field would become the team's new home.

Over the course of the South End Grounds' more than 43 years of service, baseball, the nation, and the city of Boston had all changed dramatically. At the South End Grounds, these forces of change were marked both on the field and in the stands.

Today, many aspects of the first National Association of Base Ball Players game at the site on May 16, 1871, between the Boston Red Stockings and the Troy (New York) Haymakers would seem bewildering, if not downright amusing.[4] The pitcher stood in a box some 45 feet from home and delivered the ball by means of a straight-armed submarine style motion to a batter who could both call for his preferred pitch height and, if he didn't like them, foul pitches with impunity. His catcher had no mask and typically stood several feet behind home, hoping to "[catch] the ball on its first bounce." The pitcher wore no glove; neither did any of his fielders.[5] This was baseball as the game was played by the first of its "major" professional leagues in a largely agrarian nation six years removed from a debilitating Civil War.

Over the next four decades the sport transformed itself, reflecting the fluidity of a country entering a dynamic new age of industrialization. Despite many detours along the way, by August 1914 the game had taken on nearly all of its fundamental character, as the flickering celluloid images of that era primitively attest.

At the same time, the city of Boston was growing exponentially, swelling its ranks from 250,526 (seventh largest in the country) to 670,585 (fifth) in 1910.[6] Immigrants of every stripe filled its streets, particularly the baseball-mad Irish, who during this time transformed City Hall from a bastion of Yankeedom into a virtual Irish colony.

During this era of chaotic change, Boston's baseball franchise was a source of stability and success. Indeed, for most of this period, baseball had one constant. Boston was its king.

And the South End Grounds were figuratively, and for six sweet years literally, its palace.

The South End Grounds: Home of the Braves (and the Red Stockings, Red Caps, Rustlers, Beaneaters, and, while we're at it, even the Doves)

Having seen their various amateur baseball squads suffer ignominious defeats at the hands of the professional Cincinnati Red Stockings in 1870, Boston baseball enthusiasts sprang into action after the Red Stockings disbanded once their 87-game winning streak was snapped by the Brooklyn Atlantics. In January 1871 a corporation known as the Boston Red Stockings Club was capitalized to the tune of $15,000. Ivers W. Adams was selected president, but more importantly, George and Harry Wright were recruited to put the team together, a task that they (Harry in particular) accomplished with ultimately alarming success. Harry persuaded a number of former Cincinnati teammates to join him in Boston, but his true ten-strike was signing pitcher Al Spalding from the Forest Citys.[7]

The grounds for this new team were located along the border between Boston's South End and the newly annexed town of Roxbury, which had become part of the city of Boston in 1868.[8] The site was rectangular in shape, bounded on the east by Berlin Street (which was later incorporated into Columbus Avenue), and by the tracks of the New York, New Haven, and Hartford Railroad (Providence Division) to the west.[9] The railroad proved to be a harsh neighbor. "Passing trains could be counted on to periodically rain smoke and cinders down on the third base patrons and on the field itself," a baseball historian has written. "If the wind was right and the traffic was heavy, games were halted in order to allow the haze generated by the trains to clear."[10]

A Providence and Boston Railroad roundhouse was situated to the north of the playing field, and Camden Street lay beyond that. The southern perimeter was marked by a narrow passage known as Walpole Street, giving rise to the frequently used alternative appellation for the park: The Walpole Street Grounds. "Although a concession stand was in evidence from the beginning, rest rooms were not."[11] The park was also known as the Union Baseball Grounds, Boston National League Base Ball Park, or the Boston Base Ball Grounds.

Whatever name was used, the playing grounds were unusual in shape. Left field (250 feet) and right field (255 feet) were extremely close to home plate, and a compensatingly huge center field (450 feet) gave the park many of the characteristics of the bathtub-shaped Polo Grounds. It was said the park was "like a bowling alley. It only had one field: center."[12]

The grounds were at first leased from the railroad and its associated structures were quite simple. "The pavilion looked like a big volunteer fireman's carnival booth."[13] This covered seating area "was of simple design and resembled many of the parks of the era. The main grand stand was quite boxy, containing approximately twenty five rows of seats under the cover of the overhanging roof. The roof was held up by six supports."[14] "Four rows of primitive box seats and a smaller wooden bleacher section sat in front of the grand stand behind a three foot wooden fence."[15] Fifty cents brought admission to the grandstand, while a quarter was all that was required to sit in the uncovered "bleaching seats" that paralleled the basepaths. Standing room was plentiful, particularly in the generous confines of center field. At first the park was surrounded by a 12-foot-high wooden fence. Two ticket booths stood guard on Walpole Street, directly across the street from the groundskeeper's house.[16]

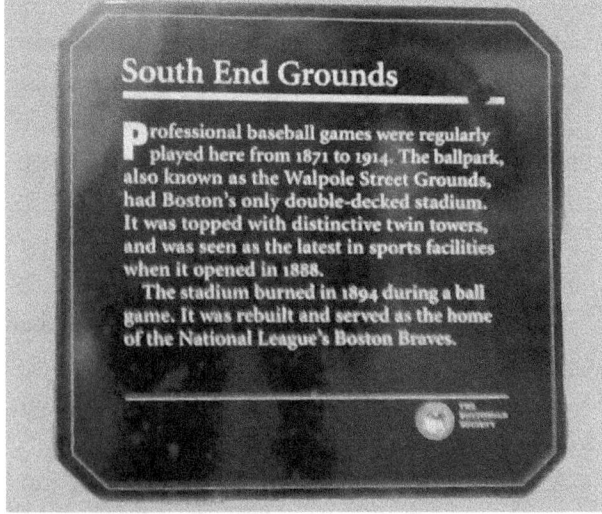

Modern-day South End Grounds plaque at Ruggles Station. Courtesy of Bob Ruzzo.

In these rather modest surroundings, the Red Stockings successfully began their professional odyssey in a match against a picked nine on April 6, 1871, before a packed house. "[A] full five thousand persons … the largest number ever assembled before in these grounds" were on hand, with some standing on top of the fence and others watching from rooftops.[17] With Spalding pitching, the professionals defeated the opposition 41-10, thereby establishing two long-term local institutions: on-field success and inventive attempts to avoid paying the entrance fee.

With Spalding leading the way, the Bostons swept to four consecutive National Association titles between 1872 and 1875. In his signature season of 1875, Spalding posted a record of 54 wins and only five losses. Boston's one-sided dominance of the National Association was a major factor in its eventual collapse. William A. Hulbert of Chicago became the driving force behind the newly formed National League.[18]

A Shift in the Balance of Power

At its core, this change represented a massive shift in power from players (in the National Association of Base Ball Players) to clubs and their owners (in the National League of Base Ball Clubs). Hulbert was also the driving force in luring Spalding along with three other Boston star players to Chicago: second baseman Ross Barnes, former catcher turned outfielder/first baseman Cal McVey, and catcher Deacon Jim White. When these "Four Seceders" came to Boston on May 30 for their first game in Chicago White Stocking uniforms, the *Boston Globe* reported that there had "never been so great a crowd at any base ball match ever played in this country, certainly not in this city."[19] The crowd of between 10,000 and 12,000 spectators, which the *Globe* described as "almost appalling," literally tore down the fences at the South End Grounds, according to one account.[20] The Four Seceders won that day, 5-1, and their defection led to a pennant for Chicago and a frustrating fourth-place Boston finish (a mere eight games over .500, landing the team in the middle of the eight-team field) in the National League's inaugural season.

The consequences of the passage of power to the owners were reflected quite clearly at the South End Grounds. By 1876 the presidency of the Boston club was vested in the hands of Nathaniel Taylor Apollonio, who was not shy about endorsing an exciting new method of protecting the security of the gate. In a postcard ad for the Washburn & Moen Manufacturing Co. of Worcester, Massachusetts, the Red Stockings president sang the praises of that company's barbed-wire fence. Installing it atop the wooden fencing "increased the size of [the] gate from $400 to $500" on the first day it was utilized.[21] Interestingly, the postcard ad also features opaque screening strung along the first-base side above the perimeter fencing in an apparent effort to thwart nonpaying spectators watching from "wildcat bleachers" on neighboring rooftops. The battle against these so-called "dead heads" was well and truly under way. It would escalate to near epic proportions in the years to come.

Three Cheers for the Triumvirs?

On-field success in the form of a pennant returned with impeccable timing to Boston in 1877, coinciding as it did with the rise of the so-called triumvirate (typically shortened to Triumvirs) of Arthur H. Soden, James B. Billings, and William H. Conant to power. According to franchise historian Harold Kaese, "Boston's threesome wielded fully as much power in the National League as their predecessors did in the Roman League and they survived to live considerably longer and happier lives."[22] At first, Boston's fans could also not have been happier, as the Triumvirs brought immediate successive pennants with them to power and secured, during the span of their collective careers, a total of eight championships.

The Triumvirs, however, had a schizophrenic quality about them. They were innovative and, upon occasion, more than willing to open their collective wallets in pursuit of glory. A prime example was the acquisition of slugger and speedster Michael "King" Kelly from Chicago in 1887 for the astounding sum of $10,000. The following season Kelly was joined by pitcher John Clarkson, a fellow refugee from Chicago. This so-called

"$20,000 battery" was showcased in the magnificent brand-new grandstand built by the Triumvirs.[23]

Although team president Soden is forever remembered as the originator of the hated reserve clause, his game-changing, free-spending approach to the practice of buying big player contracts is virtually forgotten. Truth be told, this is due to the fact that the Triumvirs were notorious penny-pinchers. "Complimentary tickets were virtually unknown," and "players were encouraged to enter the stands and wrestle fans for foul balls."[24] On one occasion Soden "ripped out the press box to make room for more paying customers. Players' wives had to buy tickets to get in."[25]

Even worse, when it came to public relations, the Triumvirs were profoundly inept. For example, when team profits declined from $120,000 in 1897 to $90,000 in 1898, team treasurer Billings lamented: "We lost thirty thousand dollars last year." In 1905 president Soden told manager Fred Tenney: "We don't care where you finish so long as you don't lose money with the team."[26] Ironically, when other teams in the League did lose money, Soden frequently provided the cash to keep other teams (and the league) afloat.[27]

Nonetheless, the relationship between fans and ownership soured over time, resulting in a "sorry exit" when the team was sold in 1906.[28] Before that occurred, the South End Grounds and its surrounding environs experienced a roller-coaster ride of highs and lows.

Sullivan's Tower

Despite, or perhaps because of, their team's successes on the field, the Triumvirs were in an almost constant battle against outlaw "dead head" spectators attempting to avoid the price of admission. The rooftops of the adjoining city streets presented an economic opportunity for enterprising individuals who were amenable to hosting large groups of visitors. At the forefront of this band of hardy entrepreneurs was one Michael Sullivan, who lived behind right field on Berlin Street, near Burke Street. His "roost," more commonly known as Sullivan's Tower, was constructed level by level over time in lockstep with the efforts of the Triumvirs to block the view. Sullivan's Tower was "an architectural monstrosity"[29] that grew over time into a Boston landmark.[30] In the view of many, "Sullivan's Roost was as much a feature of a National League game in Boston as the contest itself."[31] In its day, Sullivan's Tower was as prominent and well known as the CITGO sign in modern-day Boston; in fact, one lyrically inclined fan penned a poem in tribute to the tower that was published in the *Boston Globe*.[32]

The tower had originally been built "upon the roof of a stable, but [was later] strengthened and braced and made a separate structure."[33] The passage by the state legislature of Chapter 374 of the Acts of 1885 gave new teeth to the authority of building officials to address issues of public safety in structures of all types. Thus empowered, local officials visited or "raided" (in Sullivan's view) the edifice. Efforts to declare it unsafe under the new law failed, however, and a subsidiary effort to challenge the lack of a permit for its construction met with a similar lack of success.[34] Ironically, at one point, the *Boston Globe* reported that Soden's rather poorly constructed fence "was either blown down or helped down," and that same morning a satisfied Sullivan was observed perched on his grandstand smoking a pipe.[35] Soden quickly rebuilt.

In 1887 an adventurous *Globe* reporter paid over his 15 cents and made the trek up Sullivan's Tower. The story unfolds: "At first it was an obscure staging, modestly peeping over Mr. Soden's fence. Mr. Soden's fence was raised a few feet one day, and the next day another story had been added to Mr. Sullivan's staging." And so, on (and up) it went.

At 80 feet in height, the roost was more than double the height of the surrounding buildings. The staging was "honestly built of good timber enough of which has been employed in its construction to amply satisfy the most exacting of building inspectors," and thus compared favorably to Mr. Soden's rebuilt fence, which, incredibly, was nearly as high as Mr. Sullivan's Tower, and not nearly as well constructed. "If both were let alone the roost would be standing a dozen years after the pickets of the fence had been blown to the four winds by the blasts of springtime."[36]

As time went on, and levels were added, the viewing platform of Sullivan's Tower diminished in size. Nonetheless, it is difficult to credit accounts that "as many as 500 fans climbed [Sullivan's Tower] to see a game."[37] By 1887 the most recent "addition" to the roost, while adding eight feet of height, cut the viewing platform in half from its earlier 30 feet square. About 30 spectators were present for the late-season game attended by the *Globe* reporter, in a year in which the Bostons finished fifth.

South End Grounds II: The Grand Pavilion

The end of the 1887 season brought the curtain down on the first iteration of the South End Grounds. In September the Triumvirs announced plans to build a new facility on the site at Walpole Street.[38] The initial cost estimate was reported as $25,000.[39]

The decision was long overdue. The old familiar grounds were the only site "unchanged since the beginnings of the National Association"[40] and Soden had promised to rebuild the "shoddy grounds" as far back as the conclusion of the 1883 season, when a surprising pennant run had set new attendance records.[41]

It was worth the wait. Designed by Philadelphia architect John Jerome Deery, the new grounds consisted of an elaborate two-tiered, curving grandstand, complete with a series of towers featuring conical "witches caps."[42] The Grand Pavilion, as it came to be called, "resembled a medieval castle or fairground."[43] The *Boston Herald* proclaimed it a "grand stand unequaled for beauty and convenience in the country."[44]

The grandstand was almost never built as originally conceived. Although architect Deery assured the Triumvirs during their negotiations that the cost "would not exceed $35,000," hard cost estimates were considerably higher and, upon opening, "the actual cost [was] reported at [$]70,000." Nonetheless, the *Herald* reported that "the idea of abandoning the plan of having a new stand was not entertained for a moment." The question was whether to forge ahead or to build a less elaborate and less expensive structure instead. Not surprisingly, the *Herald* claimed it had influenced the outcome directly by pressuring the Triumvirs through the publication in mid-September 1887 of an elaborate description of Deery's master plan, complete with three drawings.[45] Just days prior, the *Globe* had publicized its estimate that the Triumvirs had made $100,000 during the 1887 season alone.[46]

Pressured or not, the Triumvirs went ahead despite the enormous costs. Optimism for the coming campaign abounded. In early April the *Boston Globe* published a cartoon entitled "Winning Cards" featuring a poker hand containing Clarkson, Kelly, and the new grandstand as three of the cards, predicting: "With this combination, the Boston Nine should be able to win a pennant and make a small fortune for the Triumvirs."[47]

The semicircular grandstand seated 2,800 persons. The lower tier accommodated 2,072 in nine sections labeled "A" (third base) through "I" (first base). Ample provision was made for "reporters and telegraphers" behind home plate. The home clubrooms were located on the first-base side, while the visitors were perched on the third-base side.

The balcony sat an additional 772 in seven sections.[48] Approximately 2,000 seats were also available in each of the two bleacher sections in left field and right field.[49] A *Boston Herald* account indicated that restaurants were located "on the extreme ends of the pavilion." "Toilet rooms were provided for the ladies with all the modern improvements." A concerted effort was made to keep the patrons of the grandstand separate from those sitting in the bleachers. The restaurants were configured so that both grandstand and bleacher patrons could be served "without in any way interfering with each other and neither can any patron of the outside seats obtain, by any subterfuge, admission to the pavilion through the restaurants."[50]

The ballpark was visually imposing. The "witches caps" sat upon four tulip-shaped columns, two at each end of the curving grandstand.[51] From Walpole Street, the full majesty of the edifice was evident. At either end sat large square brick towers with bays on the corners of their upper reaches. In between rose the central 82-foot brick and terra-cotta tower. The lower 40 feet of the tower were brick, while the upper reaches were made of terra cotta. Ticket offices were located on either side of the central tower. The Triumvirs also completed efforts to widen Walpole Street in order to improve access which provided "a good comfortable entrance" to the ballpark.[52] "While the park was complimented on its architecture ... [it was] criticized for its lack of comfort and poor sight lines."[53]

After a lengthy season-opening road trip, Opening Day festivities on May 25, 1888, were a noteworthy affair, notwithstanding the 4-1 loss to Philadelphia. "Boston's upper crust, a big slice of the lower crust and a mighty congregation of the intermediate" were on hand.[54] Dignitaries in attendance included former Governor Ames, who thought the game was "more amusing than a session of the Legislature," and the mayors of both Boston and Cambridge, numerous other elected officials, and the spouses of the famed members of the "$20,000 battery." Nearly 15,000 fans were in attendance, more than doubling the new park's 6,800-person seating capacity. The chill east wind made some spectators miserable, "but still it was a great game—for the management."[55] The season held true to this form, with the Beaneaters finishing fourth but drawing more than an estimated 300,000 paying customers to the new grandstand, bringing smiles to the faces of the Triumvirs.[56]

Those smiles truly blossomed in 1891 when second-year manager Frank Selee of Melrose, Massachusetts, and his talented roster, including Clarkson, Kelly, and pitching star Kid Nichols, took the first pennant in eight seasons home to Boston. It was the first of three consecutive pennants for the Bostons. Attendance, which had slipped as low as 147,539 in 1890, had climbed back to 193,300 by 1894.[57] While their success on the field could not be imitated, the short-lived (one year) Boston franchise of the upstart Players League had, in 1890, taken a cue from the Grand Pavilion. The club "spared no expense in planning for the new pavilion for their Congress Street Grounds" since any "baseball park [was] now incomplete without a grand pavilion," in the view of the *Boston Globe*.[58]

As 1894 dawned the Triumvirs were indeed baseball's kings, ruling from their grand castle. What could possibly go wrong?

The Great Roxbury Fire of 1894

As visually striking as the Grand Pavilion was (despite its poor sightlines and uncomfortable seats), its tenure as Boston's home grounds was brief and its end spectacular. Constructed of wood, it is unsurprising that its end came by fire. Indeed, 1894 saw a series of fires at ballparks in Baltimore, Chicago, and Philadelphia as well as Boston. Some believed that "the fires were being set deliberately, and some went so far as to hint that Sabbatarians" were to blame, seeing in the fires a conspiracy to stop Sunday baseball, which the National League had sanctioned in 1892.[59]

No such conspiracy was at work in the South End, although the precise cause of the fire on May 15, 1894, was (and perhaps remains) a matter of some dispute. The *New York Times* believed the fire was caused by "some small Roxbury boys" who had "set themselves up as rivals to Mrs. O'Leary's cow."[60] The *Boston Herald* concurred in this probability.[61] The more widely accepted account, appearing in the *Boston Globe*, told of a carelessly disposed match falling upon sawdust and timbers beneath the stands.[62]

A rotting portion of the center-field bleachers had been removed during the offseason and workers had left sawdust and debris behind, under the right-field seats.[63] Curiously, the detailed description of the careless smoker was provided by 14-year-old James Laskey who had, in the two nights following the fire, not returned home. He had been "bunking out ... just to see how it would seem."[64] Just as remarkably, the *Boston Herald* noted that the "bleachers were boarded underneath and there was no interstices, so that it would be an impossibility for a person to drop a match or cigar to the ground."[65] Despite the somewhat questionable veracity of this youthful witness, Laskey's account was embraced by most. As a result, "all theories and suspicions of incendiarism [were] wiped from the minds" of property owners and city officials.[66]

The fire began during a league match between Boston and Baltimore, in the third inning. Noticing the flames, Boston right fielder Jimmy Bannon tried to stomp out the fire with his feet. He was unsuccessful. The wind apparently shifted and "the fire roared to life."⁶⁷ The game was halted. The fire would dictate that day's winners and losers.

Within an hour, 12 acres were destroyed, 1,900 people were made homeless and the grandstand, "the handsomest in the country" in the opinion of *Sporting Life,* had been forever lost in the second worst fire in the history of the city of Boston.⁶⁸ The Triumvirs chided the Boston fire department (and police) for a slow response to the danger. Indeed, the *Boston Herald* concluded that there was one reason for such an extensive loss: "Somebody Blundered."⁶⁹ John Haggerty, the groundskeeper, tried valiantly to sound the alarm and appeared to be "the only man who acted with any sense," perhaps befitting a man whose home lay across Walpole Street from the burning grounds.⁷⁰

The franchise faced a crisis on two fronts. The immediate need to find a place to continue the still-young season was solved starting the next day by the use of the Congress Street Grounds. Located near a pier in South Boston, these were the former home grounds of the city's Players League and American Association teams.⁷¹

The second problem was more complicated. The Grand Pavilion and its associated facilities were worth $75,000, according to Triumvir Conant, but according to a list of insurance claims published two days later, the facilities were insured for only $45,000.⁷² The Triumvirs were severely criticized for underinsuring the Grand Pavilion and for the consequences that this underinsurance portended for the rebuilt ballpark.

In point of fact, the Triumvirs were hardly unique in their plight. Initial estimates (subsequently revised upward) pegged total losses from the fire at $300,000, only half of which was insured. The city of Boston lost both a school and a fire department "hose house" in the blaze. Neither the school nor the hose house was insured. According to one H.R. Turner of the Niagara Insurance Company, the fire, while "deplorable from a humanitarian standpoint," would "hardly be felt by the insurance companies," due to small tenement houses in the area. Very few "of these occupants carr[ied] any insurance." Then, in a statement callous enough to have come from one of the Triumvirs, he concluded:

"The fire could not have happened in a locality more advantageous for insurance interests."⁷³

One thing was certain. The long-running competition between the Triumvirs' fence and Sullivan's roost was over. "[T]he fire played no favorites. It leveled them both."⁷⁴

While the criticism of Triumvir penny-pinching with insurance colors the subsequent discussion of the disappointing results of their rebuilding effort, a plausible case for caution could be made. In 1894 the country was in the midst of a severe recession following the Panic of 1893; indeed, employment would not return to 1891 levels until 1900. As a result of "the disruption in the financial system, some nonfinancial businesses found it difficult to obtain the funds they needed to meet payrolls and were forced to suspend operations."⁷⁵

Thus, the Triumvirs—who after all had been willing to spend the money to construct the Grand Pavilion despite horrendous cost overruns—may have pulled back on their reconstruction efforts due to their lack of faith in the ability of *other* enterprises to keep paying (and employing) potential fans.

A more pointed—and irrefutable—criticism of ownership appeared in *Sporting Life*. The weekly chastised the Triumvirs for failing to properly police up the months-old debris in the area, and for even more egregiously failing to provide for a fire hydrant or a fire hose to be maintained on site. This "'pennywise and pound foolish' method of management" left the club unprepared for the preventable tragedy that unfolded.⁷⁶

South End Grounds III: Is It Better to Burn Out Than to Fade Away?

The combination of a lack of insurance proceeds and a lack of confidence in the overall economy produced a rebuilt ballpark on a smaller scale than its majestic predecessor. What was impressive was that it was built at a breakneck pace. The Bostons defeated New York in the rebuilt grounds before 5,206 fans on July 20, barely two months after the fire.⁷⁷

The new grandstand was a modest, single deck structure with "twin spires … suggestive of the Churchill Downs racetrack"⁷⁸ and a seating capacity of 900. The number of bleacher seats was increased to compensate for this shortcoming. "[T]he only stands in the outfield were a small set of bleachers in [right field] called the pie bleachers because they were triangular shaped, like a piece of pie."[79] "Although not as impressive as the old building, the new park had more comfortable seating and better sightlines."[80] Its seating capacity was approximately 5,000.[81]

Within a year the inadequacy of the rebuilt grounds had become apparent and the push to upgrade the facility began. In 1895 two iron wings were added, bringing the grandstand's seating capacity to 2,300.[82]

The addition was timely; the Beaneaters rebounded to win consecutive pennants in 1897 and 1898, ending the three-year dominance of the Baltimore Orioles.[83] Thereafter, the team's fortunes receded and in 1906 the Triumvirs sold the team to George and John Dovey, who had partnered with a "theatrical man named John Harris."[84] It was a poor investment decision for the new owners. The Beaneaters finished last for the first time in franchise history in 1906, the South End Grounds were in disrepair—"an ugly little wart" in the words of one description—and there was a new team in town.[85]

Five years earlier, the American League's Boston team [as of the 1908 season, known as the Red Sox] had, through the maneuverings of Connie Mack, among others, taken up residence literally on the other side of the tracks. The Huntington Avenue Grounds, built in 1901, were bordered by the New York, New Haven, and Hartford Railroad on the east, a mirror image to the South End Grounds' western boundary. The American League "park was new, neat, and larger than the South End Grounds, of which the public had grown weary."[86] The price of admission was half that at the National League park. Little wonder, then, that on the date of the upstart league's inaugural home opener, they outdrew the Nationals substantially. With the benefit of at least 70 "jumpers" from the National League, by 1902 the American League was outdrawing the National League by some 300,000 fans.[87] Among the fans attracted to the new Boston team was saloonkeeper Michael "Nuf Ced" McGreevey. McGreevey (and his Royal Rooters) had originally been supporters of the Beaneaters, and a version of the slogan for his Third Base Saloon had adorned the left-field wall at the South End Grounds.[88]

The Dovey brothers' major contribution to the physical facility at Walpole Street was the construction of new outfield bleachers for the 1908 season, although they had also supplied a new scoreboard the year before.[89] A 40-foot-wide strip across the outfield was dedicated to the new seating, with an open space retained in the vicinity of the flagpole in center field. Overall seating capacity grew to 11,000.[90] When George Dovey died suddenly, his brother John ultimately took his stead, but soon the team was sold to a syndicate headed by William H. Russell. In less than a year Russell, too, was dead and the "Doves" who had briefly become the "Rustlers" were again in search of new ownership.

In December 1911 the team was sold to a new troika of leaders, headed this time by Tammany Hall hard-charger James E. Gaffney, the club's treasurer. The franchise soon acquired a new nickname—derived from the term "Sachem," which was used to describe the leader of Tammany Hall—the Braves.

Gaffney immediately set out to improve the tired South End plant.[91] Based on the recommendations of co-owner John Montgomery Ward, a series of changes to the configuration of the South End Grounds were put through. Given the permanence of its urban boundaries, the grounds had always retained its rectangular configuration. *Green Cathedrals* reports its dimensions at LF 250 (1894), LC 445, Deepest LC 450, CF 440, Right Center 440, RF 255.[92] The addition of outfield bleachers in 1908 decreased the straightaway left-field, left-center-field and center-field dimensions by between 38 and 43 feet.[93]

Ward's changes involved removing the left-field bleachers, adding another section to the grandstand and shifting the diamond toward right field to bring "the foul line over the left-field fence at a distance of 350 feet or more than 100 feet farther down the field than at [the] present time."[94] However, the 1912-1914 left-field dimension is reported in other reputable sources as 275 feet. The 350-foot distance description quoted above was provided by Tim Murnane of the

Boston Globe, himself a former ballplayer, and has the ring of authenticity. The contemporary accounts of the *Boston Post* and the *Boston Herald* confirm that this indeed was the plan.[95]

The record nonetheless is not perfectly clear. *Sporting Life* first reported in February that "the task of changing around the old South End Grounds is greater than was at first supposed" and then in March reported "that the fielding space is increased about 15 feet."[96] Murnane tells a different story. His Opening Day 1912 account reported that all 10,000-plus spectators "enjoyed the many changes made at the park, the transformation giving about 25 percent more room for hitting."[97] Finally, Harold Kaese, author of the seminal history of the franchise in Boston, also reports a 350-foot left-field distance in 1912.[98]

In right field, what was happening was indisputable. The firm of Waitt and Bond, manufacturer of the well-known Blackstone cigar, erected a modern cigar factory (reputed to be the world's largest) at 716 Columbus Avenue.[99] The factory building, which still stood in 2013, loomed over the grounds from the opposite side of the street. Kaese wrote that Jay Kirke, a powerful left-handed hitter whose fielding was less than graceful, often launched fly balls in that direction, frequently followed by the sound of tinkling broken glass. Eventually the factory was closed and a new facility opened in New Jersey.[100]

Gaffney also made numerous cosmetic improvements to the Grounds, painting the entire plant "green with crimson trimmings" so that the facility "altogether present[ed] a very attractive appearance."[101] "The walks to the field seats on either side of the field [were] relaid in blue stones" improving the park's appearance so much that "[o]ld time patrons of the park [would] not know the place. … More money [was] spent on decorations than the Triumvirs ever spent in their lives on such things."[102]

Gaffney was in a state of perpetual motion. In the fall of 1913, he acquired a parcel at Columbus Avenue and Walpole Street that would allow for the existing grandstand to be demolished, the playing field to be enlarged, and a new modern grandstand erected.[103] In mid-January of 1914, Gaffney was reported to be returning to Boston the next week to review bids for a new concrete grandstand.[104] He also installed a new scoreboard in deep center field at the start of the 1914 season.[105]

Standing on the threshold of a major financial commitment to the four-decades-old location, Gaffney hesitated. The fateful, wonderful miracle season of 1914 began.

The End of Days

It was success that ultimately spelled the end of the South End Grounds. The maniacal climb of the Miracle Braves flooded the facility beyond its capacity. By early August 1914, Red Sox president Joseph Lannin, who had only just previously acquired a small stake in the Braves franchise, put Fenway Park at the disposal of the Braves without charge.[106] Gaffney, ever the cagey politician, initially accepted only for Saturday and holiday game days.[107] Upon their return from the road, the Braves played a Labor Day morning-afternoon doubleheader against the Giants in Fenway. Nearly 75,000 attended the two games, and the Braves never returned to the South End.[108] For the 1914 season, the combination of access to Fenway and a baseball miracle for the ages lifted Braves attendance to 382,913, first in the National League.[109]

Gaffney never looked back. Frustrated by an undersized facility plagued by "clouds of smoke from the locomotives [that] interfered with the play and the comfort of the spectators,"[110] he scoured the Boston area for sites that would accommodate his vision of

A snapshot of the site where the South End Grounds once stood, near Ruggles Station. Taken by Bob LeMoine, January 2016.

a playing field unencumbered by urban boundaries. He found just such a location on the site of a former golf course, bounded ironically by the same harsh neighbor—the railroad—that he had fled the South End to avoid.

When Gaffney's Braves moved from the Walpole Street facility, they were obliged to sell the grounds subject to an "iron bound agreement" that the land could not be used for baseball, an effort to block the grounds from falling into the hands of the Federal League.[111] And so the Braves left the familiar confines of the South End, despite the fact that to that time "[m]ore championships [had] been won on those old grounds than on any other in the world."[112]

Taking the grass from their infield with them, the Braves moved on. Moving to the expanse of Braves Field, however, "was like moving from a modern three bedroom apartment into a nineteenth century mansion."[113] The franchise was never the same, appearing in only one World Series in nearly four decades in Allston.

Today the site of the old South End Grounds barely countenances a memory of its storied past. The railroad is still there, in the form of the Southwest Corridor, and Columbus Avenue and the old cigar factory both have tales that they could tell. Now owned by Northeastern University, most of the field is occupied by surface parking and a garage. But if one goes just north beyond the garage, in the area where the old railroad roundhouse once stood south of Camden Street, there lies a trio of modest playing fields. Two of the fields are framed by small wooden stands and a larger array of concrete and aluminum seating sits there quietly as well, providing at least a distant echo to the cheers from the bleaching boards of the late 19th century.

NOTES

1. J.C. O'Leary, "13 Zeros Apiece," *Boston Globe*, August 12, 1914, 7.
2. In 1896, Chickering Station on Camden Street was closed. Prior to that time, the station was also heavily trafficked by baseball fans.
3. Ronald M. Selter, *Ballparks of the Deadball Era* (Jefferson, North Carolina: McFarland & Company, 2008), 20.
4. This was the date of the first National Association match. The first match between the Red Stockings and a picked nine took place on April 6 of that year and is described below.
5. Harvey Frommer, *Primitive Baseball* (New York: Atheneum, 1998), 61-68 (describing changes in the game from the mid-1870s to the new century).
6. census.gov/www/through_the_decades/fast_facts (retrieved June 15, 2013).
7. Harold Kaese, *The Boston Braves 1871-1953* (Boston: Northeastern University Press, 2004), 5, 7.
8. Sam Bass Warner, Jr., *Streetcar Suburbs, The Process of Growth in Boston (1870-1890)* (Cambridge: Harvard University Press, 1962), 41.
9. Alan E. Foulds, *Boston's Ballparks and Arenas* (Lebanon, New Hampshire: Northeastern University Press, published by the University Press of New England, 2005), 8. (The New York, New Haven, and Hartford Railroad leased the Old Colony Railroad in 1893, which by that time included the Boston and Providence Railroad.)
10. Bill Felber, *A Game of Brawl* (Lincoln: University of Nebraska Press, 2007), 60.
11. Foulds, *Boston's Ballparks and Arenas*, 8-9.
12. Michael Benson, *Ballparks of North America* (Jefferson, North Carolina: McFarland & Company, 1985), 39.
13. Benson, *Ballparks of North America*, 39.
14. Foulds, *Boston's Ballparks and Arenas*, 8-9.
15. Benson, *Ballparks of North America*, 39.
16. Foulds, *Boston's Ballparks and Arenas*, 8-9.
17. Kaese, *The Boston Braves*, 9.
18. Hulbert's bold maneuvering to establish the National League is described in detail in Michael Haupert's fine SABR biography, at sabr.org/bioproj/person/d1d420b3.
19. *Boston Globe*, May 31, 1876, 1.
20. Kaese, *The Boston Braves*, 19.
21. Michael Gershman, *Diamonds: The Evolution of the Ballpark* (Boston: Houghton Mifflin Company, 1993), 29.
22. Kaese, *The Boston Braves*, 22. The First Triumvirate of Rome was a political alliance between Gaius Julius Caesar, Marcus Licinius Crassus and Gnaeus Pompeius Magnus (Pompey the Great). Crassus died in battle approximately seven years into the alliance, whereupon Caesar and Pompey fought a civil war. The survivor, Caesar, ultimately was assassinated on the Senate floor.
23. *Sporting Life*, April 11, 1888, 1.
24. Kaese, *The Boston Braves*, 47, 23-24.
25. Benson, *Ballparks of North America*, 39.
26. Kaese, *The Boston Braves*, 113, 111.

27 Brian McKenna's SABR biography of Soden makes for entertaining reading on the extraordinary life of this Triumvir. sabr.org/bioproj/person/a1b2e0d0.

28 Besides their own miserliness and constant financial clashing with the team's human capital [the players], the Triumvirs' demise was hastened by poor on-field performance and the introduction of competition in the form of the American League in 1901.

29 Kaese, *The Boston Braves*, 68.

30 Peter Morris, *A Game of Inches: The Stories Behind the Innovations that Shaped Baseball: The Game Behind the Scenes* (Chicago: Ivan R. Dee, 2006), 429.

31 *Lewiston* (Maine) *Evening Journal*, July 29, 1914, 9.

32 *Boston Globe*, July 10, 1889, 5.

33 *Boston Globe*, August 1, 1885, 3.

34 *Boston Globe*, August 20, 1885, 4.

35 *Boston Globe*, August 19, 1887, 8.

36 *Boston Globe*, September 5, 1887, 4.

37 Donald Hubbard, *The Heavenly Twins of Boston Baseball* (Jefferson, North Carolina: McFarland & Company, 2008), 109.

38 *Boston Herald*, September 16, 1887, 5.

39 *Boston Globe*, August 19, 1887, 8.

40 Foulds, *Boston's Ballparks and Arenas*, 13.

41 Kaese, *The Boston Braves*, 37.

42 Unlike Fenway Park, which has evolved into a double-deck structure, the Grand Pavilion was designed and built as a two-tier facility, the only such structure in Boston baseball history.

43 Foulds, *Boston's Ballparks and Arenas*, 15.

44 *Boston Herald*, May 25, 1888, 5.

45 *Boston Herald*, May 25, 1888, 5.

46 *Boston Globe*, September 12, 1887, 8.

47 *Boston Globe*, April 8, 1888, 1.

48 *Boston Globe*, May 25, 1888, 5.

49 Lowry, *Green Cathedrals*, 108.

50 *Boston Herald*, May 25, 1888, 5; for a fascinating discussion with Tom Shieber of the Baseball Hall of Fame describing the Classic Ballpark Tours interactive exhibit featuring the South End Grounds, see: Paul Ferrante, "Travel Back in Time to Boston's South End Grounds," August 20, 2012, sportscollectordigest.com. Retrieved June 24, 2013.

51 Lowry, *Green Cathedrals*, 43.

52 *Boston Globe*, May 14, 1888, 8.

53 Foulds, *Boston's Ballparks and Arenas*, 15.

54 *Boston Post*, May 26, 1888, 2.

55 *Boston Globe*, May 26, 1888, 4.

56 Tim Murnane, "Hub Happenings," *Sporting Life,* October 3, 1888, 7.

57 Baseballalmanac.com/teamstats/roster. Retrieved July 15, 2013.

58 *Boston Globe*, February 23, 1890, 22. For an excellent history of the Congress Street Grounds, readers are directed to Charlie Bevis's ballpark biography of that facility, at SABR.org/bioproj/park/33169c79.

59 Gershman, *Diamonds: The Evolution of the Ballpark*, 53. Sunday baseball in Boston would remain controversial for decades.

60 *New York Times*, May 16, 1894, 1.

61 *Boston Herald*, May 16, 1914, 1.

62 "Was a Match," *Boston Globe*, May 18, 1894, 1.

63 Foulds, *Boston's Ballparks and Arenas*, 19.

64 *Boston Globe*, May 18, 1894, 1.

65 *Boston Herald*, May 17, 1894, 3.

66 *Boston Globe*, May 18, 1894, 1.

67 Paul Ferrante, "The Most Beautiful Ballpark Ever?" August 9, 2012, sportscollectordigest.com. Retrieved June 24, 2013.

68 *Sporting Life*, May 26, 1894, 3.

69 *Boston Herald*, May 16, 1894, 1.

70 *Boston Post*, May 16, 1894, 3.

71 Philip J. Lowry, *Green Cathedrals* (New York: Addison-Wesley, 1992), 108.

72 *Boston Globe*, May 18, 1894, 4.

73 *Boston Globe*, May 16, 1894, 5.

74 Kaese, *The Boston Braves*, 68.

75 Mark Carlson, "Causes of Bank Suspensions in the Panic of 1893," Federal Reserve Board (2002), federalreserve.gov/pubs/feds2002/200211pap.pdf. Retrieved June 11, 2013.

76 *Sporting Life*, May 26, 1894, 5; *Sporting Life*, June 2, 1894, 1.

77 Foulds, *Boston's Ballparks and Arenas*, 19.

78 Felber, *A Game of Brawl*, 60.

79 Selter, *Ballparks of the Deadball Era*, 18.

80 Foulds, *Boston's Ballparks and Arenas*, 19.

81 Selter, *Ballparks of the Deadball Era*, 18.

82 Tim Murnane, "Building Iron Wings," *Boston Globe*, January 13, 1895, 16.

83 Frommer, *Old Time Baseball*, 107.

84 Kaese, *The Boston Braves*, 115.

85 Kaese, *The Boston Braves*, 101, 113.

86 Kaese, *The Boston Braves*, 101.

87 Frommer, *Old Time Baseball*, 60.

88 Gershman, *Diamonds: The Evolution of the Ballpark*, 75.

89 Kaese, *The Boston Braves*, 115.

90 Tim Murnane, "Bleachers in Center Field," *Boston Globe*, January 7, 1908, 5.

91 Gaffney also once and for all provided the team with an enduring nickname. He chose the name Braves in deference to the Sachem, the symbol of his Tammany Hall. Previously, the franchise had been known as the Red Stockings, Red Caps, Rustlers, Beaneaters, and the Doves, as well as simply the Boston Nationals.

92 Lowry, *Green Cathedrals*, 109.

93 Selter, *Ballparks of the Deadball Era*, 20.

94 Tim Murnane, "Ward's Field Changes to Be Put Through," *Boston Globe*, January 20, 1912, 7. By the end of July 1912, John Montgomery Ward had sold his stake in the team, resigning as its president. Gaffney became the new president of the franchise.

95 *Boston Post*, January 20, 1912, 13; John J. Hallahan, "To Make Over South End Park," *Boston Herald*, January 20, 1912, 6.

96 *Sporting Life*, February 12, 1912, 7; March 30, 1912, 3.

97 Tim Murnane, "Boston Braves Play to 10,264," *Boston Globe*, April 12, 1912, 1.

98 Kaese, *The Boston Braves*, 129.

99 *Moody's Manual of Railroads and Corporation Securities: Volume 2* (New York: Poor's Publishing Company, 1921), 728.

100 Kaese, *The Boston Braves*, 125-6.

101 *Boston Globe*, March 26, 1912, 6.

102 *Sporting Life*, April 6, 1912, 7.

103 *Sporting Life*, October 18, 1913, 2.

104 *Sporting Life*, January 17, 1914, 14.

105 *Sporting Life*, April 25, 1914, 7.

106 *Sporting Life*, November 29, 1913, 3.

107 *Sporting Life*, August 8, 1914, 3.

108 *Sporting Life*, September 26, 1914, 8.

109 baseball-reference.com. Retrieved June 5, 2013.

110 A.H.C. Mitchell, "The World's Champions," *Sporting Life*, December 26, 1914, 3.

111 Tim Murnane, "Baseball Exit for South End Grounds," *Boston Globe*, December 20, 1914, 15.

112 *Sporting Life*, December 26, 1914, 3.

113 Kaese, *The Boston Braves*, 173.

BOSTON CLUB FINANCES IN THE EARLY PROFESSIONAL ERA

BY RICHARD HERSHBERGER

THE FINANCES OF THE BOSTON Club in the 1870s are uniquely well documented. Their annual financial statements were reported in the press, and some internal financial records survive in the Frederick Long papers in the Hall of Fame. Together they present a picture of baseball finances in the early professional era.

The Boston Base Ball Association was incorporated in 1871 as a joint stock company, offering 150 shares with a par value of $100 each.[1] The joint stock company was a relatively new model for baseball clubs. The early clubs had been fraternal social clubs with dues-paying members who elected officers and a board of directors. The financial demands of forming a new professional club required more startup funding. A new club needed to rent a playing ground, make improvements to the ground, and recruit players, often paying advances on their salaries. These were substantial expenses that needed to be paid before the opening of the season brought in any revenue, hence the need to raise money through the sale of stock.

The Association leased the Union Base Ball Grounds, which came to be known as the South End Grounds and would be the club's home field through 1887. The Union Grounds were first enclosed and used for baseball in 1869, and were so named because this was the result of a collective effort by several clubs. The new Boston Club took sole control of the grounds and improved the seating and added a roof.[2]

The Boston BBA's capitalization of $15,000 was generous. In part this reflected that they were doing the preliminaries right: paying for the best players and first-class amenities. But even so, the entire $15,000 was not needed up front. They therefore did not collect payment on all 150 shares. This was a common practice in this era. The par value of the shares constituted a pledge by the shareholder to pay the full amount, but this was only called upon in case of need. The problem was that this need implied that the club was in poor financial condition, which did not inspire enthusiasm. The shareholders often regarded fulfilling this commitment to be throwing good money after bad. Only 78 of the 150 shares were paid. The remaining 72 shares reflected an asset of $7,200, but this was highly theoretical. This discrepancy would result in a peculiar, unique hybrid structure.[3]

The problem was that no one actually knew what the finances of a professional baseball club would be like. The business was too new. They could project their expenses, but not their revenue. How many spectators would pass through the gate? Their model was the Cincinnati Base Ball Club of 1869-1870. This turned out to be a poor model. The Cincinnati Club with its unbroken string of victories into June 1870 drew large crowds. A more routine effort—even by a very good club such as the Bostons—wasn't the same. It is like looking at attendance in the late stages of a player's extended batting streak, and assuming that this is normal.

The results were not good. Detailed numbers are not available until 1873, but it is known that the Boston Base Ball Association finished the 1872 season about $4,000 in debt. The holders of unpaid shares showed little interest in making good, and the holders of the active shares showed little interest in contributing further. There was serious discussion of shutting down the organization. This is especially remarkable in light of their having just won the pennant. They averted this fate by putting out a call for "all friends of the club and all persons interested in base ball" to attend the annual shareholders' meeting. After the meeting was completed, an open meeting was held at which a committee was appointed "to report at a future meeting a plan or plans for assisting in paying

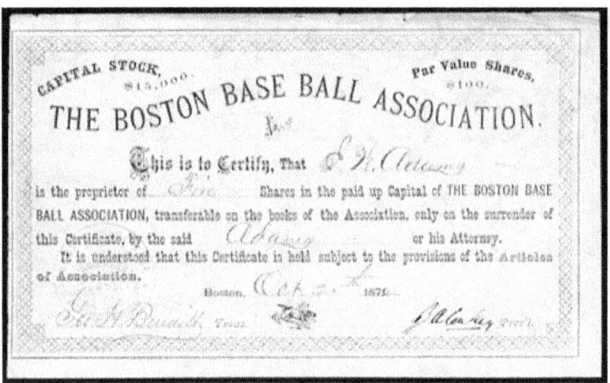

Stock certificate, 1872, Ivers Adams. (Courtesy of REA Auctions)

off the debt of the Boston Base Ball Association for 1872, and also for raising a guaranty for carrying on the club next season."[4]

The solution they arrived at was remarkable. A new organization was formed, the Boston Base Ball Club. It took over the Association's debt, as well as ownership of the 72 unpaid shares of stock—not quite a majority, but a controlling interest unless the individual shareholders voted as a nearly unanimous bloc. The membership of the Club was open to anyone for a $15 initiation fee and $10 annual dues.[5]

Over a hundred people joined. (Accounts disagree on whether the exact number was 108 or 110.)[6] What did they get for their membership fees? First was a season ticket. Season tickets typically cost about $15, so at $25 for the first year's membership, they were paying a premium, but in subsequent years they were getting a discount. Membership also carried with it access to the club rooms, apparently provided by the Association. The amenities of the earlier rooms are not clear, but in 1875 new rooms were opened just above the cigar store and billiard room run by star shortstop George Wright. These comprised a "card-room, and parlor, all handsomely fitted up and admirably lighted and ventilated."[7] The Club in essence was a replication of the fraternal baseball club as it had existed in the early professional era. The members were not playing for personal recreation and exercise, as they had in the original amateur clubs. Rather, they were sponsors of a professional club, with personal access both on and off the field. One of the first club activities was the receipt of the championship pennant for the previous season.[8] It is not too far wrong to regard it as a booster club for the Boston team.

What the Association got was both an immediate infusion of cash and a steady annual income. The Club's annual membership dues went straight into the Association's treasury. After the 1873 season this amounted to $2,730.[9] This was about 10 percent of total annual revenue, and came during the offseason, when the Association's cash flow was the tightest. In light of the reality that this was in exchange for nearly worthless stock, this wasn't a bad deal. Potentially more important was the voting power the Club's bloc of shares represented, but the Association's officers largely remained in place. They won the pennant six years out of the seven-year span of 1872-1878. The Club was happy, and wisely left well enough alone.

We have financial statements for 1873 through 1875.[10] The statement for 1873 is rudimentary, showing revenues of approximately $28,000 and expenses just $27,200. This seems to include both the funds from the Club and the retirement of the debt from the prior season. The Association went into 1874 with no debt and $767.93 in the bank.

The statement for 1874 is more detailed. It shows total assets of $31,699.10 (including the $767.93 from the previous season) and expenses of $30,865.97, giving the bottom line number of $833.73 in the bank: a profit of $65.77 for the year.[11] This year is given added interest by the trip the Boston team made with the Athletics of Philadelphia to England and Ireland in the hope of spreading the game, or at least earning a few dollars.

The 1874 revenue breaks down this way: home games 50 percent, away games 40 percent, the Europe trip 5 percent, and season tickets (i.e., Club dues) 5 percent. On the other side, the largest expense by far was player salaries, accounting for 58 percent of total expenses. Travel expenses were next, accounting for 22 percent (including both domestic and foreign travel). The Europe trip was a loss, costing $2,318.13 and bringing in but $1,660.69: a disappointment, but one they could absorb.

Revenues were up in 1875, to $37,767.06. Player salaries were modestly higher, at $20,685.00. In all, this was the club's most financially successful year, with about $2,500 in profit.

Looking over the Bostons' National Association years, their finances started out rocky. They nearly went under after the 1872 season and had to be bailed out. After that the numbers steadily improved. The club never produced massive profits—there was never any question of paying a dividend—but by the end of the NA period the treasury was slowly building up. The trends were in the right direction.

This didn't last. The post-Civil War economic boom burst with the failure in September 1873 of the banking firm of Jay Cooke & Company. This resulted in the Depression of 1873-1879. The baseball economy was a lagging indicator, but by 1875 was showing stress. The formation of the National League in 1876 can be regarded as a reaction to this. The Bostons held up well through 1875, as their continued pennant victories sustained enthusiasm. The hard times finally caught up with them in 1876. Revenue dropped by 17 percent. They were able to cut expenses and end the season with money in the bank, but revenues continued to fall.[12] This trend continued through the next several years, both for Boston and the rest of the League. This explains the rapid turnover in League franchises in these years, as well as the institution of the reserve system. The Bostons broke even in 1881 only with the help of $758 in donations. Not until 1882 did the club return to profitability.[13]

The booster Boston Base Ball Club dissolved after the 1876 season. The reason is not stated, but the team had just lost the pennant for the first time since 1871. A reasonable explanation is that a booster club is a lot more fun when it is supporting a winning team.[14] Its shares were returned to the Association, which dissolved them. Ownership of the Association was thereafter divided among the remaining 78 shares. Why were they not sold instead? The likely explanation is that they had essentially zero value. The club was not paying dividends, and had no immediate prospect of doing so. Indeed, it was an open question whether shareholders could be held liable for the organization's debt, giving shares a potentially negative value. At the same time, selling the shares would impose a liability on the Association, since shareholders at that time were entitled to season tickets. Better to sell the season tickets each year than to sell the share for a one-time payment. The next account listing voting shares comes from 1881. 77 of the 78 shares voted. The 72 Club shares were long gone and would never reappear.[15]

The Bostons have an air of inevitability to them. They were the best-run baseball club of the 1870s, both on the field and in the front office. They are the oldest baseball organization to field a team every year since 1871 to this day. They seem to be the Rock of Gibraltar of the early professional era. Yet they almost went under after the 1872 season, and only stumbled through the end of the decade. They could easily be remembered today by specialists in early baseball history as yet another of the innumerable clubs with but a fleeting existence.

Postscript: Baseball entered a boom phase in the 1880s. Albert Spalding, the Bostons' star pitcher from 1871 to 1875, maintained ties with some of the Boston organization as he established himself in Chicago, first as a player and then the president of the club and as a sporting-goods manufacturer. In 1884 he engaged in a protracted correspondence with Frederick Long, the treasurer of the Boston Association, to discreetly buy up shares. This would be a clear conflict of interest today, but would not raise an eyebrow at that time. Shares for sale were hard to find, but by April Long had scrounged 12, at par value. Spalding's reason for wanting this was straightforward: "I judge the Boston Club is making money, and a dividend might be paid one of these days."[16]

NOTES

1 *Boston Herald*, January 21, 1871.

2 *National Chronicle*, June 12, 1869; *Boston Journal*, February 20, 1871.

3 Frederick Long papers, National Baseball Hall of Fame. These include a copy of the corporate annual statement for 1873 filed with the Commonwealth of Massachusetts. It includes a list of shareholders.

4 *Boston Herald*, December 5, 1872.

5 *Boston Herald*, December 12, 1872; December 16, 1872.

6 *Boston Journal*, December 4, 1873; *New York Clipper*, December 13, 1873.

7 *New York Clipper*, April 3, 1875.

8 *Boston Herald*, January 3, 1873.

9 *Boston Evening Transcript*, December 4, 1873.

10 Respectively, *Boston Journal*, December 15, 1873; Frederick Long Papers; and *New York Clipper*, December 25, 1875.

11 Frederick Long Papers.

12 Frederick Long Papers.

13 *Boston Herald*, December 22, 1881; *New York Clipper*, December 30, 1882.

14 *Boston Herald*, December 10, 1876.

15 *Boston Herald*, December 22, 1881. One can but wonder if those 78 shares still lie buried at the bottom of the Atlanta Braves corporate structure.

16 Letters from Spalding to Long dated April 8, 1884, and May 21, 1884, Frederick Long Papers.

RED STOCKINGS FINANCES ~ A MINOR OBSERVATION

IT NOW BEING OVER 140 YEARS SINCE the Boston Red Stockings played ball, and with it not having been public information to begin with, it's not the easiest thing to determine the finances of the ballclub. Wondering about player salaries in these days long gone by, we reached out to Michael Haupert, co-chair of SABR's Business of Baseball Committee and our leading researcher in this area.

He compiled a list of 46 players in the National Association for the years 1874 and 1875, and their reported salaries, drawn from the Haupert Baseball Salary Database. His sources included the Chicago Cubs collection at the Chicago History Museum or the Cincinnati Reds collection at the Ohio Historical Society.

Dixie Tourangeau had located an article in the December 13, 1873 *New York Clipper* which, on page 291, discussed the annual meeting of the Boston Baseball Association and said, "The report of the treasurer showed that the receipts for the year had been about $23,000."

The Haupert Database provides these salaries for Boston Red Stockings players in 1874, the following year:

Ross Barnes	$2,000
Tommy Beals	$900
George Hall	$1,100
Andy Leonard	$1,800
Cal McVey	$1,800
Jim O'Rourke	$1,400
Harry Schafer	$1,400
Al Spalding	$2,000
Deacon White	$1,350
George Wright	$1,800
Harry Wright	$2,000
Payroll total	**$17,550**

Needless to say, salaries have increased significantly since 1874. The reported average salary for a major-league baseball player in 2015 was $4.25 million, with meal money alone for one player ($100.50 per day on the road) coming to about half the annual payroll of the entire Boston Red Stockings team in 1874.[1]

A personal letter Harry Wright sent to Sam Jackson along with his contract for 1871. (National Baseball Hall of Fame)

NOTES

1. http://ftw.usatoday.com/2015/04/major-league-baseball-average-salary-meal-money-2015-mlb

IVERS W. ADAMS

BY CHARLIE BEVIS

As the first president of the Boston Baseball Association in 1871, Ivers Adams was the father of professional baseball in Boston. The Association's baseball team was a charter member of the National Association during its inaugural season in 1871, played five seasons in that league, and then became the Braves franchise in the National League.

Ivers Whitney Adams was born on May 20, 1838, in Ashburnham, Massachusetts, the oldest of six children of Walter and Sarah (Whitney) Adams.[1] His father worked as a carpenter in rural Ashburnham, 50 miles northwest of Boston. Adams was educated in the Ashburnham public schools, but never attended college. Although Adams came from humble origins, he became a wealthy man in the city of Boston.

Adams left Ashburnham in 1857 to pursue a business career in Boston. Initially, he was a clerk at Houghton, Sawyer & Company, a dry-goods firm. In the mid-19th century, a clerk was an apprentice businessman, who worked for very low pay to learn the business in hopes of eventually becoming a highly compensated partner in the business. Adams left Houghton, Sawyer in 1860 to be a clerk at John H. Pray, Sons & Company, which specialized in carpets.[2] In the mid-1860s, Adams, still single, lived in a boarding house on Cambridge Street in downtown Boston near his work.[3] Since the main office of John H. Pray, Sons & Company was at 192 Washington Street, Adams was an occasional spectator at the afternoon baseball games played on the nearby Boston Common ball field by the Lowell Base Ball Club, one of the three top amateur teams in the city.

On October 4, 1866, Adams married Sarah Shepard.[4] They lived in a large house with several live-in domestic servants at 2 Delle Avenue in suburban Roxbury, which had been recently annexed to the city of Boston and renamed the Boston Highlands neighborhood.[5] Adams was still a clerk at John H. Pray, Sons & Company, but he was part of the emerging white-collar middle class that filled the void between the rich and the poor social classes.[6] Adams still watched a few ballgames played on the Boston Common on his way home from work, since he commuted to work from the Roxbury Crossing station on the Boston & Providence railroad line, whose Boston train terminal was adjacent to the Boston Common.

Before 2,000 spectators on the Boston Common on June 10, 1869, the all-professional Cincinnati Red Stockings, led by Harry Wright, trounced the amateur Lowell club, 29-9.[7] With such a large attendance, Adams saw a bright future for professional baseball in Boston and began to plot how to establish a professional team in the city.[8] Adams was not just an avid sportsman, but also a savvy businessman. He realized the potential that a professional baseball team could do for Boston's business community, to elevate Boston into the same realm as New York City and Philadelphia as one of America's leading cities that local businessmen, including Adams himself, could leverage for economic gain. It took Adams nearly two years to realize this goal and form a company to sponsor a professional baseball team.[9]

Adams had to first locate a new playing ground for Boston baseball teams. The Boston Common, once marginalized land next to the Charles River, was now valuable public land as a landfill project, begun in 1866, filled in the Charles River basin to create an elite neighborhood now known as the Back Bay. The city was issuing fewer permits to play baseball on the Common, to reduce the noise and activity that might impede the sale of house lots in the Back Bay. On June 24, 1869, the Lowell club began to play its games at the new Union Grounds, located two miles from the Boston Common on a five-acre parcel in Roxbury along the Boston & Providence railroad line.[10]

In 1870, when the Cincinnati team returned, 5,000 spectators jammed the Union Grounds on June 4 to watch Harry Wright's team crush the Harvard College team, 46-15.[11] Adams then seriously pressed forward to establish the first professional team in Boston. In November 1870, when the Cincinnati team was being disbanded, Adams recruited Wright and his brother George to form the nucleus of the new Boston team.[12] After Adams made Harry Wright the captain of the team, Wright recruited several other highly skilled ballplayers to complete the team by the time of the ballclub's first organizing meeting, on January 20, 1871, at the Parker House.

Adams was the leader of a band of five men, all in their 30s, who served as the officers and directors of that first professional baseball club in Boston. Adams, 32, was the president; Wright, 36, was the secretary; John Conkey, 31, a broker, was the vice president; Harrison Gardner, 30, a dry-goods merchant, was the treasurer; George Burditt, 38, an accountant, was the fifth director, in addition to the aforementioned four officers.[13]

At that founding meeting of the ballclub, Adams initiated a number of policies that were the foundation of Boston professional baseball for a quarter-century. First, he established the club as a corporation, which required that he marshal a bill through the state legislature.[14] Importantly, the new baseball club was called Boston, after its city location, not by a nickname that most other teams of the era used, such as the Mutual club in New York or the Athletic club in Philadelphia. Adams used his business connections to raise $15,000 in capital by selling shares in the new corporation, convincing prominent local merchants such as Eben Jordan (founder of the department store Jordan Marsh), Henry Pierce (owner of the Baker's Chocolate factory and future mayor of Boston), and John F. Mills (proprietor of the Parker House hotel).[15] The capital enabled Adams and Wright to immediately field a championship-caliber team.

Adams also established the strategy of attracting spectators to watch the baseball games: "shareholders, members of the club and those of our friends who may take sufficient interest in the success of this enterprise."[16] The operative word in the strategy was "friends," who were businessmen in the same emerging upper middle-class social status as the club's officers

Ivers Adams (Collection of Dixie Tourangeau)

and members (200 people who purchased season tickets). The laboring class was not part of the target audience. Adams bought into Wright's philosophy that the admission price to ballgames should be 50 cents, not the 25-cent fee that the Lowell club had been charging.[17] Patrons could purchase game tickets at the Wright & Gould sporting goods store, co-owned by George Wright.[18]

The strategy for the ballgrounds was also devised by Adams. He decided to rent the land where the Union Grounds were located and build "a covered building capable of seating about a thousand people," with reserved seats for the shareholders, members, and friends.[19] Bleacher seating along the baselines would come a few years later. This location later was known as the South End Grounds, where the Boston Braves franchise played its games until 1914.

Behind the capable leadership of Harry Wright, the Boston team finished the 1871 season in second place in the National Association standings, runner-up to the champion Athletic club of Philadelphia. Adams was re-elected president for the 1872 season; however, after serving as the club president for just ten months, he declined a second term since "his business engagements would not permit of his giving the proper time to the duties of the office."[20] Three weeks after stepping down as club president, Adams resigned from his position at John H. Pray, Sons & Company to start his own firm.[21] His role in establishing the ballclub had helped Adams achieve the next step in his business career; cynics would say he used the ballclub for personal gain.

However, after the Great Boston Fire of 1872 destroyed the buildings and inventory of the John H. Pray, Sons & Company, Adams returned to the carpet firm to rebuild its business. He was now part of ownership, the only nonfamily partner in the management team that had been exclusively John A. and William H. Pray.[22] His promotion from clerk to partner was lucrative because the demand for floor coverings escalated in Boston during the 1870s. Carpets were needed by residents in the new upper-class Back Bay neighborhood, but the rise of middle-class "streetcar suburbs" within five miles of downtown Boston stimulated carpet demand even more. The middle class sought to emulate the "trappings of gentility" of upper-class household furnishings, as "the carpet, the sofa, and the piano [were] all artifacts of the new middle-class way of life" in the late 19th century.[23]

While Adams was making money selling carpets, the Boston baseball team captured four consecutive National Association championships, from 1872 through 1875, and then two National League pennants in 1877 and 1878. Business was booming in Boston, as the baseball success had indeed helped turn Boston into one of America's leading cities, Adams's original goal. By the time the Boston team had won its sixth title in seven years, Adams was well on his way to becoming a millionaire as a partner at John H. Pray, Sons & Company.

In 1882 Adams retired from John H. Pray, Sons & Company as a wealthy man.[24] At age 44, he never had to work another day in his life; he, his wife, Sarah, and their five children (Alfred, Clara, Ivers S., Walter, and Mary) could live a life of leisure.[25] They moved from their home on Delle Avenue to a more upscale neighborhood in the Grove Hall section of Dorchester, building a huge house at the corner of Washington Street and Columbia Road.[26] Adams also purchased a fishing ground on the shores of the Nepisiguit River in New Brunswick, Canada.[27] He continued to dabble in the business world as a member of the board of directors at the American Net and Twine Company, the firm his father-in-law, James S. Shepard, had founded to manufacture cotton-twine fish netting to displace hemp twine.[28]

Adams rarely was in the baseball spotlight after 1871, but he did occasionally attend get-togethers. On June 21, 1897, he was a guest at a dinner given by George Wright for a touring baseball team from Australia.[29] On September 24, 1908, he spoke at a postgame dinner following an old-timer's game played at the Huntington Avenue Grounds.[30]

In his later years, Adams donated funds to his hometown of Ashburnham, to establish a water system and to erect a statue that depicts a young boy walking to school.[31]

Adams died on October 10, 1914, in Boston.[32] He is buried at New Cemetery in Ashburnham.

SOURCES

Books

Blumin, Stuart, *The Emergence of the Middle Class: Social Experience in the American City, 1760-1900* (New York: Cambridge University Press, 1989).

Devine, Christopher, *Harry Wright: The Father of Professional Baseball* (Jefferson, North Carolina: McFarland, 2003).

Sterns, Ezra, "Ivers W. Adams," in *History of Ashburnham, Massachusetts* (Town of Ashburnham, 1887), 592-594.

Tuohey, George, *A History of the Boston Base Ball Club* (Boston: M.F. Quinn, 1897).

Newspapers

"The Boston Base-Ball Club," *Boston Daily Advertiser*, January 21, 1871.

"Ivers W. Adams Dead," *Boston Globe*, October 11, 1914.

"John H. Pray, Sons & Company," *Boston Congregationalist*, April 17, 1873.

"Organization of the Boston Club as a Corporate Company," *Boston Daily Advertiser*, December 8, 1871.

Boston Daily Advertiser, 1869-1872.

Boston Herald, 1869-1870.

Archival Material

Boston Public Library, *Boston City Directory* from 1860 to 1914.

Massachusetts State Archives, marriage records prior to 1910.

US Census Bureau, federal census records for decennial years from 1860 to 1910.

NOTES

1. Ezra Sterns, "Ivers W. Adams," in *History of Ashburnham, Massachusetts* (Town of Ashburnham, 1887), 592.
2. Sterns, "Ivers W. Adams," 593.
3. *Boston City Directory*, 1865.
4. Marriage records for 1866 in the Massachusetts State Archives (Volume 190, Page 279).
5. *Boston City Directory*, 1869; the 1870 federal census (Series M593, Roll 649, Page 432).
6. *Boston City Directory*, 1870.
7. *Boston Herald*, June 11, 1869. Of the three games Cincinnati played with Boston teams in 1869, the June 10 game was the only one played at the Boston Common. In the other two games Cincinnati handily defeated the Tri-Mountain club (40-12) on June 11 in Brighton and Harvard College team (30-11) on June 12 in Cambridge.
8. George Tuohey, *A History of the Boston Base Ball Club* (Boston: M.F. Quinn, 1897), 61.
9. "Organization of the Boston Club as a Corporate Company," *Boston Daily Advertiser*, December 8, 1871.
10. *Boston Daily Advertiser*, June 24, 1869.
11. *Boston Herald*, June 6, 1870. All three games that Cincinnati played with Boston teams in 1870 were played at the Union Grounds. On June 6 Cincinnati defeated the Lowell club (17-4) and on June 9 they defeated the Tri-Mountain club (30-6).
12. Christopher Devine, *Harry Wright: The Father of Professional Baseball* (Jefferson, North Carolina: McFarland, 2003), 86.
13. "The Boston Base-Ball Club," *Boston Daily Advertiser*, January 21, 1871; *Boston City Directory*, 1871.
14. "Organization of the Boston Club."
15. Tuohey, *Boston Base Ball Club*, 62.
16. "The Boston Base-Ball Club."
17. Devine, *Harry Wright*, 12.
18. *Boston Daily Advertiser*, September 5, 1871.
19. "The Boston Base-Ball Club."
20. "Organization of the Boston Club."
21. *Boston Daily Advertiser*, January 2, 1872. A small partnership notice read: "The interest of Ivers W. Adams in our business ceases from this date. Dec. 30, 1871. John H. Pray, Sons & Co." Adams also had no occupation associated with his listing in the 1872 *Boston City Directory*.
22. "John H. Pray, Sons & Company." *Boston Congregationalist*, April 17, 1873; *Boston City Directory*, 1873.
23. Stuart Blumin, *The Emergence of the Middle Class: Social Experience in the American City, 1760-1900* (New York: Cambridge University Press, 1989), 185.
24. Sterns, "Ivers W. Adams," 594.
25. The 1880 federal census (Series T9, Roll 561, Page 482).
26. *Boston City Directory*, 1885.
27. *Boston Daily Advertiser*, June 11, 1891.
28. *Directory of Directors in the City of Boston*, 1906.
29. *Sporting Life*, June 26, 1897.
30. *Boston Transcript*, September 25, 1908.
31. *Boston Globe*, May 20, 1912, and October 13, 1912. The statue still stands today at the corner of School and Main Streets, near the entrance to Cushing Academy, a private school.
32. "Ivers W. Adams Dead," *Boston Globe*, October 11, 1914.

FAST DAY~BOSTON'S ORIGINAL OPENING DAY

BY JOANNE HULBERT

THE *NEW YORK TIMES* HERALDED the approaching start of the base-ball season in March 1871 by announcing that "the ball-fields of the metropolis will again become the scene of interesting contests—unless the weather should prove unusually inauspicious."[1] In Cleveland and Chicago, base-ball clubs and their fans also kept an impatient eye on the weather and waited for the ground to thaw and conditions to become favorable, as that all too important first game was a highly anticipated event. As reports from New York also noted, during 1863 the first game played occurred as early as March 14, and if the weather in 1871 cooperated, Brooklyn announced, a game would be played there on March 11.

But not so in Boston, where traditions ran deep and if Bostonians were to wait for the weather to cooperate, the delay could be longer than tolerated. Therefore, the first game of the season, for as long as base ball had been an essential part of life in New England, was celebrated with great fanfare on the first Thursday of April, despite what the season offered, whether in the form of rain, sleet, or even snow.

Before the calendar accumulated the holidays we celebrate today, there were only a few days during the year when Boston, along with the rest of New England, was afforded a day off from work to celebrate, commemorate a historical event, or let off some of the daily tension of simply living. One of those days was Thanksgiving, a day of celebration and commemoration, as well as a nod of respect to our forefathers, with lavish feasts and a joyful noise before Christmas joined the the calendar. In order to temper the urge toward too much celebrating and good tidings of joy, that Puritan streak in Boston's heritage produced Fast Day, traditionally held on the first Thursday in April, a day for "fasting, humiliation and prayer"—words that appeared on the formal proclamations published annually by the governor of Massachusetts. The first recorded Fast Day in New England was 1623 at Plymouth, and the last proclamation for such a day in Massachusetts would be 1893.

Last Thursday was observed as a Fast Day, and also as a Day of Humiliation and Prayer, in Massachusetts. As evidence of public repentance, there were afternoon and evening performances in all the Boston theaters, mainly for the benefit of the suburban population. As further evidence, if any were needed, there were many base-ball matches. In order to get themselves into a serious frame of mind, many members of the General Court [the state legislature] *made an excursion to Plymouth Rock. Of course, they ate no dinner, but strictly meditated upon the fasts (voluntary and involuntary) kept by the Pilgrim Fathers. There was a pleasant holiday, but no "humiliation" to speak of.*[2]

At first in the early years, there was not much of a reason to do otherwise. Most citizens were used to occasional routine moments of fasting, humiliation, and prayer, but having a day devoted to just those virtues might have been easy to swallow back then. Or not. Times change, albeit gradually. Henry David Thoreau remembered Fast Day 1830 in an April 10, 1856, diary entry: "Fast day—Some fields are dried sufficiently for games of ball—with which this season is commonly ushered in. I associate this day, when I can remember it, with games of base-ball played over behind the hills in the russet fields toward Sleepy Hollow where the snow was just melted and dried up."

Already there was a hint of where Fast Day was heading. As Thanksgiving heralded the approaching winter, Fast Day waited with hope on the arrival of spring, despite lingering climatic evidence otherwise. Today, baseball fans eagerly await the first game of the season, and our ancestors were no different. Base ball in 1870s Massachusetts held the same thrill of anticipation, and despite unreliable weather, players and fans throughout New England were ready to get outside on Fast Day, April 6, 1871, to witness amateur games and for the first time the debut of a professional base-ball club in Boston. The team included immortals George and Harry Wright, Albert Goodwill Spalding, Calvin McVey, Harry Schafer, Sam Jackson, and Ross Barnes in a game played with a picked nine in the cold wind and on a soggy field with basepaths still slippery with ice and mud. George Wright introduced the trap ball with hints of the future infield fly rule brewing. With men on first and second, the batter hit a fly ball that Wright let pass through his hands, then picked it up and threw it to third in time for it to then be passed to second, to complete a double play. The runners, it was reported, were so mystified that they hardly knew what had happened, and the crowd perceived it as a trick on the part of Wright. Thrilling!

The Red Stockings' debut wasn't the only game on Fast Day 1871. Harvard met the Lowell Club on Jarvis Field, across the river in Cambridge, and the Unas Club of Charlestown played its opening game with the Tufts College nine at College Hill. The venerable old Excelsior Club of Boston visited Waltham's Young America Club and defeated them. The score in six innings was 50-18. Games were played in Hartford, Providence, and in small towns in Vermont and Maine. Any village or town that could organize a game did so with enthusiasm, as if it were a ritual that could encourage the arrival of warmer weather.

Thursday, April 4, 1872, Fast Day, according to the governor's proclamation, instilled hope in the hearts of the devotees of outdoor sports. The extreme cold weather of the previous month had left the still frozen ground less favorable for a base-ball game, but games were played nonetheless. Due to the uncertainty of the conditions and weather that might have discouraged even the most hardy New Yorker, the invitation extended to the New York players was canceled, and

Boston Journal *advertisement for Fast Day services, April 5, 1871.*

a picked nine made up of home-grown talent thought to be better able to withstand the less than optimum climate and field conditions was organized. The Lowell Club was again invited along with several players from Harvard and the Beacon Club of Boston, and their lineup also borrowed Birdsall and Cone of the Red Stockings. About 30 loads of gravel, sand, and sawdust were used in an attempt to put the field in at least passable order. Nevertheless, the field conditions were a challenge for the players. Annan of the Picked Nine, a shortstop from Harvard, "hit a ball to the right field close to the fence, which rightfielder Ryan went for and muffed, which was quite excusable, as he slipped in a mud patch, and when he arose the purity of his nether garments had departed."[3] The stalwart crowd of about 3,000 spectators in the grandstand was "graced by the presence of a considerable number of ladies."[4] The score: Red Stockings 32, Picked Nine 0. Fasting, humiliation, and prayer went on around Boston, but just as sure as it was Fast Day, games of base ball were played everywhere.

Fast Day 1873, "in accordance with annual custom, was observed as the opening day of the base-ball season and the Boston nine made their first appearance in public since they were rewarded for their last year's exertions with the champion flag and streamer."[5] The first Thursday of April was never presumed to be auspicious for outdoor activities and watching a base-ball game was not expected to provide a comfortable atmosphere so early in the spring. The day before brought a drenching rain making the field damp and heavy with mud, though much better, reporters wrote, than the field of Fast Day 1872. Cloudy skies and a raw wind prevailed, but the conditions were not enough to discourage Boston cranks and nearly 2,500 of them turned out to watch the game and celebrate as the championship flag was hoisted over the grandstand. The picked nine of strong amateur players was captained by Cheever Goodwin, formerly of the Harvard College team. Those college boys from Cambridge had been fielding a team since 1863, and enjoyed baseball celebrity before the professionals had organized. Harvard College and the Lowell Club provided reasonably capable players who served the Boston Club well as worthy opponents on Fast Day.

A week before Fast Day 1875, the Boston Club inspected the field to see what repairs needed to be done. The game was set for Thursday, April 2, and a picked nine with players from the Beacon and Somerset amateur clubs provided the opposition. The ground was damp, the cold wind tested the fortitude of the cranks and players, and yet the crowd turned out despite the hardship, as if driven by deep-seated tradition or an inherent need to see a base-ball game, a harbinger of spring that was yet to arrive. Weather conditions did not affect the playing of the game that would naturally be played that day, but the first professional club to travel to Boston, the Philadelphias, would arrive on Saturday, April 25. The Bostons meanwhile would spend time as far south as Baltimore while waiting for warmer weather to arrive ahead of them on the home field.

> *Fast Day morning was pleasant and sunny, snow and rain at mid-day and the afternoon was leaden, cold and cheerless. The cold of the afternoon seriously interfered with the game of base ball and the aquatic sports, but the in-door amusements in the evening were well patronized.*[6]

And yet they played on Thursday, April 8, 1875, a week later than traditional, as Easter was observed on March 28, just a few days before April 1, the first Thursday in April. Having two holidays in one week was too much to endure. The grounds were in poor condition and only 500 cranks braved the cold, but they were pleased with the outcome—a shutout by Albert Spalding, Boston 8, Picked Nine 0. The game featured the debut of Arthur Latham, who played "excellently well."[7] The picked-nine lineup was filled with future stars and local favorites. George Bradley of the Graftons would join the Boston National League team in 1876 and be nicknamed "Foghorn." Tyng and Thatcher from Harvard and Briggs of the Beacon Club along with Apollonio, an outfielder from the Excelsiors, appeared on the field, adding interest to the opening game.

The appearance of "Apollonio" in the lineup of the picked-nine players adds a note of intrigue. Nicholas A. Apollonio, city registrar of Boston, had three sons—Nicholas T., Samuel, and Spencer—who were apparently smitten by the game of base ball. Which one was the player for the Excelsiors? Nicholas Taylor Apollonio is unlikely to be the candidate; he was president of the Red Stockings, and as such would likely have been recognized as a player-president— an unlikely though sporting gesture as the team's executive. Samuel achieved prominence as a stationary engineer and was not known to be connected to any base-ball business. And then there was Spencer, the youngest of the three. A newspaper article in 1908 introduced Helen Apollonio as the daughter of Spencer Apollonio "who played with the Boston Nationals 30 years ago and is well-known in baseball circles."[8] Indeed, the headline on Helen's impending nuptials heralded: "Newspaper Man Marries. James H. Holt Takes Daughter of Old Time Ball Player for Bride." There was no mention of Helen's prominence in Boston's musical circles.

Beyond 1875, Fast Day continued to herald the opening of the base-ball season in Boston. Several Fast Day games were nearly impossible to play on account of snow—not just a dusting, but knee-deep. In 1877 snow covered the field and the air was uncomfortably damp. The 1880 game was a cold, uncomfortable affair, as was the game in 1882, and yet more than a thousand cranks turned out for the game. Snow canceled the game in 1884, but what finally put an end to the ancient day of fasting, humiliation, and prayer was the encroachment of modern times and the reality that a decreasing number of citizens were attending the church services and instead celebrated the harbingers of spring—light, warmth, and base ball.

> *At Easter, London gets almost a week of rest or pleasure. Now, in America we have not more holidays in a year than the Londoner gets in a week. At a pinch, if we put in Fast Day which the unregenerate will call "Farce Day," we can lay claim to seven days in the year. Washington's Birthday, Fast day, Memorial day, the Fourth of July, Labor day, Thanksgiving day and Christmas day. At least two of these are not general, so that they have only five days that are national property, or six at the outside, and those are distributed over the 52 weeks. But your Briton is more generous to himself. His springtime is earlier than ours, and just after the great change has set in the stalwart Englisher takes a week of it, as who should say: "I have labored in the darkness of winter; now let me take for the sunny fields, and the sparkling river.*[9]

Debate over the abolishment of Fast Day began in earnest in 1893 when only a shadow of the original intent of the holiday remained. The governor "for years had been in effect the umpire in the national game, and when he set the date of Fast Day he said in effect: 'Play ball!'"[10] Debate in the Great and General Court began in 1893 with abolitionists battling the defenders of the old tradition. Neither side won that year and the battle continued into 1894, when the faction calling for abolishment won out. But this posed a problem: As the legislature soon found out, no one wanted to lose a holiday once that day had become a welcome day off from work. A replacement needed to be found and a new, practical reason for that day was required. Massachusetts was rid of Fast Day at last, but some other formal means of proclaiming the base-ball season had to be found. April 19, a day closer (cranks and players hoped) toward warmer weather, was a perfect replacement and fulfilled the proper requirement for historic value. The day commemorated the Battles of Lexington and Concord. The day also marked the shedding of first blood by the soldiers of Massachusetts as they changed trains in Baltimore on their way to defend Washington in 1861, and for good measure was also the day Governor Andros was overthrown and placed under house arrrest by the Boston militia in 1689.

The newly proclaimed Patriots Day immediately adopted the activities held most dear by the adherents of Fast Day: field sports and, in particular, baseball. Patriots Day is still a popular holiday in Massachusetts for the dramatic re-enactment of the Battles of Lexington and Concord and the running of the Boston Marathon. The first game at Fenway Park in 1912 would have been played on April 19, if rain hadn't forced postponement of that game to the next day. One constant still on the Red Sox schedule at that green cathedral, Fenway Park, is Patriots Day, with a game that starts at 11 o'clock in the morning, the hour, perhaps just coincidentally, when church services were held on Fast Day.

NOTES

1. "Base-Ball. Approaching Inauguration of the Season," *New York Times*, March 1, 1871: 6.
2. *New York Tribune*, April 8, 1871: 4.
3. "Base Ball," *Boston Journal*, April 5, 1872: 2.
4. Ibid.
5. "Inauguration of the New Season," *Boston Herald*, April 4, 1873: 4.
6. "Base Ball," *Boston Journal*, April 9, 1875: 2.
7. "The Sporting Season Opened," *Boston Daily Advertiser*, April 10, 1875: 1.
8. "Newspaper Man Marries," *Boston Herald*, January 19, 1909:3.
9. "The Easy English," *Boston Herald*, April 14, 1893: 3.
10. "The Unfortunate Career of a Small Petition," *Boston Journal*, February 8, 1893: 9.

APRIL 6, 1871
Boston Red Stockings 41, Picked Nine 10, at Boston's South End Grounds.

BY BOB LEMOINE

"WELL, BACK IN 1871, MY GREAT-great-grandmother had a boardinghouse in Boston," recounted a sparkling, white-haired lady speaking with appraiser Leila Dunbar on a PBS episode of *Antiques Roadshow*. "And she housed the Boston baseball team. Most of them had come from the Cincinnati Red Stockings and were among the first to be paid to play baseball." Her unique collection, appraised at $1,000,000, contains baseball cards and personal correspondences of the 1871-1872 Boston Red Stockings, Boston's first professional baseball team. They are also the ancestors of the Atlanta Braves and the first Boston team to wear red socks.

They had sparkled in those red and white uniforms when they came to Boston in the summer of 1870, and Boston businessman Ivers Whitney Adams took notice, particularly of baseball's Wright brothers, George and Harry, who were touring the East Coast with the legendary Cincinnati Red Stockings, the nation's first professional baseball team. Adams had begun dreaming of a professional baseball club in Boston since January of that year,[1] and was convinced that if professional baseball could be a reality in Boston, he needed these talented brothers. Adams began a correspondence and even made a trip to Cincinnati to talk further with George and Harry.[2] George Wright then arrived in Boston in November,[3] and met Adams at Boston's Parker House, shortly after the Cincinnati team disbanded. On December 3, the *Boston Journal* verified rumors of a new professional team in the works and said that "Boston shall possess a nine, composed of gentlemanly players, whose unquestionable skill and ability will make it second to none in the country."[4]

The Wrights began constructing the Boston team. They brought along first baseman Charlie Gould and catcher Cal McVey from their old Cincinnati club, then signed pitcher Albert Spalding, second baseman Ross Barnes, and outfielder Fred Cone of the Rockford, Illinois, club. They also brought along their socks. "Back in Cincinnati," historian David Voigt wrote, "not even (Harry Wright's) best friends forgave him for taking the name 'Red Stockings' to Beantown."[5]

The Boston club was officially organized at the Parker House on January 20, 1871. "Boston can now boast of possessing a first-class professional Base Ball Club," wrote the *Journal*.[6] The Boston Base Ball Association was now formed with $15,000 in stock divided into 150 shares.[7] The next step was to pay the $10 membership fee and join the new National Association of Professional Base Ball Players, organized on a rainy night in Collier's Rooms upstairs saloon at 13th Street and Broadway in New York City on March 17, 1871. The first professional baseball league was under way.[8]

The new Boston team practiced for three weeks, then on April 6 the players were ready for their first exhibition game. "With a month of steady practice," wrote the *Journal*, "they will be in a condition to contest for the supremacy with the best clubs in the country."[9]

The game was between "the new Boston professional nine and a strong nine selected from the best amateurs in this vicinity," wrote the *Journal*. The "picked nine," according to the *Boston Herald*, consisted of players from the "Harvard, Lowell, and Tri-Mountain clubs."[10] The game was played on the leased Union Grounds, then being referred to as the "Boston Grounds" by the newspapers, and was later named the South End Grounds. "The grounds were not in the best condition owing to the rains of the past ten days," wrote the *Journal*.[11]

This inaugural 1871 game stirred up huge interest in Boston. The crowd was electric, "for there assembled on the grounds of the club yesterday afternoon, full five thousand persons to witness the opening game of the Boston Nine," wrote the *Journal*, "thus being a larger number than ever assembled before on these grounds."[12] The *Herald* estimated a crowd of 6,000, and noted that the crowd was "larger than ever seen here before, and excepting the Peace Jubilee, probably the largest crowd which ever came together on one occasion in this city."[13] Fans were standing on the fence and on nearby rooftops to watch this inaugural event.

The crowd applauded as the new Boston team took the field, looking very much like the old Cincinnati club, with a white flannel shirt, knee breeches, cap, red belt, red necktie, white shoes, and the name of the club in block letters across the shirt. And we mustn't forget the red stockings, which also made their debut that day, making this "the neatest uniform yet originated," according to the *Journal*.[14]

While no play-by-play account of the game exists, it's safe to say the 41-10 Boston win was historic but not a classic. After a scoreless first inning, Boston broke out with 10 runs in the second, through some "fine heavy hits, assisted by field errors of their opponents."[15] "This was a long inning," the *Journal* elaborated.[16] Three more runs came across in the third inning, with runs from Sam Jackson, George Wright, and Barnes, and the score was now 13-0 Boston. They added 11 more runs in the fourth inning, and then the Picked Nine answered with a run of their own to cut Boston's lead to 24-1. Both teams scored six times in the sixth inning, the Picked Nine's runs mostly coming courtesy of Boston errors. The lead through seven innings was Boston 32-9, and the final score of 41-10 ended the first game of a Boston professional baseball team. Boston's George Wright had four total bases in the game and scored four runs, while Harry Wright also scored four times. Jackson scored seven runs, McVey six, and Gould five. Spalding pitched the entire game for Boston.

For the Picked Nine, third baseman Frank Barrows scored twice, as did right fielder Dave Birdsall, a Boston player who played for the Picked Nine that day. First baseman Maxson Mortimer "Mort" Rogers led the Picked Nine with three hits. Left fielder William Ellery Channing Eustis, second baseman Horatio Stevens White, center fielder John Cheever Goodwin, and shortstop Archibald McClure Bush were Harvard players. Catcher William M. "Met" Bradbury, pitcher James D'Wolf Lovett, and Rogers were players from the Lowell team. Barrows was from the Tri-Mountain club, and would later that season play 18 games for Boston, the only player of the Picked Nine to play professional baseball. "It is quite apparent," the *Journal* remarked, "that a nine picked from two or three clubs, be they ever so good players, do not do so well as in their own club."[17]

"Of course the Picked Nine were defeated," espoused the *Harvard Advocate*, "but not 'of course' as badly as the result shows. Never was the fact made equally manifest that working together constitutes a club's strongest point. The men played each for himself, and the effect was a brilliant series of abortive efforts at even medium play."[18]

Boston fans had now seen the stars of the old legendary Cincinnati Red Stockings who were now *their Boston* Red Stockings. "George Wright fully maintained his reputation as the model base ball player of the country," wrote the *Journal*. "Some of his stops, fly catches and throws Thursday equaling anything seen on a ball field. … Harry Wright also played well up to his usual standard of excellence. … McVey bids fair to succeed to the laurels of catcher *par excellence* of the country. … Spalding will rank among the best professional pitchers of the country. He has good command over the ball, which he sends into the bat at a speed somewhat less than a cannon ball."[19]

Today, Boston's MBTA subway rumbles into Ruggles Station, and busy Northeastern University students and other hurried Bostonians pass by the spot where the South End Grounds once stood. Only an overlooked, lonely plaque remains to tell us of the origins of professional baseball in Boston and of the beginnings of the Atlanta Braves franchise.

Except for a few extraordinary baseball cards.

SOURCES

Besides the sources cited in the text, the author benefited from the following sources:

Batesel, Paul. *Players and Teams of the National Association, 1871-1875* (Jefferson, North Carolina: McFarland, 2012).

Devine, Christopher. *Harry Wright: The Father of Professional Baseball* (Jefferson, North Carolina: McFarland, 2003).

Harvard Book: A Series of Historical, Biographical, and Descriptive Sketches. Harvard University Archives. Retrieved May 16, 2015, nrs.harvard.edu/urn-3:hul.arch:15010.

Harvard College Class of 1873 Ninth Report of the Secretary. Boston: Rockwell & Church Press, 1913. Retrieved May 16, 2015. books.google.com/books?id=tdglAAAAYAAJ&lpg=PA20&ots=3R3 5K_uW_d&dq=John%20Cheever%20Goodwin%20Harvard%20 class%20of%201873&pg=PA19#v=onepage&q&f=false.

Report of the Secretary of the Class of 1871 of Harvard College, Issue 11. Cambridge, Massachusetts: The Class, 1921. Retrieved May 16, 2015, books.google.com/books?id=vCZOAAAAMAAJ&dq=inauthor%3 A%22Harvard%20university.%2C%20Class%20of%201871%22&pg=P P5#v=onepage&q&f=false.

Articles

Bevis, Charlie. "Ivers Adams," The Baseball Biography Project, SABR BioProject, sabr.org/bioproj/person/813abb83#sdendnote10sym, accessed May 1, 2015.

Brooks, Jimmy. "Columbus Lot Slabbed Where Boston's Historic South End Grounds Once Stood," *Huntington News*, January 9, 2014. Accessed May 16, 2015 huntnewsnu.com/2014/01/columbus-lot-slabbed-where-bostons-historic-south-end-grounds-once-stood/.

Thorn, John. "Baseball's First League Game: May 4, 1871," ourgame.mlblogs.com/2012/02/07/baseballs-first-league-game-may-4-1871/ accessed May 12, 2015.

Voigt, David Quentin. "The Boston Red Stockings: The Birth of Major League Baseball," *New England Quarterly* vol. 43 no.4 (1970), 531-549.

Websites

"1871-1872 Boston Red Stockings Archive." *Antiques Roadshow*. Public Broadcasting System, 2014. pbs.org/wgbh/roadshow/season/19/new-york-ny/appraisals/1871-1872-boston-red-stockings-archive—201407A12, accessed May 15, 2015.

NOTES

1. Based on Adams's recollection at the founding of the team a year later. "The Boston Base Ball Club: Meeting of the Stockholders—A History of the Enterprise—Organization of the Association and Election of Officers," *Boston Traveler*, January 21, 1871.

2. George V. Tuohey, *A History of the Boston Base Ball Club ... A Concise and Accurate History of Base Ball From Its Inception* (Boston: M.F. Quinn & Co., 1897), 61 [Google Books version]. A special petition was submitted to the Massachusetts Legislature to grant a charter for a new baseball club with no less than $10,000 capital stock at $100 per share. Acquiring the services of George and Harry Wright was now the top priority. "A Boston Professional Base Ball Nine," *Boston Journal*, November 15, 1870: 2.

3. "Base Ball Matters," *Boston Journal*, November 25, 1870: 4.

4. "Boston and Vicinity: The Boston Professional Nine," *Boston Journal*, December 3, 1870: 3.

5. David Quentin Voigt, *American Baseball: From the Gentleman's Sport to the Commissioner System* (Norman, Oklahoma: University of Oklahoma Press, 1966), 34.

6. "The Boston Base Ball Club: A Permanent Organization Effected All the Players Engaged," *Boston Journal*, January 21, 1871: 1.

7. Adams was elected president of the club, along with vice president John A. Conkey, treasurer Harrison Gardiner, secretary Harry Wright, and "fifth director" G.H. Burditt. "The Boston Nine. Organization of the Boston Base Ball Association—History of the Movement—Adoption of By-Laws and Election of Officers," *Boston Herald*, January 21, 1871.

8. The Boston club was one of eight teams pay the $10 fee to join. The others were the Philadelphia Athletics, New York Mutuals, Washington (D.C.) Olympics, Troy (New York) Haymakers, Chicago White Stockings, and two teams sharing the same name: the Cleveland Forest City club and the Rockford (Illinois) Forest City club. Before the season began, a ninth club joined: the Fort Wayne (Indiana) Kekiongas.

9. "Base Ball: Opening Match of the Boston Club—The Picked Nine Defeated, 41 to 10—Other Matches," *Boston Journal*, April 7, 1871: 2.

10. "Affairs About Home: Baseball," *Boston Herald*, April 8, 1871: 4.

11. "Base Ball: Opening Match of the Boston Club." The Union Grounds opened on June 19, 1869, on the east side of the Providence Railroad track, near Milford Place on Tremont Street. The game was between the Brooklyn Atlantics and a picked nine from the Lowell, Massachusetts, and Tri-Mountain clubs. The *Boston Herald* reported that despite the large crowd the game was long and tedious as foul balls over the fence had to be chased down. See "Affairs About Home."

12. "Base Ball: Opening Match of the Boston Club."

13. "Affairs About Home: Baseball," *Boston Herald*, April 8, 1871: 4. The "Peace Jubilee" was a massive music festival in Boston organized by band leader Patrick S. Gilmore to celebrate the end of the Civil War. The celebration was held for a week in June 1869, and included thousands of instrumentalists and singers in a specially built coliseum to hold the enormous crowd. Among the celebratory masses were President Ulysses S. Grant and poet

Oliver Wendell Holmes. This was the first so-called "monster" festival in 19th century America. See Roger L. Hall. "Peace Jubilees," *Oxford Music Online,* Oxford University Press, accessed May 5, 2015, oxfordmusiconline.com/subscriber/article/grove/music/A2252160.

14 Ibid.

15 "Base Ball: Opening Match of the Boston Club"

16 Ibid.

17 Ibid.

18 "The Games on Thursday," *Harvard Advocate*, Vol. XI. No. V, April 14, 1871, 69. Retrieved May 9, 2015. books.google.com/books?id=PN3OAAAAMAAJ&lpg=PA69&ots=E3t8MgYPD&dq=%22picked%20nine%22%20%22eustis%22&pg=PA69#v=onepage&q&f=false.

19 "Base Ball: Opening Match of the Boston Club."

MAY 5, 1871

Boston Red Stockings 20, Washington Olympics 18, at the Olympic Grounds in Washington, D.C.

First regular-season game in Boston professional baseball history.

BY BOB LEMOINE

"This sort of thing isn't done in England, you know, where they have cricket, you know, and rowing, you know, but not this sort of thing, you know."
— Comments overheard from a British high commissioner in attendance.[1]

IN WHAT WOULD BE A "PRIME TIME" matchup today, the first scheduled game of the new National Association of Professional Base Ball Players was to be a match of the now-disbanded Cincinnati Red Stockings, or what the *Boston Advertiser* called a matchup liken to "When Greek meets Greek."[2] Five of the old Red Stockings (Charlie Sweasy, Asa Brainard, Doug Allison, Andy Leonard, and Fred Waterman) signed with the Washington Olympics, while four signed with Boston (Harry and George Wright, Cal McVey, and Charlie Gould), which also took the Red Stockings name. A rainout on May 4 spoiled that storybook beginning of the association, yet the matchup still, according to the *New York Clipper*, was "the principal topic of interest in base ball circles east and west."[3] The matchup of Boston and Washington, which countered with the nickname of Blue Stockings, was a battle of two teams "torn from their Western admirers," grumbled the *Cincinnati Enquirer*.[4]

"Long before the appointed time for calling play (4 P.M.), crowds could have been seen moving towards the grounds from all directions—hacks, ambulances and street-cars coming out heavily loaded … an eager and expectant multitude, numbering at least five thousand, were in waiting," the *National Republican* wrote.[5]

The Olympic Grounds were located about 13 blocks north of the White House.[6] Members of President Grant's Cabinet, congressmen, and two British high commissioners, were in attendance.[7] "The National Game of Base Ball has many admirers here at the Metropolis," wrote Benjamin Perley Poore of the *Boston Journal*, "especially among those young men who are clerks in the Departments, and who need outdoor exercise."[8] This was the first official game in Boston's professional baseball history.

Fans traveled from Cincinnati "anxious to witness the playing of those who gave the name of that pork packing metropolis such an honorable place in 1868,'69 and '70," wrote Poore.[9] There was a new team wearing red stockings with "the name 'Boston' emblazoned in scarlet letters upon the white flannel which covered their ample chests."[10]

Umpire Hicks Hayhurst failed to appear, so Hervie Alden Dobson of the Flower City club of Rochester, New York, was chosen. Dobson was the baseball editor of the *New York Clipper* and had lost a leg in the Civil War but "moves about nimbly on crutches."[11] He was also a known friend of the Washington club and "it was generally remarked on the grand stand that the Bostons were playing against the Olympics and the umpire."[12] Dobson had also written a letter in the March 11, 1871, *Clipper*, suggesting batting averages should be determined by at-bats, not games played.[13]

Pitching for Washington was Brainard, "who rivals Lord Dundreary in his faultless attire and his whiskers," Poore commented.[14] Albert Spalding pitched for Boston.

At 3:30 P.M., the flags of both clubs were hoisted up the flagpole. Harry Wright won the coin toss and elected for Washington to bat first. Washington starters Sweasy and John Glenn were unable to play due to illness.

With runners at first and second in the first inning, Washington's Doug Allison doubled on a fair-foul hit[15] past third that scored Davy Force and put Everett Mills on third. George Wright's throw of a George Hall grounder was wild, and Mills scored. Allison scored on a passed ball to make the score 3-0. Andy Leonard and the pitcher Brainard walked to load the bases, and then Harry Wright misplayed a fly ball by Henry Burroughs to center, and Hall scored. A groundball and another passed ball gave Washington a 6-0 lead over the error-prone Boston team.

Boston countered with one run in its half of the first, as George Wright walked and scored on a single by Cal McVey.

In the Washington second, Force led with a single, and Mills was hit by a pitch. Allison's fair-foul loaded the bases with no outs. A single by Hall scored Force and Mills. George Wright and Schafer collided on a pop fly hit by Leonard, and Allison scored. A single by Burroughs scored Leonard, and Washington led 10-1 after two innings.

In the Boston third, Spalding and George Wright scored on a throwing error by Allison. McVey reached on Henry Berthrong's error, and Ross Barnes scored. Gould's grounder scored Birdsall, and Harry Schafer's single scored McVey. Fred Cone walked to load the bases, and a groundout by Spalding scored Gould, making the score 10-7 Washington. George Wright hit back to the pitcher, but Schafer beat the throw to the plate. Seven runs scored on only two hits, making the score Washington 10-8.

In the fourth, singles by Hall and Brainard plus another error on George Wright loaded the bases for the Olympics. Berthrong walked, scoring Hall. Washington scored another run in the fifth to take a 12-8 lead, then added another three runs in the sixth inning, as another error by George Wright scored Burroughs and Berthrong. Barnes dropped a pop fly and Waterman scored. Washington led 15-8 after six innings.

An advertisement in the May 4, 1871 edition of the Daily National Republican *in Washington, D.C. This was the first regular-season game in Boston professional baseball history. It was rained out and played on May 5.*

In the Boston seventh, George Wright walked for the fourth time, advanced to second on a passed ball, and stole third. Barnes walked, and both runners scored on Allison's throwing error. Allison also "had his thumb split by a ball,"[16] and had to leave the game later. Birdsall scored on a single by Harry Wright, who scored on a double by Gould. Washington led 15-12.

In the Washington eighth, a groundball through George Wright's legs scored Mills and Hall. A single by Burroughs scored Leonard. Washington pushed its lead to 18-12. In the Boston eighth, Schafer reached on an error by Norton, who was now playing third. He scored on a double by Cone, who then scored on a throwing error by Waterman, now catching. Wright scored on a double steal to cut the Washington lead to 18-15. Also in the eighth, "The umpire received an ugly blow on his only leg in the eighth inning, which keeled him over on the grass, but he soon recovered," reported Poore.[17]

Boston held Washington scoreless in the ninth.

Harry Wright led off the Boston ninth with a walk and Gould singled. Both scored on Schafer's triple to center, cutting the lead to 18-17. Spalding singled in Schafer to tie the game. George Wright singled, and Barnes doubled in Spalding with what would today be the walk-off run, but back then the entire inning had to be played out. Birdsall tripled to right, scoring Barnes with Boston's 20th run for the eventual 20-18 win. Boston tallied six of its 13 hits in the ninth inning, "when Brainard had dropped his pace to accommodate Waterman, who was catching," wrote the *Clipper*.[18] In those days with smaller rosters, the lack of a qualified backup catcher proved a game-changer that day for Washington.

"The victors were loudly applauded and warmly congratulated," wrote Poore, "while the Olympics received many compliments for their plucky playing under the difficulties incident on the loss of three of their trained nine."[19]

However, umpire Dobson was lambasted in the papers. "In several instances," blasted the *Boston Herald*, "he called balls when they should have been strikes, and vice versa."[20] The *Cincinnati Gazette* declared that he "kept the bases full continually by calling every ball either as a strike or as a count, and the consequence was that the poorest batter got his base equally with the best."[21] A walk was definitely not as good as a hit in those days.

The *Clipper*, however, blamed the rule changes, not the umpire, for the chaos. "He umpired the game strictly in accordance with the letter of the new rules, never letting a ball pass after the first one, without it was either called 'strike' or a 'ball.' It is the first game so umpired here." The rule change made an immediate impact on game strategy, the *Clipper* believed. In what sounds familiarly close to modern baseball strategy of taking pitches and making the pitcher work, "the Bostonians … won the game by waiting. Harry Wright's orders were to wait for three balls, as they must necessarily come before three strikes in nine cases out of ten. … (F)orty-six strikes were called on the Boston to twelve on the Olympic, showing that the game was won by simply waiting. Truly not very scientific play."[22] Boston walked 18 times, Washington, 10.

The *Cincinnati Gazette*, not surprisingly, wasn't impressed with the new Red Stockings. "The Reds made several wretched muffs, such as dropping flies, overthrows and general bad playing. They will have to vastly improve before they will be up to the old Red Stocking discipline."[23]

NOTES

Special thanks to John Thorn for research assistance in writing this article.

1. Benjamin Perley Poore, "Base Ball at Washington. The First Match for the National Championship. The Boston Club Victorious," *Boston Journal*, May 6, 1871: 1. Note: The article is signed at the bottom with "Perley." Benjamin Perley Poore (1820-1887) was a Washington correspondent for the *Boston Journal* (1854-1883) and other newspapers, covering mostly Congress and politics. He used his trademark "Perley" on his articles. Joseph P. McKerns. "Poore, Benjamin Perley," in *American National Biography Online*, February 2000. anb.org/articles/16/16-01311.html; accessed July 24, 2015.

2. "The Red Stockings vs. Blue Stockings Base-Ball Match," *Boston Advertiser*, May 8, 1871: 4.

3. "Grand Match at Washington," *New York Clipper*, April 29, 1871: 26.

4. "Base-Ball. The Great Game at Washington. Boston Club Victorious," *Cincinnati Enquirer*, May 6, 1871: 1.

5. "Base Ball. The Great Game. Boston 20—Washington 18," *Daily National Republican*, May 6, 1871: 4.

6. The Olympic Grounds were bounded by 17th Street NW on the west, 16th Street NW on the east, and S Street NW to the south. Paul Batesel, *Players and Teams of the National Association, 1871-1875* (Jefferson, North Carolina: McFarland & Co., 2012), 196 [Google Ebook edition]. According to the *National Republican*, (January 27, 1870), work began on the new Olympic Grounds in early 1870. A block of ground bounded by 16th and 17th and R and S Streets were fenced in with an eight-foot fence. They also erected "a beautiful cottage-style club-house, painted in lavender and white, set back from the street, inclosed by a neat picket fence, to be decorated by a flower garden in front, when the season shall justify." Two tiers of seats of 125 feet long, with five rows of seats in each tier, were assembled and could hold 1,000 spectators. Between the tiers was a space of 40 feet, above which the scorers and writers would stand. The total size of the grounds were said to be 426 feet by 450 feet, with an excellent drainage system. The grounds were formally opened on April 27, 1870, for the then-amateur Washington Olympic Base Ball Club, according to the April 30 edition of the *Republican*. The fences were "colored with a wash of bluish tint," and seating accommodated over 1,000 spectators. A year later, with the Olympics becoming a professional club and acquiring an influx of new talent, the grounds were improved. The *Republican* (January 20, 1871) noted that double train tracks were to be put in place by the Washington and Georgetown Railroad Company along 14th Street to accommodate visitors. The *Republican* (April 7, 1871) noted that by the opening of the baseball season that there was a line of covered seats constructed to accommodate 2,500 spectators. The west side of the grounds contained a section seating 600, and along the north side was a section seating 1,200 along the entire width of the grounds. The grandstand was called "The Grand Duchesse." The grandstand was 60 feet long and 12 feet in width, and could accommodate 200, with front seats reserved for the press. The east side had a row of uncovered seats accommodating 500. The northwest end of the section with covered seats was a "refreshment stand provided with eatables and drinkables in abundance for the benefit of the inner man. Many persons visiting the grounds to witness a game are compelled to go with-

out their dinners, and this eating saloon, no doubt, will receive its full share of patronage."

7 The two British high commissioners were among several in Washington from February 27 to May 8 to draw up the Treaty of Washington. After the Civil War, tensions were high between the United States and United Kingdom over the latter's role in assisting the Confederacy during the war. The treaty settled various disputes between the countries. Theodore A. Wilson, "Treaty of Washington." *Salem Press Encyclopedia* (January 2014): *Research Starters*, EBSCO*host* (accessed June 14, 2015).

8 "Base Ball. The Great Game. Boston 20—Washington 18."

9 Poore.

10 Ibid.

11 Ibid.

12 Ibid.

13 John Thorn, "Chadwick's Choice: The Origin of the Batting Average." Our Game. Published September 18, 2013. ourgame.mlblogs.com/2013/09/18/chadwicks-choice-the-origin-of-the-batting-average/.

14 Poore.

15 A fair-foul hit was one that landed started fair and rolled foul, even in the infield. In baseball's early days, this was scored a hit, as opposed to the modern game's foul ball. Some batters excelled at hitting fair-fouls.

16 Poore.

17 Ibid.

18 "The Professional Championship. Boston vs. Olympic," *New York Clipper*, May 13, 1871: 42.

19 Poore.

20 "Base Ball. Boston vs. Olympic," *Boston Herald*, May 8, 1871: 2.

21 "Base Ball. The Red Stockings of Boston vs the Olympics of Washington. All in the Family," *Cincinnati Gazette*, May 6, 1871.

22 "The Professional Championship." The rules of umpires calling balls and strikes had changed, based on the action of the convention in November 1870, and both of the split amateur and professional leagues approved these in March of 1871. "The Base-Ball Guide for 1871," published after these conventions, stated in Rule II, Section II, "Should the pitcher repeatedly fail to deliver to the striker fair balls, from any cause, the umpire must call one ball; and if the pitcher persists in such action, two and three balls. When three balls shall have been called, the striker shall take the first base without being put out." Rule III, Section II stated, "The striker shall be privileged to call for either a high or low ball, in which case, the pitcher must deliver the ball to the bat as required. The ball shall be considered a high ball if pitched between the height of the waist and the shoulder of the striker; and it shall be considered a low ball if pitched between the height of the knee and the waist." (This text is taken from retrosheet.org/1871Rules.doc.) The first pitch was not called anything unless the batter swung. Strictly calling balls and strikes as the rules dictated, based on the striker's (batter's) request of "high" or "low," resulted in more bases on balls. This outraged fans as it "took the bat out of player's hands," and made for a less interesting game. Still, there was disagreement over the actual rules themselves, something not uncommon in the NAPBBP. See David Nemec, *The Great Encyclopedia of 19th Century Baseball* (New York: David Fine Books, 1997), 7-8; William J. Ryczek, *Blackguards and Red Stockings: A History of Baseball's National Association, 1871-1875* (Wallingford, Connecticut: Colebrook Press, 1992), 17; Peter Morris, *Game of Inches: The Stories Behind the Innovations That Shaped Baseball: The Game on the Field* (Chicago: Ivan R. Dee, 2006), 17-20.

23 "Base Ball. The Red Stockings of Boston vs the Olympics of Washington."

MAY 16, 1871
Troy Haymakers 29, Boston Red Stockings 14, at the South End Grounds, Boston
First regular-season home opener in Boston professional baseball history.

BY BOB LEMOINE

"THE GAME BETWEEN THE RED Stockings and Haymakers this afternoon, on the Boston Grounds," wrote the *Boston Advertiser*, "will be perfectly interesting from the fact that it is the first game between professional nines in this city."[1] Those few sentences, buried in a column of "local matters about town," are a far cry from what an opening day looks like at Boston's Fenway Park today. While Fenway Park opened in 1912 and was celebrated 100 years later, 41 years prior there had been Boston's first baseball opening day at the South End Grounds. The day was the first of its kind, and it started a tradition that has continued for over 140 years.

The night before, the visiting Troy Haymakers quartered at the United States Hotel and were "accompanied by quite a large delegation of their friends," wrote the *Boston Journal*.[2]

Both "nines made their appearance on the field, and were greeted with hearty cheers by the large crowd of spectators in attendance, numbering some 2,500," the *Journal* wrote.[3] Mortimer M. Rogers, of the Star Club of Brooklyn, was chosen as the umpire, and the game began at 3:30 PM.[4] Boston's Harry Wright lost the toss, so Boston batted first.

Al Spalding was pitching the first home opener for Boston. Spalding was off to a 2-0 start with a 4.00 ERA. Troy sent a 22-year-old John McMullin to the mound. McMullin was seeking redemption for the loss he received in his first start against Boston a week prior, although he only gave up three earned runs in a complete-game loss. Boston's George Wright was unable to play after injuring himself in a game at Troy the previous week. Left fielder Fred Cone didn't hear Wright calling for a fly ball because of a passing train, leading to a collision.[5] Wright injured his leg and would play in only 16 games in 1871.

It was an explosive first inning for both teams. Boston's Ross Barnes led off, grounding to Steve Bellan, who threw wildly to first and Barnes was safe at second. Barnes scored on a single to center by Dave Birdsall. Cal McVey doubled to left, scoring Birdsall, then moved to third on a groundout. Gould grounded to Edward Beavens at second, scoring McVey. With two outs, Harry Schafer second on another error. Fred Cone grounded to Beavens, who threw wildly to first and Schafer scored. "Spalding made two bases on a corker to left field,"[6] the *Journal* described, scoring Cone. Sam Jackson singled home Spalding, giving Boston fans the delight of seeing their club tally a 6-0 lead in their inaugural inning.

Boston was sloppy in the field, however. Mike McGeary of the Haymakers reached on a throwing error, then stole second. Charlie Gould's muff landed Tom York at first and McGeary went to third. McGeary scored when Barnes threw wild in an attempted double-play and the pitcher McMullin, batting cleanup, reached first. Steve King doubled, scoring McMullin. A Beavens' grounder would have been an easy out, "but H. Wright was pushed aside by King, just as he was fielding the ball," and King scored. Troy had cut Boston's lead in half, 6-3.

In the Boston second, Barnes scored on a passed ball to make the score Boston 7-3. The inning ended when a "splendid throw"[7] by Chipper Flynn cut down Birdsall who tagged up.

— 208 —

In the Troy third inning, Beavens singled home King on a fair-foul, then Bellan scored on Lipman Pike's triple to cut Boston's lead to 7-5. The inning also saw Craver ground out to Schafer, whose throw resulted in Gould "taking the ball high in one hand."[8]

In the Haymaker fourth inning, McGeary walked and stole second. York reached on a dropped popup by Barnes. McMullin singled home McGeary, then King reached on a single, scoring York. Beavens singled, scoring McMullen and King. Beavens scored on a passed ball. Craver singled to left, scoring Bellan. Six runs scored, and Troy now led 11-7.

Boston struck for two runs in the fifth inning. Harry Wright walked. A sharp liner by Gould was caught by Bellan, who tried to double-up Wright at first, but his throw went through Pike's hands "and injured him so as to cause a temporary suspension of the game."[9] Schafer got a broken-bat single, and both scored on wild throws by Craver and Pike to cut the Troy lead to 11-9.

In the Troy sixth, Beavens reached on a wild Harry Wright throw, stole second, and reached third "on a muff between Harry and Barnes,"[10] then scored on a sacrifice fly. Craver and Flynn reached on errors by Schafer and Barnes, then both scored on McGeary's single. McGeary scored on a Birdsall muff of a York fly ball, and after the comedy of errors, Troy had added four more runs for a 15-9 lead.

Boston countered with two runs in the seventh to cut the lead to 15-11. Gould sent a fly ball to Flynn who "took it very close to the ground." McVey ran to third base on the play. The Haymakers wanted an appeal on the catch by Flynn. Rogers ruled the batter out on the fly. Play was about to resume when Craver then asked for an appeal on McVey, "it being claimed that he failed to touch the second base before running on the play."[11] Rogers ruled McVey out for failing to touch second base, ending the inning. This must have been a replay challenge, circa 1871.

In the seventh, the Haymakers scored 11 runs in the inning, "but two or three being earned," wrote the *Journal*.[12] Beavens, Bellan and Pike all scored on a hit to short center field by Craver, who then scored on a hit by Flynn. An error by Schafer put McGeary on base, followed by a York double. McMullen, "got to his first, while Harry Wright, Barnes, and Jackson stood in a triangle watching, any which either might have taken" wrote the *Herald*.[13] McMullen and York scored on a double by King, who then was out trying to steal third. Beavens and Bellan singled, and Cone muffed a Pike fly ball to load the bases. Craver "cleared the bases and took the second by a hot grounder to left field" wrote the *Herald*.[14] Troy now had a 26-11 lead.

Boston scored two runs in the eighth, but Troy wasn't done yet. A walk and another error on Schafer led to York and McMullin scoring on King's double. Three runs came across to make the score Troy 29-13. Boston added a lonely run in the ninth, and the final score was 29-14.

"There is no mincing the matter at all," wrote the *Journal*, "our 'Red Stockings were beaten by the 'Haymakers' in the match game yesterday. It was not only a beat, but a bad beat." Fans witnessed "the rather slovenly exhibition made by the Bostons."[15] The loss of George Wright was a big factor, "but this is hardly an excuse," the *Journal* whined, "for errors in others nearly as proficient in their own positions as he most certainly is in his."[16] The first opening day was known for "muffs and errors being frequent in all parts of the field" slammed the Herald, as Boston committed 15 errors and Spalding's pitching "void of its usual effects."[17] The highly-anticipated home opener did not live up to expectations, "for the credit of Boston," wrote the *Boston Post*, "we could have wished it were played elsewhere."[18]

The *Journal* seemed to give a hint of fans sensing heartbreak in losing on opening day (something that would often be repeated in Boston baseball history).

Advertisement for the first Opening Day in Boston's professional baseball history, Boston Herald, May 16, 1871.

"To think that our boys, on whom we depend so much, who, we began to believe, were invincible, should be so thoroughly defeated on their ground, is rather tough… [George Wright's] "absence from the field seemed to demoralize to a certain extent the whole club."[19] The 29 runs allowed by the Red Stockings were the most runs allowed in a game in the 1871-1875 period. Only on two other occasions did they allow 20 or more runs in a game (20 runs on June 22, 1871, and 22 runs on June 5, 1873).

"We congratulate the Haymakers," wrote the *Journal*, "and beg to advise them that when our nine are all right again they propose to retake the wreath which they lost yesterday, and hold it to the end of the season. Meanwhile, the Haymakers had as well wear it as any other club, and we wish them joy in having so finely demonstrated their worthiness to do so."[20]

The Haymakers stayed in town another day, playing on the same field against Harvard, and losing 15-8 to the "flyers of the magenta." That evening, the Haymakers left on the 9 o'clock train on the Boston and Albany Railroad.[21]

SOURCES

Thanks to Dixie Tourangeau for research assistance in writing this article.

NOTES

1. "Local Matters. About Town," *Boston Advertiser*, May 16, 1871: 1.
2. "Base Ball. First Defeat of the Boston Club," *Boston Journal*, May 17, 1871: 1.
3. Ibid. Actual attendance accounts ranged from 2,500-8,000 spectators depending on the newspaper.
4. Maxson Mortimer "Mort" Rogers had an interesting baseball career prior to this game. A Brooklyn native, Rogers was the son of a fish dealer. In the 1860's, Rogers and his two brothers played for the Brooklyn Resolutes amateur club. He later moved to Massachusetts and played center field for the Lowell Club and was called an outfielder "ahead of his time," wrote James D'Wolf Lovett in his *Old Boston Boys and the Games They Played* (Boston: Riverside Press, 1907), 165. "There is no player who can run in to a swiftly batted liner and pick it up within six inches of the ground better than he could," D'Wolf said. Rogers and E.E. Rice became involved with the *New England Base Ballist*, a weekly sports newspaper which ran from August-December of 1868. The first edition announced "After a long and arduous experience in reporting and playing Base Ball, we have at last the pleasure of addressing the Fraternity, and friends, through the medium of the Editorial columns of a paper devoted to the interests of our National Game, other Field and outdoor Sports, Music and the Drama." The paper evolved into the *National Chronicle*, edited by Rogers, Rice, and C. Ruthven Bryan, and ran 1869-1870. In the 1870s, Rogers wrote for the *Sunday Mercury* newspaper and produced scorecards of Boston's games, the first to include photographs of the players. See Peter Morris "Clipper Base Ball Club of Lowell," in *Baseball Founders: The Clubs, Players, and Cities of the Northeast that Established the Game* (Jefferson, North Carolina: McFarland, 2013), and the *New York Clipper*, May 21, 1881: 138.
5. Harold Kaese. *The Boston Braves 1871-1953* (Boston: Northeastern University Press, 1954), 9.
6. Ibid.
7. "Affairs About Home. Base Ball. The Professional Championship — Haymakers vs. Red Stockings — The Latter Badly Whipped — Score 29 to 14," *Boston Herald*, May 17, 1871: 1.
8. "Affairs About Home. Base Ball,"
9. "Base Ball. The National Championship— Red Stockings vs. Haymakers," *Boston Advertiser*, May 17, 1871: 1.
10. "Affairs About Home. Base Ball,"
11. "Base Ball. The National Championship,"
12. "Base Ball. First Defeat of the Boston Club,"
13. "Affairs About Home. Base Ball,"
14. "Affairs About Home. Base Ball,"
15. "R Beaten!" *Boston Journal*, May 17, 1871: 4. (Note: The author isn't exactly sure if the article headline is "R" or "B," based on the poor quality of the digitally scanned version of the *Journal*. However, he is convinced it is "R" based on other examples on the page, and "R" would stand for "Red Stockings," although no experts were consulted in its analyses.
16. "Base Ball. First Defeat of the Boston Club,"
17. "Affairs About Home. Base Ball,"
18. "Base Ball. Match Between the Boston Nine and the Haymakers, of Troy— the Boston Club Badly Beaten," *Boston Post*, May 17, 1871: 3.
19. "R Beaten!"
20. Ibid.
21. "Base Ball. Credible Victory for the Harvards," *Boston Journal*, May 18, 1871: 1.

HOMESTAND FROM HELL
The Boston Red Stockings, May-June 1871

BY RICHARD "DIXIE" TOURANGEAU

LOSSES IN MAY AND JUNE COUNT as much as those in September; just ask any second-place team.

Ivers Whitney Adams's assembled dream team of Boston Red Stockings was designed to have an exciting and superior baseball season in 1871. But after winning their very first two games on the road, their initial home appearance at the South End Grounds, between Columbus Avenue and the South End railroad yards, proved disastrous. The 29-14 Opening Day thrashing there by the Troy Haymakers on May 16 shocked local fans. But who could have known that Troy's 15-run margin would be the largest Adams's stars ever suffered in their 292 NA games? Later success unknowable at the time, it was not the way to begin their inaugural "homestand" before highly expectant fans.

A few days later Boston made amends by beating pitcher-manager John Dickson McBride and his strong Athletics of Philadelphia, 11-8, behind Harry Wright's and Charlie Gould's hitting and a seven-run inning. All seemed well again. Making its debut that day at the Grounds was the ever-enterprising Max Mort Rogers' "elegant new scorecard with Harry's picture on the cover," noted the *Boston Herald*.[1] The mediocre Washington Olympics were the next visitors, featuring pitcher Asa Brainard, the iconic hurler of the Cincinnati Red Stockings with whom four of the now Boston Red Stockings played in 1869 and '70. The other half of Cincinnati's legendary barnstorming team also had signed with Washington: catcher Doug Allison, third baseman Fred Waterman, outfielder Andy Leonard, and infield sub Charlie Sweasy. Joining them was the little fireball, Davey Force, at second.

Businessman Adams had signed Cincinnati brother-stars Harry and George Wright back in January, along with catcher Cal McVey and first sacker Gould.

By late April Charlie Gould and George Wright were already in the sporting-goods business on Boylston Street. Star batsman and shortstop George Wright missed the Troy trouncing and nearly half the season because of an injury, but the other Red Stockings certainly appeared to have enough combined talent to win without him. Of note also on Boston's roster was Albert Spalding of the old Rockford Forest Citys amateurs, who was in the pitcher's box with his Rockford second baseman, Ross Barnes, behind him, while Philly native Harry Schafer played third and tough David Birdsall of the New York Morrisania club patrolled the outfield with manager Harry Wright.

Spalding was terrific for seven innings against Washington (allowed three hits) and held a 4-1 lead as Boston scored its four in the third inning. In the ninth a defensive collapse became crucial as with two outs and nobody on a few Boston errors (six total by Schafer) let Washington tie the score 4-4 just before umpire (and scorecard seller) Mort Rogers of the Lowell Club called the game because of darkness, a decision not agreed with by many of the spectators who enjoyed the exciting, small-score battle. Not only was it the Reds' only tie in 1871, it was the only NA tie game ever in Boston. Both the Olympics and Red Stockings then boarded a late train and met to play each other at Brooklyn's Union Grounds three days later in an unusual neutral site game on May 27. It is listed as a home game for Boston. The Reds jumped out to a comfy 5-1 lead before squandering it all in the final two innings and losing 6-5 to a rally sparked by ex-mates Allison, Waterman, and the pesky Force. Two sure wins were instead a very disappointing loss and tie. The Westernmost NA Rockford Forest Citys pro team then arrived in Boston. They had been thrown together in the final weeks before the National Association started and just did not have the all-around

The 1871 Rockford Forest Citys (Courtesy of the Rock River Times*)*

talent of the other clubs. Boston swept two, 25-11 and 11-10, winning in the ninth on Decoration Day, May 30, as Birdsall walked, made third on McVey's hit, and scored on Gould's single.

June brought Chicago's White Stockings to the Hub with ace thrower George "The Charmer" Zettlein. George would be as much a thorn in the Red Stockings' side as anyone for all five NAPBBP seasons. He was no stranger to four of them as Zett was the Brooklyn Atlantics hurler who beat the undefeated Cincy club in June 1870, 8-7 in 11 innings, garnering national headlines. However, on June 2, 1871, he was pounded for 10 runs in two innings and dejectedly walked to right field—replaced by third baseman Ed Pinkham. Pinkham didn't have much on the ball but the Reds suddenly had less. Though wild at first, relief man Ed held the Reds to four more runs while Spalding lost his touch completely. Manager Harry Wright did so poorly in relief trying to quell the rally that Spalding came back in a second time to allow even more runs. The Chicagomen scattered 11 unanswered runs for a 16-14 victory, thanks to Brooklynites Pinkham (three runs) and shortstop Ed Duffy (three doubles, four runs). Tied in the ninth, Chicago got two hits, a Boston error, and two groundouts that scored the winning tallies. Relief winner Pinkham, (really an infielder) pitched twice more during the year, notching one save. He did not play in the NA beyond 1871. In this giveaway Boston made 12 errors, four by Schafer at third.

Twelve days went by before Albert George Pratt came to town with the Cleveland Forest Citys, which had lost the very first NA game, 2-0 to the Fort Wayne Kekiongas. Cleveland behind the hitting of catcher James Doc White (three hits/two RBIs), first baseman Jim Carleton (three hits/two RBIs), and third sacker Ezra Sutton (four hits/one run) maintained a slight lead for "Uncle Al." In the ninth Boston needed three to win but plated just one, losing 8-7. Pratt tried for the next four years but never beat Boston again. Meanwhile the South End horror show continued as the solid New York Mutuals visited the Red Stockings. Pitcher Reinder "Rynie" Wolters gave the Reds fits, winning easily 9-3, getting two hits with one RBI himself, and getting help from Dickey Pearce (two hits/two runs) and Joe Start (three runs). Reds sub second sacker Sam Jackson had five errors of the 12 Boston committed. Only one other time in those five years would the Reds lose three consecutive South End games. (In late September of 1874 they lost three straight and five of six, but were far ahead in the standings by then.)

Fort Wayne's struggling Kekiongas paid the price for the Reds' awful showing as they played the final homestand game before Boston left town. Spalding allowed the light-hitting Indiana club only a two-out, first-inning single by Jim Foran. The contest turned out to be Spalding's best pitched NA game in terms of hits allowed, and the Red Stockings ripped the usually reliable Bobby Mathews (tosser of the league's

Opening Day 2-0 shutout of Rockford), 21-0. It was Spalding's only shutout of the year and Bobby's worst defeat in his NA career. The Reds stood at 6-5.

Still minus George Wright's bat and defensive prowess, the Reds boarded a southbound train for Philly and were beaten by McBride, 20-8, at the new Jefferson Street Grounds at 25th. They rallied and whipped Brainard in Washington, but out West in Chicago Zettlein took his revenge, 7-1, easily the fewest runs scored in one game by the Bostons that year. That sequence left Adams's Wrightmen at 7-7, their worst 14-game starting record during the five NA seasons. After George Wright rejoined the squad, the Reds were terrific and won their last seven home games, but enough damage had been done. In a close finish but behind the champ Athletics, the Reds could have/should have salvaged at least three of those home losses and tie that they suffered by blowing leads. Those victories would have given them a better final record than Philadelphia and therefore a clean sweep of all five National Association championships. Apparently the Red Stockings did learn a valuable lesson, and won 87 percent of their home games (113-17 the next 4½ years) after that hapless homestand from hell.

NOTES

[1] "Affairs About Home," *Boston Herald*, May 22, 1871: 4. The *Boston Daily Advertiser* offered more information about the scorecard: "Mort Rogers issued for the first time at the Boston-Athletic match, Saturday (May 20), his photograph score-card. Each of these cards contains the names of the players in order of striking, with their positions, and on its back a photograph of some prominent player. The card at the match, Saturday, had a capital picture of Harry Wright, by Black, and other members of the Boston club will figure on the cards for succeeding games here. It will be seen readily that a person can secure by the close of the season a record of all important games here, and a collection of photographs of the Boston club and all the leading base-ball players in the country. The idea is an excellent one, and Mr. Rogers will doubtless reap the remuneration he deserves. These cards will be sold inside the grounds." *Boston Daily Advertiser*, May 22, 1871: 1.

JUNE 21, 1871

Boston Red Stockings 21, Fort Wayne Kekiongas 0, at South End Grounds, Boston

Albert G. Spalding's Only Shutout of the Season.

BY JAY HURD

ON MAY 4, 1871, THE FORT WAYNE Kekiongas[1] opened the inaugural season of the National Association of Professional Base Ball Players with a 2-0 victory over the Cleveland Forest Citys. By the end of June the Kekiongas had compiled a 5-4 record, with two of the losses being shutouts. One of the shutouts came at the hands of the Boston Red Stockings.

The amateur Lowell Base Ball Club of Boston hosted the Kekiongas on Tuesday, June 20; the Fort Wayne nine lost by a score of either 12-2 or 10-2.[2] At 3:35 the following afternoon, the Kekiongas faced the Boston Red Stockings before a crowd of about 700 at Boston's South End Grounds. On the mound for the Red Stockings was 21-year-old right-hander Albert Goodwill Spalding, making his 12th start of the season. The Kekiongas countered with 20-year-old right-hander Bobby T. Mathews, making his 12th start of the season. Harry Wright managed and played center field for the Reds while catcher Bill Lennon managed the Fort Wayne nine. Harry Wright's brother, George, did not play in this game. M.M. Rogers of the Star Brooklyn Club assumed umpiring responsibilities.

The Reds batted first and shortstop Ross Barnes reached first on a fly to "short field."[3] He advanced to third on a passed ball and right fielder Dave Birdsall reached first on an error by third baseman Williams.[4] Birdsall stole second and scored along with Barnes on a double by catcher Cal McVey. In making a play on a popup by second baseman Sam Jackson, Kekiongas catcher Bill Lennon collided with pitcher Mathews. Mathews needed time to collect himself, but returned to the mound and completed the game. An out made by first baseman Charlie Gould ended the top of the first.

The Kekiongas sent four men to bat in the bottom of the first, and scored no runs. The top of the second began shakily for the Kekiongas as passed balls, dropped flies, and errant throws allowed the Reds to score six runs. The inning started with an error by Pete Donnelly in right field that allowed Harry Schafer to reach first. Schafer advanced to third on a passed ball. Left fielder Fred Cone walked and stole second; Lennon's poor throw allowed Cone to advance to third and Schafer to score. After Spalding popped up to Williams for the first out, Barnes singled to left, advanced to third on Foran's inaccurate throw to home plate, and saw Cone score. Donnelly muffed Birdsall's popup and Barnes scored. McVey hit to third, where Williams made a clean play and good throw to first, but first baseman Charles Bierman dropped the ball. Jackson flied out to Jim Foran for the second out, but Birdsall and McVey scored on another passed ball. Harry Wright then singled to right, advanced to third on a passed ball, and scored on Charlie Gould's hit to left. Gould stole second but was left there as Schafer flied out to Kelly. Six runs had scored. Despite errors by the Bostons in the bottom of the second, the Fort Wayne team again was unable to score. They did make changes on the field, however, with Williams moving from third base to catcher, Lennon from catcher to shortstop, and Wally Goldsmith from shortstop to third.

Each team exhibited solid fielding in innings three through six; only two runs were scored, both by the Reds. In the top of the seventh, the Red Stockings demonstrated good batting and fine baserunning. At one point, with the bases loaded and McVey at bat, Harry Schafer, who was running for Birdsall, was caught in a rundown. He managed to evade a tag until two more runs had scored. Although the Kekiongas had a baserunner reach third in their half of the seventh, they could not score and the Reds now led the contest 14-0.

The Bostons sent four men to bat in the top of the eighth, and did not score. The Kekiongas did have baserunners in the bottom of the eighth, but none were able to reach home. This inning did see a close play at first, however. Williams had reached first on an error by Barnes; he advanced to second after Mathews earned a walk. However, on the next at bat, left fielder Foran flied out to Schafer, whose quick throw to first caught Mathews, who had started to run. The umpire's call was "a doubtful decision," the *Advertiser* wrote.[5]

The Red Stockings held a commanding lead by the top of the ninth inning, but their scoring for the day was not over. After left fielder Fred Cone flied out to Bill Kelly in center field, Spalding reached on first baseman Bierman's error. He scored on Barnes's single; Birdsall hit safely and drove in Barnes. McVey singled and drove in Birdsall. Wright and Gould reached base, and after a "heavy hit"[6] by Schafer, scored. Before Cone ended the inning with an "easy"[7] hit to Mathews, Schafer scored the seventh run of the inning on a passed ball. The score was now 21-0.

The Kekiongas closed out the game, which ended two hours after it had begun, with a quick 1-2-3 inning, and, as with each inning prior, scored no runs. Al Spalding had his sixth win and his only shutout of the 1871 season, a one-hitter.

The *Boston Daily Advertiser* summarized the game thus: "The score shows this to be one of the most remarkable games of record. The deportment of the Kekiongas on the field was excellent, and notwithstanding their severe defeat they maintained a perfect composure. The impression made by them here is favorable and our base-ball men heartily wish them better luck next time."

The *Boston Journal* noted of the Kekiongas: "They are to be commended … for the plucky manner in

The Kekionga Base Ball Club, 1871 (Courtesy of John Thorn)

which they played the concluding portion of the game against such odds."

Rosters:

Boston Red Stockings	**Fort Wayne Kekiongas**
Ross Barnes (ss)	Williams (3b)
Dave Birdsall (rf)	Bobby Mathews (p)
Cal McVey (c)	Jim Foran (lf)
Sam Jackson (2b)	Wally Goldsmith (ss)
Harry Wright (mgr, cf)	Bill Lennon (mgr, c)
Charlie Gould (lf)	Tom Carey (2b)
Fred Cone (lf)	Charles Bierman (1b)
Harry Schafer (3b)	Pete Donnelly (rf)
Al Spalding (p)	Bill Kelly (cf)

SOURCES

In addition to the sources indicated in the notes, the author also consulted:

Wilbert, Warren N. *Opening Pitch: Professional Baseball's Inaugural Season, 1871* (Lanham, Maryland: Scarecrow Press, 2008).

NOTES

1. Before its settlement by French fur traders in the 17th century, the area that encompasses Fort Wayne had the Native American name Kekionga. It was the capital of the Miami nation. "History of Fort Wayne, Indiana." u-s-history.com/pages/h2273.html.
2. The *Boston Daily Advertiser* of June 22, 1871, said the score was 12-2; the *Boston Journal* said it was 10-2.
3. "Base Ball, Visit of the Kekiongas—Their Defeat by the Boston Nine," *Boston Daily Advertiser*, June 22, 1871.
4. Frank Sellman also played under the name Frank C. Williams. Sellman played third base, as did Williams in this game.
5. Ibid.
6. Ibid.
7. Ibid.

JULY 4, 1871
Boston 7, Washington Olympic 3, at Union Grounds, Cincinnati[1]

BY MICHAEL R. MCAVOY

THE JULY 4 GAME WAS PLAYED neither in Boston nor in Washington, but in Cincinnati. The Ohio city had been the home of the 1869-1870 Cincinnati Red Stockings, considered the first openly professional club—a team famous for its undefeated 1869 season and national tours.

The National Association began play in 1871. With neither a reserve nor a draft, the Cincinnati Base Ball Club had informed its players that it would not field a professional nine. The Cincinnati players soon found work with the Boston and Washington clubs, which stocked their rosters with these proven veterans. Boston manager Harry Wright took the name Red Stockings and three regulars, while manager Nick Young's Olympics, nicknamed Blue Stockings, signed the other five to contracts.[2]

The game at Cincinnati offered something akin to a homecoming for the original Red Stockings during the Fourth of July holiday. It offered the return of professional baseball to Cincinnati, a city that had a reputation for drawing a large crowd to a baseball game on Independence Day. Both Boston and Washington were in competition for the National Association championship.

From the old Reds, the Boston club started Cal McVey at catcher, Charlie Gould at first, and Harry Wright in center field. George Wright, the short stop, did not travel to Cincinnati on this trip. The Olympic club fielded Fred Waterman at third base, Doug Allison at catcher, Andy Leonard at second, and Asa Brainard in the pitcher's box. Second baseman Charlie Sweasy was on the Olympics roster but did not play

The championship game was preceded by an exhibition on July 3 when the former 1869-1870 Cincinnati Red Stockings, the "Old Reds," played a "Combination Nine," consisting of players from the Boston and Washington nines who were not on the 1869-1870 Cincinnati nine. As George Wright was not present, 1870 Cincinnati substitute Harry Deane, of the 1871 Fort Wayne Kekiongas, appeared for the Old Reds. The Old Reds lost, 15-13. The result surprised the *New York Clipper*'s writer, but he noted George Wright's absence, and observed that Charlie Sweasy was immobile fielding at second base, ineffective at bat, and someone who played for "advertising effects" only.[3]

The record for the National Association championship race showed Boston at 6-6, in sixth place, while Washington was in fourth at 9-7. The two clubs had previously played three games, each team winning one with one tie. The victor on July 4 would be in position to win their five-game series.

Living up to its reputation for drawing power on July 4, this particular day was no different, with 5,000 Cincinnati spectators ready to watch the game between the Red Stockings and the Blue Stockings.

At 3:30 P.M. Dr. John Draper of the Cincinnati Base Ball Club was selected umpire and tossed the nickel. Captains Harry Wright and Charlie Sweasy watched the nickel land in the ground; Wright selected Boston to field first.[4]

In the top half of the first inning, the Olympics batted against pitcher Al Spalding. With one out, Davy Force reached first on a low drive to left. Everett Mills hit a groundball directly to second baseman Barnes, who forced out Davy Force and threw to Gould to execute a double play. In the Boston half, Ross Barnes hit a ball hard to left, earning first base. Dave Birdsall

AMUSEMENTS.
BASE BALL.

3 1-2 O'CLOCK, TO-DAY,

Olympic
vs.
Boston.

This game was arranged to be played in this city when above Clubs were organized.

An ad in the Cincinnati Commercial Gazette *on July 4, 1871, hyping the return of several former Cincinnati Red Stockings players. The* Cincinnati Daily Times *later reported "not a single vacant seat could be found."*

hit a hopping ball to third baseman Waterman, who badly overthrew first base, enabling both Barnes and Birdsall to score. "This was a very unreasonable proceeding on Fred's part," wrote the *Cincinnati Daily Gazette*, "as he could not by any stretch of imagination have concluded that Mills could by personal exertion on the spur of the moment have added three cubits to his stature."[5] The Washingtons completed the inning with their own double play; Sam Jackson took off from first when Harry Wright hit a long fly ball, caught by John Glenn, who earned an assist when Jackson failed to get back to first base quickly enough.

In the top of the third inning, George Hall of the Olympics reached on an infield grounder to second baseman Barnes. Harry Berthrong followed with a hard ball to shortstop Jackson, who tossed the ball to Barnes at second, forcing out Hall. Waterman hit another to Jackson, who forced Berthrong at second but threw poorly to Gould at first base, and Waterman scampered to second base on the error. Washington scored when Waterman went home on two flies, first by Force—who reached on Birdsall's error—and the second by Mills, who safely recorded a base hit with a fly to short left.

Boston increased its lead to 3-1 in the bottom half of the third inning. Fred Cone made second base when he executed a hit on a high fair-foul ball that Glenn could not reach from right field. Cone advanced to third base when Brainard was charged with a balk. Spalding then hit a line drive into left field. Berthrong grabbed it on the fly with one hand and made a throw to home plate, but Cone beat the throw, if only barely, and scored.

In the fourth inning Spalding had the breath knocked out of him when Glenn drove a pitched ball into his chest. Spalding managed to pick up the ball and throw the ball to Gould at first to force Glenn out. Washington completed another double play to end the bottom half of the fourth.

Both clubs scored in the fifth inning. In Washington's half, Hall doubled on a hit to left and scored when Berthrong hit a fly ball to right. When Waterman hit a fast grounder through the left side, a good throw from outfielder Cone to Schafer caught Berthrong trying to make third. Waterman stole second base, but Mills and Force went out. In Boston's half, Spalding hit a ball hard to third baseman Waterman, who overthrew first again, and Spalding took second. Barnes hit a line drive hard to Hall, who dropped it, and Barnes took first. Birdsall advanced the runners when he "rolled the ball" to Force and was out at first. McVey hit a drive over second and scored both Spalding and Barnes. The Reds led, 5-2.

In the sixth inning, both clubs scored the rest of their runs of the game, putting Boston up 7-3. In the top half, Allison drove a pitch into left for a single and then took second when Glenn hit one at Jackson and Barnes failed to cover second. Allison moved to third when Spalding made a balk and went home on Leonard's fly out to Cone. Boston scored two runs during its half. The *Clipper's* writer particularly noted Berthrong's fielding: "Wright sent a long fly to left, which Berthrong took magnificently on the back run."6 Gould singled to left. Schafer then doubled to left with a similar hit which advanced Gould to third. Force misplayed Cone's grounder, which scored Gould, advanced Schafer to third, and placed Cone on first. The Red Stockings then executed a double steal, Cone taking second and Schafer scoring on the throw. Spalding and Barnes both grounded out.

Neither club scored the remainder of the game, although Boston ended the game with second and third bases occupied. The *New York Clipper* evaluated the 1-hour 45-minute game as a fine one, with great catching by the catchers (neither recording an error), good hitting and fielding, and fine umpiring.

Boston finished the championship season in third place with a 20-10 record, and Washington finished fourth, at 15-15. In head-to-head matchups between the two clubs, the Red Stockings won three games to the Olympics' one, and they tied one game.

SOURCES

Unless otherwise noted, the game account is from the *New York Clipper*, July 15, 1871: 116. Certain details are from Baseball-Reference.com.

NOTES

1. The Cincinnati Base Ball Club grounds were at the Union Grounds, at the foot of Richmond Street. See a reprint of the 1907 book by Harry Ellard, *Base Ball in Cincinnati: A History* (Jefferson, North Carolina: McFarland & Co., Inc., 1998), 24. The 8 acres were fenced and behind Lincoln Park near the Union Terminal. Stephen D. Guschov, *The Red Stockings of Cincinnati: Base Ball's First All-Professional Team* (Jefferson, North Carolina: McFarland & Co., Inc., 1998), 10.

2. See Guschov, 133-137; the Washington Olympics were called the Blue Stockings in the *Cincinnati Daily Gazette* account of the game. See *Cincinnati Daily Gazette*, July 6, 1871: 4.

3. *New York Clipper*, July 15, 1871: 116. A complete account of the game is recorded in the *Cincinnati Enquirer*, July 4, 1871: 4.

4. *Cincinnati Daily Gazette*, July 6, 1871: 4.

5. Ibid.

6. The writer at the *Chicago Tribune* wrote, "For the Boston's Harry Wright tremendous hard hit was taken in superb style by Berthrong, on a backward run, with his side turned toward the ball." *Chicago Tribune*, July 5, 1871: 4.

"THE STEVE BELLÁN GAME"

August 3, 1871: Troy Haymakers 13, Boston Red Stockings 12, at Haymakers' Grounds, Troy, New York

BY BOB LEMOINE

ESTEBAN "STEVE" BELLÁN WAS THE first Latin-born player in professional baseball. While Clemente, Perez, Ortiz, and Rivera, among others, are household names and heroes to both Hispanic and non-Hispanic baseball fans in the early years of the 21st century, the name of Steve Bellán is mostly unrecognized. The half-Irish, Cuban-born player was light-skinned enough to pass through the racial prejudices of the National Association of Baseball Players, which at its 1867 convention voted to bar black clubs ("any club which may be composed of one or more colored persons") from entering the league.[1] Bellán played for the Unions of Morrisania in 1868. Nicknamed "The Cuban Sylph" for his fielding skills, mainly at third base, Bellán was a weak hitter with a .251 career batting average in 60 games, but on August 3, 1871, he had the game of his life.

Some 3,000 spectators arrived at the Haymakers' Grounds with "the expectation that the occasion would be marked by one of the finest displays of the beauty of ball tossing science," wrote the *New York Clipper*.[2] George Wright returned to the Boston lineup for the first time since he injured his leg on that very field in May. Charlie Sweasy of the Washington Olympics was the umpire for the game.

The Boston Red Stockings were 10-7-1 and 4½ games from first place. Troy was 7-7-1 and six games behind. Albert Spalding of Boston would oppose John McMullin of Troy. Both pitchers started every one of their team's games that season.

Boston batted first. George Wright singled to left-center and made it to second on an error by Tom York. Ross Barnes walked. As Dave Birdsall struck out, Wright took off for third. Bellán began the game as the goat, muffing the throw from catcher Charles McGeary, ruining the double-play attempt and allowing Wright to score. Harry Wright singled to center and Barnes scored. Harry Wright scored on a double steal, and Boston had a 3-0 lead after the first inning.

In the bottom of the second, the Haymakers got a run back when Steve King reached second on first baseman Charlie Gould's error. Lipman Pike singled King to third. Bellán began his path to redemption by singling to right-center, scoring King. A double play ended the inning, with Boston leading 3-1. In the top of the third, a triple by Barnes and a single by Cal McVey gave Boston a 4-1 lead.

The Haymakers erupted for five runs off Spalding in the bottom of the third. York singled and Dickie Flowers reached on an error by Harry Schafer at third. York scored on Clipper Flynn's single, then King got a hit. Flowers scored on a passed ball by McVey, which then led to a comedy of errors. Pike hit a foul ball, but both runners, King and Flynn, "supposed that Pike was out, and started to take their fielding stations," wrote the *Troy Times*.[3] In the rules of the time, runners had to hurry back to their bases on foul balls at the risk of being put out. But a "series of wild throws to bases by Spaulding [sic]"[4] in overthrowing bases allowed both King and Flynn to score. Pike reached on a hit, and another bad throw by Spalding put him at second. Pike made third on another passed ball, and scored on Bellán's single past George Wright at shortstop. Only one run of the five was earned. Troy now led 6-4 after three innings.

Spalding was obviously having a bad day, so Harry Wright decided to pitch and moved Spalding to center field in the fourth inning. McVey, also having a bad day, was replaced behind the plate by Birdsall, McVey moving to right field. The Haymakers offense didn't let up, however, as York and Flowers both scored in the fourth, giving Troy an 8-4 lead.

The Red Stockings scored two runs in the top of the fifth, as George Wright reached second on a fair-foul hit to the left of home plate, went to third on a bad throw by McGeary, and scored on a bad throw from York to Bellán. Barnes also reached on a fair-foul, stole second, and scored on McVey's single. The inning ended as Bellán made "a magnificent running foul bound catch,"[5] that was called "*the* catch of the game" by the *Troy Times*[6] and "which called forth several rounds of applause," according to the *Troy Whig*.[7]

Not to be outdone, Troy answered with two more runs in the bottom of the inning. For whatever reason, all Boston fielders returned to their old positions, and Spalding was back on the mound. Pike tripled on a "splendid line hit to South fence," and Bellán singled him home. Troy now led 10-6 after five innings. Boston was held scoreless in the sixth, thanks again to Bellán, who caught a Spalding pop fly, then doubled off Harry Schafer scrambling back to second, "a pretty chance for a double play prettily taken," according to the *Troy Times*.[8]

Boston scored two runs in the seventh inning as Fred Cone scored on George Wright's double, Wright took third on an error, and he scored on a fly ball by Barnes. Boston had cut the lead to 10-8. Again the Haymakers countered, scoring three runs for a 13-8 lead. A muffed fly ball by Harry Wright was followed by a walk to McMullin. Bellán launched a triple to the center-field fence, scoring both runners. Bill Craver's fly ball scored Bellán.

Boston scored two runs each in the eighth and ninth innings to keep the game close. In the ninth, George Wright scored on a passed ball to cut the lead to 13-11, and Barnes scored on a groundout. In the ninth, McVey, the potential tying run, doubled past third base with two outs, but was left stranded when Harry Wright grounded out to shortstop. "The 'Mowers' escaped from being beaten by a hair's breadth," wrote the *Troy Whig*.[9]

Bellán was 5-for-5, and "made either first, second or third base hits every time," reported the *Troy Times*.[10]

Esteban "Steve" Bellán, the first Latin-born player in professional baseball, went 5-for-5 against Al Spalding, leading Troy to the win against Boston. (Ars Longa Cards)

After his brief professional baseball career (1871-1873), Bellán returned to Cuba and played in his native land's first recorded organized baseball contest in 1874. Professional baseball began in Cuba four years later, and player-manager Bellàn led Havana to the championship,[11] "warming the native people to the sport that would eventually consume a nation."[12] Maybe he told them tales of the day he went 5-for-5 in Troy, New York, and even the great Albert Spalding couldn't get him out.

NOTES

1 For more on the 1867 National Association of Base Ball Players, see MLB historian John Thorn's November 12, 2012, blog entry "The Drawing of the Color Line, 1867" in ourgame.mlblogs.com/2012/11/12/drawing-of-the-color-line/.

2 "Haymakers vs. Boston," *New York Clipper*, August 12, 1871.

3 "Thrashing the Reds," *Troy Daily Times*, August 4, 1871: 3.

4 "Haymakers vs. Boston."
5 Ibid.
6 "Thrashing the Reds."
7 "The National Game," *Troy Whig*, August 4, 1871.
8 "Thrashing the Reds."
9 "The National Game."
10 "Thrashing the Reds."
11 "Cuban Baseball Yesterday," pbs.org/stealinghome/history/.
12 Brian McKenna, "Steve Bellán," SABR BioProject, sabr.org/bioproj/person/78dbf37d.

SEPTEMBER 2, 1871
Boston Red Stockings 31, Cleveland Forest Citys 10, at the Boston Grounds

BY BILL NOWLIN

THE RED STOCKINGS WERE RIDING a scoring spree. In three of the preceding seven games, they had scored 20 or more runs, with an average of 16.57 runs per game. When the Forest City club arrived in Boston for a Saturday game on September 2, 1871, the weather was ideal and a good game was expected—Cleveland had beaten Boston 8-7 the first time they met, then lost 12-8. Between 1,200 and 1,500 spectators turned out for the game. But "it proved a one-sided and unsatisfactory contest."[1] And it was the *Boston Journal* that found the 31-10 Red Stockings victory an unsatisfactory game, not a Cleveland paper.

The *Journal* noted the quality of the actual baseball used. The lopsided result "was owing in part to the ball which the Clevelands furnished, which was known as the Van Horn dead ball, but which proved an exceedingly lively one, and as the pitching was easy to bat, the consequence was the ball was batted all over the field."[2] The defense was unusually poor. Cleveland's "catcher passed balls without number before he was changed."[3] (There were, in fact, 11 passed balls charged to Forest City's three catchers. Neither Boston's Dave Birdsall nor Cal McVey, who took over in the fifth, was charged any.) The Cleveland pitcher was necessarily changed, too, more than once, and with only 11 players on the team, and only nine in the game, the swapping around of pitchers and catchers inevitably destabilized other positions as well.

Boston scored three times in the first inning and added two more in the third. The score was 8-2 in Boston's favor after six. Then things fell to pieces, for both teams. The Red Stockings batted first (as happened at times) and scored 12 runs in the seventh, the final three of them off the left fielder (and manager) Charlie Pabor, who came in to replace Al Pratt. Both Pratt and Pabor uncorked five wild pitches in the game. Boston threw none. The score was 20-2. Al Spalding was pitching for the Bostons, as he had in every one of the prior 21 games in the championship season. He weakened, and Cleveland scored eight runs in its half of the seventh inning. Harry Wright finished the game for Spalding, swapping places with Spalding going to center field.

With 11 passed balls and 10 wild pitches, one might think Boston's batters could just stand at the plate and watch runs score, but they cracked out 24 hits, five of them (for 11 total bases, thanks to three triples—two of them in the eighth inning) by shortstop George Wright. Boston second baseman Ross Barnes tripled, too. Indeed, "they punished both Pratt and Pabor without mercy."[4]

There were errors, of course, of an uncertain number. The Red Stockings team "made less than half a dozen fielding errors, and who made three double plays."[5] The best play seems to have been the seventh-inning 6-4 double play when third baseman Harry Schafer "made a brilliant one-hand stop, and by a quick throw to Barnes assisted in making the finest double play of the game."[6] None of the box scores otherwise tallied the number of errors assessed, nor did any of the game stories.

In the eighth, Pabor was hit for 11 more runs. The score stood Red Stockings 31, Forest Citys 10. Forest City failed to score in the eighth. At that point, the *Boston Post* reported, "It was now getting late in the afternoon and the captain of the Forest Citys withdrew his nine and the ninth was not played."[7] That may have represented a biased point of view; the *Cleveland Plain Dealer* wrote, "At the end of the eighth inning, it being

The 1871 Cleveland Forest Citys, who committed 18 errors that day in losing to Boston, 31-10. (Courtesy of John Thorn)

late, the game was called by mutual consent."⁸ The game had run 2 hours and 35 minutes, exceptionally long for the era. The *Boston Journal* probably got it right: After eight full innings, "as the Clevelanders had not a ghost of a chance for winning, they requested that the contest end there, and accordingly game was called."

The final stood at 31-10. The game had been, as the *Post* allowed in understated fashion, "rather an uneven one."⁹ That there had been a lot of errors was evident. If one counted only earned runs, the score was much closer: Boston 4, Forest Citys 3.¹⁰

NOTES

1. *Boston Journal*, September 4, 1871: 4.
2. Ibid.
3. Ibid.
4. Ibid.
5. Ibid.
6. Ibid.
7. *Boston Post*, September 4, 1871: 3.
8. *Cleveland Plain Dealer*, September 4, 1871: 3.
9. *Boston Post*.
10. The earned-run totals are provided by the *Cleveland Plain Dealer* in its account.

"BUSHEL BASKET" GOULD HITS FIRST GRAND SLAM IN PROFESSIONAL BASEBALL HISTORY

September 5, 1871: Boston Red Stockings 6, Chicago White Stockings 3, at the South End Grounds in Boston

BY GREGORY H. WOLF

THE GRAND SLAM. IT IS ONE OF the most exciting, dramatic, and potentially game- and momentum-altering occurrences in baseball. Lou Gehrig hit 23 of them; Manny Ramirez 21; and the much-maligned and confessed PED-user Alex Rodriguez has hit the most (25). But the first one in professional baseball history? That honor goes to Charlie Gould of the Boston Red Stockings in 1871, in the inaugural season of the National Association.

On Tuesday, September 5, 1871, about 4,000 fans piled into Boston's South End Grounds to see what the *Boston Daily Advertiser* described as "by all odds the most interesting [game] witnessed here this season."[1] Player-manager Harry Wright's Red Stockings were in third place (13-9) and coming off an overwhelming, 31-10 victory over the Cleveland Forest Citys three days earlier in their first home contest since June 21. Their opponent, the Chicago White Stockings, was in first place (17-5), and had been victorious in nine of its last 10 games. Boston hoped to avenge losses in their first two meetings, 16-14 on June 2 and 7-1 on July 7. The pitching matchup featured two righties: Boston's 21-year-old Al Spalding, en route to a National Association-high 19 victories, and Chicago's George "The Charmer" Zettlein (so named because his supposedly ever-present smile and jolly disposition drew comparisons to "George the Charmer" in minstrel shows). Both Spalding and Zettlein had started every game for their clubs so far this season. The pitching mound was 50 feet from home plate, and pitchers threw underhand.

The game commenced at 2:30 when umpire Nick Young, pitcher-manager of the Washington Olympics, yelled, "Play Ball." The Chicagos struck first. Player-manager Jimmy Wood, the club's best hitter (.378 batting average), "earned first" and then scored on what the *Daily Advertiser* called "two loose plays" (errors).[2] Chicago threatened again in the next frame. After Tom Foley singled to right field and Ed Pinkham drew his league-high 16th walk, Charlie Hodes smashed a double into left field. With some "fast running," Foley scored, but Pinkham was thrown out at the plate by left fielder Frank Barrows.[3] The White Stockings increased their lead to 3-0 in the third inning when Fred Treacey doubled and scampered home on Joe Simmons' "daisy cutter" between second baseman Ross Barnes and shortstop George Wright.[4]

Notwithstanding Zettlein's fine hurling, the Boston nine was probably not concerned about a three-run deficit after three innings. The club averaged 12.9 runs a game, second only to the champion Philadelphia Athletics' 13.4 per game. As if on cue, Dave Birdsall and Cal McVey led off the Red Stockings' fourth with hits. Harry Shafer reached first on a two-out error to load the bases. But the first grand slam in professional baseball history had to wait as Zettlein induced Barrows to pop up to second baseman Wood.

"Every Red Stockings inning except for the fifth may be disposed of with the remark that closed fielding and brilliant catching prevented them from tallying," wrote the *Chicago Tribune*.[5] Harry Wright, Boston's number nine hitter, led off the fateful frame with a single. His brother George lofted a high fly to outfielder Tom Foley who dropped it. After Barnes lined out to left fielder Treacey, Birdsall hit a screeching liner to Wood. The *Chicago Tribune* reported that Wood handled it "prettily," pivoted, and threw wildly to shortstop Ed Duffy in an attempt to cut down George Wright at second.[6] By the time Duffy recovered the ball, Harry Wright had scored and runners were on second and third. McVey followed with one of his league-leading 66 hits (good for a runner-up .431 batting average) to drive in George Wright, and then Spalding loaded the bases with a hit to third baseman Ed Pinkham. Up stepped Charlie Gould.

At an even 6 feet and about 170 pounds, 24-year-old first baseman Gould was one of the tallest players on the Red Stockings, trailing only 6-foot-1 Al Spalding. He was affectionately called "Bushel Basket" for his long arms and reach, which made it easier for fielders to throw the ball to him. A native of Cincinnati, he got his start in Organized Baseball in 1863, and played with the legendary Cincinnati Red Stockings clubs from 1867 to 1870 piloted by Harry Wright. When Wright left the Queen City to organize a team in Boston for the inaugural season of the National Association of Professional Baseball Clubs in 1871, he took along Gould, Cal McVey, and his brother George; he also brought with him the nickname, the Red Stockings.

With the bases loaded and Boston trailing 3-2, Gould had a chance for heroics, yet few players or fans probably thought about a home run. Boston hit only three all season; two of those were by Gould, his only homers in his six-year professional career. The entire league counted just 47 round-trippers in 1871. Gould waited "until he got a nice low ball," wrote the *Chicago Tribune*. "[He] hit a terrific drive, and before it stopped on the outside of the left field fence, the bases were emptied."[7] The *Boston Daily Advertiser* praised Gould's "powerful arms" and "tremendous sweep" to give the Red Stockings a dramatic 6-3 lead.[8] Zettlein retired Schafer and Barrows, but the damage was done.

"The Chicago boys, at least those who had been playing to win, seemed to lose all heart" after Gould's bases-clearing hit, opined the *Chicago Tribune*.[9] Neither team scored or even mounted a serious threat for the rest of the game, which was described by the *Boston Daily Advertiser* as "very sharp."[10] The game was completed in two hours.

In light of the low-scoring game, newspaper reports focused on fielding. At this time, fielders did not wear gloves; they became the norm about a decade later. While each team averaged about eight errors per game in 1871, Boston committed only four while Chicago tallied eight.[11] The *Chicago Tribune* lamented that the game was lost "through loose fielding and weak hitting on the part of the Whites" and pointed to the "muffing line" of Duffy, Foley, and Wood as major reasons for the loss despite a strong outing by Zettlein.[12] "Tom [Foley]," continued the paper, "seems to have lost all control over his nerves," and suggested that he should be replaced. Hodes, on the other hand, "showed himself to be a superb catcher" by throwing out two runners attempting to steal and permitting only one passed ball. The *Boston Daily Advertiser* praised George Wright and Gould for playing the "Cincinnati style" of baseball with smooth fielding and swift, sharp throws to first base; third baseman Harry Shafer *[sic]*, gushed the paper, "distinguished himself by holding two extremely hot flies, low down, for which he was heartily applauded."[13]

The gentleman/professional ball players apparently felt no ill will toward one another after the hard-fought game. According to the *Boston Daily Evening Transcript*, the Red Stockings took their guests to the Globe Theatre later that evening for the opening of a play, *The Victims — The Forty Winks*.[14]

NOTES

1 "Base Ball—The Red Above The White," *Boston Daily Advertiser*, September 6, 1871.

2 Ibid.

3 Ibid.

4 "Games and Pastimes Defeat of the White Stockings by the Bostons, 6 to 3," *Chicago Tribune*, September 6, 1871: 4.

5 Ibid.

6 Ibid.

7 Ibid.

8 "Base Ball—The Red Above The White."

9 "Games and Pastimes Defeat of the White Stockings by the Bostons, 6 to 3."

10 "Base Ball—The Red Above The White."

11 Some contemporary newspapers claimed five errors and nine errors.

12 "Games and Pastimes Defeat of the White Stockings by the Bostons, 6 to 3."

13 "Base Ball—The Red Above The White."

14 "Local Intelligence," *Boston Daily Evening Transcript*, September 6, 1871: 4. In the September 5, 1871, edition of the *Boston Journal*, the Boston-Chicago baseball game and the performance of *The Victims—The Forty Winks* at the Globe Theatre are listed as the top two items for amusement in Boston on September 6.

SEPTEMBER 9, 1871
Boston Red Stockings 17, Philadelphia Athletics 14, at South End Grounds, Boston

BY MARK PESTANA

HAVING WON SEVEN OF THEIR nine previous matches, including a huge come-from-behind win against Chicago four days earlier, the Boston Red Stockings prepared to meet their other main rival for the National Association championship, the Athletic club of Philadelphia, on Saturday, September 9, 1871.

The two teams had met thrice previously in the season, the Reds winning at home in May, and then losing one and winning one on the Athletics' grounds in June and August, respectively. The Bostons were looking to clinch the best-of-five seasonal series with another victory.

Game time at Boston's South End Grounds was 3 o'clock. The weather was favorable and helped draw the largest crowd of the year, nearly 5,000, according to the *Boston Journal*.[1] Boston captain Harry Wright lost the opening coin toss and the home team went to bat first.[2]

Pitching to Wright's nine was 23-year-old Philly native George Bechtel, who normally shared right-field duties with George Heubel. Bechtel was making his third fill-in start for the ailing Dick McBride, and had no problems in the first inning, retiring the top of the Boston order in one-two-three fashion.

The Athletics came strong out of the gate in the bottom half, sending 10 men to the plate and producing five runs, aided greatly by three Red Stockings errors. Bechtel helped his own cause with a two-run double to left. During the inning, catcher Cal McVey suffered an injury from a foul tip off Al Reach's bat. Play was suspended for 10 to 15 minutes while the gash over McVey's left eye was bandaged. McVey "pluckily resumed his position,"[3] but to "make matters more easy for him,"[4] the softer-throwing Harry Wright came in to pitch, sending Al Spalding temporarily out to center field.

The home team got its offense rolling in the top of the second inning. McVey led off with a double and Spalding followed with a base on balls. Two more safe hits, two more walks, and an error by Heubel added up to four runs for the Reds.

Philadelphia came roaring right back in its half of the second. Ned Cuthbert, who had been at the plate in the first inning when Heubel was put out running on a foul ball, started the onslaught with a double into left. After a popout to third base, John Radcliff reached on George Wright's error at shortstop. A wild pitch, a walk, an error by third baseman Harry Schafer, and four straight singles by Al Reach, Count Sensenderfer, Levi Meyerle, and Heubel resulted in a half-dozen runs for the Athletics. Finally, Cuthbert, up for the second time in the inning, was put out on a great play by George Wright to stop the bleeding.

With the score now 11-4, McVey led off again in the Boston third. Meyerle, the Athletics' "great-hit, no-field" third baseman, made the first of his four errors in the game, allowing McVey to reach safely. Spalding whacked a ball over Meyerle's head next, sending McVey to second. The hot-corner barrage continued as Charlie Gould, too, laced a single past Meyerle, scoring McVey. But Schafer's grounder was fielded nicely by shortstop Radcliff, who cut Spalding down at the plate, catcher Fergy Malone applying the tag. The Reds loaded the bases after that but could not inflict further damage. George Wright's fly ball was nabbed by Sensenderfer in center to quell the rally.

Spalding returned to the box in the bottom of the third and blanked the visitors. The score remained 11-5 in the Athletics' favor as both teams were whitewashed in the fourth and fifth innings.

Harry Wright began the Boston sixth with a base on called balls and brother George followed with a fair-foul hit that went for two bases. After Ross Barnes' out and Dave Birdsall's infield hit, McVey knocked the Wright brothers home with a single to left. Meyerle then made his second error, on a grounder by Spalding, and base hits by Gould and Schafer drove in Birdsall and Spalding, cutting the lead to two runs. Then, when Radcliff misplayed a ball off Frank Barrows' bat, Gould and Schafer raced home and the score was tied, with five of the six Boston runs being unearned.[5]

The Reds made some changes in the field as Philadelphia went to bat in its half of the sixth. Harry Schafer had suffered a collision chasing a fly ball a week or so earlier and, apparently still feeling the aftereffects, was "obliged to withdraw."[6] McVey, who had been mercifully moved from catcher to right field earlier, made his second switch of the afternoon, replacing Schafer at third base. Fred Cone, who like teammate Frank Barrows was participating in his only major-league campaign, entered as the right fielder. Birdsall continued subbing for McVey behind the bat.

The Athletics proceeded to rough Spalding up a bit, tallying three runs—all earned—thanks to fair-foul hits by Radcliff and Fisler, and pitcher Bechtel's three-baser to left-center.

Finding themselves trailing again, 14-11, Boston's nine tried to muster something in the seventh. George Wright and Barnes reached on infield miscues. Al Reach then attempted a little trickery, purposely dropping Birdsall's popup and seemingly catching both runners out, but umpire Bob Ferguson declared that Reach had held the ball long enough and therefore the batter was out, and the runners were held at their bases.[7] The Reds, however, failed to make anything of their opportunity. The seventh and eighth went down as whitewashes for both clubs.

Leading off Boston's ninth, Captain Wright drew his fourth base on balls of the day. Brother George was up next and sent a low liner to left, which Cuthbert nearly, but not quite, caught. It went for two bases and the elder Wright crossed the plate with the Red Stockings' 12th run. Barnes garnered a pass on balls as well, and he and the younger Wright lingered on base while Birdsall and McVey were retired on foul bound catches. Meyerle then botched a grounder from Spalding, allowing George Wright to score, and Radcliff, also having a poor day in the field, saw Gould's grounder go through his legs, letting Barnes in to tie the score again. Schafer, who had returned to his position in the bottom of the seventh, now sliced a double down the left-field line, driving in both Spalding and Gould with the go-ahead runs. Frank Barrows, following, recorded his only hit of the day, a single to center that sent Schafer home with the final Boston run.

The Philadelphians had nothing left in the tank for the bottom of the final frame. The *New York Clipper* noted that they hit "carelessly at the first good balls pitched to them." Cuthbert and Radcliff both made long strikes to left that were hauled in by Barrows, and Malone fouled out to the catcher. A blank for the Athletics and a 17-14 triumph for Harry Wright's boys.

The Red Stockings thus took the important season series with the Athletics, three games to one. They had already completed—and won—their best-of-five series with the Olympics of Washington and the Rockford Forest Citys. This put them in a strong position near the front of the league, as they looked forward to completing their series with Troy, Cleveland, Chicago, and New York in the coming weeks.

NOTES

1. *Boston Journal*, September 11, 1871: 1. Philip J. Lowry's, *Green Cathedrals* (New York: Walker Publishing Company Inc., 2006) lists park capacity as 3,000. However, Retrosheet.com shows attendance for this game at 4,500, and the *Journal* states "nearly 5,000." For what it's worth, the *New York Clipper*'s report on the game says only "over two thousand."

2. This must have been a going trend, as both the *Journal* and the *Boston Daily Advertiser* of September 11 make mocking references to Wright losing the toss "of course" and "as usual."

3. *New York Clipper*, September 16, 1871: 186.

4. *Boston Journal*, September 11, 1871: 1.

5. This article follows the *Clipper* account in describing this sequence of events. In some points, such as who scored on a given hit or error—or whether a batter reached via hit or error, it differs from the account in the *Daily Advertiser*, but as

the *Clipper's* play-by-play is on the whole more detailed (and thorough, compared with the many gaps in the Boston papers' reports), we have relied on it here.

6   *Boston Daily Advertiser*, September 11, 1871: 1.

7   This was before the creation of the "infield fly" rule.

SEPTEMBER 13, 1871

Boston Red Stockings 20, Troy Haymakers 17, at South End Grounds, Boston

Harry Wright's Only Win of the Season (at least three other appearances)
Wright replaced starting pitcher Al Spalding in the seventh inning.

BY JAY HURD

THE GAME TO BE PLAYED ON Wednesday, September 13, 1871, between the Boston Red Stockings and the Troy Haymakers (aka Unions) was touted as a "Base Ball Grand Match for Championship."[1] "Championship" applied to the team with more wins in regular-season meetings. At this point in the season, Troy held a two-wins-to-one advantage over the Boston nine. Should the Red Stockings win this meeting, a fifth game would be needed to determine a champion. Tickets for this game could be purchased for 50 cents each at Wright and Gould's sporting goods shop at 18 Boylston Street in Boston.[2]

Play started at 3:00 P.M. and continued for 2 hours and 45 minutes. Pitching for the Red Stockings, making his 26th start of the season, was right-hander Albert Goodwill Spalding. John McMullin, a left-hander making his 23rd start of the season, was on the mound for the Troy (New York) Haymakers. Harry Wright, manager and starting center fielder for the Bostons, would make his ninth pitching appearance, changing positions with Spalding, in the seventh inning and would earn his only win of the season. The manager and second baseman for the Haymakers was Bill Craver. Umpiring duties fell to J.C. Goodwin of the Harvard Club. Despite "threatening weather,"[3] a crowd of nearly 2,000 gathered at the South End Grounds to witness the contest.

Troy took to the field in the top of the first and surrendered six runs, three unearned, to the Boston nine. In the bottom half of the inning, Boston also allowed six runs, all unearned. While errors dominated first-inning play, both teams did exhibit batting skills—shortstop George Wright and second baseman Ross Barnes both hit doubles, and catcher Cal McVey, Spalding, and Harry Wright each reached first. For the Haymakers, center fielder Tom York and shortstop Dickie Flowers had "3-base hits."[4]

Neither team scored in the second inning. However, fielding had improved with each team completing sparkling double plays. In the top of the second, with the Red Stockings at bat and Barnes on third, shortstop Flowers caught McVey's sharp liner and threw to third baseman Steve Bellan, who promptly put the tag on Barnes as he tried to return to third, having broken for home. In the Haymakers' half of the inning, York and Flowers singled, but Red Stockings tird baseman Harry Schafer snared Clipper Flynn's sharp grounder, stepped on third, forcing York, then quickly threw to Charlie Gould at first to catch Flynn.

The Red Stockings scored four times during the middle innings while the Haymakers scored six. Although the Haymakers "were by no means punishing [Spalding],"[5] manager Harry Wright sent the pitcher to center field and assumed the pitching duties himself. No runs were scored in the seventh inning, but the crowd saw fine fielding, including a play by Red Stockings right fielder Dave Birdsall. Troy left fielder Steve King hit to center and, when he saw the ball pass Spalding, broke for second base. Birdsall, backing up Spalding, made a "perfect throw" to second base, where Barnes tagged King out.

Harry Wright, 1872. Harry Wright pitched in 36 games for the Red Stockings between 1871-1875, starting only eight of them. (Spalding Collection)

At the end of the seventh inning, Troy had a 12-10 advantage. However, the Red Stockings put more men on base in the top of the eighth. George Wright reached first base on an error, Barnes "earned first base,"[6] and Birdsall walked. McVey then hit safely, allowing Wright and Barnes to reach home and tying the score at 12-all. By the end of the inning, with solid hitting by Schafer and left fielder Frank Barrows, the Bostons held the lead, 15-12.

The Haymakers answered the Red Stockings' five runs with one run in their half of the eighth inning as John McMullin tripled and Lip Pike drove him in. The inning ended abruptly as Bellan flied out to center, on a fine play by Spalding, and second baseman Bill Craver and catcher Mike McGreary popped up.

George Wright opened the ninth inning with a hit over the head of Pike in right field. Barnes drove in Wright and scored himself on a hit by Birdsall. Harry Wright ended the inning on a popup to Pike, and the Reds led by seven runs, 20-13.

By "wielding the bat heavily,"[7] Flowers, Flynn, Pike, and Bellan brought the Haymakers to within three runs of the Red Stockings. However, they could not score the seven runs they needed to tie, or the eight runs to win.

This game was remarkable for the many errors (28) and unearned runs (22) surrendered by both teams. Also, it was the only game of the season in which Spalding neither won nor lost, and it was the Wright's only win of the season. The Red Stockings now boasted a 16-9 record, with one tie and a four-game winning streak, and were in third place in the Association behind the Chicago White Stockings and the Philadelphia Athletics.

Boston Red Stockings	Troy Haymakers
George Wright (ss)	Mike McGeary (c)
Ross Barnes (2b)	Tom York (cf)
Dave Birdsall (rf)	Dickie Flowers (ss)
Cal McVey (c)	Clipper Flynn (1b)
Al Spalding (p, cf)	Steve King (lf)
Charlie Gould (1b)	John McMullin (p)
Harry Schafer (3b)	Lip Pike (rf)
Frank Barrows (lf)	Steve Bellan (3b)
Harry Wright (cf, p)	Bill Craver (2b)

SOURCES

In addition to the sources indicated in the notes, the author also consulted:

Wilbert, Warren N. *Opening Pitch: Professional Baseball's Inaugural Season, 1871* (Lanham, Maryland: Scarecrow Press, 2008).

NOTES

1. "Multiple Classified Advertisements," *Boston Daily Advertiser*, September 13, 1871.
2. John Thorn, *Baseball in the Garden of Eden* (New York: Simon & Schuster, 2011), 154.
3. "Base Ball—The Red Stockings Defeat the Haymakers," *Boston Daily Advertiser*, September 14, 1871.
4. Ibid.
5. Ibid.
6. Ibid.
7. Ibid.

CHICAGO BEATS BOSTON IN LAST GAME IN THE WINDY CITY BEFORE THE GREAT FIRE

September 29, 1871: Chicago White Stockings 10, Boston Red Stockings 8, at Union Base-Ball Grounds

BY GREGORY H. WOLF

THE *CHICAGO TRIBUNE* DESCRIBED the Chicago White Stockings as "disaffected, demoralized and crippled" as the club prepared to clash with the Boston Red Stockings in a match of pennant contenders on September 29, 1871.[1] With third baseman Ed Pinkham sick in bed and the club suffering from a host of other injuries, Chicago had not only lost its last two games to fall to 17-7, it had been drubbed 17-2 three days earlier by an amateur team, the Rockford Forest Citys.[2] That loss heightened growing suspicions, arising from the recent announcement of the team's roster for the 1872 season, that players who would not be returning to the club would have little incentive to help Chicago capture the championship.

Overcoming early-season injuries, Boston (18-9) was on a roll, having won 11 of its last 13 games, including the last six. The *Tribune* praised the team as "all that is hightoned and aristocratic in the professional fraternity." In perfect health and without a "sore finger or lame leg" of the squad, the Red Stockings exuded confidence. "The red-legged gentry frisked and cavorted about the field before the game," expecting to defeat Chicago as they had had on September 5, and to tie the season series at two games each.

A warm, sunny Midwestern day attracted at least 7,000 spectators to Chicago's Lake Front Park (also called colloquially White Stockings Park) to take in an afternoon of baseball. "The White Stockings," opined the *Tribune*, "undoubtedly occupied a larger share of the public attention than any other private citizens in the city." After Chicago's player-manager Jimmy Wood lost the customary coin toss to determine which team would bat first, umpire Harry McLean of the Washington Olympics called the game to order at 3:05.

Batting first, the Whites took a 1-0 lead in the first inning when striker Fred Treacey reached first on third baseman's Harry Schafer's error, stole second, and scored on another error by Schafer. In the second inning Charlie Hodes scored on Schafer's third error to give Chicago a 2-0 lead. The Reds' Al Spalding led off the second by walking, stealing second "by proxy in the person of the fleet-footed [Ross] Barnes," and tallying the visitors' first run. In the fourth inning Schafer redeemed himself by knocking in Cal McVey, who had led off with a walk, to tie the game.

Schafer, who was Boston's starting third sacker for all five years in the National Association (1871-1875), was having a bad day, and was charged with seven of the team's 11 errors.[3] In those days of playing without a glove, Schafer muffed two more grounders in the fifth inning. Those miscues, coupled with Spalding's wild pitch and McVey's wild throw, led to two more Chicago runs. But Boston, whose average of 12.9 runs per game and .310 team batting average trailed only the eventual champion Philadelphia Athletics, stormed back. George Wright (whom the *Tribune* described as Boston's "mainstay and chief reliance"), Ross Barnes, and McVey tallied safe hits leading to two runs, the first of which was the team's only earned run of the game, and tied the game, 4-4.

Catching for Chicago was Marshall King, who had not played in a game for the White Stockings since August 16 while recovering from a broken finger. He "swore to stop every ball that [George] Zettlein pitched—if not with his hands, then with his head," wrote the *Tribune* excitedly. However, in the fifth inning King suffered a "peculiarly painful and enervating injury" that forced him to change positions with Hodes (the regular catcher) in the middle of the following inning. One can only imagine what kind what injury befell the 21-year-old.

The sixth inning was the "turning point of the game," opined the *Tribune*. Tom Foley, a much-maligned outfielder, led off with a single and scored on Hodes' RBI single to left. The bases were loaded after Zettlein reached on Barnes's muff and Bub McAtee, once described as a "player of coolness and judgment good under the most trying and exciting circumstances," singled.[4] Wood (whose .378 batting average paced the club in '71) "dashed at a hip high ball," belting it to left field and clearing the bases for an 8-4 Chicago lead. A "storm of cheers," wrote the *Tribune*, "lasted for nearly five minutes."

Boston, which the *Tribune* reported was often disdainfully termed the "plug bat nine" by some pitchers in the league, cut the deficit to two by scoring two unearned runs in the sixth. Noteworthy was the first of two Chicago double plays. After Harry Wright singled, his brother George hit a grounder to second baseman Jimmy Wood. Inexplicably, Harry raced back to first. Wood threw to first sacker McAtee to nab George; McAtee then fired back to Wood, who erased Harry, caught between the bases. The Whites turned their second double play of the game (they had 16 the entire season) the following inning when left fielder Treacey made a "brilliant" running catch of Dave Birdsall's smash "just off the ground" and then doubled McVey (running for George Wright) off first.

Described as a "state of things too critical to be comfortable," Chicago tacked on an insurance run in the seventh when Foley scored after two more errors by Schafer and a hit by Zettlein. In the ninth inning Treacey smashed a "beauty over [the fence] into Michigan Avenue"; however, according to Captain Jimmy Wood's rules regarding balls over the fence, he was granted only first base. Treacey subsequently scored on a passed ball to give the Whites what appeared to be an insurmountable 10-6 lead.

According to the *Tribune*, the Red Stockings mounted a "savage and determined" comeback in the bottom of the ninth. Charlie Gould doubled to drive in Spalding and subsequently scored on a wild throw to second on a double steal to make the game 10-8. With Schafer on third and George Wright on first with two outs, Ross Barnes (who batted .401 and led the NA with 66 runs in just 31 games) was in position to tie the game with a double. However, he hit a high fly that Wood caught on the run "between the in and out fields" to secure Chicago's exciting victory.

Chicago's "nine ball players never worked harder, or more harmoniously, to win a doubtful and difficult contest," wrote the *Tribune*, suggesting that all of the pregame concerns about the players and team were for naught. "They demonstrated that they are men of pride and principle."

The *Tribune* noted many inconsistent calls by the umpire. For example, Treacey struck out in the sixth on a ball that was "positively over" the batter's head; at other times, the paper reported incredulously of consecutive balls and strikes. In defense of the umpire, who admitted that he got "all mixed up," the daily castigated spectators whose "jeers and howls at decisions adverse to the White Stockings were a disgrace to Chicago." Seeking to preserve both the gentlemanly aspect of the sport and the behavior of the spectators,

A depiction of the Great Fire in Chicago in 1871. The city would not have a baseball team again until 1874. (Library of Congress).

the *Tribune* suggested that more police are needed at games to suppress such "ruffianly demonstrations." In a dig at spectators in the City of Brotherly Love, the paper suggested that "Chicago cannot afford to acquire a Philadelphia reputation with reference to baseball crowds."

With the victory, Chicago took the season series from Boston, appeared to be the front-runner to win the National Association championship, and set up an anticipated matchup with Philadelphia. However, the White Stockings had to wait for more than two years and seven months before they played another professional game in Chicago.

Disaster struck Chicago on Sunday night, October 8, when a massive fire erupted that destroyed about 3.3 square miles of the city, including much of the central business district (the Loop) and Lake Front Park, at the intersection of Michigan Avenue and Randolph Street (now Grant Park). The two-day fire killed an estimated 300 people and destroyed 17,000 structures.

The fire decimated the White Stockings. Though no players were injured, the team lost all of its equipment and uniforms. Most of the players were left homeless and in financial ruin. Undoubtedly more concerned about their friends and family and rebuilding their lives, they agreed to play the remaining games with borrowed gear on the road, splitting two games with the Troy Haymakers on October 21 and 23. Chicago concluded the season in an anticlimactic game on October 30 by playing Philadelphia at the Union Grounds in Brooklyn to determine the championship. On a neutral field, far from the fans of either city, the game drew only 500 fans who witnessed Athletics triumph, 4-1.

When Chicago defeated Philadelphia 4-0 at the newly rebuilt 23rd Street Grounds on May 13 to open the 1874 season and re-inaugurate professional baseball in the Windy City, only two players remained from the 1871 team: pitcher George Zettlein and outfielder Fred Treacey.

NOTES

1 The play-by-play information for this game summary relies heavily on the very detailed game report from the *Chicago Tribune*. All of the quotations in this game summary are from the following edition unless otherwise noted: "Games and Pastimes. Fourth and Deciding Game Between the Whites and Red Stockings," *Chicago Tribune*, September 30, 1871: 4.

2 "Games and Pastimes. The White Stockings at Rockford—How They Scored 2 to the Forest City's 17," *Chicago Tribune*, September 27, 1871: 4.

3 The *Chicago Tribune* reported that Schafer made two errors in the first, one in the second, two in the fifth, and two in the seventh.

4 "Games and Pastimes. Composition of Next Year's White Stocking Nine," *Chicago Tribune*, September 22, 1871: 1.

NINTH-INNING COMEBACK GIVES RED STOCKINGS VICTORY IN HOME OPENER

May 11, 1872: Boston Red Stockings 4, New York Mutuals 2, South End Grounds, Boston

BY GREGORY H. WOLF

NEWSPAPERS WERE FULL OF superlatives following the Boston Red Stockings' exciting ninth-inning comeback to defeat the New York Mutuals, 4-2, in their 1872 home opener. It was "one of the most exciting games ever played in this city," gushed the *Boston Daily Evening Transcript*.[1] "[T]he play of both nine was almost near perfection as possible," mused the *Boston Post*.[2]

The formidable-looking Red Stockings were on a roll. In the previous, inaugural season of the National Association, the Bostons, as the club was often called in the press, won eight of their last nine games to finish in third place (20-10), two games behind the Philadelphia Athletics. Player-manager Harry Wright's squad began the 1872 season by playing their first seven games on the road, trouncing their opponents by a cumulative score of 98-23. Their only loss was to Philadelphia, 10-7.

After finishing in fifth place (16-17) in the nine-team NA in 1871, the Mutuals (5-2) seemed like pennant contenders. Led by player-manager Dickey Pearce, they had won five in a row before losing to Boston, 9-2, at the Union Ball Grounds in Brooklyn on May 8. "We have seen some noteworthy displays of pitching skill within the last fifteen years," opined the *Brooklyn Daily Eagle*, "but we never saw such judgment exhibited in the position than in this game."[3] Boston's strapping 6-foot-1 right-hander, Al Spalding, yielded three hits and two runs in the first inning, then shut down the Mutuals on one hit thereafter in that contest.

The first professional baseball game of the 1872 season in Boston drew approximately 4,000 spectators—"many of them ladies," noted the *Boston Journal*—to the South End Grounds on a springlike Saturday afternoon, May 11.[4] The prediction by the *Brooklyn Daily Eagle* that "baseball will not be so popular this season as last" seemed erroneous when one surveyed the wooden stands filled with a raucous, smartly dressed crowd.[5] According to the *Boston Post*, betting was brisk, with bookies taking 2-1 odds on Boston, despite the Red Stockings' loss of first baseman Charlie Gould, who had injured his hand in the previous game.[6] Gould was replaced by outfielder Fraley Rogers, while 33-year-old utilityman Dave Birdsall took Rogers's place in left field.

Harry Wright won the customary coin toss to determine which team would bat first, and chose to take the field. It was a fortuitous decision. At 2:30 umpire E. Chandler, from Boston, called the game to order.

From the outset, the game proved to be a duel between two of the best hurlers in the NA, both future Hall of Famers. The 21-year-old Spalding was the most celebrated pitcher in the earliest phase of professional baseball. Spalding led the NA in victories in all five seasons of its existence, including a 38-8 record in 1872. Weighing just 120 pounds, 23-year-old right-hander Candy Cummings is often regarded as the inventor of the curveball. The Massachusetts native baffled batters with that pitch as a member of the amateur Brooklyn Stars (1869-1871) before joining the Mutuals, for whom he won 33 games and led the league with 497 innings pitched in 1872.

After each team managed just one baserunner in the first two frames, Boston rallied in the third when George Wright, the manager's brother, reached first. He scored on a double by Ross Barnes, arguably the most dangerous hitter in the NA. Barnes paced the circuit in batting in 1872 (.430) and 1873 (.431), and finished with the highest career mark in the five-year existence of the league (.391). The right-handed hitter was also the unequivocal master of the "fair-foul" hit whereby he struck the ball in such a manner that it hit in fair territory in front of the third baseman before rolling into foul territory.

The Mutuals finally solved Spalding in the fifth when Cummings led off with a double and scored on George Bechtel's single. Bechtel subsequently stole second base and scored on rugged Nat Hicks's one-out single. When John McMullin followed with one of his team-leading 11 walks for the season, the Mutuals seemed to have Spalding on the ropes. The game's momentum took a quick and unexpected turn when John Hatfield hit a routine popup to shortstop George Wright. But with runners on first and second, the crafty infielder apparently let the ball purposely fall out of his glove. He quickly retrieved the orb, rifled a shot to third baseman Harold Schafer, who forced Hicks; Schafer threw to second baseman Barnes to complete the inning-ending double play. "[I]t was done so quick," reported the *Boston Post*, "that Dickey Pearce began to 'chin' with the umpire."[7] The *Boston Journal* noted that the sequence of events "occasioned some talk between umpire and the captains of the rival nines, but it was allowed to pass as a muffed fly."[8] [The National League instituted the infield-fly rule in 1895 to prohibit such intentional drops, which had become commonplace by then].

Stymied by Cummings since the third inning, Boston mounted a rally in the eighth. George Wright got a one-out hit, and subsequently scampered to third on Andy Leonard's two-out single. Leonard stole second, giving Cal McVey a chance to be a hero. Often overlooked on a squad that featured the Wright brothers, Barnes, Spalding, and (beginning in

Boston Herald, *May 11, 1872.*

1873) Deacon White, McVey was a dangerous hitter, finishing second in batting average (.431) and RBIs (43) in 1871, and twice leading the NA in RBIs (1874-1875). But this time McVey hit an inning-ending grounder to third baseman Pearce.

Spalding set down the "Mutes," so called by the *Boston Journal*, in the ninth. George Wright made a fine defensive play for the second out when he corralled Cummings' hot grounder after it got by third baseman Schafer, and heaved to first.

Tension mounted again in the ninth. "When Boston went to bat for the last time," wrote the *World Telegraph*, "the feeling was that they were defeated, but never was the glorious uncertainty of the game more manifested."[9] Spalding stepped to the box to lead things off. No one-trick pony, Spalding was a bona-fide hitter; his 47 RBIs led the team in '72, and his .354 batting average trailed only Barnes. At the plate with Spalding stood Barnes, who was serving for this at-bat as a designated runner—an accepted custom at the time. Spalding sent a ball sailing down the left-field line. According to the *Boston Journal*, Barnes had made it around second base before noticing that the ball was foul, and returned to the plate.[10] Playing it cautious, Cummings walked Spalding, a mistake that proved fatal with the pitcher's designated runner on the basepaths. Barnes immediately stole second

> **BASE BALL.**
> First Championship Game on Boston Grounds for 1872.
> **Mutuals, of New York,**
> vs.
> **Bostons,**
> SATURDAY, May 11th.
> Game called at 3.30.   Tickets 50 cents.

Boston Journal *May 11, 1872*

and third. Birdsall hit a "daisy-cutter" to right field to drive in Barnes and tie the game.[11] The next batter, Harry Schafer, smashed a double to deep left field. Birdsall raced around the bases to score the winning run, sending the partisan crowd into a frenzy. "The spectators seemed fairly wild," read one report about the excitement, "shouting for minutes, and throwing their hats in the air."[12] But in then-customary fashion, the teams kept playing until all 27 outs were recorded, even though the outcome had been decided. After Cummings dispatched Rogers, Harry Wright lined a single past the shortstop to drive in Schafer for the final run in the 4-2 victory.

Reports about the game focused on the excellent pitching and fielding. "Spalding sent in the balls very hot," wrote the *Boston Post* about the Red Stockings ace, who surrendered only five hits and issued one walk.[13] Since losing to the Athletics, Spalding had squashed opponents, permitting just 14 hits in his previous 31 innings. Cummings pitched almost as well, giving up eight hits and two walks, in a game that last 1 hour and 45 minutes.

The unequivocal stars of the games were the fielders, who played without gloves; the use of gloves did not become the norm until the mid-1880s. In 1872 an average of 15 errors were committed per game in the NA, but the league's two best defensive squads combined for just six (two by Boston). "[George] Wright was himself," lauded the *Post*, "sending some balls to first in a manner that did great credit to Rogers for holding them."[14] The newspaper also considered Schafer's play at third base "superb."

As courageous as the infielders were catchers Cal McVey and Nat Hicks, neither of whom allowed a passed ball despite playing without mask, glove, or any other protection. "[McVey's] play," mused the *Boston Journal*, "served to keep good his reputation as the best player at his position in the country."[15] Baseball's most dangerous position, catchers routinely suffered serious injury to the face before masks became *de rigueur* a decade later. In 1873 Hicks almost lost his right eye in a game.[16]

Boston continued its juggernaut after the dramatic victory, extending its winning streak to 19 games before suffering a home loss to the Haymakers of Troy, New York, on July 20. The Red Stockings finished the season with a 39-8 record to capture their first of four consecutive NA titles.

NOTES

1 *Boston Daily Evening Transcript,* May 13, 1872: 4.

2 "Base Ball—Red Stockings vs Mutuals—A Brilliant Victory for Boston—Cricket—Harvard vs Boston, etc," *Boston Post,* May 13, 1872: 4.

3 "Sports and Pastimes. Base Ball," *Brooklyn Daily Eagle,* May 9, 1872: 3.

4 "Extraordinary Game Between the Bostons and Mutuals of New York Saturday—Brilliant Victory of the Red Stockings—Score 4-2," *Boston Journal,* May 13, 1872: 1.

5 "Miscellaneous News," *Brooklyn Daily Eagle,* May 11, 1872: 1.

6 "Base Ball—Red Stockings vs Mutuals—A Brilliant Victory for Boston—Cricket—Harvard vs Boston, etc."

7 Ibid.

8 "Extraordinary Game Between the Bostons and Mutuals of New York Saturday—Brilliant Victory of the Red Stockings—Score 4-2."

9 *World Telegraph* quoted from "The Mutual Defeat in Boston," *Brooklyn Daily Eagle,* May 13, 1872: 2.

10 "Extraordinary Game Between the Bostons and Mutuals of New York Saturday—Brilliant Victory of the Red Stockings—Score 4-2."

11 "The Mutual Defeat in Boston."

12 Ibid.

13 "Base Ball—Red Stockings vs Mutuals—A Brilliant Victory for Boston—Cricket—Harvard vs Boston, etc."

14 Ibid.

15 "Extraordinary Game Between the Bostons and Mutuals of New York Saturday—Brilliant Victory of the Red Stockings—Score 4-2."

16 Chuck Rosciam, "The Evolution of Catcher's Equipment," *SABR Baseball Research Journal,* Summer 2010. sabr.org/research/evolution-catchers-equipment.

JUNE 10, 1872
Boston Red Stockings 3, Mutuals 2 (11 innings), at Union Grounds, Brooklyn

BY RICHARD "DIXIE" TOURANGEAU

BOSTON'S RED STOCKINGS WERE 11-1 when they arrived at Brooklyn's Union Park to play the host Mutuals (10-5) on June 10, 1872. Boston had already taken a home-and-home set, 9-2 and 4-2, from New York, scoring three winning runs in the ninth at the South End Grounds a month before. This would be the Reds' last road game before starting an eight-game homestand. They had just beaten Baltimore in a home-and-home series, 7-0, on a terrific Al Spalding two-hitter in Boston, then 15-2 behind the batting of Spalding and flychasing newcomers Andy Leonard and Fraley Rogers.

The *Brooklyn Daily Eagle* provided the best immediate coverage of the game. Despite a sound record, that media outlet was puzzled by the Mutuals' up-and-down play, saying they were "earning the reputation of being the most uncertain club in the championship arena." The 3:30 afternoon game was played in a slight drizzle and the umpire was Theodore Bomeisler, an old amateur ballplayer from Newark, New Jersey. Morning rain and dark skies did not prevent nearly 4,000 fans from gathering at Union Park to witness the clash.

Pitching foes Spalding and Candy Cummings were not at their best, but runs were still scarce in the near-two-hour span of play. It turned into a game of fielding prowess and the Reds had the edge there, making five double plays to squash repeated rallies while the Mutuals made six errors to the Reds' three. The hosts managed 13 hits off Spalding but only two runs. Dave Eggler (leading Association hit-maker that season) had two hits and George Bechtel three (with one RBI), but only "Old Reliable" Mutual stalwart Joe Start and John Hatfield scored.

Rogers, back in his native Brooklyn, was comfortable enough to get two hits and with various Mutual miscues scored both Reds runs in the first nine innings. Rogers' tying score came when Ross Barnes and Start collided at first base on a close play in the eighth. He had been 0-for-9 against his former Brooklyn Stars teammate Cummings in their first two matchups. Field conditions were poor at best, but into the 10th inning the combatants plodded. This was the first extra-inning game ever for the Red Stockings. In their 292 Association games they would play only seven (4-1-2), which included two 10-inning games, four 11-inning ones, and one 12, which was with these Mutuals in 1873. Only one was played in Boston, a 4-3 win over the Philadelphia White Stockings in August 1875.

The *Eagle* and later the weekly *New York Clipper* used few words describing the winning tally; in fact they didn't really say anything special about it. But they had much to explain about a play in the 10th inning that forced the contest to continue. In the 10th Harry Schafer made a safe hit but Rogers was put out. Harry Wright walked and brother George reached on an error, loading the bases. Here National Association rules clash with later nineteenth-century changes that we, 140 years later, take for granted. Batting wizard Barnes bounced his requested pitch to Hatfield at second base. Hatfield caught it and made a quick-witted play by tagging George as he passed by and then threw on to first baseman Start for a double play. However, Schafer had crossed home before Start caught the ball and by the rules of the day the run should have counted. According to the newspapers the rule was that because there was only "one hand" out when the ball was struck (if) the runner at third touched home base before the throw got to first base on such a play, the run counted, "regular" double play or not. Ump Bomeisler, though usually respected, was highly criticized when he disallowed Schafer's score, saying he didn't see Harry get home before the third out because he was paying attention to the plays at second and first. Reds first sacker Charlie Gould was adamant that the tally should count, but passions cooled and the visiting Boston gentlemen did not argue with Bomeisler's final verdict. The eventual outcome did not change because in the next inning with one out Cal McVey and Spalding reached base on hits, after which Schafer's single (his third safety) ended the hard-fought contest, 3-2.

Below the game account in the *Eagle* the next morning, the paper editorialized on the complete episode. In part it said, "We notice that the New York papers this morning are as abusive of the umpire as the Quaker City press is when their pets got whipped badly. While an umpire is open to criticism for errors in interpreting the rules, he is not so for poor judgment. … (Bomeisler's) errors of judgment worked against both sides. We have already few umpires enough, without driving those we have off the field." The *Eagle* also said this about Bomeisler, "He was too irregular in his enforcing the rules governing the pitcher and striker, he failing to call unfair balls on both sides. His very eagerness to watch every point, and to do the fair thing, mars his efficiency, besides which he is too excitable for the position."

The Red Stockings returned to the South End Grounds for the rest of June through Independence Day, winning eight straight games. On July 5 they were 22-1.

SOURCES

Brooklyn Daily Eagle, June 11, 1872: 2.

New York Clipper, June 15, 1872: 82.

Retrosheet.org.

BOSTON RED STOCKINGS BURY THE PHILADELPHIA ATHLETICS

June 12, 1872: Boston Red Stockings 13, Athletics of Philadelphia 4, at the South End Grounds, Boston

BY PAUL E. DOUTRICH

WEDNESDAY JUNE 12, 1872, WAS A hot, sultry day at the South End Grounds in Boston, as Harry Wright and his Red Stockings faced their rivals, the Athletics of Philadelphia. Despite the midweek date and the heat, so many Red Stockings fans flocked to the ball park that the 3:30 P.M. game time had to be delayed by 20 minutes so that ropes could be put up around the field to accommodate the overflow. Many of those unable to get inside the park climbed onto nearby roofs or stationed themselves precariously atop fences adjacent to the park. Meanwhile gamblers from both cities snaked through the grandstand offering odds to anyone interested in a wager. In the middle of it all sat the French national band, honored guests who had recently performed in Boston. Called the best national band in the world by the *Chicago Tribune*, the visitors eagerly awaited their first baseball experience.[1] By game time as many as 10,000 patrons, the biggest baseball crowd in Boston history, awaited the first pitch.[2]

The game had special significance for the Red Stockings and their supporters. Featuring several of the game's best players, the two teams were expected to contend again for the league championship. The previous year, the National Association's inaugural season, the Athletics finished two games ahead of Boston and won the championship. More importantly, in the 12 games Boston had played thus far in the 1872 season, their only loss had come six weeks earlier to the Athletics, 10-7. Meanwhile, Philadelphia entered the game with an 8-1 record.[3]

The anxious fans did not have to wait long to see what they had come for. After escaping a first-inning bases-loaded threat, the Red Stockings set the stage for the rest of the afternoon. In the bottom of the first, shortstop George Wright led off with a fair-foul double and his keystone counterpart, Ross Barnes, followed with a walk. Wright and Barnes scored when the Athletics shortstop, Dickie Flowers, "threw wide to first base," making the first of his team's 13 errors in the game.[4] Base hits by catcher Cal McVey and pitcher Al Spalding, and a stolen base that included an overthrow, put the home team up by four runs before the visitors had recorded their first out. A single by Fraley Rogers added another tally to the scoreboard and gave Boston a five-run lead after just one inning of play.

In the third inning a one-out error by the Athletics' first baseman, Denny Mack, followed by an overthrow and then an error by Philadelphia's young third baseman, Adrian Anson, accounted for the sixth Boston tally. (Anson was already recognized as one of the league's better hitters, but it would be several years before he became more famously known as Cap, after he was named captain and manager of the Chicago White Stockings in 1979. His Athletics teammates had dubbed the 20-year-old the Marshalltown Infant, after his age and his Iowa birthplace.) Anson finished the game hitless and with three errors, and this afternoon was undoubtedly one in his Hall of Fame career that Anson would have chosen to forget.

Three more Red Stockings scored in the fourth. The first two came in after a double by McVey. An out later Charlie Gould lifted a fly ball to left field. Athletics outfielder Fred Treacey misplayed the ball so badly that McVey scored easily and Gould was able to circle the bases as well. The inning ended after another Philadelphia error, a stolen base, and a single by right fielder Fraley Rogers that drove in Boston's third run of the inning.

After sailing through the first four innings, Red Stockings pitcher Al Spalding ran into his first bit of real trouble in the fifth. Down by nine runs, the Athletics strung together a one-out single by pitcher Dick McBride, an error by third baseman Harry Schafer, a walk to Flowers, and Wes Fisler's fly ball that "amid applause" plated McBride.[5] The tally had little effect on Spalding. Considered to be one of the league's top pitchers, the Boston hurler had won 19 games the previous season and was on his way to doubling that number in 1872. Over the next four years he would win 185 games, easily the best record in the National Association.

The Red Stockings matched the Athletics' fifth-inning effort with a run of their own in the sixth. After a popout to the catcher, Schafer reached base on Anson's second error. He stole second and one out later sprinted home on a single by George Wright.

Over the last three innings both teams scored three more times. Two of the Athletics' runs came in the seventh on a walk to Ned Cuthbert, McBride's second hit of the day, another free pass, and a single by Treacey. Philadelphia might have scored more runs in the inning had it not been for a defensive gem by center fielder Harry Wright. With two out, two on, and two runs already in, Anson smacked a Spalding pitch into deep right-center field. Wright galloped after the ball and made a magnificent running catch "which gained him continued applause" from the Boston fans.[6] Philadelphia's final run came in the ninth on a double by outfielder Levi Meyerle and a single by Flowers.

Weary from the long, hot, and unproductive afternoon, the Athletics gave up three final runs to the home team in the bottom of the ninth. Though they had already won the game, the Red Stockings used their last turn at the plate to add to Philadelphia's gloom. George Wright's second hit of the day, a wild pitch, and an error followed by Spalding's single added two to Boston's total. The game ended a batter later when Charlie Gould singled and then "danced between Mack and Fisler" just long enough for Spalding to scamper across the plate with his team's 13th run.[7]

With shadows beginning to stretch across the field the throng of happy Boston fans filed out of the ballpark satisfied by the afternoon's contest. Their team had outplayed Philadelphia both at the plate and in the field. During the next four months the two teams would meet again seven times, with the Athletics getting a bit of revenge by taking three of those games, with one tie. However, the Red Stockings in 1872, managed by their legendary leader Harry Wright and featuring star pitcher Spalding, went on to win the first of their four consecutive National Association championships.

SOURCES

In addition to the sources cited in the Notes, the author also reviewed coverage of the game in the *Philadelphia Inquirer*.

NOTES

1 "Amusements," *Chicago Tribune*, July 19, 1872: 6.

2 Crowd estimates ranged from 8,000 in the *Boston Journal* to "at least ten thousand" in the *Boston Globe*. All agreed it was the largest crowd on the Boston grounds.

3 Officially Philadelphia's record stood at 8-1. However, the league had voided a 7-4 loss on May 20 to the Baltimore Canaries because of a dispute with the umpire, and declared the game a tie.

4 *Boston Journal* June 13, 1872.

5 "Out-Door Sports," *Boston Globe*, June 13, 1872: 5.

6 "Base Ball: The Bostons Still Victorious. The Athletics Badly Defeated—Score 13 to 4," *Boston Journal*, June 13, 1872.

7 "Out-Door Sports," *Boston Globe*, June 13, 1872: 5.

JULY 20, 1872
Troy Haymakers 17, Boston Red Stockings 10
At The South End Grounds

BY GERARD R. GOULET

ON JULY 13, 1872, THE *NEW YORK Clipper* reported as follows: "The Boston on a Rest. On July 6th, the Boston Reds went into camp on the Island in Boston Harbor to fish, shoot, bathe and recuperate generally for the fall campaign." The island in question was Calf Island, one of the Brewsters, where, in addition to the restful activities noted above, the Red Stockings were to, "practice two hours morning and evening of each day, as well as indulge in manly sports suited to keep their muscle up."[1] Boston had faced Troy twice in May and had beaten them by scores of 4-2 and 10-7.[2] Boston had also won its last nineteen games in a row and was now sitting comfortably atop the league standings.[3] Troy, for its part, after an early start that had it leading the league as late as May 24, had won only two games since then and team members were rumored to be embroiled in internal discord. By all rights, then, a well-rested Boston nine and its fans, numbering in the vicinity of 2500, expected the same kind of easy victory as did the odds makers who had put the odds at 100-36.[4] On Saturday, July 20, however, a rusty Red Stocking team lost for only the second time this season, with Troy scoring more runs against Boston and Al Spalding than any other team had done thus far in the 1872 season. The *Herald* took the defeat particularly and sarcastically hard, "For nearly three [exaggeration] weeks previous they [Boston] had been recuperating at their summer residence and in the company of the 'sad sea waves'. Perhaps they still hankered for their seaside resort and pined for the saltness of the locality they had quitted, and perhaps to this may be partially attributed the little excursion up the historical Salt river which they took Saturday afternoon."[5] While the *Herald* admitted that luck may have played a role in the Boston defeat, it was not as philosophical as others on the topic.[6]

In many respects, it was as if two different games were played. In the first, it appeared that Boston had forgotten how to play after its long period of inactivity. Through the mid-point of the fifth inning, the Haymakers dominated play, scoring 10 runs to Boston's two, both of the latter coming in the Boston half of the fifth inning.[7] The second half was more of a contest. From the bottom of the fifth through the ninth inning, the sides were more evenly balanced with Boston scoring eight runs to Troy's seven. Although not necessarily helped by the fielding lapses of his teammates, Spalding revisited the difficulties he had had with the Troy batters in 1871, when they had scored 29, 13, and 17 runs against him in three of their five meetings. The *Herald* believed it knew why Spalding was pounded "...all over the field. The ball must have been a lively one, as the Reds claimed it was, though [Troy] Capt. Jimmy Wood protested that it was picked out of a number of dead balls and as it had the proper marks of course there was no getting around it."[8] Lively ball or not, it wasn't until Harry Wright inserted himself at pitcher and gave them some slow pitching after four Troy runs had scored in the bottom half of the fifth inning that the Troy hitters were able to be controlled.[9] "It made little difference at first, but soon had its effect, and although the balls seemed slow and all right over the plate, the Trojans could not hit them."[10] Some suggested that had Spalding been relieved earlier, the game may have been salvaged.[11]

Although numerous inconsistencies appeared in several accounts of the game reported in the Boston

A depiction of Calf Island as it looked in the 1880s. Here, the Boston players rested for a couple of weeks, then were rusty when they took the field again against Troy. (Image taken from the book King's Handbook of Boston Harbor *by Moses Foster Sweetser, 1888).*

and New York press, all were agreed that Boston was outplayed at every level by the team from Troy. Boston batters flied to the outfield "and directly into the hands of their adversaries"[12] for the majority of their outs. In contrast, the Haymakers "batted to just that particular spot which a Red could almost, but not quite, reach."[13] In the field, every Boston fielder but Andy Leonard in left field and Fraley Rogers in right, neither of whom had many chances, was guilty of errors (12 in all). While the Haymakers fielded cleanly for the first four innings, good fielding was not a highlight of the match for either team as Troy managed to commit eight errors over the last five innings of the game.

The game had a few interesting plays by both teams with Steve King throwing out Leonard trying to score on a Spalding fly in the fourth, and Harry Schafer and Charlie Gould combining for a double play in the fifth inning. While the final score of 17-10 was bad enough, it could have been worse had it not been for Harry Wright's cleverly dropping Bub McAtee's fly in the ninth, enabling Schafer and Ross Barnes to force Doug Allison and Davy Force at third and second, respectively.[14] Force and McAtee were the Troy hitting stars while Spalding and George Wright were best among the Boston batters.[15]

The irony of the final result was that it came amidst swirling rumors that the Haymakers were headed for dissolution. The *Boston Times* for July 21 reported as follows: "It is reported that the match on Saturday will wind up the Haymakers as a club hailing from Troy, as they have not received any salary for some time. They intend to try the co-operative system for a while and should this project fail the club will dissolve…. The directors of this club should not act hastily in this matter, as they have as good material in this nine as any club in the country, and the only thing that is wanted is harmony and discipline, which their present captain has not the head-work to effect. Let the Trojans take pattern from the Boston and Athletic clubs, then they will have a nine which will be a credit to their city." The following day's *Boston Evening Journal* had different sources of intelligence, "The rumor that the Troy club were to be disbanded on their return home is without foundation. The members of the club deny the statement, and also claim that they have been paid up to the present time, while some of the members are in arrears to the stockholders." As it turns out, Troy's July 20 rout of the Red Stockings was its penultimate professional game of the year. Four days later, the team was dissolved.[16]

NOTES

1. "Boston and Vicinity—Base Ball-The Haymakers Defeat the Boston Club," *Boston Evening Journal*, July 22, 1872. The Brewsters, a group of the nine easternmost islands in Boston Harbor, were named for Elder William Brewster, Plymouth's first preacher and teacher, who along with Captain Myles Standish explored the harbor in 1621.

2. "Sporting Matters—-Base Ball- Boston vs. Troy," *Boston Daily Advertiser*, July 22, 1872.

3. "The Championship Record," *New York Clipper*, July 20, 1872.

4. "About Home Matters —-Base Ball," *Boston Times,"* July 21, 1872.

5. *Boston Herald*, July 22, 1872. The reference to "sad sea waves" may be to a song written by Jules Benedict in the mid-1800s and popularized by Jenny Lind, while the allusion to the Salt River may derive from the term's use in nineteenth century politics. Brewer's *Dictionary of Phrase and Fable* described that use as follows," A defeated political party is said to be rowed up Salt River, and those who attempt to uphold the party have the task of rowing up this ungracious stream." E. Cobham Brewster, *Dictionary of Phrase and Fable*, (Philadelphia: Claxton, Remsen and Haffelfinger, 1870). Sports writers and political writers were often one and the same.

6. *Boston Daily Advertiser*, July 22, 1872; *Boston Evening Journal*, July 22, 1872.

7   Boston, although it was playing at its home grounds, had lost the coin toss and batted first. Therefore, at the mid-point of the fifth inning, Boston had batted and had just scored its two runs but Troy had not yet come to bat in the bottom of the fifth and scored the five runs that made it 15-2 at the end of the fifth.

8   "The National Game," *Boston Herald*, July 22, 1872. The Haymakers were, of course, the visiting team and responsible for providing the game ball. The Haymakers were also a team with a reputation for favoring a lively ball. While the weight and circumference of the ball were set as of 1872 at five to five-and-a-quarter ounces and nine to nine-and-a-quarter inches, respectively, the amount of rubber in the ball was not so regulated. William J. Ryczek, *Blackguards and Red Stockings: A History of Baseball's National Association, 1871-1875*, (Jefferson, North Carolina, McFarland, 1992), 43-44. See also www.baseball-reference.com/bullpen/1871_Haymakers, but also see Jeffrey Laing, " *The Haymakers, Unions and Trojans of Troy, New York, Big-Time Baseball in the Collar City, 1860-1883*, (Jefferson, North Carolina, McFarland, 2015), 87 for a view that the team's reputation does not hold up to close scrutiny. Boston's alleged concern was not merely an academic issue. In a reasonably contemporaneous account of Boston's June 12, 1872 victory over Philadelphia, the *Brooklyn Daily Eagle* correspondent went to great lengths to explain the difference in game play when a lively ball was used rather than a dead ball. The piece is worth reading in its entirety but the most cogent sentence is probably that which follows: "A 'dead' or non-elastic ball forces the batsman to depend entirely on his judgment and skill in hitting the ball 'safely' in order to secure base hits, while a 'lively' or very elastic ball admits of the heavy muscular hitter sending it to the field so swiftly that ordinary hands cannot stop it." "Sports and Pastimes—-Base Ball," *Brooklyn Daily Eagle*, June 13, 1872.

9   *Boston Herald*, July 22, 1872.

10 *Boston Evening Journal*, July 22, 1872.

11 "Base Ball," *Boston Post*, July 22, 1872.

12 *Boston Herald*, July 22, 1872.

13 Ibid.

14 *Boston Daily Advertiser*, July 22, 1872.

15 *Boston Post*, July 22, 1872.

16 Laing, 90.

BOSTON OVERCOMES SEVEN-RUN DEFICIT TO WIN IN EXTRA INNINGS

July 29, 1872: Boston Red Stockings 17, Brooklyn Atlantics 12 (11 innings), at Capitoline Grounds

BY GREGORY H. WOLF

THE BOSTON RED STOCKINGS burst out of the gate in 1872, winning 22 of their first 23 games. After they lost their next two contests, including a 9-1 defeat at the hands of their arch-rival Athletics of Philadelphia, the declared champions of the National Association the previous season, the New England press was concerned. "The Boston Base Ball Club appears to be losing the laurels so easily won in the opening season," opined the *Lowell Daily Citizen and News*."[1] The *Boston Globe* suggested that the loss to the Athletics made the club "careful."[2] The doom and gloom about baseball in general extended to Philadelphia, where the *Inquirer* pronounced, "It is coming, slow, it is true, but surely nonetheless, the new national pastime, Base ball, has grown monotonous."[3]

On paper, the matchup between Boston and the Brooklyn Atlantics on Monday, July 29, 1872, looked like a laugher. The Red Stockings had beaten Brooklyn in their three previous meetings, outscoring them 49-13. The pride of the National Association, Boston had some of the league's most acclaimed players; 21-year-old pitcher Al Spalding had led the NA in wins in '71 (19), and had notched each of the 22 Boston victories thus far in '72. Second baseman Ross Barnes and shortstop George Wright, each of whom batted in excess of .400 in the inaugural season of the NA, were arguably the most feared hitters in the league. Brooklyn, in its maiden season in the NA, lost its first nine games, and had a record of 2-10. The Atlantics had been outscored 164-65. Other than player-manager Bob "Death to all Flying Things" Ferguson (who also served as president of the NA), the club consisted almost entirely of local young, green players with no previous professional experience. James Britt, the Atlantics' pitcher, was just 16 years old, en route to leading the league in losses (9-28). Brooklyn, however, was a proud club that traced its lineage to 1855. Named after Atlantic Avenue, a major thoroughfare in Brooklyn, the Atlantics were a charter member of the National Association of Base Ball Players in 1857 and were declared the NABBP champions in 1864 through 1866, and in 1869.

The game between the Red Stockings and Atlantics took place at the Capitoline Grounds, located in the Bedford neighborhood of Brooklyn. "Now that the prestige of invincibility has fallen from [Boston], there was little curiosity to see them, but the counter argument of a close game brought out a good attendance," opined the *New York Times*, which estimated that 1,000 spectators were there for the 3:35 starting time.[4] John Hatfield, player-manager of the Mutuals of New York, served as umpire. Boston won the coin toss, and chose to take the field first.

Brooklyn, playing its first game since July 8, got on the board first when Tom Barlow reached on first baseman Charlie Gould's error, stole second, and then scampered home on what the *Brooklyn Eagle* described as "wild throwing" by catcher Cal McVey and center fielder/manager Harry Wright.[5]

After Boston tied the score, "the Atlantic boys went in lively" in the second inning, scoring five runs.[6] The hitting barrage was led by England-born Al Thake, who smashed a "splendid" triple, and Herb Worth, who rapped a double.[7] By all accounts, this was Worth's only professional game and his only hit; he also scored a run. "This sort of playing astonished the Reds," mused the *Brooklyn Eagle*.[8] The Atlantics tacked on a run in the third to make the score 7-1.

"It looked as if the Boston boys were going to be beaten badly," wrote the *Eagle*, "and the enthusiasm of the spectators was very great."[9] Scoreless for three straight frames, Boston tallied two runs each in the fifth and sixth innings to make it 7-5. A wild pitch by Britt and a dropped ball by center fielder Jack Remsen contributed to Boston's scoring.

Just as it appeared that momentum had shifted to Boston, the Brooklyn youngsters pounded Spalding in the seventh for five more runs. "The Atlantic piled the ash vigorously," wrote the *Times* excitedly.[10] Thake "came to the rescue" by walloping another triple to give the Brooklyns what appeared to be an insurmountable 12-5 lead.[11] Thake's two three-baggers proved to be the only ones in his career; the 22-year-old outfielder died tragically about a month later, on September 1, in a drowning accident while fishing.

No lead was safe when playing Boston, which averaged 10.9 runs per game, tied with the Troy Haymakers (who ceased playing after their July 23 game) for second most in the league behind Philadelphia's 11.5.

The Red Stockings stormed back, scoring six runs in the seventh. Accounts of this game in Boston newspapers were very limited, probably because it was an out-of-town game; New York and Brooklyn papers provided primarily information about the Atlantics' scoring. In the bottom of the eighth, Ross Barnes, en route to leading the NA in hitting (.430) and slugging (.583), tied the game "by his wonderful base running."[12]

The game went into extra innings after a scoreless ninth. The *Brooklyn Eagle* reported that "it was getting dusky" after a scoreless 10th, but the teams decided to continue playing. Another option could have been to declare the game a tie; Boston had one tie in 1872; Brooklyn had none.

After Spalding tossed his fourth straight scoreless frame, Boston's McVey, who finished with a .431 batting average in 1871, runner-up to Philadelphia's Levi Myerle (.492), reached first base. Spalding lined to shortstop Jack Burdock, who caught McVey off base, but his throw to first was wild, enabling McVey to scamper to third. The next batter, Charlie Gould, hit to second baseman Edward Beavens, driving in McVey for the winning run, 13-12.

"There was little interest taken in the game after [McVey scored]," wrote the *Brooklyn Eagle*.[13] As the spectators filed out of the Capitoline Grounds, the game continued until Boston recorded three outs. Anticlimactic as it was, and though it would startle later generations of baseball fans, this was the way the game was played at the time. The Red Stockings tacked on four more runs to conclude the game in 2 hours and 50 minutes.[14] It was the longest game of the season for both clubs.

"The earnestness of the contest rendered it decidedly exciting," opined the *New York Times*.[15] Boston pounded out 24 hits, led by Barnes's six; Brooklyn tallied 17 safeties, paced by Bob Ferguson's four. Leadoff hitter George Wright led all players with four runs scored.

The game was not without some tense moments between the players and umpire. "Owing to the peculiar 'fair-foul' style of batting adopted by both sides, but chiefly by the Bostons, the umpire was called upon to make many close calls," noted the *Times*.[16] In all likelihood, the *Times* probably directed its comment to Ross Barnes, the undisputed master of the fair-four hit, a legal hit in all five seasons of the NA and the inaugural campaign of the National League in 1876. Unlike most practitioners of the fair-foul, the right-handed Barnes took a hard swing at the ball, chopping it in such a way that it would land in fair territory, bounce in front of the third baseman, and then roll into foul territory.

As exciting as the hitting was, the *New York Times* lamented the fielding, which it described as "the poorest of the season, the nines being equally bad."[17] Boston committed eight errors, well above its season average of 5.8; however Brooklyn's seven miscues were considerably better than its average of 9.7 per game. The *Times* reserved its harshest judgment for shortstop George Wright, whose fielding (three errors) it described as a "weak point."[18]

The two clubs met again later that week at Boston's South End Grounds, but the games were never in doubt. On August 2 the Red Stockings exploded for 12 runs in the second inning en route to an overpowering 26-3 victory. The following day, Boston scored three in the first and coasted to an 8-1 lead behind Spalding's six-hitter. Notwithstanding the press's concern with Boston in the wake of its two-game losing streak in late July, the Red Stockings finished the season with a 39-8 record to capture their first of four consecutive National Association championships.

NOTES

1 *Lowell* (Massachusetts) *Daily Citizen and News*, July 30, 1872: 2.
2 "Out-Door Sports," *Boston Globe*, July 30, 1872: 5.
3 *Philadelphia Inquirer*, July 30, 1872: 4.
4 "Base-Ball. Atlantic vs. Boston—The Latter Wins in Eleven Innings—Score 18-12," *New York Times*, July 30, 1872: 5. [Note: The score was 17-12; the *Times* misstated it in the headline.]
5 "Sports and Pastimes. Base Ball," *Brooklyn Eagle*, July 30, 1872: 3.
6 Ibid.
7 Ibid.
8 Ibid.
9 Ibid.
10 *New York Times*.
11 According to the *Brooklyn Eagle*, Thake had two triples; according to Retrosheet, he had only one.
12 *Brooklyn Eagle*.
13 Ibid.
14 According to the *Brooklyn Eagle* and the *New York Times*, the game lasted 2 hours and 55 minutes. Baseball-Reference and Retrosheet give the game time as five minutes shorter.
15 *New York Times*.
16 Ibid.
17 Ibid.
18 Ibid.

SEPTEMBER 20, 1872

Boston Red Stockings 11, New York Mutuals 4, at South Weymouth Park, South Weymouth, Massachusetts

BY GERARD R. GOULET

ONE DAY BEFORE THE FINAL GAME in the championship series between the Boston Red Stockings and the New York Mutuals, the two teams met on September 20, 1872, in a nonchampionship contest for a purse of $300 offered by the managers of the South Weymouth Park.[1] The game was one of several events presented in conjunction with the eighth annual agricultural fair of the Weymouth Agricultural and Industrial Society. While the judging of livestock, poultry, fruit, vegetables, bread, butter, and cheese was a staple of the fair and reported on extensively in the *Boston Post* of September 21, the principal feature of the first day of the two-day fair was the baseball game.[2] The two teams had last played on September 12 in a game the *New York Clipper* regarded as "one of the best played in fielding of the whole series between the two nines."[3] Fans came out in large numbers to see the Red Stockings, who stood atop the National Association standings with a record of 33-6, play an always tough opponent.

Although Boston had won six of the eight previous contests between the two clubs in this 1872 season, the games were generally closely contested, with five decided by two runs or less.[4] Accordingly, an exciting game was expected in South Weymouth. The teams were escorted to the grounds by the South Weymouth Brass Band, and after entertaining the fans with their warm-up exercises, they began play.[5]

Apart from the Boston half of the sixth inning, the game was an even match, with each team scoring four runs, but Boston's seven tallies in the sixth were the margin of victory. The Boston burst was a combination of heavy batting coupled with loose fielding on the part of Mutuals second baseman John Hatfield, shortstop Dickey Pearce, and third baseman Chick Fulmer, the latter having already made three errors in the contest.[6] The Mutuals did succeed in keeping the score down by catching Andy Leonard attempting to steal second in the first,[7] Ross Barnes attempting to score on a hit in the third,[8] and Cal McVey attempting to score in the eighth.[9] In the field, Boston's George Wright excelled at shortstop and Leonard was stellar in the outfield.

Three events were deemed unusual by those who reported on the game. In the early going, Barnes tried to run but called upon Charlie Gould to take his place when a sprain he suffered in a game against the Athletics six days before proved troublesome.[10] In the fourth Barnes struck out—a rarity for him.[11] In the sixth Pearce reached first on called balls[12] — a rare combination of wildness on the part of Spalding and umpire discretion on the part of Mr. Burdock of the Atlantics Club of New York.[13]

In the final analysis, the game meant nothing in the championship standings but was yet another example of the importance of the business side of baseball; the two clubs, relatively well assured of a good draw, were willing to ignore the strictures against playing exhibition games before their championship series had been completed in order to compete for a significant purse.[14]

NOTES

1 "Base Ball—Bostons vs. Mutuals," *Boston Globe*, September 21, 1872.

2 "Agricultural –The Weymouth Agricultural Fair—Base Ball—The Bostons Beat the Mutuals, Etc., Etc.," *Boston Post*, September 21, 1872.

3 "Boston vs. Mutual," *New York Clipper*, September 21, 1872. New York preferred playing exhibition games against top teams rather than championship games against lesser teams. Interestingly, their record in these exhibition games (4-8-1 in 1872) suggested

that the games were not played with the same zeal exhibited in their championship contests. William J. Ryczek, *Blackguards and Red Stockings: A History of Baseball's National Association, 1871-1875* (Jefferson, North Carolina: McFarland, 1992), 90, 92.

4   Ibid.

5   *Boston Globe,* September 21, 1872.

6   Ibid.

7   Ibid.

8   Ibid.

9   "Base Ball—Prize Game Between the Bostons and Mutuals—The Reds Victorious by a Score of 11 to 4," *Boston Herald,* September 21, 1872.

10 *Boston Globe,* September 21, 1872.

11 *Boston Herald,* September 21, 1872.

12 *Boston Globe,* September 21, 1872.

13 Jack Burdock played professional baseball from 1872 through 1888, and then three games in 1891. He was asked to umpire in 22 games during his time as a player.

14 See Ryczek, 57-58, for a discussion of the problem of exhibition games generally, and Ibid., 203, for corroboration of the fact that $300 was a meaningful purse for Harry Wright.

SEPTEMBER 21, 1872

Boston Red Stockings 11, New York Mutuals 10, at South End Grounds, Boston

BY MARK PESTANA

HEADING INTO THE FINAL 10 days of September 1872, the Boston Red Stockings had just experienced their first real turbulence of the season. A five-game road trip down the Atlantic Seaboard beginning September 7 had produced but one win, along with a tie and three losses. For a team that had suffered only three losses the entire year before that point, this was indeed a jarring turn of events.

Two of those recent road losses came at the hands of New York's Mutuals, who, though still trailing Boston and Baltimore, were not completely out of the pennant hunt. Anticipation was high when the Manhattanites visited Beantown on Saturday, September 21, for the ninth and final match between the two clubs for 1872—one that certainly proved a fitting climax to the seasonal series.

Pleasant weather greeted fans and players for the 3:20 P.M. start time at Boston's South End Grounds.[1] Jack Burdock, a 20-year-old rookie infielder with the Brooklyn Atlantics of the National Assocation, was the umpire. The first inning ended with the Bostons up 2-1, but the Mutuals broke out some fireworks for the second inning.

The bad news for Boston began with the bottom of the New York order rapping four straight safeties off Al Spalding. Among this quartet was Dickey Pearce, who at 36 was the second oldest player in the NA, behind Harry Wright. The wee (5-feet-3) shortstop had starred for the great Brooklyn Atlantics in the halcyon days of the 1860s and still had another five pro seasons ahead of him. Also included was pitcher Candy Cummings, pioneer of the curveball, who had been lured out of amateur status by the Mutes[2] after being courted by a number of clubs, and whose 1872 win total was exceeded only by Spalding's.

The top of the order came around now, led by Dave Eggler, one of the finest-fielding outfielders of his day and, at least in the five seasons the NA lasted, a .322 hitter. Eggler skied one to short left field that George Wright was able to snare. A nice opportunity for a double play was missed, however, as Wright's peg to Charlie Gould at first base, though ahead of the returning runner, was too wide of the base for Gould to make the putout.

Boston's fielding jitters continued. After the next batters, John Hatfield and Joe Start, reached base, George Bechtel flied to right fielder Fraley Rogers for what should have been one out and maybe more. But Rogers was "so eager to return the ball after the catch"[3] that he dropped it entirely, and everyone was safe.

Nat Hicks followed Bechtel with a single to center and here the Bostons got their fielding act together as the ball went from Harry Wright in center to brother George at short to Cal McVey at home in time to cut down the runner at the plate.

Two were out but the Mutes weren't quite done. Pearce stepped in for the second time in the inning and waited Spalding out for a base on balls. He scored when McMullin collected his second base hit of the inning. Cummings' foul-tip out stranded McMullin but the New Yorkers had pushed eight runs across and were in the van, 9-2.

For the next three innings, Spalding and Cummings kept opposing bats quiet, the fielding sharpened up, and goose eggs went up for both clubs until the sixth. Ross Barnes led off the sixth with one of his specialty fair-foul hits, this one going for two bases. An error by Chick Fulmer at third base, a base on balls to Spalding, and a base hit by Harry Schafer produced two Reds runs. Both teams added a run in the seventh and the score favored New York, 10-5, as Boston went to bat in the eighth.

Spalding, probably the best hitting pitcher of his day,[4] led off with a double to left and came home one out later on Schafer's single. At this point, a nasty scene ensued involving umpire Burdock. The Boston and New York papers would both later complain of unfair treatment, and the *Daily Advertiser* went so far as to say Burdock was "unusually strict" and "rather severe."[5]

The boiling point was reached during the at-bat of Boston right fielder Fraley Rogers, who followed Schafer to the plate.

Two rapidly called strikes on Rogers evinced "shouts of derision, hisses and cries of 'put him out'… from the excited crowd."[6] Two pitches later, strike three was called on a ball that, according to the *Journal*, "was not over the home plate, and if anything should have been called 'a ball.'" This brought a "perfect uproar of disapproval" from the South End faithful, and play was suspended for about five minutes until calm returned.[7]

Jack Burdock, a 20-year-old second baseman for the Brooklyn Atlantics, umpired the contest and faced a "perfect uproar of disapproval" from the Boston crowd. (Spalding Collection)

The harsh reaction apparently rattled Burdock; the *Journal* said he was "not self-possessed" for the rest of the game.

But the Reds got right back to business, with the Wright Brothers due up next. After Harry took a base on balls, Fulmer made his second costly error, muffing George's hit and allowing Schafer to notch the seventh run for the home team.

The Mutuals got nothing in their half, but, leading 10-7, still appeared in good position to hand the Red Stockings a third consecutive loss for the first time in 1872.

The Boston ninth began auspiciously with a double by Andy Leonard, then singles by McVey and Spalding, the latter scoring Leonard. Gould's grounder to Fulmer forced McVey at third, but Schafer came through again, driving a double into left that chased Spalding home.

Now needing but one run to pull even, the Reds saw their hopes sink a little as center fielder Dave Eggler made a nice catch of a fly off Rogers' bat for out number two. Captain Wright was the last chance, and when he took two called strikes, things looked dim. Harry let two more pitches go by, then saw one to his liking, and sent it "way down between centre and right fields." Gould and Schafer made it home with the tying and go-ahead runs. The crowd, "mad with delight,"[8] caused another brief suspension of play, after which the younger Wright flied out to end Boston's half.

Ironically, both reporting Boston papers (the *Journal* and the *Daily Advertiser*) indicated that the fourth of Cummings' pitches to Harry Wright could just as easily have been called the other way.

According to the *Advertiser*, the pitch "appeared to be just right, and had the umpire dealt as strictly with Harry as with Leonard and Rogers, the last chance would have been gone." The *Journal* said simply that it "should really have been 'three strikes.'"[9]

Spalding blanked the Mutes in the bottom of the ninth, and the Red Stockings, thanks to a surge of strong and timely hitting in the final four innings, came away with the 11-10 victory. Perhaps an umpire's desire to give a "make-up call" played a factor as well.

Referring to the Boston-New York season series, the *New York Times* rhapsodized over "the best series of games ever played between professional clubs, every contest having been stubbornly fought from beginning to end."[10] True, they were generally good contests, with several scores of the 4-2, 3-2 variety. But in the end there was no question as to the superior nine: The Red Stockings took seven of the nine contests, never allowing the Mutuals—or any other contenders—to make any serious gains on them. Despite the ugly September road trip, and their close shave with the Mutes, Harry Wright's boys were back on track and in another month would deliver Boston its first baseball championship.

NOTES

1. *Boston Daily Globe*, September 23, 1872: 5.
2. The nickname "Mutes" for "Mutuals" appears in both the *Boston Journal* and *Boston Daily Advertiser* of September 23, 1872.
3. *Boston Daily Advertiser*, September 23, 1872: 1.
4. A career .313 hitter, Spalding batted .354 in 1872.
5. *Boston Daily Advertiser*, September 23, 1872; *New York Times*, September 22, 1872.
6. *Boston Journal*, September 23, 1872: 2.
7. Ibid.
8. *Boston Daily Advertiser*, September 23, 1872: 1.
9. Also somewhat ironically, Jack Burdock eventually earned his fame playing for the National League Boston club from 1878 to 1888, the stalwart second baseman of their pennant-winning teams in 1878 and 1883.
10. *New York Times*, September 22, 1872: 8.

APRIL 23, 1873

Red Stockings get Whites-washed

Philadelphia Whites 8, Boston Red Stockings 5, at South End Grounds, Boston, Mass.

BY MATT ALBERTSON

THE BOSTON RED STOCKINGS won the 1872 National Association championship with a record of 39-8 and finished 7½ games ahead of the second-place Baltimore Canaries and Philadelphia Athletics. Boston fans had reason to believe that Harry Wright would lead the Red Stockings to yet another title in 1873 as the addition of Deacon White bolstered both the team's offense and defense. The club included some of baseball's best players, who were in the prime of their careers—Deacon White was 25 years old, George Wright was 26, and Al Spalding was 22. The Red Stockings simply outclassed their competition in 1872 so Boston fans assumed that the improved Red Stockings would again win in 1873.

The Philadelphia White Stockings[1] were one of the National Association's new teams for the 1873 season. "The White Stockings were by far the most imposing of the NA's three new teams for 1873, because ... [they] built [an] excellent team by raiding their Philadelphia brethren."[2] Levi Meyerle, Ned Cuthbert, Fergy Malone, Denny Mack, and Fred Treacey exchanged their blue stockings for white in 1873. Pitching star George Zettlein signed with the White Stockings as well and gave the new club credibility. Philadelphians now had a team that they thought could compete with the Red Stockings, as the Athletics had in 1871.

The two clubs met for the first time on April 23, 1873, in front of 2,000 fans at Boston's South End Grounds. It was Boston's first game of the season and Philadelphia's second, the latter's first game a decisive victory over their intracity rival the Philadelphia Athletics on April 21. In Boston, Philadelphia won the coin toss and chose to hit last. The game was called at 3:10 P.M. when Zettlein's first pitch was offered to Boston's George Wright, who was promptly put out by Denny Mack. Ross Barnes drew a walk and Harry Schafer sent a fly to Fred Treacey (Tracy) who muffed the ball. Boston's early attack ended as Zettlein induced two fly balls, stranding the two Boston baserunners. In the bottom of the first inning, Ned Cuthbert sent the ball to center field, where Harry Wright had difficulty fielding the ball, and Cuthbert reached second base. Bob Addy hit a fair-foul ball[3] and was thrown out at first while Cuthbert advanced. Cuthbert eventually scored and Philadelphia led 1-0 at the end of the first inning.

The Whites kept the champion Red Stockings' offense in check through five innings with good pitching and defense and continued to pressure offensively. Boston's offense sputtered in the second with only one baserunner and the Red Stockings were retired in order in the third. In the fourth, Boston's Deacon White earned a base hit and advanced to second base on Spalding's single. With two on and one out, Boston's Harry Wright and Jack Manning were retired, ending the threat. Conversely, Philadelphia batters earned bases regularly with hits and walks.

Philadelphia continued what the *Boston Herald* called its "good execution" and scored three more runs in the fifth inning.[4] Denny Mack led off the inning with a base hit and stole second base. Zettlein flied out and Cuthbert earned first on a throwing error by Harry Schafer. What happened next is not clear. The *Boston Globe* reported that "White threw to second to cut off Cuthbert, and Mack and Cuthbert came in. Addy made a safe hit past second. ..."[5] Addy scored on a safe hit by Meyerle. However, the *New York Clipper* and *Boston Herald* wrote that after Addy's hit, Malone was thrown out at first, "Mack in the meantime coming home."6 Levi Meyerle singled, scoring Addy. Jim Devlin doubled and advanced Meyerle to third. The inning closed when George Bechtel flied out. Based on the batting order, the *Boston Globe* correctly interpreted the scoring plays while the *Herald* and *Clipper* didn't comment on Cuthbert scoring and instead misattributed an RBI to Jim Devlin. Regardless, Philadelphia scored three runs in the inning, increasing its lead to 4-0.

Boston's offense woke up in the seventh inning. Al Spalding opened the inning by reaching on an errant throw by Levi Meyerle and advanced to third on a double by Harry Wright. Jack Manning sent a dribbler between shortstop and third base that scored Spalding. With two men on base, Malone tried to throw Manning out at second but overthrew Bob Addy and Harry Wright came in to score. After Birdsall singled to left field, George Wright flied out to Jim Devlin and Manning raced home while Birdsall advanced to third. Boston's Ross Barnes singled on a groundball between first and second, scoring Birdsall and tying the game, 4-4.

With the game still tied in the ninth inning, Al Spalding hit a fair-foul ball and reached first safely After Harry Wright walked, Manning struck out but reached first when Philadelphia's Fergy Malone dropped the called third strike. Malone recovered and put Spalding out at third. Boston took its first lead of the game when Birdsall scored Harry Wright on a base hit. George Wright nearly increased the Boston lead to 6-4 when he hit the ball to third. Manning attempted to score but was put out at the plate. The inning concluded with Boston leading the Whites 5-4.

Philadelphia continued its aggressive offensive play in the ninth. Denny Mack reached first on a botched play by Harry Schafer and stole second on a poor throw by White. George Zettlein advanced Mack to third base on a base hit. Ned Cuthbert scored Mack and advanced to second base on a grounder by Bob Addy. Fergy Malone hit a single past George Wright that scored Zettlein and Cuthbert. Philadelphia continued its outburst as Levi Meyerle singled and drove in Fergy Malone. George Bachtel grounded out to end the inning and the game. Philadelphia scored four runs in the inning and won the game 8-5, ruining Boston's home opener.

Boston played the White Stockings eight more times in 1873. The teams fought for possession of first place throughout the season but Boston had trouble keeping pace with the Whites in the first half of the season. Philadelphia won 10 straight games between May 20 and June 14, including a 22-8 drubbing of the Red Stockings on June 5. Boston ended Philadelphia's streak on June 17 with an 11-6 victory in Boston but trailed the Whites by 3½ games in the standings. The Red Stockings fell even further behind when Philadelphia brushed off the loss and went on another 10-game winning streak between June 19 and July 10, defeating Boston 18-17 on July 10, and led the Red Stockings by eight games. Philadelphia was 27-3 while Boston had a 16-8 record.

It was typical for teams in this era to play few league games during July and August in favor of playing exhibitions and resting for the second half of the season. Between July 10 and August 30, Boston played nine league games, which helped it stay within reach of Philadelphia. "That's not what happened in 1873, when the White Stockings, possibly starting what would be a tradition for millions of twentieth century Philadelphians, spent almost three weeks 'Down the Shore,'" wrote baseball historian John Shiffert.7 The team did not play in any type of baseball game during those three weeks as the players celebrated their exquisite play while on vacation in Cape May, New Jersey.

When the Whites returned to resume their season in late July, the dutiful Red Stockings drubbed them, 23-10, on July 30 The Red Stockings were red-hot in August and September. After the July 30 contest, Boston won 14 games and lost 2. (They played one tie.)8 As the season wound down, Boston continued its hot streak while Philadelphia dropped crucial contests to Baltimore and the terrible Washington Nationals. The Whites blew an eight-game lead in 18 games and Boston all but sealed the pennant on October 2 when it punished the Whites, 18-7. The White Stockings lost 14 of their last 23 games, while the Red Stockings were 24-2 from the August 19 loss to the Whites until two meaningless losses to Athletic in the last two games of the year.[9] Boston was once again crowned champion of the National Association.

NOTES

1. Also known as the Whites, Philadelphias, and Phillies. See John Shiffert, *Base Ball in Philadelphia: A History of the Early Game, 1831-1900* (Jefferson, North Carolina: McFarland & Company, Inc., 2006), 77.
2. Ibid.
3. A ball that is bunted in fair territory but rolls/bounces into foul territory. These were counted as fair until 1877.
4. "The Bostons Beaten," *Boston Herald,* April 24, 1873.
5. "Out-Door Sports: Baseball: Bostons vs. Philadelphias," *Boston Globe,* April 24, 1873.
6. "Philadelphia vs. Boston," *New York Clipper,* May 3, 1873.
7. Shiffert, 78.
8. Ibid.
9. Shiffert, 80.

JUNE 2, 1873
Boston Red Stockings 5, Brooklyn Atlantics 0, at the Union Grounds, Brooklyn

BY TERRY GOTTSCHALL

THE RED STOCKINGS STARTED A 10-game road trip in early June with their first stop in Brooklyn to play the Atlantics. Boston had a 4-3 record, good for fourth place, four games behind the Philadelphia White. Brooklyn was 3-4 in fifth place, five games back. The two teams had split a two-game series in May with Boston winning the first game, 8-2, and losing the second, 11-10.

The teams played at the Union Grounds, baseball's first enclosed grounds, constructed by William Cammeyer and opened in 1862.

Al Spalding pitched for the Red Stockings with 17-year-old Jim Britt pitching for Brooklyn.

The *Boston Herald* noted that a large crowd of approximately 2,000 fans attended the game with the betting favoring Boston with odds at 6-1.[1]

The sporting crowd had correct odds as Boston easily shut out the Atlantics, 5-0. The *Brooklyn Eagle* noted, "The Brooklyn nine were, for the first time this season outfielded and outbatted." Meanwhile, "The play of the Bostons was excellent"; the reporter commended the "noteworthy" defensive play of catcher Deacon White (seven putouts, one assist) and left fielder Andy Leonard (three putouts, outfield assist, no errors).[2]

Spalding gave up just five hits. The *Boston Herald* noted, "The Atlantics worked like beavers to score a run, but all to no purpose, Spaulding's *[sic]* pitching being decidedly too much for them, backed up as it was by the sharpest kind of fielding."[3]

Boston scored its five runs against Britt on 10 hits. The Atlantics also committed 14 errors, with one writer particularly citing the poor defensive play of third baseman Bob Ferguson: "The weak point of the Brooklyn nine was at third base, in which position many of the most important errors of the season by the nine have been committed."[4]

The game also produced a controversy that perhaps reflected baseball's recent transition from pre-professional days when original rules, as envisioned by Henry Chadwick, required "gentlemanly" conduct.

The controversy occurred in the top of the second inning with Boston at bat. The Red Stockings had loaded the bases with no outs in part because of errors by Ferguson. With Jim O'Rourke at bat, catcher Tom Barlow deliberately dropped the third strike. He picked up the ball, touched home plate to force out runner Deacon White coming in from third, and then threw out O'Rourke at first. First baseman Herman Dehlman then threw to shortstop Dickey Pearce and Pearce threw to second baseman Jack Burdock, "who ran Manning out" in a rundown to complete the triple play.[5]

Umpire Theo Bomeisler disallowed the triple play, ruling O'Rourke out on strikes, calling Manning out on the basepaths for attempting to advance, and sending White back to third. Harry Wright then flied out to end the inning. Reporters described the umpire's decision as "an error of judgment" but noted that it did not affect the score.[6]

The controversy continued when team captain Ferguson confronted umpire Bomeisler. Ferguson had already complained about an "objectionable decision" in the bottom of the first when Bomeisler called an Atlantic runner out at second. Ferguson complained that second baseman Ross Barnes had missed the tag on a throw from catcher White.

According to the *Eagle*, Ferguson "came from the field [and] began to abuse the umpire for his decision [negating the triple play], and to question the integrity of his action." Bomeisler promptly "retired from the field," refusing to continue as umpire.

The article described Ferguson's actions as "insulting" and inappropriate. Ferguson, as captain, had a responsibility to "set his men a proper example in deportment and particularly in curbing an unruly temper." Since Ferguson was also president of the National Association of Base Ball Players, his job was also to "not only see that the rules of the game are strictly enforced, but especially is it requisite that he himself should obey them."[7]

After a brief delay, the Atlantics persuaded Dick Higham, an outfielder for the New York Mutuals, to come out of the stands and umpire the rest of the game.[8]

The victory was Spalding's only shutout in 1873, when he pitched in 60 games, starting 54, and ending the season with a 41-14 record.

Brooklyn pitcher Britt, on the other hand, retired after the season with a two-year record of 26-64.

NOTES

1 "Base Ball," *Boston Herald*, June 3, 1873: 2.
2 "Base Ball," *Brooklyn Daily Eagle*, June 3, 1873: 3.
3 *Boston Herald*.
4 *Brooklyn Daily Eagle*.
5 "The National Game," *New York Herald*, June 3, 1873: 4.
6 Ibid.
7 Ibid.
8 With almost poetic irony, the National League banned Higham (who had ended his playing days with the Troy Trojans in 1880) from baseball in 1882 for fixing games as an umpire.

JUNE 3, 1873

Boston Red Stockings 6, New York Mutuals 5, at Union Grounds, Brooklyn

BY MARK PESTANA

THE CHAMPS OF 1872 GOT OFF TO a slow start in 1873. Matches were few and far between in the early going: Up to their hosting New York's Mutuals in back-to-back meetings May 30 and 31, they had played only five games. By that point, the Baltimore Canaries had already seen 17 contests, the new White Stockings of Philadelphia, 13. Only the Marylands (also of Baltimore) had played fewer games: three—which turned out to be half of that franchise's entire major-league total.

But with the two-game Mutual series, things began heating up for Boston, with 14 games scheduled over 19 days—three of those 19 being Sundays, on which no ball could be played anyway. The teams split their end-of-May miniseries, New York getting the better of a close 6-4 contest, and then Boston coming back strong with a 16-9 triumph on the 31st.

After seven games at home to open the season, Harry Wright's Red Stockings traveled to New York to begin a two-week road trip that would see them visiting all their NA opponents save the Athletics and Marylands. A masterful shutout by Al Spalding against Brooklyn on June 2 put the Reds' record at 5-3 as they prepared to face the Mutuals the next day.

The Mutes were struggling, having managed only two victories in 11 decisions. Six times they had allowed their opponents 11 or more runs. On the heels of a 7-6 loss to Baltimore on May 27—their fourth defeat by that club in the season's opening month—the *New York Clipper* posed the question, "What is the matter with the Mutuals?" While noting that the club "began the season with a nine apparently equal to the best," and citing the additions of Phonney Martin and Steve Bellan as strengthening factors, the *Clipper* bemoaned "the entire neglect of those rules so necessary to insure clear judgement, keen sight, steady nerves, and full powers of endurance," asserting that the players "take not the slightest care of themselves as regards steady attention to sanitary rules"—a veiled allusion, presumably, to overindulgence in liquor and general carousing. Less than 500 New York fans turned out for the May 27 match. There was even a rumor afloat that the club might be reorganized "under the old amateur rule."[1]

Certainly the team did not want for on-field talent. In Bobby Mathews, their number-one starter, and recent acquisition Martin, the Mutuals possessed two early proponents of curveball pitching. Martin would be out of the majors after 1873, but Mathews, only 21, had another dozen seasons ahead of him, eventually compiling just a shade under 300 victories. Batterymate Nat Hicks, renowned for his durability behind the bat, had caught Candy Cummings a few years earlier with the amateur Brooklyn Stars, and made a perfect receiver for Mathews' curving tosses.

Center fielder Dave Eggler and left fielder Count Gedney both ranked high among NA outfielders defensively. Eggler had topped the circuit in outfield chances, assists, putouts, and fielding percentage in 1872. And then there was "Old Reliable" Joe Start at first base, who had been in organized ball since 1860 and would play in the big leagues until 1886, finally retiring at age 43. Player-manager John Hatfield split his time between second base and third and was one of five .300 batters on the team.

The Union Grounds in Brooklyn, opened as the first enclosed ball field by William Cammeyer in 1862, housed Brooklyn's Eckfords and Atlantics in their NA years and also served as home field for the Mutuals for all five years of their NA existence. It was there that the New York and Boston clubs met on Tuesday, June 3.

The Red Stockings went quickly three up, three down in the top of the first, and the first two New York batters followed suit in the bottom half. But Hatfield laced a Spalding pitch down into right field for a triple and then scored on Start's single. The *Clipper* made note of the "rather elastic ball," and duly pointed out that it had been "legally furnished" by Harry Wright.[2]

Both teams were blanked in the second inning, and Boston again in their third, but Bellan led off the Mutuals' third with a base hit and Hatfield, the sudden slugger, followed with a home run, giving New York a 3-0 advantage.

The Reds made up some ground in the fourth, two base hits being abetted by errors on the part of Hatfield and Hicks and resulting in two runs. The Mutes, in their half, made it a 4-2 game when Jim Holdsworth stroked a triple and was sent home on Eggler's safe hit.

The Red Stockings could manage only one base hit in the fifth, but that, in conjunction with errors by Eggler, Start, and Hicks, produced two unearned runs and tied the score at 4-4.

Manager Hatfield, perhaps for the benefit of Hicks, who was laboring with a broken forefinger, called Phonney Martin in from right field to relieve Mathews in the seventh inning, Mathews moving to right. Both teams added single runs in the seventh, thanks to errors. Eggler uncharacteristically made a second costly muff to the Mutuals' detriment, and George Wright was the culprit on the Beantown side.

Spalding and Martin kept opposing bats in check for the next two innings, and at the end of the ninth the clubs were knotted at 5-5. The 10th and 11th innings were whitewashes for both sides as well. Rowdy factions in the home crowd, meanwhile, expressed themselves "in anything but a manner creditable to the assemblage," according to the *Clipper*, booing Red Stocking attempts at fair-foul hits and targeting the ever-respectable Harry Wright in particular.[3]

Finally, in the top of the 12th, the deadlock was broken. Leadoff batter George Wright made a successful fair-foul hit and reached third on a bad pitch by Mathews, who had just returned to the box. Ross Barnes then bounced a hit to center, driving in Wright with the go-ahead Boston run.

The Mutes immediately mounted a counterattack. Holdsworth led with a double and Eggler reached on another error by George Wright. When Bellan was given first on called balls, the bases were loaded with no outs, and the New Yorkers appeared in good shape for a come-from-behind win. Hatfield, with a hot hand, was up next, and he shot a grounder to shortstop. This time Wright was up to the task, delivering the ball to catcher Deacon White in time to nip Holdsworth at the plate.

The bases were still full, with just one hand out. Hatfield took an extra-long lead off first, attempting to draw a throw and maybe make something happen, but the Reds wouldn't bite. Start was retired on a foul pop to catcher White for the second out, and Phonney Martin was the last hope for the home team. Though he hit a good one to Barnes, the ball got to first baseman Jack Manning before Martin got there, and the threat was over.

In a most exciting contest, Boston had escaped with a razor-thin victory. None of the Red Stockings' six runs were earned, though the error totals for the game were not unusually high for the era. Echoing the *Clipper's* concerns, the *Sunday Mercury* saw "lack of nerve" on the Mutuals' part and "coolness and judgement" on the Red Stockings' part as the key factors deciding the outcome.[4]

NOTES

1 *New York Clipper*, June 7, 1873.
2 *New York Clipper*, June 14, 1873.
3 Ibid.
4 *New York Sunday Mercury*, June 8, 1873.

RED STOCKINGS SHUT OUT IN BOSTON

June 14, 1873: Philadelphia Athletics 3, Boston Red Stockings 0, at the South End Grounds, Boston

BY RICHARD "DIXIE" TOURANGEAU

ACE HURLER JOHN DICKSON McBride stood in the pitcher's box in the unseasonably brisk June wind. He was again flirting with a grand accomplishment as he had twice the previous year, 1872. But this time things were a bit different; he was not at his home ballpark at 125th and Jefferson Streets in North Philadelphia. "Dick" was at rival Boston's South End Grounds, 45 feet from the powerful champs, whom he had efficiently stifled all day. It was Boston's eighth inning. They had two earlier paltry hits, by Ross Barnes and Jack Manning, and the Athletics clung to a 3-0 edge.

The year before, on July 27, 1872, McBride led 4-0 in the eighth thanks mainly to his own batting, when Fraley Rogers' second base hit scored Philly native son Harry Schafer, but the Athletics cruised 9-1. In the Athletics' final game that year, on October 7, which happened to be versus Boston, McBride led 1-0 in the eighth. Right fielder Al Reach threw out George Wright at the plate to maintain the shutout. Then 20 minutes of rain fell, leaving pools of mud and water under a dark sky. Umpire Scott Hastings (Baltimore Canaries) ruled the game should continue, as Boston had requested. With two out in the ninth a controversial base on balls was given to Barnes, a notorious "waiter" on pitches. After a passed ball moved Barnes to second, Andy Leonard followed with a clean safety and Levi Meyerle's throw home could not prevent Boston from scoring its only tally in a 5-1 loss. Twice McBride had a "chicago" (the term for shutout in those days) within his grasp versus Harry Wright's Run Machine and both times they narrowly escaped.

But those outcomes occurred on McBride's turf; he was now in the enemy's ballyard.

The pure numbers were simple and ugly for South End visitors to face. To that point in 1873, the Reds had scored an average of 11.4 runs in 96 games over two-plus National Association seasons. They touched the plate about 12 times on average in 45 home games. There had never been a game, in the Boston team's three seasons to date, in which they had failed to score.

In 13 total NA games with the near equally talented Athletics, Boston "only" scored 9.7 runs per game, but at the South End Grounds they were 6-0, averaging 13 runs off McBride. The Athletics veteran had shut out the strong Mutual bats in 1872 and again a month before this mid-June Boston game. Opposing pitchers Candy Cummings (Mutuals) and Al Spalding (Boston, end of season, two days before that 5-1 loss in Philly) each had whitewashed the Athletics in 1872, but the Red Stockings remained un-chicagoed. Not only was all this history blowing competitive-charged memories in the June gusts, but on that afternoon first-place Boston was 12-5 while Philly was 10-4. In 1872 Harry Wright's club had taken the NA championship from 1871 winner Philadelphia, and were now the defending champs. This was a grudge match on many levels.

Timely hitting by Wes Fisler, Bill "Cherokee" Fisher, and Ezra Sutton combined with two Boston errors plated two runs in the second inning and another in the seventh for the Athletics. Throughout the game, respected ump Theodore Bomeisler (Newark, New Jersey) tended to business as rain clouds threatened and temperatures fell to April-like degrees. It was then, or maybe never, for McBride, and he managed craftily to dispatch the Red Stockings batters in order in both the eighth and ninth innings for the unthinkable 3-0 victory, completed in 100 minutes in front of "a great number of spectators" (*Boston Courier*). The *Courier* also commented that it was "the worst defeat, which the present champions have ever experienced."

With no Sunday issue the *Boston Daily Advertiser* said on Monday, "The Bostons met a Waterloo on Saturday, playing the first game since their existence as an organization in which they failed to score. … There were about 2,000 persons on the grounds in spite of the cold weather and disagreeable high winds." The *Boston Herald* also had Monday words: "At last we have something 'new under the sun' to record for the Boston club in the shape of a large-sized cipher as the result of a full game." The weather was described as "extremely raw and cold" with "a high wind which interfered seriously with hard hit balls by deadening their force and causing them to fall easy victims for the outfielders." The *Boston Globe*'s Monday account echoed the competition: "The Bostons have again been unfortunate, and more unfortunate than ever before." On the weather, "The afternoon was very unfavorable to players and spectators, the air being cold and raw and the wind disagreeably high."

Dick McBride was a pioneer of early Philadelphia ball teams, first notable in 1863 with the amateur Athletics guided by Hicks Hayhurst. Though the Red Stockings eventually took the 1873 banner with a 43-16-1 record to fourth-place Philly's 28-23-1 mark, the exciting battles between these foes were the best the Association had to offer. McBride actually took that season's series five wins to four despite losing 7-6 and 8-7 in Boston. In their October 6 thriller (which ended the Athletics' campaign), he bested Spalding 12-11 in eight innings at the South End Grounds, a contest involving true "gamesmanship" by McBride. Late in the game he threw to first base several times as the sun started to set. Philly wanted the game called while they led. In the ninth inning they scored four more runs but Boston rallied in the home half and plated a run and had other runners on base when umpire Nick Young called a halt to the action at 5:10 P.M., much to the dismay of the howling crowd. But the next day Boston newspapers said it was the proper thing to do because it was just too hard to see the ball by then. The score at the end of the eighth inning prevailed.

At 125th and Jefferson in 1873, McBride won 5-4, 5-4, and 10-6 but dropped a 10-4 decision. Over the course of the five NA seasons, McBride held the Stockings to five or fewer runs a record 13 times.

SOURCES

Boston Daily Advertiser, Boston Globe, Boston Herald, and *Boston Post* of June 15 and 16, 1873.

New York Clipper, June 21, 1873.

A NOT SO GLORIOUS FOURTH

July 4, 1873 (morning): Elizabeth Resolutes 11, Boston Red Stockings 2, at South End Grounds, Boston

BY JOHN ZINN

AFTER A WIN ON JUNE 17 OVER THE Philadelphia White Stockings, Harry Wright and his Boston club had a lot of time to mull over their progress, or lack thereof, in the 1873 championship season. It would be almost two weeks before the Red Stockings were scheduled for their next championship match, a June 30 contest against the New York Mutuals. Boston's record thus far in 1873 was 13-6, which left them in third place, 3½ games behind the White Stockings, a situation not exactly meeting the expectations of the team and its fans. Not surprisingly, the players used part of their respite from championship play to take out their frustrations on a series of local clubs, beginning with a 64-6 pounding of the Lowell team. Boston even gave two other opponents five outs per inning, but it made little difference as the Red Stockings thrashed Chelsea of Massachusetts and the Olympics of Providence, Rhode Island, by scores of 36-5 and 39-6.[1]

However, neither the easy victories nor a convincing 17-6 defeat of the Mutuals could completely drive away all of the storm clouds on Harry Wright's horizon as he contemplated three early July games with the woeful Elizabeth Resolutes. Although the 1-14 New Jersey club didn't appear to pose much of a challenge on the field, the Boston leader was doubtless concerned that the gap between his club's third-place position and that of first-place Philadelphia was now at six games. Wright's worries were not limited solely to the club's performance on the field; its 1872 championship season had been a financial disaster. By the end of that season the club was over $5,000 in debt (including a balance due on players' salaries), and it took an infusion of new capital to ensure that the Red Stockings would even take the field in 1873.[2]

Attention to the club's finances was therefore a mandatory part of Wright's job and he had no illusions about the Resolutes' potential drawing power. On a recently concluded "Southern trip," Boston's share of the gate receipts for two matches with the Resolutes, including one played at Brooklyn's Union Grounds, was a paltry $124.67, less than one day's receipts with more competitive opponents.[3] To make matters worse, the three coming matches were scheduled around July 4, a major holiday in the Boston area. Independence Day itself was of special concern because of multiple competing activities, including a rowing competition in the morning, a patriotic concert, and a sailing regatta scheduled for 2:30 in the afternoon.[4] Trying to make the best of a bad situation, Wright decided to offer Bostonians two opportunities to watch base ball on a day when few people would be working, thereby creating the first professional doubleheader.[5] But the games would carry separate admission charges, based on the perhaps questionable premise that anyone would pay twice in one day to see the Resolutes.

Having to play the Resolutes in the first place was due to the National Association's dubious practice of accepting any club willing and able to pay the $10 annual admission fee. As a cooperative club dependent on gate receipts to fund players' salaries, Elizabeth had little financial wherewithal to upgrade its 1873 amateur roster beyond adding the Allison brothers, Doug and Art. Both had reputations as "hard-core complainers," which put them in good company with another Resolute brother combination, Hugh and Michael Campbell, also "renowned grumblers."[6] All of this negativity may have led the Red Stockings and their fans to overlook another fact about the Campbells. Only seven years earlier, the two had been part of one of the biggest upsets of the pre-professional period, the Irvington Club's 1866 victory over the defending champion Brooklyn Atlantics.

If those in attendance for the 10:00 A.M. first pitch thought the early start might beat the heat, they were quickly disabused of that notion; the *Boston Daily Globe* reported intense heat even in the morning. The *Boston Daily Advertiser* and the *Boston Evening Journal* agreed about the heat, but not about the crowd. The *Advertiser* reported a large crowd while the *Journal* wrote that attendance was kept down by the oppressive weather. The *Advertiser* also accused the Boston club of playing a "second-class nine," but the only change appears to have been a game off for star shortstop George Wright, allowing old Cincinnati Red Stockings luminary Charles Sweasy to play his only game for the Boston version of the Red Stockings.[7] Not surprisingly, Boston's ace pitcher, Albert Spalding, kept the Resolutes off the scoreboard in the first two innings, but the home team didn't fare much better against Hugh Campbell, managing only single runs in their first and second at-bats.

When the Resolutes came up in the third, they surprised everyone, perhaps most of all themselves, by erupting for five runs and a 5-2 lead. The visitors from New Jersey were by no means finished, scoring six more times over the last four innings. No play-by-play accounts survive, but six Resolutes had at least two hits which, combined with five Boston errors, helped build a balanced attack. Leading the Resolutes hit parade were Henry Austin (.248 batting average), Frank Fleet (.258), Art Allison (.320), and Mike Campbell (.143). These averages paled in comparison with the Red Stockings, who featured one .400 hitter and five others over .300; in fact, Boston had a team batting average of .340. All of which made Hugh Campbell's pitching performance even more remarkable as he shut Boston out the rest of the way, aided by a defense that made only two errors behind him.[8]

As they walked off the field after the last Boston batter was retired, no one could blame the Campbell brothers if they took special satisfaction in adding a second major upset to their playing record. Then, as now, the media was quick to rub in the ignominious defeat; the *Daily Advertiser* hoped the Boston club now understood "that every game of base ball is liable to be hard to win." It was rubbing salt in Harry Wright's wounds as he endured not only the apparently meager gate receipts, but also another missed opportunity to gain ground on Philadelphia.[9]

NOTES

1. *New York Clipper*, July 5, 1873: 107.
2. William J. Ryczek, *Blackguards and Red Stockings: A History of Baseball's National Association, 1871-1875* (Wallingford, Connecticut: Colebrook Press, 1992), 96.
3. Harry Wright Account and Notebooks, in Spalding Baseball Collection, Manuscript and Archives Division, New York Public Library. Astor, Lenox, and Tilden Foundations, *New York Clipper*, June 21, 1873: 90.
4. *Boston Evening Journal*, July 3, 1873: 2.
5. Ryczek, 116.
6. Ryczek, 101.
7. *Boston Daily Advertiser*, July 5, 1873: 4; *Boston Globe*, July 5, 1873: 1; *Boston Evening Journal*, July 5, 1873: 1.
8. *New York Clipper*, July 12, 1873: 117.
9. *Boston Daily Advertiser*, July 5, 1873: 4.

PAYBACK—BIG TIME

July 4, 1873 (afternoon game):
Boston Red Stockings 32, Elizabeth Resolutes 3,
at South End Grounds, Boston

BY JOHN ZINN

AFTER MIKE AND HUGH CAMPBELL helped the upstart Irvington Club pull off its historic 1866 upset of the champion Brooklyn Atlantics, they had plenty of time to enjoy the fruits of victory before a rematch. However, in the case of the Resolutes' equally shocking victory over the Red Stockings in the July 4, 1873, morning game, the time between matches was measured in hours, not days. With the first game ending about 11:30 A.M., the two clubs probably left the hot playing field looking for any shade they could find, which unfortunately gave little respite from the oppressive heat. Although Harry Wright's primary concern with the impact of conflicting events on attendance was the 2:30 regatta, all accounts agreed that a good crowd made its way to the Red Stockings grounds for the afternoon game with the *Boston Evening Journal* estimating the attendance at over 1,800.[1]

The Red Stockings probably couldn't wait to get back on the field and made only one change in their lineup: George Wright replaced Charles Sweasy, who in the morning had played his only game with Boston. There were, however, some position changes. Jim O'Rourke moved from right field to catcher, exchanging places with James "Deacon" White, who had caught the first game. Interestingly, in spite of the brutal loss and the club's relatively subpar performance thus far in 1873, Harry Wright didn't panic with his choice of pitchers. While pitchers of the era typically pitched every game, Wright appeared to have recognized that asking his ace, Albert Spalding, to pitch twice in such heat was too great a long-term risk. Instead Wright elected to make his second pitching start of the year with Spalding taking his manager's place in center field.[2]

Elizabeth, on the other hand, which probably didn't have any substitutes, not only went with the same players, but in the same positions, a decision that probably helped to determine the outcome or at least the final margin. If the Red Stockings had been guilty of taking Elizabeth for granted in the first match, they made no such mistake in the second. When a Resolute runner reached base in the first inning, O'Rourke and Ross Barnes wiped out the threat with "a good double play."[3] Barnes became especially aggressive on foul balls, retiring three Resolutes on bound catches which the crowd "greeted with rounds of applause."[4] All told, Boston made only one error in the match and the defense played a key part, especially in the early innings, in limiting the possibility of another upset, because the Red Stockings offense was still having a hard time with Campbell's pitching. Boston did manage four runs in its first four at-bats, but the Red Stockings and their fans must have got more than a little nervous when the bottom of the Resolutes order generated three runs in the fifth inning to close the score to 4-3.

By this point, however, both Hugh Campbell and his catcher, Doug Allison, must have been close to exhaustion. Boston broke through for five runs in the sixth and three in the seventh for a commanding 12-3 lead as the Resolutes couldn't generate any further offense against Harry Wright and the stout Boston defense. Finally, as the *Elizabeth Daily Journal* reported a few days later, the Resolute battery "gave out" and "Fleet had to pitch then and [A.] Allison catch."⁵ According to National Association historian Bill Ryzcek, Frank Fleet had the dubious distinction of being "the most traveled player in the league's history."⁶ Fleet was primarily an infielder, but with limited ability at any position, and pitching was clearly not his forte. This may also have been the point that the Resolutes' defense fell apart (14 Red Stockings reached base on errors over the course of the game). Having suffered an especially galling defeat in the first game of the holiday twin bill, Boston was in no mood to be merciful and gave full vent to its frustrations in the eighth inning, scoring an incredible 21 times before the side was finally retired. Umpire Thomas Mosely, who had also worked the morning game, called the contest at the end of eight innings, perhaps due to darkness; but at any rate a decision thoroughly seasoned with mercy. Mosely worked all three of the Red Stockings-Resolutes matches in July 1873; That constituted 60 percent of his professional umpiring career of five games.⁷

Newspapers in both cities recognized the magnitude of the rout. The *Elizabeth Daily Journal* informed its readers that "the Bostons ran up the score then out of all proportions."⁸ After giving due credit to Elizabeth for its opening-game victory, the *Boston Daily Advertiser* said the visitors "could not have expected to defeat the Bostons a second time on the same day but it is doubtful they anticipated the terrible drubbing of 32-3." The paper also noted that the Resolutes' "depleted treasury" had received some badly needed "replenishment."⁹ The New Jersey club's bank account doubtless received further "replenishment" the next day when Boston took the final game by a comfortable but more reasonable 13-2 score. Probably no day of baseball ended with two teams going in more dramatically different directions. Boston was now headed toward the second of four consecutive championships, while Elizabeth was sliding toward oblivion before the season even ended. And yet the *Boston Daily Globe*'s description of the July 4 holiday experience of visitors to Boston might very well have applied to both clubs—they "returned home at night, tired and cross, but satisfied [at least partially] with the day's enjoyment."¹⁰

NOTES

1 *New York Clipper*, July 12, 1873: 117; *Boston Evening Journal*, July 5, 1873: 1.

2 *New York Clipper*, July 12, 1873: 117.

3 *Boston Evening Journal*, July 5, 1873: 1.

4 Ibid.

5 *Elizabeth Daily Journal*, July 7, 1873: 3; *New York Clipper*, July 12, 1873: 117.

6 William J. Ryczek, *Blackguards and Red Stockings: A History of Baseball's National Association, 1871-1875* (Wallingford, Connecticut: Colebrook Press, 1992), 51.

7 *New York Clipper*, July 12, 1873: 117; *Boston Daily Globe*, July 5, 1873: 1; *Boston Evening Journal*, July 5, 1873: 1. The *Clipper* reported the game as lasting only eight innings while the two Boston papers had it going the full nine.

8 *Elizabeth Daily Journal*, July 7, 1873: 3.

9 *Boston Daily Advertiser*, July 5, 1873: 4.

10 *Boston Globe*, July 5, 1873: 1.

JULY 26, 1873

Baltimore Canaries 17, Boston Red Stockings 14, at South End Grounds, Boston

BY TERRY GOTTSCHALL

BOSTON LOST A HOME GAME TO the visiting Baltimore Canaries, 17-14, at the South End Grounds on Saturday, July 26, 1873, in a game marred by both poor pitching and poor fielding.

The game was Boston's 28th of the 1873 season. The Red Stockings, 17-10 (.650), entered the game in third place in the National Association, 8½ games behind Philadelphia, 27-3 (.900). Baltimore was one game ahead in second place with a 23-14 (.622) record. The two teams had played four previous games with Boston winning three out of four.

The Canaries had won three out of four on their current road trip, the last game an 11-10 loss to the New York Mutuals on July 24. Boston hadn't played since a 21-13 victory over the Philadelphia Athletics on the 16th. The nine-day layoff certainly seemed to have affected Boston's play.

Albert Spalding pitched for the Red Stockings against the Canaries' William "Candy" Cummings, the man credited with inventing the curveball.

The day's weather, according to the *Boston Journal*, affected the teams' play. Strong gusty winds transformed the simplest pop fly into a full adventure while the hot sun, in an era that lacked sunglasses and billed caps, blinded fielders and batters alike and sent cranks again and again to the concession stands for lemonade and, perhaps, something stronger, to cool the day.[1]

Baltimore led early, scoring four runs in the second, but Boston came right back in the third with eight runs and added five more runs over the next several innings to lead 14-4 by the end of the sixth. Harry Wright had scored twice in the third, "something that was never known before in one inning in a professional game."[2]

Boston faced disaster in the seventh inning. According to the *Journal*, "On going to the bat for the seventh inning, the Baltimores got on Spalding's pitching and began to make safe hits."[3] Boston's defense faltered as well with George Wright, Barnes, and Manning committing errors, allowing Baltimore to score five runs.

Although Boston came back with a single run in the bottom of the seventh to lead 14-9, disaster struck in the eighth. When Spalding quickly loaded the bases with no outs, Harry Wright took over as the pitcher. Perhaps channeling his days as a cricket bowler, Wright promptly threw a wild pitch "which went five feet over White's head," allowing two inherited runners to score. "The crowd," according to the *Journal*, "now began to get excited at seeing the victory slipping from the hands of their favorites, and cries of 'Spalding, Spalding' came from all parts of the field." In fact, before the inning ended, Baltimore scored eight runs to take a 16-14 lead.[4]

In the bottom of the eighth, Boston rallied briefly as the Wright brothers and Spalding loaded the bases with one out. "It was a forlorn hope," according to the *Journal*, "for Leonard and White failed in the critical moment, each batting out to center field and retiring."[5]

Baltimore scored a final run in the top of the ninth to win 17-14.

Published accounts of the game blamed Boston captain Harry Wright for the loss. Observers cited two mistakes: his defensive lineup and his poor performance in relief of starter Spalding.

The reporter for the *Boston Globe* criticized Wright for putting Jim O'Rourke, who usually played right field, at first base and Jack Manning, a 19-year-old rookie first baseman, in right field. Both players, now

Candy Cummings, credited with creating the curveball, had a rough outing against the Red Stockings, but still got the win. (Ars Longa Cards)

in unfamiliar positions, committed several costly errors that allowed four runs to score. The reporter noted, "Then there were disastrous errors, in critical times, on the part of men who ought not to make errors."[6] The *Journal* explained the roster switch, noting that Manning suffered from sore hands, but added, "The change was well enough as far as O'Rourke was concerned, but Manning did poorly in the field, and when the game was half through went back to first."[7] The sportswriter for the *Boston Daily Advertiser* added a second criticism, denigrating Wright's pitching when he relieved Spalding on the mound in the eighth inning.[8] Spalding had already given up 11 runs but Wright allowed five runs himself plus an additional score in the ninth to close out the game. The *Boston Journal* wrote, "The trouble was that Harry Wright pitched worse than he ever did in his life, but it was probably as much a surprise to him as it was a disappointment to the spectators and friends of the Bostons."[9]

The *Advertiser*, with a strong sense of understatement, described the game as "highly unsatisfactory for the Bostons."[10] The *Boston Globe*, on the other hand, noted, "The Baltimores deserve credit for their fine up-hill struggle, and for some brilliant individual play."[11] The *Journal* cited the defensive play of Cal McVey, John Radcliffe, and Everett Mills before noting that "George Hall's live center field catches at the close settled the fate of the Bostons."[12]

Cummings' curveball certainly failed to work; he surrendered 14 runs on 18 hits while striking out five. Nothing at all worked for Spalding and Wright, who combined to give up 17 runs on 29 hits with only three strikeouts. (Cummings finished the season 28-14 with a 2.80 ERA, while Spalding went 41-14 with a 2.99 ERA.)

Numerous errors—Baltimore committed 13 while Boston made 11—also contributed to the high score.

NOTES

1 "Base Ball," *Boston Journal*, July 28, 1873: 3.
2 "The Bostons Beaten," *Boston Daily Advertiser*, July 28, 1873: 3.
3 *Boston Journal*
4 Ibid.
5 Ibid.
6 "Base Ball," *Boston Globe*, July 28, 1873: 5.
7 *Boston Journal*.
8 *Boston Daily Advertiser*.
9 *Boston Journal*.
10 Ibid.
11 *Boston Globe*.
12 *Boston Journal*.

SEPTEMBER 6, 1873
Boston Red Stockings 23, Brooklyn Atlantics 1, at the South End Grounds

BY BILL NOWLIN

THE RED STOCKINGS WERE IN third place with a record of 22-12. In retrospect, we see they were poised to take off and go 21-4 (with a tie) the rest of the way in the 1873 season, and capture first place. Brooklyn was 15-23. The Bostons hosted the Brooklyn Atlantics on Saturday afternoon, September 6, a day when "the weather was delightful and the expectation of a fine game was universal."[1] Around 1,500 to 2,000 spectators turned out for the contest. D.P. Demorest was the umpire; it was the last of only three games he umpired, two in 1872 and just this one in 1873.

The visitors won the coin toss, and so Boston batted first, the game getting under way at 3:15. Neither team scored a run for the first two frames. "The third inning was hot work," wrote the *Boston Globe*, "but by means of two errors by [third baseman and manager Bob] Ferguson and a bad drop by [catcher Tom] Barlow, the Bostons left the bat with a score of five runs."[2]

The score was 6-0 after six innings, with a number of men left on base by both teams. Then Boston broke the game open, teeing off on 17-year-old Brooklyn pitcher Jim Britt.[3] Boston sent 15 men to the plate and scored 12 runs. "The ball was sent in succession to every corner of the field, while the visitors, who fell into a corresponding state of demoralization, were tumbling over each other, muffing and throwing wildly in a manner which called forth the merriment of the spectators."[4] It was worse. Of the first nine men to come to bat, only one failed to reach base, and there were "several" two-base hits. "So loose was the fielding of the Atlantics," continued the *Globe*, "that some of the Boston boys amused themselves by running at hap hazard from base to base, while the ball was being thrown before, after and around them, without any system, and with no effect."[5] The Red Stockings scored 12 runs. The only weak spot in the Boston offense was right fielder Bob Addy, the only player to go hitless. First baseman Jim O'Rourke had two base hits; everyone else in the lineup had three or four.

Boston added another two runs in the eighth and three in the ninth. Al Spalding allowed only three hits in the game, one each off the bats of Ferguson, Eddie Booth, and Herman Dehlman. The Atlantics scored one run, in the bottom of the eighth when Dehlman rounded the bases "on a miserable throw from [third baseman Harry] Schafer to O'Rourke, the ball being lost under the spectators' seats."[6]

The game was "a poor one," wrote the *Boston Traveler*.[7]

It was a "signal defeat" for the Atlantics, only Schafer's error "saving them from being 'Chicagoed,'" or shut out. They were, quite evidently, "out batted and outfielded."[8] The number of errors tabulated differ from one newspaper to another. Brooklyn fielders committed 14 (or 15) errors; Boston committed five (or maybe four, or eight). The Brooklyn "in-fielders did poorly, almost without exception, while the outfielders generally did well."[9] The *Post* credited Brooklyn third baseman Ferguson with "several fine pick-ups" and praised the play of Jack Remsen in center field.[10]

However many errors there may have been, the final score was not in dispute.

The two teams played again on Monday; Boston won 15-10. The Red Stockings finished the 1873 season with a very impressive .340 team batting average. Al Spalding's pitching record was 41-14.

NOTES

1 *Boston Journal*, September 8, 1873: 1.
2 *Boston Globe*, September 8, 1873: 5.
3 Britt finished the season with a 17-36 record.
4 Ibid.
5 Ibid.
6 Ibid.
7 *Boston Traveler*, September 8, 1873: 1.
8 *Brooklyn Eagle*, September 8, 1873: 4.
9 *Boston Journal*.
10 *Boston Post*, September 8, 1873: 3.

OCTOBER 2, 1873

Boston Red Stockings 18, Philadelphia White Stockings 7, at Jefferson Street Grounds, Philadelphia

BY MARK PESTANA

IN THE EARLY GOING OF THE 1873 season, the White Stockings of Philadelphia enjoyed the kind of success the Boston Red Stockings had enjoyed the previous year. The Quaker City's "second" team lost but three of its first 30 games, putting together two separate streaks of 10 consecutive victories, and spent much the better part of five months—late April through late September—in first place in the National Association. By contrast, the "veteran" Philadelphia Athletics, winners of the first NA pennant, struggled all season to do better than third place but never quite made it, fading to fifth place at the finish.

Meanwhile, it certainly appeared that the Red Stockings would be hard-pressed to retain their championship title. As of July 15, their record was a middling 16-10—not bad by any means, but far off the pace of the 1872 Boston team that did not lose its fourth game until September 7! They were nine games behind the White Stockings, with Baltimore and the Athletics in the queue ahead of them.

The Whites seesawed with the Canaries of Baltimore at the top of the pack for two weeks or so in late August, but by the end of that month the Philadelphians were back in sole possession of the lead, and stayed there through the last day of September.

After spending most of August engaged in exhibition games on a Western tour, the Boston nine began a steady, rapid climb in the NA standings. The men from the Hub chalked up 12 wins against one loss (plus one tie) in September. Defeating the Atlantics in Brooklyn on October 1, they rode a seven-game winning streak into the City of Brotherly Love for a contest with the White Stockings the following day.

The clubs were in a virtual dead heat: The Whites' record was 34-14, the Reds', 33-13-1.

On Thursday afternoon, October 2, at 25th and Jefferson Streets, a very large crowd—estimates ranged from 4,000 to 5,000—turned out in very fine weather to witness the crucial match. The park at the Jefferson Street Grounds was the first home of pro ball in Philadelphia: The Athletics had played there since the inaugural NA season of 1871.[1] It would become the site of the first game in National League history, on April 22, 1876, when the Athletics hosted (and lost to) the Boston Red Caps.

Thus far the two clubs had evenly split the season series, four wins apiece; this was to be the ninth and final match between them in 1873.

Doing the twirling for the White Stockings was George Zettlein, a right-hander who had been in organized ball since 1865 and famously was the winning pitcher for the Brooklyn Atlantics when they snapped Cincinnati's epic undefeated streak in June 1870.

For reasons still unclear, though perhaps influenced by his team's poor 2-4 record since mid-September, player-manager Jimmy Wood had held Zettlein out of the Phillies' previous two games, starting instead the team's right fielder, George Bechtel, who, with all of three games' prior pitching experience (in 1871), proceeded to lose both contests, albeit by relatively close margins (10-6 and 14-13).[2] For the highly anticipated Boston match, Wood went back to his number-one pitcher, and hoped for the best.

Things started with a bang, as each club scored four runs in its first inning. For the Quakers, who batted first after losing the coin toss, Ned Cuthbert, Levi Meyerle, Wood, and Bechtel all tallied, the production being helped by three Boston errors. In the bottom half, the home team, "[n]ot to be outdone in courtesy to the visitors … went into the muffing business"[3] as well. Two botched plays by first baseman Denny Mack aided the Reds in getting their four tallies.

The second inning saw the rivals again go halves on the scoring, as Wood for the Whites and Barnes for the Reds each scored his second run of the day.

The Phillies suffered the first "Chicago" of the game as they went one-two-three in the third. Boston took the opportunity to pull into the lead with a pair of runs, O'Rourke and Schafer contributing key hits.

In the fourth inning, rookie utilityman Jim Devlin, yet to embark on either his promising pitching career or his damnable gambling career, entered the game at first base for the Phillies, replacing the shaky Mack. Devlin reached on a hard hit to right but two grounders handled by George Wright and a fly out to left fielder Andy Leonard left him stranded.

The Bostons cranked out another four runs in the bottom half, and as with much of the scoring in this game, the cause had more to do with shame in the field than sharpness at the bat. With George Wright and Barnes having reached ahead of him, pitcher Al Spalding popped one up in the vicinity of second. Center fielder Fred Treacy came in toward the ball while second sacker Wood angled back for it. Neither succeeded in actually capturing the ball, and it dropped between them to their mutual consternation. Wright scored easily. Then, while Wood and Treacy were, in the words of the *New York Clipper*, "indulging in some chin music,"[4] Barnes bolted home all the way from second. Even the Philadelphia patrons were amused, the *Clipper* noting that this happened "amid shouts of laughter."

The slapstick wasn't over yet. Shortly after this, Wood bungled a potential double play and, no doubt completely flustered by the course of events at this juncture, simply threw the ball down "in a pet," allowing another Red Stocking to score and drawing more laughter from the spectators.[5] At inning's end, Boston led 11-5, having yet to record a single earned run.

The Quakers came back with a run in the top of the fifth, but the Reds piled on four more in the bottom. Spalding blanked Wood's crew again in the sixth, and Wright's nine refused to be kept off the board, adding two runs to their total.[6] The seventh inning saw Philadelphia again fail to diminish the Reds' lead, although Zettlein was finally able to whitewash the visitors.

In the eighth the clubs matched single runs again, the White Stockings making several changes in the field as Boston went to bat. Shortstop Chick Fulmer, possessor of even less pitching experience than George Bechtel, relieved Zettlein. The latter was installed at first, Devlin moving over to third, and Meyerle then plugging the gap at shortstop. Wood's motives, again, are unclear; the position switches made little sense … and little difference.

Harry Wright pulled one switch himself to start the ninth inning, catcher Deacon White and first baseman Jim O'Rourke exchanging places. The White Stockings, down to their last ups, came alive a bit—but all too late. They managed four runs before umpire Nicholas Young rang the curtain down on account of the creeping October darkness. Because the inning was incomplete, the score reverted to where it stood at the end of the eighth: 18-7 in the visitors' favor. Boston had wrested first place from the upstart Pennsylvanians.

As Bill Ryczek aptly puts it, the Reds and Whites, though still neck-and-neck at this point, "had merely intersected while traveling in opposite directions."[7] For the Philadelphians, the brilliant promise of the season's first half faded ignobly in the second, as they could manage only nine wins in their final 23 games. The Bostonians, on the other hand, after a so-so 18-11 start, breezed through their second half with a 25-5-1 record. They held the Phillies and the other clubs at a comfortable distance the rest of the way and brought home a second pennant.

NOTES

1 Philip Lowry, *Green Cathedrals* (New York: Walker Publishing Company, Inc., 2006), 171.

2 This Philadelphia NA team was known by various nicknames, including both White Stockings and Blue Stockings. (Since Chicago disbanded its NA club after the catastrophic 1871 fire, there was not another "White Stockings" team in competition.) They were sometimes also called the Phillies, but should not be confused with the modern-day National League Philadelphia team, which is a different franchise altogether.

3. *New York Clipper*, October 11, 1873.

4. Ibid. This "chin music" is not the modern baseball slang for a high tight pitch that brushes a batter back from the plate, but rather old American slang meaning someone "jawing" away at another, arguing, verbally harassing, etc.

5. Ibid.

6. The *Clipper* states clearly that two runs were put up by Boston in the sixth. All other accounts of the game consulted, including the *Philadelphia Public Ledger*, *Philadelphia Inquirer*, *Boston Daily Globe*, *Boston Journal*, and the *Washington Daily National Republican*, report only one run here, and give the final score as 17-7. The sketchiness of the accounts, including that of the *Clipper*, makes it unlikely the discrepancy can be resolved. The only other relevant detail provided in the papers is that the *Clipper's* box score credits Bob Addy with one run scored in the game, while all other sources give him a zero.

7. Bill Ryczek, *Blackguards and Red Stockings* (Wallingford, Connecticut: Colebrook Press, 1992), 127.

A RARE FIRST-PERSON ACCOUNT
of What Nineteenth Century Ball Players Did on An Unexpected Day Off

THOUGH THE AUTHOR OF THIS first-person *New York Clipper* piece in its May 2, 1874, issue will remain a mystery, the real provider was Mother Nature. Though several April opening-season Association games were scheduled, only three were played, two in Baltimore and one between the two Philadelphia clubs. This rare type of account gives 21st century readers a glimpse into the non-game doings of the players and some behind-the-scenes commentary which is usually not available, all because of a day off caused by bad weather.

—Richard "Dixie" Tourangeau

April 25, 1874: Boston vs Philadelphia, at Boston (postponed), *New York Clipper*

The Eastern Tour of the Philadelphians
—Special Correspondence of the Clipper—
Boston, April 25, 1874

I arrived in Boston, via the New Haven and Springfield Road, at 6 am today. While at the United States Hotel[1]—the headquarters of the visiting clubs, it being opposite the New York depot—I met the Philadelphians, who arrived by the Fall River route. Besides the club ten, Messrs. Jacobs and Gillingham were of their party, as was (Thomas) Carey[2] of the Mutuals, who came to act as umpire. The Philadelphians referred to the decisions of the umpire in the Baltimore match, and according to their account he must have queer notions in regard to interpreting the new rules. They stated that pieces of board were laid down on the ground to mark out the striker's position. That is not right. The lines of the positions on the field—pitcher's and striker's—should be laid down in chalk lines, or with some other white substance. The striker is at perfect liberty to stand anywhere within the six-feet by-three space of his position, no matter whether he stands across from the base-line running through its center of not. But I will comment on this subject at another time.

The weather on Saturday did not look promising, the sun still being under a cloud and the air chilly—in fact, it was an easterly Boston air, but it did not prevent a large gathering of spectators at the Union Grounds, though the threatening aspect of the clouds kept away who may be called the fair-weather patrons of the game. The city had been well "billed"—as the theatrical people say—for the match, the Boston Club management evidently doing things up in good business style. In the morning, the players of both clubs assembled at the Boston Club rooms, 591 Washington Street, where ball talk, gossip and friendly intercourse prevailed until near dinner-time, when the visitors returned to their hotel and prepared to go to the grounds.

At 2 P.M., while the Philadelphians stood dressed waiting for the stage to take them to the grounds, a sprinkling of snow began to fall, the wind having changed more to the northward, and half an hour afterwards all chance of playing a game was gone, as a regular March snowstorm set in. By 2 P.M. a large crowd considering the weather, had assembled at the grounds, and the champions were ready to take the field, when the snow put a stop to all further proceedings. It was unfortunate, as the ground previously was in good condition and a pretty fielding game would doubtless have been played. When the snow came down in earnest, the Philadelphians took off their uniforms, packed up their traps, and stepping across the street from their hotel, took the 3 P.M. train for

Hartford. Messrs. Gillingham and Jacobs remaining behind to arrange a game with the Bostons for Tuesday in place of visiting New Haven, which they had arranged to do, the Yale College Club being unable to play matches except on Wednesdays or Saturdays.

In the afternoon, members of the Boston nine assembled at the gymnasium of the Young Men's Christian Association, of which they are all members, and Shaffer and White practiced defending a wicket against Harry Wright's bowling, a soft rubber ball being used. O'Rourke and Leonard have developed excellent bowling powers since practicing at the gymnasium, and Spalding is rapidly becoming a good cricketer. They are all splendid fielders, and will soon be able to defend their stumps well.

While at George Wright's store I was shown a new baseball bat. It is a rather expensive bat as regards first cost, as the price was $4 but, as it is alleged that it will last a season without breaking, it is cheap. It is made with a cane fitted through the whole length of the bat, which makes it proof against breaking from hitting a ball with it, and the cane imparts an elasticity to the bat, which is a great aid in batting. The bat weighs a little over two pounds only.

Should the weather be fine on Tuesday, there will be a large crowd at the match, as all are anxious to the see the first championship match. The present nine is the strongest, I think, the "Reds" have ever laced on the field. They are in fine condition for play, and their morale is excellent. They will be a credit to America in England if they deport themselves there as they are now doing here, which they will, of course, take a national pride in doing.

On Monday morning the weather cleared off and the sun came out, and all the snow in Boston vanished like magic. In fact, the Bostons were out on their grounds, and had the Philadelphias waited

Boston's United States Hotel in 1883. (Courtesy Smithsonian Magazine)

at the United States Hotel until Monday and then telegraphed to Hartford to learn the condition of the ground, they would have been saved a trip to Hartford, and on Tuesday could have played their game in the "Hub." Now the first championship game will be that with the Mutuals on Saturday. The Philadelphians left Hartford Sunday night for New York, the snowstorm leading them to believe that play would be impossible.

NOTES

1 The United States Hotel (1826) was at Beach and Lincoln Streets (near today's Chinatown) and since 1860 was the largest Boston hotel with 500 rooms. It was about two miles from the South End Grounds.

2 Thomas Joseph Carey was a Brooklyn native. He was Ft. Wayne's second-baseman in 1871 who then became a solid Baltimore infielder for 1872 and '73. By 1874 he was the New York Mutuals' normal shortstop but had started to umpire Association games on occasion in 1873. On April 16, 1874, he oversaw the game between the city rivals in Philadelphia.

1874 RED STOCKINGS OPENER AFTER TWO WEATHER POSTPONEMENTS

May 2, 1874: Red Stockings 12, New York Mutuals 3, at South End Grounds, Boston

BY RICHARD "DIXIE" TOURANGEAU

MOTHER NATURE AND OLD MAN Winter were not yet in a "base ball" mood when the Red Stockings were supposed to begin their season in late April 1874. Two officially scheduled dates were snowed out and rained out respectively before May 2, when the Reds could finally open their season against the Mutuals of New York.

April was not completely bad: The Red Stockings started their practice regimen on April 2 before a huge crowd of 2,000 to 3,000 on a fairly nice spring day when they beat a Picked Nine, 10-8. Such a throng was unexpected but publicity about the Reds' European Tour later in the year had hiked the notoriety of and affection for the club. Fans were eager to see their two-time champions, who were now going to take their sport to England. On the "Nine" were normal subs Tommy Beals, Jack Manning, and the third Wright brother, Sam. Three days later the temperature was reported as 24 degrees in the Hub.[1]

Trying to stay in shape after that frigid spell, the next week Boston played and twice beat the Beacons, a makeshift "Field Team," and finally the Harvard boys, 24-10, in what was "not Spring-like weather" on April 22 according to the *New York Clipper*.[2] On April 25 the Philadelphia White Stockings were supposed to open the season but it snowed just as the game was about to start. (Elsewhere in this volume is a story about what the players did instead that day.) New Association entry Hartford was rained out on the 29th.

Eventually calendars turned to May in hope of better conditions. By elimination New York's solid Mutual club became the Opening Day opposition. But they got caught in a two-way trap. They played in Hartford the day before and because the Dark Blues were postponed with the Reds, it was the first-ever National Association game for a Hartford team. New York was better and made more hits, but the home crowd wildly cheered the Blues to a 10-7 win behind slugger Lipman Pike (three hits/one run/three RBIs) and Tom Barlow (two hits/three runs). Ross Barnes of the Reds was the umpire.

The next day the Mutuals were at the South End Grounds to face the pent-up Reds. The *New York Clipper* claimed, "The Bostons appeared with a nine as strong perhaps as ever fought beneath the banner of the Red Stockings on any field."[3] Even with champion manager-outfielder Harry Wright sitting down and James "Deacon" White slightly injured, the game was over quickly as Boston jumped to a 9-0 lead and won 12-3. The poor Mutuals were beaten but unbowed, as the *Clipper* noted, "(Bobby) Mathews played pluckily between the pitcher's points and 'old reliable' (Joe Start), again proved himself worthy of the title at first base. Jack Burdock covered third in fine style."[4] It was not enough.

Basking in their home glory and chilly sunshine, the Reds were nearly flawless. Al Spalding gave up New York's three runs in the eighth inning, on hits by John Hatfield (two hits/run), John Candy Nelson (two hits/run), and Burdock's triple/run/RBI. Boston's attack was paced by Cal McVey (three hits/four runs), Jim O'Rourke (three hits/two runs), and George Wright's three hits/run. The *Clipper* was terse: "The Reds put it to the Yorkers."5 Hartford's Scott Hastings, whose contract miscues helped cost the Reds the 1871 pennant, umpired the Opening Day game, likely a reciprocal favor for Barnes's work the day before.

Little Tommy Bond's Great Feat

Two days later the Reds whipped the Mutuals and Mathews, 11-4, behind the hitting of McVey again (three hits/three runs), Spalding (three hits/two runs), and George Hall (three runs). "Reliable" Start (three hits/run) and pitcher Mathews' same output were no match. Ex-Red Dave Birdsall did the umpiring. McVey would lead the NA that season in hits, runs, and RBIs, and finish second to Levi Meyerle in batting (.359). Three more pummelings gave the Reds a 5-0 mark and a huge 75-18 run differential. Excited Hartford came to town after winning its first four games by a total of 58-24. The confident Hub Stockings first crushed them 25-3 and then 8-1 back in Hartford. After another six road victories, the Reds cruised home at 13-0.

Twice they had beaten the Brooklyn Atlantics in that span, 8-2 and 6-2. Now at the South End Grounds the Atlantics shockingly repaid that debt by dragging the Reds back, briefly, to reality on May 23 and 26. Little rookie Tommy Bond had absorbed both Brooklyn losses but regained more than a little dignity and grabbed a few headlines by holding the run-crazed Stockings (averaging 14-4 wins) to just five tallies in two games, winning 9-3 and 6-2. A feat so rare as to be astounding. Brooklyn got seven runs in the first inning of the first game, while Boston managed only three hits all day. Though the Atlantics made 11 bobbles behind hero Bond they still won handily under umpire Ross Barnes's fair and square decisions. Barnes was injured and played in neither game. Three days later the Reds got seven hits but made nine errors and Tommy won again as Brooklyn hitters combined for four runs in the third inning. Brooklyn had no real standout batters in those two contests but tosser Bond did hit and score in both. The Reds took their medicine dose and then won five straight games for an 18-2 record. Warren Briggs of nearby Malden umpired that second Atlantic game, the only such game in his life.

Bond had split four decisions against the mighty Bostons in the first seven games of his career. In 1874 he topped the league in losses (32), home runs given up (15), and runs allowed (440). Tommy would later become a Boston legend when he joined the National League Bostons in 1877. He pitched for them five years and was the last hurler to win 40 games in three straight seasons. He continued to live there in quiet celebrity and operate a leather-goods business for the rest of life, passing away in January 1941.

SOURCES

"Out-Door Sports; Opening of the Base Ball Season in Boston," *Boston Daily Advertiser*, May 4, 1874: 1.

"Out-Door Sports," *Boston Globe*, May 4, 1874: 2.

"Out Door Sports. Base Ball," *Boston Journal*, May 4, 1874: 4.

New York Clipper issues for April, May, and June 1874.

NOTES

1. "Weather Report," *Boston Daily Advertiser*, April 6, 1874: 1.
2. "Boston vs. Harvard," *New York Clipper*, May 2, 1874: 37.
3. "Boston vs. Mutual," *New York Clipper*, May 9, 1874: 42.
4. Ibid.
5. Ibid.

CHICAGO DECLARES ITS INDEPENDENCE IN SURPRISING EXTRA-INNING SLUGFEST VICTORY OVER BOSTON, 17-16

July 4, 1874: Chicago White Stockings 17, Boston Red Stockings 16, at Twenty-Third Street Grounds, Chicago

BY GREGORY H. WOLF

THE CHICAGO WHITE STOCKINGS were struggling in their return to the National Association after a two-year absence precipitated by the Great Fire in the Windy City which destroyed much of the city, including the team's ballpark. The Chicago nine were 8-14, and were preparing to play the Boston Red Stockings in their first home game since June 8 after a dreadful Eastern road swing on which they lost nine of 13 contests. Three of those losses were to the two-time reigning champion Bostons who outscored them 47-15. "The recent disastrous career of the home club had lowered them greatly in public attention," wrote the *Chicago Tribune*.[1] Local fans gave Chicago little chance to defeat the Red Stockings, attested by the fact that there was "very little betting anywhere."[2] Boston appeared to be invincible. They had inaugurated the season with 13 consecutive victories, and were in first place (26-6), five games in front of the Athletics of Philadelphia. But what was foretold as a laugher turned out to be in the words of the *Tribune*, "one of the worst played and most exciting games ever seen in Chicago."[3]

Chicago seemed in disarray. Skipper Jimmy Wood had been out since before the season started suffering from a serious abscess in right leg.[4] Catcher and interim manager Fergy Malone was not with the team (he had missed the train in Philadelphia) forcing players to change positions, further suggesting that it would be an "easy victory" for Boston.[5] Boston, on the other hand, was, as the *Tribune* further said, "strong as usual and seemed like a well-oiled machine"; however, George Wright was replaced at shortstop by Andy Leonard.

On a sunny summer day an estimated 10,000 spectators packed Twenty-Third Street Grounds on Chicago's South Side.[6] Due to the late arrival of the Red Stockings, umpire William McLean of the Philadelphia Eurekas started the game at 3:35.

Having lost the coin toss, the White Stockings batted first. In an inkling of what would come, Ned Cuthbert, Davy Force, and Levi Meyerle led off with three consecutive hits off Al Spalding to score the first run. Easily the best pitcher of his era, Spalding led the NA in victories in all five years of its existence and was en route to a phenomenal 52-16 record in 1874. Two-out hits by Jim Devlin and John Peters increased Chicago's lead to 5-0; all of the runs were earned. It "began to appear that the game was worth seeing," opined the *Tribune*.[7]

Boston wasted little time tying the game. Ross Barnes, who had paced the NA in batting the previous two years (.430 and .431 respectively), led off with a hit and scored on Spalding's drive; Deacon Wright was thrown out at the plate on the play. Leonard subsequently knocked in Spalding. In the second inning, Barnes, White, and Spalding each drove in a run off hurler George Zettlein, a dependable right-hander who completed all 57 of his starts in 1874, winning 27 of them.

The White Stockings regained the lead in the fifth when Myerle, en route to leading the National Association in hitting, (.394), Paul Hines, and John Glenn led off with hits. Following Fred Treacey's one-out double to make it 7-5, Peters knocked in two more on a single. With runners on first and second, Cuttbert smashed a hard liner to Harry Schafer at the hot corner. Schafer caught it and tagged Peters, who had drifted off the base, to end the frame with the Chicagos leading, 9-5.

The sixth inning ended with the score 11-6. Miscues by catchers Cuthbert of Chicago (two passed balls and a wild throw) and White of Boston (one passed ball and a wild throw) contributed to all three runs. This was the era before players donned the "tools of ignorance"; there were no "tools" as catchers played without gloves (as all fielders did), masks, and chest protection.

"The Whites got the 'hang' of Spalding" in the seventh inning, wrote the *Chicago Inter Ocean*.[8] Following a botched double-play attempt on Cuthbert's grounder that would have ended the inning, the White Stockings scored five unearned runs. The dagger came with the bases loaded when Glenn hit a single to drive in two runs, giving the Whites a seemingly insurmountable 16-6 lead. Captain 'Arry (as the Boston papers affectionately called player-manager Harry Wright, who was born in Sheffield, England) knew his star hurler had had enough (20 hits and 16 runs, 9 earned). He switched his outfield position with Spalding, and took the mound for one of his six appearances (including two starts) that season. "The change was deadly to the Whites, who were unable to get hold of Wright's slow delivery," wrote the *Tribune*.[9] The 39-year-old Wright in his final season as an active player (though he did play in one game in each of the next three years) held Chicago scoreless through the ninth inning.

Described as "practically beaten," Boston mounted a comeback in the bottom of the seventh by scoring five runs on a combination of clutch hitting a bad defense.[10] While Treacey and Glenn dropped what the

Chicago captain Jimmy Wood, who had his leg amputated six days after the July 4 game. (Courtesy of John Thorn)

Tribune considered "easy" fly balls, and Peters made a wild throw, Jim O'Rourke, George Hall, Schafer, and Barnes all hit safely to pull Boston to within five runs, 16-11.[11] It was "the worst muffing that was ever seen," opined the *Tribune*. The *Chicago Inter Ocean* observed that "the Whites seemed demoralized."[12] Drubbed 29-6 in their last meeting with the Reds, the White Stockings were fully aware of the explosiveness of Boston's offense, which led the NA in practically every category and averaged a whopping 10.4 runs per game in 1874.

With "courage and determination," wrote the *Tribune*, Boston came to bat in the ninth trailing 16-11.[13] Boston's comeback commenced with Barnes's fifth hit of the game, a double to drive in two runs. White hit safely to knock in Barnes, and later scored to make it 16-15. Tension mounted as Boston loaded the bases with just one out. "Everyone expected to see the Whites beat," wrote the *Chicago Inter Ocean*.[14] But "Charmer" Zettlein (whose moniker derives from a minstrel of the period) reared back to retire O'Rourke on a fly that tied the score, and then Wright.

The game went into extra innings, something of a rarity in the National Association to say the least. It was Chicago's first-ever overtime contest. Boston's last extra-inning affair had been almost two years earlier when they defeated the Brooklyn Atlantics 17-12 in 11 innings on July 29, 1872. Peters led off the 10th with a double, his fifth hit of the game. He subsequently scored on Zettlein's hit and George Hall's bad throw to give Chicago the lead for good, 17-16. The inning ended when Schafer repeated his fifth-inning defensive wizardry by catching Force's hot liner and swiftly tagging Zettlein for the second double play of the game.

Taking the mound in the 10th inning for the first time in his professional career, Zettlein registered two quick outs. Up stepped Barnes with the game on the line. The 24-year-old right-handed hitter who had gotten his start in baseball in 1866 with an amateur team, the Rockford Forest Citys, for which Spalding also pitched, was the undisputed master of the fair-foul hit. He accomplished the feat by cutting down hard on the ball which would rocket toward the third baseman, hit in fair territory in front of the bag, and then bounce and curve sharply into foul territory; it was a legal hit in all five years of the NA. Barnes collected one of his specialties, stole second, and moved to third on Cuthbert's poor throw. In a do-or-die position, future Hall of Famer Deacon White popped up to Treacey to end the game in 2 hours and 20 minutes.[15]

The "batting of the Whites throughout the game was magnificent," exclaimed the *Chicago Inter Ocean*.[16] The victory over the best team in baseball gave hope to the fans, players, and, importantly, principal stockholder Norman T. Gassette and his partner, William Hulbert. (Hulbert subsequently became one of the founders of the National League, which began play in 1876.) Chicago's shortcomings thus far in 1874 had perplexed them. In their effort to challenge mighty Boston, they had raided the roster of the Philadelphia Whites near the end of the previous season and had signed Delvin, Myerle, Malone, Treacey, Wood, and Zettlein in a classic case of contract jumping. It finally appeared that their admittedly ethically questionable efforts had paid dividends. Though the White Stockings lost their next game, 12-6 to Boston, two days later, their inspirational victory on the 98th anniversary of the signing of the Declaration of Independence commenced a stretch of 14 wins in 18 games, all but the final win at home in the friendly confines of the Windy City.

Chicago's success came as skipper Jimmy Wood had his leg amputated above the right knee on July 10. According to the *Chicago Tribune*, Wood had "wasted away" and his bones became "brittle."[17] Amazingly, Wood returned as skipper just five weeks after his operation.

NOTES

1 "The Fourth. General Celebration of a Delightful Day. The White Stockings Proclaim Their Declaration of Independence," *Chicago Tribune*, July 5, 1874: 7.

2 Ibid.

3 Ibid.

4 "Local Miscellany. Baseball Gossip," *Chicago Tribune*, April 5, 1874: 5.

5 Ibid. Outfielder Ned Cuthbert took Malone's position behind the plate, second baseman Levi Myerle moved to left field, and outfielder Paul Hines moved to second base.

6 The *Tribune* estimated that 10,000 were in attendance; the *Chicago Inter Ocean* estimated the crowd at 8,000. "Sporting News. The Great White Stocking Base Ball Club Scoops the Boston Reds," *Chicago Inter Ocean*, July 5, 1874: 9.

7 *Chicago Tribune*, July 5, 1874: 7.

8 *Chicago Inter Ocean*, July 6, 1874: 9.

9 *Chicago Tribune*, July 5, 1874: 7.

10 Ibid.

11 Ibid.

12 *Chicago Inter Ocean*, July 6, 1874: 9.

13 *Chicago Tribune*, July 5, 1874: 7.

14 *Chicago Inter Ocean*, July 6, 1874: 9.

15 According to the *Chicago Tribune*, the game last 2 hours and 20 minutes. The *Chicago Inter Ocean* gave the game time as 2 hours and 10 minutes.

16 *Chicago Inter Ocean*, July 6, 1874: 9.

17 "Sporting News. Jimmy Wood Will Never Play Baseball Again," *Chicago Tribune*, July 11, 1874: 7.

SEPTEMBER 22, 1874

New York Mutuals 9, Boston Red Stockings 8, at South End Grounds, Boston

BY BILL NOWLIN

THE RACE FOR THE 1874 NATIONAL Association pennant tightened on September 21, with the Boston Red Stockings holding just a three-game lead over the second-place New York Mutuals heading into the Tuesday afternoon game on September 22. They'd been up by five games as recently as September 10, but had lost three of their last five games. (The team had been in Europe for nearly two months, not playing a championship game in the NA from July 16 through September 9.)

The Reds batted first, the contest kicking off a few minutes after 3:00 P.M. There were about 1,500 spectators at the game.

New York right-hander Bobby Mathews retired the Red Stockings 1-2-3 in the first inning. Mathews was no slouch; he won 42 games in 1874 (42-22, 1.90 ERA). It was his best season.

Al Spalding had pitched just the day before, a 10-8 loss to the Philadelphia Whites, and one of the Boston newspapers wrote, "(T)he cause of this defeat is plain: Spalding was 'off.'"[1] Red Stockings manager Harry Wright took the mound for Boston. Cal McVey caught.

Spalding had proven mortal. Though he started the season winning every one of the team's first 16 games, and posted a 52-win season (with a 1.92 earned-run average), he did ultimately lose 16 games. The September 21 game was one of them. So, as it happened, was September 22.

Spalding started 69 games in 1874; this was one of the two in which he appeared in relief. He started the game playing in center field.

New York scored twice in the first inning, and added a run in the second. Boston battled back with two runs in the third, and took a 4-3 lead in the top of the fourth. Spalding came in to relieve Wright after four innings.

He wasn't any better. The Mutuals scored three times in the fifth and twice more in the sixth. With single runs in the sixth and seventh, and two more in the eighth, the game was tied heading into the ninth. Mathews was sharp. He got Spalding to ground out to shortstop Tom Carey. McVey went down on three strikes, and Andy Leonard grounded out to the mound, Mathews throwing to first baseman Joe Start.

But third baseman Jack Burdock doubled over left fielder Leonard's head to lead off the bottom of the ninth. Center fielder Jack Remsen fouled out to Jim O'Rourke at first base. Mathews singled Burdock to third, and catcher Dick Higham lofted a sacrifice fly to Deacon White in right field "which he took handsomely" but which let Burdock score with the winning run.[2] Higham had taken over as Mutuals manager from Carey; the team had been 13-12 under Carey, but were 29-11 under Higham.

The *Boston Journal* said the Mutuals simply outplayed the Red Stockings. Boston played most of the game as an "up hill game."[3] Seven errors cost Boston some runs, though New York committed six. To the extent that luck played a role, it was "evidently against them."[4] Three of New York's runs were earned runs, including the game-winning run; two of Boston's runs were earned.

The umpire was Billy McLean of Philadelphia. The *Boston Globe* reported, "The umpiring was satisfactory, but the crowd, or a part of it, were very boisterous in expressing their disapproval of some of their rulings."[5]

The win gave New York 33 wins on the season. Boston, having lost, had 32.

The win was the 12th championship game win in a row for the New York Mutuals. Two days later the Mutuals beat Boston once again, shaving the Red Stockings' lead to just one game. New York's win streak ran to 16 games in all, but in a regular season that extended all the way to October 30, Boston went on to go 20-5 and by season's end 7½ games up over New York.

NOTES

1 "Base Ball," *Boston Daily Advertiser*, September 22, 1874: 1. Three of Philadelphia's runs had scored on wild pitches and one on a passed ball.

2 "Base Ball," *Boston Journal*, September 23, 1874: 3.

3 Ibid.

4 Ibid.

5 "Base-Ball," *Boston Globe*, September 23, 1874: 5.

ATLANTICS COMMIT 30 ERRORS

October 1, 1874: Boston Red Stockings 29, Brooklyn Atlantics 0, at South End Grounds, Boston

BY JIM WOHLENHAUS

THE SCORE OF THIS GAME IS NOT a misprint. It was a 29-0 game played between two major-league championship teams. The two biggest reasons for the lopsided score were that the Atlantics made 30 errors and that they were facing one of the best pitchers of the time, Albert Spalding.

In a bit of understatement, the *Boston Post* called it "a very one-sided affair, the champions playing it for all it was worth, an excusable passed ball by White being their only error."[1] The *Boston Globe* less kindly called it "decidedly, the funniest game of the season."[2]

It wasn't entirely poor play on the part of Brooklyn's regulars. They had previously defeated the Red Stockings three times in Boston, 9-3, 6-2, and 9-8, the last of which came just the day before, with Bond bettering Spalding. The *New York Clipper* explained that the "Atlantics attribute the result to the fact that their regular catchers were both injured, and they had no one to catch."[3] Keep in mind that in those days, passed balls by catchers were considered errors.

A play-by-play of this game has not seen the light of day. The *Boston Globe* said, "It would be impossible almost, to follow the game through its tedious course."[4] The *Globe* box score indicated that Boston received first base on errors 11 times. (Brooklyn had none.) The other 19 Atlantics errors perhaps allowed the Red Stockings to take an extra base, and possibly score.

Boston hit eight doubles, quite a number given that the team is credited with only 121 for the season—a significant percentage of the season's total in just this one game.

Bond, the Atlantics pitcher, did give up 26 hits, which means that with the 11 men who reached first due to error, 37 men got on. With only five men left on base the entire game and 29 scoring, three were put out on the bases. The box score does not mention any double plays. The *Globe* reported that the Red Stockings made seven fly catches, while the Atlantics made five.

Was this game an anomaly for Bond? A comparison of key statistics for Bond and Spalding for 1874 shows this to be not entirely true.

PITCHER	GS	W	L	R	ER	IP	ERA	RS
SPALDING	69	52	16	402	132	617⅓	1.92	10.46
BOND	55	22	32	440	112	497	2.03	5.35

Bond's ERA suggests that his pitching was arguably quite good, but that he was let down by the defense, and that his teammates were not as prolific on offense as Spalding's were, as shown by the significant difference between the runs scored.

Boston scored early and often; the only inning in which they did not get a run was the fourth. If their 13-0 lead after six wasn't enough, the Bostons scored 13 times in the seventh inning.

Brooklyn made only four hits. One of them belonged to Charlie Snow, who after catcher Jake Knowdell broke his finger in the fifth inning, came into the game long enough to play center field and collect his one and only major-league at-bat. Facing the best pitcher of the day, he singled and thus retired from big-league baseball with a 1.000 batting average. Conversely, he had three chances in the field and fumbled all three, for a career .000 fielding average. Bond was a local amateur, a native of Lowell, who was welcomed into the game so the Atlantics could field nine.

Atlantics player/manager Bob Ferguson committed seven of his team's 30 errors. (Spalding Collection)

Bob Ferguson moved from third to behind the plate, but couldn't handle Bond's pitches. He finished the game with seven errors.

Second baseman Al Martin committed six errors, and the *Globe* wrote, "Martin's muffing became the subject of so much merriment with the spectators that he was cheered whenever he held a ball, no matter from where or by whom thrown, a circumstance which happened rarely."[5] The account continued, "Martin was christened 'Lord Dundreary' by some imaginative observer, and his appearance so much resembled that of the insipid nobleman that the audience confirmed the title with a lusty cheer."[6]

The spectators weren't entirely unfair, the *Globe* said: "The crowd indulged in a good deal of merriment at the expense of the victims, although every good point they made was generously applauded."[7]

SOURCES

In addition to the sources provided in the notes, the author also consulted:

Spalding, A.G., and Lewis Meacham. *Spalding's Official Baseball Guide for 1878* (Reprint).

NOTES

1. *Boston Post*, October 2, 1874. The *Boston Daily Advertiser* and the *Boston Globe* both called it a wild pitch by Spalding, assigning him the error. The *Globe* also counted 36 errors, but lacking play-by-play, it is impossible to be fully certain how many there may have been. See also "An Extraordinary Event on the Ball Field. Defeat of the Atlantics by the Bostons by a Score of 29 to 0—Heavy and Weak Batting, Splendid Fielding and Miserable Muffing," *Boston Daily Advertiser*, October 2, 1874.
2. "Another 'Comedy of Errors'—The Atlantics Whitewashed by Champions—Score 29 to 0," *Boston Globe*, October 2, 1874.
3. *New York Clipper*, October 17, 1874.
4. *Boston Globe*, October 2, 1874.
5. Ibid.
6. Lord Dundreary is a character in the 1858 British play *Our American Cousin* by Tom Taylor. (It is the play Abraham Lincoln watched the night he was assassinated.) Dundreary is the personification of a good-natured, brainless aristocrat.
7. Ibid.

FIT TO BE TIED

October 7, 1874: Boston Red Stockings 3, Brooklyn Atlantics 3 (tie), at Union Grounds, Brooklyn

BY JOHN ZINN

AS GAME TIME APPROACHED ON October 7, 1874, a crowd estimated at 1,000 gathered at Brooklyn's Union Grounds for a match between the first-place Boston Red Stockings and the sixth-place Brooklyn Atlantics.[1] If the immediate past was prologue, it was hard to understand the fans' motivation for plunking down their hard-earned quarters to gain admission. Less than a week earlier in Boston, the Red Stockings pounded, thrashed, and humiliated the Atlantics, 29-0, in a mismatch in which the "Chicagoed" Atlantics managed only four hits. Boston's 29 runs were one part Red Stockings hits (26) and one part Atlantics errors (30). Atlantics fans could, however, draw some optimism from three earlier 1874 triumphs over the defending champions and the perhaps wishful thought that the rout was a onetime aberration. Another factor possibly boosting attendance was that while the Atlantics were playing out the string, Boston was caught up in one of the few pennant races of the National Association's five-year existence. The Red Stockings' rival for the flag was another New York club, the Mutuals, who also called the Union Grounds home. After the 29-0 humiliation of the Atlantics on October 1, Boston led the Mutuals by 1½ games, but in the intervening period, the Red Stockings briefly slipped into second before reclaiming the lead, a position they held by 2½ games on October 7.

Although there was no single cause of the 29-run disaster, one factor mentioned by the *New York Clipper* was an injury suffered by Atlantics catcher Jake Knowdell, for whom no suitable substitute was available. Knowdell was still out on the 7th so the Atlantics turned to the much-traveled Frank Fleet, who played multiple positions, none of them with any apparent success. Although the Atlantics probably had few choices at catcher, much more surprising was Boston's decision to accept Dick Higham as the umpire for the match. Not only was Higham a player for the Mutuals, his honesty both as a player and an umpire had been questioned for some time. In this case, there was plenty of fire to go with the smoke since Higham would eventually become the only major-league umpire expelled from the game for dishonesty.[2]

With the preliminaries resolved, the Atlantics lost the bat toss and went to the striker's line against Boston's ace pitcher, Albert Spalding, who continued his domination of the Atlantics by setting down the first six batters in order. Spalding was matched by the Atlantics' young sensation, Tommy Bond, who had kept the weak-hitting Atlantics in many games over the course of the season.[3] In its third turn at bat, however, the home team finally ended its 11-inning scoreless streak against Boston pitching. Red Stockings third baseman Harry Schafer gave Brooklyn a helping hand by muffing Herman Dehlman's groundball. After Pat McGee struck out and Bobby Clack singled, Jack Chapman, back with the Atlantics after starring with the club in the 1860s, hit one "dead on the line between left and centre fields," giving the crowd incentive, if they needed it, to "cheer themselves hoarse."[4] The *Clipper* reporter, probably Henry Chadwick, unkindly claimed the hit could have been a home run, but the 31-year-old's "aldermanic proportions prevented his getting farther than third base."[5] It was not only an unkind, but an unnecessary cut as Chapman shortly thereafter crossed the plate on Bob Ferguson's single.

Since they had already lost three times to the Atlantics that season, the Red Stockings most likely

— 286 —

hadn't developed any false sense of security from the 29-0 victory the week before. In its half of the third, Boston quickly put a run on the scoreboard, but the Red Stockings then tried to give the Atlantics some gift runs by making three errors in the top of the fourth. Unfortunately for the Atlantics, their fans, and the Mutuals, the home team couldn't take advantage. Given this reprieve, Boston added a second run on a single by Spalding followed by Deacon White's triple. Continuing to hold the Atlantics at bay, the Red Stockings tied the game in the sixth when Ross Barnes scored on Fleet's passed ball. Having lost the lead, the Atlantics staged their own rally in the seventh when McGee and Clack reached base with only one out. Ferguson then lifted a fly to left on which three Red Stockings converged, but let drop out of "fear of a collision."[6] Unfortunately for the Atlantics, rather than go halfway to third, McGee was "hugging second base despite Ferguson's appeals for him to run."[7] The overly cautious Atlantic was forced out at third on atrocious baserunning the *New York Herald* labeled "a piece of stupidity." Again reprieved, Boston retired the side and ended the threat.[8]

Neither team scored in the eighth, but the ninth didn't lack for drama. The Atlantics threatened to take the lead in the top of the inning, but Boston pulled off a rally-killing double play with George Wright throwing out a runner at the plate. Matching defense for defense, the Atlantics stopped Boston's attempt to win in the bottom of the ninth, keyed by "a very fine play by the old Red Stocking [Cincinnati] second baseman [Charles Sweasy]."[9] The keystone sack had been a major problem for the Atlantics all year with 13 different players, including, of course, Frank Fleet, taking a turn, but on this day at least, Sweasy had one more moment of glory. It was, in fact, a fine day for a number of veterans as the *Herald* praised not only Sweasy, but longtime Atlantic legends Bob Ferguson and Dickey Pearce.[10]

The deadlocked game headed to the 10th. The Atlantics threatened after two were out, but Boston escaped without allowing a run. With another chance to close out the game in the bottom of the inning, Boston couldn't even muster a baserunner, setting the stage for a semicomic ending in the 11th. Bond led off for the Atlantics with an infield hit, but Fleet grounded to Wright, who forced Bond and threw to first "an instant too late"[11] to complete the double play. The "instant" became even more important when Sweasy made what would have been the third out and would have given the Red Stockings another chance to close out the game without playing a full inning. Time had become important because it started raining at the beginning of the inning and with Herman Dehlman coming to bat, umpire Higham suspended play even though the *Clipper* claimed "the necessity was not remarkably urgent."[12] As a Mutual player, Higham had a vested interest in the outcome, since from the Mutuals' perspective a tie was better than a Boston victory.

The situation became even more suspicious when the rain let up and play was to resume. The Boston players apparently went onto the field without even bothering to put their full uniforms back on, but the Atlantics were "more particular about their personal appearance."[13] This was especially true of Dehlman (one of the two Atlantics needed to resume play), who reportedly "had to tie a double bow-knot in his shoe-string and comb his hair before he felt disposed to appear on the field."[14] Once on the field, the reluctant striker took extra time to find his bat, which equally suspiciously "had been carefully tied up with about twenty others."[15] By the time Dehlman finally arrived at the plate, the rain had resumed and Higham called the game "to the disgust of the Bostons and the crowd, and the delight of the Atlantics."[16]

It's impossible to know if something untoward was going on that day at Union Grounds, but the overall level of play by both teams was highly praised by the *Herald*. "Rarely indeed," the paper claimed, "have two nines put forth such efforts to win a (game)." To some degree, the *Herald* reporter seemed pleased that "neither side could claim the victory." In the end the final result didn't impact the pennant race, so the controversial ending didn't mar one of the National Association's most exciting games.[17]

NOTES

1. *New York Sunday Mercury*, October 11, 1874.
2. *New York Clipper*, October 10, 1874: 219, October 17, 1874: 229; William J. Ryczek, *Blackguards and Red Stockings: A History of Baseball's National Association, 1871-1875* (Wallingford, Connecticut: Colebrook Press, 1992), 99, 212-213.
3. Ryczek, 148; *New York Clipper*, October 17, 1874: 229.
4. *New York Clipper*, October 17, 1874: 229.
5. Ibid.
6. Ibid.
7. Ibid.
8. *New York Herald*, October 8, 1874: 4.
9. *New York Clipper*, October 17, 1874: 229.
10. Ryczek, 148; *New York Herald*, October 8, 1874: 4.
11. *New York Clipper*, October 17, 1874: 229.
12. Ibid.
13. Ibid.
14. Ibid.
15. Ibid.
16. Ibid.
17. *New York Herald*, October 8, 1874: 4.

BOSTON RED STOCKINGS CLINCH THIRD TITLE

October 20, 1874: Boston Red Stockings 14, Athletics of Philadelphia 7, at Jefferson Street Grounds, Philadelphia

BY PAUL E. DOUTRICH

NOT ALL IMPORTANT BASEBALL wins are the product of exciting, well-played games. Such was the case on October 20, 1874, when the Boston Red Stockings beat the Athletics of Philadelphia 14-7 to clinch their third consecutive National Association championship.

The day started well for the Athletics. Playing on their home field, the Jefferson Street Grounds, in front of a crowd estimated at between 1,000 and 1,500 fans, they got off to a fast start.[1] After holding the Red Stockings scoreless in the first, the home team batted around and scored five times in the bottom half of the inning. Only once before during the 1874 season had Boston been down by five or more runs after the first inning and that game had not ended well for them. On May 23 the Brooklyn Atlantics led the Red Stockings 7-0 after an inning and went on to hand the Bostons their first loss of the season.

The Red Stockings and Athletics were very familiar with each other. In addition to having already played each other eight times during the 1874 season (the Red Stockings had won six of the eight games), they had also spent the last two weeks of July, all of August, and the first week of September together in England and Ireland, where they played 14 exhibition games—and even some cricket. The tour was the brainchild of Harry Wright, the Boston manager. Born in England, Wright hoped to generate interest in baseball among his former countrymen. Reluctantly, the Philadelphia stockholders agreed to send the Athletics along as the opposition team. Wright's crew won eight of the 14 games.[2]

It was on this trip that Red Stockings pitcher Al Spalding and the Athletics star Cap Anson began a 30-year friendship. The two were fierce competitors who valued discipline and dedication both on the field and off. Over the next three decades Spalding would become the president and eventually owner of the Chicago White Stockings. While team president, he promoted Anson to the position of manager. It was a relationship that helped to establish the White Stockings as the best team in professional baseball during the 1880s.

On September 10, the day after they returned from England, the two teams resumed league play in Philadelphia. Boston beat the Athletics, 5-4. Two days later, in Boston, Philadelphia got even with a 6-5 win. Despite their journey, the Red Stockings remained comfortably atop the National Association standings, a position they had held since the first week of the season. Meanwhile, the Athletics had fallen into third place, a half-game behind the New York Mutuals.

The October 20 game was the fifth and final game in a visit by the Bostons to Philadelphia. On October 15 they had beaten the Philadelphia Whites, 6-4. On the 16th Boston played the Athletics and won, 5-1. They returned to the Jefferson Street Grounds, which the two Philadelphia teams shared, to play the Whites on the 17th, and won 5-2. After taking the Sunday off, the Red Stockings played the Whites again on Monday the 19th, this time losing, 5-2.

Despite the discouraging early deficit in the October 20 game, the Red Stockings immediately began chipping away at Philadelphia's lead. In the second inning the first two Boston hitters, catcher

Deacon White and right fielder Cal McVey, each reached base. Both scored, as did first baseman Jim O'Rourke, to pull the Red Stockings within two. An inning later Athletics right fielder Tim Murnane added a run to the Philadelphia lead but it would not be enough to counter Boston.

In the fifth inning Boston second baseman Ross Barnes, pitcher Al Spalding, and third baseman Harry Schafer tied the score. Barnes, who contributed a single, double, and triple to his team's attack, and Spalding were two of the Red Stockings' "Big Four." The other half of the Big Four was McVey and White. These four players constituted the heart of the Boston batting order and were among the most productive foursomes in the National Association. Each finished the 1874 season hitting over .300.[3] Two years later all four, along with Cap Anson, the Athletics' best player, would join the Chicago White Stockings for the National League's inaugural season.

Once the Red Stockings tied the score in the sixth, Philadelphia fell apart. Though the Bostons "did not play with their usual care in the field" and depended "more on their batting and the 'muffism' of the antagonists," they kept piling on the runs.[4] Boston went on to score four more runs in the sixth, two in the seventh, and two more in the ninth. Several crucial misplays in the outfield, two errors by second baseman John Battin, and four by first baseman Al "Count" Gedney contributed to the Red Stockings' success. In all, the Athletics committed 12 errors. Philadelphia's sloppy performance in the game was described as one that "can be eclipsed by many amateur organizations."[5] The *Boston Journal* confirmed the assessment, reporting that each team had scored only one earned run.[6] Meanwhile, pitcher Spalding and his mates limited the home team to only one more tally. For Spalding, it was his 46th win of the season, one in which he posted a 52-16 record. He threw 65 complete games.

Though "the game was a very uninteresting one in many respects," when coupled with a loss by the New York Mutuals, it brought to the Red Stockings their third consecutive National Association championship.[7] Because of the vagaries of the day, there was no official "clinching" of the pennant or scoreboard-watching as we know them today. Nevertheless, the Red Stockings were champions again.

NOTES

1 *Philadelphia Inquirer*, October 21, 1874; "Sporting News," *Chicago Daily Tribune*, October 21, 1874: 7; Retrosheet lists the attendance at 500.

2 19cbaseball.com/tours-1874-world-base-ball-tour.html.

3 Retrosheet.org.

4 "Sporting News," *Chicago Daily Tribune*, October 21, 1874: 7.

5 Ibid.

6 "Out-door Sports," *Boston Journal*, October 21, 1874: 4.

7 *Philadelphia Inquirer*, October 21, 1874.

AL SPALDING'S 50TH WIN OF THE SEASON

October 26, 1874 – Boston Red Stockings 15, Philadelphia Athletics 3, at South End Grounds, Boston

BY BILL NOWLIN

CHARLES "HOSS" RADBOURN posted a 59-12 record for the National League's Providence Grays in 1884, but that was still 10 years in the future. He'd won 48 in 1883. In his 11-year career, there were three times Radbourn won more than 30 games. Al Spalding had only a six-year career, if one excludes the 11 innings he pitched in 1877. In those six seasons, only once did he win fewer than 38 games, and that was in his first season pitching for the Boston Red Stockings, when he won 19.

Spalding had won 38 in 1872 and 41 in 1873. In 1874, he won his 41st game on October 13—but the season still had a few weeks to go. The Red Stockings had played only six regular-season games in July and none at all in August. They were busy traveling. Spalding won victory number 42 on the 14th, number 43 on the 15th, number 44 on the 16th, and number 45 on the 17th. Five days, five games, five wins, all on the road. When the road trip wound up, on October 23, Spalding had 48 wins. He beat Hartford on the 24th, and then had to take the Lord's Day off to rest. Sitting on 49 wins, he awaited the arrival of Philadelphia's team, the Whites (sometimes called the Pearls), on Monday the 26th.

Manager Harry Wright may have given it a passing thought, "Who shall I pitch against Philadelphia?" but chances are that he spent little time pondering the question. There were only three games left on the schedule and Al Spalding had already worked in 63 of the team's 67 games.

The two teams knew each other well. They had met each other eight times, with Boston winning six of the eight contests. But both teams had also traveled to England during that midseason "break" that centered on August.

Somewhere between 800 and 1,000 spectators took in the game which began at "2½ o'clock." Though Dave Birdsall had played for Boston the three prior years, he had not in 1874; Birdsall served as umpire.

The Bostons batted first and scored seven runs. The runs came thanks to a leadoff triple by George Wright and a single by Spalding, followed by a Deacon White single, and a Cal McVey "double-baser." There was a home run ("a clean drive over the fence at left field") by Jim O'Rourke, followed by another three-baser by George Wright.[1] Mixed in were two Philadelphia errors. We're not sure who reached base and who made out, nor do we know how many may have been on base when O'Rourke homered, but we do know that seven runs crossed the plate. It was written that only two of them were earned.[2] The Philadelphias got no runs in the first, but scored twice in the bottom of the second.

There had been a chance for Philadelphia to break through in the second inning, when they loaded the bases on three base hits and got a run on a ball hard-hit by striker Denny Mack that was fumbled by Boston's Harry Schafer. There was still nobody out, and Chick Fulmer at the plate. But Fulmer fouled out. The Philadelphia pitcher, Candy Cummings, singled to center, driving in the second run, but McVey's throw from center field to Deacon White at the plate cut down Tom York, who'd tried to score, and the threat was over.

Boston replied with two more of its own in the third, re-establishing the seven-run cushion.

While Philadelphia didn't score again until once in the seventh, Boston added one run in the fourth, two more in the fifth, and its 13th run in the top of the seventh. With the score 13-3 after eight, the Red Stockings added two more in their half of the ninth. Philadelphia scored no more. The final was 15-3, Boston, and Al Spalding recorded his 50th win of the season. It was already late October, and there was to be no baseball in November, but Spalding added two more wins on the following two days, only to lose his final decision of the year on October 30. His record was 52-16. He'd just turned 23 in early September.

Much of the scoring was due to differences in fielding. Boston committed seven errors in total, but Philadelphia shortstop Jim Holdsworth made six by himself, and the catcher, Nat Hicks, made four more. All told, Philadelphia was charged with 16 errors.[3]

Despite the disparity in scoring, and the relative ineptness of Philadelphia's fielding, the *Boston Daily Advertiser*'s front-page account allowed that the lead "did not appear to discourage the visitors, and all of them, excepting Cummings, who acted as if he was either sick or sulky, played with vigor and pluck."[4]

At the beginning of the sixth inning, Cummings left the game and George Bechtel came in from right field to pitch, with Pete Donnelly taking over right field. Bechtel only allowed four (or maybe three) hits in the final four innings.

The game ran 1:50.

The *Boston Globe* enthused about the weather, but said the game itself "was not remarkable in any one particular, but several brilliant plays were made."[5] The Boston papers all noted the one-handed catch the Red Stockings' Tommy Beals made, running deeper into right field to haul in the ball and them tumbling into a "heels over head" somersault with the ball firmly in hand. Philadelphia's York also made a "beautiful running catch" and their first baseman Mack was singled out for his good fielding.

None of the coverage, which included the *Boston Journal*, noted that Spalding had won his 50th game of the season. It was one of the 65 complete regular-season games he threw in 1874.

Al Spalding, 50-game winner (Spalding Collection)

After the game, both teams attended the performance at the Boston Theatre, by invitation of the management.

SOURCES

Numerous contemporary newspapers were consulted to prepare this account. Bob LeMoine checked the *Philadelphia Inquirer*, which appears to have devoted only one line to the game.

NOTES

1. *Boston Daily Advertiser*, October 27, 1874: 1.
2. Ibid.
3. The *Boston Globe* account says that Boston committed seven errors, and Philadelphia committed 16. The *Advertiser*, which sometimes had better baseball coverage at the time, agrees that Boston was charged with seven, but ascribed 20 to Philadelphia. We have simply gone with the more conservative figure here.
4. *Boston Daily Advertiser*.
5. *Boston Globe*, October 27, 1874: 5.

APRIL 19, 1875

Boston Red Stockings 6, New Haven Elm Citys 0, at Union Grounds, Boston

BY MARK PESTANA

APRIL 19, 1875, WAS A NOTABLE DATE in American history, being the Centennial of the battles at Lexington and Concord which precipitated the Revolutionary War, and lavish celebrations were held to mark the day in those Massachusetts towns. President Ulysses S. Grant attended ceremonies at both sites, Ralph Waldo Emerson spoke, commemorative poems by James Russell Lowell and John Greenleaf Whittier were heard, and Daniel Chester French's Minute Man statue was formally unveiled near "the rude bridge that arched the flood" in Concord.[1]

While the City of Boston observed the occasion by closing banks, courts, and schools for the day, there were no major Centennial events in Beantown proper. Instead, the primary excitement was in the mass exodus of city dwellers by rail out to the suburbs. Trains began running at 7 A.M., and by 9 o'clock an estimated 10,000 had passed through Boston's Fitchburg depot on their way to Concord, while the Lowell depot in Boston, which sent cars to both Lexington and Concord, carried even more. Beyond noon, thousands waited in line at the depots in hope of passage to the memorial sites.[2]

For those Bostonians left behind, there was still grand entertainment to be had, as the Boston Red Stockings were hosting the opening game of the 1875 National Association season at their South End Grounds. The Reds looked to defend their position as the NA's premier club; they had won the league championship three years running and there was no reason to believe they would not contend at the same high level in what would turn out to be the swan song of baseball's first organized league.

The team was not greatly changed from that of bygone years. Seven men in the Opening Day lineup had been regulars in 1874, and six of those had been regulars in 1873 as well. Ross Barnes, Harry Schafer, Al Spalding, and George Wright had been starters ever since 1871. Andy Leonard and Cal McVey each had three seasons with Boston under his belt, and of course they, along with George Wright and his elder brother Harry, had all been teammates on the immortal Cincinnati nine of 1869-70. This powerhouse Boston club included five future Hall of Famers: Jim O'Rourke, Deacon White, Spalding, and the Wrights, although Harry's time was now spent almost entirely on the bench, as captain and manager.[3]

Right fielder Jack Manning had been with the Reds as a rookie in 1873, and was back after spending a year with the Baltimore Canaries. The one completely new face in the lineup was George Latham. Latham, who would in time acquire the colorful nicknames Jumbo (presumably for his waistline in later years) and Juice (presumably for an affinity to the bottle), was a Utica, New York, native, signed by the Reds in February,[4] and given the nod by Harry Wright to start at first base.

The Red Stockings' Opening Day opponent was a new team from Connecticut, the New Haven Elm Citys. New Haven was the third club from the Nutmeg State to enter the NA. The Mansfields of Middletown had gone 5-19 before folding in the summer of '72. The Hartford Dark Blues debuted in 1874, finishing seventh out of eight teams, but would improve greatly on that record in '75.

The Elm City nine was a rather rough patchwork assemblage. Five of the starters were making their "big league" debuts. One was shortstop Sam Wright, the younger sibling of Boston's Wright Brothers, 22 months George's junior. He came on the recommendation of big brother Harry to New Haven captain Charlie Gould.[5] Gould, another veteran of the 1869-70 Cincinnati world-beaters, was the starting first baseman for the Bostons in 1871 and '72, and shared an infield with Jack Manning on the '74 Baltimores, a team that also included New Haven left fielder Johnny Ryan.

Second baseman Billy Geer had all of two games' prior NA experience, but would go on to play 232 games in a career lasting to 1885, more than any of the other Elm City starting nine.[6] Center fielder Jim Tipper, a Middletown native, had the unique distinction of playing on all three of Connecticut's NA clubs.

A crowd of about 1,200 braved less than agreeable conditions to witness the contest. The *Boston Post* said people "shivered and stamped in the cold,"[7] and the *New York Clipper* reported that "though the field had been rolled, and sawdust had been freely used ... still the want of the sun's rays left it unfavorable for sharp fielding."[8] Umpire Fred Cone made the "Play ball" call shortly after 3 P.M. Cone was a former player, remembered by the locals as the left fielder of the Bostons in 1871, his only big-league season.

New Haven, winning the coin toss, chose to bat second, and the Red Stockings sent George Wright, Cal McVey, and Ross Barnes to the plate in the top of the first inning. Facing them in the box was Frederick "Tricky" Nichols, a 5-foot-7 right-hander who, like Jim Tipper, was a Connecticut-bred lad, born in Bridgeport in 1850. He eventually pitched in 106 big-league games, completing 90 of his 98 starts. Here, in his first pro appearance, against three of the best hitters in the Association,[9] he enjoyed a 1-2-3 inning. In the bottom of the frame, Geer, Sam Wright, and Henry Luff for the Elm Citys went down in order against Spalding.

The Reds flexed their muscles in the second inning. Spalding and Leonard, the first batters, both reached base and subsequently scored on passed balls. White went out but Manning and Latham got base hits and Harry Schafer reached courtesy of a New Haven error. The top of the order came around now, and George Wright knocked a double, scoring Manning, while

Part of a front page ad in the Boston Traveler, *April 19, 1875.*

Latham held up at third. With McVey at bat, rookie catcher Studs Bancker allowed yet another ball to get past him, and Latham came home with the fourth Reds run. McVey, who would go hitless in the game, then ended the Boston half. The Elm Citys drew another blank in the bottom of the second.

Barnes led off the third with a double, and eventually scored on third baseman John McKelvey's error. Barnes also scored in the fifth, this time an earned run. In between, Spalding continued to keep the visitors off the board.

Except for the second inning, Nichols pitched well enough to win. He allowed only three earned runs and was sorely hurt by his batterymate's four passed balls. He even got two base hits in his own cause. But the Elm Citys could not mount a concerted attack. Geer managed two hits, while Luff and the youngest Wright got one each. Latham was kept quite busy, with 14 putouts at first base; by contrast, the Boston outfielders barely got into the action, registering just one fly ball out apiece. The last four innings went by with no scoring on either side, and the final tally stood at Boston 6, New Haven 0.

The defending champs had defeated the newcomers for the first in what became a string of 27 consecutive games without a loss to start the season.[10] Most of those wins would come in the form of lopsided beatdowns of the likes of 22-5, 14-2, 12-0, 16-2, and 13-2, against not only subpar clubs like the Nationals and Centennials, but also worthy opponents like the Athletics, Hartfords, and Philadelphia Whites. In that light, perhaps New Haven had not fared too poorly in the 6-0 loss.

The Elm Citys struggled through their only NA campaign, but they kept their collective chins up. Eighteen of their losses were by three runs or fewer, and 12 by two or fewer. They managed to get the better of some of the best pitchers of the 19th century: Candy Cummings, George Zettlein, Bobby Mathews, and George Bradley. Perhaps their most satisfying moment came July 2, on home turf, when Nichols earned his first NA victory, beating Spalding and the Reds, 10-5.

SOURCES

In addition to the sources cited in the Notes, the author also consulted the following:

Baseball-Reference.com.

Retrosheet,org.

Nemec, David. *Major League Baseball Profiles: 1871-1900, Volumes 1 & 2* (Lincoln, Nebraska: Bison Books, 2011).

_____. *The Great Encyclopedia of 19th-Century Major League Baseball* (New York: Donald I. Fine Books, 1997).

NOTES

1 *Boston Daily Advertiser*, April 20, 1875: 1; *Boston Journal*, April 20, 1875: 1.

2 Ibid.

3 Harry played one game in 1875, one in 1876, and one in 1877—the final three games of his playing career.

4 *Boston Journal*, February 15, 1875: 4

5 Wright to Gould, March 31, 1875, quoted in William J. Ryczek, *Blackguards and Red Stockings* (Wallingford, Connecticut: Colebrook Press, 1992), 182.

6 For the amusing story of Geer and teammate Henry Luff's off-field misadventures in 1875, see *Blackguards and Red Stockings*, 195-196.

7 Quoted in the *Mirror and Farmer* (Manchester, New Hampshire), April 24, 1875: 5.

8 *New York Clipper*, May 1, 1875: 37.

9 At season's end, Barnes, McVey, and Wright, along with teammate Deacon White, were all in the top five for batting average in the league.

10 Their May 27 game against the Athletics ended in a 3-3 tie.

APRIL 29, 1875

Boston Red Stockings 22, Washington Nationals 5, at the Richmond Fair Grounds, Richmond, Virginia

BY GERARD R. GOULET

ON APRIL 28, 1875, THE *RICHMOND Daily Dispatch* announced to its readership that "the famous Red Stockings of Boston (the champion club of the United States)" would play a championship game against "the celebrated Washingtons of Washington, D.C." on the next day. This was, the *New York Clipper* said, the first professional baseball game to be played south of the Mason-Dixon Line.[1]

Although Washington had just returned to the National Association after a year's absence, it was thought that a game with the Nationals would provide more of a match than one played against a local Richmond team. As the *Dispatch* indicated in its day-of-contest edition, "It is possible that a picked nine of this city will be induced to play the Red Stockings a game, though they can scarcely do so with the hope of success."[2] Notwithstanding the newspaper's realistic assessment of its local talent, it appeared to be genuinely misinformed with regard to the skill of the Washington squad which it reported "have lately increased their numbers by the addition of some of the most proficient players in the country."[3] This was news to those who more closely followed the fortunes of professional baseball. The nucleus of Washington's team resided in three position players: outfielders John Hollinshead and Art Allison (neither of whom had played professionally in 1874), and second baseman Steve Brady, who had only 27 games' experience in 1874; and the pitcher, Bill Stearns, whose professional record of 12 wins and 50 losses over the previous four years did not appear to evidence a high level of proficiency. In fact, the *Boston Advertiser* considered only two of Washington's players to be of major-league caliber.[4] The game was to be the second of the series between the Red Stockings and Nationals, the former having won the first on April 26 by a score of 8-2. Accordingly, the *Daily Dispatch* felt the game would be of "decided interest."[5] The turnout seemed to confirm that sentiment.

The match had been arranged by a local promoter, A.B. Sturgis, who guaranteed a minimum return to the teams regardless of attendance.[6] Richmond was not, however, the baseball hub it had been a decade before.[7] Thus, the crowd of spectators was surprisingly large. The weather cooperated. It was clear, mild, and pleasant with brisk southerly winds and temperatures in the mid-60s.[8] This was a far cry from what the Boston team could have expected had it instead scheduled its games for its home grounds for this weekend. As reported in the *Daily Dispatch*, "Fifteen hundred persons paid their way through the gates. ... at least five hundred men of economical and enterprising turn of mind clambered over the fence, and thus 'dead-headed'[9] themselves in," and "a goodly number of ladies were present." As if the press of people was not sufficiently problematic, the roadways of the grounds were "pretty well lined with hacks and other vehicles."[10] Railcars did not run from the city to the grounds as had previously been the case. This was because of a city ordinance passed in 1873 prohibiting any steam-propelled vehicle of any kind of the Richmond, Fredericksburg and Potomac Railroad Company from traversing Broad Street, the most important and populous street of Richmond.[11] Thus, the relief from vehicular traffic that railroads afforded in other major cities where baseball was played was not available in Richmond for this game.

Not only were the crowds and vehicles constantly encroaching on the field, but both teams were hampered by the "imperfect field appointments and roughness of the ground."[12] Nevertheless, the playing in the match "surpassed anything of the kind ever witnessed in Richmond."[13]

Boston's battery, Al Spalding and Deacon White, each collected four hits, while Hollinshead and John Dailey led Washington with two hits apiece. Spalding and Jack Manning each collected a three-base hit for Boston as did Washington's Hollinshead. The result—a 22-5 Red Stockings victory—was probably more one-sided than the locals had expected, with the game all but decided by the end of the second inning, during which Boston scored 12 runs.

In the field, in addition to George Wright's overall excellence at shortstop, Boston delivered a Wright-to-Ross Barnes-to-Jumbo Latham double play in the fifth inning as a further testament to the team's fielding prowess. Meanwhile, as a corollary to Boston's fine hitting, Washington's left fielder, Bill Parks, treated the crowd to a fine demonstration with six catches on the fly and the chance for an additional two had not carelessly parked vehicles interfered.[14]

As reported in the local press, despite (or perhaps because of) the clear superiority of the Boston team, the crowd seemed to favor the Washingtons and "notwithstanding the fair and generally correct decisions of the umpire, Mr. Beale, behaved in a most shameful manner towards that gentleman."[15] The *New York Clipper*'s account of the game, although apparently largely derived from that of the *Daily Dispatch*, seemed to expand unreasonably beyond the treatment of the umpire to describe an almost hostile environment that had not been mentioned in the local reporting: "From the report in the *Richmond Dispatch* of the day following, we should judge that it was about as partisan a gathering as any country village could present, the crowd behaving like city 'roughs' towards the gentlemanly umpire, while their prejudices were shown in their exhibition of favoritism for Washington, or what they considered as the 'Southern nine' against the Northern or Massachusetts players. The minority of the better class present, of course, resented this rural style of thing; but the shouts of the majority ruled supreme. If this is to be the result of the playing of games in Richmond, the Northern nines had better keep away.

We thought that in the baseball arena sectional ill-will was something all would refrain from."[16] This bit of editorializing was followed only a sentence away by a report that the "spectators were delighted" by the superior play. There is an inconsistency in this report that suggests another agenda.[17]

In any event, baseball experienced a rebirth in Richmond in 1875.[18] Whether this was an effect of the professionals coming to Virginia as claimed by the *Clipper*[19] or simply the fact that events that had plagued the city and its economy from 1867 to 1874 had finally abated sufficiently to allow the game to prosper as it had in 1866 and 1867 are matters of debate.[20] In either case, the Red Stockings had come to town and shown the locals how the game could be played and enthusiasm for baseball in the Richmond area was rekindled.

NOTES

1 "The Champions in Virginia—Boston vs. Washington," *New York Clipper*, May 8, 1875. The *Clipper* called it "the first professional championship match ever played in the South."

2 Corroboration of that fact came within a very short period of time. The newly organized Pacific Club of Richmond won most of its games in July 1875, and gained a reputation as one of the city's finest clubs. The Washington Nationals, with a record of 5 wins and 23 losses in professional championship games through July 4, 1875, invited the Pacific Club to Washington for a game. The Pacifics lost 22-5. Clearly, the Richmond baseball clubs were not yet a match for even a second-tier professional nine. Ryan Swanson, *When Baseball Went White—Reconstruction, Reconciliation & Dreams of a National Pastime* (Lincoln: University of Nebraska Press, 2014), 166.

3 *Richmond Daily Dispatch*, April 28, 1875.

4 William Ryczek, *Blackguards and Red Stockings: A History of Baseball's National Association, 1871-1875* (Jefferson, North Carolina: McFarland, 1992), 181.

5 *Richmond Daily Dispatch*, April 28, 1875. This was not a foregone conclusion, however, as baseball had been on the wane in Richmond since 1867. Swanson, 128.

6 Ryczek, 204.

7 Baseball flourished in Richmond in 1866. Although no team played more than 10 games, at least 30 clubs played in the city during the 1866 season. See Swanson, 30. In August 1867 the city council voted to limit baseball activity on the Old Fair Grounds, and beginning in 1868 and continuing into early 1875, baseball games declined by nearly 75 percent from their 1867

levels. Swanson, 128, 165. In that context, the turnout was quite unexpected.

8 "Local Matters—The Base Ball Match Yesterday—The Red Stockings Victorious," *Richmond Daily Dispatch,* April 30, 1875.

9 Viewed the game for free.

10 *Richmond Daily Dispatch,* April 30, 1875.

11 historyengine.richmond.edu/episodes/view/3681; caselawfindlaw.com/us-supreme-court/96/521.html.

12 *Richmond Daily Dispatch,* April 30, 1875.

13 Ibid.

14 Ibid.

15 Ibid. The umpire was actually Tommy Beals of the Boston team, who umpired eight games during the course of his playing days, the April 29 game being the first of five in 1875.

16 *New York Clipper,* May 8, 1875.

17 See Swanson, 168 for one explanation of the Northern prejudices and expectations buried in the *Clipper's* own seeming intemperance.

18 Swanson, 165.

19 "The effect of the visit of the professionals to Virginia was the organization of a new club in Richmond, called the Pacific Club, by a number of young gentlemen residents of Broad street, on Thursday evening, April 29." *New York Clipper,* May 8, 1875.

20 The 1867 commercial lease of the Old Fair Grounds, continual Reconstruction trials, poverty, racial tensions, the flood of 1870, and the Panic of 1873, with its impact on the railroads and banks, were all adversities that made the playing of baseball a more difficult challenge in Richmond than in other parts of the country during this period. Swanson 128, 158.

MAY 18, 1875

Boston Red Stockings 10, Hartford Dark Blues 5 at Hartford Base Ball Grounds, Hartford, Connecticut

BY DAVID ARCIDIACONO

IN THE 1870S IT WAS HARTFORD, NOT New York, that was Boston's biggest diamond rival. As with the Yankees-Red Sox rivalry of recent vintage, a dislike existed between the Hartford and Boston clubs and charges of buying the pennant were alleged against each. The pinnacle of this rivalry occurred on May 18, 1875, when the Red Stockings and Dark Blues entered the game with perfect records. Hartford had 12 wins in as many tries, while Boston was even better, with 16 wins against no losses.

Boston's manager, Harry Wright, wanted the game (and its accompanying big payday) to take place in Boston, but since the National Association did not have a predetermined league schedule, this was open to negotiation. Hartford's corresponding secretary, Ben Douglas, felt the game should be played in Hartford, since the clubs' first match, in 1874, was played in Boston. When Douglas informed the venerable Wright of his position, Wright scoffed at his boldness.[1]

Douglas held firm, though, and when the big day arrived, fans from all over New England and New York arrived in Hartford, not Boston. A holiday atmosphere prevailed in the city as Connecticut baseball enthusiasts believed this would be the year their team would snatch the pennant from the mighty Red Stockings, champions three years running. Nearly every business in the city displayed a team photo in the window and many stores were selling a new brand of cigars called the "Captain Bob," featuring a picture of Hartford's Bob Ferguson on the label. Many local factories, including the Colt gun factory, closed shop early to give employees the rare opportunity to watch a game. The enthusiasm even reached the State Capitol, where the House and Senate adjourned early so as not to miss the contest.[2]

Shortly after noon, Hartford streets were deserted, as those who had tickets—and many who did not—headed for the ballpark. By 2 P.M., every general-admission seat was occupied. Those too late to find seats stood in the outfield grass, corralled behind long ropes. As the mass of humanity swelled, the skimpy ropes had no hope of retaining the crowd and scores of fans spilled onto the playing field as overmatched policemen attempted in vain to push them back. Twelve thousand spectators, reportedly the largest crowd ever in New England, filled the grounds, which seated about 4,000. Most of Hartford's most prominent residents, including Samuel Clemens, a/k/a Mark Twain, were in attendance.[3] The spectators weren't all Hartford supporters, though: More than 200 men had made the trip from Boston to see their club defend its championship.[4]

Polite applause greeted the ballplayers as they appeared on the field. The last to enter was Dark Blues Captain Ferguson, and the Hartford crowd welcomed him with a tremendous roar. The throng was especially partisan this day, knowing that Al Spalding had recently belittled their hometown club in a preseason newspaper interview. In the article Spalding acknowledged that Hartford had an excellent collection of talent, yet dismissed their chances of taking the pennant from his Boston team, saying, "They are an unruly set of fellows. They want more of the qualities which carry us on to glory every year. I mean brains. ..."[5]

Boston won the coin toss and sent Hartford to bat first. Leadoff batter Doug Allison selected one of Spalding's offerings and looped what looked to be a sure base hit over second base. Ross Barnes had other ideas, however, and to the chagrin of the huge crowd, Boston's speedy second baseman made a fine running catch. Jack Burdock aroused the crowd with a clean single to center, but the joy was short-lived as he was immediately cut down attempting to steal second. Tom Carey followed with another base hit, but was quickly retired after failing to return promptly to his base after a foul ball. (In 1875 a foul ball became live again when it was returned to the pitcher's hands. If a runner had not returned to his base by that time, he could be put out.[6])

Hartford then sent William Arthur "Candy" Cummings, all 120 pounds of him, and his "terrible parabolic curves" to the pitcher's box.[7] George Wright found one to his liking and stroked a single. Barnes then launched a long drive to right field that was neatly run down by Tommy Bond. Connecticut's own Jim O'Rourke followed with a single. But Cummings retired Andy Leonard on a comebacker to the box. It appeared the game would remain scoreless when Boston slugger Cal McVey tapped an easy groundball to shortstop Tom Carey. The smooth-fielding shortstop gathered the ball in cleanly and fired straight and true across the diamond. The Hartford crowd cheered loudly when first baseman Ev Mills caught the ball, believing the side was retired. But before the last "hurrah" had expired, Al Spalding was jawing with the umpire, claiming Mills had not touched first base. "Helping" the umpire was nothing new for the Boston club. Their champion status and Harry Wright's extensive knowledge of the rules often allowed them to intimidate an unsure umpire. Sure enough, umpire Alphonse Martin, a former pitcher known as "Old Slow Ball" in his playing days, ruled McVey safe and Wright was home. The huge Hartford crowd loudly let Martin know what they thought of his decision. It was never good policy to give the powerful Red Stockings extra outs, and this occasion was no exception. Spalding followed with a base hit, plating two more runs and giving Boston a 3-0 lead.[8]

Two innings later, another controversial call by Martin had Hartford fans jeering again. Andy Leonard made an infield hit that scored Ross Barnes and advanced Jim O'Rourke to third. During the play, Martin quietly called time out and then just as quietly called time back in. But no one, including O'Rourke, heard him. Martin ruled O'Rourke out for failing to retouch second after time had been called. Spalding immediately reappeared on the field and the two men spent 15 minutes thumbing through the rulebook while the impatient Hartford crowd shouted, "Read it out loud!" and "Pass it around and let us all read it!" In the end, Martin let O'Rourke reoccupy second base as if nothing had happened. The mood in the stands turned ugly, especially when McVey singled to center, scoring O'Rourke and giving the champs a 5-0 lead.[9]

The protracted dispute seemed to rouse the Dark Blues. Doug Allison led off the fourth inning with a single. Jack Burdock then sent a slow grounder to third. Jim O'Rourke fielded it cleanly but his throw to second flew wildly into right field, leaving runners on second and third with nobody out. Carey popped out, but Cummings broke the shutout by scoring Allison with a long fly ball. Two more hits and another Boston error cut Boston's lead to 5-3 and Hartford still had two men on base. Ev Mills then made up for his earlier miscue with a single over George Wright's head, driving in his two mates and knotting the score, 5-5. As Remsen crossed the plate with the tying run, the crowd was delirious; men tossed their hats in the air, women waved handkerchiefs, and young boys jumped about and shouted wildly.[10]

The score remained tied until Boston added a pair of runs in the seventh inning on consecutive hits by Jack Manning, George "Jumbo" Latham, and George Wright. Spalding had no trouble holding the lead, and

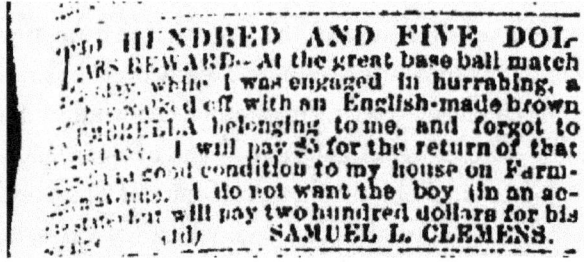

This ad from Samuel Clemens (Mark Twain) appeared in the May 20, 1875 Hartford Courant, *offering a $205 reward for the return of his umbrella and the remains of the boy who took it during the game.*

when Hartford was retired in the top of the ninth, the vast crowd streamed onto the field despite the best efforts of the police. Once the field was cleared, Boston added three superfluous runs to make the final result 10-5.[11]

When news of the Red Stockings' victory reached Boston, team headquarters were flooded by fans who were "nearly frantic with delight."[12] On the train ride home, the ballplayers got wind of the impending celebration and remained alert for the first signs of a welcome. At about 10 P.M., about 400 revelers, including a 20-piece German band, marched to the train station to greet their conquering heroes. The Red Stockings disembarked to loud cheers while the band serenaded them with "Hail to the Chief." The crowd escorted the team back to its headquarters, where a large banquet was served.[13]

NOTES

1. Wright's stinging reply to Douglas dated April 20, 1875: "As the champion club we consider ourselves entitled to the first game of the series on our grounds. ... In arranging with you we were willing, as friends and neighbors, to comply could we mutually agree on dates, but we did not expect that it would be compulsory for us to accept dates named by you under the plea that they were 'the only ones left.' If that is the case they must certainly be of great value to you, particularly so when they 'are being rapidly taken up.' We would be sorry to deprive you of the 'last of the lot' to replete our stock, nor will we be compelled to accept remnants." Harry Wright Correspondence, Albert G. Spalding Collection, New York Public Library.

2. *Hartford Courant*, April 21 and May 19, 1875; *Meriden Daily Republican*, May 18, 1875.

3. While he was at the game, Twain's umbrella was stolen and the following classified ad appeared in the May 20 *Hartford Courant*: TWO HUNDRED AND FIVE DOLLARS REWARD—At the great base ball match on Tuesday, while I engaged in hurrahing, a small boy walked off with an English-made brown silk UMBRELLA belonging to me and forgot to bring it back. I will pay $5 for the return of the umbrella in good condition to my house on Farmington Avenue. I do not want the boy (in an active state) but will pay two hundred dollars for his remains. SAMUEL L. CLEMENS. Twain's humorous ad nearly backfired on him when a local medical student reportedly had some fun at his expense. The imaginative student left one of his case studies—the corpse of a boy—on Twain's porch, along with a note claiming the reward money. A nervous Twain was concerned he'd be suspected of murder, until the janitor of the medical college came to claim the subject and clear the author's name. *Brooklyn Eagle*, August 18, 1875; *Seaside Gazette* (Vineyard Grove, Massachusetts), August 17, 1875.

4. *Hartford Courant*, May 19, 1875; *Hartford Times*, May 19, 1875; *Chicago Tribune*, May 19, 1875.

5. Arthur Bartlett, *Baseball and Mr. Spalding—The History and Romance of Baseball* (New York: Farrar, Straus and Young, Inc., 1951), 48.

6. *Hartford Courant*, May 19, 1875; *New York Clipper*, May 29, 1875.

7. *Hartford Times*, May 19, 1875; *Hartford Post*, May 19, 1875.

8. Ibid.

9. William Ryczek, *Blackguards and Red Stockings: A History of Baseball's National Association, 1871-1875* (Jefferson, North Carolina: McFarland, 1992), 205-207; *New York Clipper*, May 29, 1875.

10. *Hartford Courant*, May 19, 1875; *Boston Herald*, May 19, 1875.

11. *Hartford Courant*, May 19, 1875.

12. *Hartford Courant*, May 20, 1875.

13. *Boston Herald*, quoted in *Hartford Courant*, May 20, 1875.

THE UNBEATABLE RED STOCKINGS

June 3, 1875: Boston Red Stockings 10 vs. St. Louis Red Stockings 5, at Red Stocking Base Ball Park, St. Louis

BY BILL NOWLIN

THE BEST WINNING PERCENTAGE the New York Yankees ever enjoyed was .714 (110-44) in their 1927 world championship season. The Yankees would have had to improve to 139-15 to match the .899 winning percentage (71-8) of the Boston Red Stockings in 1875. It was as good a year as any team has ever had.

Boston won every one of its 37 home games, and went 34-8 on the road. The Red Stockings started the season with a 26-0-1 record, not losing a game until June.

Boston's dominance in 1875 was no surprise, for the team had won National Association championships in 1872, 1873, and 1874 with a cumulative record of 134 wins and only 42 losses. The Red Stockings possessed four future Cooperstown selectees—catcher Jim "Deacon" White, outfielder Jim O'Rourke, pitcher Al Spalding, and shortstop George Wright—in their starting nine. A fifth Hall of Famer, George Wright's brother Harry, was the manager. Much of the rest of the Boston lineup, notably second baseman Ross Barnes and first baseman Cal McVey, were considered among the game's elite.

The streak began with a 6-0 Opening Day shutout at home against New Haven. The Red Stockings outscored the Washington Nationals 54-7 in a three-game series, and by May 11 they were 11-0, Spalding having won all 11. Their other pitcher, Jack Manning, didn't start a game until the 12th game of the season—but he won, too. On May 27 in front of 5,000 people in Philadelphia, a 3-3 tie ended the Red Stockings' win streak at 22 games.[1]

Boston beat the Mutuals of New York on May 28 and 29, the latter their 24th win against the lone tie. Few of the games had been close. To that point, Boston had scored 288 runs and allowed only 74. Al Spalding was 22-0 and already a 20-game winner.

The team headed out by train to St. Louis, to play the Brown Stockings on June 2. Spalding won 10-3 in front of 6,000 who flocked to Grand Avenue Park. The *Boston Globe* headline the next morning ran in Latin: BOSTON OMNIA VINCIT (Boston Conquers All).

Spalding planned to pitch the next day against the other St. Louis team, the Red Stockings (also known as the Reds), who figured to be easy. It was their first and only year in the National Association, and they had played just nine games, winning two of them. Even within St. Louis itself, the Reds were the second team. The Brown Stockings, also playing their first season, were the local favorites, eventually finishing fourth at 39-29. The St. Louis Reds would wind up 10th at just 4-15.

Charlie Sweasy, a 27-year-old second baseman who doubled as the Reds manager, selected right-hander Joe Blong to face Spalding. Blong got a rough greeting. Boston scored three runs on three St. Louis errors and a double by McVey in the top of the first.

The Red Sox (so the St. Louis team was dubbed in the Boston papers—the *Globe*, *Herald*, and *Advertiser*) scored one in the second and another in the third. But Boston put up a fourth run in the top of the fourth, and added a decisive four more in the top of the fifth. Barnes singled and O'Rourke drove a hard-to-handle ball through third baseman Joe Ellick. Andy Leonard tripled, McVey singled, and Spalding doubled. The

Aerial view of the St. Louis baseball grounds. (Ballparkhistory.com)

Reds came back with two of their own in the bottom of the inning on three hits and had the bases loaded with one out. But George Wright's fielding produced a force out at home plate, and a second force out halted the rally. Boston added a run in the sixth, St. Louis one in the eighth, and then Boston put up a final run in the top of the ninth that made the score 10-5. Boston had run its record to 26-0.

Spalding was far from his best. The Bostons were outhit for just the second time all year, 13-12. The correspondent for the *Advertiser* wrote that while Boston prevailed, "it was not by any very brilliant display at the bat or in the field." They'd won the game "by their superior base-running and the many errors of their opponents."[2]

Those errors mounted up, with Boston making six of them (three by Spalding) and St. Louis committing 16. St. Louis catcher Silver Flint made six all by himself. There were so many errors that the on-scene accounts differ. The *St. Louis Republican* box score claimed Boston had committed seven errors and the Red Sox had committed 19, with just one earned run by each team. The *Daily News* had eight Boston errors and 14 by St. Louis.

Boston catcher White had no errors, but did have to leave his position in the sixth inning after injuring his thumb. He didn't leave the game; his finger was "straightened and tied up in a rag" and he moved to right field the following inning.[3]

Crowd estimates ranged between 1,000 and "at least" 2,000 reported by the *Republican*. That newspaper conceded that interest might have been lessened because "[I]t was looked upon as a foregone conclusion that the Bostons would achieve an easy victory." The newspaper added that "the 'striplings' ... gave them a good game."[4] The *Daily Times* described the losers as "not nearly so badly defeated as they themselves expected to be."

The win boosted Spalding to 24-0 for the season. He eventually won 54 games in the 79-game schedule, if one can call it a schedule when some of the games were really arranged as the weeks passed by.

Despite Spalding's staggering statistics in wins and losses, Boston's success was primarily due to offense. Their .321 team batting average ranked far above the second-place Athletics at .290, who were in turn well above the .260 average shared by the Chicago White Stockings and Hartford. Boston also led in on-base plus slugging, .737 to .677 for the Athletics. The 1.87 team ERA was good enough to rank fourth in the league. Boston's .870 fielding average ranked third.

The Red Stockings (with catcher White in a hospital) finally lost on June 5, the Brown Stockings defeating Spalding 5-4. The *Advertiser* headline read: THE BOSTONS MEET A WATERLOO AT LAST.

After the 1875 season, Spalding, White, Barnes, and McVey all signed on with the Chicago White Stockings in the new National League—and won the 1876 pennant. Playing a 66-game season, Spalding was 47-12, with a 1.75 ERA. Barnes hit for a .429 average.

Thanks to Maurice Bouchard, Dwayne Isgrig, and Jeff Kittel.

NOTES

1 The Red Caps were 22-0 when they saw the May 24 game end in a tie. But it wasn't a fair tie. Boston scored three runs in the top of the 10th, taking a 6-3 lead. The first two Athletics hit safely in the bottom of the 10th, but then a play happened on which accounts differ. Boston argued that Cap Anson had shoved second baseman Barnes and should be ruled out for interference. Umpire William McLean agreed, and so did the Athletics after some discussion. As Anson was leaving the field, he "made some remarks" and the umpire walked off the field. The crowd flocked onto the field and play was impossible, so McLean called the

game—rather than forfeit it—and it reverted to the tie it had been at the end of nine. *Boston Herald*, May 28, 1875.

2   *Boston Advertiser*, June 4, 1875. Perhaps unsurprisingly, accounts vary from newspaper to newspaper. The *Daily Times* box score, for instance, showed 12 hits for each team and had St. Louis scoring its first run in the first inning, not the second.

3   The quotation about the treatment of the finger comes from the *Daily Times*. Bill Ryczek offers a note from the *New York Clipper* of June 12, 1875, which says that White subsequently had to be hospitalized for a week. "McVey is a fine catcher, but not Jim White—for James stands alone," declared the *Clipper*. The book *Blackguards and Red Stockings* by William J. Ryczek (Wallingford, Connecticut: Colebrook Press, second printing 1999) provides an invaluable history of the National Association.

4   The *St. Louis Daily Times* cited the size as 2,000. A good source dedicated to 19th-century St. Louis baseball is Jeff Kittel's site thisgameofgames.blogspot.com.

JUNE 28, 1875
Boston 10, Philadelphia Athletic 10, at Philadelphia Athletic grounds (25th & Jefferson)

BY MICHAEL R. MCAVOY

THE *BOSTON POST* SUMMARIZED the game succinctly:

"The base ball match here to-day between the Boston and Athletic clubs resulted in a drawn game of 10 to 10. A tenth inning was commenced, the Bostons having made two runs, and the Athletics having two men out and two on bases, when the game was suspended on account of the excited crowd encroaching on the field, and before the field could be cleared the rain prevented the completion of the game."[1]

Preston Orem observed more than 80 years later that when a home club could not win, then its own crowd could assist to avoid the loss.[2]

After a decisive loss to the Athletic at their field two days earlier, the Boston season record was 35 wins and 3 losses, while the Athletic were 25 wins and 7 losses, seven games behind Boston and second in the standings. The game scheduled for Monday, June 28, 1875, at the Athletic grounds was the sixth in their 10-game series, in which Boston led with three wins, one loss, and one tie. A Boston win almost ensured a series victory over a powerful rival and an easier path to the national championship. The game outcome represented the peak of the tensions surrounding the conflation of the annual convention proceedings and the Davy Force case.[3]

"Hot and sultry" rain fell for an hour after 2:30 P.M., but it improved the playing field conditions.[4] Shortly after 4:00 P.M., with the odds about even and the "gambling toughs" present, 5,000 spectators watched as Dick McBride, the Athletic captain and pitcher, won the coin toss and selected the Boston nine to bat first.[5] Albert Spalding pitched for Boston.

Through the top of the fourth inning, Boston built a sizable lead. In the first inning, Boston scored two runs. Ross Barnes, batting second, successfully executed a fair-foul single. The Athletic scored one run. In the second, the Athletic twice loaded the bases, but were unable to score a run. In the third inning, Boston scored two runs on hits by Andy Leonard and Cal McVey, and errors by George Bechtel and John Clapp. In the fourth, Boston scored three unearned runs to increase its lead to 7-1. Boston ran the bases aggressively and capitalized on poor fielding by Bechtel in right field for two consecutive at-bats and George Wright stole home on a poorly thrown ball by Clapp.

In a big fourth inning, the Athletic scored five runs on a walk, a stolen base by Davy Force, and errors by Leonard and Barnes. They tied the contest at 7-7 in the sixth, drawing "loud shouts" from the crowd when Clapp scored from second base on a wild pitch. The Athletic took an 8-7 lead amid loud applause in the seventh, when Ezra Sutton singled, Barnes missed a double play, and scored from third base when McVey made an error on Bechtel's hit.

The lead changed again in the top of the eighth, when Boston scored three runs on four hits. *The Times* reported that with the score 9-8, umpire Charlie Gould ruled a hit by McVey foul, although Athletic captain McBride appealed that Wes Fisler had fielded the ball on its first bound.[6] McVey then went out at first on strikes, but Barnes scored on the play. (*The Philadelphia Inquirer* reported that Tommy Beals, Harry Schafer, and Leonard had scored the runs.)

In the bottom of the ninth the Athletic tied the score again. Bill Craver hit a line drive single, then scored on Sutton's triple. Sutton scored when George Hall flied out to right. The crowd exhibited "tense excitement" from the action and from a storm that approached from the southwest.[7]

The game reports vary for the Boston half of the 10th. The *Chicago Tribune* wrote that Boston scored two unearned runs due to errors by Clapp and Bechtel. The *Boston Globe* said two runs scored on five hits, and added that Barnes was erroneously ruled out when a spectator stopped his hit and threw it to Bechtel. The *Boston Daily Advertiser* reported five safe hits. The *Times* wrote that Clapp missed Schafer's ball hit foul on the bound, Schafer then singled to right, Bechtel made an error fielding the ball, which passed him, and Schafer made it to third base; Schafer scored on a single by Barnes; Barnes scored when George Wright hit a ball for a double. The *Philadelphia Inquirer* wrote that White hit a triple and scored on a hit by Wright, who in turn scored on a hit by Barnes.[8]

Whichever sequence was correct, they agreed that Boston led 12-10. In the Athletic half of the inning, leadoff batter Dave Eggler flied out and Force fouled out to White. Clapp reached first on an error by Barnes. Fisler hit the ball into the crowd, which was beginning to encroach on the playing field along the right-field line, for a "safe foul," and took first base, and Clapp went to second base. The *Boston Daily Advertiser* provided the report for what occurred next:

> "The crowd by this time had encroached within ten feet of the foul lines, and the feeble attempts of the policemen to keep them back was futile, and it was plainly evident that they were bent on breaking up the game. ... had Craver taken his position promptly as striker when the umpire called for him, the game would no doubt could have been play out, but his failing to do so cause some unnecessary talk, whereupon the crowd rushed in and put a stop to further proceeding. ..."[9]

The *Times* of Philadelphia said of the crowd on the playing field: "The more respectable portion of the spectators remained in their seats, but a large mob of half-grown boys and roughs poured on the grounds, and in a few minutes spread over the infield."[10]

The police together with the Athletic players were unable to move the crowd back. When rain poured for half an hour, spectators continued to occupy the field rather than take cover in the pavilions. After the rain ceased, both the Boston and Athletic players were willing to complete the game, but Gould refused to continue it because the ground was "soaked" and play "impossible."[11] Nevertheless, spectators continued to occupy the playing field, until an hour later when Gould officially returned the game to the ninth inning with the score tied 10-10.[12]

The *Boston Daily Advertiser* provided the tension present: "... (I)t was one of the most exciting games ever played in this city. ... The excitement ran high when the Athletic tied the game in the sixth inning, increased when they took the lead in the seventh, and was at fever heat when the tenth inning was commenced."[13] Any number of factors in combination likely heightened spectator frustration. The *Times* noted poor play, with too many errors by Bechtel and incorrect calls by Gould, who was unable to keep his composure under the stress of challenges for his decisions.[14] Indeed, the Athletic management believed that Gould's decisions gave Boston three unearned runs.[15]

The *New York Clipper* noted the lack of preparation by the Athletic management even though a crowd had previously occupied the field to prevent the completion of a game on May 27.[16]

The June 28 game was one of a series of confrontations involving Boston or the Athletic home crowds. The *New York Clipper* observed that Boston club followers were often loud and directed harsh words to the visiting nine. Philadelphia sportswriters often fanned the flames against visiting clubs, particularly Boston. It attributed the spectators' bad behavior to partisanship favoring the home club.[17] The *Times* of Philadelphia did not disagree; "(I)t was simply the spontaneous movement of an overwhelming multitude that carried all before it by its own weight."[18]

The *Clipper* declared that the clubs controlled behavior within their parks and should offer sufficient security and eject ill-behaved spectators. It said club managements should guarantee visiting teams a fair playing field and act to end rowdy behavior, which included "discreditable partisan comments, this howling at a player when he misses a ball, and the derisive cheers when any error is committed, while every play of the local nine is lauded, be it good, bad or indifferent, so that it help the local nine."[19]

In the aftermath, the Athletic management promised to provide a "clear field" to the Boston club. In turn, N.T. Apollonio, Boston club president, committed the Boston Association directors to improve the public discourse within their own grounds.[20]

NOTES

1. *Boston Post*, June 29, 1875: 2.
2. Preston D. Orem, *Baseball (1845-1881) From the Newspaper Accounts* (Altadena, California: Self-published, 1961), 220.
3. The Force controversy was adjudicated during the NA annual convention, held in Philadelphia in March 1875, ruling in a dispute between Chicago and the Athletic over claims to Force's services. Although it did not directly involve the Boston club, the outcome upset manager Harry Wright, who found himself entangled in his own public dispute with the Athletic club. As the facts behind the Force dispute became known, the *New York Clipper* published its opinions and letters from Chicago and Philadelphia interests alongside Wright's views. The *New York Clipper* supported the 1875 Judiciary Committee's interpretation of the NA contracting rules, and the Force decision. As the dispute continued, the *Clipper* advised the clubs to cease their public conflict and refused to print further related correspondence. Instead, the dispute carried into other pages, and Wright circulated a request that clubs boycott games with Athletic, but he was not broadly supported. See William J. Ryczek, *Blackguards and Red Stockings: A History of Baseball's National Association, 1871-1875* (Jefferson, North Carolina: McFarland, 1992), 186-191. This account is also summarized by Christopher Devine in *Harry Wright: The Father of Professional Base Ball* (Jefferson, North Carolina: McFarland, 2003), 118-119. See also *New York Clipper*, March 13, 1875: 395, 397; March 20, 1875: 403; and April 17, 1875: 18.
4. Unless otherwise indicated, the account of the game is drawn from the *Philadelphia Inquirer*, June 29, 1875: 3, and the *Times* (Philadelphia), June 29, 1875: 1.
5. *Chicago Tribune*, June 29, 1875: 5. *New York Clipper*, July 10, 1875: 115.
6. This is the same Charlie Gould who had played with the Red Stockings in 1871 and 1872. In 1875, Gould was the player-manager for the New Haven Elm Citys.
7. See also *Boston Globe*, June 29, 1875: 5.
8. *Chicago Daily Tribune*, June 29, 1875: 5; *Boston Globe*, June 29, 1875: 5; *Boston Daily Advertiser*, June 29, 1875: 1.
9. *Boston Daily Advertiser*, June 29, 1875: 1.
10. The *Times* (Philadelphia), June 29, 1875: 1.
11. Ibid.
12. Gould relied upon Section 7 of Rule 7, NA rules: "If a game cannot be fairly concluded, it shall be decided by the score of the last equal inning played." *New York Clipper*, June 5, 1875: 77. The *Philadelphia Inquirer* observed that the decision "satisfied the crowd," which then began to slowly exit the field. See also *Chicago Tribune*, June 29, 1875: 5.
13. *Boston Daily Advertiser*, June 29, 1875: 1.
14. The *Times* (Philadelphia), June 29, 1875: 1.
15. *Chicago Tribune*, June 29, 1875: 5.
16. *New York Clipper*, July 10, 1875: 115. The *Boston Daily Advertiser* (June 29, 1875: 1) editorialized: "That a game should be broken up twice by an unruly crowd in the same season, on the grounds of a club that claims to be one of the first in the country, is not only a disgrace to that club, a downright insult to their opponents, but a severe blow to the interests of the game, not only in this city, but elsewhere." The May 27 game was at the Athletic field, between the Athletic and Boston, and ended in an official tie. As on June 28, spectators entered the field in the bottom of the 10th. During the top of the 10th, Boston scored three unearned runs. With one Athletic out and a runner on second base, the crowd rushed the field when the umpire left (he claimed to need a drink of water). When he returned, he was unable to clear the field and ended the game with the score reverting to the score at the end of nine innings, 3-3. See also *Chicago Tribune*, May 28, 1875: 8, and Orem, 215.
17. *New York Clipper*, July 10, 1875: 115.
18. The *Times* (Philadelphia), June 29, 1875: 1.
19. *New York Clipper*, July 10, 1875: 115.
20. Ibid.

AUGUST 4, 1875

Boston Red Stockings 4, Philadelphia 3 White Stockings 3, at South End Grounds, Boston.

BY DAVID C. SOUTHWICK

"THE CHICAGOES WERE NOT, AS aforesaid, able to make a clean hit," wrote the *Philadelphia Inquirer* of what it said to be "the first game on record in which such has been the case in a professional game."[1] The first no-hitter in professional baseball was thrown on July 28, 1875, by 21-year-old Joe Josephs, an amateur who had been signed by the Philadelphia White Stockings, who were desperate for pitching help. His name really wasn't Josephs, a pseudonym created so his baseball-disapproving family wouldn't see his name in the newspaper accounts. Neither was it his other pseudonym, Nedrob, a reversal of his true last name, Borden. Joe Borden, whatever name he used, had burst on the scene as the new White Stockings pitching ace, throwing the no-hit gem against the Chicago White Stocking after two miserable starts. "The threatening appearance of the weather deterred many from witnessing one of the best games ever played," said the *Chicago Tribune*. "From the effective pitching of Josephs the Chicagos were unable to make a base hit throughout the entire game,—a thing unparalleled in the annals of base-ball."[2]

A week after his gem, Borden faced a tough challenge coming to Boston to face the champion Red Stockings team, which was a dominating 48-4 and was riding a 28-game home winning streak. Boston would not lose a home game the entire season, on their way to its fourth straight pennant. The Red Stockings' ace pitcher, Albert Spalding, Borden's mound foe, had won 43 games. A small crowd of between 500 and 1,000 spectators was there, "the threatening weather doubtless keeping many away," wrote the *Boston Globe*.[3] Fred Cone, a Boston outfielder in 1871, was the umpire. Cone had been a member of the Forest City club of Rockford, Illinois, along with future Red Stockings players Spalding and Ross Barnes.

The game opened with two scoreless innings, with John McMullin contributing the only hit for Philadelphia. Spalding and Harry Schafer both hit safely in the second, almost breaking the ice before some bad coaching resulted in Spalding being thrown out at home on Schafer's hit.[4]

Philadelphia's Tim Murnan scored the game's first run in the third inning when he and John McMullin singled, and Murnan scored when right fielder Jack Manning lost a fly ball in the sun.[5] Boston quickly tied the game in the bottom of the inning as Deacon White singled, went to second on a passed ball, to third on an error by Pop Snyder, and home on a groundout by Jack Manning.

Fergy Malone led off the fourth for the visitors with a two-base hit and came home on Chick Fulmer's single to center to reclaim the lead.

Neither team could accomplish anything in the fifth, but each scored a run in the sixth. For Philadelphia, Fulmer and Fred Treacey singled, and Fullmer came home on an error in shallow center by Boston shortstop George Wright. This gave Philadelphia a 3-1 lead. Boston stayed within one run in its half of the inning. Ross Barnes doubled, stole third, and came home on Andy Leonard's grounder to first.

Philadelphia would not cross the plate again on this day; in fact, only two more batsmen reached first base. Boston's fielding by this stage was practically perfect, making it more difficult for the White Stockings to reach safely. After a quiet seventh inning, Boston tied the score in the eighth. Barnes reached on an error and stole second. With Andy Leonard at the plate,

— 308 —

Borden gave Boston "a present of a run"[6] and overthrew to Malone at first, allowing Barnes to scamper home.

After Philadelphia went quickly in the ninth, Boston tried in earnest to pull out a win. Cal McVey's leadoff single got things started, and when the ball rolled through McMullen's legs, that put the potential winning run on second. McVey went to third on a putout to first, but he was left stranded there as White and Schafer grounded out, second baseman Murnan making a great defensive play to hold the runner. "The audience seemed delighted with the idea of a longer game," wrote the *Globe*, "and at times it was hard to tell whether the game was being played before a Philadelphia or Boston audience."[7]

Philadelphia almost went ahead in the 10th inning when Levi Meyerle tripled to "extreme left field,"[8] but the blow was wasted as he was stranded by the next batter, Fergie Malone. Boston went out one-two-three in its half.

In the visitors' 11th, a single by Snyder brought the Quaker City's hopes up, but George Wright and Ross Barnes's double play kept the team off the board.

For Boston the time was now. Leonard opened the inning by lining out to Malone at first. The next batter, O'Rourke, tripled to the same spot in deep left field where Meyerle had hit. He brought home Boston's 49th victory on a grounder by Cal McVey to Murnan at second. Al Spalding then ended the game with an easy grounder to first.

Boston outhit Philadelphia, 9 to 8, with Boston's Jim O'Rourke and Philadelphia's Chick Fulmer leading their respective nines with two hits apiece. The game was played in threatening weather in front of just 500 spectators in 1 hour and 50 minutes. The *Boston Traveler* called the game "the most exciting contest ever witnessed in Boston."[9] The *Globe* agreed, writing, "(T)hose that did take the chances of the weather were more than pleased with the afternoon's entertainment."[10] The win extended Boston's lead over the second-place Philadelphia Athletics to 10½ games in the National Association. With the loss, the White Stockings remained in fourth place with a 23-22 record, 22 games behind the Red Stockings.

"Josephs showed himself to be a pitcher of no mean ability," wrote the *Globe*, "and his first appearance before a Boston audience certainly made a very favorable impression."[11] The *Boston Daily Advertiser* called the win a "hair-breadth escape of the Bostons From Defeat on Their Own Field," and the paper recalled that "the Bostons have had occasion to pull themselves out of a good many deep holes and through a good many narrow crooks, but they never rescued a game that was nearly lost as that with the Philadelphias yesterday."[12]

SOURCES

In addition to the sources cited in the Notes, the author also consulted:

"Athletic Sports—A Great Game on the Boston Grounds," *Boston Daily Advertiser*, August 5, 1875: 1.

"The Bostons and Philadelphias Meet on the South End Grounds," *Boston Post*, August 5, 1875: 3.

NOTES

1 "Base Ball. Philadelphia vs. Chicago—the Chicagoes Fail to Make a Run," *Philadelphia Inquirer*, July 29, 1875: 2.

2 "The White Stockings Beaten by the Philadelphias, and the St. Louis Browns by the New Havens," *Chicago Tribune*, July 29, 1875: 5.

3 "Yesterday's Sports: The Bostons Beat the Philadelphias After Eleven Innings," *Boston Globe*, August 5, 1875: 5.

4 Ibid.

5 Tim Murnan later changed the spelling of his surname to Murnane, and joined the Boston team the following season. He managed, umpired, and—most notably—became baseball editor of the *Boston Globe* for more than 30 years, until his death in 1917.

6 "Yesterday's Sports: The Bostons Beat the Philadelphias After Eleven Innings."

7 Ibid.

8 Ibid.

9 "Base Ball—The Most Exciting Game in Baseball," *Boston Traveler*, August 5, 1875: 1.

10 "Yesterday's Sports: The Bostons Beat the Philadelphias After Eleven Innings."

11 Ibid.

12 "Athletic Sports—A Great Game on the Boston Grounds," *Boston Daily Advertiser*, August 5, 1875: 1.

"FOR AULD LANG SYNE"

October 30, 1875: Boston Red Stockings 7, Hartford Dark Blues 4, at South End Grounds, Boston

BY JOHN ZINN

THE FINAL DAY OF THE 1875 BASE ball season was one of those rare occasions when the weather matched the mood, not just of the game, but of the entire season. Conditions at the Boston Red Stockings' grounds on the next to the last day of October were described by the *Boston Evening Journal* as "cold and cheerless," "raw," and "disagreeable," reason enough to limit the crowd to a "few hundred spectators."[1] The dismal weather, however, was not the only reason the Red Stockings faithful found something else to do on that gray Saturday afternoon. After all, the weather wasn't that much better the day before when the Boston and Hartford clubs played the first of a home-and-home set in the Connecticut capital, but with a crowd estimated at 2,000 in attendance. The Connecticut fans were rewarded for their perseverance, witnessing a come-from-behind 9-8 win, the home team's first win in nine outings against the Red Stockings.[2] Hartford's lack of success against the defending National Association champions was hardly unique and that too helped explain the lack of excitement and energy at the next day's match in Boston.

The winners of three straight National Association championships, the Red Stockings had been so dominant in 1875 that the pennant race was effectively over in June. That made the final game the last of a string of meaningless games that had lasted three months. A championship team closing out its season at home might still have been cause for a communitywide celebration, but this was a bitter championship for Red Stockings fans. Back in July, long before such matters were usually resolved, word came out that four of Boston's stars—Deacon White, Cal McVey, Ross Barnes, and pitcher Albert Spalding—had signed their 1876 contracts not with Boston, but to play in Chicago. Continually seeing or reading about the exploits of their soon-to-be-former players could only serve as a reminder to fans of what they were about to lose. So the combination of bad weather, another unimportant game, and a final painful reminder of a far less bright future was more than enough to keep most Red Stockings fans at home or work.[3]

The game had equally little meaning to the players who at the end of another long season were playing back-to-back games in two cities. Once the October 29 game was called for darkness in the top of the eighth, the two clubs made for the train station and the uncomfortable overnight trip to Boston. With its come-from-behind win, the Hartford club had capped off a good season. After an unsuccessful inaugural campaign in 1874, Hartford still had enough of its startup funding left to acquire veteran players like Jack Burdock and Jack Remson of the New York Mutuals and Bob Ferguson and Tommy Bond of the Atlantics. Regardless of the outcome of the final act, the Hartford players and their fans had enjoyed 54 victories and a second-place finish. Whether it was because of the much smaller rosters of the day or the desire to give the Boston fans one last chance to see their heroes, Harry Wright and his club opted to play their regular lineup. Although doubtless well intentioned, little came of the move as the game was dismissed by the Boston papers as "devoid of interest."[4]

Based on the surviving box scores, the game was no classic, with both teams reaching double figures in errors. One run that was definitely earned was a home run by Boston's Ross Barnes, which cleared the left-field fence. Boston got off to an early 5-1 lead, added two more in the sixth, and held on for a 7-4 victory in a game called after eight innings. Hartford's last three runs came in their last at-bat, but the *Globe*, apparently unwilling to allow the visitors even a modicum of respect, dismissed the three tallies as scored "in the dark."[5] The *Hartford Courant*, on the other hand, proudly noted that the local club had outhit the champions, 14-10, and attributed the loss to "poor base running" and "errors."[6] Baserunning blunders may have indeed been significant as Hartford reportedly had two runners thrown out at the plate.[7] Eight innings were apparently enough for a game that marked Boston's 71st win, 54 of which were credited to the strong right arm of Albert Spalding. Hartford ended the season with only one win in 10 tries against Boston, due in large measure to the Dark Blues' anemic .205 team batting average in those 10 games.[8]

Hartford was not alone, however, in faring poorly against the Red Stockings. Boston's record against the six teams immediately below them in the standings was a resounding 48-7. None of this was surprising, given Spalding's 54-5 record with a 1.59 ERA, not to mention a batting order with six hitters over .300 and a team batting average of .321. It's no wonder Boston finished the season with a 71-8-3 record, 18½ games ahead of a Hartford club that had a solid .659 winning percentage of its own. Also not surprisingly, a league so dominated by one team was not a healthy one, to the point that only five teams finished the season. A perceptive observer attending the final game or even reading about it in the newspaper might have wondered if the National Association would survive. Any such ponderings would prove prophetic when William Hulbert of the Association's Chicago club took not only Boston's four stars, but the five surviving Association franchises into the new National League. Throughout almost all of the National Association's brief existence, the Boston Red Stockings had been the league's most dominant team and while their last game was no classic, it was fitting that Boston won the Association's not so grand finale.

NOTES

1 *Boston Evening Journal*, November 1, 1875: 4.
2 *Boston Globe*, October 30, 1875: 5.
3 William J. Ryczek, *Blackguards and Red Stockings: A History of Baseball's National Association, 1871-1875* (Wallingford, Connecticut: Colebrook Press, 1992), 216.
4 Ryczek, 182; *Boston Globe*, November 1, 1875: 3.
5 *Boston Globe*, November 1, 1875: 3.
6 *Hartford Courant*, November 2, 1875: 2.
7 Ibid.
8 *Hartford Courant*, November 16, 1875: 2.

THE RUMORS BEGIN ABOUT THE 1876 SEASON

The Prospective Cincinnati Club and the Boston Nine
Boston Daily Advertiser, July 19, 1875

It was announced in the Advertiser a few days ago that a movement was afoot to organize a professional club in Cincinnati. Now, a special dispatch to New York from Cincinnati says that Col. Keck and J. T. Joyce head the movement; that the last-named gentleman is on his way to Boston to secure the old Red Stocking players now in the Boston nine; and that Harry Wright has made "overtures" to the Cincinnati club and agreed to play with the new nine next year. It is very probable that the Cincinnati managers desire, and perhaps they intend, to secure the old Red Stocking players who now represent Boston so creditably, but however proud these players may be of the glories of the Cincinnati nine they know they have made a record here beside which the famous "clean score" of 1869 dwindles almost into insignificance. There is authority for saying that not only has Harry Wright not made "overtures," but that up to Saturday night he had not heard from the managers of the new enterprise. It can be said further that he is here to stay, being even now a Bostonian in full fellowship and good standing. As to the rest of the nine, some have already renewed their engagements, or expressed a desire to do so. It is not the wish or intention of the managers of the Boston club to make changes, although if two or three of the present players should decide to seek new situations next year several very desirable men are ready to step into their places here.

THE BOSTON NINE
Secession of Spalding, White, Barnes and McVey—
Their Engagement by the Chicago Club for 1876
Boston Daily Advertiser, July 23, 1875

Four of the best players of the Boston club—Spalding, White, Barnes and McVey—have determined to desert the champion colors and will try to take the pennant to Chicago for 1876. Precisely how this was brought about only the high contracting parties know, the negotiations having been conducted with remarkable secrecy. While the Red Stockings were dining at Taunton, on Tuesday last, McVey said to Captain Harry that he had concluded not to play ball in Boston next year. Harry laughed, thinking it was merely a jest, but his amusement was turned into surprise after dinner, when White told him, in answer to a question about playing here next season, that he had given his word to go to Chicago, and that Spalding, Barnes, and McVey had also bound themselves verbally to the same club. The managers of the Boston club were naturally astonished at this intelligence. They had been informed in plain terms by White and Spalding very recently that they had no intention of leaving Boston, and it was understood that White fully designed to remain and was exerting himself to persuade Sutton to come here next season. The four seceding players have never complained of insufficient salary or unfair treatment, and yet they engaged themselves to play in Chicago without even giving the Boston club a hint of what was going on until the affair was settled. Of course they were not bound, except in courtesy, to notify the club, but their failure to do so, and the studied concealment of the matter, threw a shadow of suspicion on the whole transaction. It should be said, however, that Barnes and McVey have not attempted to mislead the managers by professing an intention to stay, it being generally understood that they would play ball wherever they could get the most money. It was the wish of the seceders, for obvious reasons, to keep the matter quiet until the close of the season, but Chicago couldn't repress its exultation and the news came back here by telegraph Tuesday morning. The Tribune isn't connected with Spalding, White, Barnes and McVey, as will be seen by the following article:—

The management of the White Stockings, in the engagement of new players, have, acted with the most commendable promptness. The effects of delaying until the season was far advanced was seen last year. When Wood then went East in quest of players he found that the best of them had already been engaged. It was only after much difficulty that he was able to engage a nine at all. Events in the ball season, thus far, have proved that it was a poor nine, by no means what Chicago desired, and entirely unworthy to uphold her reputation in base ball, either at home or abroad. As soon as it met the professionals of the East it showed signs of weakness not before suspected. Taking the field early, the managers have been able to engage a club which, as the names will show, is well nigh invincible. As the Bostons will disband at the close of the season, the Wrights going to Cincinnati to form a club there, they have been successful in engaging the best players of that nine, in spite of a very strong competition on the part of the Wrights and others. The Athletics, also, have been levied upon for their best man. With these, and Peters, Devlin, Hines and Glenn, the flower and strength of the White Stockings, they have formed a nine which ought, in all reason, to carry off the championship of 1876. Below are appended the names, which cannot fail to be heartily approved by every admirer of the game:—

Pitcher—Spalding, Boston
Catcher—White, Boston
First base—Devlin, Chicago
Second base—Barnes, Boston
Third base—Sutton, Athletic
Short Stop—Peters, Chicago
Left field—Glenn, Chicago
Centre field—Hines, Chicago
Right field—McVey, Boston
Substitute—O'Rourke, Boston
Substitute—Golden, Chicago
Substitute—Warren, Chicago

Excepting a few trifling inaccuracies, the article is quite true. In the first place, it seems to a great many people that the present Chicago team is eminently worthy to "uphold her reputation in base ball." In the next place, there is no intention of disbanding the Boston club at the close of the season. Third, the Wrights do not propose to go to Cincinnati, and for this, and another reason which is unnecessary to state, did not compete very strongly for the "best players" of the Boston club. And, last of all, O'Rourke, with Leonard and Beals, has signed papers to play in the Boston nine of 1876.

"What are you going to do about it?" is the question everybody will ask the managers of the Boston club. Just at present they do not know, except that as long as the life and soul of the club—the Wright brothers—remain, there will be a nine and a good one. It is safe to say that the base ball fraternity of Boston will, under the circumstances, accord to the new nine even a heartier support than it has given to the champions, and that Captain Harry will organize out of this adversity a team which will within two seasons bring back to Boston the emblem which may be wrested from us.

NOTE: On that very day, the *Daily Advertiser*'s "ABOUT TOWN" chit-chat column on various topics was directly to the right side of the above noteworthy base ball news. Among the topics covered were these little jabs at Chicago.

"White Stockings are so apt to get dirty, you know, James." (Meant for Jim White).

"The tug war in the ball field next year will be between the red, white and blue."

"Wonder if Chicago has already ordered the flag-pole from which to fly the champion pennant next year."

A Base Capture
Boston Daily Advertiser,
July 23, 1875 — Editorial

The time *is* out of joint. (Boss) Tweed is escaping from the penalty of his crimes, there are bad crops in Europe, the democratic party is marching rapidly under its soft money flag, the monarchists are gaining victories in the French Assembly, — and now the famous Boston nine has been assaulted and captured by Chicago. There is probably no paragraph of news this week that has caused so much real vexation out of doors in Boston as this last.

The pride of Boston in its base ball team has been something unique. It was compounded of confidence and admiration, both fully justified by the skill and character of the men composing it. We have not only felt sure that they could beat all other clubs but that they would do their best. The wonderful record of this year's victories has increased the popularity of the nine. We believe that there has been mutual satisfaction, the men having had nothing to complain of in the treatment accorded them by Boston base ball goers, and the latter having the respect for the players which one feels for manly and fair-dealing gentlemen.

The break up of the team is therefore announced to the sincere regret of all in this community who take an interest in the sport, with the sole exception of the players who are going away. The manner in which the negotiations have apparently been conducted between the young men and the Chicago managers leaves much to be regretted. There is, of course, no chance for a charge of bad faith, as the men only contracted for this season, and their time is their own after November. But the Boston public would have been better pleased if the men who have been trusted and admired so much had given at least an opportunity to test the desire that they should remain.

There is no use in disguising the fact that the loss of the Boston club is irreparable. There is no "pitcher" in the country who will be a substitute for Spalding, and no "catcher" who is White's equal behind the bat. The places of the others may be fairly supplied, but we do not believe they are likely to be filled with men as good in the field, with the bat and at base-running as Barnes and McVey. Moreover, the Chicago club has obtained further strength by capturing (Ezra) Sutton, the incomparable third-baseman of the Athletics, and retaining the best men of its present nine it has secured a team that seems to be far superior to any club that can be organized in opposition, as is the Boston nine of last year.

However, it is a part of the faith of base ball men that Captain Harry Wright "knows what he is about," and that the extraordinary discipline maintained by him accounts for many a victory snatched from the jaws of defeat. There will be an excellent opportunity to put this article of the creed to the test next year. Meanwhile it is best to preserve all the cheerfulness possible under the disastrous blows given by the lavish city that supports the White Stockings, — which are "so apt to get dirty," in the language of one of the seceding players.

NOTE: On the morning this Editorial appeared the Reds were in the middle of hosting a series with St. Louis, and were 46 and 4.

SPORTING MATTERS
Base Ball
Red Stockings and White Stockings—
Letter from Mr. (James L. Deacon) White of the Boston Club
Boston Herald, July 27, 1875

Mr. James White of the Boston champions sends us the following letter concerning the engagement of four of the Red Stockings with the Chicago club for next season.

Editor of the Herald: Since my decision to play ball in Chicago next season next season has become known, several articles have appeared in the Boston papers conveying the impression that I was under obligations to remain another season with the Boston club and after reading the last article in the *Daily Advertiser* I deem it is my duty to define my position in the matter and correct the erroneous impression above mentioned. A day or two before starting on our late western trip, I met Mr. (Nicholas) Apollonio at the club room, at his request, and the conversation that ensued was in substance as follows:

He desired to close a contract with me for a one or three year's engagement, urging as his reasons for so early an engagement that I was about going west and might receive some flattering offers for my services there; that the Boston club were desirous of retaining me with them, but gave me to understand in plain terms that their salary list was as high as they could afford to pay, and to use his own words, "they could not and did not propose to compete with 'fancy' western prices." The only promise I made him, or any one else, was to the effect that I would not receive or open any negotiations with any club manager on *that* trip, which promise I have kept to the letter. Nearly a month after my return from this trip, during which time nothing further was said to me, I met the management of the Chicago club in Boston, who offered me the 'fancy' price that the Boston club did not propose to compete with, and under these circumstances I did not feel like *forcing* the Boston club, as they claim others have done, to pay me any "fancy" price.

James White

From the pages of the *New York Clipper*: July 24, 1875 (page 133):

The New Cincinnati Nine — The revival of baseball about Cincinnati, Ohio, has been very marked, and a few days ago a move was made to reorganize the old Cincinnati (Red Stockings) nine. Eight acres of ground have been leased on Spring Grove Avenue just north of the stock yards, and a large force of men have been put to work grading and preparing buildings, etc. $5,000 stock was subscribed in one day, and the intention is to fit the grounds up in first-class style. Col. John P. Joyce, the former secretary of the old Red Stockings, started for New York on the 14th to engage a professional nine. It is intended to have both the nine and the grounds on playing order by August 1.

July 31, 1875 (page 139):

The Centennial Chicago Team — We have authority for stating that Mr. Spalding of the Boston Club is to be engaged—he has not yet been so, of course—as captain of the centennial team of Chicago for 1876, which will be as follows: White c, Spalding p, Anson 1b, Barnes 2b, Sutton 3b, Peters ss, Glenn lf, Devlin cf, McVey rf, with Devlin, Hines, and Warren as subs. The question is how long will it take to make the party a good working team?

July 31, 1875 (page 139):

The Boston Seceders — Alluding to the secession of several of the champion nine, *The Boston Herald* of the 25th inst. says "About this time everybody wants to know what the Boston Club is going to do about it, and who they will get to fill the vacancies next year. Leonard, O'Rourke and (Tommy) Beals are re-engaged, the former for three years, with the understanding that he is to play third base. Beals will probably play second. Who they get for pitcher, catcher and first-baseman remains to be seen. There are plenty of good players anxious to come to Boston. Among them (Herman) Dehlman of the St. Louis Club for first base, and (Edgar Ned) Cuthbert of the same nine for the outfield. It would not be strange if Captain (Harry) Wright should secure some one of the several promising amateur pitchers in this vicinity, and train up a second Spalding. Harry has a sharp eye for the good points in a player, and there is no fear but he will have first-class men when the time comes. Spalding denies ever having made any promises to stay in Boston. It is well known to the Boston Club managers that he has several times been on the verge of going to Chicago, having been offered more every year than he ever received here. Two years ago he even gave up his place here, and went to New York to meet Mr. Gassett and sign with the Chicagos; but owing to some disagreement, he returned to this city and the Boston Club."

July 31, 1875 (page 139):

Breaking-Up the Boston Team.

In 1873, when the then new Philadelphia Club nine was in the height of a successful career, promising to result in the winning of the championship emblem, the entire demoralization of the team, with its sequence of their defeat as successful contestants in the race for the pennant, was accomplished through the medium of the

Chicago Club management in securing the services of their best players in the very midst of the season. Then there was no existing law of the Professional Association, as there is now, preventing such a course of procedure; but the evil results of such a course were made so apparent that, at the ensuing meeting of the Association, laws were adopted to prevent anything of the kind again; and at the last Convention these laws were amended, with a view to still further preclude this interference with club-management, by attempting to induce the players of a successful organization to join one which was quite the reverse.

It would appear, however, that not even the printed laws of the Professional Association are effective in preventing this demoralizing conduct on the part of the managers of rival clubs in trying to break up a successful organization. Having tried in vain for years to defeat the Boston Red Stockings on the field, it would appear as if an effort were to be made to break up the club altogether, as the only way of ever being able to get hold of the coveted pennant. Is there no law of fair dealing that suggests to club-managers that this violation of the spirit of an Association rule is discreditable? By years of labor in training up a baseball team to work together as much for the honor and credit of the club they represent as for third yearly salaries, the Boston Club have secured a corps of players whose success is due not to the superiority of their team in its individual strength, but to the excellent discipline, the effective training, and the judicious management of the club, both on and off the field. This is the secret of the Boston Club's four years of championship success; and not that they possess this pitcher or that catcher, or this or other occupants of the other important positions in the field.

The Philadelphia Club, which was organized to defeat the city champion Athletics in 1873, entered the arena under circumstances which occasioned them to play better together as a whole nine than any other club except the Bostons, and hence the success they met with. The Chicago Club, in securing the services of the principal players of this team, failed to secure the incentive to their unity of play which had been the secret of their success; and before half the season of 1874 was over, the then much-vaunted team of Chicago was fourth in the race for the pennant. There is a fair and honorable was of getting a team together, and there is another way which is quite different. The *spirit* of the Association laws on the subject of engaging players for the ensuing season is that no club-manager or agent shall approach players to negotiate for their services for the next year until the close of the present season. How is the letter of the law to prevent the demoralizing influence of this business, if the spirit of the rule is to be broken?

Will players care for the interests of the club they are playing with, when they know that their services are secured at advanced rates for another club before half the season is over? Away will go the power to enforce discipline, and discord will be likely, to enter where harmony and good feeling had previously prevailed. An instance of this kind presents itself in the case of the Atlantic Club and Mr. Joyce. That gentleman's agents approached the Atlantic players on the subject of joining the Cincinnati Club. And what has been the result? Simply, that the Atlantic team has become a discontented one, inasmuch as the refusal of their club-manager to release them, so that they may get higher pay in another club, causes them to be in a measure indifferent to their work. Why has such publicity been given to this matter of breaking up the Boston Club? That organization has been a model one in every respect. It has done much to make professionalism reputable, and to offset the effects of the discreditable conduct of the minority of those who at one time threatened to destroy professional play altogether.

By way of reminder to club-managers, we give below the existing rule bearing upon the subject of the eligibility of players and their engagement:

Rule III

Eligible Players.

Section 1.—In playing matches, nine players from each of the contesting clubs shall constitute a full field, and these players must be regular members of the club they represent. They must also not have been members of any other club belonging to the Professional Association for sixty days prior to the date of the match they play in; except the club they were previously members of shall have been disbanded, and their written engagement with such club shall have been duly canceled. The sixty days, however, shall not date back prior to April 1 of the season they play in.

[By this rule professional can avail themselves of the services of any players who are not members of other clubs belonging to the Association; and players of professional clubs are thereby allowed to participate in the games of amateur or other clubs not belonging to the Professional Association.]

Playing in a Regular Match.

2. Every player taking part in a regular match game, no matter what number of innings be played, or whether he be an actual member or not, shall be regarded as a member of the club he plays with; and all match-games shall be considered "regular" in the meaning of this rule in which nines of two contesting clubs of Professional Association take part.

[No game is regarded as "regular" in the meaning of the professional code unless the contesting sides are players belonging to two professional clubs.]

Ineligible Players.

3. No person who shall have been legally expelled from another club for dishonorable conduct shall be competent to take part in any match-game until reinstated by the Judiciary Committee of the Professional Association.

["Legally expelled" means after a regular trial or investigation of charges which have led to expulsion.]

Players Violating Contracts.

4. No player who is under an existing and valid contract to play baseball with any club belonging to the Professional Association shall be allowed to play in the nine of any other club of the Association, in any regular match game, until such contract has been duly canceled. *And any player who shall, while a legal member of a Professional Association club, bind himself, without the written consent of said club, to serve as a player in any other professional organization, whether belonging to this Association or not, before November 1st of the same year in which his contract expires, shall forfeit the amount of his salary due, and be liable to expulsion from the Association, at the option of the Association Judiciary Committee, before whom the case shall be heard.*

[By the amendment made to this rule no player can sign a contract—which will be valid—with any club without, in the first place, the written consent of the officers of the club he belongs to; and secondly, if this is not forthcoming he cannot sign said contract until November 1 of the year he plays in.]

Agreements To Be In Writing.

5. No contract between club and player shall be deemed valid, except it be signed by the player who is engaged and the president or manager of the club which engages him: and except also it be signed by two witnesses, one each party.

Judging from the facts that have come to our knowledge, it would appear that so great is the desire on the part of Chicago to bear off the palm of superiority in baseball playing—or rather in having the champion team emanate from the West—that they have come to the conclusion to spare no pains or expense in securing a regular representative Western team. Hence, probably, their desire to secure the services of such men as Spalding, McVey, Barnes and Anson—all four Western men. But how about White and Sutton, New York State men? A Western nine would include: Hastings, Spalding, McVey, Barnes, Sutton, Peters, etc.; but Glenn, Devlin, Warren, Sutton, White, Hines, and others mentioned are all from the East. That in Spalding they will secure a man competent to act as captain there is no doubt, and that is what the Chicago Club have all along wanted. They have had good nines enough to act in the position in one respect, but not in all. We shall have something more to say on the subject when we learn the character of the new management.

Boston Club in 1876
New York Clipper, August 7, 1875 (page 147):

A letter from the veteran Harry Wright informs us that he is going to remain in Boston, and he proposes to organize a team of Red Stockings in 1876 which, he hopes, will do as much credit to the club as the existing team has hitherto. There has been, each season, a general desire on the part of professionals to get an engagement in the Boston team, for well-known reasons. In the first place the organization is controlled by well-to-do Boston merchants, admirers of the game, who treat their professionals not as mere hired servants, but as they would like to be treated themselves under similar circumstances. Secondly, the Boston press act very liberally towards the players, giving them due credit for their work well done and being lenient when censure is necessary. Thirdly, the players are placed under the command of a captain who stands alone in the manner in which he trains his men. No harsh orders like those of a military martinet, no open rebukes of the men on the field, no ebullitions of ill-temper before the public, but simply kind consideration for their errors and warm praise for their skill, together with a general interest in their personal welfare. Under such circumstances is it surprising that Harry Wright should be able to command a choice of men at fair salaries? The nucleus of the Boston Centennial team—it's going to be a grand year for baseball, is 1876 — are Harry and George Wright, Leonard, Beals, Manning and O'Rourke. Here are three basemen, a shortstop and two outfielders including to two change-pitchers to begin with. Long before this year is out Harry will have secured a new pitcher and catcher, and, with two more men to fill up with, a team will be raised which will trouble even Captain Spalding's Western White Stockings to whip. How these two clubs will go for each other, and the Athletics will also join in to do their best to polish off Chicago! Then, too, there will be the Western rivals of St. Louis and Cincinnati. The fact is, things will be hot and lively next year, in professional circles, both East and West. After all, what appears to have been a misfortune for the "Reds" may turn out, pecuniarily, to be the best thing could have happened. There is nothing like a splendid rivalry. Hitherto Boston has somewhat "monopolized things," and it had come to be monotonous to hear of the Boston victories. Next year things will not be one-sided. All will admire Harry's fidelity to Boston, and his pluck in being equal to the emergency.

HUB KIDS BID FANS ANEW: THE RED STOCKINGS IN CANADA, 1872-1874

BY DAVID MCDONALD

"The Boston Club were immediately surrounded by an admiring crowd, as the 'professionals' were decidedly the finest and most athletic lot of players that have ever visited this city. Their loose dress uniform of light brown flannel, with red stockings and red belts, appeared to be admirably adapted for the active play of the sinews and muscles. On their arrival at the grounds, the Club at once proceeded to practice with their ball, pitching and catching with an expertness that opened the eyes of the spectators. The sinewy arms of the players sent the ball almost with the velocity of a musket shot, without describing a curve, but straight and true to the hands of the catcher. ... The 'Red Stockings' are all heavy men, very strong and active, in fact, picked men. They are paid regular salaries of from $1,800 to $2,500 per annum each, by the Boston club, to do nothing else but to play base ball, and they go from one city to another through the United States and Canada, playing matches for the gate money and for large stakes."
—*Ottawa Free Press,* August 28, 1872.[1]

ON AUGUST 19, 1872, BEFORE 300 fans in Cleveland, the powerhouse Boston Red Stockings beat the Forest Citys 12-7 to push their National Association-leading record to 30-3. Afterward, facing a two-week hiatus in championship play, Harry Wright's elite band of mercenaries headed north to pick up some extra cash in the baseball boondocks.

It was as if their successors, the Atlanta Braves, showed up to play your slow-pitch team. In Michigan, the Red Stockings cruised through their first two matches, crushing Ypsilanti 40-3 and Empires of Detroit 35-2.

From Detroit, Wright's boys crossed the border at Windsor, into the crucible of Canadian baseball, Southwestern Ontario, where the game had been played informally even before Abner Doubleday mythically invented it in 1839. The first organized teams there had popped up in the mid-1850s and had soon adopted the New York rules over an earlier, distinctively Canadian version of the game. Ontario teams had been playing exhibition games against American competition since as early as 1860.

Their first stop was London, where, on August 22, 1872, the Red Stockings played their first-ever match on foreign turf, against the Tecumsehs, a club that had been formed four years previously. The result was unequivocal, a 52-3 pasting. The next morning, the Bostons traveled to Guelph to take on the then-perennial Canadian champion Maple Leafs in an afternoon game.

Battle of the champions

The "amateur" ("semiprofessional" would probably be a more apt designation) Maple Leafs were no strangers to big-time competition. Earlier that summer, in fact, they had hosted the Baltimore Canaries of the National Association and beaten them, 10-9.

In mid-August, the Maple Leafs had embarked hopefully on an ambitious road trip to further test their mettle against Association clubs. The results were sobering. They dropped all three of their matches on the East Coast, 25-5 to the Canaries in Baltimore,

35-8 to the Athletics in Philadelphia, and 9-4 to the Mutuals in New York. This final game, at the Union Grounds, drew only 300 fans, which the *Brooklyn Eagle* blamed on "a threatening storm"[2] and a premium 50-cent ticket price.

The Maple Leafs had been exposed for what they were, namely, an excellent amateur club, one of the best on the continent perhaps, but still a notch below the American professionals.

Still, the *Eagle* was impressed with their showing. "The Maple Leafs have a nine that can get away with anything outside the professional arena," said its correspondent. "[They] are nearly all Scotchmen, and a fine athletic and active set of players; they are, too, excellent catchers and good throwers, and they play a game that makes the best men work to beat them. … They play the Reds next week at Guelph, and if this Boston nine play no better than they did here this week the Canadians will stand a good chance to win. …"[3]

Now, a week later in Guelph, while some among the 2,500 in attendance no doubt clung to hopes of a David-Goliath upset, most were simply satisfied to see the legendary Red Stockings in the flesh. Before they had even completed their Globetrotteresque warm-up, the visitors had won over the crowd. "[A]ttractive and amusing were the many pranks they indulged in in the handling of the base ball," said the *Guelph Mercury*, "… the tricks of the Wright brothers being particularly amusing."[4]

The game started at 2:45. The Maple Leafs showed some pop at the plate, touching Al Spalding for 17 hits, only four fewer than the Red Stockings managed. But the amateurs couldn't hold a candle to the Bostons in the field. The pros took advantage of numerous errors, scoring in every inning en route to a 29-7 win.

Scratched and daunted

The next afternoon, August 24, in Toronto, Wright's team took the field at the Cricket Ground for a match against the three-year-old Dauntless club. The Toronto boys were facing their first professional opposition. It was awe at first sight.

"When the Red Stockings went into the field, their build stood out in marked contrast to the men of the Dauntless Club," said the *Toronto Mail*. "They were large brawny fellows, their arms tanned up to the elbows, and stood, with very few exceptions, half a foot at least over their opponents."[5]

Said the rival *Toronto Globe*: "These circumstances seemed to have impressed themselves so deeply on their opponents, that they went to work resigning themselves to their fate without, almost, an effort to avert it."[6]

The *Mail* correspondent had this analysis of the fundamental differences between the amateur and the professional defensive games: "At the start it looked as if the Dauntless stood a chance of making at least a respectable show, but before long the great disparity of the two clubs was easily discernible. The Canadians were not up to their work in hardly any particular, and at times when a man should be on a base, he was found to be several yards away from it. On the other hand, the Red Stockings were always in the right place at the right time and worked together like clock work. …

"The style of throwing adopted by the clubs was entirely different. The Americans sent the ball in a straight line to the man it was intended for, but the Canadians threw it high in the air thus frequently losing an opportunity of putting a man out.

"The pitching of Spaulding [*sic*] of the Red Sox [*sic*] was very swift and very true. It seemed to be his desire that the batter should send the ball into the field, for as sure as he did he was a gone man."[7] Indeed, Charlie Gould made 16 putouts at first base in support of Spalding's one-hitter.

The line score conveys the gulf between the clubs.

										R	H	E
BOS	3	4	5	17	1	3	17	7	11	68	59	4
TOR	0	0	0	0	0	0	0	0	0	0	1	20

Boston accumulated 94 total bases in 105 at-bats. The Wright brothers scored 10 runs apiece, with George Wright and Roscoe Barnes each going 9-for-12 at the plate.

Independents day

After an off-day Sunday, the Red Stockings returned to the Toronto Cricket Ground. Their op-

Advertisement for the game against the Dauntless club. (Collection of David McDonald)

ponents this day were the Independents, a team from Dundas, a town 45 miles west of Toronto (and now part of the city of Hamilton). The game, starting at 10:30 A.M., kicked off a day of sporting events marking a civic holiday.

Boston jumped to a quick 12-0 lead, but the Independents plated four in the bottom half of the third, largely due to an uncharacteristic cluster of miscues by shortstop George Wright, first baseman Gould, and third baseman Harry Schafer. Overall, though, said the *Globe*, "(T)he wonderful catching of the Red Stockings, and the remarkable judgment with which their men played, was a marvel to the numerous spectators present."[8]

Schafer also "smote a ball so sorely as to drive it through the windows of a house to the eastern side of the ground, causing much and natural excitement among the occupants of the house to which the window appertained. Somebody, we opine, will have to make good the damage done...."[9]

Overall, the *Mail* judged "the playing of the Americans ... by no means as good as it was on Saturday last [vs. Dauntless]."[10] Not that it made much difference. Every member of the Boston team scored at least as many runs as the entire Dundas team. The final total was 52-4.

"The 'Red Stockings,'" said the *Globe*, "are now on their way making their tour through the Canadas, and if they find no 'foements' more worthy of their steel than those they have met in Toronto, they will go home with the idea that they are in reality, as they claim to be, the 'Champions of the World.'"[11]

The Cincinnati kids

After the game, the travelers boarded a train for the 250-mile trip northeast to Ottawa, population 21,545. Even next to the fresh-faced opposition Boston had encountered in Southern Ontario, the Ottawas were a team of neophytes—one with a strong connection to the Boston team.

In the spring of 1870 a 27-year-old Ottawa blacksmith and lacrosse player, Tom Cluff, had gone to Cincinnati for a couple of months to visit his older brother Ned, later a prominent American insurance broker and captain of the New York Lacrosse Club. There, on July 4, Tom Cluff is said to have attended his first baseball game, possibly the holiday match at the Union Base Ball Grounds between Harry Wright's Cincinnati Red Stockings and the Forest City Club of Rockford, Illinois. If so, Cluff would have seen the Red Stockings beat a 20-year-old right-hander from Byron, Illinois, named Al Spalding, 24-7.

A short time later, Cluff attended a picnic near Norwood, Ohio, and witnessed up-close a demonstration of baseball skills by three members of the Red Stockings. "Mr. Cluff was swept away in the excitement," the *Ottawa Free Press* later reported, "and after making acquaintance with the base ballers received some guidance of the manner in which he could learn the sport's finer points and return with them to his native city."[12]

The following year, as Harry Wright reconstituted the Red Stockings in Boston, Tom Cluff took what he'd learned in Cincinnati and organized his hometown's first baseball club. His collection of novices included a couple of hoteliers, a surveyor, a builder, a post-office clerk, and Tom's younger brother Harry, a refrigeration dealer. Now, in just his second summer of play, Tom Cluff had the opportunity to go head to head with some of the very players who had first fired his passion for the game.

"The Ottawa Base Ball Club are entering into the cultivation of this strictly national game of America with a zeal and enterprise which is destined to do good service to the 'cause,'" the *Free Press* proclaimed.[13]

Tuesday, August 27, 1872, in the capital might have been the greatest confluence of bat-and-ball talent in Canadian history. Not only were the Red Stockings in town; so, too, were the touring English Gentlemen eleven, featuring Dr. W.G. Grace, the Babe Ruth of cricket. The cricketers were at Rideau Hall, the Governor General's residence, for a gimmick match against a team of 22 local players.

In honor of the day's big sporting events, the city declared a civic holiday, one from which the fast, brash American game would emerge ascendant in the capital over its stuffy, class-bound British cousin.

Several unnamed Red Stockings—we can probably guess the identities of some—insisted on taking in some of the morning cricket action.[14] "The 'Reds' thought the batting very fine, but remarked that the game was 'darned slow,' and lost 'time enough in making overs to grow a nation,'" said one reporter, apparently under the illusion that the Wrights and company, being Americans—and ballplayers—were not already intimately acquainted with the English game.[15]

In the afternoon, Red Stockings went by carriage to the Ottawa Base Ball Club's new 10-acre grounds on the edge of the city. The field had just been leveled and enclosed with a seven-foot wooden fence.

"The great international base ball match,"[16] as it was billed, got under way at 3 P.M., with about 1,000 spectators (some estimates said up to 3,000) who had arrived "in carriages and on foot."[17] "Ample refreshments" were available, but no "spirituous (sic) liquors."[18] The Garrison Artillery band played throughout the 2½-hour game, which was effectively decided before it started.

"The few minutes play previous to the commencement of the match convinced all who were present that the Ottawa club would have no show against the professionals, and there were very few even of the most sanguine of the Ottawa men who would bet one to ten that our club would obtain a single run," wrote the cold-eyed correspondent for the *Ottawa Citizen*.[19]

The Ottawas actually acquitted themselves respectably at the plate, knocking Spalding for seven hits, including a single and a double by Harry Cluff. But they failed to score any runs. Barnes, meanwhile, hit a pair of two-run homers for the visitors and scored eight runs. "The 'slaughter of the innocents' was wholesale," the *Ottawa Times* remarked.[20] The score was 64-0.

Again, the biggest disparity between the teams was on defense: The Ottawas committed 24 errors, leading to 46 unearned Boston runs, while the visitors made just two muffs. "The extraordinary fielding of 'the short stop,' Mr. G. Wright, who, in this position, is excelled by none, was watched with eagerness," said the *Citizen*. "The wonderful velocity with which he delivers a ball to the first baseman is marvellous."[21]

"Nicely entertained"

The Red Stockings departed Ottawa the following day and crossed the border to Ogdensburg, New York, where they pasted the Pastimes, reputed to be the best amateur club in northern New York state, 66-1.

From there, they hopped back into Canada, capping off a long road trip with a Thursday-afternoon game on August 30 in Montreal. Baseball in the Quebec metropolis had sprung up in the 1865-70 period, introduced not from other parts of Canada, but by Franco-Americans who came to study in Quebec colleges. The Montreal Base Ball Club itself was formed in the early 1870s.

The game, in front of a small crowd at the Lacrosse Grounds, unfolded pretty much as expected. "The second innings," said the *Montreal Herald*, "displayed the wonderful expertness of the Red Stockings as batsmen, for not only were their hits splendid, but they took advantage of every flaw in the fielding of the Montrealers, and stole runs that less skillful players would not have been able to obtain."[22]

The final score was 63-3. Later, George Wright wrote that he and his teammates "were nicely entertained by the club of that city."[23]

In six games against Canadian opponents, the Red Stockings had scored 328 runs, an average of 54.7 a game, and given up 17, or 2.8 a game, for a run differential of 51.9 a game. Clearly, the Canadian clubs had some catching up to do.

Return engagement—1873

By their own standards, the Red Stockings struggled mightily through the first half of the 1873 championship season. On August 19, they fell 9-4 to the Athletics in Philadelphia. The loss dropped them to 19-12 in championship play, 6½ games behind the first-place Athletics.

Harry Wright had arranged a total of 46 in-season exhibition games to supplement the 59 championship games they would play that year, and that included another Northern swing into Michigan and Ontario during the August break. After again rolling over the Empires in Detroit, the Red Stockings took the train to Guelph for a rematch with the Canadian champs. Unfortunately, the Bostons' baggage got off in Sarnia, Ontario.

The Guelph supporters rallied behind their guests. Members of the local cricket team loaned them shoes, and a local woolen mill outfitted them in their customary red hose. And so the Red Stockings were able to take the field at 2:30 in "comparatively neat costume,"[24] to wow the big crowd with their usual pregame legerdemain.

The locals had beefed up in the offseason, adding some American mercenaries to their lineup. They included George Keerl, who would play briefly for the Chicago White Stockings two years later, and Harry Spence, later manager of the National League Indianapolis Hoosiers. The imports did not receive a salary, but rather a share of the club's financial "surplus" at the end of the season.[25]

With ace hurler Billy Smith still suffering from a rib injury, the Maple Leafs didn't fare much better than they had the previous summer, losing 27-8 before 4,000-5,000 civic holiday fans. This contest, one noted baseball historian believes, was the inspiration for Zane Grey's "The Winning Ball," one of the entries in his classic collection *The Redheaded Outfield and Other Baseball Stories.*[26]

After the game, the victorious Red Stockings were feted with a supper at the Royal Hotel. The next morning, they caught a train to Toronto for a 3:40 P.M. rematch with the Dauntless club, whom they had held to a lone hit the summer before. This time the Toronto team put up a fight.

"Hard hitting … was the order of the day, and the driving of a ball to the utmost limit of the enclosure soon came to be regarded as a matter of course," the *Globe* reported.[27] Schafer, Barnes, and Andy Leonard hit home runs for Boston, while Adams hit one for Toronto. The Red Stockings were forced to turn at least five double plays to keep the score at 45-10.

"We can't see how the Toronto club batted ten runs with the superior fielding of the Americans," the Guelph *Mercury* sniffed.[28]

Sky-creepers and coal mines

From Toronto, the Red Stockings took the train to Kingston to take on the St. Lawrence team in an afternoon contest before more than 2,000 fans at the Cricket Ground. The Kingston club was in only its second year, but already baseball, according to one newspaper, had become a "mania"[29] in the city of about 13,000, with cricket increasingly losing ground in a struggle for control of local playing fields.

The Bostons more than lived up to their hype. "The champions are lissom, active fellows, strongly inured to the game, and capable of doing almost anything they liked with amateur players," said the *Kingston News*.[30]

The rival *British Whig* concurred: "The Red Stockings are a fine set of fellows, well set-up, with muscles like smiths, and hands hardened like steel by constant punishment from the ball. Their play was really beautiful to those who understood the niceties of the game, and commanded the applause of even those whose acquaintance with Base-ball is of the slightest. …

"The by-play of the visitors during the intervals of the game was the most attractive part of it—a youngster remarking that 'he'd rather see them Red fellers coddin' with the ball nor watch the match.' Their exhibition catches, running and behind the back, and their beautiful and accurate throwing, elicited great admiration from all who had the pleasure of seeing them. ..."[31]

The *Whig* correspondent was particularly impressed with the defensive play of the professionals: "The pitcher [Spalding], a fine strapping athlete—showed to what perfection the art of pitching could be brought. … Their catching and fielding was simply perfect, a fly being taken, it seemed into whatever out of the way place it went, as easily and safely as if fell into a coal mine. Only one muff of a catch was made by the Red Stockings, and that, it is more than suspected, was an 'accident on purpose.' The fielding could not be surpassed—clean and sure, fielders always being where they were wanted and covering an astonishing deal of ground. Nor was their throwing less admirable, the farthest shies being as straight as arrows. ..."[32] The "ground fielding" of the St. Lawrence club, meanwhile, was found "painfully deficient."[33]

The *Whig* also had praise for the Boston hitters. "The batting of the Red Stockings was on par with their play on the field, magnificent striking and artful placing of the ball frequently distinguishing it," the reporter said. "Sky-creepers, sent out beyond the reach of a deep field, and low drives too hot for a comfortable handling ran up their scores rapidly. ..."[34]

Up to 55, in fact. The tally included a 17-run nose-rubbing in the ninth, when, as the *News* reported, there was "lots of fooling in the parts of the batsmen, who seemed to take everything very easy. ..."[35]

For the Bostons, recently acquired Bob "The Magnet" Addy, from Port Hope, a town 100 miles west of Kingston, played right field and scored six times. Deacon White added eight runs. Utilityman Jack Manning pitched the final three innings in relief of Spalding. Harry Wright, taking the day off from playing, umpired.

"The game could not be properly called a match," the *Whig* concluded, "as the local club had not a ghost of a chance of defeating the visitors, and the only speculation as to the result was confined to guesses as to how many runs the Kingston men would secure."[36]

They managed 10 runs, which, given "the fearful odds," was deemed "a very fair make."[37]

If the lopsided outcome was a slap in the face, it was, the *Whig* surmised, a decidedly bracing one. "The visit of the players from the Hub cannot but have a most beneficial effect on local players, giving them an opportunity … of seeing Base-ball played by the ex-champions of the world, and awakening in them an emulative spirit which will improve their love and knowledge of the game."[38]

Bucky, Juice, and Dink

From Kingston the Red Stockings headed north for a return match on August 26 with the Ottawas, who were now into their third season. Like the Maple Leafs and some other Ontario clubs, they had added a few imports to their lineup.

The recruits included two buddies from Utica, New York, 20-year-old second baseman George "Juice" Latham and teenage hurler-third baseman William "Dink" Davis, along with catcher Mike "Bucky" Ledwith, who seems to have hailed from Brooklyn, New York. Improbably, two of these men would see big-league action within two years.

Ledwith would play one game with the National Association Brooklyn Atlantics in 1874 (although there is some confusion as to whether it might have been another Mike Ledwith), while Latham would eventually play for five major-league teams and manage two.

Davis, meanwhile, would make headlines across the U.S. in the 1880s and '90s, not for his baseball prowess, but for his talents with a deck of cards. In the early 1880s he was said to have pocketed $100,000 during a 48-hour Faro binge in New York City.

How the Ottawas enticed these players north is unclear. It's highly unlikely the club would have been in a financial position to pay them much, if anything. Perhaps it provided them opportunities for employment. Indeed, during his time in Canada, Latham reportedly worked in a factory and as a baggage man on a train.

Even with Bucky, Juice, and Dink in the lineup, the Ottawas, in blue and white, were still no match for their opponents in their "white cricketing flannel shirts and knickerbockers faced with scarlet, and their traditional scarlet stockings."[39]

"The Ottawa players are all slim, lithe young men, but they look weak and puny beside the fine brawny fellows against whom they were pitted," the *Ottawa Times* commented.[40] The final score, under dark and drizzly skies, was 44-4.

Among the locals, Latham stood out, the *Citizen* calling his play "equal to anything on the side of the Bostons."[41]

Fifty-five years later, an elderly former Ottawa resident wrote the *Citizen* and offered this glimpse into the kind of showmanship Boston brought to the game. "One peculiar incident … recurs to my mind," he said of the Red Stockings' 1873 appearance in the capital. "A short but very high fly was knocked towards Harry Wright. He took off his cap and held it as if to catch the falling ball, but dropped it when the sphere seemed about a foot or two away and caught the ball in his efficient hands."[42]

"Hurriedly got up"

With a day to fill before heading to Ogdensburg, the restless Wright arranged for a cricket match the next morning against a patchwork eleven "hurriedly got up"[43] by the Ottawa Cricket Club.

The day was hot and the pitch lumpy, but, said the *Times*, "Harry Wright at once showed himself an expert batsman. At times he played rather wildly, but on the whole his batting was brilliant and easy, and his style of putting the ball over the field was somewhat trying to his opponents. The fielding of the [Red Stockings] was, of course, splendid, and much admired, while on the other hand, their handling of the willow was scarcely what lovers of the game delight to witness."[44]

Nevertheless, Boston, with the Wright brothers sharing the bowling, came out on top, 110-62, "the large score run up by them … undoubtedly due to the wretched fielding of the Ottawa men."[45]

After lunch, the Red Stockings returned to the Base Ball Ground, where, in front of a small weekday crowd, the visitors and their hosts formed two nines, with Harry Wright's picks taking on Spalding's. It turned out to be the first remotely competitive match the Bostons had played on Canadian turf. The Wrights scored two in the ninth to win 19-18. The *Citizen* called it "the finest match ever witnessed in Ottawa."[46]

Again, Latham's play earned praise. Playing first base for the Spaldings, he showed "himself a quick catcher and a steady batter."[47]

Canadian sunrise

Due in substantial part to the Canadians having recruited a number of more experienced American players, the Red Stockings faced significantly stronger opposition in 1873 than they had the previous summer. In four games (not counting the split-squad affair in Ottawa—or the cricket match), the Red Stockings scored an average of 42.75 runs, while surrendering 8, for a run differential of 34.75. That marked a 17-run decline in their margin of victory over the previous year. The Canadian clubs were improving, but still far from competitive.

The next morning, August 28, 1873, the Red Stockings grabbed the 7:15 train for Ogdensburg for an afternoon game against a similarly improved Pastimes club. Boston won that one, 37-6. On August 29 they arrived back home, having been on the road for two weeks.

The previously underperforming Red Stockings seemed to right themselves on their 1873 Northern journey. Returning to championship play, they won 24 of their final 28 games, with one tie, to capture their second straight National Association flag.

Dominion Day - 1874

Make it a third straight. The start-to-finish National Association champs in 1874, perhaps with their focus on their overseas expedition in July, played just two games in Canada that year. In late June the Red Stockings, 26-6 in championship play, journeyed from Chicago to Brantford, Ontario, for a game against Guelph.

The winner, in this third annual battle of national champions, would take home $150 in gold.

Before 2,000-3,000 fans, the Maple Leafs jumped to a 4-1 lead after 2½ innings. But the Red Stockings bounced back with seven runs in the bottom of the third. They survived the physical collapse of their bench in midgame and went on to win 26-6. They outhit the Canadians 32-14.

The next day, July 1, Dominion Day, the two clubs returned to Guelph for a contest in celebration of Canada's seventh birthday. (The Maple Leafs themselves were six years older.) Later, the Maple Leafs' owner, brewing magnate George Sleeman, would boast that 10,000 fans—more than the population of Guelph—flocked to the big game.[48]

No doubt Sleeman exaggerated, but probably not by much: The *Guelph Mercury* estimated more than 8,000 in attendance. Unquestionably, it was the biggest crowd yet to see a ballgame in Canada. Even for the well-traveled Red Stockings it was an extraordinary event. Apart from a game earlier that season in Chicago, it was probably the largest crowd they had ever performed for.

"The immense mass of people presented an imposing spectacle," said the *Mercury* of the holiday turnout, "and the alteration of the red coats of the soldiers and the ordinary clothing of the civilians was a very pleasing feature."[49]

The Red Stockings conducted their usual pregame razzle-dazzle. Play started at 2:42 P.M. After three innings, Boston led only 5-2, but broke the game open with six in the top of fourth.

As the afternoon wore on, the mass of standees around the field began to encroach on fair territory, making the last few innings difficult for the fielders. The final score was 20-4, the Red Stockings having outhit the Maple Leafs 23-5. Deacon White himself matched the home team's hit total.

The Maple Leafs lost the game, but were winners at the gate. They took their $562 share of the gate and put it toward the costs of entering a tournament billed as the "nonprofessional (read 'semipro') world's championship" the following week in Watertown, New York. There, they beat the Flyaways of New York City, the Chelseas and Nassaus of Brooklyn, the Eastons of Easton, Pennsylvania, and the Ku Klux Klan team from Oneida, New York, to capture the "world" title and a $450 first prize. The Guelph "amateurs" earned $65 apiece for their victory, with star players pocketing a little more.

Takeaways

Four observations one might make from the Red Stockings' three sorties into Canada, 1872-74:

1. These guys worked up a sweat even when they didn't have to. The "got up" cricket-baseball doubleheader in Ottawa in 1873, toward the tail end of a long road trip, is indicative of how much the boys from Boston lived to play.

2. The unwritten rule that a clearly superior team shouldn't go out of its way to run up the score had not been written yet. In 12 games in Canada, the Red Stockings racked up 545 runs and gave up 59. Average score: 45-5.

3. What the Red Stockings lacked in mercy, they made up for in showmanship and branding savvy. Their much anticipated appearances in Canada drew huge numbers of highly appreciative fans and helped stoke the baseball fever that swept Southern and Eastern Ontario in those years.

"One great feature of the Bostons' playing," noted the *Guelph Mercury* in 1873, "is the good humour that they always appear to be in when they come to tackle our boys, which in a great measure no doubt draws such a large amount of spectators, and wins good opinions from all Canadians with whom they come in contact."[50]

4. Above all, the Red Stockings set the bar for how well the game could be played. Their appearances north of the border in those years were a major catalyst in the rapid professionalization of the pastime in Canada, mostly through the importation of talent from south of the border.

Postscript

A Boston club would not venture north again until May 1877, when the Red Stockings, now of the National League, came to play the London Tecumsehs, now an all-professional entry in the fledgling International Association. This time, it took Boston 10 innings to eke out a 7-6 win.

Compare this nailbiter to Boston's 52-3 drubbing of London in 1872, and it shows how far Canadian baseball—due largely to the influx of American professionals—had come in five years. In 1877 that same Tecumsehs club would capture the IA championship, while the Red Stockings would do the same in the NL.

NOTES

1 "The Civic Holiday," *Ottawa Citizen,* August 28, 1872: 4.
2 "Sports and Pastimes," *Brooklyn Daily Eagle,* August 16, 1872: 3.
3 Ibid.
4 *Guelph Mercury,* August 24, 1872: 1.
5 "Base Ball," *Toronto Mail,* August 25, 1872: 1.
6 "Base-Ball Match," *Toronto Globe,* August 25, 1872: 1.
7 "Base Ball," *Toronto Mail,* August 25, 1872: 1.
8 "International Base-Ball Match," *Toronto Globe,* August 27, 1872: 1.
9 Ibid.
10 "Base Ball & Lacrosse Matches," *Toronto Mail,* August 27, 1872: 1.
11 "International Base-Ball Match," *Toronto Globe,* August 27, 1872: 1.
12 *Ottawa Free Press,* undated clipping.
13 "Base Ball," *Ottawa Free Press,* August 23, 1872: 3.
14 For Harry and George Wright, the cricket match in Ottawa afforded an opportunity to scout an English eleven they would face that September in New York as members of a 22-man team fielded by the St. George's Cricket Club. Despite solid performances from both Wrights on that occasion, the Englishmen would win handily.
15 "The Civic Holiday," *Ottawa Citizen,* August 28, 1872: 4.
16 "International Match," *Ottawa Free Press,* August 28, 1872: 3.
17 Ibid.
18 "Base Ball," *Ottawa Free Press,* August 23, 1872: 3.
19 "The Civic Holiday," *Ottawa Citizen,* August 28, 1872: 4.
20 "Base Ball," *Ottawa Times,* August 29, 1872: 3.
21 "The Civic Holiday," *Ottawa Citizen,* August 28, 1872: 4.
22 "International Base Ball Match," *Montreal Herald and Daily Commercial Gazette,* August 31, 1872.
23 George Wright, *Record of the Boston Base Ball Club, Since Its Organization, With a Sketch of All Its players For 1871, '72, '73 and '74, and Other Items of Interest* (Boston: Rockwell & Churchill, 1874), 52.
24 *Guelph Mercury,* August 23, 1873: 3.
25 Alan Parker, "Rewind: The 1874 World Baseball Champion Guelph Maple Leafs," blogs.canoe.com/parker/news/rewind-the-1874-world-baseball-champion-guelph-maple-leafs/, August 1, 2012.
26 Zane Grey, *The Redheaded Outfield and Other Baseball Stories* (New York: Grosset & Dunlap, 1920).
27 "Base Ball Match," *Toronto Globe,* August 25, 1873: 4.
28 *Guelph Mercury,* August 25, 1873: 3.
29 "Base Ball," *Kingston British Whig,* June 23, 1873: 2.
30 "Grand Base Ball Match," *Kingston Daily News,* August 26, 1873: 1.
31 "Base Ball Red Stockings v. St. Lawrence," *Kingston British Whig,* August 26, 1873: 2.
32 Ibid.
33 Ibid.
34 Ibid.
35 "Grand Base Ball Match," *Kingston Daily News,* August 26, 1873: 1.
36 "Base Ball Red Stockings v. St. Lawrence," *Kingston British Whig,* August 26, 1873: 2.
37 Ibid.
38 Ibid.
39 "Base Ball Match," *Ottawa Times,* August 27, 1873: 2.
40 Ibid.
41 "The Base Ball Match," *Ottawa Citizen,* August 27, 1873: 4.
42 "Another Version of Famous Red Stockings-Ottawa Match," *Ottawa Citizen,* Aug. 11, 1928: 1.
43 "Cricket," *Ottawa Times,* August 28, 1873: 2.
44 Ibid.
45 Ibid.
46 "Base Ball," *Ottawa Citizen,* August 28, 1873: 4.
47 "Base Ball Match," *Ottawa Times,* August 28, 1873: 2.
48 Brian Martin, *The Tecumsehs of the International Association: Canada's First Major League Baseball Champions* (Jefferson, North Carolina: McFarland & Company Inc., 2015).
49 *Guelph Mercury,* July 2, 1874.
50 *Guelph Mercury,* August 23, 1873.

ZANE GREY AND THE MYSTERY OF THE WINNING BALL

BY DAVID MCDONALD

BEFORE FINDING ENORMOUS success as an author of Western novels—more than 100 million copies sold, more than 110 cowboy movies spawned—Zane Grey, son of a Zanesville, Ohio, dentist, wrote a number of stories about his first love, baseball. Grey himself had played at the University of Pennsylvania and had kicked around low-level professional circuits like the Iron and Oil League before taking up a writing career.

Borrowing on his own experiences and those of his brother, Romer "Reddy" Grey, an Eastern League stalwart and a one-game major leaguer with the 1903 Pirates, Grey spun a Lardneresque series of tales later collected in *The Redheaded Outfield and Other Baseball Stories* (1920). One of them, "The Winning Ball," first published in *Popular Magazine* in May 1910, is an account of a hastily arranged exhibition game, on what was supposed to have been an offday, between the top team in the Eastern League and an amateur team in Guelph played before a comical assortment of "Indians, half-breeds, French-Canadians [and] huge, hulking, bearded farmers or traders, or trappers, whatever they were."

"We had never heard of Guelph," grouses Grey's narrator, Reddy, a fictionalized version of his brother.[1] "We did not care anything about rube baseball teams. Baseball was not play to us, it was the hardest kind of work and of all things an exhibition game was an abomination."

The jaded pros slip a juiced ball into the game when they're batting. (It is the first known occurrence of "rabbit" ball in print.) The ruse backfires: The pros are unable to recapture the rabbit. The rubes knock it all over the park en route to an upset victory.

There has long been speculation whether events described in "The Winning Ball" have any basis in reality or whether they are strictly the product of Grey's imagination.

Historian William Humber, for one, believes the story was inspired by the Boston-Guelph match of August 22, 1873. In support of his theory, Humber leans heavily on a contemporary newspaper account which notes "that the ball seemed a great deal more lively than the 'dead ball' generally used. Are we right or not? For an analysis of the game see the score. ..."[2]

If, as Humber surmises, the Bostons snuck a "rabbit" into the game—never mind the clearly superior Red Stockings' lack of impetus to do so—it would seem they had more success than Grey's fictional Rochesters did in retrieving it. Not only did the putative cheaters win the game, they won by a score, 27-8, that's remarkably consistent with the results of the other Boston-Guelph contests of those years. In other words, the alleged lively ball apparently had no discernible impact on the outcome of the game. That does little to buttress a presumption that talk of such an incident floated around the baseball ozone for almost four decades before Grey put it to paper.

No cigar

But what if we consider "The Winning Ball" not as an echo of an event many years in the past but as something much more simultaneous with its writing? What if we consider the elements of the story more or less at face value?

Grey's narrator, Reddy, identifies himself as a member of the "Rochester club, leader in the Eastern League." The month is July, the year unspecified.

The real-life Reddy Grey did play for the Rochester Bronchos of the Eastern League for part of 1901 season and all of 1902. If we accept the premise that "Reddy's" teammates in the story are thinly disguised versions of actual Bronchos—that the fictional Gillinger is

Brothers Zane, R.C., and Lane Grey, ca. 1913 (Collection of David McDonald)

indeed the real-life Ed "Battleship" Gremminger; that "Deerfoot" Browning is "Deerfoot" Barclay; that Lake is Billy Lush; that "Crab" Bane is Joe Bean, and so on—that would pinpoint the setting as 1901, because all these players are gone from the club by 1902. Could, then, the game described in "The Winning Ball" actually have occurred in July 1901, as a literal reading of Grey would suggest?

Alas, no cigar. I can find no mention (there are, problematically, some gaps in the microfilm record) of an exhibition game between Rochester and Guelph in July, or in any other month, of 1901.

But there is a pretty close match. On August 3, 1899, Rochester, then "leader in the Eastern League," traveled to Guelph to take on the Maple Leafs, then the last-place club in the "amateur" Canadian League.[3] And, sure enough, on that day the rubes upset the pros. The surviving game accounts are sketchy, but there is no mention of a livelier-than-usual ball. And the score, 8-5, would hardly suggest one.

Rabbits, skyrockets, and punks

With no particular game to tap with confidence as inspiration for "The Winning Ball,"[4] we are perhaps left with a broader notion that double-dealing baseballs might have been part of the game's roomy bag of tricks from the start. Indeed, that seems to be the case.

In the game's formative, less financially flush years, the home club was responsible for supplying the game ball, and would, naturally, offer up one best suited to its style of play. "Ball selection was a key strategy and a critical benefit of home-field advantage. Visiting teams with big hitters would, more often than not, find themselves playing with a 'dead' ball."[5]

Of course, the impulse to get a leg up on one's opponent didn't end there. The game evolved a whole set of ball dodges, common-enough occurrences, it would seem, to have spawned their own vocabulary. There was the "rabbit" and the "skyrocket," but there was also the "punk," "a ball that defies being hit solidly; one that is soft and flabby."[6] The practice of switching balls, as circumstances warranted, even had its own verbs, "to work in" or "to ring in," as in: "They rung in a lively ball on us, and when they were at bat our fielders sat on the fence, so they could get the ball quicker when it went over."[7]

The Sporting News dubbed this sort of chicanery the "double-ball racket," and pointed to the 1876 St. Louis Brown Stockings as accomplished practitioners of the art. As evidence, *TSN* cited the three consecutive

The Popular Magazine, cover. (Collection of David McDonald)

shutouts—the final being the NL's first-ever no-hitter—thrown by the Brown Stockings' George "Grin" Bradley against the Hartford Dark Blues between July 11 and 15. "… It had a very demoralizing effect on the team, and did more than anything else to keep the Hartfords from winning the championship of that year."[8]

Partly in an attempt to defuse this ruse, the National League adopted an official ball in the fall of 1876. But as long as the home team controlled the ball supply, there was still plenty of opportunity for underhandedness. (It wasn't until the early 1900s that umpires took charge of game balls, a measure that eliminated much, but certainly not all, of the tampering.) In 1878 the *Chicago Tribune* reported that the company supplying offical balls to the International Association was surreptitiously providing punks or rabbits according to the customer's preferences.[9]

Of course, shenanigans of this sort always carry with them the tantalizing possibility of comeuppance. In 1891 *Sporting Life* ran a story about an American Association meeting in Philadelphia between the Athletics and the eventual pennant winners, the Boston Reds. In the top of the seventh, with his team down 8-4 (the Athletics had chosen to bat first), Philadelphia manager Bill Sharsig "rang in" a lively ball—in this case, a Keefe & Becannon[10] model left over from the more offensive-minded Players League of 1890.[11]

"But," as *Sporting Life* reminds us, "man proposes and God disposes."[12] Athletics first baseman Henry Larkin immediately fouled the rabbit over the grandstand, and the regulation Reach ball was tossed back into the game. However, leading off the bottom of the inning, Boston second baseman "Cub" Stricker knocked the Reach ball out of play, and the rabbit returned.

"Then followed a fusillade of doubles, triples and home runs, such as is seldom witnessed, and when the inning was ended the Bostons had scored ten runs. It was one of the greatest batting exhibitions ever given."[13] The final score was 22-7. "There have been some heavy batting games so far this season," pondered *Sporting Life*. "Has the trick been worked before?"[14]

Zane Grey in batting pose. (Collection of David McDonald)

No doubt before, and no doubt for many years after. An unidentified player told *The Sporting News* in 1893 that "whenever a new ball was thrown out last season and we were in the field it was tossed to the pitcher, who would put his private mark on the same, so the visitors could not change the ball."[15]

In 1899 Washington Senators manager Arthur Irwin singled out John S. Barnes, manager of the Western League Minnesota Minnies in the mid-1890s, as one who kept a "stack of springy balls on tap in his ice chest. The refrigerator warped the rubber in the sphere and when it met the bat, it sputtered feebly into the hands of an infielder like the last dying kick of a Fourth of Juy skyrocket." Irwin also claimed another team's captain would drop "half a dozen balls into a

Reddy Grey and Zane Grey. (Collection of David McDonald)

flour sack and pounded them with an ax" to deaden them.[16]

In 1906 several managers in the Southern Association complained publicly about New Orleans Pelicans manager Charlie Frank, who allegedly kept a supply of balls for all occasions—old and new ones, doornail-dead and extremely lively ones—in a closely guarded valise beside him during home games.[17]

According to longtime player, coach, and umpire Arlie Latham, Frank would deaden balls by hanging them in a "dry refrigerator" for a few days, after which "you could slam them on the ground with all your might and they wouldn't bounce half an inch. ..." When Frank needed runs, said Latham, he "worked another ball. He generally had one of those rubber skyrockets on tap. ... Crack! When a batter hit one of those things he sent it into the next county."[18]

Montgomery manager Dominic Mullaney claimed to have cut open one of the latter and found "a wrapped rubber mixture about five times the size of the ordinary rubber [center] used in a Reach ball. The yarn inclosing the rubber is not more than a fourth as thick as the yarn in the Reach ball."[19]

Official league balls were supposed to remain in sealed boxes until introduced into a game, but Frank was a master at distracting umpires and opponents from the fact that the seals on some of the containers—and the balls in them—had been breached.

Such discussion could hardly have escaped a baseball-savvy writer like Zane Grey. It is highly improbable he would have had to dig back to 1873 for inspiration for "The Winning Ball" (or "The Manager of Madden's Hill"). It was there, in the sports section of the daily paper.

But Guelph? Why then did he choose to set "The Winning Ball" in Guelph? Perhaps it's no more complicated than Grey seizing on this oddly named outpost somewhere in the Canadian hinterland as the most rube-sounding baseball destination he could think of.

NOTES

1. The real Reddy Grey, having spent three seasons with the Toronto Canucks/Maple Leafs of the Eastern League and a couple more in Buffalo, would certainly have heard of Guelph and might even have played there once or twice.

2. From an undated newspaper clipping in the files of William Humber.

3. Bronchos skipper Al Buckenberger had more than a passing familiarity with Guelph, having managed and played there in 1886. Buckenberger's boss was George Sleeman, who was also one of the backers of the 1873 club. Thus, there are only three degrees of separation between Zane Grey—Reddy Grey-Buckenberger-Sleeman—and the 1873 lively-ball game, which might be seen as evidence, however faint and circumstantial, in support of Humber's theory.

4. Or for another of Grey's *Redheaded Outfield* stories, the often overlooked "The Manager of Madden's Hill," which also relies on a lively-ball twist. As the titular manager tells his team at a crucial point: "This game ain't over yet. ... Last innin' Bo's umpire switched balls on us. That ball was lively. An' they tried to switch back on me. But nix! We're goin' to git a chanst to hit that lively ball. An' they're goin' to git a dose of their own medicine."

5. Jimmy Stamp, "A Brief History of the Baseball," smithsonian.com, June 28, 2013.

6. Paul Dickson, *The Dickson Baseball Dictionary* (New York: W.W. Norton & Company, 2009), 676.

7   Cumminsville (Ohio) Blue Stockings second baseman Alec Voss, in describing an 1876 game between his team and the NL Hartford Dark Blues; quoted by Ren Mulford Jr., "Cincinnati Chips," *Sporting Life*, February 15, 1888: 8.

8   "… They would have a lively ball to bat, but when their opponents were at the bat a dead ball would be worked in on them. This ball the club had made especially for its own use." "Tricks of the Game," *The Sporting News*, March 10, 1888: 1.

9   9 *Chicago Tribune*, September 1, 1878, quoted in Peter Morris, *A Game of Inches: The Stories Behind the Innovations That Shaped Baseball* (Chicago: Ivan R. Dee, 2006), 328.

10 Made by a company founded by New York Giant Tim Keefe and former New York Metropolitan "Buck" Becannon. Even Keefe, a 33-year-old pitcher, found his own ball "too lively." Charlie Bevis, "Tim Keefe," Society for American Baseball Research, at sabr.org/bioproj/person/6f1dd1b1.

11 In 1890 the PL recorded a .274/.351/.378/.729 slash line, compared with the NL's .254/.329/.342/.671 and the AA's .253/.330/.332/.662. How much of the difference in offense was due to the ball is, of course, impossible to ascertain.

12 "A Trick Which Plagued the Inventor," *Sporting Life*, May 9, 1891: 9.

13 "Athletics vs. Boston at Philadelphia April 30," *Sporting Life*, May 1, 1891: 4.

14 Op. cit., *Sporting Life*, May 9, 1891: 9.

15 *The Sporting News*, January 21, 1893, quoted in Morris, 328.

16 Gerard S. Petrone, *When Baseball Was Young: The Good Old Days* (San Diego: Musty Attic Archives, 1994), 118.

17 "Baseball Was Full of Rubber: More Evidence of the Unfair Methods of Southern League Manager," *Pittsburgh Press*, June 27, 1906: 14.

18 Quoted by John Thorn, "Over the Plate: Arlie Latham's Own Baseball Stories, No. 2," ourgame.mlblogs.com/2015/08/, August 24, 2015. Latham also identified Hall of Famer Buck Ewing, Cincinnati's manager from 1894 to 1899, as a devoted baseball tamperer.

19 *Pittsburgh Press*, June 27, 1906: 14.

THE 1874 BOSTON RED STOCKINGS' WORLD TOUR

BY ERIC MIKLICH

HARRY WRIGHT PLANNED ON returning one day to his native England. He drew on the success of the All-England cricketers touring in North America in 1859 and 1868 and the success his Cincinnati Baseball Club experienced from 1867 to 1869 to convince the Red Stockings officials to allow the team to travel to Britain with a second professional baseball team. He also hoped, if nothing else, to cover all expenses. Wright, born in Sheffield, England, in 1835, felt that the American game of baseball would be politely attended if a fellow countryman was the driving force behind the historic event. In January of 1874, he sent his 23-year-old star pitcher, Albert Spalding, and Warren Briggs, a Harvard student, to Britain to arrange a series of baseball matches in the summer of 1874. The plans included the possibility of matches in Scotland, Ireland, and France, although the bulk of the tour would take place in England.

Spalding was the best pitcher in professional baseball, having compiled a 98-32 record in his three seasons as the Red Stockings' ace. He and Briggs, a member of the Beacon Club of Boston, met with Charles W. Alcock, the secretary of the Surrey Cricket Club. After a long conversation on the possibilities and logistics of Americans playing baseball in England, the two engaged in the first American baseball game played on British soil, on February 27, 1874, at the Cricket Oval at Lords (London). Spalding and Alcock headed teams made up of local cricketers. Spalding pitched for one side and Alcock the other with Briggs as his catcher. The match was halted after six innings by rain. Alcock's side won, 17-5, and he thus joined the relatively exclusive list of pitchers who had defeated Spalding. After a second meeting between the two teams the next day, Alcock agreed to become the promoter of the American baseball tour.

Alcock appeared to be a solid choice. He would be later known as the Father of Modern Sport in England for his work with the English game of football, including the founding of the Football Association (FA) Cup, the introduction of international soccer matches, and his writing and reporting on cricket.

While Spalding and Briggs were overseas, Harry Wright was busy looking for a club to accompany the Red Stockings, and persuaded the Athletic of Philadelphia Club to make the trip. While Wright may have been happy, the Boston club's stockholders were not. Many of them felt that the trip would be a financial disaster, as well as a deterrent in the club's quest for a third straight National Association of Professional Base Ball Players championship.[1]

Spalding and Briggs returned to America relieved that they could report to Wright that a relatively important figure was to take care of the tour particulars, and they handed Wright a tentative schedule. The tour was to begin in England at the end of July. Spalding did his best to hide the fact that at Alcock's request the baseball players would also play cricket at each place they visited. Wright wanted the main focus of the tour to be baseball and was unhappy to learn that cricket matches were included, as he knew that they would become the focus of the Britons. Soon after Spalding left England, Alcock hurt his thigh badly during a soccer match, an injury that severely hindered his efforts to secure grounds for baseball games and to promote the Americans' arrival. After the injury healed, he failed to truly immerse himself in the job. He eventually was able to gain access to playing fields, but his efforts to promote the summer event remained weak.

To open time for the trip to England, Wright had canceled the Red Stockings' Canadian tour for 1874, playing just one date in Brantford and one in Guelph.[2]

The Athletics and Red Stockings played "farewell" matches, one in Boston and one in Philadelphia before leaving in the middle of the National Association season. On Monday, July 13, at the South End Grounds, Boston won 7-6 in front of large and enthusiastic crowd. It was Boston's fourth win in a row over the Athletics. The two clubs then headed to Philadelphia. En route, the Red Stockings stopped in New York on July 14 and defeated the Mutuals, 9-8, giving Al Spalding his 30th win of the season. On July 15, the Athletics defeated Boston, 6-4, in front of an estimated 10,000 spectators at the Jefferson Street Grounds.[3]

On Thursday, July 16, the two clubs, stockholders, reporters, and friends boarded the steamship Ohio and headed to England. The rosters were as follows:

Red Stockings of Boston Roster
Cal A. McVey - Catcher
Albert G. Spalding - Pitcher
Jim O'Rourke - First Base
Ross C. Barnes - Second Base
Harry C. Schafer - Third Base
George Wright - Short Stop
Andy J. Leonard - Left Field
Harry Wright - Center Field (Captain)
George W. Hall—Right Field
Thomas L. Beals—Substitute
John F. Kent—Change; First Base (Harvard Col. BBC)
Sam Wright, Jr.* - Substitute

Athletic of Philadelphia Roster
John E. Clapp - Catcher
Dick McBride - Pitcher (Captain)
Weston D. Fisler - First Base
Joseph Battin - Second Base
Ezra B. Sutton - Third Base
Mike H. McGeary - Short Stop
Alfred W. Gedney - Left Field
John F. McMullin - Center Field
Adrian C. Anson - Right Field
John P. Sensenderfer - Substitute
Tim Murnane - Substitute
Al Reach ** - Substitute

Recruited primarily for his knowledge of cricket, Sam Wright did not begin his professional baseball career until the 1875 season with the New Haven Elm Citys of the National Association.

**Al Reach, originally selected, declined the invitation to oversee the growing sporting-goods business he founded in Philadelphia in 1865.*

The Philadelphia riverfront was filled with hordes of people bidding the travelers goodbye on the night of July 16. McClurg's Silver Cornet Band of Philadelphia enthusiastically played as tugboats started the ship left for England on its journey. By the next morning many of the players and guests had succumbed to seasickness and could be seen "admiring the waves over the side of the steamer."[4] To help pass the time, some played games like shuffleboard, ring of the pegs, chess, cribbage, pinochle, checkers, seven up, euchre, and forty-fives, while others took tours of the steamship. The evening of the 20th featured a concert presented by some of the players. The acts included sentimental singing by George Hall and Andy Leonard of Boston,

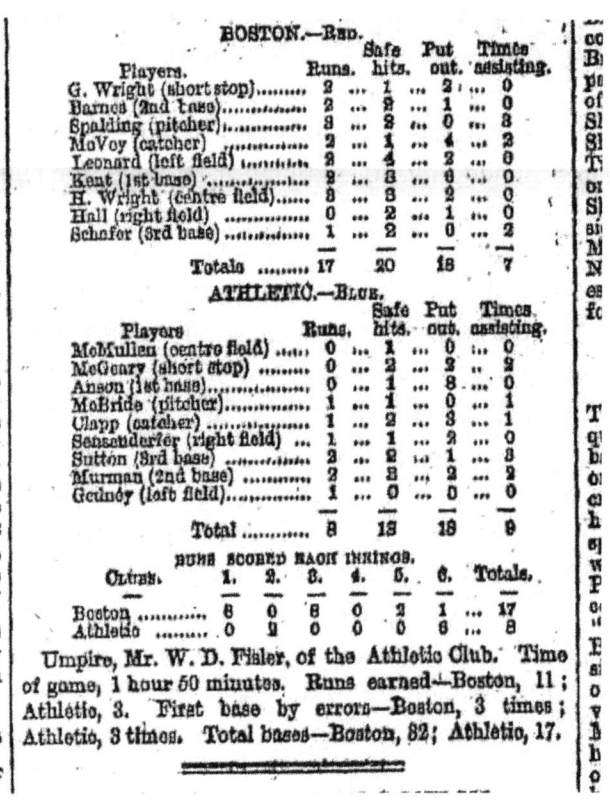

A match between Boston and Philadelphia on the Lord's Cricket Grounds in London in 1874 (Library of Congress).

comical singing by John McMullin of Philadelphia, and piano solos by John Sensenderfer and Albert Gedney of the Athletics.

On Friday, July 24, the weather became rough and the Ohio was caught in heavy swells. The seas became calmer in the evening and the ballists staged a second concert. Saturday produced the roughest seas of the journey. At times the waves were so high that they reached the ship's deck. A shoal of dolphins swam with the ship all day. On Sunday the 26th at 10:00 A.M., Red Stockings president Charles Porter held a religious service on the deck. When the Irish coast became visible at about 3:00 P.M., the entire party cheered with joy.

The travelers transferred to a tender outside Queenstown, Ireland, at 11:00 P.M. bound for Liverpool, which they reached at 10:30 P.M. on Monday, July 27. The Americans went straight to the Washington Hotel. The *New York Times* reported that some members of the party went to London but would return for the match on July 30.[5]

Before the first match, the teams held short practices on July 28 and 29 at Edgehill, the grounds of the Liverpool Cricket Club. As the Americans would see, the venues they would play in were maintained and manicured to levels far better than they were used to. The fields were green, usually level, and very firm. The hardness of the ground caused the era's dead ball to become very lively.

George Mortimer Pullman, the inventor of the sleeping car, granted the entourage free use of his cars while in England. The previous January Pullman had introduced his sleeping cars to England, on the Midland Railway.

The first match was scheduled for July 30. The players arrived at Edgehill before 2:30 P.M., to lay out and mark the playing field. With only about 500 spectators appearing at the historic event, Alcock's

Sam Wright, with cricket bat, and son Harry. (Matthew Brady photograph, Boston Public Library)

scheduling was immediately questioned. Wright could not have been more disappointed with the turnout. Boston won the toss and sent the Athletic to the bat. The Red Stockings scored six runs in the bottom of the eighth inning and tied the score, 9-9, but Philadelphia won in 10 innings, 14-11. The English press covered the match extensively. The *Liverpool Daily Albion* printed the most detailed and insightful article on the occasion. "The match fixed for yesterday came off on the ground of the Liverpool Cricket Club, at Edgehill. There were not many spectators to witness the introduction of the new game, not from any lack of interest attaching to the event, but because the public do not seem to have been properly informed that the match was coming off."[6] Descriptions of the uniforms, equipment, player positions, and strategies were offered.

Sounding a theme that would be repeated in almost every article covering the Americans as they moved around England, the *Manchester Guardian* wrote, "Base ball, as we were prepared to find, is an American modification, and, of course, an 'improvement' of the old English game of 'rounders,' or, as it is called in the West Riding, 'touch ball.'"[7]

The next day on the same grounds, only 200 spectators braved the rain to see the Red Stockings even the series with a 23-18 victory in a sloppily played match.

The players took a one-hour train ride from Liverpool to Manchester on August 1 and proceeded directly to the field to play the third match of the tour. The baseball game, scheduled for 1:00 P.M., was played at Old Trafford Grounds, home of the Manchester Cricket Club and as of 2016 still in use by Lancashire County Cricket Club. Before the game, players explained to the crowd how to lay out a baseball field, and put on demonstrations of throwing and catching the ball. Crowds more to the liking of Harry Wright and the Americans turned out; 2,000 people watched the two-hour match. Included among the spectators was the "American Consul with several American ladies and George W. Taylor,"[8] part owner of the upscale Lord & Taylor department stores. Philadelphia won, 13-12.

After the game the clubs headed for London and arrived on Sunday at 4:00 A.M., ending up at the Midland Grand Hotel. The players were given a day off to rest and relax.

The next day, August 3, was a Bank Holiday, and the clubs played in both a cricket match and a baseball game before a large crowd on the Ground at Lords. The cricket match, between the Marylebone Cricket Club and the 18 Americans, began at 12:15. It was halted at 3:00 P.M. and the base ball game began, with Boston winning the toss and sending the Athletics to bat. After the game ended, the cricket match was resumed and was played until darkness forced it to end. Between 4,000 and 6,000 spectators attended the "doubleheader," paying one shilling each (all proceeds going to the Americans). For their money they witnessed a subpar baseball game. The Athletics made nine errors, four by second baseman Joe Battin. (The Red Stockings made one.) The Greounds' extremely hard surface produced four Boston home runs, one each by Al Spalding, Andy Leonard, Jim O'Rourke, and

George Wright, all off Athletics pitcher Dick McBride. Adrian "Cap" Anson hit one for Philadelphia off Al Spalding in the 24-7 drubbing by the Bostons. After the match it was announced that the trip to Paris was canceled, reportedly due to the dearth of playing fields. More likely, it was due to Alcock's lack of interest in his job as promoter. The cricket match was completed the following day, in front of a much smaller crowd.

The players received the afternoon off as the base ball game was canceled because of "unfavorable weather."

Only 200 spectators attend the second match in London, on August 6, and 1,000 braved showery conditions in Richmond two days later. Large crowds showed up for two games at Crystal Palace, but one of them, on August 10, was shortened by rain. The clubs

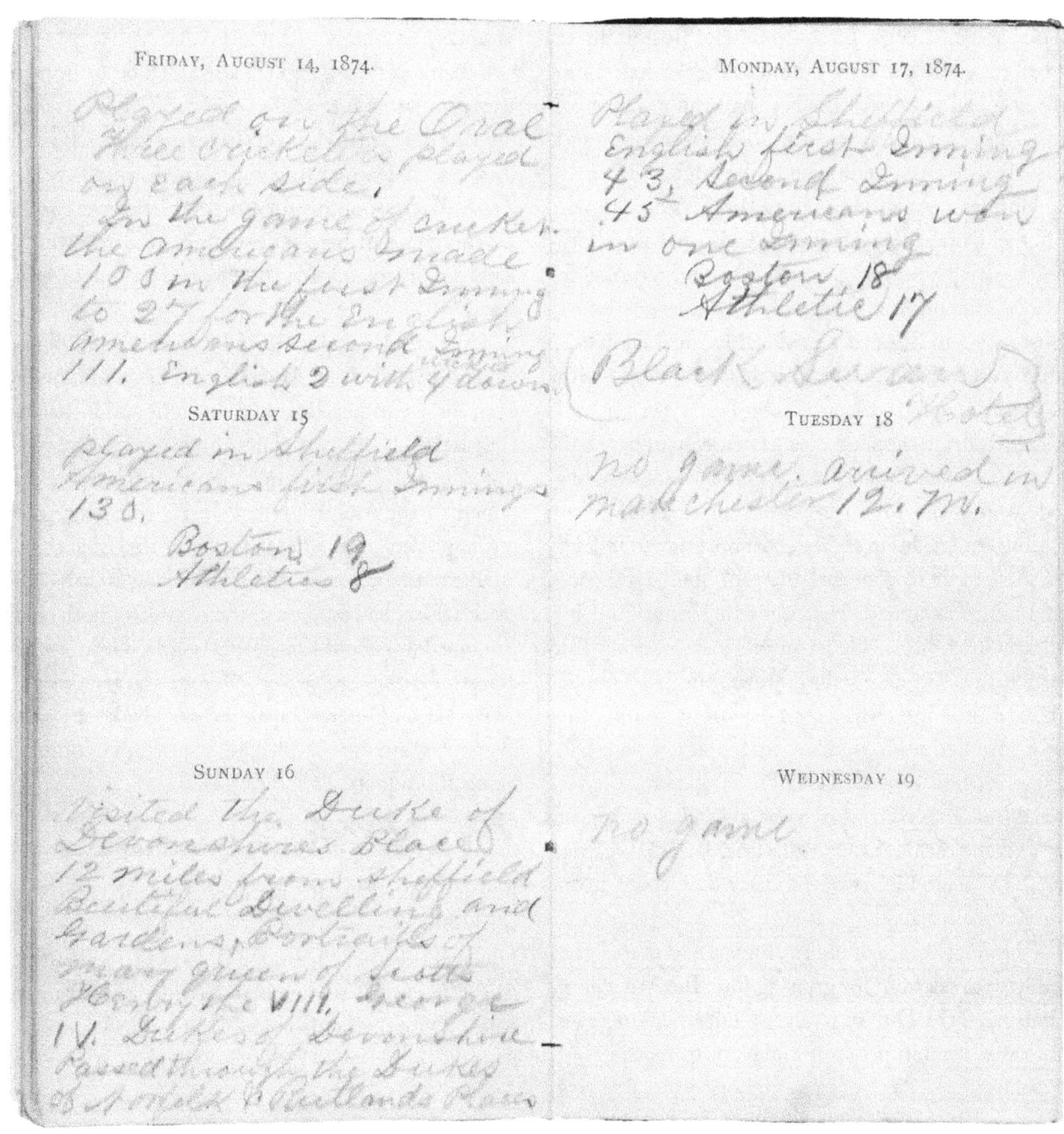

Two pages from Leonard's diary, depicting events from August 14 through 19. Images of the entire diary were provided to SABR courtesy of Heritage Auctions.

and their entourages headed to Kennington, each club having won four games.

The first day first at Kennington, August 13, began with a cricket match against the Surrey Cricket Club. After the lunch break the baseball game was played and then the cricket match resumed until it was stopped by darkness. The cricket match resumed the next day, in front of 4,000. During the afternoon break a long-distance throwing exhibition was held, then the base ball game begn. Jim O'Rourke of Boston threw a ball 122 yards and Ezra Sutton of the Athletic Club threw a ball 120 yards. The base ball game were a bit of a break for the Americans. Sides were split and captained by Al Spalding and John McMullin.

Both games played in Harry Wright's hometown, Sheffield, drew very small crowds. Boston won both and took a 7-5 lead in the series. The tour returned to Manchester on August 20, with the Athletics beating Boston 7-2 in front of a predictably small audience, after a cricket match. The next day again began with a cricket match. In the afternoon Harry Wright and Dick McBride captained teams made up of base ball players and Manchester Cricket Club players. Wright's side won 14-9, with no cricketer scoring a run.

The Americans made the short boat ride to Ireland on August 22 to conclude the tour. John Lawrence of Dublin arranged the games in Ireland and by all accounts did a wonderful job in promoting the Americans and base ball; however, the Irish public showed little interest. After a day off in Dublin, the tour resumed with a cricket match and a base ball game. Boston beat Philadelphia 12-7, taking an 8-5 series lead. The cricket match was concluded on August 25 and the Athletics won the final base ball game, 15-4. The matches in Ireland drew only about 1,500 spectators in all.

The final day in Dublin, August 26, offered the ballists a break from the grueling tour. The Americans challenged the Dublin Cricket Club. The American side was made up of nine players from the Red Stockings and Athletics and the opposing side was five members of the Dublin Cricket Club, plus George Wright as pitcher, Harry Wright as catcher, John Kent at first base, and the Earl of Kingston. The Ireland Nine were allowed five outs per inning and the Americans three. The "Americans" still won the contest, 12-6.

After a break the Americans played a "scratch game" before a large gathering. The Athletics were captained by John McMullin and the Red Stockings by Al Spalding. Unfortunately for Athletic pitcher Dick McBride, he broke his thumb during the game.

The Americans left Queenstown, Ireland, on August 27 on the Abbotsford and arrived in Philadelphia on Thursday, September 10 at 8:15 A.M. At 3:55 P.M. the two teams played a regular-season game in front of 2,500 spectators at the Jefferson Street Grounds, which the Red Stockings won 5-4. Two days later in Boston, they played again at the South End Grounds before a crowd of 4,000; this time the Athletics won 6-5.

The game of base ball was not well received in England or Ireland. The crowds were disappointingly small.

Cricket was too popular in Britain allow a different game, especially from America, to achieve a following even for a summer. Boston won eight and lost six to Philadelphia; the two clubs combined to achieve a 6-0-1 record in cricket matches against various opponents. (The Americans had one big advantage; they put 18 players on the field instead of the usual 11.[9])

The tour was not successful financially, as each club's stockholders had predicted. The red ink for both clubs combined was about $2,500, affecting each team's profit margin for the 1874 season. Despite the failures and general lack of interest, Spalding would take the game overseas again in 1888-1889, in an attempt peddle his baseball products.

Full results of baseball matches played:

July 30 (Thursday) at Liverpool: Athletic 14, Boston 11 (10 innings)
July 31 (Friday) at Liverpool: Boston 23, Athletic 18
Aug. 1 (Saturday) at Manchester: Athletic 13, Boston 12
Aug. 3 (Monday) at London: Boston 24, Athletic 7
Aug. 6 (Thursday) at London: Boston 14, Athletic 11
Aug. 8 (Saturday) at Richmond: Athletic 11, Boston 3
Aug. 10 (Monday) at Crystal Palace: Boston 17, Athletic 8

Aug. 11 (Tuesday) at Crystal Palace: Athletic 19, Boston 8
Aug. 13 (Thursday) at Kennington: Boston 16, Athletic 6
Aug. 14 (Friday) at Kennington: Spalding's Nine 14, McMullin's Nine 11
Aug. 15 (Saturday) at Sheffield: Boston 19, Athletic 8
Aug. 17 (Monday) at Sheffield: Boston 18, Athletic 17
Aug. 20 (Thursday) at Manchester: Athletic 7, Boston 2
Aug. 21 (Friday) at Manchester: Wright's Team 14, McBride's team 9
Aug. 24 (Monday) at Dublin: Boston 12, Athletic 7
Aug. 25 (Tuesday) at Dublin: Athletic 15, Boston 4
Aug. 26 (Wednesday) at Dublin: American Nine 12, Ireland Nine 6 Spalding's Nine 9, McMullin's Nine 8

SOURCES

The research for this article comes from Eric Miklich's forthcoming book *The World Tour of '74*.

NOTES

1. William J. Ryczek, *Blackguards and Red Stockings: A History of Baseball's National Association, 1871-1875* (Wallingford, Connecticut: Colebrook Press, 1992), 137, See also *New York Clipper*, April 4, 1874, and *Boston Daily Advertiser*, July 13, 1874.
2. Ryczek, 137.
3. The attendance is reported in *New York Clipper*, July 25, 1874: 131.
4. "On the Ocean Wave," *Brooklyn Daily Eagle*, August 12, 1874: 3.
5. "The American Base-Ball Clubs in Liverpool," *New York Times*, July 29, 1874.
6. *Liverpool Daily Albion*. Reprinted in *Leeds Mercury* as "Base Ball in England," August 1, 1874.
7. *Manchester Guardian*. Reprinted in the *Birmingham Daily Post* as "The Americans Base Ball Players," August 1, 1874.
8. *New York Clipper*, August, 22, 1874: 163.
9. Why did the American sides field 18, instead of the customary 11? Spalding said it was because even though they were accomplished athletes, most of the Americans had never seen cricket played. Spalding later wrote, "As we had eighteen men—and I urged that no one wanted to be left out of the cricket games—it was agreed that we should, in all cricket matches, play at the odds of eighteen to eleven in our favor, which, considering the fielding ability of the Americans, was greatly to our advantage." See Albert G. Spalding, *America's National Game* (Lincoln, Nebraska: Bison Books, 1992, reprint of 1911 edition), 180.

SELECTIONS FROM THE BRITISH NEWSPAPER COVERAGE OF THE VISIT OF THE AMERICAN BASEBALL PLAYERS

BASE-BALL IS A MODIFICATION, and of course as improvement, of the old English game of rounders, or as it is called in the West Riding, touch-ball. The children in these districts play it without a bat or club they strike the ball with the open hand, and have posts or stones at the corners of the playground, which correspond to the "bases" of the American game. If the ball is caught before it reached the ground, or the fielder could hit the striker with it before he reached the "touch" he was out. In the American game the ball if made extremely hard, and the use of a bat therefore became necessary. The players used a round club, about the same length as a cricket bat, but round and much thicker at the lower end than in the handle. Armed with this weapon, the striker takes his stand at one corner of a square; 18 or 20 yards distant, near the centre of the square, is the "pitcher" or bowler of the opposite party; at each "base," or corner of the square, a fielder is stationed and in the long field, on and off, and at leg, others are on the look out for catches. There is no wicket, but the striker stands within a square marked upon the grass, Behind him is the "catcher" of the cuts, who is next in importance to the "pitcher." He combines in his own person the wicket-keeper or the long-stop at cricket. The judge is stationed behind the striker, and it is his duty to decide, without being appealed to, all the points of the game. The "pitcher" delivers the ball as swiftly as the underhand style will admit of, and the striker has to meet it with his before it has touched the ground. Herein is one of the essential points in which base-ball differs from cricket.

[The ball] flies straight from the hand of the pitcher, and it is obvious that great quickness of hand and eye are necessary to enable the striker to use his club with effect. Another peculiarity of the game is that the striker may allow the ball to pass him without attempting to score, but the judge has the power to order the striker out if he misses the balls from which in his (the judge's) opinion a hit should have been made. The sides of the square, 30 yards in length, are defined by a broad white mark, and the ball must be struck over this line at some point, or the judge calls "foul." This rule excludes "cutting," and good hits to leg are frequently lost because the ball is struck out of the square. The striker cannot score from hits behind the wicket, but he is out if the catcher manages to secure the ball either direct from the club or on the first rebound from the turf. The remaining points of the game are pretty clear of comprehension. The striker must run to the first base if he hits the ball fairly, and the object of the fielders is to gather the ball and throw it to the keeper of the base before the striker can reach it. If they succeed and the base keeper holds the ball, the striker is out; if they fail, he remains at the base, and his place at the wicket is taken by another player on his side. If this player makes a hit, he runs in his turn to base No. 1, and his comrade makes the best of his way from No. 1 to No. 2. The quickness and dexterity of the players, both runners and fielders, elicited universal admiration on Thursday. In several instances the keeper of second base fielded the ball so cleverly that he not only put out the player who was running from first to second base, but returned it to the keeper of the first base in time to put out the player who was running thither from the wicket, and both men were run out. The game becomes highly interesting when the "ins" have men at more than one base, for the "outs" have then not only to watch the striker, but also his partner, who will inevitably "steal" a base if there be the slightest relaxation in the vigilance with which he is watched.

—*The Morning Post* (London), August 1, 1874

The game, which is more lively and more exciting than cricket, is very much akin to what is generally known as "rounders...."

Having struck the ball, the object is to make the base in safety. The game calls for the greatest agility, its success being mostly owing to excellent fielding, and anyone who saw the game played on Saturday, must give the Americans great credit for being good hands at a catch, it can be at all obtained…Some capital play was exhibited by both sides....

—*Manchester Courier and Lancashire General Advertiser*, August 3, 1874

The bulk of the spectators were thoroughly holiday seekers, fond of sport, and ready to give the base-ball men a leg up for their pluck in coming such a long way for the cause of sport. The affair is not a speculation of Barnum or any other entrepreneur, but a genuine attempt to show us in England that the Americans have a national game and can play at it well.

At first sight the placing of the fields strikes the spectator as an improved form of rounders; and so it is, but the rules and scientific addenda have been increased so as to almost obliterate our old notions of the village-green rounders, in which the chief fun consisted in corking—i.e., shying the ball and hitting the runner as he ran from one base to another.

…Behind the striker stands the catcher, almost as important a post as the pitcher. He performs the double office of long-stop or wicket-keeper. When there is no other of the side on the bases he stands back; when, however, there are men on the bases he stands up close, so as to be ready to put one down. Each of the bases has a field attached to it, and it is the duty of the fields to watch their bases and be ready in case of the batter's running to catch the ball thrown up and put the base down: if the man has got his foot off it the fielder can put him out by touching him with the ball in his hand. The players are allowed to overrun the first base but none of the others. It was curious to notice how rapid the fielding was, and how all the throwing was full pitch; in fact, when the long-fields threw up, they generally threw hard to a man half-way, who passed it on with the same hard low throw, instead of shying up for the wicket keeper as we do at cricket to take it on the first bound....

The umpire, who stands behind the striker, calls out strike when it is what he considers a proper ball, and if the striker fails to hit it in three trials he is put out, if the catcher can catch the ball from the pitcher…The pitcher has to be very quick in his delivery, and also to look out for squalls, as a ball hit hard back to him goes like lightning, and hits hard where it touches. In like manner the catcher not infrequently may get a bat flying out of the striker's hand in uncomfortable proximity to his head—this with ill-tempered or careless players.

…The captain of the side places the men in the field according to the peculiarities of the strikers, and the umpire is sole judge of any disputed point in the game....

It was evident that the Athletics were off play for the day, and in fact their fielding was at times slack, compared to that of Boston, who stopped hot ones and returned them with a rapidity almost astonishing. The fly catches were invariably well made by both sides—no butter-fingers, and the precision of their throwing was marvelous.

—*London Evening Standard*, August 4, 1874

We are reminded…that there was an old rustic game in England called base-ball, which is mentioned by Shakespeare, and was still practiced in the last century. The American game is something like what we call "rounders." Its name is derived from the bases, which serve the purpose of wickets at cricket.,,,

—*Illustrated London News*, August 15, 1874

Base ball is to Americans what cricket is to the athletes of the old country....

Base-ball proved to be a most attractive game, and the American players speedily showed themselves splendid athletes. For something with which to compare base ball we are driven to cricket, and in some respects base ball seems an improvement on our national game. It is very much quicker in its action—two hours are enough to complete the 18 innings, which finish a game. Play never drags: the movements of every player are ceaseless, consequently it is to the spectator much more exciting than cricket.

If a Lancashire county eleven could combine their present batting powers with such fielding as that of the American base-ball players, they would need to fear no rivals.

—*The Manchester Weekly Times*, August 8, 1874

Their striking was exceedingly good and the fielding was worthy of all praise. It is seldom, even in the best cricket fields of England, that better catches or quicker returns are made, while the backing up of the Americans is simply admirable. There were remarkably few cases of overthrows, or chances missed on either side.

—*The Daily News* (London), August 11, 1874

Thanks to SABR member Andrew Arends of London for gathering a selection of newspaper clippings of the tour from the United Kingdom, from which these excerpts were compiled.

TIM MURNANE'S ACCOUNT OF THE 1874 BASE BALL TRIP TO EUROPE

A LITTLE MORE THAN 40 YEARS after Tim Murnane had taken part in the trip to Europe as a member of the Philadelphia Athletics, he offered some recollections to the *Boston Globe*, where he had worked for many years as a sportswriter.

First came a foreshadowing of his intent to put down some of his memories:

My trip to Europe with the baseball combination is worth a story or two later on. Imagine two of the leading teams of the American or National Leagues, or better still, the leading team of each league, abandoning their scheduled games in the last of July for a six weeks' trip to England, to there play exhibition games on open fields with the chances of very little gate money, for the purpose of creating an interest in the game in foreign lands.

The players were given this delightful outing, while still under salary, and returned to the country to play several weeks before the season was over....

—"Murnane's Baseball Stories," *Boston Globe*, January 10, 1915: 39.

On the eve of the 11th of July, 1874, the elegant rooms of the Athletic Baseball Association of Philadelphia were brilliantly lighted and filled with friends of the ball players. These friends congratulated the boys on their splendid victory over the great Boston team that day, and pledged their good wishes for the success of the trip across the water which was to begin on the morrow.

The Boston players were stopping at the Colonade Hotel, and were being handsomely entertained by friends from Boston and their admirers in Philadelphia. McClurg's band gave a concert in front of the hotel.

The two ball clubs were the strongest exponents of our National game, and were going over 3000 miles from home during the most interesting part of the championship season.

The next morning a large crowd had gathered at the wharf, where lay the American steamship Ohio, which had been chartered to take our party to Europe. As the time drew near for the departure, the crowd had increased until the dock was black with humanity, as was the rigging of all neighboring vessel. Salutes were fired from a gun on one of the tugboats, and McClurg's band on board the Ohio made things lively until 11 o'clock. When the boat steamed out of the dock into the river, the Athletic boys were called together and managed to climb to the upper deck, where, in full view of the vast crowd on shore, they drank several bottles of champagne.

The Boston players were grouped together on deck, thinking, no doubt, that they would have been given a very different farewell if they had sailed from Boston.

Bound for Liverpool

The first day on board ship the boys talked over the lively times they had passed through during the last five days, when they had played two of the most exciting games in their history, one at Boston, which was won by the Reds after a hard fight, and the other played the day before our departure in Philadelphia and won by the Athletics.

We were bound for a new country, and our ambition was to defeat all comers at their own game, if possible. We had practiced cricket considerably during the Summer and were not so ignorant of the game as our friends across the pond thought us to be.

Our passage down the Delaware was a continuous ovation. While the musicians were down in the cabin enjoying a luncheon, the players secured their instruments and marched up and down the deck, led by John Clapp, who played the bass drum.

Champagne was opened for those who cared to indulge. Ezra Sutton was scored as the first sick man on the boat. He had picked out his stateroom and was occupying it when he was discovered with his head out the porthole as we passed the town of Chester, where the last of the crowd on shore could be seen.

It was the wine, and not the water, however, that laid out our smiling third baseman, who was around all right for supper that evening with a good appetite.

The tug chartered by the Orion Club, crowded with friends of Dick McBride and floating a streamer bearing the inscription in large white letters, "Farewell, Dick," and the Bruce, a tug kindly furnished by Mr. Flannagan of Philadelphia for the friends of both clubs, accompanied the steamer until after 6 o'clock, when we were on the broad ocean. The three boats came to a standstill in smooth water, and the whistles screamed in chorus a parting farewell. As the Orion tug was steaming off, Dick McBride threw a new ball among the party on deck, which they knocked overboard, so eager was everybody to get it. One of the party threw off his coat and hat, jumped into the water, got the ball and was hauled on deck at the end of a rope.

Most of Them Were Seasick

The first night out was clear and calm, with a full moon. A good night to rest was followed by a clear, bright morning, and every one was up and ready for breakfast. Only four of the players remained at the table to finish their meal, however, and for three days thereafter crackers and cheese on deck was the favorite diet for most of the party, and the baseball questions of the day were passed up.

But two men out of the whole party of ballplayers were over 30 years of age. They were Harry Wright and Dick McBride. Men were not overworked in those days, the playing of three games a week being about the average.

Dr. Pope, the Boston amateur, was induced to give an exhibition of his pitching on the boat's deck

The "First Nine" image is from a cigar label representing the England Tour. Courtesy of John Thorn.

every day. All the hard hitters, such as Jim O'Rourke, McVey, Barnes, Anson and Sutton, were apparently at his mercy. Not one of them could hit the curves of the great Dr. Pope. He would strike them out, one after the other—because they let him do so—until one day Cal McVey forgot his instructions and smashed the ball once for luck. Away it went for about 100 yards out to sea and put a stop to our fun in that line.

The doctor considered himself a great pedestrian also. He took a special delight in defeating George Wright and offered to give George one lap in eight around the boat. F.B. Wilkie, London correspondent of the Chicago Times, came to the front with a betting proposition. He said he was willing to back the doctor for any amount, and a match was arranged to take place the following morning.

Mr. Wilkie insisted on taking personal care of his man through the night. The doctor was given several hot drinks and put to bed for a sweat. Blankets were heaped upon him until he could not turn in his bunk. When morning came he could not respond to the call of time, and the referee declared all bets off, although

George Wright was conceded by all to be the great "Ped" in the party, much to the discomfiture of Dr. Pope.

Trip Took More Than 11 Days.

The second Sunday out we were informed by the captain that we might look for land during the day, so, after breakfast, the entire party got in the bow of the steamer, and with the aid of field glasses soon observed the outline of what appeared to be a black cloud rising out of the horizon. The captain assured us it was land, and in two hours more we were passing the extreme end of Cape Clear. We arrived off Queenstown at 11 o'clock, and passed a very interesting afternoon sailing along close to the Irish coast.

At about 8 o'clock of a pleasant Summer evening, on July 27th, the Ohio cast anchor in the River Mersey at Liverpool, just 11 days and four hours after we left Philadelphia.

Harry Wright had the honor of landing first on his native shore, and in his hurry to do so he had a narrow escape from an accident, for he slipped on the wet dock as he jumped off the boat.

Our party, all told, numbered about 50 strong.

As the papers took very little notice of our arrival we felt as though the trip would be a financial failure. It was very evident that the English people had no interest in our National pastime.

On July 30 we dressed for our first game. Both clubs wanted to win this game above all others. When the two nines made their appearance on the sidewalk in new uniforms, the crowds gathered round and looked us over with a great deal of curiosity, but when we arrived at Edgehill Cricket Grounds not 50 persons were present.

First Game in England

The diamond was laid out on the cricket field and the game commenced on time, with John Sensenderfer of the Athletics as umpire.

The players for the Athletics were: McBride, McMullen, Clapp, Fisler, Battin, McGeary, Murnane, Gedney, Sutton and Anson; for the Bostons, Spalding, McVey, O'Rourke, Barnes, Schafer, G.Wright, Leonard, H. Wright and Hall.

The Athletics scored eight runs in the third inning, but the Boston Reds were fighters and never gave up until the last man was out. They kept the Philadelphia boys from scoring again until the seventh inning, when they made one run, making the score 9 to 3 in favor of the Athletics.

The Boston boys pulled themselves together in the eighth inning and by some good hitting and a fumbled grounder by McGeary, managed to make six runs and tie the score. Both teams were blanked in the ninth.

In the 10th Boston scored two runs but the Athletics went to work in earnest. McMullen and Anson hit safely; McBride hit a low one to Leonard in left field, which was misjudged owing to the sun shining in his eyes. Fisler followed with a single. McGeary and Sutton hit weak ones to the pitcher, and went out. All depended on John Clapp. McGeary, who had given Boston the chance to tie the score by his error, sung out to Clapp: "Say, John, if you bring in two men I will give you a sovereign." Clapp was the right man at the right place, for many a time this player had pulled his club out of close places by his timely hitting.

Spalding was working Clapp for all he was worth, but John was a good waiter and a hard man to fool. Spalding could not give him his base on balls, for that would tie the score with a forced run, so he grooved one, trusting to his field.

Clapp caught the ball fair and sent it on a line far over the center fielder's head for an easy home run, winning the first game of this trip.

Talked About "Rounders."

After the game was over I heard a great deal of talk about rounders, the Englishmen claiming that baseball was an adaptation of their ancient game of rounders. While in some respects, baseball in its early stages accepted many of the best features of rounders, yet as a whole the American game was about as much like rounders as it was like cricket.

On the following day we played our second game on the same ground and this time Boston won by a score of 23 to 18, the Athletics scoring nine runs in the last inning.

Another small crowd was present, confirming our belief that Liverpool, Eng. was lacking in hospitality to foreigners and had little or no love for outdoor sports.

We were entertained royally by some well-known American actors during our stay in that city. J. K. Emmett was playing "Our Cousin German" at a local theatre, W.H. Rice, the famous female impersonator, was drawing the crowds at another theatre, while the most popular place of amusement in the city was Sam Hague's Minstrels, an American institution, that was then playing a yearly engagement at Liverpool.

The ball players were well acquainted with J. K. Emmett, W. H. Rice, and Sam Lucas, an American negro, one of the finest all-round minstrel performers ever seen on a stage.

Leaving Liverpool for Manchester, we had our first experience of traveling in small apartment cars, which proved very unsatisfactory to the Americans, who were forced to divide into small squads and were often forced among strangers.

Manchester Was Different.

A morning ride of 60 miles brought us to Manchester, in just short of five hours. That afternoon we played our third game of baseball before a fairly good crowd on a splendid field. The Philadelphia boys won by a score of 13 to 12. The spectators were very generous with their praise and spoke in the highest terms of our remarkable playing.

They asked all sorts of questions, and wanted to handle the balls and bats. They gave us much encouragement, and we found, after all, that Liverpool poorly represented the lovers of sport in England.

We found Manchester delightful, and left there at 9 o'clock on Saturday evening for London, 200 miles away, which we reached in the fast time of five hours.

In London we put up at the Midland Grand Hotel, just being finished at that time, where we were to remain for the next two weeks. Our stay turned out to be extremely interesting, if not profitable. The remainder of the trip is well worth another story.

—"Murnane's Baseball Stories," *Boston Globe*, February 14, 1915: 36.

Professional baseball was introduced to London on Aug. 3, 1874, by the Marylebone Cricket Club, an organization known all over the world, and especially favorably known in Philadelphia, where its team had been royally entertained on several visits to the United States.

The ball game between the Bostons and Athletics was played at Lord's Grounds before a crowd of 5000 persons, and was won by Boston, 24 to 7. Both pitchers were hit freely, the Boston men turning in 25 safe hits, George Wright, Spalding and McVey clipping off four each.

The game was played late in the afternoon, after we had defeated the Marylebone cricketers at cricket. The agreement was that the players from the States should be permitted 18 men, while the cricket club was only allowed 12 players.

This handicap was allowed the ball players, who were supposed to know little or nothing about cricket.

In the match the Englishmen scored 105 runs in their two innings, and it looked like an uphill game for the American youngsters, but their own game had taught them to play hard while there was a chance in sight.

Harry Wright and Dick McBride, who had played cricket before taking up baseball, went to the wickets first and after scoring two runs Harry Wright was bowled out, and our stock dropped considerably. Al Spalding was sent in and smashed the first ball for four, which brought a cheer from the ball players. Spalding scored 23 runs before he lost his wicket on a slow twister.

George Wright, out star, was next sent in and scored 12 runs.

The ball players were instructed to cut loose and not try to block the ball straight on to the wickets. They had scored 35 runs with three weak batsmen to come. George Hall, Harry Schafer and Thomas Beals managed to squeeze out 12 runs and we had won our first cricket match with an inning to spare, not by

Tim Murnane spent eight seasons as a baseball player, but his lasting contribution to the game was as a writer for the Boston Globe.

good form, but by using our baseball knowledge at the bat and cutting loose at the round-arm lobbing of the bowlers.

That evening we were given a fine banquet by the members of the Marylebone Cricket Club. Pres Charles Porter of the Boston club made the hit of the evening with a speech full of wit and wisdom. Mr. Porter was for years the Mayor of Quincy, Mass. and was well known to Boston insurance men. He was connected with the Boston club of the Players' League in 1890.

Met the Prince of Wales.

Our next appearance was at the Prince's ground, London, when we had the pleasure of meeting the Prince of Wales, later King Edward VII, who enjoyed a little cricket and appeared to be delighted at our ball playing, especially our fielding.

Here we had very little trouble in disposing of our opponents at cricket, as they scored only 60 runs in their two innings, while the American ball players scored no less than 110 runs in one inning, winning by an inning and 50 runs. The ball game that day was won by the Boston club by a score of 14 to 11.

We remained in London until the evening of Aug. 14 giving daily exhibitions of baseball at the Crystal Palace, Richmond and the Kensington Oval, playing cricket at the oval and at Richmond.

I have a very pleasant recollection of that visit to Richmond. There were about 1000 persons at the grounds when play started, and the number increased gradually until we started our ball game, at 4 o'clock.

Here we found several extra fine cricketers to oppose us. Our boys scored 100 runs in the first inning, and as the Richmond team showed splendid form, the game could not be finished. We were royally entertained at a banquet at the clubhouse that evening and returned to London quite late.

We had a great deal of time on our hands during our stay in foggy old London and paid a visit to the Tower of London, the House of Commons, Westminster Abbey, St. Paul's, the grounds around Buckingham Palace and Hyde Park. While strolling through this park one evening with A. C. Anson we were stopped by a military-looking man who, in a very polite manner, asked if we would not like to join the English Army. He said there was a fine chance for bright young men to make a name for themselves.

"My friend," said Anson. "I am afraid you are badly mistaken, for when we do any fighting it will be for the Stars and Stripes of the good old U.S.A."

A thousand apologies were offered and we had a half-hour's very interesting conversation with the English military man, who expressed the highest regards for the United States.

We found London a very dull, uninteresting city, but with a great love for outdoor sports, and while the Londoners were not willing to concede the fine points of baseball as compared to their game of cricket, they could easily understand that our American game was especially adapted for young men, while cricket was the game for middle-aged men.

Anson Given A Surprise.

A.C. Anson was one of those clever athletes that did well most everything he undertook in the line of sport. He was a crack shot, could box, toss quoits, play cricket, wrestle and was a fine billiard player.

Anson went into the billiard room of the Midland Grand Hotel, followed by several of the players, one evening.

Accosting the young man in charge of the room, Anson asked if he would play a game of billiards.

"I will, sir," answered the young man.

Anson won the game of 100 points, then suggested they play one more game for the drinks and cigars for the party.

"I'm agreeable, sir," was the Englishman's answer.

Anson defeated his opponent by 10 points. Then he remarked as he put up his cue, "I guess that will be enough for tonight," and, with a twinkle in his eye, was about to pass out of the room, followed by the players, when he was handed a check, calling for the amount due on account of the billiards and refreshments.

Anson took the check, looked at it and said, "Why, I beat you both games, the whole thing is on you."

Much to his surprise, the Englishman said, "Why, it is our custom to play with any gentleman who invites us. I was simply accommodating you, sir."

Anson saw the point as well as the pronounced smiles on the faces of his comrades.

He paid the check and insisted that another game be played. The ball players felt that something was coming off and returned to their seats in the billiard room.

The game was about half over when a tray of empty glasses was placed on a stand about three yards from the head of the billiard table. Anson maneuvered until he got his cue ball in range with the glasses. Then, hitting the ball well underneath, he executed a jump shot and sent the ivory ball spinning among the glassware.

With a look of surprise on his face he apologized to the man in charge.

Anson paid his bill and it was taken for granted that the breaking of the glassware was purely accidental.

The best part of a bright new sovereign was left to pay for the lesson in English etiquette.

London to Sheffield.

We left London for Sheffield on Aug 14 by a special train, in which there was a pullman sleeping car. This through the kindness of George Pullman, who was in London at the time introducing his sleeping cars. He was very well acquainted with several of our ball players and seemed delighted to have us as his guests to Sheffield.

We arrived at 4:30 in the morning, and put up at the Imperial and Black Swan Hotel on Snig Hill. I noticed that most of the people walking in the middle of the street, and that nearly all of the men wore aprons. Women in the streets with babies in their arms was very common. I visited the famous race track where the great Sheffield handicap has taken place annually for nearly 100 years. The cinder path was the most perfect thing of the kind that I have ever seen, and the interest in sprint running was fully as great as is shown during a post season baseball series in this country.

Our party was taken through the famous cutlery works in Sheffield and our reception from first to last in this English city was very cordial. In the two ball games played there, Boston won the first by a core of 19 to 8, and the second game by a score of 18 to 17.

We defeated the Sheffield club at cricket, by a score of 130 to 88, the Americans having one inning to spare.

In commenting on the game the next day the Sheffield Daily Telegraph said: "It was generally anticipated before the arrival of the Americans in England that their bowling would be underhand and easily playable, but better bowling has not often been witnesses at Bramall Lane."

In this match, Harry Wright and George Wright did the bowling.

By a special request of the Duke of Devonshire the party paid a visit to Chatsworth House, about 12 miles from Sheffield. One pleasant Sunday morning the large party started out in wagonettes. When about half the distance had been covered it commenced to rain very hard and we pulled up at an inn, where the inner man was refreshed. We started once more with the rain still falling, and it came down in torrents before we finally reached the massive gates at the entrance to the Duke's grand domain.

There were no celebrities at home, but the players were escorted from cellar to roof of the house and through the wonderful garden. The ride back to town was a delightful one, passing over the hills and down through the valley. It was by all odds the most delightful country that I have ever gone through, even to this date.

Beat Englishmen at Cricket.

From Sheffield, we went to Manchester, where we played one game of ball, the Athletics winning by a score of 7 to 2, and where we beat the Manchester Cricket Club by a score of 221 to 95 in a full game.

In commenting on the work of the Americans at cricket a Manchester paper said the next morning: "The extraordinary ability of the American ball players has been sufficiently acknowledged, but we are not satisfied with their form in cricket. What is technically called slugging is their one notion of what batting should be. Almost without exception the men hit out heavily at every ball, whether it to be straight or crooked, pitched well or badly. By this process a small average of runs is generally secured, and sometimes a really good ball which would have troubled a scientific batter like Grace is knocked clean out of the grounds.

"The fielding, as one might have expected, was wonderfully close and good, and with the advantage of 18 men on the field it was a matter of the greatest difficulty to get the ball through the Americans. The really important stand was that made by Watson, who batted in masterly style for his score of 25 and was then caught out from a grand hit. His out would, with ordinary English fielding, have been a piece of hard luck. To the Americans it was merely a matter of course. The Yankees are perfect marvels at fielding. Kittens are dull and apathetic by comparison."

The catch made off Mr. Watson that was called hard luck for the batter was on a long high drive to deep centerfield that I timed and, judging the ball perfectly, turned around just in time to make the catch. It was a tremendous drive. Observing that the man was a free hit, I played a very deep field. Another play in that game I shall never forget. It was made by John Kent, the Harvard first baseman, who accompanied the Boston team and played their first base during the trip.

Mr. Kent was a very tall athlete with a long reach, and while playing cricket that same day he made a one-hand catch from a cricket bat that not only surprised the natives, but forced the ball players to acknowledge that it was one of the finest pieces of fielding that ever came under their observation.

For years Mr. Kent has been the principal of the high school at Concord, N.H., will no doubt smile when he reads this brief notice of a one-handed stab of a cricket ball in Manchester, Eng., 40 years ago.

We left Manchester at 10 o'clock one Saturday morning, Aug 22, for Ireland, by way of Holyhead crossing the channel by boat. We arrived in Dublin at 10 o'clock Sunday evening.

I think Ireland will be a lovely place to rest up until I start my next story from the little old green isle.

—"Murnane's Baseball Stories," *Boston Globe*, February 21, 1915: 47.

We paused in our narrative last week at the point where our party landed in Ireland.

We put up at the Shelborn Hotel, and found Dublin a most interesting city, very much up to date. We made good use of the four days spent in the Irish metropolis by visiting many places of historical interest, including Dublin Castle and Trinity College. Mr. James Lawrence, a Dublin sportsman, anxious that the American athletes should have an opportunity to demonstrate their game, guaranteed the two teams a certain sum for the two days' sport. The games were played at the Irish Champion Athletic Grounds, the cricket game first, and winding up the afternoon with a game of baseball. The attendance was fairly good, and the spectators very generous with their applause.

While walking to the grounds on the first day we noticed the people standing along the sidewalks, the men holding their hats in their hands. Blasts from a bugle told us that's something unusual was coming, so we lined up on the side of the street to enjoy a one-man parade. It was the Lord Lieutenant of Ireland, in all his glory, escorted by out-riders in advance, and in the rear, enough for a county fair horse show. The big chief smiled and tipped his headgear to the Americans and we returned the salute. His Lordship was at the ball grounds when we arrived, taking a little cricket practice, and later he seemed to enjoy our games of baseball. Duke of Abercon, Knight of the Garter, was the gentleman's title.

Two Days in Ireland.

In the first inning of the cricket game, the Americans scored 71 runs to the Irishmen's 47, and Boston won the ball game by a score of 12 to 7. The second day the Americans scored 94 runs to the home players 32, giving the ball players the victory with 86 runs to spare, making it a clean slate of victories in our cricket games on the trip.

In the last game of ball the Philadelphia players hit like fiends and won out by a score of 15 to 4.

A.C. Anson won the prize, with the highest score for the day at cricket.

We found the boys and men bubbling over with witty sayings. In offering thanks for some little favor I heard a youngster remark, "May you never die until a dead horse kicks you."

Early one morning we left Dublin by rail for Cork, passing through the town of Templemore. I left the train and pulled down a branch of ivy from an old stone wall and brought it back to America, to give to a very old man whom I had often heard mention the name of his native town of Templemore.

The thanks I received was worth the trouble, for with tears in his honest eyes the old man pressed the ivy to his lips and said, "God bless you, my boy."

We spent one night in Cork and enjoyed the ride to Queenstown immensely. We spent several hours at Queenstown, a beautiful city, and there on the wharf we made a great hit with the old women who were selling blackthorn sticks. The players purchased freely of sticks and laces, and just as the small boat was pushed out from the dock all the sticks that had not been purchased were thrown on the boat deck with a chorus of "Good luck to you fine American gentlemen" from the old women.

Seven Weeks On Trip.

As we sailed down the beautiful Queenstown Bay to big ship pulling her anchor in the Atlantic Ocean, I know one heart that throbbed at the thought of his parents taking the same trip in '48. This time crossing the big pond in 10 weeks in a packet ship which landed at Castle Garden, New York. It was a delightful change from a slow sailing ship to a fine American built steamship that landed us at Philadelphia, Sept. 9. We had been away seven weeks.

The trip back was smooth enough with the exception of one day, when there was a fearful storm and for a time it looked to be all off for the wandering ball tossers.

We passed within a mile of an iceberg one afternoon that we were told was five times as large as the boat.

We had funeral services at sea one evening, as the sun was dropping down below the western horizon.

To sum up the trip abroad, the clubs lost money, besides the salary of the players, but much of the deficit was made up by drawing extra large crowds on the home grounds before our departure, as well as after our return, and the promoters of the trip had accomplished something in the way of introducing the game in England.

Records on the Tour.

The following is a record of the Boston and Athletics clubs in their contests of baseball and cricket on English soil, July 30 to Aug 25, 1874:

BASEBALL

	Boston	Athletics
Liverpool	11	14
Liverpool	23	18
Manchester	12	13
Lord's Ground, London	24	7
Prince's Ground	14	11
Richmond	3	11
Crystal Palace, London	17	8
Crystal Palace, London	8	19
Kennington Oval, London	16	6

CRICKET

Aug 3 and 4, Lord's Cricket Ground, London—Eighteen of America 107; Marylebone twelve, 105; won in first inning.

Aug 6 and 7, Prince's Ground, London—Eighteen of America, first inning, 110; Prince's club, first inning, 21, second inning 39, won in one inning by 50 runs.

Aug 8, at Richmond—American twenty-one, 45 with six wickets down, Richmond thirteen, 108, drawn game.

Aug 13 & 14, Kennington Oval, London—American eighteen, first inning, 100, second inning, 111; Surrey Club, first inning, 27, second inning 2, with four wickets down, won in first inning by 73 runs.

Aug 15 & 15, Bramall Lane, Sheffield—American eighteen, first inning. 130; Sheffield club, first inning, 43, second inning 45, won in one inning by 42 runs.

Aug 20 & 21, Old Trafford Grounds, Manchester. American eighteen, first inning 121, second inning 100; Manchester club, first inning, 42, second inning 53. Won by 126 runs.

Aug 24 & 25—Irish Champion Athletic Club Ground, Dublin—American eighteen, first inning 71, second inning 94; All Ireland eleven, first inning 47, second inning 32. Won by 86 runs.

THE INDIVIDUAL SCORES AT CRICKET

	Games	Not Out	Runs	Largest inn'g	Largest score	Avg per inning
G. Wright	7	0	129	50	61	14.33
Leonard	7	0	106	28	31	11.53
H. Wright	7	0	75	28	24	8.33
Barnes	7	1	81	24	30	8.10
Sheffield			19	8		
Sheffield			18	17		
Manchester			2	7		
Dublin			12	7		
Dublin			4	15		
Totals			183	161		
Spalding	7	0	74	23	24	7.50
O'Rourke	7	0	59	18	13	5.90
McGeary	6	0	51	16	18	5.66
Anson	7	1	48	27	17	4.80
S. Wright	7	0	43	9	11	4.77
McVey	7	0	41	11	11	4.53
Fisler	4	0	22	6	12	4.40
Beals	6	1	34	8	12	4.25
McBride	6	0	30	9	11	3.75
Sutton	7	1	33	18	13	3.66
Schafer	6	0	28	12	13	3.50
Hall	7	1	26	12	12	2.88
Murnane	6	2	23	9	9	2.87
McMullin	5	1	17	5	10	2.88
Kent	3	2	12	4	4	2.40
Clapp	1	0	1	1	1	1.00
Battin	5	0	4	4	4	0.57
Sensenderfer	2	0	0	0	0	0.00

Seven Have Passed On.

Of the 22 players who took an active part in the games in England and Ireland in 1874 only seven have passed away to more glorious fields, viz, Harry Wright, Andrew Leonard, Ross Barnes, Ezra Sutton, John Clapp and John Sensenderfer, four Philadelphia and three Boston players.

At the time of our trip to England baseball was really in its infancy, even the American daily papers allowed but little space to the game.

The New York morning papers, especially, practically ignored the National game and it was on Philadelphia and Boston in the East and Chicago and Cincinnati, in the West, that the promoters of the sport were forced to depend upon for what little advertising the game received at that time. In fact New York was the last city in the country to appreciate professional baseball, although the game was invented by a New Yorker and played for the first time on a lot in New York where the Murray Hill Hotel now stands.

Owing to this lack of recognition by the daily papers of this country it was no wonder that the two American teams were very poorly received as they went through England and Ireland. A trip of the same magnitude at the present time would receive ten times the attention by the press and public than was given in 1874.

—"Murnane's Baseball Stories," *Boston Globe*, February 28, 1915: 39.

"AND GOD BLESS US EVERY ONE!"
Baseball on Christmas Day, 1873

BY BOB LEMOINE

"THE DAY, THOUGH RATHER cloudy, was not chilly, and not stormy, and thus there was no reasonable cause for failure to make the most of the religious and social privileges provided as part of the day's enjoyment," wrote the *Boston Globe*. "In nearly all the churches, elaborate preparations were made and appropriate services held—all being largely attended."

Some 500 Bostonians, however, went to see a baseball game at the South End Grounds on Christmas Day, December 25, 1873. Harry Wright and Al Spalding chose two teams of 10 players and played a 10-inning game. "All players wishing to take part are requested to be on hand in good season," prompted the *Boston Post*. The game began at 10:30 A.M. and was over in time for a hearty Christmas dinner. The admission was free and the *Globe* promised that "an interesting game is sure to occur."

Spalding took the mound and had Dave Birdsall at catcher and Fred Cone at first. It also appears that a young Arthur Soden, future baseball executive and owner of the Boston Beaneaters, was patrolling center field. He would also travel with the team on their voyage to England in 1874. Harry Wright was the opposing pitcher, and he had his brother George at shortstop, Jack Manning at first, Charlie Sweasy at second and Bob Addy at third. There was also an S. Wright Jr. catching, who was probably the Wrights' younger brother Sam.

The Harry Wright side won 18-16, the *New York Clipper* commenting, "The closeness of the contest may be judged from the fact that the game was a tie at the close of the third, eighth, and ninth innings, Wright's side obtaining the winning run in the tenth."

Other teams had already experimented with the 10-10 structure. Henry Chadwick was convinced the idea was good for baseball and presented his opinions at the March 1874 baseball winter meetings. The motion was defeated by the delegates.

While it would be unheard of to see major-league ballplayers today play a game "just for fun" (and with free admission), it was common in that day. "The boys were amateurs at heart," wrote Harold Kaese.

SOURCES

"A Ten Innings Game," *New York Clipper*, January 3, 1874: 315.

Boston Post, December 25, 1873.

Kaese, Harold. *The Boston Braves: 1871-1953*. (Boston: Northeastern University Press, 2004), 13.

"Merry Christmas. Its Celebration in Boston and Vicinity," *Boston Globe*, December 27, 1873: 1.

Morris, Peter. *Game of Inches: The Story Behind the Innovations That Shaped Baseball*. (Chicago: Ivan R. Dee Publishers, 2010), 502-503.

"The City. Notes of the Day About Town," *Boston Globe*, December 25, 1873: 8.

Box score from the New York Clipper

OFF THE BEATEN PATH: VARIOUS RED STOCKING EXHIBITION TRAVELS, 1871-1875

BY BOB LEMOINE

"The Boston nine are just scooping things their own way, and as a consequence are tiptilting their athletic nasals to the surrounding ether."
— *Daily Inter Ocean* (Chicago), June 7, 1874

IN ADDITION TO REGULAR-season games (called "championship" games at the time), the Boston Red Stockings played well over 100 exhibition games between 1871 and 1875, which included tours to Canada and England. But they also traveled around New England and beyond, often drawing large crowds who would never see the baseball champions otherwise. While the author is not attempting a comprehensive list, below are several exhibition games of note the Red Stockings played "away," and while they didn't count in the standings, they were often significant in the places they stopped. Some, however, probably wished a "mercy rule" had been in effect.

Providence, Rhode Island, June 23, 1871.
Boston 24, Brown University 3

"The Brown boys play in the field was for the most part good," wrote the *Providence Evening Press*, "but in batting they were far inferior to their strong opponents." A crowd of 2,500 came and watched the spectacle, no doubt rooting hard for the underdogs. The Boston victory did not dampen the spirits of Brown, as "they seemed to be well satisfied with even so severe a defeat against so strong a nine as the Bostons."[1]

Hamilton, Ohio, June 30, 1871

Boston 27, Hamilton Resolutes 0

The Boston victory at Hamilton, "that sanguinary village" in the words of the *Cincinnati Daily Gazette*, featured excellent Boston fielding, some "heavy batting" by Cal McVey, and a double play started by Harry Wright that was called "a nice piece of workmanship."[2]

Worcester, Massachusetts, August 2, 1871
Boston 35, Worcester Mazeppas 3

A crowd of 300 saw the Red Stockings breeze by the Worcester team at the Agricultural Park. "The playing was not very brilliant," noted the *National Aegis*, while the *Springfield Republican* commented that the "Worcester people think the game was rather uninteresting."[3]

RED STOCKINGS.	O.	R.	MAZEPPA.	O.	R.
G Wright, s s,	2	4	Foley, l f,	4	0
Barnes, 2 b,	4	5	O McCann, s s,	3	1
Birdsall, r f,	5	3	Coulter, c,	3	0
McVey, c,	1	5	Conlon, 2 b,	2	0
H Wright, c f,	3	3	Moore, c f,	3	0
Gould, 1 b,	3	3	Cronan, 3 b,	4	0
Schafer, 3 b,	2	5	Finnera, 1 b,	3	0
Cone, l f,	3	4	Tower, p,	3	1
Spaulding, p,	4	3	A. McCann, r f,	2	1
Total,	27	35	Total,	27	3

INNINGS.

	1	2	3	4	5	6	7	8	9	
Red Stockings,	5	3	1	13	4	0	1	1	0	—35
Mazeppa,	0	0	2	0	0	1	0	0	0	— 3

A Trip "Downeast," September 18-22, 1871

The Red Stockings "went on an invitation tour 'down east,' we would call it," remarked the *New York Clipper*, "but the Reds call it a northern tour." Neither description was fitting for the first stop, Athol, Massachusetts, located in Worcester County, west of Boston. The Red Stockings did go "downeast," however, in the old New England phraseology, with stops in Maine that included Portland, Lewiston, and Brunswick. "Everywhere they were most cordially received," wrote the *Clipper*, "as the most gentlemanly exponents of professional ball playing the opposing clubs had ever met with, and the fine exhibition of the beauties of the game made by the Reds on their tour, has done much to advance the game in popularity in all the cities and towns they have visited."[4]

Athol, Massachusetts, September 18, 1871
Boston 50, Summit 1

"The Summits of Athol were whipped," remarked the *Springfield Republican* on the 50-1 loss to the Red Stockings; and "that in a dead ball game," the *Clipper* commented. However, "the game was witnessed by an immense crowd."[5]

BOSTON.	A.B.	R.	1B.	P.O.	A.	SUMMIT.	A.B.	R.	1B.	P.O.	A.
G. Wright, s s.	10	5	6	3	3	Allen, s s.	4	0	0	1	5
Barnes, 2d b.	9	5	6	3	3	R. Merrill, c f.	4	0	0	0	0
Birdsall, c.	11	3	4	5	2	Garfield, r f.	4	0	2	2	0
McVey, r f.	10	8	4	1	0	H. Merrill, 1st b	4	0	2	8	0
Spalding, p.	10	6	3	2	3	Goodrich, l f.	3	0	0	0	0
Gould, 1st b.	9	6	5	9	0	L. Merrill, 2d b.	4	0	0	6	5
Schafer, 3d b.	9	5	5	2	2	Snow, 3d b.	3	1	2	6	3
Cone, l f.	11	5	4	2	1	F. Merrill, p.	3	0	0	0	3
H. Wright, c f.	10	7	5	1	1	D. Merrill, c.	4	0	0	4	2
Totals.	89	50	44	27	12	Totals.	33	1	6	27	19

INNINGS. 1st 2d 3d 4th 5th 6th 7th 8th 9th
Boston .... 8 7 5 1 6 16 1 4 2—50
Summit .... 0 0 0 0 1 0 0 0 0— 1

Umpire—S. W. Sawyer, Gardner Club. Time of game—1 hour and 55 minutes.

Portland, Maine, September 19, 1871.
Boston 27, Portland Resolutes 2

Just the announcement that the Red Stockings were coming to town, reported the *Portland Daily Press*, "was sufficient to draw a large number of spectators to Forest City Park." Mainers were able to see firsthand "the famous brothers, George and Harry Wright, the former being universally recognized as the champion base ball player of America." Not much was expected of their opponent, the "junior" Portland Resolutes, who would not "be able to contend with their distinguished rivals." Yet, a "gallant fight" was put forward by the Resolutes, who exceeded expectations.[6]

The game began at about 3:00 P.M. and the Resolutes held Boston scoreless for two innings of the game, or "they choked the 'Reds' twice, amid the tumultuous applause of the spectators." When the Resolutes scored their first run of the game, in the sixth inning "the entire concourse of spectators broke forth into the wildest demonstrations of joy, hats were thrown up and there seemed to be no limit to the pleasure of the moment." But while Portland "played an excellent field game," their batting was noted as being far inferior to Boston's, which "displayed that remarkable skill and ability which has gained for them so many victories over the famous clubs of the country, and has made their name a household word in all points of the United States." The Resolutes proved no match, as it "was evident that the superior strength, skill and practice of the Red Stockings was too much for their younger and more inexperienced opponents."[7]

The *Portland Advertiser* had fun describing the play of Boston's Sam Jackson: "Jackson, a jolly fat boy to appearance, but the flesh which so lavishly clothed his skeleton, was all muscle, and it appeared that he was wanted to run for two or three men who were lame. His short fat calves flew from base to base so rapidly that, like old Fezziwig in the *Christmas Carol*, he appeared to wink with his legs."[8]

Spalding pitched a "straight, swift ball, at which the Portland boys struck after it had passed them, until they got used to it," wrote the *Advertiser*. Then, to totally confuse the batters, Harry Wright came in to pitch, throwing "slow twisters, deceitful and desperately wicked." Boston catcher Cal McVey was called "the coolest fish that ever picked a ball from the end of a bat, his eyes on every part of the field at once, his whole attention nevertheless fixed on the flying pigskin." It was McVey who started a quadruple play to end the game, when the batter struck out and McVey "stopped it with his open palm, giving the striker his run and forcing men from all the bases, and then stepped instantly to the home base, and passing the ball to third, second and first, ending the game by a *coup de main*.[9] (Often in exhibition games, the Red Stockings would give amateur teams four or five outs per inning, although the accounts do not mention this here.) The *Advertiser* estimated that the Boston players averaged between 160 and 180 pounds, and 21 to 25 years of age, "models of manly symmetry, and—it is fair to add—of gentlemanly bearing."[10]

September 21, 1871, Lewiston, Maine
Boston 41, Androscoggins 7

This game in Lewiston drew a large crowd at the Androscoggin Driving Park, which saw the Red Stockings "bat gently" at first, but eventually "they gave very hard raps. Their playing is very fine in all respects," wrote the *Lewiston Evening Journal*. The Androscoggin team, according to the *Journal*, "played well considering that they are out of practice."[11]

September 22, 1871, Bowdoin College, Brunswick Maine
Boston 24, Bowdoin College 1

"The Boston Red Stockings paid us a visit," wrote the Bowdoin College newspaper *The Orient*. The game was played at the Sagadohoc Fairgrounds (later known as the Topsham Fairgrounds) at 10 A.M.[12] "This was the best contested game played by the Bostons during their Eastern tour," *The Orient* claimed.[13]

Belfast, Maine, August 6, 1872.
Boston 35, Belfast Pastimes 1

The reader may be surprised to learn that this romp over the local team has lasting influence on baseball history, yet "it was the lore, not the score, that lives on to this day," wrote Walter Griffin of the *Bangor*

Daily News.[14] In Belfast, Robert Patterson Chase was the home-team official scorer who introduced the Belfast players to the crowd as they came up to the plate, while a Boston scorer did the same on the other side. Chase, with the flair of the local coastal town in him, announced the players this way: "Moody at bat, Boardman *on deck*, Dinsmore *in the hold*." These nautical terms (the "hold" was the area of the ship below the main deck) appealed to the Boston scorer, who brought them with him back to Boston, where they became part of the regular jargon of baseball. This story was largely forgotten to history until Jay Davis, the editor of the *Waldo Independent* newspaper in Belfast, was on vacation in Houston, Texas, and encountered the story on a scorecard at the Astrodome in the 1980s. Davis discovered a 1937 article about Chase in the *Republican Journal* in Belfast, a story which also ran in *The Sporting News* in 1938. Chase himself thought the terms were long since forgotten until hearing a World Series radio announcer using them. Chase wrote to George Wright, then the last surviving member of the Red Stockings, who recalled the 1872 game and the amusement the Boston players received at Chase's descriptions.

The 35-1 loss to the Red Stockings meant "all the Maine town got out of that contest was the distinction of being a contributor to the lexicon of the game."[15]

August 16, 1872, Oil City, Pennsylvania
Boston 9, Oil City Senecas 3

The 9-3 Boston victory was cut short after six innings due to rain. "The Oil City Boys have demonstrated that they can play a rattling game of baseball," wrote the *Cleveland Plain Dealer*. "We hope they will come this way again and can promise them a good audience if the rain does not interfere."[16]

August 21, 1872, Detroit, Michigan
Boston 35, Detroit Empires 2

On their last stop before entering Canada, the Red Stockings visited Detroit and beat the Empires 35-2, in a game the *Detroit Free Press* expounded upon in a lengthy front-page recap. "There was considerable curiosity to see this club," the *Free Press* wrote, "as the Red Stockings, whether of Cincinnati or of Boston, had never been in Detroit." The physical strength of the Boston players impressed those fans of the amateur Empires. "They are an exceedingly fine-looking and athletic body of men," the *Free Press* account said. "The contrast between the Bostons and the Empires, in point of size and weight, was particularly striking, the latter appearing mere boys by the size of the former, while the Bostons looked physically like giants in comparison." Boston turned a triple play when the Empires anticipated George Wright dropping a pop fly (one of his tricks until the infield fly rule was created) amid shouts of "drop it, drop it!" with the bases loaded in order to double up the runners. Instead, Wright caught it, and two runners who were too far off their bases were doubled up.[17]

```
                          SCORE.
      BOSTONS.                      EMPIRES.
                   O. R.                         O. R.
G. Wright, s. s....... 2  5 | Spence, 3 b.......... 5  0
Barnes, 2 b........... 2  5 | Smith, c. f.......... 3  0
Leonard, l. f......... 2  5 | O'Leary, c........... 4  0
McVey, c.............. 4  2 | Hull, 1 b............ 3  0
Spalding, p........... 4  3 | Sheeran, s. s........ 3  0
Gould, 1 b............ 3  4 | Kinney, p............ 2  1
Schafer, 3 b.......... 3  4 | Sprague, r. f........ 1  1
Rogers, r. f.......... 4  2 | Campbell, l. f....... 3  0
H. Wright, c. f....... 3  4 | Collins, 2 b......... 3  0

Total................27 35 | Total................27  2
            RUNS MADE EACH INNING.
Bostons..............2  2  8  5  0  5  8  0  5—35
Empires..............0  0  1  0  0  1  0  0  0— 2
```

A return match in Detroit on August 21, 1873, proved little had changed, as Boston won that contest 37-4.[18]

New Haven, Connecticut, May 7, 1873
Boston 23, Yale 0

The game at Hamilton Park saw the Yale nine suffer a "humiliating defeat," but "they consoled themselves with the reflection that they are not the first club the Bostons have used so badly," wrote the *Hartford Courant*.[19]

St. Louis, Missouri, August 13, 1873
Boston 37, Turners 3

"The event of the season," in the words of the *St. Louis Times*, took place at the ballpark on Grand Avenue in St. Louis, and a great amount of local interest was expressed at the arrival of the Red Stockings, "these most formidable knights of the 'bat and ball.'" Seven of those "formidable knights," however, arrived at the ballpark a mere two hours before game time, having been delayed in Columbus, Ohio. Both teams also wore nearly identical uniforms, except St. Louis "wore white hats instead of caps," and "the Bostons are, to a man, a hardy, athletic looking set."[20] Boston scored 15 runs in the ninth inning.

Despite the lopsided score, it was apparent that Boston showed little enthusiasm in the game, wrote the *Times*. Weather and travel were certainly factors. The 400 fans found it "almost impossible to find a shady spot, as the sun shone directly into the faces of the spectators, the seats being arranged so as to face west. An improvement might be made in this respect by placing the seats on the westside of the grounds."[21]

BOSTONS.	R.	O.	TURNERS.	R.	O.
Wright, s. s.	3	5	Graser, p.	1	3
Barnes, 2d b.	4	4	White, 3d b.	0	3
Spaulding, p.	5	3	John, s. s.	0	4
Leonard, l. f.	5	3	Joseph, 1st b.	0	4
White, c.	3	4	Keller, c. f.	0	3
O'Rourke, 1st b.	4	2	McMahon, 2d b.	1	2
Addy, r. f.	3	3	Schrader, c. f.	1	1
Schafer, 3d b.	6	0	Bradey, c.	0	3
H. Wright, c. f.	4	3	Miller, r. f.	0	4

INNINGS.

	1	2	3	4	5	6	7	8	9	
Bostons	3	2	3	3	1	6	2	2	15	—37.
Turners	0	2	1	0	0	0	0	0	0	—3.

Rockford, Illinois, August 18, 1873
Boston 22, Philadelphia White Stockings 2

There was much anticipation for this game as "three of the Boston club are old Rockford boys (Al Spalding, Ross Barnes, Bob Addy) whose reputation as gentlemen and base ballists has suffered no decrease since they left the Forest City," wrote the *Rockford Daily Register*.[22] The game was also a crucial contest as Boston was in third place behind front-running Baltimore and the second-place White Stockings. (Although Baltimore had more wins than Philadelphia, the White Stockings had a better winning percentage.) Both teams had split their previous six games. However, Philadelphia's Levi Meyerle was away for a death in the family, and Denny Mack suffered a freak injury.

Staying at the Holland House, Mack decided to go for a ride with George Wilson, clerk at the hotel. The horses were brought from the livery stable and both Mack and Wilson got into the carriage. Before the reins were secured, one of the horses sprang forward. Wilson reached out to grab the horse by the head, but a kick sent him to the ground. The horses became frightened and "started up Wyman Street at a furious rate dashing over stone heaps and boxes in a manner that threatened at every moment to demolish the buggy and throw out the remaining occupant." The carriage crashed upon making a sharp turn, with Mack thrown to the ground. "The violence of the shock had rendered him almost insensible," and he was helped back to his hotel room. Mack suffered a bruised left leg and hip.[23]

With being shorthanded, Johnny Ryan, "considerably out of practice," played third base and Boston had to lend the opposition catcher Dave Birdsall, a move that now made this game an exhibition. While the 800 spectators were naturally disappointed, "the unfortunate combination of circumstances which attended the Philadelphias may form some excuse," wrote the *Daily Register*.[24]

Ludlow, Kentucky, June 1, 1875
Boston 17, Ludlow 5

Around 3 o'clock in the afternoon, the Red Stockings arrived on a four-horse omnibus, ferried over the Ohio River. The sun was "boiling down"[25] in the words of the *Cincinnati Commercial Tribune*, while the *Cincinnati Daily Gazette* commented on the inadequate grounds in Ludlow. "A high hill on its southern aspect is supposed to be the favorite place from which to view a game, being shaded by umbrageous elms," the *Tribune* wrote, "but the visitor is much disappointed on taking his seat to find that he cannot get a view of but a small portion of the grounds, and is obliged, after all, to go out into the glaring sun and stand up."[26] Harry Wright, perhaps feeling nostalgic for his days in Cincinnati just over the river, wore a "C" on his uniform. The game was never in doubt for Boston, but as the 1,200 spectators were leaving, "a violent rain-storm came, catching the whole crowd in its fury, and thoroughly quenching all the enthusiasts engendered by the festive field support."[27]

THE SCORE:

RED STOCKINGS.	Total.	LUDLOWS.	Total.
G. Wright, s. s.	3	Dillon, c.	1
Beals, c.	1	Baker, 3 b.	2
O'Rourke, r. f.	0	E. Walker, r. f.	1
Leonard, l. f.	1	Burke, s. s.	0
McVey, 1 b.	0	Stiles, c. f.	0
Spalding, 3 b.	3	Williams, p.	0
White, 2 b.	4	Cullom, 2 b.	0
H. Wright, c. f.	3	Drain, 1 b.	0
Franklin, p.	2	Wm. Walker, l. f.	1
Total	17	Total	5

	1.	2.	3.	4.	5.	6.	7.	8.	9.	Total.
Bostons	0	6	3	0	2	1	2	0	3	17
Ludlows	0	0	0	2	1	0	1	0	1	5

A much closer contest was played on August 13 when the Red Stockings rested Al Spalding and Andy Leonard while also playing regulars in different positions. When the score was 7-7 after seven innings, changes were made and the Red Stockings escaped with a 9-7 win.[28]

Manchester, New Hampshire, July 29, 1875
Boston 22, Manchester Atlantics 5

A "big time" was anticipated, and posters were distributed around Manchester, reported the *Mirror and Farmer*, as the Red Stockings were coming to town to play against the amateur Manchester Atlantics.[29] The Red Stockings were on their way to Canada to play the Guelph Maple Leafs, and a stop in Manchester was on the itinerary. "Everybody who knows anything of ball will want to see the 'Reds,'" the *Mirror and Farmer* wrote. Although the game would not be of high interest like a championship game, "it will be a good deal to see Spalding pitch and Wright play short-stop."[30]

The *Mirror and Farmer* wrote that the game "was a disappointment to anyone who expected to see the 'Reds' play sharp," and "from their play here, no correct idea could be formed of their power and skill when working against a professional club." The score was 22-5, Boston, yet the Red Stockings "could easily have whitewashed their opponents and run up their own score to a surprising number." The reporter believed the Red Stockings were muffing plays on purpose and would only "trot along around the bases," becoming easy outs. George Wright was seen "several times throwing to first base without care," and the team as a whole was "evidently not caring to make much exertion." Even when they attempted brilliant plays in the field, it was "merely to amuse the lookers-on," which numbered around 600.[31]

INNINGS.	1	2	3	4	5	6	7	8	9	Total
Bostons	2	3	4	5	0	4	1	2	1	22
Atlantics	0	2	0	0	0	1	0	1	1	5

Umpire—Mr. Chandler of Boston.
Time of game—3 hours.

BOSTONS.

	R.	1 B.	P. O.	O.
Wright, s. s.	3	4	1	2
Barnes, 2d b.	3	2	3	3
O'Rourke, c. f.	2	3	1	2
Leonard, 3d b.	1	1	2	5
McVey, 1st b.	3	4	7	2
Spaulding, p.	2	1	1	4
White, c.	4	3	8	2
Manning, r. f.	2	3	0	4
Beals, l. f.	4	2	4	3
Total	22	23	27	27

ATLANTICS.

	R.	1 B.	P. O.	O.
Burke, p.	0	0	1	4
Logan, l. f.	1	1	2	2
Foley, 2d b.	0	1	4	3
Mahoney, r. f.	1	0	2	3
Hennessey, c.	0	1	7	4
Shehan, 1st b.	2	0	6	3
Ryan, s. s.	1	0	0	3
Whalen, 3d b.	1	0	4	2
Gillis, c. f.	0	0	1	3
Total	5	3	27	27

Ludlow, Kentucky, August 16, 1875

Boston Red Stockings 14, Cincinnati Reds 5

> **BASE BALL.**
> **THE REDS IN THE FIELD!**
> **LUDLOW GROUNDS.**
> 4 P. M. TO-DAY.
> **BOSTON CHAMPIONS**
> vs.
> **REORGANIZED CINCINNATIS.**
> Avoid the Rush at the Gate.
> Secure tickets at John Davis', Hawley's, John Donovan's, Ludlow Ferry, or on board: Nick Longworth, foot of Walnut street.

The advertisement for the game with the newly reorganized Cincinnati club.
(Cincinnati Daily Gazette, August 16, 1875)

Very few exhibition games could match the intensity of this contest as "the spirit of '69 blazed up brightly in the hearts of Cincinnatians yesterday, and caused a general pilgrimage to Ludlow," wrote the *Cincinnati Daily Gazette*. They were flocking to see their newly rebuilt Cincinnati Reds, and the "cars on the Third and Fourth street line were crowded to overflowing with sweltering humanity, every individual apparently impressed with the idea that his future happiness depended upon his getting to the base ball field as soon as possible."[32] The game seemed to be more symbolic than anything for the fans of Cincinnati to show the rest of the baseball world they still were a baseball city. An estimated crowd of 5,000 to 8,000 crammed into every square inch. The new Cincinnati team got its old Red Stockings name back in 1876, moved into a new ballpark, and joined the new National League.

Boston led 6-1 in the fifth inning when a fight broke out in the stands. Jim Garman, the deputy marshal of Ludlow, was trying to enforce order but instead wound up getting into a fistfight with "a Covington rough." The marshal grabbed a bat and was going to hit the man with "a blow which might have proved fatal," when a Cincinnati policeman named Mr. Mitchell grabbed his wrist and prevented the blow. Garman and his assistants grabbed Mitchell and led him out of the park.

With Boston leading 14-5 in the eighth inning, "the crowd had become unmanageable and very disorderly, encroaching on the play-ground of the catcher and right field so as to leave the players in their positions insufficient room to play," wrote the *Gazette*. In remembering the Cincinnati Red Stocking glory years of 1869-1870 "there was no scene so humiliating as this," the *Gazette* lamented. The paper blamed the scene on the small park, lack of Ludlow police, and the fact that the "noisy, fighting crowd of Kentuckians learned long since that Cincinnati officers are destitute of all color of authority on the sacred soil where the bloodless and friendly contests are waged."[33]

The game actually ended on a close play at first base in the eighth inning, which led to fans crowding around the players in anticipation of an argument with the umpire, Ham Avery. Seeing the chaos and the impossibility of continuing, Avery called the game.

THE SCORE.

BOSTON REDS.	T.	1B.	TB.	R.	O.	PO.	A.	E.
G. Wright, s. s.	5	1	1	2	3	1	2	1
Barnes, 2d b.	5	2	2	2	2	5	1	1
Leonard, l. f.	5	1	1	1	4	2	0	3
O'Rourke, c. f.	5	4	7	3	1	2	1	1
McVey, 1st b.	5	2	6	1	4	7	0	1
Spalding, p.	5	0	0	0	4	0	2	0
White, c.	4	3	5	2	2	5	3	2
Schaefer, 3d b.	4	1	1	2	2	0	3	3
Beals, r. f.	4	1	3	1	2	2	0	1
Totals	42	15	26	15	24	24	12	13
CINCINNATI REDS.	T.	1B.	TB.	R.	O.	PO.	A.	E.
Gould, 1st b.	5	2	2	1	4	6	0	2
Snyder, r. f.	4	1	1	0	3	3	0	2
Radcliffe, s. s.	4	1	1	0	3	1	1	1
Fisher, p.	4	1	1	1	2	2	3	1
Clack, c. f.	4	1	1	1	3	4	1	1
Field, 2d b.	4	2	4	1	2	1	2	0
Wardell, l. f.	4	0	0	0	2	0	0	0
Pierson, c.	4	1	1	0	3	5	2	1
Nichols, 3d b.	4	1	3	1	2	2	0	2
Totals	37	10	14	5	24	24	9	10

RUNS SCORED.

Innings	1	2	3	4	5	6	7	8
Boston Reds	2	1	0	3	0	4	1	3—14
Cincinnati Reds	0	0	1	0	1	0	3	0—5

RUNS EARNED.

Innings	1	2	3	4	5	6	7	8
Boston Reds	1	0	0	2	0	0	1	2—6
Cincinnati Reds	0	0	0	0	0	0	0	1—1

First base on errors—Boston, 5; Cincinnati, 5.
Fly balls caught—Boston, 9; Cincinnati, 11.
Fly balls missed—Boston, 1; Cincinnati, 1.
First base on called balls—Boston, 1; Cincinnati, 0.
Left on bases—Boston, 3; Cincinnati, 5.
Passed balls—White, 2; Pierson, 2.
Struck out—Boston, 2; Cincinnati, 2.
Strikes called—Boston, 31; Cincinnati, 33.
Balls called—Boston, 15; Cincinnati, 6.
Home runs—Boston, 2, McVey and O'Rourke.
Run out—Boston, 0; Cincinnati, 1.
Umpire—Mr. Ham. Avery.
Time of game—2:21.

NOTES

1. "The Great Ball Game. Brown University vs. Boston Red Stockings," *Providence Evening Press*, June 23, 1871: 3.

2. "Base Ball. Bostons Defeat Resolutes of Hamilton, Ohio—Score, 27 to 0," *Cincinnati Daily Gazette*, July 1, 1871: 4.

3. "Base Ball—Boston Nine vs. Mazeppas," *National Aegis* (Worcester, Massachusetts), August 5, 1871: 4; "New England News Items," *Springfield* (Massachusetts) *Republican*, August 5, 1871: 8.

4. "The Red Stocking Tour North," *New York Clipper*, September 30, 1871: 205.

5. Ibid; "New England News Items," *Springfield Republican*, September 20, 1871: 8.

6. "Base Ball. The Red Stockings of Boston and the Resolutes of Portland," *Portland Daily Press*, September 21, 1871: 3.

7. Ibid.

8. The *Portland Advertiser* article, "The Red Stockings in Portland," appeared in the Lewiston (Maine) *Evening Journal*, September 21, 1871, page 3.

9. A *coup de main* is a sudden attack, according to Merriam-Webster.

10. "The Red Stockings in Portland."

11. "City and County," *Lewiston Evening Journal*, September 22, 1871: 3.

12. "Base Ball," *Portland Daily Press*, September 23, 1871: 3.

13. "Bowdoin's Baseball History," *The Orient*, March 11, 1872: 250.

14. Walter Griffin, "Belfast Museum Gussying It Up for Big Season," *Bangor* (Maine) *Daily News*, June 16, 2007: C2.

15. Edgar G. Brands, "Between Innings," *The Sporting News*, March 24, 1938: 4; Paul Dickson, "at bat, on deck, in the hold." *Dickson Baseball Dictionary* 3rd ed. (New York: W.W. Norton & Co., 2011), 31-32; see also Belfast Historical Society & Museum belfastmuseum.org/museum_exhibits.html.

16. "Sporting News. Base Ball," *Cleveland Plain Dealer*, August 17, 1872: 3.

17. "Base Ball. The Bostons Defeat the Empires By a Score of 35 to 2," *Detroit Free Press*, August 22, 1872: 1.

18. "Base Ball. The Boston Red Stockings Against the Empires, of Detroit," *Detroit Free Press*, August 22, 1873: 1.

19. "News of the State," *Hartford Courant*, May 9, 1873: 2.

20. "Base Ball at St. Louis," *St. Louis Times*, August 14, 1873, printed in the *Cincinnati Daily Gazette*, August 15, 1873: 10.

21. Ibid.

22. "Base Ball," *Daily Register* (Rockford, Illinois), August 18, 1873: 4.

23. "Disastrous Runaway," *Daily Register*, August 18, 1873: 4.

24. "Base Ball," *Daily Register*, August 19, 1873: 2.

25. "The Ludlows and Boston Red Stockings," *Cincinnati Commercial Tribune*, June 2, 1875: 8.

26. "Base Ball. Match Game Between the Red Stockings, of Boston, and the Ludlows, of Ludlow," *Cincinnati Daily Gazette*, June 2, 1875: 3.

27. "The Ludlows and Boston Red Stockings."

28. "Base Ball. Bostons vs. Ludlows—Close and Exciting Game—Ludlows Defeated by a Score of 9-7," *Cincinnati Daily Times*, August 14, 1875: 4.

29. "A Big Time," *Mirror and Farmer* (Manchester, New Hampshire), July 17, 1885: 8.

30. Ibid.

31. "Base Ball. 'Bostons' and 'Atlantics'—22 to 5," *Mirror and Farmer*, July 31, 1875: 2.

32. "Base Ball. The Battle of the Red Stockings," *Cincinnati Daily Gazette*, August 17, 1875: 8.

33. Ibid.

EXHIBITION GAMES PLAYED BY THE BOSTON RED STOCKINGS, 1871-75

This spreadsheet presents a list of in-season exhibition games of the Red Stockings from 1871-1875. It is adapted from a much larger chart of all in-season exhibition games from 1871-1920, compiled and arranged by Walter LeConte and others, and is available on the Retrosheet website: http://www.retrosheet.org/Research/LeConteW/InSeasonExhibitionGames1871-1920.htm

While the chart possibly contains errors here and there and is by no means considered complete, this chart is the best source available for documented exhibition games the Red Stockings played. The chart proved valuable in our own research for this book.

Date		Runs	Opponent	RA	Place
May 8, 1871	Red Stockings	25	Atlantics (of Brooklyn, NY)	0	Brooklyn
May 13, 1871	Red Stockings	30	Picked 9	13	Boston
June 9, 1871	Red Stockings	29	Clippers (of Lowell, MA)	3	Boston
June 10, 1871	Red Stockings	15	Brown	5	Boston
June 30, 1871	Red Stockings	27	Resolutes (of Hamilton, OH)	0	Hamilton, Ohio
July 8, 1871	Red Stockings	13	Picked 9	3	Chicago
July 11, 1871	Red Stockings	10	Aetnas (of Chicago, IL)	4	Chicago
July 15, 1871	Red Stockings	10	Troy Haymakers NA	16	Boston
August 4, 1871	Red Stockings	4	Eckfords (of Brooklyn, NY)	6	Brooklyn
August 5, 1871	Red Stockings	11	Eckfords (of Brooklyn, NY)	1	Brooklyn
August 12, 1871	Red Stockings	13	Eckfords (of Brooklyn, NY)	8	Boston
Auust 17, 1871	Red Stockings	11	Rockford Forest Citys NA	7	Boston
September 11, 1871	Red Stockings	35	King Phillips (of East Abington, MA)	0	South Weymouth, Massachusetts
September 18, 1871	Red Stockings	50	Athol Summits (of Athol, PA)	1	Athol, Massachusetts
September 19, 1871	Red Stockings	27	Resolutes (of Portland, ME)	2	Portland, Maine
September 20, 1871	Red Stockings	27	Resolutes (of Portland, ME)	2	Portland, Maine
September 21, 1871	Red Stockings	41	Androscoggins (of Lewiston, ME)	7	Lewiston, Maine
September 22, 1871	Red Stockings	24	Bowdoin College	1	Brunswick, Maine

THE 1871-75 BOSTON RED STOCKINGS

October 10, 1871	Red Stockings	8	Eckfords (of Brooklyn, NY)	6	Brooklyn
October 14, 1871	Red Stockings	16	Harvard	8	Boston
April 20, 1872	Red Stockings	7	Harvard	1	Boston
April 24, 1872	Red Stockings	43	Tufts College	5	Boston
April 27, 1872	Red Stockings	26	Harvard	2	Boston
April 29, 1872	Red Stockings	15	Olympics (of Philadelphia, PA)	8	Philadelphia
June 1, 1872	Red Stockings	31	King Phillips (of East Abington, MA)	0	Boston
June 27, 1872	Red Stockings	25	George M. Roths (of Philadelphia, PA)	0	Boston
July 26, 1872	Red Stockings	9	Resolutes (of Elizabeth, NJ)	1	Waverly, New Jersey
August 16, 1872	Red Stockings	9	Senecas (of Oil City PA)	3	Oil City, Pennsylvania
August 20, 1872	Red Stockings	40	Ypsilanti	3	Ypsilanti, Michigan
August 21, 1872	Red Stockings	35	Empires (of Detroit, MI)	2	Detroit
August 22, 1872	Red Stockings	52	Athletics (of London, ON)	3	London, Ontario
August 23, 1872	Red Stockings	29	Maple Leafs	7	Guelph, Ontario
August 24, 1872	Red Stockings	68	Dauntless (of Toronto, ON)	0	Toronto
August 26, 1872	Red Stockings	52	Dauntless (of Toronto, ON)	4	Toronto
August 27, 1872	Red Stockings	64	Ottawa	0	Ottawa
August 28, 1872	Red Stockings	66	Pastimes (of Ogdensburg, NY)	1	Ogdensburg, New York
August 29, 1872	Red Stockings	63	Montreal	3	Quebec, Quebec
September 28, 1872	Red Stockings	9	Boston Juniors (Spalding was pitcher)	8	Boston
September 30, 1872	Red Stockings	16	Boston Juniors (Spalding was pitcher)	3	Boston
October 8, 1872	Red Stockings	7	New York Mutuals NA	7	Brooklyn
October 10, 1872	Red Stockings	3	Philadelphia Athletics NA	11	Brooklyn
October 11, 1872	Red Stockings	8	New York Mutuals NA	6	Brooklyn
October 14, 1872	Red Stockings	10	Philadelphia Athletics NA	10	Brooklyn
October 15, 1872	Red Stockings	5	New York Mutuals NA	7	Brooklyn
October 17, 1872	Red Stockings	7	New York Mutuals NA	3	Brooklyn
October 19, 1872	Red Stockings	5	Philadelphia Athletics NA	9	Philadelphia
October 21, 1872	Red Stockings	19	New York Mutuals NA	7	Philadelphia
April 15, 1873	Red Stockings	32	Excelsiors	0	Boston
April 16, 1873	Red Stockings	31	Atlantics	7	Boston
April 19, 1873	Red Stockings	22	Harvard	0	Boston

April 21, 1873	Red Stockings	22	Excelsiors	1	Boston
April 22, 1873	Red Stockings	21	Excelsiors	1	Boston
April 25, 1873	Red Stockings	42	Atlantics	6	Boston
April 26, 1873	Red Stockings	12	Harvard	4	Boston
April 29, 1873	Red Stockings	32	Williams College	2	Boston
May 1, 1873	Red Stockings	17	Boston Juniors	5	Boston
May 5, 1873	Red Stockings	20	Chelseas (of Brooklyn, NY)	2	Boston
May 7, 1873	Red Stockings	23	Yale	0	New Haven, Connecticut
May 10, 1873	Red Stockings	17	Harvard	6	Boston
May 14, 1873	Red Stockings	34	Tufts College	3	Boston
May 19, 1873	Red Stockings	29	Atlantics	2	Boston
May 20, 1873	Red Stockings	32	Clippers	8	Webster, Massachusetts
May 21, 1873	Red Stockings	14	Harvard	7	Boston
May 22, 1873	Red Stockings	13	Beacons	5	Boston
May 28, 1873	Red Stockings	14	Harvard	2	Cambridge, Massachusetts
June 13, 1873	Red Stockings	17	Lowell (of 1868)	3	Boston
June 20, 1873	Red Stockings	64	Lowell	6	Lowell, Massachusetts
June 23, 1873	Red Stockings	36	Chelseas (of Brooklyn, NY)	5	Boston
June 25, 1873	Red Stockings	39	Olympics (Champions of Rhode Island, Providence)	6	Boston
June 26, 1873	Red Stockings	27	Harvard Freshmen	6	Boston
June 28, 1873	Red Stockings	5	New York Mutuals NA (teams swapped pitchers & catchers)	3	Boston
July 1, 1873	Red Stockings	20	Resolutes (of Portland, ME)	4	Boston
August 1, 1873	Red Stockings	33	Lynn Live Oaks	3	Lynn, Massachusetts
August 3, 1873	Red Stockings	27	Chelseas (of Brooklyn, NY)	5	Boston
August 5, 1873	Red Stockings	21	Chelseas (of Brooklyn, NY)	5	Boston
August 6, 1873	Red Stockings	40	Clippers	13	Worcester, Massachusetts
August 7, 1873	Red Stockings	27	Fitchburg	17	Fitchburg, Massachusetts
August 8, 1873	Red Stockings	35	Modocs (Josh Hart's Theatre Comique Company)	17	Boston
August 11, 1873	Red Stockings	35	Enterprise (of Alleghany, PA)	5	Pittsburgh
August 13, 1873	Red Stockings	37	Turners (of Saint Louis, MO)	5	Saint Louis

August 14, 1873	Red Stockings	22	Enterprise (of Saint Louis, MO)	4	Saint Louis
August 18, 1873	Red Stockings	22	Philadelphia White Stockings NA	2	Rockford, Illinois
August 20, 1873	Red Stockings	43	Mutuals (of Jackson, MI)	7	Jackson, Michigan
August 21, 1873	Red Stockings	35	Empires (of Detroit, MI)	4	Detroit
August 22, 1873	Red Stockings	27	Maple Leafs	8	Guelph, Ontario
August 23, 1873	Red Stockings	48	Dauntless (of Toronto, ON)	10	Toronto
August 25, 1873	Red Stockings	55	Saint Lawrence	10	Saint Lawrence, Ontario
August 26, 1873	Red Stockings	44	Ottawa	4	Ottawa, Ontario
August 28, 1873	Red Stockings	37	Pastime	6	Ogdensburg, New York
September 24, 1873	Red Stockings	22	Chelseas (of Brooklyn, NY)	2	Boston
September 30, 1873	Red Stockings	12	New York Mutuals NA	5	Brooklyn
October 18, 1873	Red Stockings	10	New York Mutuals NA	3	Brooklyn
November 1, 1873	Red Stockings	18	Harvard	21	Boston
April 16, 1874	Red Stockings	34	Picked 9	9	Boston
April 18, 1874	Red Stockings	18	Scrub 9 (listed in narrative)	7	Boston
April 22, 1874	Red Stockings	24	Harvard	10	Boston
June 6, 1874	Red Stockings	18	Empires (of Saint Louis, MO)	1	Saint Louis
June 13, 1874	Red Stockings	17	Picked 9 (given 5 outs per inning!)	3	Worcester, Massachusetts
June 15, 1874	Red Stockings	24	Middletown Mansfields	3	Boston
June 18, 1874	Red Stockings	19	Harvard	7	Cambridge, Massachusetts
June 22, 1874	Red Stockings	24	Rollstones (of Fitchburg, MA)	10	Fitchburg, Massachusetts
June 30, 1874	Red Stockings	26	Maple Leafs	6	Brantford, Ontario
July 1, 1874	Red Stockings	20	Maple Leafs	4	Guelph, Ontario
July 2, 1874	Red Stockings	5	Middletown Mansfields	10	New Haven, Connecticut
July 30, 1874	Red Stockings	11	Philadelphia Athletics NA	14	Liverpool, UK
July 31, 1874	Red Stockings	23	Philadelphia Athletics NA	18	Liverpool, UK
August 1, 1874	Red Stockings	12	Philadelphia Athletics NA	13	Manchester, UK
August 3, 1874	Red Stockings	24	Philadelphia Athletics NA	7	London
August 5, 1874	Red Stockings	14	Philadelphia Athletics NA	11	London
August 7, 1874	Red Stockings	8	Philadelphia Athletics NA	15	London
August 8, 1874	Red Stockings	3	Philadelphia Athletics NA	11	Richmond, UK
August 10, 1874	Red Stockings	17	Philadelphia Athletics NA	8	London

August 11, 1874	Red Stockings	8	Philadelphia Athletics NA	19	London
August 13, 1874	Red Stockings	16	Philadelphia Athletics NA	6	London
August 14, 1874	Red Stockings	14	Philadelphia Athletics NA	11	London
August 15, 1874	Red Stockings	19	Philadelphia Athletics NA	8	London
August 17, 1874	Red Stockings	18	Philadelphia Athletics NA	17	London
August 24, 1874	Red Stockings	12	Philadelphia Athletics NA (members of the Dublin Cricket Club)	7	Dublin
August 25, 1874	Red Stockings	4	Philadelphia Athletics NA	15	Dublin
September 24, 1874	Red Stockings	16	Middletown Mansfields	1	New Haven, Connecticut
October 28, 1874	Red Stockings	10	Middletown Mansfields	7	New Haven, Connecticut
October 29, 1874	Red Stockings	3	Philadelphia Athletics NA	2	Worcester, Massachusetts
October 30, 1874	Red Stockings	11	Hartford Dark Blues NA	17	Worcester, Massachusetts
October 31, 1874	Red Stockings	13	Hartford Dark Blues NA	5	Boston
April 30, 1875	Red Stockings	46	Old Dominion	3	Petersburg, Virginia
May 6, 1875	Red Stockings	12	Lynn Live Oaks	0	Lynn, Massachusetts
May 7, 1875	Red Stockings	17	Harvard	8	Boston
May 21, 1875	Red Stockings	27	Actives (of Reading, PA)	11	Reading, Pennsylvania
June 1, 1875	Red Stockings	17	Ludlows (of Kentucky)	5	Ludlow, Kentucky
June 25, 1875	Red Stockings	20	Trenton	5	Trenton, New Jersey
July 1, 1875	Red Stockings	17	T. B. F. U. S. (of Bridgeport, CT)	4	Bridgeport, Connecticut
July 15, 1875	Red Stockings	24	Lowell	3	Boston
July 16, 1875	Red Stockings	20	Lowell	7	Lowell, Massachusetts
July 20, 1875	Red Stockings	30	Taunton	4	Taunton, Massachusetts
July 28, 1875	Red Stockings	6	Lynn Live Oaks	2	Lynn, Massachusetts
July 29, 1875	Red Stockings	7	Beacons	5	Boston
August 5, 1875	Red Stockings	4	Rhode Island	0	Providence
August 6, 1875	Red Stockings	23	Blue Stockings (of Cincinnati, OH)	4	Concord, New Hampshire
August 7, 1875	Red Stockings	5	Howard Juniors	0	Brockton, Massachusetts

THE 1871-75 BOSTON RED STOCKINGS

August 9, 1875	Red Stockings	17	Syracuse Stars	1	Syracuse, New York
August 11, 1875	Red Stockings	8	Keystone	2	Erie, Pennsylvania
August 13, 1875	Red Stockings	9	Ludlows (of Kentucky)	7	Ludlow, Kentucky
August 14, 1875	Red Stockings	8	Covington Stars (of Kentucky)	1	Cincinnati
August 16, 1875	Red Stockings	14	Cincinnati Reds	5	Cincinnati
August 18, 1875	Red Stockings	17	Louisville Eagles	1	Louisville
September 16, 1875	Red Stockings	19	Stars (of New London, CT)	1	New London, Connecticut
September 17, 1875	Red Stockings	15	Lynn Live Oaks	7	Lynn, Massachusetts
September 23, 1875	Red Stockings	12	T. B. F. U. S. (of Bridgeport, CT)	0	Bridgeport, Connecticut
September 30, 1875	Red Stockings	9	Dexter Juniors (of Providence, RI)	2	Providence
October 4, 1875	Red Stockings	4	New York Mutuals NA	6	Troy, New York
October 5, 1875	Red Stockings	9	New York Mutuals NA	10	Troy, New York
October 12, 1875	Red Stockings	14	Lynn Live Oaks	12	Lynn, Massachusetts
October 20, 1875	Red Stockings	20	Picked 10	3	Boston
October 23, 1875	Red Stockings	0	Chicago White Stockings NA (Players from 1875 & 1876 clubs)	14	Boston
October 27, 1875	Red Stockings	15	Harvard	6	Boston
	Totals	3384		878	

1871 -- 18-2
1872 -- 22-3-2
1873 -- 45-1
1874 -- 23-8   excluding the 9-6 European trip, their record was 14-2
1875 -- 28-3

Totals…136-17-2

BOSTON'S "HOME GAMES" PLAYED IN OTHER CITIES

BY BILL NOWLIN

THE HOME GROUNDS FOR THE Boston Red Stockings were the South End Grounds.[1]

But there were five other venues where they played "home" games as well. Here is the list of such games:

1871

May 27—Washington Olympics 6, Boston Red Stockings 5, at **Union Grounds**, Brooklyn, New York. Despite the new 50-cent admission charge, about 2,000 people turned out for the game, which the *New York Herald* proclaimed "one of the most brilliant contests of the season."[2] Boston's George Wright was unable to play due to lameness, but the Washingtons (also known as the Blue Stockings or Olympics) were even more battered by injury. The *Brooklyn Daily Eagle* rained down superlatives, with a subhead calling it "the most brilliant contest on record."[3] It was 5-1 in Boston's favor after three innings, and the score remained such after seven. The Olympics rallied with three in the eighth and two more in the ninth, to win the game.

The *New York Tribune* concurred, perhaps with a bit of hyperbole in calling the game "the finest exhibition of ball playing ever witnessed in this vicinity" but added that some of the luster was taken away by "[Andy] Leonard's unfair and illegal act in preventing Spaulding *(sic)* from catching a ball in the last inning."[4] Though there was no suggestion of anything nefarious regarding umpire Mills (of the New York Mutuals team), the *Daily Eagle* criticized Leonard for "willful obstruction," citing the rule book, and declaring his action "as plain a violation of the rules as it was unfair play, unworthy an honorable ball-player."[5]

1873

July 16—Boston Red Stockings 21, Athletics (Philadelphia) 13, at **Hampden Park Race Track**, Springfield, Massachusetts. The 2:00 P.M. game was linked to another draw, and seen as "an auxiliary to the regatta sports" that had brought in crews from Harvard, Yale, Cornell, Columbia, Brown, and other colleges.[6] The *Springfield Republican* grumbled that the ballplayers showed up late, the designated umpire never did, and that despite a crowd of about 2,500—featuring many collegians—there was "poor playing on both sides." In the third inning, the paper reported, "the only entertaining feature was a strong foul by Barnes that sent the ball flying into the river."[7]

August 16—Boston Red Stockings 11, Athletics (Philadelphia) 8, at **23rd Street Park**, Chicago. The Philadelphias were also known as the White Stockings. As the *Chicago Times* observed, the "club is apparalled *(sic)* in a very tasty uniform. The pantaloons are of a drab color, hanging loosely downward to the knee, where they are fastened into the white-stocking which have given the club their well-known name."[8] Some 6,000 turned out for the contest, despite neither team coming from Chicago. Philadelphia won the coin toss and elected to bat last; the Athletics scored five runs in the bottom of the first. The lead changed hands, and in the ninth, Boston added four runs to take an 11-5 lead, holding on as Philadelphia scored three times in the bottom of the ninth, but fell short.

Note: the same two teams faced off at the same park three days later, this time the Athletics deemed the home team. Perhaps due to home-team advantage, the Philadelphia team prevailed, beating Boston 9-4.

1874

October 30—Hartford Dark Blues 17, Boston Red Stockings 11, at **Worcester Driving Park Grounds**,

— 368 —

Worcester, Massachusetts. Hartford had held a 9-2 lead after the first three innings, and they continued to press their advantage. Al Spalding was hammered for 17 runs, but the playing surface was a rough one, and only one of the runs was earned: Boston committed 18 errors and Hartford 14. Some 500 attended the game, the last official game of the 1874 season. The *Boston Daily Advertiser* noted that the Bostons were the "only club which completed all its series, having played in all seventy championship games."9

There had been an exhibition game on the 29th, Boston 3, Athletics 2. Then the game against Hartford on the 30th. Boston played Harford again the very next day, the 31st, winning 13-5. Locally, there seemed more attention in Worcester accorded the Grafton/Live Oak game, also at the Driving Park on the 31st.

1875

May 14—Boston Red Stockings 13, Washington Nationals 1, at **Hampden Park Race Track**, Springfield, Massachusetts. Somewhere between 1,500 and 2,000 people watched the game; the Holyoke, Massachusetts, band furnished music before and throughout. It was a one-sided contest with Boston taking an early lead, and the lone Washington run coming in the sixth.

June 22—Boston Red Stockings 11, Brooklyn Atlantics 0, at **Adelaide Avenue Grounds**, Providence, Rhode Island. The two teams played a game in Boston on June 21, Spalding beating Brooklyn's John P. Cassidy, 8-7. Then, the next morning's *Daily Advertiser* advised readers, "Today the Bostons and Atlantics go together to Providence, where they play a game on the new grounds in that city. They play here again tomorrow."10 An estimated 1,400 people, "including many ladies," saw Boston score two in the third, one in the fourth, five in the seventh, and three in the ninth.11 Brooklyn committed 10 errors, Boston only three. Though the box score does not reflect it, the special dispatch to the *Globe* says, "O'Rourke caught to Manning's pitching the last innings." That would be Jack Manning (16-2 on the season) pitching to center fielder Jim O'Rourke, who is indeed listed by Retrosheet as catching in one game in 1875. After the "whitewash" (the *Boston Traveler* used the phrase, too) on June 22, the two teams squared off again in Boston, with Spalding pitching against Cassidy for the third consecutive day, and winning for the third time, 15-1. Cassidy finished the season with a record of 1-21, despite a 3.03 ERA.

The Red Stockings' record as the home team in out-of-town ballparks was 4-2.

What were these ballparks?

Both the Brooklyn Eckfords (1871 and 1872) and the New York Mutuals (1871-75) used the Williamsburg section **Union Base Ball and Cricket Grounds** as their ballpark.12 It is noted as the "first enclosed ball field to charge admission."13 The park hosted what is considered the "first major-league postseason championship game," on October 30, 1871.14 During the winters it was an ice skating rink for the Union Skating Club.

The **Hampden Park Race Track** hosted a game in 1873 and another in 1875. It had also served as the home park to the National Association's Middletown Mansfields on July 23, 1872. The teams that played baseball there played on the "south end of mile-long oval bicycle race track, running along NW-SE axis."15

Chicago's **23rd Street Park** was, perhaps unsurprisingly, at 23rd Street, at the corner of State. About 6,000 people turned out for the Boston/Philadelphia game.

The venue in Worcester drew 500 fans, "many of them sitting in trees or on fences." The facility was more formally known as the **Agricultural County Fair Grounds Race Track (I)**, host to an annual fair each September. During the Civil War, it had served as a "training and recruiting camp for Union soldiers."16 Baseball had to contend with a somewhat beat-up playing surface, and even a tree growing in left field.17 From 1880 through 1882, it was the home park of the National League's Worcester Brown Stockings. After the team drew only 18 fans to its September 29, 1882, game, there has been no more major-league baseball played in Worcester, though in 1902 and 1910, Boston's American League team played preseason exhibition games there. They played in-season exhibition games at Worcester in 1908, 1910, 1927, and 1929. The Red Sox played exhibition games against Holy Cross at Worcester in 1934, 1936, 1937, 1938, 1939, 1941, 1942, and 1947.18

Little can be found in the standard ballpark reference books about Providence's **Adelaide Avenue Grounds**. Michael Gershman's *Diamonds* has nothing. Philip Lowry's book informs us that the park was located on Adelaide Avenue (little surprise there), and also bounded by Broad Street, Hamilton Street, Sackett Street, and Elmwood Avenue. It was used as a neutral site by the Hartford Dark Blues (home team) and the New Haven Elm Citys on June 12, 1875, and by the Boston Red Stockings (home team) and Brooklyn Atlantics 10 days later, on June 22, 1875.

NOTES

1 The Red Stockings' principal home park is often rendered in books on ballparks as South End Grounds (I), to distinguish it from South End Grounds (II) and South End Grounds (III)—also known as Walpole Street Grounds (I), which of course differed from Walpole Street Grounds (II). All of those parks were on the same location, and just to complicate matters a little, the "II" park was also known as the Grand Pavilion, the Union Baseball Grounds, and the Boston Baseball Grounds. The "III" Park was sometimes called the South Side Grounds. See Philip J. Lowry's SABR book *Green Cathedrals* (New York: Walker & Company, 2006).
2 "The National Game," *New York Herald*, May 28, 1871: 6.
3 "Sports and Pastimes—Base Ball," *Brooklyn Daily Eagle*, May 29, 1871: 9.
4 "Out-door Sports: Base-Ball," *New York Tribune*, May 29, 1871: 2.
5 *Brooklyn Daily Eagle*.
6 *Lowell Daily Citizen and News*, July 17, 1873: 2.
7 "The Boston-Athletic Match," *Springfield Republican*, July 17, 1873: 5.
8 "The Boston and Philadelphia Baseball Clubs Play in Chicago," *Chicago Times*, August 17, 1873: 4.
9 "The Fall Sports—End of the Base Ball Season," *Boston Daily Advertiser*, November 2, 1874: 1.
10 "Summer Pastimes—The Base Ball Field—Another Boston Victory," *Boston Daily Advertiser*, June 22, 1875: 1.
11 "Base Ball—The Bostons Whitewash the Atlantics," *Boston Globe*, June 23, 1875: 1.
12 The opening of the grounds is detailed in the *Brooklyn Eagle* of May 16, 1862.
13 Michael Gershman, *Diamonds* (Boston and New York: Houghton Mifflin, 1993), 2.
14 Ibid., 12
15 Lowry, 221.
16 Alan E. Foulds, *Boston's Ballparks & Arenas* (Boston: Northeastern University Press, 2005), 146.
17 Ibid.
18 Bill Nowlin database of Red Sox exhibition games.

MCBRIDE & ZETTLEIN – THORNS IN RED STOCKINGS' SIDE

BY RICHARD "DIXIE" TOURANGEAU

LITTLE BOBBY MATHEWS (ALL OF 5-feet-5½ inches) twirled a gem of a ballgame to initiate play of the National Association of Professional Base Ball Players. But the Fort Wayne Kekiongas' fantastic 2-0 victory over Cleveland on May 4, 1871, was not a harbinger of scores to come as it was soon proved to be a fascinating anomaly. Though nine Association teams battled through another 126 games that inaugural season, no contest came close to that low a run total.

That was especially true in games played by the Boston Red Stockings, whose bats were lethal to opposing pitchers. The average score of a second-place Red Stockings game was 13-10, and that did not decrease much over the next four NA championship campaigns, despite better pitching and all-around play. Completely shutting down the Bostons was thought impossible; even allowing them just a single run was extremely rare, even in theory. About a dozen opposing hurlers had their isolated moments of such glory during the Association's five years, but two stood out with several grand feats against the original Big Red Run Machine. Philadelphia's manager-pitcher John Dickson McBride and Brooklyn native George Zettlein (who hurled for four teams of that era, mostly Chicago) were the sharpest thorns in Boston's side.

Civil War Union Navy veteran Zettlein had history with some Boston players, since four of them played for the famous Cincinnati Red Stockings of 1869-70. At Brooklyn's Capitoline Grounds on June 14, 1870, it was George "The Charmer" who snapped the iconic Porkopolis boys' string of 71 wins, proving Cincy's squad was slightly mortal by edging them, 8-7 in 11 innings.

McBride was no surprise newcomer to the Red Stockings, either. He was a fixture in Philadelphia base ball since the early 1860s as an infielder and crack pitcher. There were five workhorse hurlers in the Association during its stint from 1871-75. Boston's Albert Spalding (2,346⅔ innings), Bobby Mathews who hurled for three clubs (2,221⅔), McBride of the Athletics (2,049), Zettlein of Troy, Brooklyn, Chicago, and Philadelphia (1,942⅔) and Candy Cummings of four teams (1,778 frames in four seasons).

Boston's Stockings were held to four runs or fewer 44 times in five years (15 percent of their 292 games). Fifteen of those games belonged to McBride (9) and Zettlein (6). What was most telling of the twosome was that each of the seven games in which Boston made only one run (four times) or no runs (chicagoed in three) were pitched by George or Dick. Statistically the records of both tossers versus only the Bostons were poor, McBride 13-24-3 and Zettlein 10-22, but in comparison to all others who tried, they looked very good. Boston won 79 percent of its games thanks to the better fielding and hitting they put forth on the diamond. Though Spalding benefited greatly because of this talent, he was a stellar pitcher in his own right. It was a depressing combination to oppose year after year. Against McBride and Zettlein, Boston won 66 percent of its games. When the "thorns" faced each other, just about the same amount of excitement was generated as when they played Boston. Zettlein had the upper hand, winning 13 of 22 games with one tie. His winning record was due mostly to 1873, when he defeated McBride seven straight times, two games by one run, one in 13 innings, and another by two tallies. All these games were in McBride's Philly ballpark. As the Association was ending in 1875, the fading star duo matched up only once, October 4, with McBride winning 19-10. In their 23 career matchups, the run totals were 189-182 in Zett's favor. Strangely symmetrical, there were only three games in which both sides scored the normal 10 or more runs, their first match in 1871, the last in 1875, and a game in June 1873 that was played in rain, sawdust piles and the dark, according to the *New York Clipper*. Zett won, 27-17. As for the other NA "horses," Mathews was 8-30 versus Boston while Candy posted a 7-19 mark.

During the first three NA seasons, both McBride and Zettlein fought the Reds to a near-standoff, as McBride was 10-10-1 and Zett, 7-9. In the following two years Harry Wright's Stockings got better despite efforts by a few clubs to sign better players to curb the Reds' domination. In 1874-75 McBride was just 3-14-2 and George was humbled at 3-13, his wins being two shutouts and a 17-16, 10-inning victory versus Harry Wright, not Spalding. The average score in 40 McBride-Reds matches was 9-6, while for Zettlein it was 10-7. It must be remembered that in August 1874 McBride pitched many more exhibition games versus the Reds during the famous barnstorming trip to England, so Boston was even more familiar with his style of pitching.

It was true that constantly losing the close games caused both hurlers much consternation. Each lost four one-run games to Boston, and McBride a two-run game and two by three-run margins. Zettlein bowed twice by two runs and thrice by three. They would have needed to win three-quarters of those games to emerge with a 35-34 combined record against the mighty Reds.

On the opposite end of the pitching spectrum was poor William Eckloff "Bill" Stearns of Washington. He hurled 700 innings for the various Washington entrants and the Hartford Dark Blues (1874). His tenacity and dedication to the game is unquestionable, but his pitching prowess was always very suspect, and having no offense behind him solidified the results. No one in the NA pitched more against Boston and came up winless than Stearns, 0-18.

As a teenager in June 1871 Stearns subbed for Olympics starter Asa Brainard twice and won both games quite easily, 16-3 and 13-8, but such success was not to come in the future as Bill ended his career at 13-64. He allowed the Reds 20-plus runs six times, including the opening game of 1872 (26-3). Half of his Red Stocking decisions were decently close, the

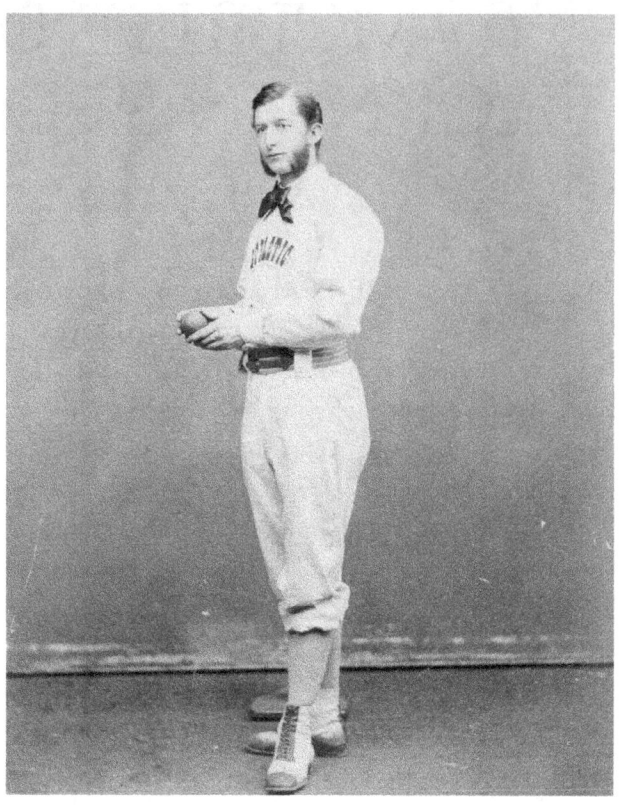

Dick McBride (Spalding Collection)

other half were plain routs. The average score was 15-5, but he did lose twice by one run, 9-8 in 1873 and 7-6 in 1874 (at Hartford). In both, his club had a good chance to beat the Reds but failed. In consecutive games on October 5 and 6, 1874, Stearns lost 7-4 and 7-6. William "Cherokee" Fisher was the regular starter for Hartford in 1874, but by August third baseman Bill Boyd was injured and Fisher often played third, Stearns getting more starts. Fisher was the sixth NA pitcher to notch 1,000 innings (1,087⅔) but was 1-9 against Boston. In the 7-6 loss on October 6, infielder Fisher was 0-for-5 and made five errors. In the last of the ninth, Hartford rallied for two runs but Spalding closed them and Stearns down. Days later Stearns took another Boston defeat at the South End Grounds, 11-8.

It is sad that he couldn't have come up with a single win against the repeating champions because Bill Stearns, a government clerk, was a double war hero. Born in 1853 and not yet even a teenager, he served in the Civil War in several capacities and later volunteered for service in Puerto Rico in the Spanish-American War. Various stomach illnesses he suffered there and while returning home by ship caused his death on

December 30, 1898.[1] He and his son (William E. Jr., died 1933) are buried in Arlington National Cemetery.

SOURCES

Pitching record methodology: The author followed the Red Stockings game-by-game via the Retrosheet Game Log dates and, by consulting daily newspapers throughout, developed a running account of the Reds versus various pitchers whom they faced most often. This was also done for the 23 matchups between John McBride and George Zettlein over their five NA years.

Boston newspaper (*Herald, Globe, Post,* and *Daily Advertiser*) game accounts, *Hartford Courant, Washington Post,* and *Philadelphia Inquirer.*

New York Clipper, selected game texts.

Retrosheet.org for box scores and team game logs.

NOTES

[1] baseballsgreatestsacrifice.com/biographies/stearns_bill.html.

FOLLOWING THE BOSTON RED STOCKINGS IN THE EARLY 1870S

BY DONNA L. HALPER

BEING A MEMBER OF RED SOX nation in our modern era is easy: if you can't attend the games, you can watch them on TV, listen to them on the radio, read about them in magazines or newspapers, or do all of the above on the Internet, as well as participate in fan sites. But in 1871, when the Boston Red Stockings came into existence, none of those options was possible. At that time, there was only print journalism—which meant newspapers and magazines; and unfortunately for anyone trying to find out who won yesterday's game, not all of these publications covered baseball (or reported on any sports at all). And even in the ones that did report on how the Red Stockings were doing, it was usually necessary to look through the entire paper to find the results. There was no such thing as a sports section (or "sporting section," as it was then called), and the game summary might be anywhere.

But a small number of publications did make time for baseball, and they provided information the fans were eager to read. One of the most popular was the *New York Clipper*. Founded in 1853, it soon made a name for itself as a reliable resource for news from the world of sports—and not just the games that took place in New York. The *Clipper* looked like a typical weekly newspaper, but it was unique for its era: Within its eight pages, readers could find extensive coverage of sporting events, and the baseball news was generally located on one or two specific pages, making it easier for readers to locate. Long before the debut of such publications as *Sporting Life* (1883) or *The Sporting News* (1886),[1] the *Clipper* filled an important niche. While it also covered other kinds of entertainment, such as stage plays, the majority of its stories were about the athletic competitions from the previous week, including national news about baseball, horse racing, aquatics (swim meets, yacht races), prize-fighting, chess, cricket, and other sports and games of the era. By April 1859, the banner and logo at the top of the front page identified the *Clipper* as a "sporting and theatrical journal," and by April 1868, the banner said it was the "Oldest American Sporting and Theatrical Journal." Only a few other publications of the 1860s and early 1870s, including the *Brooklyn Daily Eagle*, *New York Times*, and *Chicago Tribune*, devoted as much time and energy to covering baseball as the *Clipper* did. It is not surprising that fans all over the United States made sure to subscribe: Not only was the reporting thorough, but the *Clipper* also published letters to the editor, making it one of the few publications that allowed the readers to express their opinions.[2]

The years immediately after the Civil War saw so much interest in baseball that newspapers began remarking on how "base ball fever" was sweeping the country, as amateur and semipro teams sprang up in cities of all sizes.[3] Some newspaper reports predicted that interest would soon die out, as with any other fad. But the love of baseball endured, and large crowds continued to attend the games, proving it wasn't a fad after all.[4] However, this turned out to be a mixed blessing for the press. Although interest in both amateur and professional baseball continued to grow, most newspapers still did not place much emphasis on regular coverage of the games. In fact, compared to the in-depth reporting and analysis from today's baseball writers, the newspapers of the early 1870s offered very little information: a typical write-up ranged from a couple of sentences to a couple of paragraphs.

There were several reasons why the accounts were so brief. For one, there was no system of "beat reporters" yet, and some newspapers had no writers with expertise in baseball. This meant sending a writer who could offer little more than the basic facts. Also, as baseball continued to grow in popularity through the 1860s and into the early 1870s, there weren't enough reporters to cover all the teams and all the games in the region.[5] Sometimes, newspapers would call upon someone from the club's management to report on what happened. The editor also might ask a local fan who had attended a recent game to give a quick write-up; or a young reporter might get some experience by going to a game and providing a few sentences about it.[6]

Another factor in keeping the stories brief was that reporters still had to rely on the telegraph to transmit the scores and game summaries back to their newspaper. (The telephone would not come along till the late 1870s, and the *Boston Globe* is said to be the first newspaper that used it for receiving news, a report of a lecture by Alexander Graham Bell telephoned to the *Globe* newsroom in 1877.)[7] While the telegraph had certainly become more efficient since its inception in the mid-1840s, well into the 1860s many smaller cities still did not have enough telegraph lines,[8] and sending messages from these distant locations could be expensive.[9] As a result, stories had to be kept short, in order to stay within budget. (Some reporters, especially with the weeklies, mailed their stories to their newspaper, which saved money and allowed them to write a longer article.)

If you lived in greater Boston in 1871, you probably got your information about baseball by reading the *Boston Journal*, the *Daily Advertiser*, the *Post*, or the *Herald*. Many of the newspapers in smaller cities like Quincy or Lowell were mainly following the local amateur teams,[10] but some newspapers outside Boston also covered the professional clubs, including the Red Stockings, among them Worcester's *Aegis and Gazette* in central Massachusetts and the *Springfield Republican* farther west. But when the Red Stockings made their official debut in May, you couldn't read about it in the *Boston Globe*, since that newspaper wouldn't publish its first issue until early March 1872. And no matter which newspaper you were reading, including the *New York Clipper*, you did not know who wrote the stories of the games, since reporter bylines were not yet in common use. (The lack of bylines meant that even the most famous journalists of that era received little credit for their stories. This applied even to one of the most respected sports reporters of that time, Henry Chadwick. He wrote many of the baseball articles for the *Clipper* and was its baseball editor for more than 20 years.[11] A prolific writer, Chadwick was also the editor of a widely used reference book, *Beadle's Dime Base-Ball Player*, which contained summaries of the previous season, including the accomplishments of the best teams and players.)

In the early 1870s the language of sportswriting was quite different from what we are accustomed to seeing today. The publications that covered sports in the early 1870s referred to what the Red Stockings played as "base ball" or "base-ball." The word "team" was seldom used—the Red Stockings were called a "club" or referred to as a "nine." And reporters didn't always call them the Red Stockings: often they were just referred to as the "Bostons." There were few if any slang terms to describe the loyal followers of the game: the word "fan" wasn't seen at all, and wouldn't be used until the late 1880s, around the same time that another word, "crank," became popular with reporters.[12] The same was true for the word "rooter," which was also not in common use until the late 1880s.[13] In 1871 people who attended the games were generally described by journalists as "spectators," or there was mention of the size of "the gathering" or "the crowd"—and given that most of the ballparks were much smaller than today, a good day's attendance was between 2,000 and 3,000,[14] although at certain important games, the newspapers reported more than 5,000 in the stands, and the new ballpark in Chicago was built to seat 7,000 White Stockings fans.[15] And speaking of ballparks, this word too was not commonly used yet: The places where the games took place were often referred to as either the "grounds" or the "ball grounds."

In downtown Boston, the part of Washington Street that would come to be known as Newspaper Row was still a work in progress in 1871. By the late 1880s, it had become a center of publishing. Of Boston's nine daily newspapers, six were clustered on Washington Street, close to one another as well as a number of weekly and monthly publications.[16] (This part of Boston would become very important for the fans: They could gather on Newspaper Row and await the reporters coming back from the games, get the scores from chalkboards set up outside each newspaper, and talk baseball with each other.) But in 1871 the Boston newspapers were not yet concentrated in one central location. This left fans with only limited options. Sometimes those who couldn't get into the game might gather outside the park—the Union Base Ball Grounds, at Milford Place in the South End,[17] and try to find out what was happening inside. Or sometimes they might try going to the nearest Western Union telegraph office in hopes that a reporter might stop by to receive information from a distant city where a game had been played. In some cities, a local team might host a get-together at a hotel,[18] or fans could gather at their favorite local establishment to have a few drinks and talk sports. (It should be noted that only men were expected to engage in this activity; while women could, and often did, attend the games, they were not supposed to spend time in taverns or saloons if they wanted to preserve a good reputation.) However, given that fans of the early 1870s had no expectation of instant information the way we do today, they were undoubtedly accustomed to waiting for their favorite newspaper to come out so they could find out how the Red Stockings and other clubs were doing.

Several of the Boston newspapers wrote extensively about the Red Stockings' May 2, 1871, opener against the Washington Olympics, although the news didn't get published until several days later. The *Herald* and the *Journal* were especially thorough. The *Herald* provided an inning-by-inning description of every play, as well as the box score. (Boston won, 20-18.) One interesting fact about the reporting of the game might seem remarkably modern: the unnamed correspondent took the umpire to task, saying he had done a terrible job of calling balls and strikes.[19] (That much-maligned umpire was Henry A. Dobson, a veteran baseball writer for the *New York Clipper*, and a Civil War veteran who had lost a leg during that conflict, but refused to let it stop him.) As a reporter for the *Boston Journal* noted in a story that was reprinted by the *Aegis and Gazette* of Worcester, Dobson "moves about nimbly on crutches." But while admiring the umpire's determination, the reporter also had harsh criticism for his work, noting that he clearly favored the Olympics and always gave them better calls than he did the Boston club.[20]

After the *Boston Globe* made its debut in 1872, local fans had one more place to read about the Red Stockings. In addition to covering some of the games, the *Globe* was soon providing news and commentary about the players, information about the activities of the club's executives, and schedules of where and when the Red Stockings would be playing next. And like several other local newspapers, the *Globe* published advertisements announcing when a game at the Union Base Ball Grounds was due to take place; admission was 50 cents.[21]

A particularly lengthy road trip in August 1873 kept the Red Stockings away from Boston for three weeks, as they traveled by train to games in the East and Midwest, and then played in Ontario, Canada.[22] Many Americans of that time were surprised to learn that baseball was already quite popular in parts of Canada, and had been as far back as the 1860s.[23] Thus, when the Red Stockings played against the Dauntless club of Toronto, Canadian newspaper reporters were excited to cover the game. By 1873 the Red Stockings had a reputation for winning, and Toronto fans turned out in great numbers, according to the *Toronto Globe* (today the *Globe and Mail*), including "a large number of ladies." And while the Toronto fans hoped their team could hold its own against what they recognized was a far superior Boston club, the attendees "showed their appreciation of the scientific display made by the Red Stockings." There was also lots of scoring, and in this case, no controversies about the umpire. The final score was 45-10, with the Red Stockings winning decisively.[24]

Another trip, this one by boat, did not go nearly as well. In July 1874, the Red Stockings, along with the Athletics of Philadelphia, arrived in Liverpool, England, in hopes of introducing British fans to baseball and perhaps winning them over. (Harry Wright, the manager of the Red Stockings, had been born in England and was still very skilled at the game of cricket. His hope was that the exhibitions by two of the best American baseball teams would create some new fans and help the sport to spread overseas.)[25] But while reporters from both countries covered the matches (as the British press called them), attendance was poor, and British spectators seemed puzzled by baseball. They were polite in praising the skills of the players, but couldn't seem to figure out the rules, even when British journalists tried to explain them. Said one British reporter, "The game is so entirely unknown in this country that it will doubtless be some time before the various points are fairly understood and appreciated."[26] That was an understatement. The trip not only did not win over many fans, but it was also a financial disappointment, as the *New York Clipper* acknowledged.[27] And as Athletics player (and later baseball writer for the *Boston Globe*) Tim Murnane recalled, the trip also interrupted the season, and deprived the league of its two best teams for about six weeks.[28]

But other than the frustrations of the trip overseas, the Boston Red Stockings provided the fans with plenty of positive news. In fact, from 1871 to 1875, there were many occasions when the club gave its followers something to talk about. Led by Harry Wright, and the pitching wizardry of Albert Spalding, the club nearly won the pennant in 1871. And from 1872 to 1875 no team in the National Association of Professional Base Ball Players[29] was more dominant. The Red Stocking won the championship four years in a row.[30] And even without the convenience of radio, television, or social media, the fans of the early 1870s still found many ways to support the team, thanks in large part to the newspapers and magazines that kept everyone informed.

SOURCES

In addition to the sources cited in the notes, the author also consulted:

"A Model Game of Base-Ball," *New York Times*, May 28, 1871: 8.

"The Boston Base Ball Club," *Boston Journal*, January 21, 1871: 1.

"The Boston Base Ball Club: Interesting Details, the Grounds, Uniform, &c.," *Boston Journal*, February 20, 1871: 2.

"The Bostonians Defeat the Nationals," *Fort Wayne Daily Gazette*, May 4, 1871: 1.

NOTES

1 John Rickards Betts, "Sporting Journalism in Nineteenth-Century America," *American Quarterly*, Spring 1953: 49.

2 Harold Seymour, *Baseball: The Early Years* (New York: Oxford University Press, 1960), 41.

3 "City News: Base Ball," *Cleveland Daily Leader*, April 12, 1866: 4.

4 "The National Game," *New York Herald*, June 29, 1869: 1.

5 R. Terry Furst, *Early Professional Baseball and the Sporting Press* (Jefferson, North Carolina: McFarland Press, 2014), 20-21.

6 Betts, "Sporting Journalism in Nineteenth-Century America": 52.

7 Marianne Salcetti, "The Emergence of the Reporter," in *Newsworkers: Toward a History of the Rank and File* (Minneapolis: University of Minnesota Press, 1995), 50.

8 "Telegraph Lines from Jackson to Lansing City Improvements," *Detroit Free Press*, August 3, 1866: 2.

9 John Rickards Betts, "The Technological Revolution and the Rise of Sport, 1850-1900," *Mississippi Valley Historical Review*, September 1953: 238.

10 For example, throughout the early 1870s, the *Quincy Patriot* published game accounts of the Actives, as well as other amateur teams from the Quincy and Braintree area.

11 "Fiftieth Year of Journalism," *Brooklyn Daily Eagle*, December 23, 1900: 5.

12 David Shulman, "On the Early Use of Fan in Baseball," *American Speech*, Autumn 1996: 330.

13 "Psychic Force," *Brooklyn Daily Eagle*, July 25, 1889: 6.

14 "The Most Brilliant Contest on Record," *Brooklyn Daily Eagle*, May 29, 1871: 9.

15 David Quentin Voigt, "The Boston Red Stockings: The Birth of Major League Baseball," *New England Quarterly*, Vol. 43, No. 4 (December 1970): 537.

16 Herbert A. Kenney. *Newspaper Row: Journalism in the Pre-Television Era* (Chester, Connecticut: Globe Pequot Press, 1987), 6.

17 "Grand Opening of the Union Base Ball Grounds," *Boston Herald*, June 18, 1869: 3.

18 "Town and Country," *Harrisburg* (Pennsylvania) *Daily Telegraph*, March 14, 1871: 3.

19 "Base Ball: Boston vs. Olympic," *Boston Herald*, May 8, 1871: 2.

20 "Interesting Game—Boston Red Stockings vs. Olympics of Washington," *Aegis and Gazette*, (Worcester, Massachusetts), May 13, 1871: 6.

21 See, for example, the advertisement for the Thursday, June 6, 1872, game, Baltimore vs. Boston in the *Boston Globe*, June 6, 1872: 1.

22 "The Beacons Beat the Mutuals," *Boston Globe*, August 11, 1873: 5.

23 William Humber, *Diamonds of the North* (New York: Oxford University Press, 1995), 4.

24 "Baseball Match: Interesting Game Between the Torontonians and Bostonians," *Toronto Globe*, August 25, 1873: 4.

25 John W. Bauer, "New Game in the Old Country," in *Inventing Baseball: The 100 Greatest Games that Shaped the 19th Century* (Phoenix: Society for American Baseball Research, 2013), 84.

26 "The American Base-Ball Players," *The Week's News*, London August 1, 1874: 974.

27 "Baseball in England," *New York Clipper*, August 15, 1874: 154.

28 Tim Murnane, "Murnane's Baseball Stories," *Boston Globe*, January 10, 1915: 39.

29 Voigt, 532.

30 Henry Chadwick, "On the Death of Harry Wright," in *Spalding's Base Ball Guide and Official League Book for 1896* (American Sports Publishing Company, 1896), 163.

THE DAWN OF ATHLETE ENDORSEMENTS

BY JOHN THORN

Red Stockings Cigar.

TODAY MANY ATHLETES EARN FAR more from their endorsement deals than from their efforts on the playing field. As the table below demonstrates, Tiger Woods is the king of active player endorsements, last year raking in $65 million compared to his $13.1 million in prize money from golf tournaments. As a retired player, Michael Jordan is not counted, yet if former athletes were in the mix, Jordan would top everyone with his $80 million in royalties from his own brand. Yet for ratio of endorsement dollars to athletic ones, the king among sport's top 100 earners is perhaps a surprise: Usain Bolt, who garnered only $200,000 on the track but $24 million off it. (Endorsement income is an estimate of product/service sponsorship deals, appearance fees, and licensing fees for the twelve months through June 2013, as tabulated by *Forbes* in its annual survey of the 100 highest-paid athletes.)

Many high-salaried athletes had negligible endorsement income (Floyd Mayweather, for example, earned $34 million in the ring and not a penny outside it). Among the 27 baseball players on the list, of prime interest to the readership here, no one gained more off the field than on it, and the highest earners via endorsements were Derek Jeter with $9 million and Ichiro Suzuki with $6 million.

Athletes Who Earned More via Endorsement than Sport

Tiger Woods $65M to $13.1M
Roger Federer $45M to $7.7M
Phil Mickelson $44M to $4.7M
Lebron James $42M to $17.8M
David Beckham $42 M to $5.2M
Kobe Bryant $34M to $27.9M
Mahendra Singh Dhoni $28M to $3.5M
Usain Bolt $24M to $200K
Maria Sharapova $23M to $6M
Lionel Messi $21M to $20.3M
Derrick Rose $21M to $16.4M
Rafael Nadal $21M to $5.4M
Sachin Tendulkar $18M to $4M
Rory McIlroy $16M to $13.6M
Ernie Els $16M to $3.5M
Li Na $15M to $3.2M
Novak Djokovic $14 M to $12.9M
Dale Earnhardt $13M to $13M
Serena Williams $12M to $8.5M

You would not be wrong to think that athlete endorsements were few and far between until the pioneering efforts of Babe Ruth and his agent, Christy Walsh. But who was the first ballplayer to endorse a product and, presumably, be paid for the persuasive power of his celebrity? Authors Bernard Mullin, Stephen Hardy, and William Sutton suggest, in their 2007 book *Sport Marketing*: "According to Bert Sugar, the first recorded instance of a modern

George Wright, by Warren

athlete's leasing his name (to endorse a sports product) occurred on September 1, 1905, when Honus Wagner ... of the Pittsburgh Pirates gave the J.F. Hillerich & Son Company permission to use his name on its Louisville Slugger bats for a consideration of $75."

This is surely incorrect. A poster from 1874, featuring Hall of Famer George Wright of Boston promoting the Red Stockings Cigar, tops Honus with three decades to spare. A splendid lithograph from the firm of J.H. Bufford & Sons, the only example known to survive, has now emerged from a private collection to be placed at auction in the spring. That it is handsome you may judge; that it is important in the history of baseball and sport altogether—as the earliest tangible evidence in any sport of an athlete endorsing a commercial product—permit me to describe. There are three stories to tell here: that of the ballplayer, another of the lithographer, and the last about the cigar and its makers.

Before Babe Ruth rolled his own cigars or endorsed candy and tobacco products, before he became the baseball hero of the nation with 54 home runs in 1920, his first season with New York, there was another titan whose name was synonymous with the emerging national game: George Wright. Although he was elected to the Baseball Hall of Fame two years before that institution opened its doors to the public, George Wright is not a name that, like Ruth's, shines as brightly as ever.

His stats are readily available for the years since the debut of the game's first professional league in 1871, but he was already a legend by then. In the undefeated 1869 campaign of the Cincinnati Reds, in the 57 contests that came against National Association clubs, George Wright's bat produced an average of five hits and ten total bases per game; he collected 49 home runs

First Nine of the Cincinnati Red Stockings

among his 304 hits and batted .629. To the argument that the opposition was frequently soft: In the club's 19 games against fellow professionals (the Reds won all, of course), he hit 13 home runs and batted .587.

Selling his services to the highest bidder each year, he had played for the top club in the country in nearly every year since the end of the Civil War: the Unions of Morrisania; the Nationals of Washington, DC; the Cincinnati Red Stockings; the Boston Red Stockings; and the Providence Greys. Indeed, from 1866 through 1879 only three times was his club not the champion, and one of these years was 1871, when despite an outfield collision that limited him to half of his club's scheduled games, he hit a resounding .413.

In the *New York Evening Journal* of 1911, four decades after Wright played his last game, Sam Crane declared, "There have been many great shortstops, but for all-round ability there has been none who ever played the position who has been able to force George Wright from the top-notch rung of the ladder of fame." Crane, a second baseman who began his career in the National League as George was winding down his, wrote this at a time when Honus Wagner was at the height of his powers: "I have known them all and have seen them all play, but to George Wright I give the credit of being the best ever."

He was so popular a figure in his Boston years that he became the first player to author (or, more probably, affix his name to) a book: *Record of the Boston Base Ball Club, Since its Organization, With a Sketch of All its Players for 1871, '72, '73, and '74, and Other Items of Interest*. Rockwell and Churchill of Boston published the 52-page book in 1874, surely recognizing the value

Red Stockings Cigars, 1870s

of attaching George Wright's name. This was also the year in which George and his teammates, along with the Philadelphia Athletics, crossed the Atlantic to introduce America's new game to England.

And 1874 was also the year when the fledgling firm of Nichols & Macdonald, Boston cigar makers, secured an image of George Wright for a 14- by 10-inch advertising poster. Produced for them by the venerable lithographer and job printer J.H. Bufford's Sons of 490 Washington Street, it is a graphic and historic landmark. Wright's image within the poster dates to 1871 or '72, when Warren's Photographic Studios of Boston issued it as a cabinet card. The address listed for Bufford in the city directory for 1875 is 666 Washington, so we may deduce the date of the poster as no later than 1874. The young cigar makers are not listed before 1874, so there we have the date of issuance with certainty.

The lithographic house of John Henry Bufford (1810–1870), and its successor entities run by his sons, went back to 1829, when he began as an apprentice of William S. Pendleton in Boston. He labored alongside Nathaniel Currier, who had started with Pendleton one year earlier. Bufford worked under his own name in New York from 1835 to about 1840, sometimes working under commission for George Endicott and for Currier (Currier and Ives would not form until 1852). He then returned to Boston where, from 1845, J.H. Bufford & Co. became a major lithographic establishment of the period. If Bufford is less highly regarded today than his contemporaries, it may be because where Currier early on tilted toward "framing prints," Bufford continued as a multipurpose job printer who sometimes

Union Pond, Williamsburgh, L.I.

co-published works with other companies. Bufford ran the firm until his death in 1870, after which his sons—Frank Gale Bufford and John Henry Bufford, Jr.—took over operations, continuing until about 1910.

Starting as an apprentice, Bufford appreciated not only the practice of lithography but also the need to employ apprentices with artistic talents. Of these, none went on to greater fame than Winslow Homer, who trained with Bufford from 1855 to 1857. While with Bufford, he produced a group of undistinguished sheet music covers. In 1862, working on commission for Thomas & Eno, he produced his only image with baseball associations—a spectacular lithograph of "Union Pond, Williamsburgh, L.I." This site became the Union Base Ball Grounds of Brooklyn, to which patrons were charged ten cents for their admission.

Testifying to the senior Bufford's interest in sports are four magnificent lithographs produced under his aegis. The earliest is "The Eleven of New England: Cricket Match at Boston, September 18th, 1850." Another is a beautifully detailed litho, with 250 recognizable portraits, of "The International Contest Between Heenan and Sayers at Farnborough, on the 17th, of April 1860." A third is "Camp of the 37th Mass. Vol's. near Brandy Station, Va." with a detail showing soldiers playing wicket. And the last is well known to advanced baseball collectors: "The Base Ball Quadrille" of 1867, dedicated to the Tri-Mountain Base Ball Club of Boston—pioneers of the New York Game—and depicting its top player, Frank Prescott Norton. After John H. Bufford's death in 1870, his sons gave even more attention to sport—particularly baseball—by publishing trade cards, handheld-fan illustrations, and of course this momentous poster from 1874.

Messrs. Nichols and Macdonald were not the first to name a product for a baseball club—that distinction goes to Ohioan Fred Burrell, who manufactured a Red Stocking cigar in 1869 or '70 to honor the unbeaten Cincinnati nine. A generic baseball player adorns

Burrell's Cincinnati Red Stocking Cigar Box

the cigar-box label; its model may have been either Harry Wright or Charlie Gould, as they were the only two Red Stockings to sport a goatee. But the image is sufficiently indistinct to presume that neither was paid for the use of his likeness.

When the Cincinnati Red Stockings disbanded after the 1870 season, manager Harry Wright took the name and several key players—brother George, the aforementioned Gould, Dave Birdsall, and Cal McVey—and formed a club in Boston to compete in the new National Association of Professional Base Ball Players. Harry also brought the discarded nickname to Boston; the Red Stockings are today, in an unbroken line of descent, the Atlanta Braves.

The Eleven of New England, Morgan, Bufford, 1851

David L. Nichols, as a career salesman and the older partner in the firm of Nichols and Macdonald, is probably the one who came up with the idea to create a Boston version of Burrell's "Red Stockings Cigar" and to promote its sale through a highly recognizable George Wright. As Crane would recall in 1911, "he had a thick crop of dark curly hair, a small mustache and a dab on either cheek for a bluff at 'siders' … his prominent teeth would gleam and glisten in an array of white molars that would put our own Teddy Roosevelt and his famed dentistry establishment far in the shadow."

Born in West Newbury, MA in 1836, Nichols fought in the Civil War with Company F of the 18th Massachusetts Infantry and with Company D & M of the 2nd Massachusetts Heavy Artillery. He was mustered out on September 3, 1865. Little more than two years later, on January 14, 1868, he married Mary M. Carter, daughter of Isaac Carter and Maria Manson Carter. Upon her husband's death, Maria married again, in 1843, to Hugh Macdonald (also

David L. Nichols, 1863

spelled as McDonald); in 1850 they produced Frederick William Macdonald. In short: David L. Nichols would join in cigar-making partnership with his brother-in-law, Frederick. So close were the two that they shared the same household in Cambridge, with Maria Macdonald, who had been widowed once more.

Nichols and Macdonald sold their Red Stocking cigar at 114 Broad Street in Boston in 1874 and 1875, but at some point in 1876 the firm failed. Nichols was reduced to becoming a seller of butter and cheese at Faneuil Hall Market. At 2 PM on October 9, 1878, wrote the *Boston Journal* of the following day, he took a room at the Carlton House, No. 5 Hanover Street,

stating that he wanted to sleep a couple of hours, and leaving orders to be called at 4 o'clock. An hour or so after he entered the room the report of a pistol shot was heard.… At 4 o'clock the occupant was found dead on the bed, with a bullet hole in his head. A new pistol was lying by his side on the bed, also a box of cartridges, one of the cartridges

Red Stockings Cigar, ca. 1905

only having been removed. There were two or three letters in the room, left by deceased.…

David L. Nichols' widow continued to live in the Macdonald household until her death at age 78, in 1916. She was buried alongside her husband in West Newbury.

In 1884 Fred Macdonald, now married to Theresa A. Brown of Cambridge, reappears in the Boston city directory as a cigar manufacturer or seller at 15 Oliver. In that year a design patent taken out by Nichols and

Macdonald in 1874 was transferred to Macdonald alone, though the Red Stocking (no longer plural) Cigar may actually have been revived in the previous year. (*The Cambridge Chronicle* reported September 15, 1883 that "Bailey's Key West and Red Stocking Cigars are the best 10 cents cigar in town.")

The Red Stocking brand's identification with the national pastime was reinforced in 1886 by the issuance of sample cards that are among the greatest rarities in the hobby. Only three Red Stocking Cigar cards are known: Charlie Buffinton, John Morrill, and Hoss Radbourn.

For the rest of his life, Fred Macdonald was a success in the cigar-making line and so was his Red Stocking brand, by now a somewhat wistfully obsolete reference, as Boston's National League ball club was no longer called by that name. A notice by Ren Mulford in the *Cincinnati Post* of May 18, 1905, testified that the brand was a nostalgic one: "The Red Stocking cigar is a Boston weed named for the Beaneaters." The twentieth century label for the Red Stocking Cigar features the Bufford background of 1874 but replaces George Wright with an unidentified Boston NL player of the 1901–1905 period, given the lace front of the jersey; I think it's Fred Tenney.

In 1889 another instance of player endorsement predating Honus Wagner was memorialized in a fine lithographic advertisement for E. and J. Burke's ale and stout. According to Charles Zuber of the *Cincinnati Times-Star*:

There is only one case of record where ball players received a large remuneration for acting as models for an advertisement. Those players were Capt. Ewing and 'Old Man' Anson. It was before the Brotherhood War, when Ewing was in the very zenith of his glory. A certain ale manufacturing concern wanted a taking ad. for its goods and decided that a base ball picture was the best thing. So when the Chicagos came to New York this firm arranged for Ewing and Anson to sit in front of a tent on which the ad of the company was emblazoned. Barrels and cases of the product were placed in close proximity and Ewing and Anson, in their uniforms and each with a glass of ale poised graceful in his hands, were in the foreground. The ad made a big hit and Ewing and Anson received $300 and a case of ale each. It was quick and easy for them.

In 2008 this baseball advertising piece sold at auction for $188,000. What will the Red Stockings Cigar poster bring?

NOTE: The item sold for $189,600.

This article first appeared at: http://ourgame.mlblogs.com/2014/01/20/the-dawn-of-athlete-endorsements/

Thanks to John Thorn for permission to include it in this volume.

Anson and Ewing promoting ale and stout.

SOME RED STOCKINGS STATS

IN FIVE FULL SEASONS, THE BOSTON Red Stockings only featured 22 different ballplayers. The entire 1871 team had just 11 men. Every one of them appeared in at least 16 games, however. They made do with just two pitchers all season long. It was kind of like what you might call a one-man rotation – Al Spalding actually started every game all year. Harry Wright relieved in nine.

In 1872, they made do with 10 players. Andy Leonard and Fraley Rogers joined the team, but Frank Barrows, Fred Cone, and Sam Jackson departed. The one-man rotation held; Spalding started every game. Harry Wright relieved in the seven games Spalding didn't go the distance.

There were five first-timers who joined the squad in 1873: Bob Addy, Jack Manning, Jim O'Rourke, Charlie Sweasy, and Deacon White. Gould and McVey had left. For the first time, Spalding didn't start every game. He only started 54 of the 60 games. Harry Wright started the other six, but Spalding pitched in every one of the games Wright began. They couldn't keep Al off the mound. They featured a baker's dozen players – 13. That was as large as the roster ever became. In 1874, there were 11 Red Stockings, and in 1875, they again had 13.

The 1874 team had seen two new men – Tommy Beals and George Hall.

The two new players on the '75 team were Frank Heifer and Jumbo Latham.

Over the course of the five seasons of the Red Stockings, one notes some unusual statistics. For one thing, the existing historical record doesn't show that even one batter was hit by a pitch at any time over the half-decade.

Red Stockings batters totaled 1,372 at-bats in 1871, but only struck out 17 times. They drew 60 walked that year, but over the five seasons averaged a team 44.4 walks (in 1872, they walked a low of 27 times.)

The team batting average ranged from a low of .243 in 1872 to a high of .340 the very next year. But they won the pennant both years.

There wasn't a lot of slugging. The team slugging average in 1872 was .275. (As a point of interest, the lowest slugging percentage for Don Buddin of the Red Sox was .342. Mario Mendoza, for whom the "Mendoza line" was named, had a career slugging percentage of .262.) The Red Stockings team as a whole hit 55 home runs over the five seasons – from a low of three homers in 1871 to a high of 17 in 1874.

Red Stockings pitchers gave up five home runs in 1873, but only five in the other four seasons combined – not one homer in 1872 and only one in 1874.

One might think that batters were particularly adept at dancing away from pitches. Hit by Pitch totals show that Red Stockings batters never got hit by a pitcher, nor did a Red Stockings pitcher ever hit anyone. There was a reason for that, though. As Tom Ruane from Retrosheet explains, "Hit by pitches didn't exist until 1884 in the American Association and 1887 in the NL. Before that, if you got plunked with a pitch, it just counted as a ball."

The team ERA was:

1871	3.36
1872	1.85
1873	2.99
1874	1.92
1875	1.87

This wasn't because there were a lot of shutouts. There was only one shutout thrown in 1871 and one in 1873. There were three in 1872, four in 1874, and eight shutouts in 1875. One of the shutouts in 1875 was thrown by Jack Manning. (There were some combined shutouts where two pitchers combined on a game without allowing a run; those aren't recorded as shutouts.)

Of course, one of the reasons the ERAs were so low was due to the large number of unearned runs scored by opponents. The totals were a little staggering, but reflected the conditions of the various fields, the lack of baseball gloves, and any number of other factors.

Errors per year:

1871	245
1872	303 (with the acknowledgement that records are incomplete)
1873	472
1874	591 (with the acknowledgement that records are incomplete)
1875	483
TOTAL	2094

The most errors committed in any one game by an opponent were the 30 (!) errors committed by the Brooklyn Atlantics on October 1, 1874. Boston won, 29-0. There were three other games in which the opposition helped Boston by erring 21 or more times: May 7, 1872, May 12, 1874, and June 27, 1874.

The most errors the Red Stockings committed in a game were 18, on October 30, 1874, the last game of the season. The Hartford Dark Blues won, 17-11. Next most were the 17 errors in the September 28, 1874 game – a game they won, beating Baltimore, 14-7.

Runs vs. earned runs, per year:

YEAR	RUNS	EARNED RUNS
1871	303	109
1872	236	89
1873	460	183
1874	415	136
1875	343	152
TOTAL	1757	669

Thus, overall, just shy of 45% of the runs scored were unearned.

One reason the Red Stockings won four pennants in a row, and only feel two games short in 1871 is because they scored a lot more runs that the opposition.

YEAR	RUNS SCORED	RUNS ALLOWED
1871	401	303
1872	521	236
1873	739	460
1874	735	415
1875	831	343
TOTALS	3227	1757

The most runs scored in any game was a total of 32 – something the team did twice in 1873: July 4 (32-3), in the second game of a doubleheader against the Elizabeth Resolutes (they had bounced back after losing the first game, 11-2), and on October 13, beating Baltimore 32-13. The July 4 doubleheader in 1873 was the only doubleheader the team played in the five years of its existence.

That second game against the Resolutes constituted the largest margin of victory (29 runs) they ever had, but it was matched by arguably an even more lopsided win, the aforementioned 29-0 win over the Brooklyn Atlantics on October 1, 1874.

Note: All the above figures were taken from Retrosheet.org. The status of statistics is sometimes uncertain. For instance, in calculating the most errors in a game, Retrosheet lacks boxscores for the games in 1873 and 1875. There may have been bigger error totals in some of those games than the ones reported. There are other times that figures don't seem to cross-foot correctly, leaving one in doubt about the totals presented. For instance, the team totals for 1872 say that Al Spalding threw three shutouts, and no one else threw one, for a total of four. The game logs do show four shutouts by Spalding.

SOME NEWSPAPER COVERAGE OF THE 1874 EUROPEAN TOUR OF THE RED STOCKINGS AND ATHLETICS

THE NATIONAL ASSOCIATION OF Professional Base Ball Players was baseball's first attempt to organize as a professional business and break away from its long amateur heritage.

"From its creation in 1871 to its crash five years later," wrote baseball historian John Thorn, "the National Association had a rocky time as America's first professional league. Franchises came and went with dizzying speed, often folding in midseason. Schedules were not played out if a club slated to go on the road saw little prospect of gain. Drinking and gambling and game-fixing were rife.… But from the ashes of the National Association emerged the Boston Red Stockings' model of success and the entrepreneurial genius of Chicago's William Hulbert."

In the summer of 1874, the Boston Red Stockings and Athletics of Philadelphia set sail for England and embarked on the first comprehensive European baseball tour. Material from the Boston Herald's coverage of the tour was gathered and re-typed from the original newspaper stories by Bill Nowlin, in 2016, to accompany publication of the SABR book Boston's First Nine: The 1871-75 Boston Red Stockings.

Click here to download the 1874 Boston Herald coverage of the Red Stockings-Athletics baseball tour (PDF; 44 pages)

Or visit: http://sabr.org/research/1874-boston-herald-red-stockings-tour

CONTRIBUTORS

MATT ALBERTSON is a Bloomsburg, Pennsylvania native who currently resides outside of Philadelphia. He holds two Bachelor of Arts degrees from Bloomsburg University (2012) and a Master of Arts in History from Villanova University (2014). He joined SABR in 2015 and is active in Philadelphia's Connie Mack Chapter and has contributed to several SABR publications. Matt is also the historical columnist for Philliedelphia.com. His future side projects include a book on the 1915 Philadelphia Phillies and working on placing a Pennsylvania Historical Marker at the site of the original Jefferson Street Grounds in Philadelphia. Matt is currently a Project Manager at an electrical distributor in the Philadelphia region.

DAVID ARCIDIACONO, of East Hampton, Connecticut, is a member of the Society for American Baseball Research (SABR), specializing in nineteenth-century baseball research. He is the author of three books on nineteenth-century baseball in Connecticut, including his latest, *Major League Baseball in Gilded Age Connecticut: The Rise and Fall of the Middletown, New Haven and Hartford Clubs*. Mr. Arcidiacono's articles have also appeared in many SABR and Vintage Base Ball Association publications.

ANDREW ARENDS is an American from New York, now long-time resident in England. He holds degrees from Oxford and Harvard universities and is a research fellow at the University of London currently writing an economic history of Association football (soccer). He is a lifelong Boston Red Sox fan.

CHARLIE BEVIS is the author of six books on baseball history, most recently *Tim Keefe: A Biography of the Hall of Fame Pitcher and Player-Rights Advocate*. A member of SABR since 1984, he has contributed more than three dozen biographies to the SABR BioProject as well as the SABR books *The 1967 Impossible Dream Red Sox*; *New Century, New Team: The 1901 Boston Americans*; and *Red Sox Baseball in the Days of Ike and Elvis: The Red Sox of the 1950s*. He teaches research writing at the University of Massachusetts Lowell and lives in nearby Chelmsford with his wife Kathie and their dog Kasey.

CHRISTOPHER J. DEVINE is an Assistant Professor of Political Science at the University of Dayton, in Dayton, Ohio. He is the author of two baseball books: *Thurman Munson: A Baseball Biography* (2001), and *Harry Wright: The Father of Professional Base Ball* (2003). In 2001, he won SABR's Jack Kavanagh Memorial Youth Baseball Research Award. In subsequent years, Devine's research interests shifted to politics, and he earned an MA and PhD in Political Science from The Ohio State University. He is the co-author of *The VP Advantage: How Running Mates Influence Home State Voting in Presidential Elections* (2016), and he has written on the subject of vice presidential candidacies for *Time*, Politico, and the *Washington Post*. Baseball and politics are his favorite sports, and his favorite party—er, team—is the Cleveland Indians.

PAUL E. DOUTRICH is a professor of history at York College of Pennsylvania. While his specialty is the American revolutionary era and early nineteenth century he also teaches a very popular course on baseball history. Among his monographs is *The Cardinals and the Yankees: 1926* (McFarland). He has also contributed several pieces to other SABR projects, has written articles about early America that have been published in various scholarly journals, and he has curated six major museum exhibits including two for the state of Pennsylvania.

BRIAN ENGELHARDT is a native of Reading, Pennsylvania where he resides with his wife, Suzanne, who is a good sport about any number of things. They raised three daughters to be Phillies fans, although the one now living in Pittsburgh seems to favor the Pirates as well. He is the author of the recently released book, *Reading's Big League Exhibition Games*, as well as of several SABR biographies and articles appearing in SABR publications. A regular contributor to the *Berks County Historical Review* on things baseball plus other local historical matters, he has also written for the Reading Phillies website. The collapse of the 1964 Phillies and his mother throwing out his baseball cards that same year stunted his emotional growth at age 13.

CHARLES F. FABER is a native of Iowa currently living in Lexington, Kentucky. He holds degrees from Coe College, Columbia University, and the University of Chicago. A retired public school and university teacher and administrator, he has contributed to numerous SABR projects, including editing *The 1934 St. Louis Cardinals*. Among his publications are dozens of professional journal articles, encyclopedia entries, and research reports in fields such as school administration, education law, and country music. In addition to textbooks, he has written 10 books (mostly on baseball) published by McFarland. His most recent work, co-authored with Zachariah Webb, is *The Hunt for a Reds October*, published by McFarland in 2015.

SCOTT FIESTHUMEL of Clinton, New York, is author of the self-published 2001 book *Barnstorming Champions - The 1920 Adirondack Stars - A First Hand Account of a Bygone Era*.

TERRELL (TERRY) D. GOTTSCHALL teaches German and European history at Walla Walla University. He alternates research projects between late 19th-century town teams in the interior Pacific Northwest and German naval operations in East Asian waters before 1914. His current work focuses on the role of German naval infantry in the Seymour Expedition during the Boxer Rebellion in June 1900. He has published several articles in *Base Ball: The Journal of the Early Game* as well as a biography *By Order of the Kaiser: Otto von Diederichs and the Rise of the Imperial German Navy, 1865-1902* (Naval Institute Press, 2003).

GERARD R. (GERRY) GOULET, of Warwick, Rhode Island, is now semi-retired after forty years in health care regulation as an analyst and attorney. Although he has been a member of SABR for 28 years, this is his first attempt at researching and writing about something as important as baseball history. A lifetime Red Sox fan, his juvenile enthusiasms for that organization have been tempered over time by the influence of his wife of 42 years, Julie, a lifetime Yankees fan. After many failed attempts at effecting her conversion, he has moved on to their two grandchildren who, at this point, have potential as, at age 3 and 1 1/2 respectively, they are still too young to have developed allegiances.

DONNA L. HALPER is an Associate Professor of Communication at Lesley University, Cambridge, Massachusetts. A media historian who specializes in the history of broadcasting, Dr. Halper is the author of six books and many articles. She is also a former broadcaster and print journalist.

RICHARD HERSHBERGER writes on early baseball history and rules. He has published in various SABR publications, and in *Base Ball: A Journal of the Early Game* and is currently writing a book on the development of baseball's rules to be published by Rowman & Littlefield. He is a paralegal in Maryland.

JOANNE HULBERT is co-chair of the Boston chapter, co-chair of SABR's Baseball Arts committee, and is a collector of baseball poetry. She resides in Holliston, Massachusetts, and its venerable neighborhood, Mudville, where the early history of baseball bloomed and produced ball players of minor repute. Lest we forget, let us continue to dig deep into baseball's glorious past.

JAY HURD, a longtime member of SABR, is a librarian and museum educator. He studies and presents on the Negro Leagues and is a regular attendee of the annual Jerry Malloy Negro League Conference. Jay has contributed articles to the SABR BioProject and SABR publications. A fan of the Boston Red Sox, he has recently relocated from Medford, Massachusetts to Bristol, Rhode Island and looks forward to attending meetings of the Lajoie-Start Chapter of SABR, and to enjoying AAA baseball at McCoy Stadium, the home of the Pawtucket Red Sox.

BILL LAMB is the editor of *The Inside Game*, the newsletter of SABR's Deadball Era Committee.

BOB LEMOINE came up with the idea for this book while researching the beginnings of professional baseball in Boston, wondering "How did all of that come together?" He often daydreams about time traveling to the 19th Century too see early baseball games, horse and buggies, and meet the legendary stars. Actually, he'd just like to see a game for 25 cents. Bob works as a high school librarian and lives in Barrington, New Hampshire.

LEN LEVIN has been following Boston teams for a long time, but certainly not as far back as the Red Stockings. A retired newspaper editor in Providence, Rhode Island, he currently spends a lot of time editing articles for SABR books and for BioProject.

MICHAEL R. MCAVOY is an Assistant Professor of Economics at the State University of New York College at Oneonta. Mike graduated from the University of Illinois at Urbana-Champaign with an A.B. and a Ph.D., both in Economics. Growing up a life-long Cubs fan, Mike has become a student of the club's 19th century origins and history. A SABR member since 2013, Mike is a member of the 19th Century Committee and enjoys attending the FRED. He has collected information on the salaries of the American Association Cincinnati Reds, and has written a paper on the pricing of the baseball cards of players selected for the Hall of Fame.

DAVID MCDONALD is a writer, filmmaker, and broadcaster, who grew up in Toronto and now lives in Ottawa. His writing about baseball has appeared in the *The National Pastime*, *The Baseball Research Journal*, *The Globe and Mail*, the Ottawa *Citizen*, and in the Canadian baseball anthologies *All I Thought About Was Baseball* (University of Toronto Press) and *Dominionball: Baseball Above the 49th* (SABR). He has been a member of SABR for more than 20 years.

WILLIAM MCMAHON is a retired professor of philosophy at the University of Akron. He received an A.B. and Ph.D from Notre Dame and an M.A. from Brown. Growing up in Chicago, he is a diehard Cubs fan. He has been a SABR member for more than 30 years. He chairs the Farm Club Subcommittee of the Minor League Committee, is also on the Nineteenth Century and Womens' Committees, and contributes to Retrosheet. His baseball publications include articles in *Nineteenth Century Stars*, *Baseball's First Stars*, and the *Dictionary of American Sports-Baseball*. In addition to his wife of 53 years, Mary Louise Owens McMahon, he has a son Coleman (SABR member) and daughter Elizabeth.

ERIC MIKLICH has written for SABR and John Thorn's *Base Ball: A Journal of the Early Game*. In 2014, he co-authored *Forfeits and Successfully Protested Games in Major League Baseball: A Complete Record, 1871-2013*, with David Nemec and has been a contributing author to other Nemec publications. He is a member of SABR's Nineteenth Century Committee and has served on the Executive Board of the Vintage Base Ball Association (VBBA) from 2009 to the present, seven years as its Historian. Eric owns 19C Base Ball Inc. and maintains its website, www.19cbaseball.com. He was a Volunteer 19th Century Base Ball Coordinator at Old Bethpage Village Restoration (Long Island), the re-birthplace of 19th century base ball in North America, from 2000-2009. Eric has competed in close to 800 19th century base ball matches throughout the US and currently pitches for the Eckford of Brooklyn BBC. He is from and still lives on Long Island.

PETER MORRIS is a baseball historian who lives in Haslett, Michigan.

DAVID NEMEC is a novelist and baseball historian. He has written *The Great Encyclopedia of Nineteenth Century Major League Baseball*; *The Beer and Whisky League*, a history of the American Association's 10-year sojourn as a rebel major league; *Major League Baseball Profiles: 1871-1900*; and many other baseball history and memorabilia books. His most recent novel, *The Picture Maker*, was translated into Czech and published in April 2016 in the Czech Republic under the title *Zajatec Predstav*. Nemec's contributions to the 1871-75 Boston Red Stockings' book are expanded and updated versions of biographies that originally appeared in *Major League Baseball Profiles: 1871-1900.*

BILL NOWLIN was born in Boston, but well after the glory days of the Red Stockings. In December 1907, when the successor Boston Braves decided to move to wear blue stockings, the Boston Americans quickly grabbed red for their "sox" and the American League franchise had a new name. Bill has followed the Red Sox since sometime in the 1950s, and written extensively on them when not working for Rounder Records. He has been on SABR's board since 2004.

MARK PESTANA has been a SABR member since 1990, and a baseball fan since 1967 when he moved to the Boston area during the summer of the Impossible Dream Red Sox. He currently lives in rural Dunstable, Massachusetts, and his focus is on 19th Century baseball history. His previous work for SABR publications includes contributions to *Inventing Baseball: The 100 Greatest Games of the 19th Century* and *Braves Field: Memorable Moments at Boston's Lost Diamond*, as well as to the forthcoming *From the Braves to the Brewers: Great Games and Exciting History at Milwaukee's County Stadium*, and the Deadball Era Committee's book on World Series of the Deadball Era. His most recent efforts are chapters for SABR's two volumes on Baseball's 19th Century Winter Meetings.

MIKE RICHARD is a lifelong Red Sox fan who still counts the Impossible Dream season of 1967 as his greatest baseball thrill. He retired as a guidance counselor from Gardner (Massachusetts) High School and is a sports columnist for the *Worcester Telegram & Gazette* and also a sportswriter for the *Barnstable Patriot*. A Massachusetts high school sports historian, he has authored two high school football books: *Glory to Gardner: 100 Years of Football in the Chair City*, and *Super Saturdays: The Complete History of the Massachusetts High School Super Bowl*. He has also documented the playoff history (sectional and state championships) of all high school sports in Massachusetts. He lives in Sandwich on Cape Cod with his wife Peggy. They are the parents of a son Casey, a daughter Lindsey, and have a grandson Theo.

BOB RUZZO is an attorney practicing real estate and affordable housing law at Holland and Knight, LLP in Boston. Before becoming a Red Sox fan, his father rooted for the Boston Braves, and so the spirit lives on. Bob's articles about Braves Field and the Federal League have appeared in SABR's *Baseball Research Journal*.

WILLIAM J. RYCZEK has written a trilogy on 19th century baseball: *Baseball's First Inning, When Johnny Came Sliding Home,* and *Blackguards and Red Stockings*. The latter is a history of the National Association that covers the period when the Boston Red Stockings dominated major-league baseball. He has also written on baseball and football during the 1960s, including books on the Yankees, the Mets, and the American Football League's New York Titans. Bill is a finance professional who lives in Wallingford, Connecticut.

MARK SOUDER is from Fort Wayne, Indiana which he represented in the United States Congress for 16 years. Now mostly retired, in addition to doing political commentary in Indiana media, he has been working on a multi-year project on the history of baseball & politics. SABR's 2015 *The National Pastime* published his article "Why did Wrigley, Lasker, and the Chicago Cubs Join a Presidential Campaign?" In 2015 at SABR's 19th Century Conference in Cooperstown (the FRED) he presented "The French Connection: Government Baseball in Washington" and in 2016 was chosen to present "Baseball, Tammany Hall, and the Battle of Bull Run." His interest in the interaction between baseball & politics was stimulated by comments during his participation as a lead questioner in Congressional Steroid Hearings. His version of a perfect day was spending his 50th birthday in the Chicago White Sox co-owner's suite and having his name appear on the scoreboard, all while raising money for his campaign and watching baseball.

DAVID C. SOUTHWICK is former publicity coordinator of the Boston Chapter of SABR. He conceived and initiated SABR's first team book for BioProject, on the 1975 Red Sox: *'75: The Red Sox Team That Saved Baseball*. When his beloved Red Sox are out of season, he is a dedicated follower of his alma mater's sports teams, the North Quincy (Massachusetts) High School Red Raiders. David presently resides in Dorchester, Massachusetts.

MARK S. STERNMAN works in Boston and, though a diehard fan of the New York Yankees, holds a partial season-ticket plan for the Boston Red Sox. He has enjoyed writing for various SABR outlets about six Boston players: Jack Burdock, Ben Cardoni, Scotty Ingerton, Mike Stenhouse, Fred Tenney, and Sam Wise. He has also written game recaps for SABR books on the 1914 Boston Braves, 1967 Red Sox, and 1975 Boston Red Sox.

JOHN THORN is the Official Historian of Major League Baseball and the author/editor of many books.

RICHARD "DIXIE" TOURANGEAU was the creator/author of the "Play Ball!" wall calendar for Tide-Mark Press from 1981 to 2005, for which he wrote more than 250 player biographies. As the 21st century began he felt an urge to know more about 19th century teams and players. While becoming comfortable with them he was credited with finding the gravesites of Mort and Fraley Rogers for the Biographical Committee and confirming those of Dave Birdsall (cleaning his headstone) and John Dickson McBride (unmarked). Dixie, SABR 1981, lives a mile from both Fenway Park and where the South End Grounds and Huntington Avenue Grounds were located. While researching the Red Stockings creation he realized that in 1870, Ivers Whitney Adams lived a third of a mile from his house, in the Highlands, now the Mission Hill section of Boston. He has written for *The National Pastime* and biogs and game accounts for the SABR Braves Field and County Stadium books.

JOSEPH C. (JOE) WILLIAMS has been a SABR member since 1990. He was the chair of SABR's 19th Century Overlooked Baseball Legends Project from 2008-2013 and still contributes as a member. His area of expertise is the National Baseball Hall of Fame in Cooperstown, New York and has attended the past 30 induction ceremonies. He also contributes to Seamheads.com and his football website Leatherheads of the Gridiron. In his professional life, he is a senior manager for a large law firm overseeing the firm's Information Resource Center. A Poughkeepsie, New York native, Joe roots for the Mets. Other than the Mets winning the World Series in 1986, his most memorable baseball moment is being thanked by Deacon White's great grandson in White's induction speech in 2013.

JIM WOHLENHAUS is a retired Federal Government worker who hopes he was not a modern age Lord Dundreary. He has been a SABR member off and on since 1975. He recently discovered he had over 800 baseball books.

A lifelong Pirates fan, **GREGORY H. WOLF** was born in Pittsburgh, but now resides in the Chicagoland area with his wife, Margaret, and daughter, Gabriela. A professor of German studies and holder of the Dennis and Jean Bauman Endowed Chair in the Humanities at North Central College in Naperville, Illinois, he edited the SABR books *"Thar's Joy in Braveland!" The 1957 Milwaukee Braves* (2014), *Winning on the North Side. The 1929 Chicago Cubs* (2015), *A Pennant for the Twin Cities: The 1965 Minnesota Twins* (2015), and *From the Braves to the Brewers: Great Games and Exciting History at Milwaukee's County Stadium* (2016). He is currently working on a project about Sportsman's Park in St. Louis and co-editing a book with Bill Nowlin on the 1979 Pittsburgh Pirates.

JOHN ZINN is an independent historian with special interest in the history of baseball as well as the Civil War. He is the chairman of the board of the New Jersey Historical Society and was the chair of New Jersey's Committee on the Sesquicentennial of the Civil War. John is the author of three books including two about the Brooklyn Dodgers as well as numerous essays and articles. He also writes a blog on baseball history entitled "A Manly Pastime." John holds BA and MBA degrees from Rutgers University and is a Vietnam veteran. He is also the score keeper for the Fleminton Neshanock vintage base ball team. John lives in Verona, New Jersey with his wife Carol. They are the parents of Paul Zinn and the grandparents of Sophie and Henry Zinn.

SABR BioProject Team Books

In 2002, the Society for American Baseball Research launched an effort to write and publish biographies of every player, manager, and individual who has made a contribution to baseball. Over the past decade, the BioProject Committee has produced over 6,000 biographical articles. Many have been part of efforts to create theme- or team-oriented books, spearheaded by chapters or other committees of SABR.

THE 1986 BOSTON RED SOX:
THERE WAS MORE THAN GAME SIX
One of a two-book series on the rivals that met in the 1986 World Series, the Boston Red Sox and the New York Mets, including biographies of every player, coach, broadcaster, and other important figures in the top organizations in baseball that year. .
Edited by Leslie Heaphy and Bill Nowlin
$19.95 paperback (ISBN 978-1-943816-19-4)
$9.99 ebook (ISBN 978-1-943816-18-7)
8.5"X11", 420 pages, over 200 photos

THE MIRACLE BRAVES OF 1914
BOSTON'S ORIGINAL WORST-TO-FIRST CHAMPIONS
The other book in the "rivalry" set from the 1986 World Series. This book re-tells the story of that year's classic World Series and this is the story of each of the players, coaches, managers, and broadcasters, their lives in baseball and the way the 1986 season fit into their lives.
Edited by Leslie Heaphy and Bill Nowlin
$19.95 paperback (ISBN 978-1-943816-13-2)
$9.99 ebook (ISBN 978-1-943816-12-5)
8.5"X11", 392 pages, over 100 photos

SCANDAL ON THE SOUTH SIDE:
THE 1919 CHICAGO WHITE SOX
The Black Sox Scandal isn't the only story worth telling about the 1919 Chicago White Sox. The team roster included three future Hall of Famers, a 20-year-old spitballer who would win 300 games in the minors, and even a batboy who later became a celebrity with the "Murderers' Row" New York Yankees. All of their stories are included in Scandal on the South Side with a timeline of the 1919 season.
Edited by Jacob Pomrenke
$19.95 paperback (ISBN 978-1-933599-95-3)
$9.99 ebook (ISBN 978-1-933599-94-6)
8.5"x11", 324 pages, 55 historic photos

WINNING ON THE NORTH SIDE
THE 1929 CHICAGO CUBS
Celebrate the 1929 Chicago Cubs, one of the most exciting teams in baseball history. Future Hall of Famers Hack Wilson, '29 NL MVP Rogers Hornsby, and Kiki Cuyler, along with Riggs Stephenson formed one of the most potent quartets in baseball history. The magical season came to an ignominious end in the World Series and helped craft the future "lovable loser" image of the team.
Edited by Gregory H. Wolf
$19.95 paperback (ISBN 978-1-933599-89-2)
$9.99 ebook (ISBN 978-1-933599-88-5)
8.5"x11", 314 pages, 59 photos

DETROIT THE UNCONQUERABLE:
THE 1935 WORLD CHAMPION TIGERS
Biographies of every player, coach, and broadcaster involved with the 1935 World Champion Detroit Tigers baseball team, written by members of the Society for American Baseball Research. Also includes a season in review and other articles about the 1935 team. Hank Greenberg, Mickey Cochrane, Charlie Gehringer, Schoolboy Rowe, and more.
Edited by Scott Ferkovich
$19.95 paperback (ISBN 9978-1-933599-78-6)
$9.99 ebook (ISBN 978-1-933599-79-3)
8.5"X11", 230 pages, 52 photos

THE TEAM THAT TIME WON'T FORGET:
THE 1951 NEW YORK GIANTS
Because of Bobby Thomson's dramatic "Shot Heard 'Round the World" in the bottom of the ninth of the decisive playoff game against the Brooklyn Dodgers, the team will forever be in baseball public's consciousness. Includes a foreword by Giants outfielder Monte Irvin.
Edited by Bill Nowlin and C. Paul Rogers III
$19.95 paperback (ISBN 978-1-933599-99-1)
$9.99 ebook (ISBN 978-1-933599-98-4)
8.5"X11", 282 pages, 47 photos

A PENNANT FOR THE TWIN CITIES:
THE 1965 MINNESOTA TWINS
This volume celebrates the 1965 Minnesota Twins, who captured the American League pennant in just their fifth season in the Twin Cities. Led by an All-Star cast, from Harmon Killebrew, Tony Oliva, Zoilo Versalles, and Mudcat Grant to Bob Allison, Jim Kaat, Earl Battey, and Jim Perry, the Twins won 102 games, but bowed to the Los Angeles Dodgers and Sandy Koufax in Game Seven
Edited by Gregory H. Wolf
$19.95 paperback (ISBN 978-1-943816-09-5)
$9.99 ebook (ISBN 978-1-943816-08-8)
8.5"X11", 405 pages, over 80 photos

MUSTACHES AND MAYHEM: CHARLIE O'S THREE TIME CHAMPIONS:
THE OAKLAND ATHLETICS: 1972-74
The Oakland Athletics captured major league baseball's crown each year from 1972 through 1974. Led by future Hall of Famers Reggie Jackson, Catfish Hunter and Rollie Fingers, the Athletics were a largely homegrown group who came of age together. Biographies of every player, coach, manager, and broadcaster (and mascot) from 1972 through 1974 are included, along with season recaps.
Edited by Chip Greene
$29.95 paperback (ISBN 978-1-943816-07-1)
$9.99 ebook (ISBN 978-1-943816-06-4)
8.5"X11", 600 pages, almost 100 photos

SABR Members can purchase each book at a significant discount (often 50% off) and receive the ebook edtions free as a member benefit. Each book is available in a trade paperback edition as well as ebooks suitable for reading on a home computer or Nook, Kindle, or iPad/tablet.
To learn more about becoming a member of SABR, visit the website: sabr.org/join

THE SABR DIGITAL LIBRARY

The Society for American Baseball Research, the top baseball research organization in the world, disseminates some of the best in baseball history, analysis, and biography through our publishing programs. The SABR Digital Library contains a mix of books old and new, and focuses on a tandem program of paperback and ebook publication, making these materials widely available for both on digital devices and as traditional printed books.

GREATEST GAMES BOOKS

TIGERS BY THE TALE:
GREAT GAMES AT MICHIGAN AND TRUMBULL
For over 100 years, Michigan and Trumbull was the scene of some of the most exciting baseball ever. This book portrays 50 classic games at the corner, spanning the earliest days of Bennett Park until Tiger Stadium's final closing act. From Ty Cobb to Mickey Cochrane, Hank Greenberg to Al Kaline, and Willie Horton to Alan Trammell.
Edited by Scott Ferkovich
$12.95 paperback (ISBN 978-1-943816-21-7)
$6.99 ebook (ISBN 978-1-943816-20-0)
8.5"x11", 160 pages, 22 photos

FROM THE BRAVES TO THE BREWERS: GREAT GAMES
AND HISTORY AT MILWAUKEE'S COUNTY STADIUM
The National Pastime provides in-depth articles focused on the geographic region where the national SABR convention is taking place annually. The SABR 45 convention took place in Chicago, and here are 45 articles on baseball in and around the bat-and-ball crazed Windy City: 25 that appeared in the souvenir book of the convention plus another 20 articles available in ebook only.
Edited by Gregory H. Wolf
$19.95 paperback (ISBN 978-1-943816-23-1)
$9.99 ebook (ISBN 978-1-943816-22-4)
8.5"X11", 290 pages, 58 photos

BRAVES FIELD:
MEMORABLE MOMENTS AT BOSTON'S LOST DIAMOND
From its opening on August 18, 1915, to the sudden departure of the Boston Braves to Milwaukee before the 1953 baseball season, Braves Field was home to Boston's National League baseball club and also hosted many other events: from NFL football to championship boxing. The most memorable moments to occur in Braves Field history are portrayed here.
Edited by Bill Nowlin and Bob Brady
$19.95 paperback (ISBN 978-1-933599-93-9)
$9.99 ebook (ISBN 978-1-933599-92-2)
8.5"X11", 282 pages, 182 photos

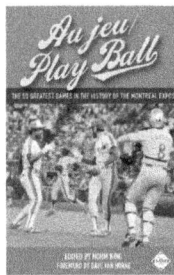

AU JEU/PLAY BALL: THE 50 GREATEST GAMES IN THE
HISTORY OF THE MONTREAL EXPOS
The 50 greatest games in Montreal Expos history. The games described here recount the exploits of the many great players who wore Expos uniforms over the years—Bill Stoneman, Gary Carter, Andre Dawson, Steve Rogers, Pedro Martinez, from the earliest days of the franchise, to the glory years of 1979-1981, the what-might-have-been years of the early 1990s, and the sad, final days.and others.
Edited by Norm King
$12.95 paperback (ISBN 978-1-943816-15-6)
$5.99 ebook (ISBN978-1-943816-14-9)
8.5"x11", 162 pages, 50 photos

ORIGINAL SABR RESEARCH

CALLING THE GAME:
BASEBALL BROADCASTING FROM 1920 TO THE PRESENT
An exhaustive, meticulously researched history of bringing the national pastime out of the ballparks and into living rooms via the airwaves. Every play-by-play announcer, color commentator, and ex-ballplayer, every broadcast deal, radio station, and TV network. Plus a foreword by "Voice of the Chicago Cubs" Pat Hughes, and an afterword by Jacques Doucet, the "Voice of the Montreal Expos" 1972-2004.
by Stuart Shea
$24.95 paperback (ISBN 978-1-933599-40-3)
$9.99 ebook (ISBN 978-1-933599-41-0)
7"X10", 712 pages, 40 photos

BIOPROJECT BOOKS

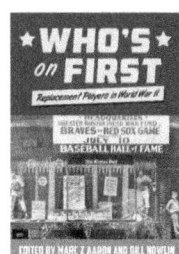

WHO'S ON FIRST:
REPLACEMENT PLAYERS IN WORLD WAR II
During World War II, 533 players made the major league debuts. More than 60% of the players in the 1941 Opening Day lineups departed for the service and were replaced by first-timers and oldsters. Hod Lisenbee was 46. POW Bert Shepard had an artificial leg, and Pete Gray had only one arm. The 1944 St. Louis Browns had 13 players classified 4-F. These are their stories.
Edited by Marc Z Aaron and Bill Nowlin
$19.95 paperback (ISBN 978-1-933599-91-5)
$9.99 ebook (ISBN 978-1-933599-90-8)
8.5"X11", 422 pages, 67 photos

VAN LINGLE MUNGO:
THE MAN, THE SONG, THE PLAYERS
Although the Red Sox spent most of the 1950s far out of contention, the team was filled with fascinating players who captured the heart of their fans. In *Red Sox Baseball*, members of SABR present 46 biographies on players such as Ted Williams and Pumpsie Green as well as season-by-season recaps.
Edited by Bill Nowlin
$19.95 paperback (ISBN 978-1-933599-76-2)
$9.99 ebook (ISBN 978-1-933599-77-9)
8.5"X11", 278 pages, 46 photos

NUCLEAR POWERED BASEBALL
Nuclear Powered Baseball tells the stories of each player—past and present—featured in the classic Simpsons episode "Homer at the Bat." Wade Boggs, Ken Griffey Jr., Ozzie Smith, Nap Lajoie, Don Mattingly, and many more. We've also included a few very entertaining takes on the now-famous episode from prominent baseball writers Jonah Keri, Joe Posnanski, Erik Malinowski, and Bradley Woodrum
Edited by Emily Hawks and Bill Nowlin
$19.95 paperback (ISBN 978-1-943816-11-8)
$9.99 ebook (ISBN 978-1-943816-10-1)
8.5"X11", 250 pages

SABR Members can purchase each book at a significant discount (often 50% off) and receive the ebook edtions free as a member benefit. Each book is available in a trade paperback edition as well as ebooks suitable for reading on a home computer or Nook, Kindle, or iPad/tablet.
To learn more about becoming a member of SABR, visit the website: sabr.org/join

Society for American Baseball Research

Cronkite School at ASU
555 N. Central Ave. #416, Phoenix, AZ 85004
602.496.1460 (phone)
SABR.org

Become a SABR member today!

If you're interested in baseball — writing about it, reading about it, talking about it — there's a place for you in the Society for American Baseball Research. Our members include everyone from academics to professional sportswriters to amateur historians and statisticians to students and casual fans who enjoy reading about baseball and occasionally gathering with other members to talk baseball. What unites all SABR members is an interest in the game and joy in learning more about it.

SABR membership is open to any baseball fan; we offer 1-year and 3-year memberships. Here's a list of some of the key benefits you'll receive as a SABR member:

- Receive two editions (spring and fall) of the *Baseball Research Journal*, our flagship publication
- Receive expanded e-book edition of *The National Pastime*, our annual convention journal
- 8-10 new e-books published by the SABR Digital Library, all FREE to members
- "This Week in SABR" e-newsletter, sent to members every Friday
- Join dozens of research committees, from Statistical Analysis to Women in Baseball.
- Join one of 70 regional chapters in the U.S., Canada, Latin America, and abroad
- Participate in online discussion groups
- Ask and answer baseball research questions on the SABR-L e-mail listserv
- Complete archives of *The Sporting News* dating back to 1886 and other research resources
- Promote your research in "This Week in SABR"
- Diamond Dollars Case Competition
- Yoseloff Scholarships
- Discounts on SABR national conferences, including the SABR National Convention, the SABR Analytics Conference, Jerry Malloy Negro League Conference, Frederick Ivor-Campbell 19th Century Conference
- Publish your research in peer-reviewed SABR journals
- Collaborate with SABR researchers and experts
- Contribute to Baseball Biography Project or the SABR Games Project
- List your new book in the SABR Bookshelf
- Lead a SABR research committee or chapter
- Networking opportunities at SABR Analytics Conference
- Meet baseball authors and historians at SABR events and chapter meetings
- 50% discounts on paperback versions of SABR e-books
- 20% discount on MLB.TV and MiLB.TV subscriptions
- Discounts with other partners in the baseball community
- SABR research awards

We hope you'll join the most passionate international community of baseball fans at SABR! Check us out online at SABR.org/join.

SABR MEMBERSHIP FORM

	Annual	3-year	Senior	3-yr Sr.	Under 30
U.S.:	☐ $65	☐ $175	☐ $45	☐ $129	☐ $45
Canada/Mexico:	☐ $75	☐ $205	☐ $55	☐ $159	☐ $55
Overseas:	☐ $84	☐ $232	☐ $64	☐ $186	☐ $55

Add a Family Member: $15 each family member at same address (list names on back)
Senior: 65 or older before 12/31 of the current year
All dues amounts in U.S. dollars or equivalent

Participate in Our Donor Program!

Support the preservation of baseball research. Designate your gift toward:
☐ General Fund   ☐ Endowment Fund   ☐ Research Resources   ☐ _____
☐ I want to maximize the impact of my gift; do not send any donor premiums
☐ I would like this gift to remain anonymous.

Note: Any donation not designated will be placed in the General Fund.
SABR is a 501 (c) (3) not-for-profit organization & donations are tax-deductible to the extent allowed by law.

Name _____

E-mail* _____

Address _____

City _____ ST_____ ZIP_____

Phone _____ Birthday _____

* Your e-mail address on file ensures you will receive the most recent SABR news.

Dues $_____
Donation $_____
Amount Enclosed $_____

Do you work for a matching grant corporation? Call (602) 496-1460 for details.

If you wish to pay by credit card, please contact the SABR office at (602) 496-1460 or visit the SABR Store online at SABR.org/join. We accept Visa, Mastercard & Discover.

Do you wish to receive the *Baseball Research Journal* electronically?: ☐ Yes   ☐ No
Our e-books are available in PDF, Kindle, or EPUB (iBooks, iPad, Nook) formats.

Mail to: SABR, Cronkite School at ASU, 555 N. Central Ave. #416, Phoenix, AZ 85004

www.ingramcontent.com/pod-product-compliance
Lightning Source LLC
Chambersburg PA
CBHW081332080526
44588CB00017B/2599